Principles of
Estate Planning

Second Edition

Carolynn Tomin
Colleen Carcone

National Underwriter Academic Series

FOREWORD

Technically, Estate Planning encompasses the process of accumulation, conservation, and distribution of an estate in the manner that most efficiently and effectively accomplishes the client's goals. In short, almost everyone has some estate and every one of those estates are planned – either by the dictates of state law – or by a person or couple who takes deliberate and conscious control of the process.

But money and assets are not the whole story. Estate planning is very much about people, the accomplishment of their dreams and hopes, and the vanquishing of their fears. In fact the "people problems" are every bit as – if not more so – challenging than the technical tax and other legal aspects. This is why the subject of estate planning is so very important.

Practitioner-educators Carolynn Tomin and Colleen Carcone are uniquely qualified to guide you through your first look at this intellectually, psychologically, and financially rewarding field. They have succeeded in taking a highly complex and astoundingly broad body of information and distilling it into an organized, clear, crisp, and concise tool to help you quickly master the basic concepts. Each term of art is both defined and illustrated by examples. Carolynn and Colleen have provided you with a Rosetta stone to the language of estate planning.

Look at the contents of this book as a door to a mansion filled with fine art. Walk in and wander through the rooms and you will be awed by the treasure that you will find – not just to enrich others' lives – but also to enrich your own and your family's.

Stephan R. Leimberg
April 2015

SECOND EDITION

Since we wrote the first edition of this book in 2012, we have seen new legislation implemented in the form of the American Taxpayer Relief Act of 2012 (ATRA) that made permanent some of the tax code provisions pertaining to estate planning, while changing some other provisions. These changes have produced a more stable tax environment than what we had in 2012; the estate tax exemption amount is now stable and indexed for inflation, and most practitioners seem to expect tax rates to stay where they are for at least the near future.

Principles of Estate Planning, Second Edition reflects the very latest tax code laws, rates, and exemptions enacted with ATRA. We have also updated the text to reflect other changes that are relevant to estate planning professionals. These include the creation ABLE accounts, the increased use of trust protectors, and of course the rise in the legal recognition of same-sex marriage. These changes are important from a "nuts and bolts" perspective, but they also remind us that the practice of estate planning involves more than just taxes. Estate planning is about helping your clients take stock of what they have accomplished and decide what kind of legacy they will leave behind for those that they care about. We hope you will find this updated version of the first edition most useful in understanding the comprehensive subject of Estate Planning.

Carolynn B. Tomin, CFP®
Colleen Carcone, JD, CFP®
April 1, 2015

PREFACE

Throughout our many years of experience in teaching estate planning we recognized the need for a textbook that would assist students in learning the complex principles and techniques of estate planning. We observed that students were easily confused by certain legal terms and tax concepts and that they struggled to understand some of the more advanced estate planning strategies they were expected to know. This led us to continually search for effective teaching methods and materials that would help students understand these difficult estate planning topics.

We also tried to find the right textbook for our students, but after reviewing several of them, we could not find one that met our standards and criteria. Therefore, we spent a great deal of time developing ancillary class notes and supplemental materials to provide our students with the critical information that we felt was missing from textbooks. Over time, and through experience, we developed better teaching practices and materials that have helped our students with their studies. We decided to share our format, the organization of our materials, and the many client situations and practitioner tips we developed with students and instructors whom we hope will benefit from our work.

The Importance of Learning Estate Planning

Sometimes a student wonders why he or she needs to learn estate planning when a licensed attorney is the only professional who has the authority to practice law and provide comprehensive estate planning for clients. We explain that estate planning involves the coordination of expertise and special skills of all members of the client's estate planning team, which often includes financial planners. Financial planners must recognize clients' estate planning issues and they should understand how alternative solutions can affect a client's overall financial plan. Every member of the estate planning team is obligated to be aware of the tools and techniques of estate planning, to understand their limitations as well as their problem-solving potential, and to be knowledgeable enough to discuss them in general terms with clients and their other advisors.

It is important for students to understand that estate planning knowledge can add tremendous value to a client's life and also to a client relationship. A former student, Thomas C. Schwab CFP® of Santa Fe, New Mexico, contributed this explanation:

"In many client engagements, I have found estate planning knowledge and the ability to make meaningful contributions to a client's estate planning the most significant aspect of the relationship. This area of knowledge often sets CFP® practitioners apart from other financial advisors, creating opportunities to engage and collaborate with the other important professionals in the client's life. It also demonstrates to our clients that we are committed to helping them manage and find solutions to often complex intergenerational issues that touch upon their hopes, desires, and values. Because estate planning usually integrates fundamental aspects of our other areas of expertise, such as tax planning, investment planning, and insurance planning, it also creates an opportunity to organize the many pieces of the planning puzzle together with the client into a coherent, comprehensive plan.

"Estate planning inevitably touches upon many (sometimes deeply charged) emotional areas of the client's life—their family relationships, their charitable motives, their wish to leave a legacy, and their acceptance of their own mortality. Therefore a CFP® practitioner who is skilled in estate planning knowledge can forge a deep and intensely meaningful professional relationship with clients and their families. In my practice, it is not at all unusual for clients to express deep gratitude for the sensitive handling of all of these issues.

"Clients are often surprised, having initially contacted me for investment advice, that there is so much more that a knowledgeable CFP® practitioner can contribute to their overall planning. Some clients report feeling immense relief, confidence, and peace of mind that this area of their planning has been addressed thoughtfully and comprehensively. In the process, I often get to know the client's children and grandchildren and this is a source of enrichment for me and for my clients. In some cases, I am treated as a trusted member of the family. All of this makes a solid grounding in estate planning not only a necessity, but it also creates opportunities for truly intellectually and emotionally stimulating experiences in financial planning that can be life changing for my clients and for myself. I have no doubt that this has contributed to my being considered a trusted member of the professional community and, through word of mouth, has brought many new clients into my practice."

Unique Features of Principles of Estate Planning

Principles of Estate Planning is written specifically for students enrolled in financial planning programs and for financial planning practitioners who want to provide greater value for their clients by offering more comprehensive financial planning services.

This textbook is, in essence, a financial planner's guide to estate planning. The most important aspect of this book is that it addresses all of the CFP® Certification Examination Principle Topics and subtopics related to estate planning at the highest academic level. Our objective is not only to explain the topics in great detail but to emphasize their practical application in financial planning situations and in the context of a comprehensive financial plan. Each topic is broken down into smaller components and illustrated with client situations to reinforce the concepts and facilitate the student's learning experience.

Learning objectives are provided for each chapter. They emphasize the most important information that students need to know. Chapter learning objectives have specific learning outcomes linked directly to CFP Board principal topics. Students should test their understanding of chapter material by using the learning objectives as academic benchmarks in their studies. Many of the learning objectives are taken from the CFP Board resource document *Student Centered Learning Objectives based upon CFP Board Principal Topics*.

Financial Planning Practice Standards describe best practices relative to the six steps in the financial planning process. We have presented the *Practice Standards* where appropriate in each chapter so that students can understand how topic information is applied in relationship to specific steps in the financial planning process. All of the *Practice Standards* are included in Appendix C and students must become familiar with them.

Client situations are interspersed throughout the book and are intended to demonstrate how topic information is applied to financial planning situations. Students often find that topic content is difficult to understand, but when an explanation is combined with a client situation, the material is better understood. Client situations in this book are not necessarily based on real-life examples, but they can be applied to real-life financial planning situations.

Practitioner tips are included throughout the textbook because they provide advice and practical guidance to students and financial planning practitioners when working with clients. We want our readers to understand how the information is used in a financial planning practice and have emphasized points that a practitioner would want to know.

Chapter highlights emphasize the most important material presented in the chapter and are included at the end of each chapter. Students must have a thorough understanding of the information presented here and can use this feature as a summary and a review of chapter information.

Key terms are bolded throughout the text and are listed in alphabetical order at the end of each chapter. The meaning of these terms can be found in the context of the chapter material, and definitions can be found in the glossary.

Review questions are the last component of each chapter and are intended to test a student's knowledge of the chapter information. We encourage students to test themselves on the questions provided, because practice questions will help students understand the material better. The answers are provided in Appendix A, located in the back of the book, so that students can read an explanation of the correct answer and understand why other answer options are incorrect.

Finally, for simplicity's sake, we have opted to use the pronoun *he* in this book, to represent both genders.

We believe that the format and structure of our textbook will allow students to learn not only the estate planning concepts essential for practitioners to know, but it will provide them with an understanding of how these concepts work in the real world of financial planning. We are proud of this textbook and hope that our readers will be educated and enlightened by it.

 With best wishes for your professional success,

Carolynn B. Tomin, CFP®
Colleen Carcone, JD, CFP®
April 1, 2015

ABOUT THE AUTHORS

Colleen Carcone, CFP® is a financial planning professional and attorney specializing in comprehensive estate and tax planning matters. Since 2008, Ms. Carcone has taught estate planning at Boston University's Program for Financial Planning. Ms. Carcone also serves as a Wealth Planning Strategist for TIAA-CREF, where she provides wealth transfer, estate planning, and tax planning services for the company's client needs.

Prior to joining TIAA-CREF, Ms. Carcone worked with Atlantic Trust Company, where she advised high-net-worth clients on all aspects of estate planning including basic planning, asset ownership, charitable gifting, multigenerational transfers, and other sophisticated estate planning strategies while working with clients' outside advisors to implement these techniques. Formerly Ms. Carcone worked with Atlantic Benefit Group, an insurance firm, advising high-net-worth individuals and business owners and providing assistance with the implementation of advanced estate and business planning techniques utilizing life insurance.

Carolynn B. Tomin, CFP®, specializes in financial education. She is the Program Director for Boston University's classroom and online financial planning programs and has augmented curriculum for the online program for twelve years. She has taught estate planning courses, virtual reviews, and CFP® Certification Exam reviews for twenty years at colleges in Massachusetts and Florida, and for many banks and financial service companies in both states.

As cofounder of a financial education company, Beacon Hill Financial Educators, she has presented continuing education courses to many financial service corporations and financial planning organizations.

Ms. Tomin served as a member of CFP Board's *Council on Education* from 2009 - 2012, and was appointed Chair in 2012. She has also served on the board of directors for the southwest Florida chapter of the Financial Planning Association (FPA). She is a former member of the Boston Estate Planning Council.

ABOUT THE PUBLISHER

Kelly B. Maheu, J.D., is Managing Director of the Professional Publishing Division of The National Underwriter Company, a Division of ALM Media, LLC. Kelly has been with The National Underwriter Company since 2006, and served in editorial, content acquisition, and product development roles prior to being named Managing Director.

Prior to joining The National Underwriter Company, Kelly worked in the legal and insurance fields for LexisNexis®, Progressive Insurance, and a Cincinnati insurance defense litigation firm.

Kelly has edited and contributed to numerous books and publications including the *Personal Auto Insurance Policy Coverage Guide, Cyberliability and Insurance, The National Underwriter Sales Essentials Series*, and *The Tools & Techniques of Risk Management for Financial Planners*.

Kelly earned her law degree from The University of Cincinnati College of Law and holds a BA from Miami University, Ohio, with a double major in English/Journalism and Psychology.

ABOUT THE MANAGING EDITOR

Richard H. Cline, J.D., is the Manager, Tax and Insurance Content for the Professional Publishing Division at The National Underwriter Company. He is responsible for both the print and online versions of Tax Facts as well as developing new tax products for our customers.

Richard has over twenty-five years of tax editing and publishing experience. Prior to joining The National Underwriter Company, Richard worked for Lexis-Nexis, CCH, Inc., and PricewaterhouseCoopers.

He has a B.S. degree from Franklin and Marshall College in Lancaster, Pennsylvania, and earned his law degree from Tulane University in New Orleans, Louisiana.

ABOUT THE EDITOR

Jason Gilbert, J.D., M.A., is an assistant editor with the Professional Publishing Division of The National Underwriter Company, a division of ALM Media, LLC. He edits and develops publications related to tax and insurance products, including titles in the *Advisor's Guide* and the *Tools & Techniques* series of investment and planning products. He also develops content for National Underwriter's other financial services publications and online products. He has worked on insurance and tax publications for more than nine years.

Jason has been a practicing attorney for more than a dozen years in the areas of criminal defense, products liability, and regulatory enforcement actions. Prior to joining National Underwriter, his experience in the insurance and tax fields has included work as a Westlaw contributor for Thomson Reuters and a tax advisor and social media contributor for Intuit. He is an honors graduate from Wright State University and holds a J.D. from the University of Cincinnati College of Law as well as a master's degree in Economics from Miami University in Ohio.

EDITORIAL SERVICES

Connie L. Jump, Manager, Editorial Operations

Patti O'Leary, Editorial Assistant

ACKNOWLEDGMENTS

Writing a textbook is a very time-consuming process. Once we started writing this book we found that all of our precise planning and self-imposed deadlines were quickly overturned as events in our lives took center stage and demanded our full time and attention. We both experienced the deaths of loved ones, the illness of close friends, and the birth of two special nieces. These events made us recognize how truly important estate planning is and appreciate what it can accomplish, as we dealt with estate planning issues within our own families.

We want to extend a very special thank you to our families, who have supported us and encouraged us throughout the writing of this book. Carolynn would especially like to recognize and thank her husband, Nigel Tomin. Without the love, understanding, and support of our families, this book would never have been written.

We wish to further acknowledge the many colleagues who provided us with advice and especially acknowledge the following individuals who made significant contributions to this book: Lisa McGrath, William B. Reeve, Thomas C. Schwab, Joanne Snider, and Alicia Waltenberger.

We have been very fortunate to work with our editor, Jane Garwood, of Asclepion Publishing. Jane skillfully guided us through the writing process and also provided us with much-needed encouragement along the way. We are also grateful to the folks at the National Underwriter Company for the support and confidence they have shown in us and in this project.

We want to specifically acknowledge CFP Board for allowing us to reprint their materials in this textbook.

Finally, we want to extend a very sincere and special thank you to Stephan Leimberg, who graciously allowed us to adapt and incorporate into this textbook parts of *The Tools & Techniques of Estate Planning*.

SUMMARY TABLE OF CONTENTS

DETAILED TABLE OF CONTENTS

Introduction to Estate Planning

CFP® CERTIFICATION PRINCIPAL TOPIC COVERED IN THIS CHAPTER:

Fiduciaries

- Types of fiduciaries
  - Executor/Personal representative
  - Trustee
- Duties of fiduciaries
- Breach of fiduciary duties

Learning Objectives

- Explain the importance of estate planning and what it can accomplish.

- Describe the unauthorized practice of law.

- Identify the financial planning practitioner's role and responsibilities in the estate planning process.

- Define fiduciary duties and identify the parties that would be subject to them.

Chapter Contents

OVERVIEW

Estate planning is the process of planning for the accumulation, conservation, and distribution of an estate in a manner that most efficiently and effectively accomplishes a person's goals. The purpose of an estate plan is to provide personal protection and financial security to an individual and his family. Most people spend a lifetime accumulating assets and want to distribute them to their loved ones in a manner that reduces transfer taxes and distribution costs. They also want to protect their assets from financial, economic, and creditor risks that might diminish value and affect their ability to achieve their financial planning goals. These common estate planning objectives are addressed in the estate planning process through the development of a comprehensive estate plan that is integrated with a client's overall financial plan and personal goals.

Financial planners have an important role to play in the estate planning process, and they can provide better service and greater value to their clients by understanding the fundamental principles of estate planning. This knowledge will help planners recognize deficiencies in a client's estate plan that can be addressed in collaboration with the client's estate planning team. Planners can also use their knowledge to assist clients in determining realistic estate planning goals and priorities, and they can ensure that the estate plan is properly implemented and monitored once recommendations have been developed.

The financial planner is one of several members of a client's estate planning team. The estate planning attorney is the person primarily responsible for developing the plan and for drafting the legal documents. Other professionals, such as insurance specialists, trust officers, and accountants also serve the client with specialized expertise. Planners can contribute to the development of an estate plan with their unique knowledge of a client's personal and financial situation and their grasp of estate planning techniques and strategies. The client is best served when all team members work together to formulate, execute, and maintain a plan that meets a client's needs and accomplishes his estate planning objectives.

Practice Standard 200-1

Determining a Client's Personal and Financial Goals, Needs and Priorities

The financial planning practitioner and the client shall mutually define the client's personal and financial goals, needs and priorities that are relevant to the scope of the engagement before any recommendation is made and/or implemented.

WHO NEEDS AN ESTATE PLAN?

An **estate** is defined as the rights, titles, or interests that a person, living or deceased, has in property. The manner in which assets are owned determines how they will pass at death, and to whom they will pass. Without proper planning, property could pass to the wrong person in the wrong manner. And if there is no will, individually owned property will pass to others according to state distribution rules, known as **state laws of intestacy.** Therefore, every adult older than age 18 should have an estate plan.

Estate planning is essential for people who want to care for and provide financial support for spouses, domestic partners, minor children, parents, or other relatives or dependents during their lifetime and after their death. Proper estate planning can preserve a client's assets for the benefit of others. Estate planning is especially needed for:

- spouses, partners, children, or other dependents who cannot handle or do not wish to handle money, securities, or a business;

- children, spouses, or other dependents who are emotionally or mentally challenged, emotionally disturbed, or physically handicapped;

- spouses, children, or other dependents who are expected to have their own significant wealth;

- elderly parents who are financially—and perhaps emotionally—dependent on their children to provide them with support and care; and

- pets that need to be cared for after an owner's death.

Estate planning is also needed to prepare for incapacity. Legal documents such as durable powers of attorney, health care proxies, living wills, and trusts can be used to make legal, financial, and healthcare decisions for the benefit of an incapacitated person. **Trusts** are important estate planning instruments because they can provide continuity of income and asset management in the event the trust creator, the **grantor,** becomes incapacitated. In the absence of documents such as a power of attorney, the courts will appoint a guardian or a conservator to make these types of decisions on behalf of an incompetent person.

SITUATIONS THAT REQUIRE ADVANCED ESTATE PLANNING

A simple will may be appropriate to meet many clients' needs, but more sophisticated planning is indicated for people who own substantial assets. A common estate planning goal is to reduce taxes when property is transferred to others. Such taxes take the form of gift taxes, estate taxes, and generation-skipping transfer taxes. Because the estate tax exemption amount has increased significantly over the past several years, many clients will focus on income tax planning within their estate plans. Estate planning is essential for individuals with:

- Estates that exceed $5,430,000 in 2015. Estate planning can minimize estate taxes and consequently transfer more family wealth to beneficiaries.

- Highly appreciated or other unique assets. Understanding the income tax consequences of transferring assets during life or at death will be an important component of planning.

- Closely held business interests. Estate planning can provide for the orderly transfer of a business to a key employee or a competent family member.

- Charitable objectives.

- Property owned in more than one state.

- Special property such as fine art or a coin, gun, or stamp collection.

- Asset protection concerns for heirs.

- Estates that need sufficient liquidity to pay debts, expenses, and taxes owed at death.

THE ESTATE PLANNING PROCESS

There are six steps in the financial planning process:

1. Establishing and defining the relationship with a client

2. Gathering client data

3. Analyzing and evaluating a client's financial status

4. Developing and presenting financial planning recommendations

5. Implementing the financial planning recommendations

6. Monitoring the plan

Each step in the financial planning process is related to the CFP Board's *Financial Planning Practice Standards,* which are intended to:

- assure that the practice of financial planning by CERTIFIED FINANCIAL PLANNER™ professionals is based on established norms of practice;

- advance professionalism in financial planning; and

- enhance the value of the financial planning process.

The *Practice Standards* provide a framework for the professional practice of financial planning and apply to practitioners engaged in performing the tasks of financial planning.

The estate planning process follows the same steps as the financial planning process; therefore, the *Financial Planning Practice Standards* can be applied to the development of a client's estate plan. See Appendix C for a complete listing of the CFP Board's *Financial Planning Practice Standards.*

Step 1: Establishing a Relationship with a Client

The financial planning practitioner and the client must mutually determine the scope of engagement, which identifies the services to be provided and each party's responsibilities in developing and implementing the financial plan. This step refers to services that the financial planner will provide with respect to a client's estate plan, and these responsibilities should be coordinated with other members of the client's estate planning team. For example, only an attorney can draft legal documents, including estate planning documents, and the planner might be involved only in implementing the client's estate plan.

Step 2: Gathering Client Data

The practitioner and the client mutually define the client's personal and financial goals, needs, and priorities. The practitioner obtains sufficient quantitative information and documents pertaining to the engagement. Data includes legal documents such as wills, powers of attorney, trusts, etc., in addition to tax returns, insurance policies, deeds, and account statements for investment, bank, and retirement accounts. Beneficiary designation forms are also very important for planners to review.

Practitioner Tip: The ability to gather accurate, comprehensive, and useful information in a logical and orderly manner is most efficiently developed through the use of a data-gathering system.

Step 3: Analyzing the Client's Financial Status

The planner must assess a client's current and future financial situations to determine the likelihood of meeting his financial planning and estate planning goals. Deficiencies should be identified and the client should be informed of how assets are scheduled to transfer, and at what cost, under the current estate plan.

Step 4: Developing Recommendations

A financial planner should work with a client's estate planning attorney to develop alternatives to the existing estate plan in an effort to reasonably meet the client's estate planning objectives and priorities. Recommendations are developed based on selected alternatives to the current course of action. Techniques that do not meet the client's goals are eliminated, as are techniques that are inconsistent with the client's financial needs and priorities. A planner can identify problems with a client's current situation that might affect the proposed recommendations. Recommendations should be communicated to the client in a manner that will help him make an informed decision about implementing the plan.

Some factors that can affect the selection of a particular estate planning technique include:

- the current and projected value of a client's estate;

- the net amount of estate or gift tax liability;

- the client's health and life expectancy;

- the client's financial needs during lifetime;

- the types of property the client owns and how it is owned;

- the beneficiaries' ability to manage transferred assets;

- the client's marginal income tax bracket; and

- the laws of the client's state of **domicile** (permanent residence).

Step 5: Implementing the Recommendations

The client, the planner, and members of the estate planning team determine implementation responsibilities for the plan. The planner helps the team select products or services to implement the recommendations that are suitable for the client and consistent with the client's goals, needs, or priorities.

Step 6: Monitoring the Plan

The practitioner's role in monitoring the estate plan must be clearly defined. The plan might need to be revised if changes occur that render it or certain provisions ineffective or outdated. Circumstances that can affect an estate plan include:

- changes in a client's personal objectives;

- changes in a client's personal situation, such as the birth of a child or grandchild, divorce in the family, illness, death of a beneficiary, etc.;

- relocation to another state or accumulation of property in another state;

- substantial changes in a client's wealth, income, or business interests; and

- changes in federal or state tax laws.

Practitioner Tip: A client's estate plan should take into account his current financial situation and projected financial needs. The estate planning recommendations and techniques selected for implementation should be appropriate to accomplish both the client's tax and non-tax estate planning objectives. Finally, the estate plan should be flexible enough to include amendments or revisions that will accommodate a client's changing personal circumstances as well as changes to future tax laws and policies.

THE UNAUTHORIZED PRACTICE OF LAW

An attorney who specializes in estate planning is the most important member of a client's estate planning team. The attorney must be able to relate well to the other team members and the client. The attorney should take the lead in developing plan recommendations and establishing implementation priorities. The estate planning team can work together with the client to ensure that recommendations are completed in a timely manner.

It is sometimes difficult to draw the boundaries of professional responsibility in an area as complex and sophisticated as estate planning. Special skills and learning are necessary prerequisites not only for the attorney but also for a CFP® practitioner, CPA, ChFC, CLU, trust officer, or other individuals serving a client in an advisory capacity.

Yet it is clear that regardless of how knowledgeable an advisor is only an attorney is legally authorized to practice law. The practice of law is regulated and limited for a number of reasons.

- The public needs and deserves protection against advice by nonattorneys who have been neither trained nor licensed to practice law.

- Many nonlawyers who are highly skilled in specific areas such as tax law might lack the broader viewpoint and depth provided by law school or legal experience.

- The preparation of an estate plan involves the proper coordination of how assets are distributed. This process requires specialized training and knowledge, and this task is best coordinated by a lawyer.

Estate planning is an art, not a science; it involves the coordination of special skills and expertise from all members of a client's estate planning team. The very idea of an estate planning team implies that each member serves the client. It is often the financial planner who motivates the client to take action—and then follows through to make sure the plan is implemented. However, when any member of the team usurps the province of another, the client loses.

What can—and cannot—be safely discussed with a client? There are few redline tests, but practitioners can follow some common-sense guidelines. Essentially, when a statute or legal interpretation has become so well-known and settled that no further legal issue is involved, there should be no problem in suggesting its simple application on a general basis. This is known as the "general-specific" test; no violation arises from the sharing of legal knowledge that is either generally informatory or, if specific, is so obvious as to be common knowledge.

Only when legal rules (which are general in nature) are applied to specific factual situations is the line crossed. Providing advice involving the application of legal principles to a specific situation is clearly the "practice of law" under the general-specific test. When the application of basic legal principles to specific and actual facts or the resolution of controversial or uncertain questions of law is required in an actual case, the practice of law is involved. Each state has the right to decide—independently from all other states—what is meant by the "unauthorized practice of law."

No safety can be found in an argument that the nonlawyer is both a specialist and an acknowledged expert in the field. The rationale is that the public interest is not protected by the narrow specialization of a person who lacks the broad perspective and orientation of a licensed attorney. That dimension of skill and knowledge comes only from a thorough understanding of legal concepts, processes, and the interaction of all the branches of law. In other words, the nonlawyer may have learned the rules, but often the full meaning and import of the rule and its components—and the impact of that rule on other seemingly unrelated rules—may not be fully understood by someone who is not a licensed attorney. For instance, a proposed arrangement might "work" in terms of its tax implications, but it could violate other laws such as ERISA or securities laws.

Almost everyone agrees that the actual drafting of a will or trust or the preparation of the instruments and contracts by which legal rights are secured is the practice of law. Definitive solutions, i.e., the choice of which specific tools or techniques to use in a given case or the decisions regarding how they should be used, must be considered only by the client, together with his attorney. Likewise, the drafting or adoption of instruments needed to execute the techniques or utilize the tools discussed in this book is exclusively the province of a lawyer.

Practitioner Tip: Practitioners should avoid most problems by working closely with a client's attorney at the earliest opportunity.

Every member of the estate planning team is obligated to be aware of the principles of estate planning and to understand the problem-solving potential of specific tools and techniques, as well as their limitations. Financial planners must be knowledgeable enough to discuss them in general terms with clients and with a client's other advisors.

THE FINANCIAL PLANNER'S ROLE

CFP Board Rule 4.2 of the *Rules of Conduct* states, "A certificant shall offer advice only in those areas in which he or she is competent to do so and shall maintain competence in all areas in which he or she is engaged to provide professional services."[1]

The single most important skill of a financial planner is the ability to understand who the client is, where that client stands in relation to the objectives he may have, and what things have to be done to move the client closer to the realization of these goals. Knowledge of the client, his fears, hopes, and dreams, and his family circumstances and relationship to other family members is essential for the financial planner to apply this skill.

The estate planning interview is important far beyond the data gathered, because it is probably the first time in a client's life that he will be confronted with his property, his loved ones, his mortality, and the relationship of each to the others. The planner must actively listen to the client to gain a thorough understanding of what is truly important to him.

Practitioner Tip: The goal of the financial planner should be to help his client come to his own realizations and conclusions.

The financial planner should work with a client to help formulate estate planning goals that are measurable, relevant, and realistic considering the client's resources and time frames, and he should help the client prioritize his goals.

When constructing a financial plan or reviewing an existing plan, the planner should review the client's legal, financial, and tax documents to ensure coordination and compliance with the client's goals. This review also serves to identify any weaknesses in the current estate plan. If problems are discovered, the planner can inform the client about the consequences of not taking corrective action and persuade him to obtain legal advice. If necessary, the planner can assemble a team of experts to work with the client, the planner, and the client's attorney to develop alternative estate planning solutions that reflect the client's wishes.

Practitioner Tip: The planner may need to assume a counselor's role when encouraging a client to make changes to his current plan or convince him that the proposed estate planning recommendations are suitable and appropriate for his needs.

Financial Planner Responsibilities

There are many actions a financial planner can take to implement, or assist in updating, a client's estate plan. The financial planner can:

- Ensure the client understands the intricacies of his current estate plan and the tax and non-tax aspects of the plan.

- Work with the client to correct improper or outdated beneficiary designations found on life insurance policies, investment accounts, IRAs, or other retirement accounts.

- Offer to assist the client in funding revocable trusts to avoid probate and to obtain professional management of trust assets in the event of the client's incapacity.

- Determine the value of the client's assets and liabilities to determine whether the estate has a federal or state estate tax liability.

- Review life insurance policies to determine whether there is sufficient coverage for family protection and estate liquidity needs. Determine the effect the death benefit will have on the client's estate tax liability.

- Review all insurance policies including disability and long-term care policies to determine whether coverage and benefits are sufficient to protect the client, his family, and his assets.

- Work with the client to divide jointly owned property into individually owned assets if this is needed to fund specific trusts that save estate taxes for the client and his spouse.

- Review the client's will, trusts, asset titling, and deeds to ensure that bequests of property and titles of ownership are coordinated.

- Review the will to determine whether beneficiaries, executors, or guardians need to be changed or contingent executors or guardians added.

- Make sure all property interests the client owns can pass by will, trust, or automatically to a joint owner.

- Create spreadsheets that show how assets are currently owned, how they are transferred to beneficiaries at death, how much each beneficiary will receive, and the net amount of the client's and spouse's estate tax liability.

- Provide the client with a written summary of the documents included in his estate plan and a list of all of his financial accounts.

- Assist in implementing estate planning recommendations.

- Monitor the client's progress in implementing the plan.

- Conduct periodic reviews of the estate plan to identify whether updates are needed based on changes in tax laws and the client's goals and personal circumstances.

Practice Standard 500-1

Agreeing on Implementation Responsibilities

The financial planning practitioner and the client shall mutually agree on the implementation responsibilities consistent with the scope of the engagement.

Practice Standard 600-1

Defining Monitoring Responsibilities

The financial planning practitioner and client shall mutually define monitoring responsibilities.

Practitioner Tip: Financial planners might prefer to refer clients to estate planning attorneys to handle all of their estate planning needs. But planners have invaluable personal knowledge of a client and his financial situation, and when that information is combined with the planner's knowledge of estate planning, the client is better served. Knowledge of estate planning increases a planner's level of competency and distinguishes the planner as a valuable advisor to his clients. This can also give the planner a competitive edge over other advisors, because attorneys prefer to work with competent professionals who understand estate planning issues.

FIDUCIARIES

Clients need to carefully select the right people whom they trust to execute their estate plan. These people are known as *fiduciaries* and they have specific responsibilities and roles in executing an estate plan. Fiduciaries often include executors, trustees, guardians, and agents.

A **fiduciary** has a responsibility to place a beneficiary's interests first, before his own. Fiduciaries have the authority to perform special acts or specific duties for others. Depending on the type of fiduciary selected and the scope of his authority, fiduciaries can carry out directives set forth by a **principal** to manage that person's property or affairs.

Practitioner Tip: CFP Board Rule 1.4 of the *Rules of Conduct* imposes a fiduciary duty on CFP certificants. Rule 1.4 states, "A certificant shall at all times place the interest of the client ahead of his or her own. When the certificant provides financial planning or material elements of the financial planning process, the certificant owes to the client the duty of care of a fiduciary as defined by CFP Board."[2] CFP Board defines a fiduciary as "one who acts in utmost good faith, in a manner he or she reasonably believes to be in the best interest of the client."[3]

Fiduciaries must perform their duties with utmost care and loyalty toward the beneficiaries they serve. Fiduciaries who manage property interests should make every effort to preserve and protect the property and make prudent investment decisions with the goal of increasing the property's value. Fiduciaries can be sued for breach of fiduciary duty in civil and criminal courts.

The proper selection of a fiduciary begins with an understanding of the tasks and duties of each member of the client's estate planning team and how each fiduciary interacts with others.

Executor Responsibilities

An **executor** is a fiduciary designated under a will to serve as the client's personal representative. An executor is responsible for collecting and valuing estate assets, paying the decedent's debts and taxes, and distributing assets to the beneficiaries named in the will. The probate process typically lasts from nine months to two or three years, and an executor must be willing to serve throughout that period until the estate has been probated.

A person may want to choose a close relative or another caring individual to serve as his executor who is sensitive to the emotional and financial needs of the beneficiaries. A trusted family member is preferable in this role but only if the person selected has the skills and abilities to handle the responsibilities of administering an estate. If family members do not have the necessary skills, a person should know which professional to turn to for help. Family members chosen as executors must remain impartial and should avoid taking actions that provide them with distinct advantages over other estate beneficiaries.

In some circumstances it may be necessary or appropriate to name a corporate fiduciary as executor. Corporate fiduciaries, such as banks and trust companies that specialize in estate administration can be named as executors or co-executors under the will. These entities should be considered for administering large or complex estates because they can provide professional management for all types of property interests, including businesses, investments and real estate.

Practitioner Tip: It is the executor's responsibility to choose an attorney to probate the estate. Any attorney that specializes in estate planning can be selected for this role—it does not have to be the same attorney that drafted the will.

Trustee Responsibilities

Trusts have many uses and often provide assets or income to trust beneficiaries. The **trustee** is a fiduciary who holds title to the trust assets and manages them on behalf of the beneficiaries according to the terms specified in the trust instrument. A trustee is chosen by a grantor and can be an individual or a **corporate trustee**. A trust can also have co-trustees, for example, one or more family members can serve as co-trustees with an institutional trustee, such as a bank or a trust company.

An advantage to having a corporate trustee is its availability to serve for many generations, whereas individual trustees cannot. Corporate trustees can also provide professional investment management, business advice, tax-planning expertise and accounting services that individual trustees may not be capable of providing.

Practitioner Tip: It certainly makes sense to choose a corporate trustee rather than an individual trustee when a client has complex investments and extensive property holdings.

As part of the selection process, a grantor should consider the manner in which a beneficiary might be permitted to remove a corporate trustee and appoint successor trustees. The grantor should also name successors to step in should the original trustee be unavailable or unable to serve. The trust document should address conditions and circumstances that would lead to the trustee's dismissal.

Practitioner Tip: Often, changes within corporations can change the nature of the relationship between a corporate trustee and individual co-trustees or beneficiaries. For example, a bank named as corporate trustee might merge with a larger bank and the manner in which they handle a trust could change. For this reason it may make sense to allow trust beneficiaries the flexibility to remove the corporate trustee and replace it with another corporate trustee.

Chapter Highlights

- Estate planning is the process of planning for the accumulation, conservation, and distribution of an estate in a manner that most efficiently and effectively accomplishes a person's goals.

- An estate is defined as the rights, titles, or interests that a person, living or deceased, has in any property.

- Estate planning is essential for people who want to care for and provide financial support for spouses, domestic partners, minor children, parents, or other relatives or dependents during their lifetime and after their death.

- Advance planning is needed to protect an individual and his property in the event of incapacity or untimely death.

- Estate planning can minimize gift and estate taxes, protect assets, transfer a business or other property interests to others in a proper manner, accomplish charitable objectives, and plan for the final distribution of a person's estate.

- Six steps are involved in the financial planning and estate planning process, and they are aligned with the CFP Board's *Financial Planning Practice Standards.*

- The financial planning practitioner must avoid the unauthorized practice of law and must work with the client's estate planning attorney at the earliest opportunity.

- The financial planner can help the client determine estate planning goals and priorities and spot weaknesses in a current estate plan. The financial planner can help assemble a team of professionals to make estate planning recommendations and identify specific circumstances that might adversely affect those recommendations. Other members of a client's team might include an accountant, an investment manager, an insurance agent, and, of course, an attorney.

- The planner should take action to implement any recommendations that he has agreed to, and he should monitor the implementation of the plan.

- The types of fiduciaries involved in estate planning include executors, trustees, guardians, and agents who are holders of powers of attorney.

Key Terms

corporate trustee	grantor
domicile	principal
estate	state laws of intestacy
executor	trust
fiduciary	trustee

Review Questions

1-1. Which of the following statements correctly describes what estate planning can accomplish?

A. Estate planning can provide financial support and security for spouses, partners, children, and other dependents.

B. Estate planning is needed only for individuals with estates that exceed $5,430,000.

C. Estate planning ensures that the courts will select proper guardians and conservators to manage an incapacitated person's affairs.

1-2. Which of the following situations does not constitute the unauthorized practice of law?

A. When a nonlawyer is both a specialist and an acknowledged expert in the field.

B. When legal rules are applied to specific client situations.

C. When a statute or legal interpretation has become so well known and settled that no further legal issue is involved.

D. When the resolution of controversial or uncertain questions of law is required in an actual case.

1-3. Which of the following statements does not correctly describe the financial planner's role in the estate planning process?

A. The practitioner and the client mutually define a client's personal and financial goals, needs, and priorities that are relevant to the scope of the engagement.

B. The planner must assess a client's current and projected future financial situation to determine the likelihood of meeting his financial planning and estate planning goals.

C. The financial planner must analyze a client's current estate plan and make recommendations to correct any known deficiencies.

D.   The financial planner can assemble a team of experts to work with the client, the planner, and the client's attorney to develop alternative estate planning solutions that reflect the client's wishes.

1-4. Which persons or institutions have a fiduciary responsibility to the client?

A.   A CERTIFIED FINANCIAL PLANNER™ professional.

B.   A bank trustee.

C.   An agent with a durable power of attorney.

D.   An executor.

1-5. The financial planner can assume all of the following responsibilities in an estate planning engagement, except:

A.   Gather the client's personal, financial, and tax information.

B.   Act as captain of the financial planning team.

C.   Calculate the value of the client's assets and liabilities to determine whether the estate has a current or projected federal estate tax liability.

D.   Assist in implementing the estate planning recommendations.

1-6. Which of the following statements correctly pertains to a trustee?

A.   The trustee manages trust assets according to directives in the trust document.

B.   An institutional trustee in conjunction with a co-trustee who is a family member can make distributions of trust assets to a beneficiary.

C.   The trustee must collect a decedent's assets at death to pay debts, taxes, and expenses attributable to the decedent's estate.

D.   A trustee typically specializes in estate administration.

Notes

1.   www.cfp.net/learn/rulesofconduct.asp#4.

2.   www.cfp.net/learn/rulesofconduct.asp#4.

3.   Go to www.cfp.net/Downloads/FAQ_(FP_Board's_Revised_Standards.pdf.

Chapter 2

Property Interests

CFP® BOARD CERTIFICATION EXAMINATION TOPIC COVERED IN THIS CHAPTER:

Characteristics and Consequences of Property Titling

- Sole ownership
- Tenancy in common
- Joint tenancy with right of survivorship (JTWROS)

- Tenancy by the entirety
- Trust beneficiaries: Income and remainder

Learning Objectives

To ensure that you have a solid understanding of the various forms of property ownership and how titling affects transfer taxes and probate, the following learning objectives are addressed in this chapter:

- Compare and contrast the most common forms of property ownership and how they affect the gross estate, the probate estate, marital deductions, and step-up in basis.

- Recommend the appropriate property titling mechanism given the client's lifetime and estate distribution objectives and tax situation.

- Understand the implications of how property ownership affects the manner in which assets will be distributed at a decedent's death.

- Explain how the contribution rule applies to property titled JTWROS.

Chapter Contents

OVERVIEW

Asset ownership is one of the most important—and often, one of the most overlooked—aspects of an estate plan. A client may have the most intricate estate plan; however, if asset ownership has not been coordinated with the plan, then estate planning objectives will not be met. To plan an estate, it is necessary for a financial planner to understand the ways in which property is owned and how it is transferred. The way in which property can be transferred depends on the form of ownership, and there may be certain limitations on how a person can transfer property based on how the property is owned. A person must not only own property to make gifts during his lifetime or to dispose of an asset at death, but the form of ownership must also allow him to transfer his interest at death.

The financial planner must recognize the income tax, gift tax, and estate tax implications of property ownership to recommend the most appropriate titling to meet his clients' objectives.

Practice Standard 300-1

Analyzing and Evaluating the Client's Information

A financial planning practitioner shall analyze the information to gain an understanding of the client's financial situation and then evaluate to what extent the client's goals, needs, and priorities can be met by the client's resources and current course of action.

SOLE OWNERSHIP

Sole ownership is the simplest form of ownership. The owner has complete lifetime and testamentary control of property that he owns; it is outright ownership of the asset. When someone owns an asset in his own name, he owns the property in **fee simple** or **fee simple absolute**. This is the most comprehensive form of ownership, and there are no restrictions on how the property holder can use the asset while he is alive. This includes the owner's ability to make gifts of the assets to others or to charity. For example, if you own a bank account, you can withdraw assets from the account and the money is yours to spend as you wish or to give away to others. Solely owned assets are subject to creditor claims unless they are transferred into creditor protection trusts.

Just as an individual can do whatever he wants with the assets that he owns during his lifetime, he can leave the asset to whomever he wishes at death. The owner of an asset has testamentary disposition of assets at death. The asset will pass per the terms of his will; if he does not have a will, it will be transferred per his state's laws of intestacy, and therefore the property will be subject to probate.

Income Tax Considerations

When an individual owns an asset, all income from that asset is attributed to him and reported on his federal income tax return. The income is taxed according to the individual's marginal tax bracket.

Estate Tax Considerations

The full fair market value of an asset is included in an owner's gross estate at death and subject to probate.

Practitioner Tip: Solely owned property located in a state that is not the owner's state of **domicile** is subject to ancillary probate at the owner's death. Out-of-state property may be owned by trusts to avoid ancillary probate.

Client Situation

Andrea has a bank account and a mutual fund account. She can spend money from these accounts as she wishes. She can also give these assets to whomever she wants, or to whichever charities she chooses. Each year, Andrea must report the income generated from her bank account and the capital gains from her mutual fund account on her income tax return. At Andrea's death, the value of her bank account and her mutual fund account will be included in her gross estate. The assets will pass per the terms of Andrea's will, if she has one, or they will pass per the terms of her state's laws of intestacy if she does not have a will.

TENANCY IN COMMON

Tenancy in common is a form of co-ownership of property. Tenants in common own an undivided right to possess property. Each tenant owns a separate, fractional interest in the same property. When individuals own an asset together as tenants in common, that ownership can be either equal or unequal.

Client Situation

Sid, Ben, and Jacob are brothers who own 40-foot fishing boat together as tenants in common. Sid paid 50% of the purchase price, and Ben and Jacob paid 25% each. The brothers have unequal ownership of the fishing boat. If the brothers had contributed equally when they bought the boat, then they would have equal ownership.

As with individual ownership, each tenant can use and has full control of his fractional interest both during his lifetime and at his death. Each tenant is generally .o transfer his interest in the property as a lifetime gift or as a bequest at death homever he chooses. There is no obligation to transfer the property to the other ants in common. When property is held as tenants in common, there is some loss of control over the asset. For example, it may be more difficult to sell, transfer, or mortgage a **fractional share** of property.

Income Tax Considerations

Income is received and taxed based on each individual's fractional share of ownership. If ownership is not split equally but income is split equally, a gift is made to the tenant(s) receiving more than his (or their) fractional share of interest.

Client Situation

Sid, Ben, and Jacob occasionally rent their fishing boat to a captain who takes his friends deep-sea fishing. The income the brothers receive from these excursions is not split equally among them, because they have unequal ownership of the boat. However, if Sid were to split the income equally with his brothers, he would be making a gift of the extra income to Ben and Jacob.

Gift Tax Considerations

If an individual owns property in sole title and converts that ownership to tenancy in common, then the value of the property transferred to the other property holder(s) is a gift.

An individual can also make gifts of his fractional interest in property that he owns as tenants in common during his lifetime. Transfers are subject to gift tax rules.

Client Situation

Sid gifted his interest in the boat to his son David; this was subject to gift taxes. Now the new owners of the boat are David (50%), Ben (25%), and Jacob (25%).

Estate Tax Considerations

At death, the fair market value of the decedent's fractional interest in property held as tenants in common will be included in his estate. The fractional share will receive a step-up in basis at the owner's death. As with individual ownership, the decedent's interest in an asset is subject to probate and will pass per the terms of the owner's will or according to his state's laws of intestacy.

Client Situation

John and his brother Jeff own an apartment building as tenants in common. The value of the building is $200,000. John and Jeff each own a 50% interest. As rental income is received, John and Jeff split it equally. Each must report his proportionate share on his income tax return.

John wishes to make a gift of one-half of his interest in this property to his son, Sam. When John transfers one-half of his interest to Sam, he has made a gift of $50,000 (one-half of John's interest in the property). John, Sam, and Jeff are now tenants in common, and their respective ownership interests are 25%, 25%, and 50%. As rental income is received, it is to be split proportionally.

At John's death, his interest in the rental property will pass per the terms of his will. His will indicates that all property is to be split equally between his daughter Jennie and his son Sam. Following John's death, Jennie will own 12.5% of the building, Sam will own 37.5% of the building, and Jeff will continue to own 50% of the building, as tenants in common.

JOINT TENANCY WITH RIGHT OF SURVIVORSHIP

Another form of co-ownership of property is a **joint tenancy with right of survivorship. Joint tenants** have an undivided right to the enjoyment of property. Unlike a tenancy in common, joint tenants own a property equally, even if there are more than two joint owners. Joint ownership is a very common form of ownership; however, certain considerations should not be overlooked both during the property holders' lifetimes and at the time of their deaths.

Considerations during Lifetime

While a joint tenant is alive, he can generally sever (or divide) the joint tenancy or transfer his interest to another person without the consent of the other joint owners. This will form a tenancy in common between the remaining property owners. If the proportional interests remain the same, there will be no gift tax consequence. Although a joint owner has the ability to dissolve the joint tenancy or to sell his interest in the property, he will need the other joint tenants' consent to sell the property or to take a loan against it.

A further consideration with regard to joint tenancies is that one tenant's undivided interest can be reached by creditors. If property is held in joint tenancy, and one owner gets sued, liability will attach to the property. The joint owner's interest will be attached as well. If the jointly held asset is a bank account or securities, only the tenant who was sued will be affected.

Client Situation

Steve is a physician. He and his wife Jane own their home jointly with right of survivorship. If Steve wishes to take a mortgage out on the house to buy office space for his medical practice, he will need Jane's consent to take the loan. If Steve is sued by a patient and the judgment exceeds the limits of his malpractice policies, the creditor can place a lien on Steve and Jane's home to satisfy Steve's debt.

Considerations at Death

Unlike a tenancy in common, when a joint tenant dies, that person's interest in the property passes by operation of law rather than by will or intestacy to the remaining joint tenant or joint tenants. Assets that are held jointly with right of survivorship do not pass according to the terms of an individual's estate plan and are not subject to probate. At the first joint owner's death, the asset automatically passes to the surviving owner(s), and the surviving owners(s) become(s) the sole owner(s) of the property. This can save administrative costs and the delays commonly associated with probate; however, it can sometimes interfere with a decedent's estate planning objectives.

Client Situation

Tom has a prized possession: the 1965 Mustang that he spent years rebuilding with his son Jack. Tom owns the Mustang jointly with his wife Kathy, with right of survivorship. Tom knows how much he and Jack enjoyed rebuilding the car together and wants Jack to have the car when he dies. Tom's will leaves the Mustang to Jack; however, because Tom owned the car with Kathy, at Tom's death Kathy will become the owner. The Mustang will pass by operation of law to Kathy and not to Jack, as Tom's will stipulated.

Another consideration with jointly held property is that the asset that passes to the joint property holder will not be available to pay for any estate taxes, debts, or expenses of the estate. This can create a liquidity issue for the decedent's estate once the asset is owned solely by the surviving joint property owner.

Income, gift, and estate tax considerations differ depending on whether the joint property holders are married or not married. Let's take a look at the differences that the relationship of joint property holders has on these different types of taxes.

JOINT TENANCY WITH RIGHT OF SURVIVORSHIP WITH SPOUSES

When an asset is held jointly with right of survivorship between spouses, it does not matter which spouse purchased the property, or whether both spouses contributed to purchasing the property. The property is presumed to be owned one-half by each spouse, regardless of who actually purchased it, for income, estate, and gift tax purposes. This is a major distinction from property that is owned jointly with right of survivorship between two or more nonspouses.

Client Situation

Arthur and Doris bought a cottage on a lake in 1960 for $20,000. Arthur paid $15,000 and Doris paid $5,000, and they titled the property jointly with right of survivorship. Each spouse owns 50% of the cottage for income, gift, and estate tax purposes, and each spouse will retain 50% of the purchase price as his original basis in the property.

Income Tax Considerations

If a couple files income tax returns as "married filing jointly," the entirety of the income will be included on the joint return. There will be no income splitting. If a couple files their tax returns as "married filing separately," one-half of the income will be included on each spouse's tax return.

Gift Tax Considerations

When one spouse owns property individually and changes the title to joint tenancy with right of survivorship, naming his spouse as co-owner, he has made a gift to his spouse. Because of the unlimited marital gift tax deduction, there is no gift tax liability, assuming his spouse is a U.S. citizen.

When joint property is used to make a gift to others, it is deemed that the gift was made one-half by each spouse.

Estate Tax Considerations

One-half of the value of property held jointly with right of survivorship will be included in the decedent spouse's estate. Because the asset will automatically pass to the surviving spouse, the estate will be able to claim a marital deduction for the value of the property that was included in the decedent's estate. If there is a mortgage on jointly held property, one-half of the mortgage will be included on the decedent's estate tax return as an expense of the estate. At death, only one-half of the decedent's property will receive a step-up in basis and the surviving spouse's original basis will not be stepped up to fair market value.

Client Situation

Jeff purchased a home for $200,000 with a mortgage of $100,000. Shortly after he purchased the home, Jeff and Michelle were married. Jeff changed the title on the house to joint tenancy with right of survivorship. Because they were married, the gift was eligible for the unlimited gift tax marital deduction, so there was no taxable gift. When Jeff died, the property was worth $400,000 and the mortgage was $50,000. The house automatically passed to Michelle. Jeff's interest in the house ($200,000) was included in his gross estate. Jeff's half of the mortgage ($25,000) was deducted as an expense from his gross estate, and the balance ($175,000) was allowed as a marital deduction. Michelle's basis in the property is now $300,000. (Michelle retains her basis of $100,000, and Jeff's interest in the home will receive a step-up in basis to the date-of-death value of $200,000.) If Michelle sells the house for $500,000 three years after Jeff's death, she will have a gain of $200,000, subject to the $250,000 capital gains exclusion.

> Michelle had stock certificates that were worth $120,000 with a basis of $100,000. She deposited these stocks into a jointly held brokerage account with Jeff after they got married. Michelle made a $60,000 gift to Jeff, but because they were married, the gift was eligible for the unlimited gift tax marital deduction. If Michelle predeceases Jeff when the stocks are worth $150,000 and Jeff sells the stocks, Jeff will realize a capital gain of $25,000. (Jeff's basis is $50,000 plus the stepped-up basis on Michelle's $75,000 interest in the stock.)

Practitioner Tip: When spouses own property together, jointly with right of survivorship, neither spouse has complete control over the asset because each owns only one-half of the property. If a spouse becomes mentally incapacitated, then his or her share of the property is not accessible to the other spouse and cannot be gifted or sold unless the competent spouse has a durable power of attorney or is named guardian or conservator by the probate court.

JOINT TENANCY WITH RIGHT OF SURVIVORSHIP WITH NONSPOUSES

All property that is owned jointly with right of survivorship is owned equally by all joint tenants regardless of whether the property is owned by spouses or nonspouses.

Income Tax Considerations

Income that is earned on jointly held property is deemed to have been earned equally among all joint tenants. This allows for income splitting. For example, if two people jointly own an account that produces $10,000 of income per year, each joint tenant will report $5,000 of taxable income. Or if both tenants sell an asset that has a basis of $20,000 for $100,000, each joint tenant will report a capital gain of $40,000. Neither joint tenant will bear the full responsibility of the income tax liability.

Gift Tax Considerations

If a property owner converts an individually titled asset to a joint asset, or if one joint tenant purchases property as joint tenants and pays for the entire value of the property, the purchaser has made a taxable gift equal to one-half of the value of the property minus the amount of the available annual exclusion. Once property is either transferred to a joint account or purchased in joint name, a gift has been made which cannot be rescinded without the consent of the joint property holder.

Further, if the original owner continues to pay all expenses associated with the property—for example, mortgage or maintenance expenses on a house—one-half of the ongoing payments is deemed a gift to the joint tenant each time a payment is made.

Finally, if joint tenants sell property, each is deemed to have received half of the proceeds of the sale. For example, if joint tenants sell property for $100,000, each should receive $50,000. If one of the joint tenants receives $70,000 and the other joint tenant receives $30,000, the joint tenant receiving $30,000 has made a gift of $20,000 to the other joint tenant.

Client Situation

Mary Ann and Rob had owned their home together for 55 years jointly with right of survivorship. When Rob died last year, Mary Ann became the new owner of the home. She added her daughter Christine to the deed and retitled the property jointly with right of survivorship. Mary Ann was unaware that she had made a gift to Christine of one-half of the home's fair market value when she changed the deed. Furthermore, Mary Ann paid to have the house painted this year, and she pays all of the landscaping bills. The home improvement and maintenance bills that Mary Ann pays are gifts to Christine for of one-half of the expenses, which may be subject to gift taxes.

Estate Tax Considerations

IRC § 2040 provides that the value of a decedent's gross estate shall include the entire value of property that the decedent held at the time of his death, with two exceptions.

- The joint property holder contributed to the purchase of the property.

- The decedent and the remaining joint property holder(s) received the property by inheritance or gift.

This means that the entire fair market value of the property will be included in the first decedent's estate unless it can be proved that the surviving owner contributed to the purchase of the asset. This is known as the *Contribution Rule*, which applies only to property owned jointly with right of survivorship with nonspouses.

The amount that will be included in a decedent's gross estate is determined by his proportional contribution to the purchase of a property. For example, if two persons purchased property for $100,000, but one party contributed only $20,000, then when that person dies, only one-fifth of the fair market value of the property will be included in his estate. The amount that is included in the decedent's estate will receive a step-up in basis. The surviving joint tenant will add this inherited basis to his original basis, resulting in a new basis for the property.

Practitioner Tip: When assets are titled jointly with right of survivorship between two people who are not spouses, it is important to track contributions to the property. Otherwise, the full value of the asset will be included in both the first decedent's estate and the second decedent's estate.

Client Situation

Cynthia and her sister, Sally, own a vacation home jointly with right of survivorship. They rent the home out for several months of the year and receive $20,000 of rental income. Cynthia and Sally each report $10,000 of rental income on their income tax returns each year.

Cynthia paid for the entire value of the house and took out a mortgage for $100,000. Cynthia pays the mortgage and Sally does not contribute. When Cynthia titled the house jointly with Sally, she made a taxable gift to Sally. Further, each time Cynthia makes a mortgage payment, she is making a gift to Sally. The full value of the gifts will be subject to gift tax, but Cynthia can use the annual exclusion to offset the value of the taxable gift.

At Cynthia's death, the house is worth $500,000 and will automatically pass to Sally. The house will not be subject to probate and will not be transferred according to the terms of Cynthia's will. The $500,000 value of the house will be included in Cynthia's estate; however, the outstanding mortgage will be an expense of the estate. Sally's new basis in the property will be $500,000.

If Cynthia and Sally had inherited the home from their mother and shared any expenses equally, the gift and estate tax consequences would be different. Cynthia and Sally would have equal ownership interests for estate tax purposes so that only $250,000 would be included in Cynthia's estate.

As noted, the value of the house is included in Cynthia's estate; however, because the asset passes automatically to Sally, the value of the house will not be available to Cynthia's estate to pay for expenses or taxes. When Sally dies, the full fair market value of the home will be included in her taxable estate because she is the sole owner.

Practitioner Tip: There are many benefits to owning an asset jointly with right of survivorship. Joint ownership is a simple way of ensuring that assets will automatically pass to the joint owner without the delay and expense associated with probate. Avoidance of probate may be an advantage, but there are also disadvantages. If assets automatically pass to the joint property holder, they are not available to fund trusts or to meet other estate planning objectives. Assets passing to a nonspousal beneficiary will be included in a decedent's gross estate, but because the asset passes automatically to the beneficiary, the decedent's estate will not have access to that asset to pay for any estate tax liability or debts of the estate—or even for the estate tax attributed to that asset. The client's overall estate plan should be examined, and the effect of assets titled jointly with right of survivorship should be carefully considered.

TENANCY BY THE ENTIRETY

Tenancy by the entirety is a form of joint tenancy that can be held only by husband and wife. While both spouses are alive and married to each other, one spouse cannot terminate a tenancy by the entirety without the consent of the other spouse. The advantage of this type of ownership is that the creditors of one spouse cannot attach the other spouse's interest in the property. This is in contrast to joint tenancy with right of survivorship, where a creditor of one owner can attach the debtor's interest in the property. Although a lien can be attached to property held as tenants by the entirety, a creditor cannot force liquidation of the property, and any claim against the property can be satisfied only when the property is sold.

Similar to property that is held jointly with right of survivorship, when one spouse dies, the property owned as tenants by the entirety will automatically pass to the surviving spouse. One-half of the value will be included in the decedent's gross estate, subject to a marital deduction in the decedent's estate, and the surviving spouse will receive a step-up in basis on one-half of the value of the property.

Client Situation

Chet and Bonnie titled their home as tenants by the entirety. When Bonnie died, the fair market value of their home was $800,000. Therefore, $400,000 was included in Bonnie's gross estate, but a marital deduction of $400,000 was available to offset Bonnie's estate tax liability. Chet received an inherited basis of $400,000 that he added to his original basis in the property, which was half of the acquisition cost. As the sole owner of the home, Chet will include the fair market value of the home in his gross and probate estates, unless he sells or gifts the property to others.

LIFE ESTATES AND REMAINDER INTERESTS

Sometimes outright ownership in property can be split into a life estate and a remainder interest. In this type of arrangement, ownership is divided on a time line basis, where one person owns the property for a period of time (the **life estate**), and another person owns the property after the first time period ends (the **remainder interest**). This is a split-interest transfer. A person with a life estate is generally free to use the real property or to receive income from the property or trust for life. The life tenant's rights end at his death and the property then passes to the remainder beneficiary, known as the **remainderman**.

Life estates can be gifted or bequeathed to another person. The primary beneficiary may use the property or receive distributions of income, but the beneficiary has no right to withdraw principal. The life tenant has no control over the property and cannot determine who the remainder beneficiary of the property will be. When the life tenant dies, the property will either pass to a designated beneficiary or will revert to the donor.

A life estate can also be created by a person who has sole ownership of real property and who wants to live in, use, or enjoy that property for the remainder of his life. A person can also create a life estate in a trust by transferring his own money into the trust and receive all of the trust income for life. In either situation, the creator of the life estate will select one or more remainder beneficiaries to receive the property at his death. The creator of a life estate has retained control in this form of property ownership; therefore, the value of the property will be included in his gross estate at death.

Practitioner Tip: The gift and estate tax implications are very different when a life estate has been given to someone as opposed to when it is intentionally created by a property owner or the grantor of a trust. Life estates will avoid probate if they are included in the life tenant's gross estate.

> **Client Situation**
>
> Mike owns a house. When Mike dies, he leaves the house to his sister Sarah so she can live in it for the rest of her life. Sarah has received a life estate from Mike. When Sarah dies, the property will pass to Mike's nephew Bob. Mike has given Bob a remainder interest in the house.

> **Client Situation**
>
> Bill transfers $200,000 into a trust today, and he will receive all of the trust income for the rest of his life. He names his son Alex as the remainder beneficiary of the trust. When Bill dies, Alex will receive the trust's income and principal and Alex can designate the beneficiary of this trust in his will. In this situation, Bill has created a life estate for himself in the trust.

The Life Tenant's Interest

The beneficiary of a life estate has certain rights and responsibilities. The life tenant cannot be forced out of the property or be required to give up his current interest in the property regardless of the misfortunes of the remainder beneficiary. A homestead may be declared in the life estate, preventing a forced sale by the life tenant's creditors. If the transfer was valid, the remainder interest is protected from a life tenant's creditors, because the life tenant's interest is limited. The life tenant's responsibilities include maintaining the property, paying property taxes, and maintaining proper insurance coverage. If the life tenant fails to meet these responsibilities, the remainder beneficiaries may have a cause of action against him.

The Remainder Beneficiary's Interest

Unlike the remainder beneficiary of a trust, the remainder beneficiary of a life estate has an immediate vested interest in the property. The remainderman can sell or give away his interest in the property without the consent of the life tenant; however, the buyer's interest in the property will have to wait until the death of the life tenant.

If the remainder beneficiary dies before the life tenant, he has the right to bequeath his remainder interest to his heirs, who will someday receive the principal. The value of this remainder interest is calculated under the same rules as annuities, remainders, and life estates and can be determined using valuation tables.

Income Tax Considerations

The life tenant is responsible for reporting any income from the asset on his tax return. The remainder beneficiary has a vested interest in the trust, but he is not the current income beneficiary; therefore, he does not report any income. When the remainder beneficiary actually receives the property (and any income generated from the property), he will then have to report the income on his tax return.

If the property is sold during the lifetime of the life tenant, a portion of the gain will be taxed to the life tenant and a portion will be taxed to the remainderman. In the case of real property, if the life tenant has lived in the home for two of the previous five years, the gain will qualify for the $250,000 primary residence exclusion, but the remainderman's gain will not qualify.

Gift Tax Considerations

If a person gifts or bequeaths a life estate to another person, he is making a split-interest transfer of the present interest and the remainder interest. The gift of the current income interest and the gift of the remainder interest are both taxable gifts. The annual exclusion can be used to offset the value of the taxable gift for the income beneficiary; however, the annual exclusion will not be available to offset the gift of the remainder interest, because a remainder interest is a future interest in the trust.

Practitioner Tip: A person who creates a life estate for himself in real property or in a trust is making a future interest gift to the remainderman of the present value of the property's remainder interest. The gift tax value would be calculated actuarially using valuation tables.

Estate Tax Considerations

If someone creates a life estate for himself from solely owned real property or trust income, he has retained a right to live in the property until death, or he has the right to receive all income from the trust for life. As such, under IRC § 2036, the fair market value of the property or trust will be included in his gross estate at death because he retained too much control over the property. If the donor or grantor filed a gift tax return, then the value of the taxable gift will not be included as an adjusted taxable gift on the estate tax return. The remainderman will receive a full step-up in basis of the property at the life tenant's death.

If someone receives a life estate in real property or trust income, he does not have any control over the disposition of the asset at his death, because the person who gave him the life tenancy has decided who will receive the remainder interest in the property. Therefore, the value of the life estate would not be included in the life tenant's gross estate at death.

Practitioner Tip: Be aware that there are some circumstances that would cause the property to be included in the life tenant's estate. One example is when a life tenant is given a general power of appointment over the trust property, and another is when the decedent spouse's executor qualifies the property for a marital deduction in the decedent's estate.

Client Situation

Sam has a vacation home that he and his family have enjoyed for many years. He wants to make sure that his family continues to enjoy it. Sam gives his brother Mike a life estate and his sister Cara a remainder interest in the home. At the time Sam transfers the house, he has made two gifts: a life estate to Mike and a remainder interest to Cara. Sam can use his available annual exclusion to offset the taxable gift to Mike, but because Cara's interest is not a present-interest gift, he cannot use his available annual exclusion for Cara. At the time the gift is made, Cara has a vested interest in the house when Mike dies. Cara may sell that interest, but the buyer will not take possession of the house until after Mike dies. Mike is responsible for keeping up the home. He must pay real estate taxes and maintain insurance on the house. If he does not, Cara can sue him. Because Sam has retained no interest in the property it will not be included in his estate when he dies.

If Sam had retained a life estate for himself, giving the remainder interest to his brother Mike, the value of the house would be included in Sam's gross estate.

ESTATE FOR A TERM OF YEARS

An *estate for a term of years* functions very much as a life estate does; however, instead of the current beneficiary having an interest in the property for his lifetime, the interest is limited to a term of years. A term of years can be for any number of years that is less than a lifetime interest. Similar to a life estate, the current beneficiary's interest is limited and he cannot determine the remainder beneficiary of the property. If a current beneficiary dies before the term is up, he can appoint by will another tenant to use the property or to receive the income until the term ends.

Client Situation

In the preceding example with Sam, if Sam had given Mike the right to enjoy the property for five years, with the property passing to Cara at the end of the five-year term, it would have been an estate for a term of years. The gift tax consequence to Sam is that he made a gift to Mike of the present value of the five-year income interest. This gift is a present interest and Sam can offset the gift tax with an annual exclusion. Mike's responsibility to maintain the house and pay for taxes and insurance remains the same. Cara's right to the property will vest in five years rather than when Mike dies.

Chapter Highlights

PROPERTY TRANSFERS AT DEATH

Property	How Passed?	Probate	Gross Estate	Marital Deduction	Heirs New Basis
Solely owned	Will/intestacy	100%	100% FMV	If passed to spouse	FMV at death
Jointly (w/ spouse)	By operation of law	No	50%	50%	50% FMV at death + basis
Tenants by the entirety	By operation of law	No	50%	50%	50% FMV at death + basis
Jointly (w/a nonspouse)	By operation of law	No	100% (with no proof that other joint tenant contributed)	No	% of FMV at death +basis
Tenants in common	Will/intestacy	Yes - % owned	% of FMV owned	If passed to spouse	% of FMV at death +basis
Community property	Will/intestacy	Yes— decedents' 50% interest	50%	If passed to spouse	FMV at death
Create a life estate	Automatically to remainder beneficiary	No	100% FMV	No (unless passed to spouse)	FMV to remainder beneficiary
Receive a life estate	Automatically to remainder beneficiary	No	No	No	FMV to remainder beneficiary
Life insurance policy – Decedent is owner and insured	By beneficiary designation	No	Death benefit	If spouse is beneficiary	Proceeds not subject to income tax
Life insurance policy – Decedent is owner and not insured	Will/intestacy	Yes	Replacement cost/ cash value/FMV	If spouse is new owner	Not taxed

- The manner in which property is owned determines how it can be gifted during life and how it will be taxed and transferred at death.

- Individually owned property can be gifted during life. At death, the full fair market value of his fractional interest will be included in the decedent's gross estate. It can be transferred by will, or if there is no will, by intestate succession.

- When someone owns property held as tenants in common, he can gift his interest in that property during his lifetime. The fair market value of his interest will be included in his estate and transferred by will or intestate succession.

- Assets that are held jointly with right of survivorship automatically pass to the surviving owner at the first owner's death. When the joint property owners are spouses, it is presumed that each party contributed equally to the property, so one-half of the value will be included in the first spouse's estate at death. Tenancy by the entirety is a form of ownership that can be held only between spouses.

- When joint property owners are not spouses, the amount that will be included in the first spouse's estate is his fractional interest based on the amount that he contributed to the property.

- A life estate and an estate for a term of years are split-property interests. In both arrangements there is a current (income) beneficiary and a remainder beneficiary. The property is not included in the current beneficiary's estate, unless he created the life estate for himself. The remainder beneficiary will receive the property either following the income beneficiary's death or after a set term of years.

Key Terms

domicile	remainder interest
fee simple or fee simple absolute	remainderman
fractional share	sole ownership
joint tenancy with right of survivorship	tenancy by the entirety
joint tenants	tenancy in common
life estate	

Review Questions

2-1: Jane bought a condo for $150,000 for her son Keith to live in while he attends graduate school. She titled the property jointly with right of survivorship and has paid for all of the home maintenance expenses and property taxes. Assume that Jane dies today when the condo is valued at $160,000. Which of the following statements is/are correct?

A. One-half of the condo ($80,000) is included in Jane's gross estate.

B. The value of the gift that Jane made to Keith when she put his name on the deed is the fair market value of the property at the date of the gift.

C. Keith receives a complete step-up in basis in the property, and if he sells the condo today, he will not need to report any capital gains.

D. Based on the contribution rule, all of the home maintenance expenses and property taxes that Jane paid will be included in her gross estate.

2-2: Alan and Jill bought their father's home six years ago to help him out financially. The fair market value of the home was appraised at $300,000, and they titled the property jointly with right of survivorship. Alan paid $180,000 for 60% of the home and Jill paid the remaining $120,000. Jill died unexpectedly this year, and the house was appraised at $360,000. Which of the following statements is *in*correct?

A. Alan made a gift to Jill of 10% of the purchase price of the home, because each joint tenant must own one-half of the property in equal shares.

B. Jill's gross estate will include $144,000 based on her contribution to the purchase price of the home.

C. Alan will inherit Jill's stepped-up basis in the property, for a new basis of $324,000 in the home.

D. The value of the home included in Jill's estate will not go through probate.

2-3: Kim and Sal married in 1974. Sal worked throughout their marriage, and Kim stayed home and raised their children. When Sal died in 2011, Sal and Kim had a house worth $450,000 that was titled jointly with right of survivorship and a joint investment account worth $725,000. Which of the following statements is/are correct?

A. Because Sal contributed all monies to purchase the house and to fund the investment account, the entire value of those assets will be included in his estate.

B. Because Sal and Kim are married, only one-half of the value of the house and the investment account will be included in his estate.

C. Sal can bequest his half of the house to his daughter Marie.

D. Sal will have to leave these assets to Kim in his will if he wants her to keep them.

2-4. Jack and Jane are married. At the time of his death, Jack holds the following assets:

Residence (JTWROS with Jane)	$1,000,000
Common stock (Jack)	$900,000
Municipal bonds (Jack)	$300,000
Investment real estate (Jack's revocable trust)	$500,000
Life insurance (owned by Jack, Jane is beneficiary)	$1,000,000
Mutual funds (Jane)	$400,000
IRA (Jane is beneficiary)	$550,000

What is the amount of Jack's gross estate if he dies?

A. $4,250,000

B. $3,750,000

C. $2,750,000

D. $2,200,000

2-5: All of the following statements regarding property held as tenants by the entirety are correct except:

A. Neither party can unilaterally transfer his interest.

B. Each party holds an undivided interest in the whole property.

C. The property passes automatically to the survivor at the time of the first death.

D. Either two spouses or a parent and child may hold property as tenants by the entirety.

Chapter 3

Community Property

CFP® CERTIFICATION EXAMINATION PRINCIPAL TOPIC COVERED IN THIS CHAPTER:

Characteristics and Consequences of Property Titling

- Community property vs. non-community property

Learning Objectives

To ensure that you have a solid understanding of community property interests and the implications of an asset being treated as community property, the following learning objectives are addressed in this chapter:

- Describe how community property affects property ownership, the manner in which assets will be distributed at a decedent's death, and the inclusion of an asset in the decedent's estate.

- Identify the types of property that are community property interests and those that are not.

- Understand the implications of moving from a community property state to a non-community property state and vice versa.

Chapter Contents

OVERVIEW

Community property laws generally provide that all property acquired by a married person during a marriage is communal in nature. Excluded from this are assets owned prior to marriage or acquired by gift, bequest, devise, or descent. States that recognize community property laws include Alaska, Arizona, California, Idaho, Louisiana, Nevada, New Mexico, Texas, Washington, and Wisconsin. Some of these states are pure community property states, and others are **quasi-community property** states. In Alaska, spouses can elect community property as a form of property ownership, but in the other states listed it is the default form of ownership.[1] It is important for financial planners to identify community property interests and understand the implications of this form of property ownership. Even if the planner is not practicing in a community property state, once an asset is classified as community property, it remains that way, even when the client relocates to a non-community property state.

Financial planners must understand the income, gift, and estate tax implications of the community property ownership of an asset.

Practice Standard 300-1

Analyzing and Evaluating the Client's Information

A financial planning practitioner shall analyze the information to gain an understanding of the client's financial situation and then evaluate to what extent the client's goals, needs, and priorities can be met by the client's resources and current course of action.

COMMUNITY PROPERTY INTERESTS

In **common-law states**, each spouse can retain individual property. The presumption is that the manner in which property is titled is the manner in which it is owned. In community property states, however, there is a presumption that assets acquired following marriage are **community assets** that belong one half to each spouse. In a community property state, a couple's earnings or one spouse's earnings are considered community property; therefore, each spouse owns a one-half interest in property acquired with such earnings during marriage. (In Alaska, on the other hand, property is not community property unless the couple agrees that property acquired during marriage is the community property of the spouses.)

Community property can include residences, stocks, bonds, bank accounts, personal property, and life insurance policies if these assets were purchased with money earned after the marriage. It does not matter whether the assets are titled in individual name or in joint name: if the asset is purchased in a community property state with community income, it will be deemed a community property asset.

In many ways, community property functions as a tenancy in common in that each party has an undivided interest in his share of an asset. The difference is that all income and assets acquired with that income is deemed one-half owned by each spouse, regardless of who earned the income or contributed to the property.

NON-COMMUNITY PROPERTY INTERESTS

Certain property is not considered community property even if a couple lives in a community property state. The following assets are considered to be separate property:

- Property acquired by one spouse by gift or inheritance

- Property acquired before marriage, unless it is **commingled** with community **property**

- Property acquired by one spouse after marriage with the proceeds of a **separate asset**

- Property acquired by court order, including recovery for personal injuries

---

Client Situation

Matt and Jen live in California. Before marrying, Matt owned a home. After they got married, he sold his home and used the proceeds to purchase a larger home for Jen and him to live in. The new home will remain separate property. Jen's great-uncle Chris died and left her $100,000. This inheritance is Jen's separate property.

Spouses are generally free to make agreements regarding community property. For example, the spouses can agree that what would otherwise be community property is not community property. Generally, such agreements must be in writing.

Practitioner Tip: A prenuptial or marital agreement can be effective in most states to overcome presumptions of community property. In view of the increasing frequency of divorce and remarriage, the use of prenuptial and marital agreements is encouraged by most estate planners.

TAX CONSIDERATIONS

Income Tax Considerations

Income earned by spouses in a community property state is considered to be earned one-half by each spouse. Similarly, income produced by any community asset is deemed to be earned one-half by each spouse.

For the most part, income earned on a separate asset remains income attributable to the spouse who owns that asset. Four states, however, recognize income derived from separate property as community income: Idaho, Louisiana, Texas, and Wisconsin.

> **Client Situation:**
>
> Matt is a salesman who earns a high income. The money he earns after marrying Jen is community property and is considered one-half Matt's and one-half Jen's. Income that Jen earns on the investment portfolio that she started with her $100,000 inheritance is Jen's separate income.

Gift Tax Considerations

Each spouse is generally free to transfer his one-half interest in the property at death as he wishes. However, while both spouses are alive and married to each other, one spouse cannot dispose of the community property without the consent of the other spouse. When a gift is made to a third party from a community property asset, the gift is deemed to have been made one half by each spouse, even when only one spouse made the gift. In situations where both spouses consent to making the gift, this is often the intention. If, on the other hand, one spouse gifts his entire interest in a community property asset to a third party and his spouse does not consent, then the donor spouse may be liable to his spouse for one-half of the value of the gift.

Some states allow one spouse to make a "reasonable" gift of community assets to a third party without the other spouse's consent. What is considered a reasonable gift is determined by state law. In Wisconsin, for example, a spouse is allowed to make a gift of community property of $1,000, "or a larger amount if, when made, the gift is reasonable in amount considering the economic position of the spouses." If one spouse makes a gift that is unreasonable, the other spouse has a claim against him.

Likewise, in a separate property state, the owner of separate or individual property in a community property state can make gifts of or sell that property without his spouse's consent. The owner of separate property in a community property state also has complete testamentary control.

> **Client Situation**
>
> Matt deposits his earnings in his bank account, which is titled in his name. He makes a gift of $10,000 to his son Max. Jen and Matt are presumed to have made one-half of the gift (or $5,000) each. Matt is required to get Jen's permission to make this gift, or Jen may have a claim against him. Jen can, however, make a gift from the account funded with her inheritance to whomever she wishes, without obtaining Matt's consent.

Estate Tax Considerations

There is a major distinction between community property states and common law states regarding the inclusion of assets for estate tax purposes and for the purpose of making bequests. Although community assets can be titled in a manner similar to other assets—individually, as tenants in common, or even jointly—one-half of the value of all community assets is includible in the deceased spouse's estate, regardless of titling. Community property is includable in the estate of a decedent to the extent that it represents the decedent's one-half interest in community property.

Client Situation

Carl and Joyce grew up in Arizona and lived there throughout their 32-year marriage. All of their property was acquired after marriage and titled in Carl's name. When Carl died last year, the value of his assets totaled $3 million, but only $1.5 million was included in his gross estate. If Carl and Joyce had lived in a common-law state, then $3 million would have been included in Carl's gross estate as an individual owner of the marital property.

One of the main differences in estate planning with community property is that when a community property asset is bequeathed to a surviving spouse, the entire asset—both the decedent's and the surviving spouse's interests—gets a step-up in basis to the date-of-death value of the asset.

Client Situation

Dave and Dorothy bought their home in Nevada for $160,000 two years after they were married. Dave worked full time and the couple was able to purchase the home from Dave's earnings. Dorothy worked as an unpaid volunteer at a women's shelter and did not contribute toward buying the home. Dave died suddenly last year and his will bequeathed all of his property to Dorothy. The home was valued at $280,000; therefore, $140,000 was included in Dave's gross estate. Dorothy inherited Dave's new basis of $140,000 and, although she did not contribute to buying the home, her basis was also stepped up to $140,000. Dorothy is now the sole owner of the home and will not have a capital gain if she sells the home for $280,000.

Community property assets pass similarly to assets in common law states. If the asset is jointly titled or has a beneficiary designation, it passes by operation of law or by beneficiary designation, respectively. If an asset is simply titled as community property or is titled in an individual's name, it passes by will. If there is no will, the decedent's half of the asset passes per state laws of intestate succession.

Similar to individually titled assets, each individual can bequeath his interest in community property to whomever he wishes. However, it is important to note that only the decedent's interest can be bequeathed. Assets that are bequeathed to a spouse may qualify for the estate tax marital deduction.

Client Situation

At the time of Matt's death, Matt and Jen had the following assets:

- Bank account in Matt's name: $100,000—funded with community earnings

- Home in Matt's name: $500,000—purchased with Matt's separate property

- Investment account in Jen's name: $300,000—funded with Jen's inheritance

- Mutual fund account in Jen's name: $500,000—funded with community earnings

- Joint investment account: $200,000—funded with community earnings

At Matt's death, only one-half of the bank account in his name will be included in his estate. He can bequeath only one-half of that account, because the other half belongs to Jen.

The full value of the home will be included in his estate and he can bequeath the full value of the home to whomever he wishes.

The investment account in Jen's name is not a community property asset and is not included in Matt's estate.

One-half of the mutual fund account in Jen's name will be included in Matt's estate. He may bequeath his one-half interest in Jen's investment account.

One-half of the joint investment account will be included in Matt's estate, but it will pass automatically to Jen by operation of law.

To the extent he does not dispose of his interest in the community assets by will or trust, it will pass per intestate succession.

If he bequeaths the assets to Jen, or if they pass to Jen by operation of law, the full value of the asset—not Matt's interest alone—will get a step-up in basis to the date-of-death value.

If Matt had established a Transfer on Death designation for his bank account, naming his sister, Susie, as the beneficiary, Jen would have a claim against both Susie and against Matt's estate.

MOVING BETWEEN COMMUNITY PROPERTY STATES AND NON-COMMUNITY PROPERTY STATES

Common-law states rely on the title of an asset to determine ownership. In community property states the titling of property does not determine ownership, but the character of the property—whether it is community property or separate property—determines ownership. When property is acquired in a community property state and the couple later moves to a non-community property state, the character of the property does not change. Once an asset is classified as community property, it will always be community property. When proceeds of a community asset are used to purchase an asset in a common-law state, the new asset is still considered community property.

Client Situation

If John and Megan move from California to New Jersey and use the proceeds of their community investment accounts to purchase a new home in New Jersey, the home would be considered community property. It does not matter if the house is titled in one of their individual names, titled jointly with right of survivorship, or titled as tenants in common; the home would still be considered community property.

Practitioner Tip: Spouses may choose to divide community property into separate property when they move from a community property state to a non-community property state; however, they should consider the tax consequences of doing so. It is not advisable to commingle community property assets with non-community property assets.

Likewise, when a couple moves from a non-community property state to a community property state, the character of the separate property does not change (except in the case of quasi-community property states, discussed below).

Client Situation

If John and Megan had started out in New Jersey, where the house was titled in John's name alone and was his separate property, when they moved to Texas and bought their new home using the proceeds of the New Jersey home in John's name alone, their home in Texas would remain John's asset, and Megan would have no claim to the house.

Practitioner Tip: Practitioners often suggest that a client consolidate accounts for ease of administration. However, because community property assets will receive a full step-up in basis for the entire asset, not the deceased spouse's interest alone, it may make sense to keep these assets segregated from non-community property assets. If a client commingles community property assets with non-community property assets, this step-up in basis may be lost.

Practice Standard 400-2

Developing the Financial Planning Recommendation(s)

The financial planning practitioner shall develop the recommendation(s) based on the selected alternative(s) and the current course of action in an effort to reasonably meet the client's goals, needs and priorities.

Practice Standard 400-3

Presenting the Financial Planning Recommendation(s)

The financial planning practitioner shall communicate the recommendation(s) in a manner and to an extent reasonably necessary to assist the client in making an informed decision.

QUASI-COMMUNITY PROPERTY

California, Idaho, Washington, and Wisconsin are quasi-community property states. Arizona is considered a quasi-community property state in the case of divorce. The major difference between a pure community property state and a quasi-community property state is that property acquired in a separate property state that would have been considered community property if it had been acquired in a community property state is treated as community property. Property that would not have been treated as community property when acquired will not be treated as community property.

Client Situation

In the preceding example where John and Megan owned a home in John's name in New Jersey, if they had moved to California instead of Texas, the home would be considered community property if community funds had been used to purchase it, even though it was titled and remains titled in John's name.

Client Situation

Tom and Sue lived in Ohio, a common-law state, and they bought their home soon after they were married. Years later Tom and Sue sold their home and moved to California, a quasi-community property state. The new home in California is considered community property. Why? Because the home in Ohio would have been community property had they originally acquired it in California, because it was purchased with marital assets.

Practitioner Tip: Assume that Tom had titled the home in Ohio in his name and that he also titled the new home in California in his name. The new home is still considered community property when the couple moves to California because the home in Ohio was originally acquired with marital assets. It does not matter how the home is titled.

> ### Client Situation
>
> Ryan and Denise were married and living in Michigan. Denise inherited money from her grandfather and bought a home in Detroit. Five years later, Ryan was offered a job in San Diego, so they sold the home and moved to California. The new home in California remains Denise's separate property. Why? Because the home in Michigan would have been separate property if Denise had originally acquired it in California. A gift or inheritance is the recipient's separate property in a community property state.

Practitioner Tip: Property from a common-law state becomes community property in a quasi-community property state if it was acquired after marriage—unless it was acquired as a gift or an inheritance. Always look back to see how the property was originally acquired!

COMMUNITY PROPERTY CONSIDERATIONS WITH LIFE INSURANCE

Where community property funds are used to purchase an insurance policy and there has been no agreement otherwise affecting the ownership of the policy, the policy is owned by the community and therefore belongs one-half to each spouse. In most cases, even though the insured may be shown on the policy as "Owner," the policy is considered the community property of both spouses in the absence of any evidence that there was an agreement between the spouses that it would be separate property.

Thus, if a policy on the husband is community property and the beneficiary is someone other than the wife, a transfer subject to both estate tax in the husband's estate and gift tax from the wife to the third party will occur when the insured dies, and the proceeds will be payable to that third person. The amount of the gift will be one-half of the proceeds, which represents the wife's one-half community interest in the policy.

Practitioner Tip: Financial planners should note the ownership and beneficiary designations of insurance policies so they can consider any gift tax problems that might exist.

> ### Client Situation
>
> While John and Megan live in California, John purchases a life insurance policy on his life, and names his son Danny the beneficiary. John pays the life insurance premiums with community assets. At John's death, the $100,000 death benefit is paid to Danny. Fifty-thousand dollars of the proceeds will be included in John's estate and will be subject to estate tax; $50,000 will be a taxable gift from Megan to Danny.

Chapter Highlights

- For a summary of the tax, probate, and estate tax implications of community property interests, see the chart - Property Transfers at Death at the end of Chapter 2.

- Community property is a unique form of ownership recognized by 10 states.

- One-half of all community assets are considered to be owned by each spouse.

- Once an asset is community property, it retains that character, even if a couple moves to a non-community property state.

- Assets acquired in common-law states remain separate assets when moving to a community property state.

- If a couple moves from a non-community property state to a quasi-community property state, assets that were acquired in the non-community property state may become community property.

- From an estate planning perspective, one-half of all community property assets are included in a decedent's estate, regardless of how they are titled.

- Because the full value of a community property asset that passes to a surviving spouse will receive a step-up in basis to the date-of-death value, planners should exercise caution when advising clients with respect to commingling assets.

Key Terms

common-law state   community property

commingled assets   quasi-community property

community asset   separate asset

Review Questions

3-1. All of the following are true with respect to community property except:

A. Only 10 states have this form of property ownership between spouses and nonspouses.

B. Community property retains its character even if the spouses move to a non-community property state.

C. At death, it is easy for spouses to transfer their interest in community property without the consent of the other spouse.

D. Assets acquired by a spouse prior to marriage are not community property assets.

3-2. Assume that Jake and Jane are married. They used to live in Florida, and now they live in Texas. Identify the community property interests.

A. Jake and Jane live in Texas and Jake inherits a summer house from his parents.

B. Jane purchases an automobile with monies from their joint checking account.

C. Jane owned a house before she and Jake married. She sold the house and invested the proceeds in mutual funds.

D. Before moving to Texas, Jake invests $50 from each check in a savings account titled in his name. He keeps these funds in a separate savings account when he and Jane move to Texas.

E. Jake and Jane move to California, and Jake keeps his separate savings account titled in his name alone.

3-3. Carol and Dick were married in New York, where they lived and acquired all of their property after marriage. The company Dick worked for relocated to California, and they moved there five years ago. The value of their property interests before moving to California was $1.6 million and they have subsequently acquired an additional $700,000 in property interests since moving to California. Dick and Carol have decided to divorce. For property settlement purposes, all of their assets are community property assets.

True or False?

3-4: Lester and Naomi lived in a common law state and titled their marital assets in Lester's name. Lester died shortly after moving to California; for estate purposes, the assets will be treated as belonging solely to Lester.

True or False?

3-5: Amy and Shawn have moved from Alaska (a community property state) to Florida (a common law state). Which of the following assets will retain community property character?

A. An account in Shawn's name that was funded with assets he inherited from his mother while he was living in Alaska.

B. A savings account in Amy's name that she funded with money from her paycheck each week.

C. An investment account that they opened up after they moved to Florida and funded with excess cash flow.

D. An investment account that Shawn had before he married Amy. It remained titled in his name alone.

Notes

1. AlaskaStat. § 34.77.010–34.77.995.
2. Wis. Stat. §§ 766.53 and 766.70.

Chapter 4

Methods of Property Transfer at Death

CFP® CERTIFICATION EXAMINATION PRINCIPAL TOPIC COVERED IN THIS CHAPTER:

Methods of Property Transfer at Death

- Transfers through the probate process
- Transfers by operation of law
- Transfers through trusts
- Transfers by contract

Learning Objectives

To ensure that you have a solid understanding of how property transfers at an owner's death, the following learning objectives are addressed in this chapter:

- Identify property interests that pass by probate.

- Explain the characteristics and consequences of using alternative methods of transferring property at death, including contracts, trusts, and property passing by operation of law.

- Select the most appropriate property transfer mechanism for a client's situation.

Chapter Contents

OVERVIEW

Understanding the manner in which property will pass at death is an integral part of understanding, analyzing, and organizing a client's estate plan. The income, gift, and estate tax implications of the various forms of property ownership are examined here. Following is a closer look at the manner in which various types of assets pass upon a property holder's death. This includes property that will pass by **probate, operation of law**, contract, and trust. (See Figure 4.1.)

Figure 4.1 Property Transfers at Death

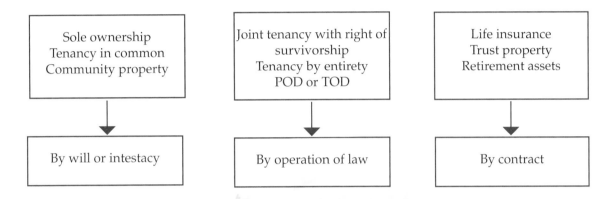

The manner in which property passes is a very important aspect of client planning. Although clients can establish an estate plan that disposes of their assets in the manner they wish, if the assets are passing by **beneficiary designation** or by contract, the plan may never be funded and the intended heirs may not inherit. Also, any tax planning intended might not be effective.

Financial planners should review a client's estate planning documents and coordinate asset titling to ensure that property passes as intended.

Practice Standard 300-1

Analyzing and Evaluating the Client's Information

A financial planning practitioner shall analyze the information to gain an understanding of the client's financial situation and then evaluate to what extent the client's goals, needs, and priorities can be met by the client's resources and current course of action.

Practice Standard 400-2

Developing the Financial Planning Recommendation(s)

The financial planning practitioner shall develop the recommendation(s) based on the selected alternative(s) and the current course of action in an effort to reasonably meet the client's goals, needs, and priorities.

ASSETS THAT PASS BY PROBATE

Probate is the court-supervised process of settling a decedent's estate. Certain assets owned at death pass through probate, and other property interests avoid the probate process. Financial planners must recognize which assets will be subject to probate when their clients die, because probate is an additional expense to the estate.

Property Transferred by Will

Any property transferred under a decedent's will is subject to probate. This includes all individually or solely owned property, a decedent's interest in property held as tenants in common, and a decedent's interest in community property.

A common estate planning strategy is to implement a **pour-over will** that directs any property that the decedent owned at the time of his death to pour-over into his **revocable trust**. Another common estate planning strategy is to establish a **testamentary trust** funded by assets that flow from a decedent's will at death. In both situations, the assets first pass under the decedent's will before they are transferred into the trusts; therefore, they are subject to probate. The terms of each trust, not the will, dictate how and when the assets will be distributed to the trust beneficiaries.

Typically, when we think about assets that a decedent owns, we think about bank and investment accounts, stock certificates, savings bonds, and personal property. Another asset that we may not often think about or plan for is life insurance that a decedent owns on another person's life. At the decedent's death, if no contingent owner was named, the life insurance policy will be subject to probate and will pass by will to the decedent's heirs.

Client Situation

Carmine has a will that indicates that any property he owns at the time of his death is to pour over into his revocable trust. Carmine has a bank account and an investment account titled in his name alone. Carmine also owns a life insurance policy on his wife, Marie. At his death, the bank account, investment account, and insurance policy on Marie's life will all pass under his will to his trust. The assets will be subject to probate.

Intestacy

If a person dies without a will, he is said to die **intestate**. Each state has enacted laws that provide for the disposition of a decedent's assets if he does not have a will. These laws are called *laws of intestacy*. Each state's laws are different. The persons who will inherit, and the amounts inherited, typically are based on a number of factors, including but not limited to whether the decedent was married at the time of his death, whether he had children, and whether there are more remote heirs such as parents or siblings.

Laws of intestacy rarely provide the intended disposition of assets. For example, if a decedent is survived by a spouse and minor children, the spouse may inherit only a fraction of the assets, and the minor children may inherit the remaining assets. Often clients in this situation would prefer that the surviving spouse have access to all of the assets, rather than only the portion designated by the court. Additionally, the courts may need to appoint a guardian or a conservator to manage or supervise a minor's assets, and this person might not be the surviving parent. Minors will receive equal shares of the decedent's property and take possession of the assets when they reach their state's age of majority.

Assets passing per intestacy are subject to probate. The probate court determines the takers under the estate.

Practitioner Tip: It is important to understand the laws of intestacy in your own jurisdiction so that you can explain them to your clients. Otherwise, the default estate plan that each state has put in place may not accomplish your clients' goals. It is important that clients have a current estate plan in place that complements their goals and is reviewed at least annually.

Assets Paid to the Estate

Normally life insurance and retirement assets are paid to the designated beneficiary, but if no beneficiary is named, or if the "Estate" is named as the beneficiary, the assets are subject to probate.

Client Situation

At the time of his death, Carmine had an IRA. He had not named a beneficiary, so the IRA was paid to his estate and was subject to probate.

Dower, Curtesy, and Homestead

Dower is a widow's right to a life estate in a portion of her husband's property. Curtesy is the equivalent right of a widower. Historically, the purpose of dower and curtesy was to protect the surviving spouse against disinheritance or from creditors' claims consuming assets in common law states. Community property states provide for the surviving spouse by giving each spouse a one-half interest in community assets; therefore, dower and curtesy typically are not applicable in community property states. Only six states still recognize dower and only four states still recognize curtesy. Several other states have grandfathered dower and curtesy for marriages or plans that were put in place before the statutes abolishing these statutory rights. Dower and curtesy rights are typically asserted during the probate process.

Instead of dower and curtesy, many states have enacted a **homestead** statute, which offers certain rights and protections to a surviving spouse. The amounts protected under the homestead allowance vary by state. Typically, homestead statutes protect the surviving spouse's residence. With respect to the homestead allowance, a surviving spouse is typically granted a life estate in the decedent's real property. The property is protected from the decedent's creditors' claims. Some states also provide for a **family allowance**, which provides the surviving spouse with money from the decedent's estate to pay for living expenses.

Elective Share

No state allows a spouse to disinherit his or her surviving spouse. All of the common law states have implemented some form of **elective share statute**. Community property provides for surviving spouses by treating property as one-half owned by each spouse. An elective share statute permits the surviving spouse to elect to receive an amount prescribed by state law. There is great variation regarding which property is eligible and how much a spouse can claim by asserting the elective share statute. Furthermore, a spouse who elects against her deceased spouse's may give up her rights to any property bequeathed to her.

Client Situation

Carmine and Marie transferred ownership of all assets to Carmine. In his later years, Carmine started to dislike Marie. On his death, he left all of his assets to his children. Marie was left with nothing. Marie can elect against Carmine's will, and she will be granted the amounts allowed under her state's elective share statute.

ASSETS THAT PASS BY OPERATION OF LAW

A number of different assets pass by operation of law. These assets bypass probate. Many of the rules regarding the transfer of assets by operation of law are governed by state law. We will discuss the general rules; however, the financial planner should learn the nuances of any particular state's law.

Jointly Held Assets and Tenancy by the Entirety

Assets held jointly with right of survivorship or as tenants by the entirety automatically pass to the surviving joint property owner. The decedent's interest in these assets will be included in his taxable estate at death; however, the assets will not be subject to probate. As a matter of law, these assets automatically flow to the joint property holder.

When a government savings bond is jointly owned, upon the death of the owner, the surviving owner becomes the sole owner as a matter of law. Alternatively, a sole owner can name a beneficiary of the savings bond, who will receive the bond upon his death.

Client Situation

Marie and Carmine own their house as tenants by the entirety, and they have a joint bank account. At Carmine's death, the house and the bank account will automatically pass to Marie by operation of law. Carmine's interest in these assets will be included in his gross estate at death, but they will not be subject to probate. Because Marie and Carmine were married, Carmine's interest is presumed to be one-half of the value of the property.

Carmine also owns a fishing boat jointly with his son Gene. The boat will automatically pass to Gene at Carmine's death. Unless Gene actually contributed to the purchase of the boat, the full value will be included in Carmine's estate.

Life Estates and Estates for a Term of Years

The remainder interest in a life estate or an estate for a term of years will also, as a matter of law, pass to the remainderman. Assuming that the holder of the present interest is not the original owner of the interest, the asset subject to the life estate or term of years will not be included in the life beneficiary's gross or probate estates. Upon the death of the life tenant, or upon the expiration of the term of years, the interest will automatically pass to the remainderman.

Client Situation

Carmine also owned a beach house. At death, he gave Marie a life estate in the beach house and bequeathed the remainder interest to their two sons, Gene and Frank. At Marie's death, the property will pass to Gene and Frank by operation of law. The beach house will not be subject to estate tax or probate in Marie's estate.

Totten Trust, POD, TOD

Totten trusts, payable-on-death (POD) accounts, and **transferable-on-death** (TOD) accounts are available in most states. All of these provide for the automatic transfer of certain types of property at death to a named beneficiary, while avoiding probate.

For a Totten trust, a person can deposit money into a bank account in his own name as trustee for another person. Generally, such a transfer is revocable until such person provides otherwise (e.g., gives a passbook to the donee) or dies. If the person dies without having revoked the Totten trust provision, the donee receives the bank account.

A POD account is quite similar. A person deposits money into a bank account in his own name and designates that the account is payable at his death to a named person. The transfer to the account is generally revocable. If the person dies without having revoked the POD provision, the donee receives the bank account.

A TOD account is similar to a POD account, except that TOD provisions are used for stocks, mutual funds, and other accounts that hold securities.

POD and TOD designations function for nonqualified accounts, very much like beneficiary designations on qualified accounts. Not all states allow POD and TOD designations, and some have restrictions on the way in which they can be used.

Practitioner Tip: Although a Totten trust is called a trust, it is not a trust at all. It is simply a bank account whereby the account holder holds the account for the benefit of another. The use of the term trust in this type of account can sometimes be misleading.

TRANSFERS THROUGH TRUSTS

All property owned by a trust will be transferred to the trust beneficiaries per the terms of the trust. When a client creates a trust and transfers assets to it, the trust spells out who receives the corpus (trust property) and when they will receive it. Each state has rules regarding the formality with which a trust must be executed.

One of the most common estate planning strategies consists of establishing a pour-over will and a revocable trust. This not only ensures that a client's assets pass to the intended beneficiaries and that efficient tax strategies are implemented, but it also provides a means of avoiding probate. For this strategy to be effective, the client must coordinate asset ownership with his revocable trust. For example, a client can transfer ownership of individually owned assets to his revocable trust, or he can name his trust as beneficiary by POD or TOD. If the client keeps assets titled in his individual name, although the pour-over provisions of the will ensure that the assets eventually get to the trust, the assets will be subject to probate, which can cause unnecessary delay and expense.

Practitioner Tip: One of the most often overlooked aspects of a client's estate plan is the coordination of asset ownership with the actual estate plan.

Client Situation

Following Carmine's death, Marie implemented her own estate plan. Marie executed a pour-over will and a revocable trust. Marie changed the title of her bank and investment accounts to the trust, but she forgot to change the title of her home. The bank and investment accounts will not be subject to probate and will automatically pass per the terms of her revocable trust. The home, however, will pass through Marie's will and be subject to probate before it passes to her trust.

TRANSFERS BY CONTRACT

Assets That Pass by Beneficiary Designation

A number of assets are transferred by contract. Assets that are transferred by contract avoid probate if they are payable to a named beneficiary. The most common examples of this include life insurance; IRAs, 401(k), 403(b), and other retirement or pension plans. Annuities that have joint annuitants are payable to the joint annuitant by the terms of the annuity agreement.

Practitioner Tip: It is important to review a client's beneficiary designations and to ensure that they meet a client's planning objectives. Often, clients forget to name a beneficiary for their retirement accounts, or they might forget to update beneficiary designations after a marriage, divorce, or the birth of children. Imagine having to tell a client's second spouse that his first wife was named as the beneficiary of an IRA!

> **Client Situation**
>
> Carmine had a 401(k) from his employer. He named Marie as the primary beneficiary of his 401(k) and Gene and Frank as the contingent beneficiaries. Marie will receive the 401(k) at Carmine's death. Carmine also has an older whole-life insurance policy. He named his parents as the beneficiaries of the policy. Both of his parents have died, and no contingent beneficiary was named. The death benefit will be included in his gross estate and will pass through probate. The policy will be distributed as part of Carmine's estate according to his state's law of intestacy, but the portion that passes to Marie will receive a marital deduction in Carmine's estate.

Prenuptial and Postnuptial Agreements

Prenuptial and postnuptial agreements are a type of contract that spells out the parties' rights to property. A **prenuptial agreement**, also known as an antenuptial agreement, is an agreement entered into before marriage. A **postnuptial agreement** is an agreement entered into after marriage. Pre- and postnuptial agreements can dictate the amounts that a surviving spouse will receive after the decedent spouse's death. Because of the increasing frequency of divorce, these are very common contracts—especially in the case of a second marriage.

> **Client Situation**
>
> After Carmine's death, Marie falls in love with a much younger man. She wants to make sure that her children, Gene and Frank, still inherit all assets, and that her soon-to-be new husband does not inherit any of the wealth that she built with Carmine. Marie asks her fiancé to sign a prenuptial agreement, stating that he forfeits all rights under her estate. At her death, her second husband will have no claim to her estate.

Buy/Sell Agreements

Business owners frequently enter into buy/sell agreements that lay out the disposition of a business owner's interest upon his death. Buy/sell agreements allow for surviving business owners to purchase the deceased business owner's interest, or for the company to purchase the deceased business owner's interest. Such agreements are will substitutes that keep the deceased business owner's stock or partnership interests from passing through probate.

Deeds of Title

Deeds of title are contracts that dispose of real property at a property owner's death. Typically, the property owner or donor will deliver the deed to an escrow agent, who will then deliver the deed of title to the donee or beneficiary at the donor's death. The deed must deliver present title to the escrow agent at the time of delivery. Title must pass during the grantor's lifetime (so that the grantor no longer owns the real property at the time of his death) for the asset to avoid probate.

Chapter Highlights

- For a summary of the methods of property transfer, see the chart - Property Transfers at Death at the end of Chapter 2.

- It is very important for the estate planner to understand the manner in which a client's assets will pass at death. This determines whether the asset is subject to probate and whom the asset will pass to.

Key Terms

beneficiary designation	payable on death (POD)
curtesy	postnuptial agreement
dower	pour-over will
elective share statute	prenuptial agreement
family allowance	probate
homestead	revocable trust
intestate	testamentary trust
laws of intestacy	Totten trust
operation of law	transferable on death (TOD)

Review Questions

4-1. Identify the assets that will pass through probate:

A. Life insurance payable to the decedent's surviving spouse.

B. An IRA payable to the decedent's estate.

C. A bank account titled jointly with the decedent's daughter.

D. The decedent's interest in a beach house owned as tenants in common with his brother.

E. A mutual fund account that the decedent held in his own name.

F. A home that the decedent leaves to his wife in his will.

G. A brokerage account that passes to the decedent's revocable trust under the pour-over provisions of his will.

H. A stock account owned by the decedent's revocable trust.

I. A life insurance policy owned by the decedent's irrevocable life insurance trust.

J. A money market fund that is held for the benefit of the decedent's children in his testamentary trust.

4-2. Jack and Jane hold the following assets:

Residence (jointly with Jane)	$1,000,000
Common stock (Jack)	$900,000
Municipal bonds (Jack)	$300,000
Investment real estate (Jack's Revocable Trust)	$500,000

Life insurance (owned by Jack; Jane is beneficiary)	$1,000,000
Mutual funds (Jane)	$400,000
IRA (owned by Jack; Jane is beneficiary)	$550,000

What is the amount of Jack's probate estate if he dies?

A. $3,150,000

B. $2,250,000

C. $1,200,000

D. $1,700,000

4-3: Which of the following assets will not automatically pass to Jane at Jack's death?

A. Their residence

B. Jack's life insurance

C. Jack's IRA

D. The trust-owned investment real estate

4-4: Which of the following statements regarding the probate of certain property interests is/are correct?

1. Property owned as tenants in common will be subject to probate.

2. Property owned jointly with right of survivorship will be subject to probate.

3. Individually owned property will be subject to probate.

4. Assets owned by a Revocable Trust will be subject to probate.

A. 1 and 3

B. 1, 2, and 3

C. 1, 3, and 4

D. 1, 2, 3, and 4

4-5: Which of the following assets would be subject to probate at Caitlyn's death?

A. A vacation home that she owned as tenants-in-common with her brother.

B. Her 401(k) account - she named her husband as beneficiary.

C. Her investment account owned jointly with her husband.

D. A life insurance policy with a trust for her son named as beneficiary.

Chapter 5

The Probate Process

CFP® CERTIFICATION EXAMINATION PRINCIPAL TOPIC COVERED IN THIS CHAPTER:

Transfers through the Probate Process

- Testamentary distribution
- Intestate succession
- Advantages and disadvantages of probate

- Probate avoidance strategies
- Ancillary probate administration

Learning Objectives

To ensure you have a thorough understanding of the probate process, the following learning objectives are addressed in this chapter:

- Describe the probate process, its advantages, disadvantages, and costs.

- Explain the various ways to avoid probate.

- Recognize the implications of ancillary probate.

Chapter Contents

OVERVIEW

Probate is the court-supervised process of settling a decedent's estate. The process consists of many steps that can vary from state to state and even within a state from court to court. Often, probate is perceived negatively and is viewed as a step that should be avoided to the extent possible because it can be a lengthy and expensive process. However, there are also advantages to the probate process. Financial planners should understand the steps involved in the probate process, the responsibilities of the executor, and ways to avoid probate.

Practice Standard 400-1

Identifying and Evaluating Financial Planning Alternative(s)

The financial planning practitioner shall consider sufficient and relevant alternatives to the client's current course of action in an effort to reasonably meet the client's goals, needs and priorities.

STEPS IN THE PROBATE PROCESS

An **executor** is the person (and/or institution) named in a valid will to serve as the personal representative of a testator when his or her will is being probated. When death occurs, the executor must locate and probate the decedent's will (i.e., prove that it was the decedent's will and that it was in fact his last will). The executor must then collect the decedent's property; pay debts, taxes, and expenses; and distribute any remaining assets to the beneficiaries specified in the decedent's will.

One of the disadvantages of the probate process is that there are many steps involved, and it can take a long time to finalize a decedent's estate. An executor's responsibilities typically last from nine months to two or three years. In rare instances (such as when a will is contested or the estate remains open for tax or other reasons) the executor's duties can continue for several years.

A decedent's property subject to probate includes real or personal property that the decedent owned in his sole name or as tenants in common, community property, and any property passing to a testamentary trust or to a trust per the "pour-over" provisions of a will. Also subject to probate are life insurance, retirement assets, or annuities payable to the decedent's estate.

Appointment of the Personal Representative

Before the executor can begin probate proceedings, he must be formally authorized or empowered by the court to do so. Being named as executor in a will is not adequate authority. The will must be recorded in the office of the local register of wills of the county in which the decedent was domiciled (often the clerk of the county court), and the court will issue either *letters of administration* to the administrator or *letters testamentary* to the executor. These "letters" are proof of the legal authority of the personal representative to collect and deal with the assets of the decedent's estate. Financial institutions will not release information about the decedent's assets absent this legal authority. The executor or administrator is then able to assume title to the decedent's property and act on behalf of the estate. (See Executor's Primary Duties in Appendix 5A.)

Practitioner Tip: Although there are many different terms, the executor, administrator, and personal representative are all essentially the same. An *executor* is the person appointed in the will of the decedent. In some jurisdictions, the person named as executor in the will has limited or no authority to act until his appointment is approved by the appropriate court. If the decedent left no will, if the will is invalid for some reason, or if the named executor is unable or unwilling to serve, then either the surviving spouse, another relative of the decedent, or one or more of the persons entitled to his or her estate may be appointed as the *personal representative*. In some jurisdictions, a creditor or any other "person" may be appointed if no one of higher priority is able or willing to serve. If not named in the will, the personal representative is called the *administrator* of the estate.

In most situations, unless the will specifically excuses the executor from providing bond, he will be required to post a bond with the appropriate court. The bond is a way of protecting the beneficiaries' interests in the event the executor fails to manage the estate appropriately. The amount of the bond is related to the value of the estate. Requirements for the amount of the bond vary from state to state. When creating their wills, many testators will excuse or waive the requirement that their executor post bond.

Practitioner Tip: Depending on the executor's financial acumen and the size of the estate, the executor may wish to hire an attorney to help him through the probate process.

Practitioner Tip: The appropriate court is determined by state or local law. In some states, it will be the *register of probate* or *registrar of probate*; in others it will be simply the *probate court*. It is important for a financial planner to understand the specifics of local law and the procedures in place in his jurisdiction.

Client Situation

Erin and Ryan are married and live in New Haven, Connecticut. They have established an estate plan consisting of pour-over wills and revocable trusts. In his will, Ryan named Erin as his executor. Upon Ryan's death, Erin will have to go to the local probate court with a copy of Ryan's will, and she will have to be appointed executor by the probate court. Once she has received the letters testamentary, she may begin the steps of collecting Ryan's assets.

Providing Notice to Creditors

One of the requirements of the probate process is that the executor notify potential creditors of a decedent's death so that creditors or other persons who might have an interest in the decedent's estate will have public notice of his death and thus have time to present any claims against the estate to the executor. The exact requirements of the notice are defined by state or local law; typically, this will be an official legal notice published in local newspapers. The public notice gives creditors warning that claims must be made before a certain date or else future claims will be barred.

If notice is advertised and the prescribed period of time elapses from the first date of publication, then the executor files his final account with the court. Only after the specified period of time elapses and the executor has accounted for what came into the estate, what went out, and what was paid to the beneficiaries can the executor be discharged of all responsibility for handling the estate.

Client Situation

Erin will have to provide notice to Ryan's potential creditors that he has died and that they must assert any claims against his estate within a certain period of time. Erin may do so by posting a legal notice in the local newspaper.

Collecting the Assets

Once an executor has been appointed, he will need to take an inventory of the decedent's assets to determine how they will pass and whom they will pass to. When the executor is the decedent's spouse or someone who was close to the decedent, he may have a good idea of what the decedent's various assets are; however, it is important to locate all of the assets. If the executor is not a family member, it is very important that the executor work with the decedent's family to assemble the inventory of the estate.

One strategy is to review the decedent's past income tax returns, cancelled checks, and mail to determine whether there are any purchases, accounts, securities, or other assets of which the executor might not otherwise be aware. Prior income tax returns, for example, might list interest from bank accounts or dividends from securities of which the executor has no knowledge. From this information, the executor can trace the present location of the assets and determine whether those assets were owned by the decedent at the time of his death. In addition, the executor must try to collect all outstanding claims that the decedent had against others at his death. In one case, a court held the executor responsible for failing to make a claim that the estate was the beneficiary of—and therefore entitled to—monies from another estate.

Practitioner Tip: There is no special sequence in which an executor must collect a decedent's assets, but it is usually logical to collect the decedent's life insurance as soon as possible. Life insurance proceeds are generally received fairly quickly, and it is an easy way to provide liquidity to the estate if the policies are payable to the estate. There are also forms for collecting Social Security and the U.S. Department of Veterans Affairs (or VA) benefits. Sometimes unpaid salary, as well as other fringe benefits, must be collected. The executor should arrange to have the decedent's safe-deposit box opened and make a list of its contents.

> **Client Situation**
>
> Following Ryan's death, Erin contacts all of the institutions where he held accounts and files claims for his life insurance, retirement assets, and Social Security benefits. While she believes that she knows about all of his accounts, she examines their past tax returns to ensure that she has contacted all of the institutions that sent him tax forms. She also reviews the files in his office to see whether she can find any paperwork on old accounts or life insurance policies that she may not be aware of. She found a small savings account that Ryan had at a local bank.

Valuation of the Estate

As assets are collected, they should also be valued. This means an appraisal must be made of the real property and of any personal property that the decedent owned, such as jewelry, clothing, automobiles, and household furniture and effects. And, of course, a value has to be placed on any business interest of the decedent. In some jurisdictions, all assets other than cash or cash equivalents must be appraised by court-appointed appraisers. With respect to bank accounts and securities, the fair market value will be included.

If the decedent held real estate in his own name, in addition to determining the fair market value of the property, the executor must be certain that the property is protected, that appropriate amounts of insurance are obtained or maintained, and that adequate safeguards are instituted to maintain the security of the property. If it is decided that the property should be sold, the executor is responsible for making sure that the sale is conducted properly and a fair price is received. It is also necessary for the executor to have court approval for the sale of real estate unless that power is specifically given to him in the will.

Practitioner Tip: Although the probate process formally covers only the assets subject to probate, one of the executor's responsibilities is to file any necessary federal or state estate tax returns. Therefore, it is important that he obtain the value of all assets that the decedent had an interest in at the time of his death, and ascertain whether they will be subject to probate or they will pass in some other manner.

> **Client Situation**
>
> Erin has contacted all of the institutions where Ryan had accounts and has determined the date-of-death value of the assets. Ryan owned a home in Florida, which he had inherited from his father. Erin hires a local real estate appraiser to obtain the fair market value of the house as of the date of Ryan's death. Erin has not yet decided whether she should keep the home or sell the home. She does not anticipate traveling to Florida without him, but the real estate market is depressed and she does not think she will be able to sell the home for as much as it is worth. While she makes this decision, she will have to maintain homeowners and flood insurance on the home.

Managing the Estate

It is the executor's responsibility to manage a decedent's estate. This includes not only opening an estate checking account and maintaining investments and real estate in the name of the estate during the probate process, but also filing appropriate income tax returns.

The executor should take steps to ascertain that the assets are properly invested. An executor is required to exercise the same degree of judgment that a reasonable person would exercise in the management of his own estate. For this reason, an executor who is not particularly financially astute should consider hiring someone to manage the estate's investments, if he is enabled to do so by will or by state law.

Where the decedent owned property as tenants in common with other individuals, the decedent's share passes under the decedent's will or by **intestacy**—not to the other owners. This is different than property that the decedent owns jointly with right of survivorship with other property holders. The executor represents the decedent's interests in his proportionate share of the property. In some cases, questions can arise regarding what the decedent's interest actually is, and these situations require extreme caution on the part of the executor.

Client Situation

Erin has opened an estate checking account and has used it to pay the expenses of Ryan's estate. She deposited the proceeds of a life insurance policy that was payable to Ryan's estate into this checking account and is using the funds as needed to pay attorney fees involved in settling the estate. Erin has also retained an accountant to help determine which tax returns must be filed. Because Erin is not a sophisticated investor, she has also hired ABC Investment Management Co. to help her manage the investments in a prudent manner.

Payment of Taxes, Debts, and Expenses

The executor is responsible for paying all of the taxes, debts, and expenses of an estate. Typical debts that a decedent might have outstanding at death include loans, credit card balances, day-to-day household bills, and income and property taxes. Expenses commonly incurred when administering an estate include probate costs, legal fees, executor's or administrator's fees, fees for appraisers, costs inherent in selling real estate and personal property, costs arising on account of the decedent's last illness, and the costs involved in winding up the executor's business.

Numerous categories of taxes must be paid in the process of settling an estate. In many estates, the executor must pay two categories of death taxes: state inheritance and estate taxes and the federal estate tax. The executor is also responsible for the payment of federal and state income taxes, and any personal property or real estate taxes. In many cases there are additional taxes to be paid and other forms to be filed. For example, income taxes have to be paid on the income that the decedent earned prior to his death. Tax also has to be paid on the income generated from the assets in the estate. Options are available to the executor in regard to the timing of the estate's income tax return, and the executor should make this determination after a thorough review of the entire tax situation of the decedent, the estate, and the beneficiaries.

Practitioner Tip: A decedent's assets often must be converted relatively quickly into cash to pay expenses, debts, and taxes. Because no two decedents own exactly the same property, no two estates will be handled in an identical manner. There is very little demand for some of the personal property that people own. Therefore, it is hard to realize cash from such assets. Of course, assets such as the proceeds from life insurance, certificates of deposit, and Treasury bills may be available to take care of the estate's liabilities. Listed securities can also be quickly converted to cash, but the market value at the time that funds are needed or other circumstances might preclude or inhibit the feasibility of their sale at that time. Assets such as real estate and business interests are not readily convertible into cash, and it might take months, or even years in the case of business interests, to realize cash from these assets. Therefore, the executor has to analyze the assets of the estate after they have been assembled, determine what amounts of cash will be needed to cover the debts, expenses, and taxes of the estate, and then develop a plan to make the necessary funds available when required.

Client Situation

When Erin was going through Ryan's office in an attempt to locate all of his assets, she also found several credit cards that were in Ryan's name alone. She did not know about these accounts and was surprised to find that one carried a rather large balance. She was able to add this to the list of Ryan's debts.

Distributing Remaining Assets

Once an executor has assembled the decedent's assets and paid appropriate debts, expenses, and taxes, he must distribute any remaining assets according to the decedent's will or under state intestacy laws. In the case of a very small estate where the spouse might be the executor and sole beneficiary, distribution can be accomplished by turning the property over to the beneficiary and accepting a *receipt and release* to the executor of any liability to the beneficiary. However, although this is certainly the most expedient and inexpensive way of concluding an estate, the executor could remain liable for any unpaid debts and taxes and be responsible for any number of other problems that might arise.

If the executor wishes to be formally discharged from his duties, responsibilities, and liabilities, then it is necessary to prepare a final account of administration with the court. Unpaid creditors and beneficiaries are given notice of the filing of the account. When the court is satisfied that all of the procedures in handling the estate have been complied with, then the account is approved, a formal schedule of distribution is presented and approved, and the executor distributes the assets to the beneficiaries and is discharged from his responsibilities. When trusts have been established in the decedent's will, assets are transferred from the executor to the trusts so that these trusts can be immediately funded, if assets have not already been so transferred.

Complications when making distributions often occur because the people mentioned in the decedent's will are not all available to receive it, or assets that are supposed to pass to named beneficiaries are not in the decedent's estate at the time of his death, or they are there in a different form. For example, if a decedent leaves his estate equally to his two brothers, and subsequent to the writing of the will but prior to his death the two brothers die, with one leaving two children and the other survived solely by his wife, how should the executor distribute the proceeds? The answer depends upon an interpretation of the decedent's will, or the law of the state of domicile, or perhaps a combination of both.

Practitioner Tip: Wills should name primary and contingent beneficiaries as well as a contingent executor to avoid unintended complications and delays in probating the estate.

Ademption and Abatement Statutes

Additional complications arise when a decedent has bequeathed specific assets that are no longer in his estate at the time of his death. For example, bequests of "all my money in my savings account at XYZ Bank to my brother" and "all of my stock certificates to my sister" would be complicated if, before his death, the decedent had closed out his bank account and used part of the funds to purchase securities and part to purchase an automobile. A state's **ademption** statutes determine which assets may be used to satisfy a bequest when the bequeathed asset is no longer in existence.

Client Situation

Ryan left his 1977 Mustang convertible to his son Shawn. At the time of Ryan's death, he had sold the 1977 Mustang convertible and purchased a 1965 Ford Thunderbird. Relying on ademption, Shawn will receive the Thunderbird instead of the convertible.

A final issue with respect to the distribution of assets under a decedent's will can occur when the deceased makes bequests of a greater amount of assets than currently exist under his will. The state's **abatement** statutes then provide an alternative distribution of the assets.

Client Situation

Ryan had provided for Erin and their children in his revocable trust and for his two sisters, Jill and Danielle, in his will. He left $500,000 to each sister. At the time of his death, however, his probate estate was valued at only $750,000. Jill and Danielle might each receive 50% of the probate estate ($375,000) instead of one receiving $500,000 and the other receiving $250,000.

Practice Standard 400-1

Identifying and Evaluating Financial Planning Alternative(s)

The financial planning practitioner shall consider sufficient and relevant alternatives to the client's current course of action in an effort to reasonably meet the client's goals, needs and priorities.

Practice Standard 400-2

Developing the Financial Planning Recommendation(s)

The financial planning practitioner shall develop the recommendation(s) based on the selected alternative(s) and the current course of action in an effort to reasonably meet the client's goals, needs and priorities.

ADVANTAGES AND DISADVANTAGES OF PROBATE

The disadvantages of probate are fairly evident. The many steps involved in the administration of an estate can take significant time to complete. It is not uncommon for a probate proceeding to last from nine months up to two years. Probate can also be quite costly. Although the actual fees charged by the probate court may not be exorbitant, when an executor hires an attorney to help settle an estate, an accountant to file appropriate tax returns, appraisers, and other professionals as needed, the fees can add up quickly. It is not uncommon for these fees to exceed 5% of the value of the estate. Probate is also a public proceeding. The value of assets passing through probate is a matter of public record with the probate court, and anyone can look up the value of a decedent's estate.

> ### Client Situation
>
> Although Erin did much of the legwork herself, she had her estate planning attorney help with all paperwork, had her accountant file the appropriate tax returns, and ABC Investment Company manage the estate assets. It took 26 months from the time Ryan died for his estate to finally close. The value of Ryan's probate estate was $2.6 million, and the value of his gross estate was $3.9 million. The total cost of all legal and other administrative fees was $110,000.

Despite these negative implications, a probate proceeding has certain advantages. When the probate court is involved in settling an estate, there is court supervision of the manner in which property is distributed to heirs. This can be important if there is the possibility of a will contest or other challenges to the decedent's estate. Probate proves the validity of a will and documents the title to property. Furthermore, probate offers protection to creditors (by ensuring that all debts are paid) and heirs (by barring future creditor claims against the estate). The requirement of providing notice of a decedent's death protects not only a creditor's interests but also those of the heirs. Probate is a distinct advantage in such cases because the same creditor protection does not exist for assets that pass by trust.

Client Situation

After Ryan's estate had been settled and all assets had been distributed from the estate, a former business associate, Kevin, came forward and claimed that Ryan owed him $10,000. Kevin attended Ryan's funeral and knew that he had died. Because notice had been published and the time for claiming against the estate had passed, Ryan's heirs were protected against this claim.

ANCILLARY PROBATE

Personal property is probated in the decedent's state of domicile. Real property is probated in the state where it is located (**situs**). **Ancillary probate** is a separate probate proceeding where property that is located outside of the decedent's state of domicile is subject to a separate probate proceeding in the state where the property is located. This is often an unintended consequence of holding property in another state, and it can be both time consuming and expensive. Ancillary probate can be avoided either by transferring the ownership of out-of-state real estate to a trust or titling the asset as jointly held with right of survivorship. The property can also be gifted or sold during life.

When a decedent owns real estate located in a state different from that of his domicile at the time of death, the state in which the real estate is located has the right to tax the property. This often leads to problems, especially in cases where two states are trying to tax the same property.

Practitioner Tip: When a client has assets in multiple states, the financial planner should discuss the implications of ancillary probate. Local law determines the ways in which property can avoid probate. The use of a trust may be the best solution because property titled jointly with a spouse will avoid probate for the decedent spouse, but the property will be solely owned by the surviving spouse and subject to ancillary probate at that person's death.

Client Situation

Ryan's home in Florida is subject to ancillary probate in Florida. To avoid this, Ryan should have either transferred ownership of his home from his name to a trust or other entity while he was alive, or he could have gifted the property to his children while he was still alive. Because he did not, Erin, as executor, will have to go through the steps of the probate process not only in Connecticut but also in Florida.

INTESTATE SUCCESSION

When a decedent dies with a valid will in place, he is said to have died *testate*. When a decedent dies without a valid will (or with no will) in place, he is said to have died *intestate*, and his property will pass per state laws of intestacy. Laws of intestacy vary from state to state and likely will not accomplish the decedent's wishes. For example, if a decedent is survived by a spouse and children, many states will split the assets in near equal proportions for the spouse and the children, even though most decedents would prefer the assets to pass outright to their spouses.

> **Client Situation**
>
> Eric and Rose were domiciled in Connecticut at the time of Eric's death. They had three children together, and Eric died without a will. Rose would take the first $250,000 of the estate and one-quarter of the balance. If they were domiciled in Florida at the time of Eric's death, Rose would take $60,000 plus one-half of the intestate estate.

Practitioner Tip: Intestate property that passes to a surviving spouse receives a marital deduction in the decedent's estate, just as testate property would, to reduce the decedent's estate tax liability.

PROBATE AVOIDANCE STRATEGIES

Financial planners should discuss the advantages and disadvantages of the probate process with clients. In some situations, the clients may determine that it would be advantageous to avoid probate to the extent possible by using **will substitutes**. There are several ways to do this:

Operation of Law

Property can be titled jointly with right of survivorship with the person the decedent wants to take the property at his death. The decedent's interest in these assets is still included in his estate; however, the asset will automatically pass to the survivor and will not be subject to probate. Property titled as tenants by the entirety with spouses will also avoid probate.

Practitioner Tip: If a decedent intended to use his assets to fund a credit shelter trust, titling the asset in this fashion could prohibit the use of the assets in this manner. Further, when property is titled jointly with right of survivorship with a nonspouse, there may be unintended estate and gift tax implications.

Beneficiary Designations

To avoid probate, primary and contingent beneficiary designations can be used to transfer assets to the intended beneficiaries for many different types of accounts. For retirement benefits, annuities, or life insurance, traditional beneficiary designations are commonly used. For bank or investment accounts, TOD or POD designations may be used. It is important to note that if the named beneficiary is the estate, then the assets will be subject to probate. Furthermore, it is important to carefully coordinate these designations with the client's overall estate planning goals.

Practitioner Tip: Government savings bonds can also designate either a joint owner or a beneficiary, which would also avoid probate. Many states allow real property to be transferred by deed. Valid prenuptial agreements and postnuptial agreements are contracts that supersede state laws; therefore, property transferred subject to such agreements would also avoid probate.

Trusts

Assets owned by a revocable trust or an irrevocable trust are not subject to probate and pass per the terms of the trust, which will dictate who is to receive the trust property and when they are to receive it. For this strategy to be effective, it is important that the client transfer assets into the trust before the date of his death.

Probate cannot be avoided when a revocable trust is established but is not funded. For example, one of the more common estate planning techniques is to establish a pour-over will with a revocable trust. The will directs any property that the decedent owns at the time of his death to "pour" from his will to the revocable trust. The property passing into the trust will avoid intestacy, but it will not avoid probate.

Chapter Highlights

- There are many steps in the probate process. It is imperative that the executor understand these steps and that a financial planner be able to explain them to clients.

- Often an executor will require the assistance of a team of professionals to help settle an estate. This can cause significant expense, and probate can also cause delay.

- Probate is a public process, without privacy. However, certain protections are afforded to both creditors and heirs by having the court involved in overseeing the probate process.

- Being an executor is serious business. In addition to having to understand incredibly complex state and federal tax laws, the executor must also be accountable to the decedent's family, beneficiaries (if they are not members of the decedent's family), creditors, business associates, various branches of government for the myriad taxes for which the executor is responsible, and finally to the court for the proper performance of the executor's duties.

- For these reasons, financial planners should work with clients to establish an estate plan that accomplishes their goals and to the extent possible, avoids probate, unless the client has a compelling reason for wanting court involvement.

Key Terms

abatement

ademption

ancillary probate

executor

intestacy/intestate succession

probate

situs

will substitutes

Review Questions

5-1. What is the duty of the executor?

1. Must collect the decedent's assets.

2. Is responsible for filing an estate tax return.

3. Must make sure that assets are distributed to the heirs entitled to receive the property.

A. 1 only

B. 2 only

C. 3 only

D. 1 and 3

E. All of the above are duties of the executor.

5-2. Probate is

A. Meaningless if the decedent dies without a will.

B. A court proceeding to determine the validity of a will.

C. A private matter dealing with the administration of an estate.

D. A simple, inexpensive process in all cases.

5-3. Amy's estate is comprised of the following assets: $400,000 residence owned as a tenancy by the entirety; $300,000 brokerage account payable on death to her surviving spouse; $50,000 bank account; $200,000 life insurance policy payable to her surviving spouse. Amy's will transfers all assets to her surviving spouse. What is the value of Amy's probate estate?

A. $0

B. $50,000

C. $350,000

D. $750,000

5-4. What is the best definition of probate assets?

A. An asset that must be owned by the decedent on the date of death.

B. An asset that is included in the decedent's gross estate.

C. An asset that transfers under the provisions of the decedent's will.

D. The executor determines what is considered a probate asset.

5-5. Which of the following is not considered a benefit of probate?

A. Creditors are given notice of the decedent's death and have a limited time frame in which to file claims against the estate.

B. Probate can be quite lengthy and sometimes expensive.

C. The court will oversee the manner in which property is distributed to heirs.

D. The validity of the will is proven by the court.

Appendix 5A

Executor's Primary Duties

An executor has many responsibilities in settling a decedent's estate. It is important that the executor understand his responsibilities. As a financial planner, it is helpful to review these responsibilities with your clients while they are still alive so that all parties are prepared for what is expected of them after a decedent's death, and the appropriate persons are named as personal representatives and beneficiaries.

ESTATE DUTIES

1. Probate will.

2. Advertise Grant of Letters.

3. Notify the beneficiaries of the estate, along with immediate members of the decedent's family (to the extent required by local rules).

4. Open estate checking and savings accounts.

5. Write to banks for date-of-death value.

6. Value securities.

7. Appraise real property and personal property.

8. Obtain three years of U.S. individual income tax returns and three years of cancelled checks.

9. Obtain five years' financials on business interests plus all relevant agreements.

10. Obtain copies of all U.S. gift tax returns filed by decedent.

11. Obtain evidence of all debts of decedent and costs of administering estate.

12. File personal property tax returns—due February 15 of each year the estate is in administration.

13. Determine whether the estate is subject to ancillary administration.

14. Determine whether administrative expenses and losses should be claimed as an income or estate tax deduction.

15. File inventory: check local law for requirements and due date.

16. Apply for tax waivers.

17. File account or prepare informal family agreement.

18. Prepare audit notices and statement of proposed distribution/obtain waiver of accounting.

19. File schedule of distribution, if applicable.

INCOME TAX DUTIES

1. File IRS Form 56, Notice of Fiduciary Relationship with the Internal Revenue Service.

2. Determine whether any of the decedent's medical expenses were unpaid at death.

3. Determine whether the estate has received after-death income taxable under IRC § 691.

4. Consider requesting prompt assessment of the decedent's U.S. income taxes.

5. File final U.S. and state individual income tax return (IRS Form 1040), due April 15 of the year after the year in which death occurs, and gift tax returns, due by the time the estate tax return is due.

6. Apply for federal tax identification number if estate will file U.S. income tax returns.

7. File U.S. Fiduciary Income Tax Return (IRS Form 1041), choice of fiscal year.

ESTATE TAX DUTIES

1. Prepay state inheritance tax; check state law to determine whether this is permissible, the advantages, and applicable deadlines.

2. Obtain alternate valuation date values for federal estate tax return, if applicable.

3. Consider options for paying the estate tax, if any. Consider election of extension of time to pay U.S. estate or generation-skipping transfer tax (IRC § 6161 or § 6166); must be filed on or before due date of U.S. estate tax returns including extensions. In addition, determine whether tax returns should be filed to document the deceased spouse's unused exclusion amount. This

determination relates to the portability of the estate tax exemption and applies to estates of individuals who die in 2011 and 2012.

4. Make sure that appropriate required minimum distributions from retirement assets are taken in the year of death if the decedent has not already taken such distributions.

5. Consider election to defer payment of inheritance tax on remainder interests; where permitted, determine deadline for election.

6. Consider election for special valuation of farm or business real estate under IRC § 2032A; must be made with timely filed U.S. estate tax return.

7. Elect (or do not elect) to qualify certain terminable interest property for marital deduction.

8. Ascertain whether credit for tax on prior transfers is allowable.

9. File state inheritance or estate tax return and federal estate tax return. Federal tax is due within nine months of death; extensions may be requested. Check local law for due date and possible extensions.

10. Consider requesting prompt assessment of U.S. estate tax return.

11. Consider requesting prompt review and approval of decedent's income tax returns.

12. Consider Deceased Spousal Unused Exclusion Amount election.

OTHER DUTIES

1. Inventory safe deposit box.

2. Claim life insurance benefits. Obtain IRS Form 712 from insurance company.

    a.   Consider mode of payment.

3. Claim pension and profit-sharing benefits.

    a.   Consider mode of payment.

    b.   Obtain copies of plan, IRS approval, and beneficiary designation.

4. Apply for lump sum Social Security benefits and VA benefits.

5. Consider redemption under IRC §303.

Chapter 6

Wills

CFP® CERTIFICATION EXAMINATION PRINCIPAL TOPIC COVERED IN THIS CHAPTER:

Estate Planning Documents

Wills

- Legal requirements
- Types of wills
- Modifying or revoking a will
- Avoiding will contests

Learning Objectives

To ensure that you have a solid understanding of how a will coordinates with an estate plan, the legal requirements of a will, and the different types of wills, the following learning objectives are addressed in this chapter:

- Identify the manner in which assets will pass per the terms of a will.

- Recognize the provisions that a will should contain.

- Understand the legal requirements of a will.

- Distinguish the different types of wills.

- Understand the grounds for contesting a will.

- Understand the manner in which a will can be modified or revoked.

- Identify the estate, generation-skipping transfer tax, and income tax consequences of property passing by will.

Chapter Contents

OVERVIEW

A will is a legal instrument by which a person leaves certain instructions for others after his death. A will is generally used to dispose of a decedent's real and personal property in accordance with state laws. However, a will can also address other important matters, such as naming an executor or a guardian for minor children, and determining how debts and taxes should be paid at death.

Although only an attorney can draft a will, the financial planner and all other members of a client's planning team must understand the provisions included in it and ensure that it is coordinated with the client's other property interests. Planners must ascertain the manner in which a client's property will pass to others and understand how certain provisions, such as tax provisions, can affect the overall estate plan. Financial planners need to review their clients' wills periodically as their circumstances change to identify and resolve any particular problems associated with the will and to ensure that their clients' wishes will be realized at their death.

Practice Standard 300-1

Analyzing and Evaluating the Client's Information

A financial planning practitioner shall analyze the information to gain an understanding of the client's financial situation and then evaluate to what extent the client's goals, needs and priorities can be met by the client's resources and current course of action.

AN INTRODUCTION TO WILLS

The person who executes or makes the will is known as the **testator**. When an individual dies with a will, he is said to die **testate,** and any property that he owns at the time of his death will pass to others as directed by the terms of his will. When an individual dies without a will, he dies **intestate** and property will pass according to his state's laws of intestate succession, or intestacy.

A will does not become operative until a decedent's death, and it is revocable during his lifetime. This means that the testator can change any of the provisions of the will or rewrite it as often as he likes while alive. If a testator wishes to change only a portion of his will, he can execute a **codicil** instead. A codicil is a legal document that is executed to address minor changes in a will.

DISPOSITION OF PROPERTY UNDER A WILL

When a testator leaves property under a will, he is making a **bequest** to a **legatee.** Property can be bequeathed in several ways. It is fairly common for a testator to dispose of **tangible (personal) property** separately from other **intangible property** (bank and investment accounts) that pass through his estate. For example, a will might leave "all tangible personal property to my wife Rachel, if she survives me. If Rachel does not survive me, I leave all tangible personal property to my children." Most often, the testator's tangible personal property is the subject of a **specific bequest**. For example, the will might leave "my 1962 Corvette to my niece, Heather." If the property that is the subject of a specific bequest does not exist at the testator's death, in most states, the legatee receives nothing. For example, if the Corvette does not exist at the testator's death, Heather gets nothing, subject to the state's **ademption** statute.

Practitioner Tip: When reviewing a client's will, ensure that any property that is specifically bequeathed to an individual is currently owned by the testator. In the preceding example, the planner should ensure that the client still owns the 1962 Corvette. It should also be confirmed that all named beneficiaries in the will (Heather in this example) are still alive.

A **general bequest** disposes of a certain amount or value of property. For example, a will might leave "$10,000 to my nephew Ralph." If there is $10,000 of property remaining after specific bequests have been satisfied, Ralph will get $10,000 even if property must be sold to satisfy that bequest.

A **residual bequest** disposes of all property that has not been disposed of by specific or general bequest. In other words, a residual bequest disposes of everything that is left after all other bequests have been satisfied. The residuary beneficiary can be an individual, a trust, or an institution. For example, the will might provide "the rest and residue of my estate will pass to my wife Jane." Frequently, the residual legatee is a primary beneficiary, such as the testator's spouse or children, or a trust. The testator should take into consideration that the residual legatee may get nothing if the estate should shrink and the specific and general bequests wipe out the estate.

Practitioner Tip: A **residuary clause** should be included in a will to dispose of property that was acquired after the execution of the will or other property that has not been specifically disposed of. If a will does not contain a residuary clause, the estate could potentially be subject to partial intestacy.

If a specific or general legatee is not alive at the time of the testator's death, the specific or general bequest lapses and passes under the residuary clause as part of the residue of the decedent's estate. Some states provide that a specific or general legacy for certain persons related to the testator does not lapse but instead goes to descendants of the legatee. If the testator does not want this result, he can provide that a specific bequest is conditioned on the legatee surviving him.

Client Situation

At the time of his death, Chris had a valid will that left $100,000 to each of his sons, Grant and Lachlan, and the rest of his estate to his wife Hillary. When Chris created the will, he had $1 million of assets and anticipated that Hillary would receive $800,000. At the time of his death, he had only $250,000. Because he had left specific bequests to his sons, Hillary will receive only the remaining $50,000.

If Grant predeceased Chris, the bequest to Grant would lapse and Hillary would inherit $150,000.

If Hillary predeceased Chris, the residue of his estate would pass per his state's law of intestate succession unless Chris provided a contingent residuary beneficiary in his will.

Per Capita and Per Stirpes

A will allows the testator to make alternative provisions in case some of the heirs predecease him. For instance, if a child dies, the testator may want to leave that share to the child's siblings, or perhaps to the child's issue. The language used to describe the manner in which assets pass to heirs is very important in determining who will ultimately inherit assets and how much they will inherit.

If assets are left to beneficiaries **per capita,** each of the intended beneficiaries will inherit equally. For example, John has three children: Andrew, Ben, and Colin. Colin has three children: Dan, Ed, and Frank. John leaves $1 million in his will to "my children that survive me, or if a child has predeceased me, to his issue per capita." Colin predeceased John. Because assets are left to Andrew, Ben, and Colin's children— Dan, Ed, and Frank "per capita"—each beneficiary will inherit $200,000.

When assets are left **per stirpes,** descendants are not treated equally; rather, they inherit by right of representation when one or more descendants have predeceased the decedent. In the preceding example, if assets were left per stirpes instead of per capita, Andrew would inherit $333,333 (1/3), Ben would inherit $333,333(1/3), and Colin's children would split $333,333 (1/3). (See Figure 6.1.)

Figure 6.1 Per Capita and Per Stirpes

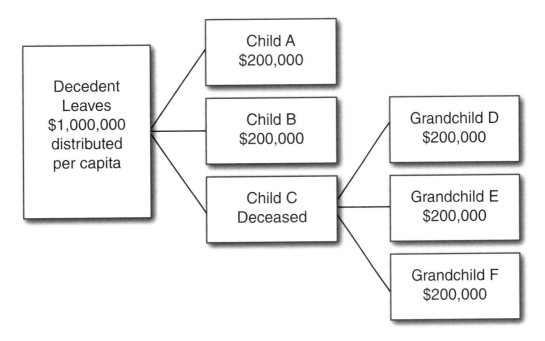

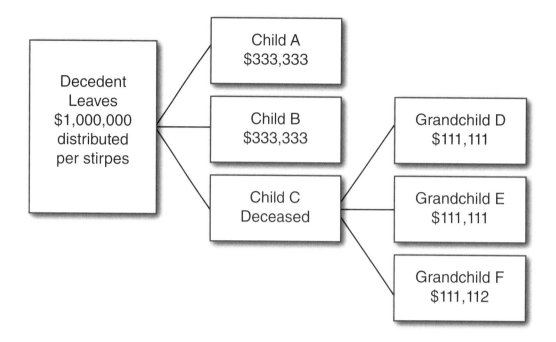

Client Situation

At her death, Hillary leaves $600,000 to her children, Grant and Lachlan. Grant has no children. Lachlan has two children, Molly and Hannah. If Lachlan predeceased Hillary, and Hillary left the bequest to "my children or to the issue of a predeceased child per capita," then Grant, Molly, and Hannah would each inherit $200,000. If Hillary had left the same bequest per stirpes instead of per capita, Grant would receive $300,000 and Molly and Hannah would each receive $150,000.

Practitioner Tip: Because of the variation in the amounts that heirs of different generations can inherit based on whether the assets are left per capita or per stirpes, it is imperative that financial planners not only understand the difference, but identify the distribution scheme and communicate the implications to a client.

Practice Standard 400-3

Presenting the Financial Planning Recommendation(s)

The financial planning practitioner shall communicate the recommendation(s) in a manner and to an extent reasonably necessary to assist the client in making an informed decision.

LIMITATIONS OF WILLS

Property Passing by Will

A will can dispose only of property that a decedent owned in his own name at the time of his death. A will does not dispose of property that was owned jointly with right of survivorship or that was owned as a tenancy by the entirety between spouses, nor can it direct assets that are held by a trust. Retirement assets or a life insurance policy pass by beneficiary designation and will not pass through the will unless the estate is named as the beneficiary of these contracts.

Client Situation

At the time of his death, Tom had the following assets:

- Bank account titled jointly with his wife Kathy: $100,000

- Retirement account with Kathy named as beneficiary: $530,000

- Mutual fund account titled jointly with Kathy: $275,000

- Life insurance with $1 million death benefit. Tom's sons, Tim and Jack, are named as beneficiaries.

Tom had a valid will at the time of his death; however, because he had no property titled in his name alone, no assets would pass under his will. Instead, the bank account and mutual fund account would pass to Kathy by right of survivorship, the retirement assets would pass to Kathy by beneficiary designation, and the life insurance proceeds would pass to Tim and Jack by beneficiary designation.

Practitioner Tip: It is important to coordinate asset ownership with a client's overall estate plan. If asset ownership is not coordinated, the estate plan may not work, and property will not pass to the intended beneficiaries.

Community Property Considerations

Assets held as community property are owned equally by spouses. At death, each spouse has testamentary power of distribution over his half of the community assets. The will of the deceased spouse may affect the survivor's half of the community property. For example, the decedent's will may purport to give all of the community property assets (the shares of both husband and wife) to a trust for the benefit of the surviving spouse and the children. If so, the survivor must elect whether to take under the will (thus assenting to the decedent's disposition of the survivor's one-half community property interest) or to take his one-half of the community property outright (denying the decedent's power to dispose of the survivor's community property interest).

Pretermitted Heirs

There are certain limitations on how a decedent can dispose of his property at death. No state allows one spouse to disinherit another, whereas in all states except for Louisiana a parent can disinherit his child. The majority of states provide that if a spouse or child is not named in a will, such a person is deemed to be a **pretermitted heir**. Regardless of what the will says, such person will take the share of the estate that would be given to him under the state's rules of intestacy.

Practitioner Tip: If a client intends to disinherit a child or provide for his surviving spouse by some other means, he should express this in his will so that his heirs cannot claim to be overlooked by the testator.

In most states, a child born or adopted after the execution of a will is entitled to share in the estate if provision is not otherwise made for the child. In some states, a child alive at the time of the execution of a will who is omitted from the will is entitled to share in the estate unless it appears the omission was intentional.

ELECTIVE SHARE STATUTE

Under state law, a surviving spouse is generally given a right to elect to take against a will. The elective share statute allows a spouse to receive a prescribed share of the decedent's estate, even if the decedent provided otherwise.

Practitioner Tip: Sometimes the application of these rules can be complicated. It is important to have an attorney calculate whether a spouse would be better off making this election or accepting the property that the spouse is entitled to receive from joint assets and beneficiary designations.

A spouse's right to elect against the will can be waived by agreement during life. For example, the right to elect could be waived in a postnuptial agreement. Some states provide that a will executed before marriage is revoked upon marriage. A few states provide that such a will is revoked unless other provisions are made for the new spouse. Conversely, most states hold that provisions in a will for a former spouse are revoked upon divorce.

WILL PROVISIONS AND CLAUSES

Although only an attorney can draft a will, it is imperative that all members of a client's financial planning team, including the financial planner, understand how to review a will. It is important to be able to ascertain the manner in which property will pass based on the provisions contained in a will. It is also important to understand the significance of certain provisions, such as tax provisions, to ensure that a client's wishes will be realized following his death.

Introductory Clause

The introductory clause of a will should identify the testator and establish the state where the decedent lives. This identifies the state laws that will govern the validity of a will. Furthermore, because a testator can revoke or amend his will any number of times during his lifetime, his will should specify whether the will is intended to revoke all prior wills or whether some previous will still contains valid provisions and the document being executed is simply a codicil.

An example of such an introductory clause follows:

> I, Edward Grieg, a resident of and domiciled in the city of Bryn Mawr in Montgomery County, Pennsylvania, declare this to be my last will. I revoke all wills and codicils made prior to this will.

Practitioner Tip: The state identified as the client's domicile is the state that will have legal jurisdiction for the purposes of determining the validity of a will and interpreting its provisions. If a client has multiple residences, the financial planner should ascertain whether the stated domicile is the correct one.

- For tax or other planning purposes, would it make sense to begin to document a different domicile?

- Will the will meet all the statutory requirements of the stated domicile?

- If a client spends a great deal of time in more than one residence, could the address mentioned in the will trigger a "double domicile" problem (e.g., where more than one state claims the decedent was a domiciliary of the state and therefore has the right to impose a death tax)?

Payment of Expenses, Debts, and Taxes

A will should establish the source of and provide instruction regarding the payment of debts, expenses, and taxes. The executor will be instructed regarding which property should be used to pay any debts and taxes. For example, the executor can be instructed to pay all debts, expenses, and taxes from the residue of the testator's estate, or from a specific asset or source. It is important that a financial planner review the debt and tax clause in a client's will for a number of reasons: first, to ensure that the client has adequate assets to cover any anticipated liabilities. Furthermore, the executor will need to pay debts, expenses, and taxes in a relatively short period of time (often within nine months). It is important to ascertain whether the client has adequate liquid assets to cover these expenses. Finally, this clause can substantially affect the amount received by any legatee. In the absence of such a provision, most states would apportion the death taxes among all legacies. A few states would charge the death taxes to the residuary estate.

Following is an example of the payment of debts clause:

> I direct all of my lawfully enforceable debts (including any expenses of my last illness) and my funeral expenses to be paid.

Here is an example of a tax clause:

> I direct that all inheritance, estate, transfer, succession, legacy, and other death taxes on property required to be included in my taxable estate, whether or not passing under this will, except transfer taxes levied pursuant to the provisions of Chapter 13 of the Internal Revenue Code of 1986, relating to "generation-skipping transfers" or any similar state law, and taxes on property held in trust under the will (or any revocable trust) of my spouse, and any interest and penalties thereon, shall be charged against and paid from my residuary estate passing under Article *FOURTH* of Part I of this my will.

Practitioner Tip: The payment of debts, expenses, and taxes must be addressed in a will because many assets, such as assets titled jointly with right of survivorship or assets passing by beneficiary designation, pass outside the provisions of the will and are not available to the testator's estate to provide for such payments. It is important to plan for who will pay the tax on these assets and designate the sources of payment.

Specifically, a planner should consider the following:

- State "apportionment" statutes. If there is no tax clause in the will or if it does not adequately address the payment of a particular death tax, state law will allocate the burden of taxes among the beneficiaries. Many states require beneficiaries to pay a share of estate taxes unless the will provides otherwise. The result is often an inappropriate or unintended reduction of the shares of certain beneficiaries or adverse tax consequences. (For instance, suppose you wanted a child to receive $100,000 of your client's $2 million estate free and clear. Without special provision, that child would be forced to pay his share of taxes, or 1/20 of the total federal and state death taxes. With a special tax clause, the child will receive the entire $100,000.

- Does the client expect or want property passing outside the probate estate to pay its share of tax if the disposition of that nonprobate asset generates tax? For instance, assume $1 million of pension proceeds (or life insurance) is payable to a client's two oldest children and $1 million of cash is payable to the client's two youngest children. Who is to pay the tax on the $2 million? The will should specify who pays taxes on both probate and nonprobate property.

- Assume a sizable amount of property will pass through a revocable living trust. Is the tax clause in that instrument coordinated with the tax clause in the will, or are they incompatible? Who is to pay the tax on a generation-skipping transfer? Absent a contrary direction, the taxes will probably be payable from the assets of the fund subject to the tax.

- Are there adequate liquid assets in the estate to pay for anticipated debts, expenses, and taxes? If not, the financial planner should discuss ways in which the estate may need to generate liquidity. For example, should the client consider purchasing life insurance?

Powers Clauses

A will should contain a provision granting certain powers to the executor (and trustee, if the will establishes a testamentary trust). The purposes of the powers clause are to:

- give the executor (and trustee) specific powers and authority over and above those provided by state law to enable the executor to conserve and manage the property;

- limit, where desired and appropriate, the executor's power and authority (for instance, the client may not want the executor to make certain investments);

- provide authority to continue a business (or handle other property with special management or investment problems) and the special flexibility necessary to accomplish that objective; and

- protect the executor from suits by other beneficiaries by specifying the powers necessary to accomplish the executor's role.

Practitioner Tip: The planner should ensure that the will contains adequate powers to allow the executor and trustee to administer the decedent's estate appropriately. For example, if a decedent held an interest in an S-corporation or a closely held company, specific powers should allow the executor to handle these business interests. Note also that a will cannot change the terms of a trust. With a revocable trust, only the grantor can change the terms of the trust while he is still alive.

Appointment of Fiduciaries

In a will, the testator should name the *personal representative* or *executor* of the estate. A person or institution can be named to act as executor and can be appointed to carry out the directions in the will and to dispose of property according to the testamentary provisions. If a will contains trust provisions, a trustee should also be named.

Practitioner Tip: The named personal representative is often a relative or close friend. But if the estate is large or complicated, the testator should consider appointing either a professional or an institution, such as a bank, that is accustomed to dealing with assets and with the sometimes complicated rules of probate.

Guardian of Minor Children

Another important provision of a will allows parents to name a guardian and a contingent guardian for their minor children. This is often the biggest concern for parents, allowing them to ensure that in the event of their death they designate the individuals they want to take care of their children. When there are minor children, the will can nominate a guardian of both the "person" and the "estate" of each child. A "guardian of the person" generally provides for the custody and care of the child. A "guardian of the estate" manages the child's assets.

State laws generally require a court to give significant weight to a nomination by a parent who has custody of a child. Without such a provision, the court names the guardian upon the death of the parent(s) based on available information and often depending on who volunteers for guardianship. In some cases, a client may wish to leave the personal custody of a child to one person and leave the management of the child's assets to another. It is important to ensure that the person handling the management of the child's assets is not only financially astute, but understands the financial values of the parents.

Practitioner Tip: Even when an estate is modest, it is important to name a guardian for both the person and the estate of the client's children. A client may have very strong feelings that a close friend is the best person to care for the children, and if those wishes are not expressed the children may end up in the custody of relatives or others who would not have been chosen to deal with the children and/or their assets.

LEGAL REQUIREMENTS

The legal requirements for creating a will are established by state law; however, there are some commonalities among the states. Typically, a will must be in writing, signed by the testator (or in the testator's name by some other person in the testator's presence and at his direction), and must be witnessed, or attested to, by at least two persons.[1]

Practitioner Tip: The purpose of witnesses is to attest to the testator's capacity to make a will. This is important should the will be contested.

Testamentary Capacity

A person must have the capacity to make a will at the time that the will is executed. The law ordinarily requires less mental capacity to make a will than to make a contract. An individual can make a will even if sick, elderly, weak, or of low mental capacity. A person can be declared legally incompetent to manage his affairs and still have sufficient capacity to execute a will. Capacity means that the testator must (1) be of legal age, (2) understand the extent of his property, (3) understand the natural objects of his bounty, and (4) understand the nature of his dispositions.

The general rule is that any person 18 or more years of age who is of sound mind can make a will; however, a few states have a different minimum age requirement.[2]

Understanding the extent of his property means the testator has to have a general understanding of what property he owns. For example, he must know in general that he owns a home in Ohio and a home in Florida, two life insurance policies, retirement benefits, two bank accounts, three mutual funds, household possessions, etc.

The testator must understand his relationship to the natural objects of his bounty. This means that he must understand, for example, that he is married and has two sons, a sister, and a brother.

The testator must also understand the nature of his dispositions, for example, that his spouse Mary gets the house; his brother Tom gets $10,000; his sister Janet gets the antique ring; his estranged son Mike gets nothing; and Mary gets everything else.

TYPES OF WILLS

Most commonly, each individual creates his own will, complying with the formalities prescribed by state law. There are a number of different types of wills.

Practice Standard 400-2

Developing the Financial Planning Recommendation(s)

The financial planning practitioner shall develop the recommendation(s) based on the selected alternative(s) and the current course of action in an effort to reasonably meet the client's goals, needs and priorities.

It is fairly common for a married couple to execute **reciprocal wills** in which each spouse's will leaves property to the survivor. Alternatively, a married couple or others who own property together can execute **mutual wills,** in which each party agrees to bequeath a particular property to the other. In certain circumstances, two individuals, typically a married couple, can execute a **joint will**, where one will is created for both persons. This is not a common practice, and some states do not recognize a joint will.

One of the more common estate planning structures consists of a **pour-over will** and trust. A pour-over will designates a testator's previously established trust (often a **revocable trust**) to receive the remainder of a decedent's property. The trust provides the terms for distributing assets to beneficiaries. When implementing this type of estate plan, typically assets should be transferred to the revocable trust during a testator's lifetime. When assets are transferred to the trust during life, they are not subject to probate and will pass per the terms of the trust. Assets that pour into the revocable trust via the pour-over provision in the will are still subject to probate.

Practitioner Tip: Even where an individual has a revocable trust that holds most of the individual's assets to avoid probate, it is still very important to have a will that will pour over into the previously established trust any assets that were not already transferred to the trust. If an individual does not have a will to accompany his revocable trust, any assets that have been acquired after the trust's execution may be subject to intestate succession.

Alternatively, a will can also contain testamentary trust provisions. A testamentary trust is one created under a will at the testator's death. Because the trust is established and funded after a testator's death, the property is included in the testator's estate and subject to the estate tax. Therefore, property passing from the will into the testamentary trust will go through probate.

Approximately half the states recognize a **holographic** or handwritten **will**. A will that is not effective under other provisions may be effective as a holographic will, whether or not it is witnessed, if it is dated and the signature and the material provisions are in the handwriting of the testator.[3] In some states, printed or typed material on a holographic will can invalidate it.

Less than half of the states recognize oral (**nuncupative**) **wills**, that is, wills declared or dictated by a testator during his last illness before a sufficient number of witnesses, and later put in writing. In some states, such wills are valid only under certain circumstances. For instance, they may be valid only to transfer a limited amount of personal property.

WILL CONTESTS

A **will contest** can be initiated during the probate process. Wills can be contested for number of reasons. When a will is contested it may be deemed invalid by the court. Typically a will contest is initiated by a pretermitted heir (a spouse or child not provided for in the will). It can be contested by an interested or aggrieved party on many different grounds, including the following:

1. The testator lacked sufficient mental capacity.

2. The testator was unduly influenced at the time the will was drafted.

3. The will was not executed according to statutory formalities.

4. The will offered for probate was revoked.

5. The will offered for probate was a forgery.

6. The will is the result of fraud. The heirs tried to deceive the testator.

7. There are mistakes in the clauses of the will.

Practitioner Tip: Will contests can be costly and take significant time. Financial planners should discuss the potential for will contests with their clients and help them think about ways in which they can be avoided.

MODIFYING OR REVOKING A WILL

A will should be reviewed periodically and may need to be updated. As time passes, a person's financial and family situations can change. The will itself can provide for changing circumstances by making provisions for successor beneficiaries and/or executors in the event of the death of any named beneficiaries and/or executors. A will can be amended or revoked anytime during a testator's lifetime. It is possible to revoke a will in full and to create a new will, to revoke only a portion of a will, or to add new provisions by means of a codicil. The codicil must be executed with the same formality as the will.

Reasons for Reviewing a Will

When determining whether it is appropriate to update a will, a testator should consider the following:

- Have there been any major life changes? Has the testator or any of his beneficiaries gotten married? Divorced? Had children? Have any beneficiaries died? Has the testator moved to a new state?

- Has his financial situation changed? Has wealth increased or decreased substantially? Are there any newly acquired assets that the testator would like to specifically bequeath? Has the testator previously disposed of property bequeathed in his will? Has the testator acquired real property in another state?

- Have his overall financial goals changed? Does he still wish to benefit the same individuals in the same manner?

- Have there been any changes to federal or state tax law that would affect the structure of his financial plan?

TAX IMPLICATIONS OF WILLS

Estate Tax

Property passing by will is part of a testator's probate estate and will be included in his gross estate. If property passes to a surviving spouse by will, a marital deduction may be available to offset the value of the property included in the estate. If property passes to a qualified charitable organization, a charitable deduction may be available to offset the value of property included in the estate. Both the marital and charitable deductions are available only to the extent that property is included in the taxable estate.

Property passing by will to grandchildren or more remote descendants is subject to the generation-skipping transfer tax.

Income Tax

For income tax purposes, a probate estate is a separate taxable entity. A federal fiduciary income tax return (IRS Form 1041), and often a state income tax return, must be filed annually during the period of administration if sufficient income ($600 or more for the federal return) is received during a 12-month period, or if the trust has a beneficiary who is a nonresident alien.

Chapter Highlights

- A will is the legal document that disposes of a decedent's property. If a decedent does not have a will, or does not provide for the disposition of all of his property by will, property will pass by intestate succession.

- There are many ways in which property can be disposed of by will. Tangible personal property is often the subject of specific bequests. Cash or other intangibles may be left to specific individuals by general bequest. Any assets not bequeathed by specific bequest pass as part of the residue of a decedent's estate. A will should contain a residuary clause to dispose of any property that has not been bequeathed to named beneficiaries.

- Careful attention should be paid to the manner in which assets are bequeathed. As the value of a decedent's estate fluctuates, the amount bequeathed also fluctuates. When a will contains specific bequests, the amount passing as part of the residue is affected by fluctuations in net worth.

- Only property that an individual owns in his individual name passes according to the terms of a will. Asset ownership should be carefully coordinated with an estate plan.

- Although only a client's attorney should draft a will, all members of the client's financial planning team should know how to review a will and understand the implications of will provisions.

- The debts and tax provisions of a will direct the manner in which liabilities are paid from the estate. It is important that a client pay attention to these provisions because they can reduce the amounts passing to an intended beneficiary.

- Each state's laws establish the legal requirements for executing a will. Careful attention should be paid to the formalities of execution to ensure the validity of a will.

- The level of capacity required for creating a will is less than that required for entering into other contracts. The testator must be of the age of majority and understand the nature of his property, his familial relationships, and the nature of the disposition of assets under his will.

Key Terms

ademption	intangible property
bequest	intestate
codicil	joint will
executor	legatee
general bequest	mutual will
holographic will	nuncupative will

per capita

personal representative

per stirpes

pour-over will

pretermitted heir

reciprocal will

residual bequest

residuary clause

revocable trust

specific bequest

tangible (personal) property

testate

testator

will contest

Review Questions

6-1. All of the following are requirements of a will except:

A. Must be signed by the testator.

B. Must be signed by at least two (2) witnesses.

C. The testator does not have to be competent.

D. A nuncupative will is an oral will.

6-2 and 6-3. Decedent dies owning the following assets: $250,000 real estate owned equally as a tenancy in common with his brother; $500,000 residence owned jointly with right of survivorship with his wife; $250,000 individual retirement account payable half to spouse, half to kids; $1 million life insurance policy payable in equal shares to wife, kids, the decedent's college.

6-2. The decedent's will provides that half of his estate will pass to his wife and half to his children. What is the value of the decedent's estate passing to his wife under the provisions of his will?

A. $0

B. $ 62,500

C. $520,833

D. $583,333

6-3. The testator has had a change of heart and would like to change his will so that all of his assets will pass to his wife. What is the best method by which the testator can change his will?

A. Tell his wife.

B. Cross out the section he wants changed within the will and insert the correction.

C. A codicil to the will.

D. Move to another state.

6-4. With respect to when it is appropriate to consider updating a will, all of the following are true except:

1. Whenever federal and/or state law changes.

2. Whenever the testator moves to another state.

3. Whenever there is a change in the family circumstances of the testator.

A. 1 only

B. 2 only

C. 3 only

D. 1, 2, and 3

E. None of the above.

6-5. Which of the following statements is true concerning the review of a will?

A. Only an attorney has the ability to review a will.

B. It is the unauthorized practice of law for a nonattorney to review a will.

C. Every member of the estate planning team should be able to review a will.

D. Only an attorney can determine whether there is a problem with an existing will.

6-6. The fiduciaries clause of a will does not appoint which of the following?

A. The executor.

B. The trustee of the Living Trust.

C. The trustee of the testamentary trust.

D. A guardian for minor children.

Notes

1. Uniform Probate Code § 2-502. All states except for Vermont require two witnesses. Vermont requires three witnesses.

2. In Georgia, the minimum age for executing a will is 14. In Louisiana, the legal age for executing a will is 16. In Kentucky, the legal age for executing a will is 18, unless the testator is married, in which case the legal age is 16.

3. Uniform Probate Code § 2-502(b).

Chapter 7

Incapacity Planning

CFP® CERTIFICATION EXAMINATION PRINCIPAL TOPIC COVERED IN THIS CHAPTER:

Incapacity Planning

- Definition of incapacity
- Powers of attorney
  - For health care decisions
  - For asset management
  - Durable feature
  - Springing power
  - General or limited powers

- Advance medical directives (e.g., living wills)
- Guardianship and conservatorship
- Revocable living trust
- Medicaid planning
- Special needs trust

Learning Objectives

To ensure that you have a solid understanding of the importance of planning for incapacity and the manner in which various estate planning documents accomplish the goal of incapacity planning, the following learning objectives are addressed in this chapter:

- Identify the different documents that provide for incapacity planning.

- Compare the different types of powers of attorney.

- Describe the provisions that should be contained in a power of attorney.

- Recognize the importance of coordinating special needs trust planning with available government benefits.

- Understand the need to coordinate Medicaid planning with state law.

- Describe the challenges of guardianship and conservatorship proceedings.

Chapter Contents

OVERVIEW

Much of estate planning focuses on disposing of assets in a tax-efficient manner and ensuring that assets will be distributed to whomever a client wishes in the manner he wishes. Planning for incapacity is a very important aspect of an estate plan that warrants thought and attention to ensure that a client's health and financial assets are taken care of in the event of **incapacity**. An incapacitated person is someone who is legally deemed unable to make or communicate responsible decisions regarding his health, medical or personal care, property, legal, or financial affairs.

Incapacity can occur because an individual lacks capacity because of advanced age or minority, unconsciousness or coma, physical illness, mental deficiency, or mental illness. An incapacitated person cannot make legally binding contracts such as real estate purchases, sales, or refinances, and he cannot purchase consumer goods or use credit cards, make investment decisions or banking transactions, nor make wills or personal health care decisions.

Financial planners must communicate the importance of planning for incapacity to their clients and ensure that the necessary estate planning documents are in place. This planning should always be undertaken when, by reason of age or health, there is a real possibility that a client will become mentally or physically incapacitated and unable to manage his own affairs.

Practice Standard 400-1

Identifying and Evaluating Financial Planning Alternative(s)

The financial planning practitioner shall consider sufficient and relevant alternatives to the client's current course of action in an effort to reasonably meet the client's goals, needs and priorities.

DOCUMENTS TO PLAN FOR INCAPACITY

Individuals can prepare for their possible future incapacity in a number of ways. When a client executes a **revocable trust**, it typically contains provisions addressing the grantor's incapacity. **Powers of attorney** are documents that specifically authorize the named agent to act on an individual's behalf. Powers of attorney can name someone to deal with financial matters, or to make health care decisions if the principal cannot make these decisions for himself. **Special needs trusts** are a type of trust designed to provide financial security for disabled individuals who receive government assistance.

Revocable Trust

Often, provisions pertaining to incapacity are contained in an individual's estate planning documents, such as a revocable trust. There are three parties to every trust; the grantor who creates the trust, the trustee who manages the trust assets, and the trust beneficiaries. Typically, a revocable trust contains provisions that allow for the distribution of assets to a trust beneficiary, who is also the grantor, during his lifetime and in the event of his incapacity. Further, a revocable trust typically provides that the grantor is the trustee of the trust during his lifetime and names a successor to step in and serve as trustee following the grantor's death or incapacity. When these provisions are contained in a revocable trust, the successor trustee is empowered to handle the management and distribution of the assets held by the trust. For this reason, the revocable trust should be funded with the grantor's assets before the grantor becomes incapacitated. This avoids delays in locating the grantor's assets and transferring them into the trust to be managed by the successor trustee.

Practitioner Tip: A standby trust is a type of revocable trust designed to become effective upon a grantor's subsequent incapacity. The standby trust functions similarly to a revocable trust, except that the grantor's incapacity triggers the successor trustee's duties. Like a revocable trust, the standby trust should be funded prior to the grantor's incapacity.

> ### Client Situation
>
> Ned created a revocable trust and transferred all of his investment assets into it. Ned named himself the trustee and the beneficiary of this trust, and he named his brother Dennis the successor trustee. Ned has complete control over his investment assets while he remains competent. If Ned's doctor declares in writing that Ned is mentally incompetent, then Dennis will manage the trust assets for Ned.

Practitioner Tip: A revocable trust gives the trustee certain powers to manage the assets owned by the trust. Because these powers are limited to property that is held in the trust, any assets held outside of the trust (retirement assets or other assets that have not been transferred to the trust) will not be subject to the trustee's control. It is, therefore, important to provide for the management and distribution of assets held outside the trust. Thus, although a revocable trust should contain provisions pertaining to incapacity, it is likely that other documents such as a power of attorney and heath care proxy should also be executed.

Powers of Attorney

Powers of attorney are fairly common documents that most individuals execute; they are prepared by an estate planning attorney. In some states, statutory powers of attorney and powers of attorney for health care have been created. A properly executed power of attorney can help avoid legal proceedings to establish a legal guardianship or conservatorship for an individual who may face short- or long-term incapacity. Although the power of attorney is appropriate for most clients, it is particularly important in certain circumstances:

- When the principal is elderly and there is a significant chance that he will become senile or otherwise mentally incapacitated. A broadly drawn durable power of attorney could eliminate the need to petition the local court for appointment of a guardian or conservator to handle the principal's assets.

- When an individual is suffering from a physical disability or illness, the effect of which could lead to a permanent or long-term incapacity.

Client Situation

Maggie took an early retirement to care for her mother Doris, who had signs of early dementia. Maggie began paying her mother's bills but quickly realized she needed to make financial decisions for her mother, because Doris was not fully capable of making them for herself. Maggie took Doris to an estate planning attorney and had a durable power of appointment and other estate planning documents drawn up. Now Maggie can sign documents, manage her mother's bank and investment accounts, and make financial and real estate decisions on her mother's behalf.

Powers of Attorney for Financial Matters

Legal documents such as a power of attorney allow agents to make legal and financial decisions for individuals who are incapacitated. A power of attorney is a written document that enables an individual, the **principal** (person creating the document), to designate another person or persons as his **attorney-in-fact**, or **agent**, to act on the principal's behalf. The scope of the power can be **limited** or **nondurable** and can allow the agent to act only in a very specific capacity, for example "only to pay my utility bills." A nondurable power of attorney ceases when the principal becomes incapacitated.

Client Situation

Mark, a journalist, was in the process of buying a new home when his employer sent him overseas to cover a breaking news story. Before Mark left, he had his attorney create a nondurable power of attorney. He named his sister Denise as his agent so that she could attend to the real estate closing on his home and handle other financial transactions for Mark while he was away. Denise did not have the power to act on Mark's behalf once he returned to the United States, and at that time her powers were permanently revoked.

Alternatively, the powers can be durable or **general powers,** which can be quite broad, enabling the agent to act in all matters that the principal can; for example, "all the legal powers I myself have, including but not limited to the following –." Any trusted person, such as a spouse, relative, or friend, may serve as an attorney-in-fact or an agent. The named individual need not be an attorney. It is a good idea to have an alternative or successor attorney-in-fact to serve if the agent of first choice cannot serve for any reason.

Practitioner Tip: Because the principal is conferring significant power on the agent, he should be certain that the agent is someone who is trustworthy and has some level of financial acumen. Typically an individual will name his spouse to serve as the primary agent. The power can also be drafted to require two agents to act either jointly or individually (severally). Careful consideration should be given when naming two agents to act jointly. Practically speaking, this may cause complications if, for example, the two agents do not live near each other or the principal, or if the agents do not agree on the best course of action for the principal.

Durable Power of Attorney

A **durable power of attorney** is a power of attorney that is not terminated by subsequent disability or incapacity of the principal. All states have recognized some form of durable power of attorney. The vast majority of such states have either enacted in total the durable power of attorney provisions of the Uniform Probate Code (UPC) or drafted their own statutes in conformity with the provisions of the UPC.[1]

A durable power of attorney typically contains language indicating that the powers remain intact through the principal's disability. For example, "This power of attorney shall not be affected by subsequent disability or incapacity of the principal, or lapse of time," or "This power of attorney shall become effective upon the disability or incapacity of the principal," or similar words showing the intent of the principal that the authority conferred on the agent shall be exercisable notwithstanding the principal's subsequent disability or incapacity. Unless the power of attorney states a time of termination, the passing of time will not invalidate its powers. The durable power of attorney continues until it is revoked by the principal or upon the death of the principal.

> ### Client Situation
>
> Enzo had executed a durable power of attorney, which gave his wife Alicia unrestricted powers to act on Enzo's behalf. Although Alicia, as Enzo's agent, could have used her powers to transact financial, business, or legal matters for Enzo once the document was executed, she did not exercise her powers until Enzo became mentally disabled, 20 years later. In contrast, if Enzo had executed a nondurable power of attorney, then Alicia's powers would have ceased once Enzo was declared incompetent.

Practitioner Tip: Financial institutions quite often raise the problem of "staleness," even though there is nothing in state law suggesting that the mere passage of time dates a power. For this reason, all powers of attorney should be revised every three years or less. Although banks and other financial institutions should honor a power of attorney, it is good practice to check to see whether that institution has its own specific power of attorney form or required wording. The principal should re-execute these powers periodically to keep them current while he is legally competent.

Springing Durable Power of Attorney

The typical durable power of attorney takes effect upon execution. Clients who are reluctant to grant another person wide powers to act at a time when the principal is capable of acting may prefer to use a **springing power of attorney**. A springing power does not become effective until the occurrence of a specified event such as physical or mental incapacity.

Some states define the contingencies under which the springing power becomes effective by statute, and other states require that the contingencies be specified in the document. All states require that the instrument name the person or persons who are to determine whether the contingency has occurred. For instance, if the contingency is incapacity, a doctor or group of doctors should be named to make such a determination. The attorney-in-fact may be the person making the determination.

Client Situation

Derek executed a springing power of attorney naming his wife Tracy as his attorney-in-fact, and his children Liam and Lily as successors. Tracy passed away five years ago. Derek has started showing signs of diminished capacity. Per the terms of the power of attorney, Liam and Lily have received documentation from Derek's treating physician indicating that he is no longer competent to make legal or financial decisions. Liam and Lily can handle his financial affairs under the power granted to them in the power of attorney.

As with all tools and techniques, there are costs and downsides. The major drawback of a springing power is the potential difficulty in determining whether the contingency has occurred. There may be family disputes over whether a disability has in fact triggered the springing power. This puts a premium on clear and precise language defining the contingency in the document and creating an objective mechanism for determining whether it has actually occurred. An even greater potential problem is the reluctance on the part of banks, brokerage firms, hospitals, and other institutions to accept a document granting broad powers over property if that document was executed a number of years prior to the date that it "springs."

Practitioner Tip: Durable powers of attorney—whether regular or springing—are effective only during the principal's lifetime. Because the power of attorney authorizes an agent to act in the manner that the principal can act with respect to the listed activities, once the principal dies he can no longer act, and neither can the agent.

An Agent's Powers

The extent of the powers conferred by the principal upon the attorney-in-fact is limited only by the desires of the principal. Appendix D.1 is an example of a broad general power of attorney in which the principal attempts to confer upon the attorney-in-fact the right to act to the same extent the principal would have acted if the principal were present and able to act.

The attorney-in-fact can be given the power to make gifts on behalf of the donor, although this is the one area involving the use of durable powers that has resulted in the most tax controversy. The powers must specifically authorize the attorney-in-fact to make gifts, or state law must allow the attorney-in-fact to make gifts. Further, any power allowing an agent to make gifts to himself must be limited in the power of attorney, or the assets could be included in the agent's estate.

Note that if the durable power of attorney is drafted to permit the attorney-in-fact to make gifts, consideration should be given to whether the power holder can make gifts to himself. Bear in mind that the attorney-in-fact is often a close family member. If that person can make gifts to himself, this power could be deemed a general power of appointment for federal tax purposes, and the failure to exercise the power could constitute a taxable gift. (See Appendix D.2.)

Client Situation

Rita, who is very wealthy, has a durable power of attorney that names her husband Will as her agent. Will has been given the power to make all financial, legal, business, and real estate decisions for Rita if she becomes incapacitated, and he can also make gifts to himself from Rita's property interests. Because Will has been granted a durable power of attorney with such sweeping powers, Rita's assets can be included in Will's gross estate at death, as if Will has a general power of appointment over Rita's property. This would ruin Rita's existing estate plan and would substantially increase her estate tax liability.

Table 7.1 Advantages and Disadvantages of Powers of Attorney

Advantages of Powers of Attorney	Considerations with Powers of Attorney
Allows an individual's desires to provide for the continuity of the management of the individual's assets in the event the individual is unable to manage such assets for either a short or long duration of time because of physical or mental incapacity. The durable power of attorney permits an individual, when competent, to make a determination of who will handle his affairs.	An agent can undertake only those powers expressly conferred by the document. The lack of flexibility in the document could prohibit the agent from exercising a power that needs to be exercised, but which cannot be. For example, if the document is drafted so that the agent can enter into certain contracts relating only to personal property, but the needs of the disabled principal require that his real estate holdings be liquidated, the power of attorney may be of no benefit to the principal.
Unlike a guardianship, which requires a legal declaration that the disabled person is both legally and mentally incompetent, a power of attorney can be used without the stigma of a declaration of incompetency.	In many states, the power of attorney is referred to as being durable, meaning that the document is binding at the time it is executed, even if the principal is not incapacitated at that time.
The POA is relatively inexpensive to administer and its form is quite simple.	Many lending institutions will not accept a durable power of attorney. Furthermore, the institutions that do accept them may do so only if the power meets certain specific guidelines established by the institution itself.
No implied powers may be inferred from the fiduciary role that the agent undertakes because the agent cannot undertake additional powers without the consent of the principal. However, state law can expand or contract powers that are not clearly articulated or delineated within the power of attorney.	A bank or a brokerage firm may not accept a durable power of attorney because it is not current enough according to their standards. The principal should re-execute these powers periodically to keep them current while the principal is legally competent.
Often, only one document needs to be drafted and the agent can exercise only the powers expressly contained in the document.	An agent has a fiduciary duty to act in the principal's best interest, but he is not held to the same fiduciary standards as a trustee, because he or she does not hold legal title to the principal's property. The agent can be held liable for using the powers contrary to the principal's best interest.
	Durable powers of attorney cannot be used after death to dispose of property omitted from a will.

Powers of Attorney for Health Care

A **power of attorney for health care** or **health care proxy** designates an individual to make decisions regarding medical treatment in the event the principal is not legally competent. The extent of the permissible powers varies according to state law. In general, the principal authorizes the agent or attorney-in-fact to make certain decisions regarding medical treatment on behalf of the agent. Some of the responsibilities of the agent include conferring with medical professionals to determine where the principal should be treated, the extent of medical treatment that should be provided, whether surgery should be performed or medications should be administered, and whether life support (or which type of life support) should be administered. A principal can also limit the agent's authority and specify under what circumstances the agent can act on the principal's behalf.

One of the most important and controversial aspects of this document is the extent to which it authorizes the attorney-in-fact to terminate treatment or even terminate life support when the principal is terminally ill or is in what is called "a persistent vegetative state," meaning the principal is in a permanent coma and the best medical opinion is that the principal will never recover.

In some states, the durable power of attorney for health care is a separate legal document (from the power of attorney for financial matters) and requires more formality in execution than the durable power for management of property. In other states, the two powers are combined in a single document. (See Appendix D.3.)

The Health Information Portability and Accountability Act of 1996 (HIPAA) was amended in 2003 to provide greater protections regarding confidential medical information. A health care provider must receive express written permission to disclose any information regarding a patient's health condition or care. There is some concern in the legal field that unless HIPAA provisions are included in a power of attorney for healthcare (or a separate HIPAA disclosure is executed) a physician could potentially be prohibited from releasing information regarding a patient to his named attorney-in-fact. For that reason, the power of attorney for health care should contain HIPAA provisions (or a separate HIPAA release should be executed).

Client Situation

Derek executed a health care proxy naming Tracy as his attorney-in-fact and his son Liam as her successor. Because Tracy passed away, Liam will be responsible for consulting with Derek's physicians to determine appropriate medical treatment for Derek as his condition worsens.

Practitioner Tip: As with all estate planning documents, health care powers of attorney should be updated periodically. A copy of the health care power of attorney should be given to the principal's doctors and agent, and the original should be kept in a safe place that is easily accessible to the agent. Unless the agent has access to the principal's safe deposit box, the document should not be kept there.

Living Will

A **living will**, also called an **advance directive** or a **natural death declaration**, enables an individual to direct in advance what kind of health care he desires or rejects in the event he becomes so ill he cannot at the time communicate his desires with respect to life-sustaining medical treatment. The living will enables an individual to choose what kind of medical care he wants or does not want under specified circumstances. Many states have statutory living will forms (a form of living will designed by a state legislature) designed for use specifically in terminal illness situations, but living wills are not recognized in all states

---

Practitioner Tip: One disadvantage of a living will is that it is brief and may contain vague language that is not written in medical terms. Consequently, it may not be detailed enough to provide sufficient medical directives in particular situations, and it might not address all treatment options available to an individual. This lack of information can result in differing interpretations of an individual's wishes. Therefore, physicians and family members should be informed in writing of the extent of medical treatment that an individual desires before a serious illness occurs.

A **do-not-resuscitate declaration (DNR)** authorizes health care providers to withhold CPR or other measures to restart a patient's heart or breathing. Unlike a living will, a DNR is appropriate only for a small group of people who are in the final stages of a terminal illness or who are suffering from a serious condition such that they do not want to receive emergency treatment.

A health care proxy can include living will provisions and also name an agent to make health care decisions. Although the living will is usually concerned only with directives concerning the withdrawal or withholding of life-sustaining medical treatment in the event of a terminal illness, the durable power of attorney for health care can address itself to any range of health decisions desired by the principal. (See Appendix D.4.) In the absence of either a living will or a health care proxy, an incapacitated patient's desires with respect to life-sustaining treatment can be determined and communicated by a court-appointed surrogate or guardian. Once a guardian is appointed, he is the sole advocate for the patient's wishes as they were conveyed to others by the patient prior to incapacity. Because there is no hard evidence as to an incapacitated patient's desires in the absence of a living will or health care proxy, the patient's wishes may sometimes go unfulfilled because of the high standard of proof required by most states in such cases.

Client Situation

In addition to his health care proxy, Derek has executed a living will expressing that he does not want life-sustaining medical treatment. If he is in an accident and requires life-sustaining medical treatment, his attorney-in-fact and his physicians should refer to this document and respect his wishes.

Special Needs Trusts

A special needs trust is a type of trust established by clients who have children or other beneficiaries who have a disability and are receiving Social Security benefits or other forms of state or federal assistance. Disabled individuals who receive Social Security Disability Insurance (SSDI), Supplemental Security Income (SSI), and Medicaid benefits need to maintain these benefits that provide them with monthly cash payments and comprehensive medical insurance. Individuals who qualify for SSI have very limited financial resources and receive only small cash payments each month to cover their basic living expenses. Special needs trusts are intended to permit the donor to furnish some economic benefits to the beneficiary without disqualifying him for public assistance. The trust may also be used to provide for elderly persons who are disabled, such as a parent.

The purpose of the special needs trust is to permit payments by the trustee to cover the needs of the disabled person that do not affect his eligibility for public assistance. Trust assets are available to provide services for disabled beneficiaries that are not covered by Medicaid or other public assistance programs. The special needs trust does not intentionally provide for basics such as food, clothing, shelter, and in particular, medical care. Special needs trusts should always be coordinated with public assistance programs, because the trust corpus cannot be used to replace public benefits. It provides only for non-necessaries such as birthday and holiday gifts and comforts of life that cannot be considered basic needs. Assets can also be used to improve the beneficiary's living situation by paying for communication services such as computers, Internet access, cable television and telephone services, and for basic household furnishings.

The guidelines for which assets can be considered resources available to the disabled person are determined by state law. If the assets in the trust are available for the basic needs of the disabled person, it could result in the denial of public assistance, or the appropriate government agency might even seek to compel reimbursement of public assistance payments from the trust assets.

On the other hand, property held in such a trust does not count as a resource of the disabled person if access to the trust assets is restricted. In general, such trusts should follow a discretionary or protective trust format used for asset protection, but it must be even more restrictive. For example, if the trust provided that the trustee could use trust assets only for the "support" of the disabled person, it would count as an available resource.

Such trusts should specifically provide that the trustee cannot make any payments that cover items provided by public assistance programs. The trust must be irrevocable, and an independent trustee is preferred. It may be part of the basic estate plan of the parents, either in a will or living trust that takes effect at death. Although the trust could be created irrevocably while the parents are alive, this is generally discouraged. It could have gift tax consequences, and government officials must be informed whenever a disabled person becomes the beneficiary of an irrevocable trust.

To guard against attacks from the providers of public assistance, these trusts can provide for contingent beneficiaries, such as other children, who could become the exclusive beneficiaries of the trust if such an attack is launched. The trust may also have a destruct clause, providing that if the providers do attempt to reach it or use it to disqualify the disabled person it will terminate and be distributed entirely to contingent beneficiaries, such as the other children.

Client Situation

Derek's daughter Lily has a special needs son, Sam. Derek wants to provide for his grandson but wants to be certain that any inheritance does not disqualify his grandson from the government benefits he is currently receiving. Derek has created a special needs trust for Sam's benefit that will only pay assets to Sam for certain circumstances, such as for supplemental attendant care and additional therapies. He has named an attorney specializing in disability planning as the trustee and is confident that the trust will be administered in a way that will not disqualify Sam from his current benefits.

ABLE Act

The Achieving a Better Life Experience (ABLE) Act was signed into law Dec. 19, 2014 which expanded section 529 of the Internal Revenue Code to allow the creation of tax favored accounts for disabled individuals. These accounts are available for persons with a documented onset of disability prior to age 26 and are intended to supplement the benefits they currently receive from SSI, Medicaid and private insurance.

An ABLE account will function very similarly to a 529 account, however, there are some very distinct differences between an ABLE account and 529 account. First, only one account can be opened per beneficiary, and the account must be opened in the state that the beneficiary resides. Further, contributions are capped at the annual gift tax exclusion amount, which is $14,000 per beneficiary in 2015. Balances in the ABLE account, up to $100,000, is exempt from the $2,000 resource cap on personal assets that ordinarily affects eligibility for Medicaid and Supplemental Security Income (SSI) benefits. Beneficiaries will lose their eligibility to receive monthly SSI benefits, but not Medicaid benefits, when the account exceeds $100,000. Each state will determine the total contribution limits for these accounts based on limits they have previously established for 529 education plans in their states, which is typically $300,000 or more per plan. Similar to 529 plans, account contributors or designated beneficiaries may change the way money is invested in the account up to twice a year.

Distributions from the account will be tax-free if the money is used for "qualified disability expenses". Examples include expenses for education, housing, transportation and health care and these accounts can also cover expenses related to employment training and support, assistive technology, personal support services, financial management and administrative services. Note that when an account beneficiary dies, states would be able to recoup some expenses through Medicaid.

There are several advantages and disadvantages when comparing ABLE accounts to special-needs trusts.

- Special-needs trusts can hold an unlimited amount of assets to cover supplemental expenses not covered by Medicaid while ABLE accounts can only hold up to $100,000 before SSI benefits are suspended.

- Money distributed to a disabled beneficiary from a special-needs trust is considered taxable income while qualified distributions from ABLE accounts are tax-free. Keep in mind that any undistributed trust income that exceeds $12,300 in 2015 is taxed at 39.6% but ABLE accounts are not taxed.

- There are legal costs associated with establishing a special-needs trust and a trustee controls and manages the assets, whereas with an ABLE account, it is less expensive to open an account and the account owner can control the assets within the account.

Practitioner Tip: Parents can establish both a special-needs trust and a 529 ABLE account for their disabled child to accomplish different planning objectives.

MEDICARE AND MEDICAID PLANNING

A number of federal programs are available to assist in providing health care for the elderly and disabled, including Social Security Disability, Supplemental Security Income, Medicare, and Medicaid.

Social Security Disability

Social Security Disability provides benefits when an individual is unable to engage in gainful employment by reason of medically established mental or physical impairment that must be expected to last until death or continuously over a period of at least 12 months. Supplemental Security Income, often called SSI, provides for needy persons who are elderly, blind, or otherwise disabled. Medicare provides medical benefits on the basis of a person's age without regard to need. Medicaid provides medical assistance to the needy regardless of age.

Medicare

In general, taxpayers who are age 65 and eligible for Social Security, or who are age 65 and whose spouses are eligible for Social Security, are eligible for Medicare. Part A of Medicare provides hospital insurance at no cost except for deductible and coinsurance amounts that must be paid by the patient. Part A also provides limited coverage for care in a skilled nursing facility, in a hospice, or post-hospital home health services. Part B of Medicare primarily covers physician's services and is voluntary. Premiums are required under Part B. Certain individuals over age 65 who are not covered by Part A can elect voluntary coverage by paying premiums if they are enrolled in Part B. Certain disabled persons under age 65 can also be eligible for Medicare benefits.

Medicaid

Medicaid is a joint federal and state program that provides assistance for health care to certain aged, disabled, or blind individuals. The intent is to provide help to needy individuals. In some cases, this is integrated with the requirements for SSI, described above. Each state establishes its own eligibility standards; determines the type, amount, duration, and scope of services; sets the rate of payment for services; and administers its own program. Many states impose an income cap based on SSI requirements. These tests depend heavily on state law. There are also special requirements for nursing home benefits.

For Medicaid purposes, *resources* are assets owned or available to an individual that are tested against threshold levels determined by each state within federal guidelines. Individuals whose resources exceed a certain amount will be ineligible for certain benefits like nursing home care. Resources often include the income of the individual and spouse and assets owned by the individual and the spouse.

When one spouse is in a nursing home, the law permits the other spouse, who is called the "community spouse," to retain assets of a certain value. The amount varies from state to state. In this regard, revocable trusts can cause substantial problems. If the trust language permits the use of trust assets for the support of the institutionalized spouse, the trust will be considered an available resource. Further, the community spouse may not be able to claim any exemption for the trust assets because they are not in his name. The revocable trust should contain specific language dealing with these issues.

State law determines whether an individual's personal residence counts as an asset for purposes of Medicaid eligibility. For example, in California, the residence is exempt even if an individual is in a nursing home if the individual indicates he intends to return to his home at some point in time. When the home is exempt, it can be transferred without penalty and without affecting eligibility for Medi-Cal benefits.

Congress has imposed and continues to impose strict limits on the transfer of assets to achieve Medicaid eligibility. In addition, the Deficit Reduction Act of 2005 made changes designed to thwart planning in this area. For example, the value of any assets transferred within 60 months before an individual makes an application for Medicaid will be considered an available resource.[2] Penalties are in the form of denial of Medicaid benefits for a period of months depending on the value of the property transferred. There are exceptions, including one for transfers to children who are "caretakers" for their parent. There are other exceptions for transfers to spouses, minor children, trusts for disabled children, etc. Check the law for the effective dates of this look-back period.

For assets transferred to trusts, the look-back period is still 60 months from the date the individual makes a Medicaid application or the date the individual enters a nursing home. Assets transferred to trusts within 60 months prior to these dates are considered an available resource.[3] This includes trusts—other than trusts created by will—that are created by the individual, his spouse, and certain third persons, such as conservators and trustees. The purpose for which the trust was created is irrelevant.

Assets in a revocable trust are presumed to be available resources regardless of when the trust was created. Additionally, if any assets are transferred from the revocable trust to another individual within the 60-month period, that transfer is also subject to the 60-month look-back period.

Assets in an irrevocable trust are also deemed to be available resources if payment could be made to the individual from the trust. There are various exemptions, and the statutes are confusing regarding the extent of availability.

LEGAL ASPECTS OF INCAPACITY PLANNING

Very often family members want to become involved in making medical and personal care decisions for their loved ones, but they may not have the time or expertise to manage the incompetent person's finances, property, business, or legal affairs. Further, if an individual has not previously planned for these circumstances, family members or other caregivers will have to be appointed guardians or conservators by the court system. This can result in high costs, delays, and ongoing court supervision. For these reasons, it is imperative that clients anticipate and plan for their incapacity.

Practitioner Tip: Many married couples believe that if one spouse becomes incapacitated, the other spouse will automatically care for them and manage their property interests as well. This is a serious misconception because guardianship of person and property is determined by the probate court. Without proper legal planning, the court will appoint individuals to care for an incapacitated person and their property, who may or may not be their spouse, nor the person whom the incapacitated individual would have selected as guardian.

Guardianship

Guardianship is a fiduciary relationship created by the law for the purpose of enabling one person, the **guardian**, to manage the person or estate, or both, of another person, the **ward**, when the law has determined that the ward is incapable of managing his person or estate himself. Wards fall into two general categories: (1) minors; and (2) adults who have been legally adjudged incompetent to act for themselves.

The term *guardian* is used to refer to both the guardian of the person of the ward and the guardian of the ward's property. The guardian of the person takes custody of the ward, looks after his personal needs, and in general performs the duties performed by the parents of a minor (except the duty of support). The guardian of a ward's property, sometimes known as a **conservator**, a **curator**, or a **committee**, is charged with the responsibility of investing and managing the estate of the ward. One who is appointed a guardian, without any further words of limitation, is held to serve in both guardianship capacities (**plenary guardianship**).

Unlike a trustee, a guardian does not take title to the ward's property. Title to the ward's property remains in the ward; the guardian takes custody and control of the ward's property as an officer of the court under whose supervision he acts. Whereas a trustee derives his powers from the trust instrument, a guardian derives his powers from the law. Limited guardianships can be awarded to manage only specific aspects of an incompetent person's care, giving the individual some control over his circumstances.

Conservatorship

Conservators have the authority under the Uniform Probate Code to manage and distribute the ward's property for the support, education, care, or benefit of the protected person and his dependents.[4] Typically, courts and state laws restrict a conservator to making only a limited number of conservative investments, and permission from the court is required to engage in most property transactions. Restrictions are also placed on the use of the ward's assets and on the ability to make gifts of the ward's property.

Wills cannot be created for the incompetent individual. Limited conservatorships further restrict the management of property and number of transactions a conservator can make on behalf of an incompetent individual.

The court that normally has jurisdiction to appoint a guardian is the court in the state of the ward's domicile that has jurisdiction of probate matters. Because a guardian's powers at common law do not extend outside the state in which the guardian is appointed, and because a guardian functions as an officer of the court that appointed him, courts are reluctant to appoint as guardian anyone not a resident within the jurisdiction of the court.

Guardianship proceedings are determined by state law, and a high cost and time delay are often associated with the proceedings. States vary in the manner in which they appoint guardians; however, there are some commonalities. Typically a petition will be filed with the appropriate court indicating that a ward has become incompetent. The court will appoint a guardian *ad litem* to represent the ward and protect his rights. Court proceedings are public matters, and interested parties may testify with respect to the ward's mental state. If the court determines that the ward is incompetent, it will appoint a guardian. The court will exercise ongoing supervision and control.

Practitioner Tip: Courts are reluctant to determine that an individual is incompetent. Furthermore, the subject of a guardianship proceeding typically does not desire the control of his person and possessions to be granted to another. This can be a highly emotionally charged area, and to the extent possible it should be avoided by proper planning.

Some states have statutes that require guardians appointed within the state to be residents of the state. Sometimes, therefore, an ancillary conservator of the estate will be appointed in the state (outside the ward's domicile) where the ward owns property. In many cases, however, the state (outside the ward's domicile) where the ward actually resides or where his property is located will, as a matter of comity, recognize the authority of the guardian appointed by the state of the ward's domicile. But "full faith and credit" requirements of the U.S. Constitution do not appear to hold much sway in guardianship; if a local court thinks the welfare of the ward requires the appointment of a local guardian, such action is likely to be taken whether or not a guardian was appointed in the state of the ward's domicile. Some courts will, if necessary and if statutes permit, appoint nonresident guardians.

Chapter Highlights

- An incapacitated person is one who is legally unable to make certain decisions regarding his health care or to manage his finances. Incapacity planning allows an individual, before he becomes incapacitated, to designate the person or persons he wants to ultimately handle his affairs in the event of incapacity.

- Durable powers of attorney are documents that name an agent or attorney-in-fact to handle a principal's financial affairs. The durable power of attorney may be effective upon execution or spring into effect upon the occurrence of a specific event (typically the principal's incapacity).

- Durable powers of attorney can confer very broad or very limited powers on an agent. Durable powers remain in effect after a principal becomes incompetent.

- Health care proxies or health care powers of attorney are documents that name an individual to make health care decisions on the principal's behalf in the event of his incapacity. A living will is the document outlining a principal's wishes with respect to the type of medical care he wishes to receive.

- Special needs trusts are trusts established for individuals who are receiving some sort of government assistance. Special needs trusts should be coordinated with state law to ensure that payments made would not disqualify a beneficiary from receiving government benefits.

- Medicaid is a joint federal and state program that provides medical benefits to certain individuals. Eligibility requirements restrict the amount of assets that an individual may have while qualifying for Medicaid. These limits vary from state to state. There is a five-year look-back period that affects eligibility for Medicaid.

- Guardianship and conservatorship are court-determined proceedings wherein an individual is named to care for an incompetent person's property and person. These proceedings can be time consuming and costly; therefore, proper attention should be paid to incapacity planning before disability occurs.

Key Terms

advance directive

agent

attorney-in-fact

committee

conservator

curator

do-not-resuscitate declaration (DNR)

durable power of attorney

general power of attorney

guardian

guardianship

health care proxy

incapacity

limited power of attorney

living will

natural death declaration

nondurable power of attorney

plenary guardianship

power of attorney

power of attorney for health care

principal

revocable trust

special needs trust

springing power of attorney

ward

Review Questions

7-1. There are several advantages to using a durable power of attorney rather than a conservatorship for managing an incompetent person's property. Which statement is incorrect?

A. A durable power of attorney avoids the need for a public court hearing that would declare a principal incompetent.

B. A durable power of attorney avoids the need for ongoing court supervision and the payment of legal fees to manage a principal's financial affairs.

C. With a durable power of attorney, the principal, rather than the courts, appoints a fiduciary to handle his financial affairs.

D. With a durable power of attorney, the principal does not retain title to his own property because the title is transferred to the attorney-in-fact. Similarly, the courts award a guardian legal title to a ward's property.

7-2. Which of the following statements best describes the purpose of a special needs trust?

A. To avoid the look-back period when transferring assets into a Medicaid trust.

B. To pay trust income to the beneficiary for food and shelter.

C. To preserve the beneficiary's eligibility for government benefits and public assistance programs.

D. To shelter the disabled person's assets for Medicare eligibility.

7-3. Which statement regarding a springing durable power of attorney is correct?

A. A springing power of attorney ends once the principal becomes incompetent.

B. A springing power of attorney remains in effect after the principal's death.

C. A springing power of attorney is activated once the principal is declared incompetent by his physicians.

D A springing power of attorney is activated when the document is executed.

7-4. Which of the following statements pertaining to health care powers of attorney and living wills is incorrect?

A. A living will can appoint a health care agent to make end-of-life decisions for the principal.

B. State statutes dictate provisions in living wills, and living wills are not recognized in all states.

C. Under a health care proxy, an agent can make decisions concerning whether surgery should be performed and medications should be administered to the principal.

D. A principal can limit the agent's authority in the health care power of attorney document.

7-5. The difference between a durable power of attorney and a springing power of attorney is:

A. The durable power of attorney takes effect immediately; the springing power of attorney takes effect only upon the occurrence of a specified event.

B. The durable power of attorney takes effect only on the occurrence of a specified event; the springing power of attorney immediately springs into effect.

C. Both the durable power of attorney and the springing power of attorney take immediate effect.

D. Both the durable power of attorney and the springing power of attorney take effect upon the occurrence of a specified event.

Notes

1. UPC §5-501.
2. 42 USC §1396p(c)(1)(B)(i).
3. *Ibid.*
4. UPC §5-425.

Chapter 8

Trusts

CFP® CERTIFICATION EXAMINATION PRINCIPAL TOPIC COVERED IN THIS CHAPTER:

Types, Features, and Taxation of Trusts

- Classification
  - Simple and complex
  - Revocable and irrevocable
  - Inter-vivos and testamentary

Types and basic provisions

- Spendthrift trust
- Pour-over trust
- Sprinkle and spray provisions

Trust beneficiaries: Income and remainder

Rule against perpetuities

Estate and gift taxation

Learning Objectives

To ensure you have a solid understanding of the various types of trust and planning strategies available, the following learning objectives are addressed in this chapter:

- Define and describe the uses of the four types of trusts, including revocable, irrevocable, inter-vivos, and testamentary.

- Describe the basic components of trusts, including identifying the parties to a trust.

- Recognize various trust provisions and their purpose within a trust.

- Identify and explain the operating terms of a trust and the dispositive provisions of a trust.

Chapter Contents

OVERVIEW

A trust is a fiduciary relationship in which property is held by one (or more) person(s) for the benefit of one (or more) person(s). The person creating the trust is generally called a **settlor**, **trustor**, or **grantor**. The grantor typically executes a trust document and transfers property to the person who will be responsible for administering the terms of the trust, who is called a **trustee**. The trustee receives title to the trust property and generally manages and distributes income according to the terms of the trust. The person for whose benefit the trustee administers the trust is called a **beneficiary**. The beneficiary receives the direct or indirect benefit of the use of income from and/ or principal of the trust property. The property held in trust is often called the **trust corpus** or **res**.

There are many different types and features of trusts. A trust can provide for the management of property, the accumulation or distributions of income to beneficiaries, the distribution of the trust corpus to beneficiaries, the withdrawal powers of beneficiaries, and other powers of appointment.

It is important for financial planners to understand the different types of trusts and the common provisions of trusts, which are very common estate planning instruments. To understand a client's estate plan, a financial planner should be able to review a client's trust and recognize the various tax and other planning strategies. The planner will also need to understand the different types of trusts to make appropriate recommendations to clients. Although only an attorney can draft a trust instrument, it is imperative that financial planners understand how to review a trust.

Practice Standard 400-1

Identifying and Evaluating Financial Planning Alternative(s)

The financial planning practitioner shall consider sufficient and relevant alternatives to the client's current course of action in an effort to reasonably meet the client's goals, needs and priorities.

PARTIES TO A TRUST

Grantor

The grantor or settlor is the person who establishes a trust. There may be more than one grantor to a trust, for example with a joint trust. The grantor is the party responsible for establishing the terms of the trust, including the dispositive provisions (i.e., who gets what and when they get it). The grantor also determines other parties to the trust.

Trustee

The trustee is the person (and/or institution) named in a trust agreement to carry out the objectives and follow the terms of the trust. More than one trustee may serve (**co-trustees**). A trustee can be an individual (professional or nonprofessional) or a **corporate fiduciary**. Because trusts can be complex legal instruments that require scrupulous attention to detail, the grantor should take great care in selecting a trustee. If the trust is an irrevocable trust, trust income tax returns may need to be filed on an annual basis, which will be the trustee's responsibility. Moreover, a grantor typically establishes a trust to provide for a particular planning objective. He may wish to accomplish estate tax or income tax planning, to provide for the security of his beneficiaries, to protect assets from creditor claims, or provide for a special circumstance. The trustee is the party responsible for ensuring that the purpose of the trust is met and that the terms of the trust are upheld.

The type and size of assets to be placed into the trust, as well as a client's goals, are important considerations when selecting a trustee. A trustee should possess business judgment, honesty, and integrity. The trustee must be able and willing to exercise a high degree of care over trust property. Investment skill is necessary. Under the "prudent person" rule, a trustee will be liable to the beneficiary for losses unless he exercises the same care and skill that a person of ordinary prudence would exercise in dealing with his own property. But the Uniform Probate Code, now in effect in some form in most states, raises this standard for professional trustees by providing: "If the trustee has greater skill than that of a man of ordinary prudence, he is under a duty to exercise such skill."

Practitioner Tip: There are significant advantages and disadvantages to naming a family member or friend as trustee. The obvious advantage is that such a person may have a working knowledge of the client and the family. A nonprofessional trustee may be indicated where the minimum fee charged by local professional fiduciaries is higher than it is feasible to pay or where the trust has relatively simple provisions or a smaller principal.

A corporate fiduciary (with or without individuals as co-trustees) is indicated when it is likely that the trust will span more than one generation. Corporate fiduciaries are also indicated when the amount placed into the trust is large and/or will require skillful and constant attention. If there is a likelihood of family conflict, corporate fiduciaries can make decisions on a more objective, disinterested basis than family members.

One common strategy is to name an **individual trustee**, such as a family member or friend, to serve as co-trustee with a corporate fiduciary. This allows the individual trustee to address the personal considerations of the trust while the corporate trustee addresses business decisions.

Practitioner Tip: Because a trust can be operative for many years—often for the lifetime of a younger generation such as children or grandchildren—it is a good idea to provide flexibility for changes that may occur in the future. One way to do this is to allow the beneficiaries to remove and replace a trustee. This is particularly important if a corporate trustee is serving. Although a client may have a strong relationship with a current trustee, changes in the family situation or within the corporation can make this relationship less desirable in the future.

Client Situation

Kathy and Artie have established a trust that will benefit their children and grandchildren. The trust is designed to last through the grandchildren's lifetimes. Kathy and Artie funded the trust with $1 million, and they anticipate that the value of the trust will grow significantly. Because the trust has significant value and none of their children or grandchildren are financial professionals aware of the importance of managing this asset, Kathy and Artie name their local bank as trustee. They are worried that the small bank they are working with may merge with a larger bank, or that their children might leave their hometown, making working with the bank they have selected less attractive. Kathy and Artie give their children and grandchildren the ability to remove the bank and name another corporate trustee after both Kathy and Artie have died.

Trust Protectors

A **trust protector** is not a required party to a trust but is sometimes used in trust planning. A trust protector may also be referred to as a *special trustee* or *trust advisor*. A grantor can name a trust protector to provide greater flexibility for carrying out trust provisions in the future. The trust protector can adapt various trust provisions as determined when the grantor establishes the trust to provide for changes in tax law or beneficiary circumstances. Some of the powers that a trust protector may be given include the ability to terminate the trust, reduce or accelerate distributions to a beneficiary, name additional beneficiaries, remove beneficiaries, remove or replace a corporate trustee, make changes to the trust to take advantage of changes in tax laws, or change the situs or location of the trust to a jurisdiction that is more favorable for asset protection, or terminate the trust.

Trust protectors are beneficial when a trust will not be funded until after a grantor's death, will continue past the grantor's death, or in an irrevocable trust where the grantor has not retained the right to change trust beneficiaries. The trust protector can make personal decisions for the trust or beneficiaries in lieu of the grantor. Appointing a trust protector to make such decisions enables the grantor to have these changes made without bringing the assets back into the grantor's estate. However, if the grantor is actually controlling the disposition of trust assets through the trust protector, then there is a risk that the assets will be included in the grantor's estate.

Trust Beneficiaries

Trust interests are often split into an **income interest** and a **remainder interest**. A beneficiary with an income interest generally receives income from the property for a fixed period of years, for life, or until the occurrence (or nonoccurrence) of a particular event. The beneficiary with the remainder interest is the ultimate beneficiary of trust property and receives the property when the income interest ends.

Income Beneficiary for a Term of Years

The income beneficiary of a trust has the right to receive trust income for a number of years, as stipulated in the trust document. The income interest is a present-interest gift, and the donor can use an annual exclusion to offset a taxable gift based on the present value of the income interest.

Client Situation

Ann transfers $150,000 into a trust today. The trust has two beneficiaries, Ann's sister Janet and her son Bill. Income will be distributed to Janet annually for the next 10 years. After that, the trust corpus and income interest will be available to Bill. Janet is the income beneficiary and Bill is the remainder beneficiary.

To calculate each party's respective interest, the present value of Bill's remainder interest will be subtracted from Ann's gift. Using an HP12C Calculator, and assuming a 4% interest rate, the calculation can be performed as follows:

FV = $150,000, n = 10, i = 4.0, PV = $101,335.

The present value (PV) of the remainder interest gift to Bill equals $101,335. This is a future-interest gift that cannot be reduced by Ann's annual exclusion. An annual exclusion is available to a person making a gift to reduce the tax on the gift by $13,000. But it cannot be used if the person receiving the gift has to wait to use the property, which is the case with a remainder interest gift.

Janet's income interest is determined by subtracting the remainder interest from $150,000 ($150,000 – $101,335 = $48,665). Ann can apply an annual exclusion of $13,000 to reduce the gift tax on the income interest in the trust to $35,665. In making this gift to the trust, Ann has made a total taxable gift of $137,000 ($101,335 + $35,665).

A beneficiary who dies after his income interest ends will not have the trust assets included in his estate. If the beneficiary dies before the income term ends then his remaining interest will pass either as appointed or by will.

Income Beneficiary with a Life Estate

A beneficiary can also receive a life estate in a trust, which entitles him to receive all trust income for life. The income interest ends at the life tenant's death and is not included in his estate.

Client Situation

Today Paul and Rose transfer $150,000 into a trust with two beneficiaries: Paul's father Jake, age 72, and their daughter Heather. Income will be distributed annually to Paul's father for the remainder of his life. When Jake dies, Heather will receive the remainder of the trust property.

To calculate the value of Jake's income interest, assuming a 9.6% interest rate, the Single Life Valuation Table must be consulted (see Exhibit 8.1).

Exhibit 8.1 Example of Income Interest

TABLE S (9.6)
SINGLE LIFE FACTORS BASED ON LIFE TABLE 2000CM

9.6% INTEREST							
Age	Annuity	Life Estate	Remainder	Age	Annuity	Life Estate	Remainder
72	6.2356	0.59862	0.40138				

Calculate the PV of Jake's income interest by finding his age on the valuation table. Because Jake's income interest is a life estate factor, the amount transferred into the trust should be multiplied by the life estate factor ($150,000 × .59862 = $89,793) to calculate the value of the father's income interest.

The remainder interest passing to Heather can be calculated in two ways:

1. Multiply the remainder factor: 0.40138 × $150,000 = $60,207

2. Subtract the income interest: of $150,000 – $89,793 = $60,207

Remainder Beneficiaries in Trust

A remainder beneficiary can have either a **vested remainder interest** or a **contingent remainder interest**. A vested remainder interest is a fixed and absolute interest. If the beneficiary dies before receiving the remainder interest, it will pass by will. With a contingent remainder interest, the right to receive trust property depends on the occurrence of a specific event.

Client Situation

In the preceding example, Heather had a vested remainder interest. Heather was the remainder beneficiary following Jake's death. If Paul and Rose indicated that Heather would receive trust property only if she survived Jake, she would have had a contingent remainder interest.

Practitioner Tip: When property that is the subject of a split-interest transfer is real property, the remainder beneficiary has an immediate vested interest in the property and can sell or gift the remainder interest without the life tenant's permission. The buyer or donee of the property will have to wait until the expiration of the life tenant's interest before he can enjoy the property.

TRUST CLASSIFICATION

A trust can be classified under several categories: simple or complex, revocable or irrevocable, inter-vivos or testamentary. A trust will fall into one or more of these categories. For example, a trust can be a testamentary, irrevocable complex trust.

Simple Trusts versus Complex Trusts

A trust is classified as simple or complex based on its distribution provisions. A **simple trust** is one where all trust income must be distributed in the year it is earned. The trustee cannot distribute trust principal or make charitable gifts. Alternatively, a **complex trust** can accumulate income, distribute corpus, and make gifts to charities. A complex trust qualifies as a separate tax entity that deducts income distributed and pays tax on income retained.

Client Situation

Casey and Tom have established a trust for their daughter Caroline. The trust provides that all income is to be paid to Caroline annually. No other distributions are permitted. This is a simple trust. They have also established a trust for their daughter Grace. The trust for Grace allows the trustee to distribute income or principal at his discretion. This is a complex trust.

Revocable Trusts versus Irrevocable Trusts

Trusts created during a grantor's lifetime are either revocable or irrevocable; a trust created at death is irrevocable. A revocable trust is a trust in which the grantor retains the right to revoke the trust; upon revocation, property in the trust is returned to the grantor. A trust that is not revocable is irrevocable.

Practitioner Tip: Whether a trust is revocable or irrevocable is clearly defined in the trust document. It is important to recognize whether a trust is revocable or irrevocable because of the tax consequences.

Revocable Trusts

Revocable trusts can be funded or unfunded. This means that the grantor can transfer property to the trust either upon execution or at some later date. Revocable trusts are inter-vivos trusts, which are trusts created during a grantor's lifetime. The grantor retains the right to revoke or amend the trust at any point in time and retains total control over trust assets. A revocable trust becomes irrevocable when the grantor, during his lifetime, relinquishes title to property placed in the trust and gives up all right to alter, amend, revoke, or terminate the trust, or when the grantor dies.

Planning with a revocable trust. The use of a "pour-over" will and revocable trust is a very common estate planning strategy. Typically, a pour-over will directs that following the grantor's death, any assets passing by will pour into the trust. When this strategy is used, the goal is to transfer any individually titled assets from the owner's name to the name of his trust. As long as the individual is alive, the assets remain his and he can use them as he wishes. At death, the trust becomes irrevocable and assets are disposed of per the terms of the trust. The trust contains the dispositive provisions of the decedent's estate plan.

Although a will can be used to dispose of assets at a decedent's death, there are a number of benefits to using a revocable trust instead of a will to transfer assets at a client's death. Any assets that pass by will are a matter of public record. A revocable trust provides privacy in the administration of a decedent's affairs. Further, any assets passing per the trust are not subject to probate. This can be particularly attractive if the client lives in a state that has a more challenging probate process. It is also very attractive if the client owns property in multiple states: transferring ownership of that real property to a revocable trust will avoid ancillary probate in the second state.

Using a revocable trust during a client's lifetime also confers certain benefits. Revocable trusts can provide for the management of the grantor's assets or beneficiaries' assets if they become incapacitated. A revocable trust also allows the grantor to name a trustee to manage assets, enabling the grantor to see whether professional management by a corporate trusetee is preferred, or if the assets are managed competently by an individual trustee.

As with any planning strategy, certain considerations can offset these advantages. There may be costs associated with establishing a trust: attorney fees, transfer costs for changing title to property, and trustee fees for managing assets if the grantor elects professional asset management. Such costs can be greater than the costs of establishing a will. A revocable trust offers no creditor protection because the grantor retains too many rights and powers. The assets held in a revocable trust are subject to any creditor claims.

A revocable trust is appropriate in a number of situations; it should be used when the grantor would like:

- someone else to accept management responsibility for all or a portion of the grantor's property;

- to ensure continuity of management and income flow of a business or other assets in the event of death or disability;

- to protect against the investment and asset management problems that would be brought on by his own physical or mental incapacity or legal incompetency, or the physical, mental, or emotional incapacity or legal incompetency of beneficiaries;

- privacy in the handling and administration of his assets during lifetime and at death;

- to minimize estate administration costs and delay at death by avoiding probate;

- to see how efficient, competent, and costly the trust (and the trustee) is in operation;

- to avoid ancillary administration of assets situated in other states by placing title to those assets in the trustee of a revocable living trust;

- to reduce the potential for an election against, or a contest of, the will. However, in some states, the statutory estate that can be elected against is expanded to include revocable living trusts; or

- to select the state law under which the provisions of the dispositive document will be governed.

Tax consequences of the revocable trust. Because the grantor of the revocable trust retains the right to revoke or amend it, he still maintains control of the trust principal; therefore, all income generated by the property held in trust is taxable to the grantor. No gift tax is generated by establishing or funding a revocable trust because the gift is not completed until the trust becomes irrevocable. Because the grantor has not irrevocably disposed of any assets, the entire trust corpus is included in the grantor's estate for federal estate tax purposes.

Client Situation

Kim has established an estate plan consisting of a will and a pour-over trust. Kim transfers ownership of her home and her investment account to her trust. She has not transferred ownership of her money market account at her local bank to her trust. Following her death, the money market account will pass to her trust per the terms of her will. This asset will be subject to probate. Kim's home and her investment account will not be subject to probate because they are already owned by her trust. All assets will pass to the beneficiaries named in Kim's trust. While she is alive, Kim has to pay income tax on income earned on her investment account because it was held in a revocable trust. All assets will be included in Kim's taxable estate.

Irrevocable Trusts

Unlike a revocable trust, an irrevocable trust must be funded to legally exist. An **irrevocable trust** is created by a grantor during his lifetime and is funded during his lifetime. When a grantor creates an irrevocable trust, he no longer owns the trust property, he retains no control of the trust property, and he cannot change the terms of the trust.

Although irrevocable trusts generally cannot be changed, some states permit changes to the trust if all of the people who have an interest in the trust agree, or if a court approves the change. In some states, the trustee may be permitted to make administrative changes as well.

Planning with an Irrevocable Trust. Irrevocable trusts are used to accomplish many different planning objectives. Some of the more common types of irrevocable trusts include:

- An irrevocable life insurance trust (ILIT), which holds life insurance policies on an insured's life;

- A Crummey trust, which can be used as the recipient of annual exclusion gifts or larger taxable gifts;

- A qualified personal residence trust (QPRT), which is used to transfer a grantor's primary residence or vacation home;

- A grantor retained annuity trust (GRAT), which is used to transfer the appreciation on an asset to children or other relatives;

- A special or supplemental needs trust (SNT), which is used to preserve a beneficiary's government assistance;

- A dynasty trust, which is used to leave assets in trust in perpetuity for many generations; and

- An intentionally defective grantor trust (IDGT), which is used to transfer assets to children or other beneficiaries while allowing the grantor to retain certain powers or control over trust property.

Tax Consequences of an Irrevocable Trust. The grantor of an irrevocable trust generally makes a gift upon transfer of property to an irrevocable trust. Assuming the grantor has not retained any control over the trust, the value of the assets will not be included in the grantor's estate. Whether the grantor is taxed upon trust income or whether the irrevocable trust is includable in the grantor's estate generally depends on what interests the grantor has in the irrevocable trust. Under certain circumstances, property that a grantor gifts to an irrevocable trust can be included in the grantor's estate at his death. Some of these circumstances include:

- When the grantor retains a life estate, a right to trust income, or a right to use or enjoy trust property. (Code section 2036).

- When the grantor retains a reversionary interest valued at greater than 5%, the value of the reversionary interest will be included in the estate (Code section 2037).

- When the grantor retains a general power of appointment over trust assets either during lifetime or at death.

- When the grantor dies within three years of transferring a life insurance policy to a trust, or if the grantor has retained any incidents of ownership in a policy that is owned by the irrevocable trust.

- When the grantor retains the right to change trust beneficiaries, add new trust beneficiaries, or alter a beneficiary's interest (Code section 2038).

- When trust principal or income can be used to discharge the grantor's legal obligations, such as child support.

If the trust is a grantor trust as classified by Code sections 674–677, income will be taxed to the grantor and may be included in the grantor's estate. If the trust is not a grantor trust, income generated by trust assets will be taxed to the trust and distributions to the beneficiaries are taxable to the beneficiaries.

Inter-vivos Trusts versus Testamentary Trusts

A **testamentary trust** is a trust created at the decedent's death per the terms of his will. Assets passing by will to a testamentary trust are subject to probate at the grantor's death and potentially continuing after death, and any assets passing by testamentary trust are a matter of public record. Assets passing from the decedent's will to the testamentary trust are included in the decedent's probate estate.

On the other hand, trusts created during lifetime (**inter-vivos trusts**) are established during the grantor's lifetime (when the grantor is alive). Assets passing by inter-vivos trust generally are not subject to probate. Assets may be taxed in the decedent's estate depending on whether the trust is revocable or irrevocable. An inter-vivos trust can be established for a limited period of time and last until the occurrence or nonoccurrence of a specific event, or it can continue after the death of the grantor.

COMMON TYPES OF TRUSTS AND TRUST PROVISIONS

Distribution Provisions

Assets in trust can be left to beneficiaries in many different ways. A grantor should carefully consider the manner in which he wishes to leave assets to his beneficiaries. Factors to consider include the beneficiary's financial position, financial knowledge, and ability to handle the receipt of assets. The trustee is the party responsible for making distributions to beneficiaries. If a trustee has the discretion to make distributions to beneficiaries, the grantor should provide guidance for the trustee. For example, the trustee may be permitted to make distributions of principal or income for a beneficiary's health, education, maintenance, or support (HEMS). This is an example of a **discretionary provision** known as an *ascertainable standard*.

The trustee may also be instructed to make distributions to support the beneficiary. When a trust contains **support provisions**, the trustee will distribute as much income or principal as necessary to discharge the grantor's legal obligation of support for the trust beneficiaries. Support trusts are used in divorce situations to provide a fixed stream of income to the custodial parent on behalf of the children, and it ends when the youngest child is 21.

Trusts can also provide **sprinkle** and **spray provisions**. A sprinkle provision in a trust gives a trustee discretionary authority to allocate income to beneficiaries in an equal or unequal manner. A spray trust authorizes a trustee to distribute some or all of the income or corpus to beneficiaries in equal or unequal amounts.

Spendthrift Provisions or Spendthrift Trust

In a broad sense, a **spendthrift clause** is a provision in a trust in which the grantor attempts to provide funds to a beneficiary while limiting the ability of the beneficiary to squander the funds or creditors of the beneficiary from reaching the funds. Spendthrift provisions could include any of the following: (1) prohibiting the beneficiary from transferring the beneficiary's interest; (2) forfeiting a beneficiary's interest if the beneficiary attempts to transfer that interest; (3) distributions of income or principal to a beneficiary are limited to the beneficiary's support (possibly, limited to distributions on behalf of the beneficiary for support rather than distributions directly to the beneficiary); (4) distributions to a beneficiary at the trustee's discretion; or (5) a prohibition against creditors reaching the beneficiary's interest.

States differ considerably as to when a creditor of a beneficiary can reach the beneficiary's trust interest. Unless the trust document or state law provides otherwise, a creditor of a beneficiary can generally reach the beneficiary's trust interest.

State laws generally attempt to restrict a grantor's ability to prevent creditors from reaching a beneficiary's interest in one of the following ways: (1) no restriction, creditor can reach trust interest; (2) creditor can reach amount not needed by beneficiary for support; (3) creditor can reach amount above some dollar amount; or (4) creditor cannot reach trust property.

Trust Jurisdiction or Situs

Theoretically, the law of any state with which a trust has contact could apply. Such states could include the state where the grantor resided upon creation of the trust, where the trustee is located or resides, where trust property is located (especially with regard to real estate), or where the beneficiaries reside. The grantor may specify in the trust document the state whose laws are to be applied to the operation and termination of the trust. Also, the grantor can permit the trustees to "move" the trust to another state, in which case the laws of the new state will apply. This is called changing the **situs** of the trust.

Rule Against Perpetuities

Some states allow for **perpetual** or **dynasty trusts** that can last indefinitely. However, many states limit the duration of trusts. The **rule against perpetuities** is a statutory limit on the duration of trusts that provides that a beneficiary's interests in a trust must generally vest within the period allowed. For example, all members of a class must generally be ascertainable immediately or within the period allowed for in the rule against perpetuities. And a beneficiary must generally be born within the period allowed for in the rule against perpetuities.

The common-law version of the rule against perpetuities generally provides that interests in property must vest no later than a life in being plus 21 years (plus a gestation period, if necessary). This means that the trust must terminate no more than 21 years plus 9 months after the death of the last trust beneficiary alive at the time the trust was created. Interests that did not vest within the rule against perpetuities at the creation of a trust would be void. Many states have a version of the common-law rule against perpetuities (sometimes codified). Other states have adopted a "wait-and-see"' approach; that is, an interest is void only if the interest actually fails to vest within the perpetuities period. The Uniform Statutory Rule Against Perpetuities (1990) (some version of which is in effect in approximately one-half the states) provides that a non-vested interest is invalid unless (1) as of the date of the creation of the trust, the interest is certain to vest or terminate within a period measured by a life in being plus 21 years (plus a gestation period, if necessary); or (2) the interest either vests or terminates within 90 years of its creation. Some states have eliminated the rule against perpetuities.

Trusts should be drafted to comply with the rule against perpetuities if applicable in the state whose laws govern the trust documents. A clause may also be inserted that provides that any interest must vest within the time provided by the rule against perpetuities.

Pour-over Trust

A **pour-over trust** is a revocable or irrevocable inter-vivos trust created to receive and consolidate assets passing from a decedent's will or property outside of probate (such as life insurance death benefits, pension plans, and IRA assets).

Chapter Highlights

- A trust is a legal entity. The parties to a trust have a fiduciary relationship. The grantor transfers property to the trustee, who manages the assets and distributes trust property to the beneficiaries per the terms of the trust.

- A grantor should carefully select a trustee based on the terms of the trust, the trust property, and the beneficiaries' needs and capabilities.

- Trust beneficiaries can have an income interest or a remainder interest.

- Trusts can be revocable (meaning the grantor can change all or part of the trust and can take all assets out of the trust) or they can be irrevocable and cannot be changed.

- Revocable trusts are common estate planning instruments that accomplish many goals including privacy, avoidance of probate, control over distributions to beneficiaries, and terms for continued control and management of assets.

- Income generated from assets held in a revocable trust is taxed to the grantor. There is no gift tax consequence for a grantor funding a revocable trust because he has not given up control of the trust property. Assets held in a revocable trust are included in a grantor's estate at his death.

- When an irrevocable trust has been funded, the grantor has made a completed gift to the trust that may be subject to gift tax. Income generated from assets in the trust will be taxed to the grantor if the trust is a Grantor Trust, or to the trust. Distributions to beneficiaries are taxed to the beneficiaries.

- Inter-vivos trusts are created during a grantor's lifetime, and assets passing per the terms of the trust will not be subject to probate. Testamentary trusts are established under the terms of a decedent's will, and assets are subject to probate.

- Trusts outline the terms of distribution of trust property. Property may be distributed on a discretionary basis; the trustee can sprinkle or spray trust income among trust beneficiaries.

- Spendthrift provisions may be added to a trust to protect trust assets from being exhausted by beneficiaries or the creditors of beneficiaries.

- The rule against perpetuities is a statutory limitation on the duration of a trust. The common-law rule against perpetuities allows trusts to last for 21 years and 9 months after the death of the last trust beneficiary.

Key Terms

beneficiary

complex trust

contingent remainder interest

corporate fiduciary

co-trustees

discretionary provision

dynasty trust

grantor

income interest

individual trustee

inter-vivos trust

irrevocable trust

perpetual trust

pour-over trust

remainder interest

res

revocable trust

rule against perpetuities

settlor

simple trust

situs

spendthrift clause

spray provision

sprinkle provision

support provision

testamentary trust

trust corpus

trust protector

trustee

trustor

vested remainder interest

Review Questions

8-1. All of the following statements concerning a testamentary trust are correct except:

A. Its provisions are included in a decedent's will.

B. It saves probate costs.

C. It is revocable until the death of the testator.

D. It becomes irrevocable once it becomes operative.

8-2. Which of the following is not an advantage of a revocable trust?

A. Assets passing per the terms of a revocable trust will not be subject to probate.

B. Assets passing per the terms of a revocable trust will not be included in a decedent's gross estate.

C. A revocable trust offers privacy.

D. A revocable trust may provide for incapacity.

8-3. Which of the following is an example of a discretionary provision?

A. The trustee is instructed to distribute income to the beneficiaries annually.

B. The trustee is instructed to distribute a certain dollar amount of principal annually.

C. The trustee is instructed to make distributions for a beneficiary's health, education, maintenance, or support.

D. The trustee is directed to pay income or principal upon the beneficiary's request.

8-4. A financial planner notes the following during a meeting. Her client's estate planning goals are to provide for her two children. One of the children is a successful physician and was recently sued by a patient for medical malpractice. The other child has a gambling problem and is having a hard time managing his assets. Which of the following strategies is most appropriate to provide for her needs?

A. A trust giving the trustee the ability to sprinkle and spray trust property.

B. A trust containing spendthrift provisions.

C. Outright distribution of trust property to the children.

D. Passing all assets to a Pour-over Trust.

8-5. Which of the following statements is correct?

A. Only individuals can be beneficiaries of a revocable trust.

B. Assets transferred to a revocable trust cannot be used by the grantor of the trust.

C. An irrevocable trust allows the grantor to change trust terms as he wishes.

D. A testamentary trust becomes irrevocable at the decedent's death.

Chapter 9

Income Taxation of Trusts, Estates, and Beneficiaries

CFP® CERTIFICATION EXAMINATION PRINCIPAL TOPICS COVERED IN THIS CHAPTER:

Income in Respect of a Decedent (IRD)

Assets qualifying as IRD
Calculation for IRD deduction

Income Tax Treatment

Simple and complex trusts
Distributable net income (DNI)

Grantor Trusts

Learning Objectives

To ensure that you have a solid understanding of the income tax considerations that relate to a client's trust and estate, the following learning objectives are addressed in this chapter:

- Recognize the income tax consequences of simple versus complex trusts.

- Explain the concept of distributable net income.

- Identify a grantor trust.

- Identify the most common income that can be classified as IRD, including pay, interest, dividends, and business income.

- Describe the tax consequences for both the decedent and heir/beneficiary for income included in a decedent's gross estate and/or final income tax return.

- Calculate the IRD deduction for one or more sources.

Chapter Contents

OVERVIEW

Although much of estate tax planning focuses on the estate tax, certain income tax considerations come into play in a client's overall estate plan. Trusts and estates are treated in the tax law as separate taxpayers that are required to file annual federal income tax returns. Congress chose to adopt a hybrid approach for estates and trusts known as the **sharing concept**. The general rule is that the trustee or executor pays income tax on the amount of income the trust or estate retains. Beneficiaries pay tax on the income of the trust or estate actually distributed to them. In some circumstances the grantor of a trust is deemed the owner of a trust for income tax purposes, and income tax on assets held in trust is assessed to the grantor of the trust rather than to the trust itself or to trust beneficiaries.

An additional income tax consideration pertaining to trusts and estates is the concept of **income in respect of a decedent**, or **IRD**. The concept of IRD provides that assets that would have been subject to ordinary income tax by a decedent if he had received the income prior to his death are subject to tax when received by a trust or beneficiary. However, if these assets were subject to estate tax in the decedent's estate, the beneficiary (or trust) would be permitted to deduct the estate tax attributable to that asset.

Further, the current estate tax exemption amount makes estate tax planning less of a concern for many, and the need to consider both the client and beneficiaries' income tax situations more of a planning concern.

The estate planner or financial planner must attain a degree of familiarity with the income taxation of estates and trusts, and IRD, to properly service clients. Members of the estate planning team must have a working knowledge of the income tax ramifications of various trust arrangements to perform properly.

Practice Standard 400-2

Developing the Financial Planning Recommendation(s)

The financial planning practitioner shall develop the recommendation(s) based on the selected alternative(s) and the current course of action in an effort to reasonably meet the client's goals, needs and priorities.

INCOME TAXATION OF TRUSTS AND ESTATES

A trust is a tax-paying entity. The taxable income of a trust (or an estate) is computed in basically the same manner as that of an individual; however, there are several important distinctions. The tax brackets for trusts (and estates) are much more progressive than for individuals. (See Appendix B.1.) In other words, given the same amount of income, a trust or estate will pay a much higher tax for income it retains than an individual would pay. Also, in computing tax liability, multiple trusts are treated as one trust, and their incomes are aggregated if the trusts have substantially the same grantor or grantors and substantially the same primary beneficiary or beneficiaries and if a principal purpose for the existence of the trusts is the avoidance of federal income tax.

Practitioner Tip: You cannot cut income taxes by creating cookie-cutter replica trusts for the same beneficiaries.

Generally, for tax purposes trusts are treated as separate entities from the grantor, the trustee, and the beneficiary. The basic question in the income taxation of trusts is, "Who will be taxed on trust income—the trust, the beneficiary, or the grantor?" Generally, the burden of taxation falls on either the trust itself or the beneficiary. But it is possible for the income of the trust to be taxed to the grantor in a so-called **grantor trust** where, for income tax purposes, the trust is deemed the alter ego of the grantor.

A trust is not allowed a standard deduction.[1] Further, the personal exemption is limited to $300 for a simple trust and $100 for a complex trust.[2] (If a trust is required to distribute its income to a beneficiary, it will not lose the $300 exemption even if it distributes corpus or makes a charitable contribution in a given year and thus is considered complex for all other purposes.)[3]

Practitioner Tip: Income tax rates for trusts increase much more quickly than income tax rates for individuals. For example, a trust is taxed at the highest rate of 39.6% when income exceeds $12,300 in 2015, but an individual generally does not reach the 39.6% income tax bracket until income exceeds $413,200. Further, under the Health Care and Education Reconciliation Act of 2010, trusts that are in that top tax bracket will pay the 3.8% Net Investment Income Tax (NIIT) on the lesser of net investment income or modified adjusted gross income exceeding the threshold. Individuals do not face the 3.8% net investment income tax until they have $200,000 of income if single or $250,000 if married.

Taxation of Simple Trusts

Trusts are categorized for income tax purposes as either *simple* or *complex* trusts. Either type of trust can also be a grantor trust. A simple trust requires that all income be distributed to the beneficiaries annually and does not allow for any other distributions. If all income does not have to be distributed currently, or if the trust can make distributions from principal, or if it can make charitable gifts, it will be deemed a complex trust for that taxable year.

A **simple trust** is treated as a separate tax entity. As such, it has the same deductions as an individual, subject to certain exceptions. It also has a special deduction for income that is distributable to its beneficiaries. The net result is that a simple trust does not pay tax on income it pays out. The beneficiary of a simple trust reports the income that he receives or that is receivable by him. In other words, a simple trust acts like a funnel—a true and complete conduit for passing the trust income from the grantor to the beneficiaries.

> ### Client Situation
>
> Sue is the beneficiary of a trust created by her father. The trust holds $500,000 invested in a bond portfolio. The trust provides that all income is to be paid to Sue annually and does not provide for distributions of principal. The trust has generated $20,000 of income this year; it will distribute the income to Sue and she will claim it as income on her income tax return. The trust will file an informational income tax return showing that the income was distributed to Sue and that no income is attributable to the trust.

Taxation of Complex Trusts

A second type of trust is known as the complex trust. A **complex trust** is any trust that is not a simple trust. That is, a complex trust is one in which the trustee either must or may accumulate income.[4] The trustee of a complex trust, unlike the trustee of a simple trust, can also distribute corpus (principal) or make gifts to charities.

A complex trust, like a simple trust, is a separate taxable entity. It is allowed a special deduction for actual distributions of income but pays tax on any income it does not distribute. Generally, the same rules that govern complex trusts also apply to the income taxation of a decedent's estate.

Distributable Net Income (DNI)

When a complex trust distributes assets to a beneficiary, the general rule is that the trust or estate pays income tax on the amount it retains and the beneficiaries pay tax on the income of the trust or estate actually distributed to them. This result is obtained by applying the **distributable net income (DNI)** concept. Thus, income is taxed only once. Under the concept of DNI, to the extent that a trust has income and distributes assets to beneficiaries, the distributions are deemed income first, and as a return of principal to the extent the distribution exceeds the income received by the trust.

The concept of DNI is used to achieve three main results: First, it ensures that the trust or estate receives a deduction for amounts distributed and provides a limit for that deduction.

> ### Client Situation
>
> Ethan is the sole beneficiary of a trust. Assume the trust earns $10,000 in income and distributes $6,000 of that income to Ethan. The trust would be taxed on the amount it retains, $4,000, and it would deduct $6,000 for the amounts distributed. The $6,000 actually distributed would be taxed only once, as income to the beneficiary.

Second, DNI limits the portion of distributions that is taxable to beneficiaries.

Client Situation

If the trust in the preceding example distributed $12,000 to Ethan, it would be allowed to deduct $10,000 (i.e., the amount it received in that year as income), and the trust would have no tax liability (because the $10,000 deduction it takes wipes out the $10,000 of income it received). Ethan would be taxed on only $10,000 of the $12,000 he received because only that amount was attributable to income. The remaining $2,000 distributed to Ethan is considered a tax-free distribution of trust corpus.

Practitioner Tip: Under the concept of DNI, the characterization of distributions and the breakdown into income and corpus are not left to the trustee to decide. Under the **income first rule**, the trustee's classification of a distribution as *income* or *corpus* is ignored; instead, all amounts distributed are deemed to be income to the extent of DNI.

Client Situation

Assume a trust had interest income of $10,000 that a trustee decided to accumulate. In the same year the trustee decided to distribute $10,000 of corpus to one of the beneficiaries. If the trustee made the distribution, the beneficiary would be deemed to have received $10,000 in income, even though in actuality the trustee might have been distributing an amount from corpus.

The third function of DNI is to ensure that the character of distributions to a beneficiary remains the same as in the hands of a trust or estate. Tax-exempt interest received by a trust and distributed to a beneficiary retains its character as tax-exempt and is exempt from ordinary income taxation to the beneficiary or heirs.[5] Likewise, what enters the trust or estate as ordinary income remains ordinary income when received by beneficiaries or heirs. This is known as the **conduit theory**.

Client Situation

Anne is the beneficiary of a trust that allows the trustee to distribute trust principal and income for her health, education, maintenance, or support. The trust has $20,000 of taxable income and $15,000 of tax-exempt income in 2015. The trust distributes $45,000 to Anne in 2015. On her income tax return, Anne will realize $20,000 of ordinary income and $15,000 of tax-exempt income. The trustee will be allowed to deduct these amounts as distributions on the trust's income tax return. The remaining $10,000 distributed to Anne will be a return of principal. The trust will not be allowed to deduct this amount; however, Anne will not realize this amount as income on her income tax return.

Grantor Trust Rules

In some cases the trust itself is disregarded as a taxable entity. A grantor trust is either a simple or complex trust in which the trust is disregarded as a taxable entity. Generally, in the case of either a simple or complex trust, the trust or its beneficiary is taxable on the income of the trust. However, in some cases the grantor is taxed on the trust income whether or not the grantor actually receives the income. Under the **grantor trust rules**, when the grantor of a trust is treated as the owner of a portion of the trust corpus for income tax purposes, items of income, deductions, and credits that are attributable to that portion of the trust are deemed to be the grantor's. Accordingly, the grantor of the trust is deemed to be the recipient of trust income and is allowed a deduction to the extent that there are trust expenses and/or credits. The grantor trust rules are found in I.R.C.§§ 671–677.

A trust is deemed a grantor trust if the grantor or the grantor's spouse:

- retains a reversionary interest in either the trust corpus or income exceeding 5% (of the value of the trust's principal or income interest);[6]

- can control the beneficial enjoyment of a trust;[7]

- retains certain administrative powers such as

  - the power to purchase, exchange, or otherwise deal with or dispose of the corpus or income of the trust for less than adequate consideration in money or money's worth;[8]

  - the power to borrow trust corpus or income without adequate interest or security;[9]

  - certain administrative powers, including the power to vote stock of a corporation in which the grantor or the trust has a significant voting interest, the power to control investment of the trust funds, and the power to reacquire the trust corpus by substituting other property of an equivalent value;[10] or

- can revoke the trust;

- can receive distributions of trust income; or

- income can be held or accumulated for future distribution to the grantor or grantor's spouse, or applied to the payment of premiums on life insurance policies on the life of the grantor or the grantor's spouse.[11]

Client Situation

Seth established an irrevocable trust and transferred his life insurance policy to the trust. The beneficiary of the trust is his wife, Maddie. Seth owns and rents two storage units, which he also transferred to the trust. The rental income from his units will pay for the annual premiums on his life insurance policy. This irrevocable life insurance trust is subject to grantor trust rules because the trust income is used to pay the insurance premiums on Seth's life. In this case, the income the trust receives from the storage units is taxable to Seth and not to the trust.

Although a poorly drafted trust could unintentionally include these provisions, often the inclusion of grantor trust provisions is intentional. This is known as an **intentionally defective grantor trust (IDGT)**. The trust must still file an income tax return (IRS Form 1041); however, income will not be taxed to the trust, but will be taxed to the grantor instead. Trust assets may or may not be included in a decedent's estate at death depending on the type of powers or rights the grantor retained.

INCOME TAXATION OF ESTATES

An executor or administrator has the duty to file two different types of income tax returns for a decedent. He must file a decedent's last income tax return and an estate's income tax return.

A decedent-taxpayer's tax year ends with the date of his death. For example, if John dies on March 30, an income tax return must be filed for the short year of January 1 to March 30. The return must be filed on the regular due date, April 15th, of the following year.[12] The amount of income and deductible expenses that must be reported depends on the deceased taxpayer's regular method of accounting.

For cash-basis taxpayers, only income actually or constructively received must be reported. Deductions can be taken only for expenses actually paid. If the decedent was on the accrual method, the return will show all income and deductions accrued through the date of death.[13] Any income received following the decedent's date of death will be considered IRD.

As a taxable entity, an estate must pay tax on its income.[14] If the income of the estate consists of dividends from stock and interest from bonds, these items comprise the gross income of the estate. Likewise, if there is rental income, royalty income, income from the sale or exchange of property, or income from a business carried on by the executor or administrator, then the income of the estate includes those items as well.

Because an estate is considered a separate tax entity, it has not only income but also deductions. An estate can deduct reasonable amounts paid for administration costs including executor's fees, legal fees in connection with the administration of the estate, and expenses of preparing the income tax return of the estate.[15] If the estate manages a business, it is entitled to deduct ordinary and necessary business expenses.

Practitioner Tip: Some expenses, such as administration expenses including executor fees and legal fees, can be taken on either the income tax return of the estate or as deductions from the gross estate to obtain the net estate for federal estate tax purposes. However, the same expense generally cannot be taken as a deduction on both the estate income tax return and the estate tax return.[16] In such cases, the executor would have to weigh the relative advantages and take the deduction where it would be most advantageous. If an estate is not subject to estate tax it could make sense to take the deductions on the income tax return for the estate (IRS Form 1041) rather than on the estate tax return (IRS Form 706).

> ### Client Situation
>
> Marie died in 2015. Her estate consisted of a $500,000 home, a $1 million stock portfolio, and a $250,000 IRA. The total value of her estate is $1,750,000, which is less than the available estate tax exemption in 2015 of $5,430,000; therefore, her estate will not be subject to estate tax. Marie's estate has administrative expenses of $150,000. Her executor should elect to take this deduction on her estate's income tax return rather than the estate tax return because her estate will not have an estate tax.

An estate is also entitled to a deduction for amounts of income distributed.[17] An estate can take a $600 personal exemption.[18] As previously mentioned, to the extent that the estate retains income, it is taxed, and to the extent that the beneficiaries receive income, they are taxed. The estate might have income and DNI available to distribute to beneficiaries. The only beneficiaries who will not pay income tax on distributions of income from estates are those who receive specific bequests under the will.

> ### Client Situation
>
> Assume that Marie's will states, "I bequeath $5,000 to my grandson Eddie, and all the rest, residue, and remainder to my granddaughter Chrissy." During the first year of the administration of the estate, assets held by the executor generate $16,000 of income. The executor distributes $5,000 to Eddie and $11,000 to Chrissy. Because Eddie's $5,000 was a specific bequest, he is not taxed. This amount is considered a distribution of estate corpus. In this case, Chrissy would be taxed on the $11,000 she received, and the estate would be taxed on the remaining $5,000 of income.

INCOME TAXATION OF BENEFICIARIES

Once assets are received by a beneficiary, either through gift or through inheritance, there may be income tax considerations for that beneficiary. For example, if assets are given outright to a beneficiary, rather than to a trust for a beneficiary, then any income earned by those assets will be taxed directly to the beneficiary on his Form 1040. The timing and manner that assets are transferred to a beneficiary will impact the income tax.

In addition to ordinary income or capital gains tax, taxpayers should consider the impact, if any, of the 3.8% net investment income tax imposed under Health Care and Education Reconciliation Act of 2010. Single taxpayers with greater than $200,000 of modified adjusted gross income or married taxpayers with greater than $250,000 of modified adjusted gross income will pay an additional 3.8% tax on the lesser of net investment income or modified adjusted gross income exceeding the threshold.

> ### Client Situation
>
> James is a successful single. James has earned income of $150,000 and investment income of $100,000. James will be subject to a 3.8% net investment income tax on $50,000. If James had earned income of $300,000 and investment income of $100,000, then $100,000 would be subject to net investment income.

Practitioner Tip: A CFP® practitioner should understand the income tax impact that gifts or bequests will have not only on the donor of the property, but also on the recipient of the property. Comprehensive planning will help both the donor and recipient prepare for these tax planning issues and make adjustments as necessary.

Basis Considerations

When a beneficiary receives assets, and those assets generate taxable income, the beneficiary will have to pay income tax. When that beneficiary sells the underlying asset, there may also be further income tax considerations depending on whether the beneficiary received that asset by lifetime gift or by bequest. When a donor makes a gift of property to a beneficiary during the donor's lifetime, the beneficiary will receive the donor's basis in that property. If that same property is transferred to the beneficiary upon the donor's death, and it was included in the donor's estate at death, that property will receive a step-up in basis to the date of death value.

Client Situation

Amy is meeting with her financial planner to discuss certain gift and estate planning strategies. Amy purchased a beach house in 2000 for $350,000. The value of this house has appreciated, and is now worth $500,000. Amy wants her daughter Riley to have the house. Her financial planner explains that if Amy gives the house to Riley while Amy is still alive, Riley's basis in the home will be $350,000. However, if Amy bequeaths the asset to Riley at Amy's death, Riley's basis in the home will be $500,000. Assuming Riley will sell the home following Amy's death, it may make sense for Amy to bequeath the property to Riley (rather than to give it to her during lifetime) so that Riley will enjoy the step-up in basis and will face less of a capital gains tax on the value of the home when it is sold.

The type of property that is transferred will also have an impact on the income tax consequences. When a beneficiary inherits IRA or other retirement assets, for example, he will have to pay income tax on any amounts distributed from those accounts. There is no step-up in basis on these assets. The beneficiary will, however, be allowed to deduct on his income tax return any estate tax that was paid and attributable to that asset. This may impact the type of assets that a client wishes to give or bequeath to individuals or to charity both during lifetime or at death.

Client Situation

In addition to the beach house, Amy has a $1 million IRA and a $1 million mutual fund account. Amy tells you that she wishes to leave one-half of these assets to Riley and the balance to her favorite charity. You explain to Amy that if Riley receives the IRA assets, she will have to pay income tax when she takes distributions from the IRA. However, if she leaves Riley the mutual funds, Riley will inherit those funds with a stepped up basis. Riley can sell the mutual funds with no capital gain.

Practitioner Tip: It is important to consider the income tax implications to beneficiaries receiving different types of property in order to advise clients which types of assets are best to leave to each beneficiary.

INCOME IN RESPECT OF A DECEDENT

There are a number of situations where an individual earned income but had not yet been taxed on the income because he did not actually or constructively receive the income by the date of death.[19] For example, an insurance agent's renewal commissions paid after death cannot be included in his last income tax return. Other examples of IRD include interest on certain U.S. Savings Bonds or accrued interest on other bonds, deferred compensation, and retirement plan or IRA assets that have not been distributed from the retirement plan as of the decedent's death. These assets may not have been subject to income tax as of the date of the decedent's death, but they would have been taxable to the decedent had he received them. These sources of income will not escape taxation.

It is important to know what types of assets are deemed to be items of IRD. Capital assets, such as bank accounts, CDs, stocks, bonds, mutual funds, real estate, and business assets are not. The beneficiary of these assets receives as his basis in the property the fair market value (FMV) of the asset at the time of the decedent's death. These assets typically receive a step-up in cost basis.

Taxation of IRD Assets

Income in respect of a decedent is taxed to the recipient of the payments. In other words, the estate or the beneficiary who receives IRD pays tax on it in the same manner that it would have been taxed to the decedent. If it had been ordinary income to the decedent (had he lived), it would be ordinary income to the estate or beneficiary.[20] What would have been return of capital to the decedent remains tax free when recovered by the estate or beneficiary. There is no step-up in basis at death for IRD.[21]

The problem with respect to IRD items is that they are included in the decedent's taxable estate and subject to estate tax, and then they are also subject to income tax when the estate or beneficiary receives the assets. The estate that includes or beneficiary who receives an IRD item is entitled to a deduction on the same income tax return for the amount of additional federal estate tax attributable to inclusion of that item in the decedent's federal estate tax return.[22] This precludes the beneficiary paying income tax on an asset that was already subject to (and presumably had the value reduced by) estate tax.

To calculate the income tax deduction that the beneficiary will be allowed, the estate tax attributable to the asset must first be calculated; this includes the value of the IRD items. Next, the estate tax must be calculated subtracting the value of the IRD items. The difference represents the estate tax attributable to the IRD items.

Client Situation

Walter had an estate valued at $10 million. An estate tax of $1,900,000 was assessed on Walter's estate and was paid from liquid assets in his estate. Walter named his daughter Catey as the beneficiary of his $1 million IRA and his $1 million beach house. When Catey inherits the beach house, she will receive a step-up in basis and no income tax will be due if she sells the house for $1 million.

The beach house is not an IRD item. The IRA is considered an IRD item, and Catey will not receive a step-up in basis on the IRA; further, she will have to pay income tax when she takes distributions from the IRA. Catey will be able to deduct the estate tax attributable to the inclusion of the IRA in Walter's estate when she takes distributions from the IRA.

If the IRA was not included in Walter's estate, the estate tax would have been $1,500,000; therefore, the estate tax attributable to inclusion of the $1 million IRA in Walter's estate is $400,000. As Catey takes distributions from the IRA, the estate tax will be deducted pro rata and distributions of the retirement assets she receives as a beneficiary will be treated as income. This deduction would be taken on Catey's IRS Form 1040 Schedule A line 28 as a miscellaneous itemized deduction not subject to the 2% floor. In general, an income taxable distribution of $100,000 would be offset by a $40,000 deduction for estate tax.

Chapter Highlights

- Trusts and estates are considered separate (from individuals) tax-paying entities with separate tax brackets that apply to the income tax earned by trusts and estates. A number of rules pertain to the income taxation of trusts and estates.

- A simple trust is a trust that requires that all income be paid to the beneficiary and that allows no other trust distributions. The income distributed to a beneficiary is taxed to the beneficiary, and the trust will have no taxable income.

- A complex trust is a trust that allows distributions from income and/or principal. A complex trust can deduct from income any amounts paid to a beneficiary, but it will be taxed on any income the trust retains.

- The concept of DNI applies to any distributions made from a complex trust to a trust beneficiary. DNI provides that any distributions be made first from trust income, regardless of whether a distribution is actually made from trust income or trust corpus.

- If the grantor of a trust retains certain powers or rights over the assets transferred to a trust, the trust is deemed a grantor trust for income tax purposes. All income generated by the trust is taxed to the grantor rather than to the trust.

- The executor is responsible for filing both the federal estate tax return and any income tax returns for the estate. A number of deductions can be taken on either the estate tax return or the estate's income tax return. The executor should determine where the deduction will afford the greatest tax benefit.

- A decedent may have earned income that was not realized prior to death. Such income (IRD) is subject to estate tax in the decedent's estate and income tax will be assessed to the estate or beneficiary that receives it. If the income property was subject to estate tax in the decedent's estate, the recipient of such income can deduct the estate tax attributable to the distribution on his income tax return.

Key Terms

complex trust

conduit theory

distributable net income (DNI)

grantor trust

grantor trust rules

income first rule

income in respect of a decedent (IRD)

intentionally defective grantor trust (IDGT)

simple trust

sharing concept

Review Questions

9-1. Which of the following is an income tax ramification associated with simple trusts?

A. Because all income is required to be paid, the trust beneficiary is subject to income tax liability.

B. Because payment of income is not required, the trust is responsible for the income tax liability.

C. A DNI calculation is required to ascertain the income tax liability of the beneficiary and the trust.

D. The grantor is always responsible for the payment of income tax.

9-2. All of the following are items of IRD except:

1. Unpaid life insurance commissions

2. Unpaid life insurance cash value

3. Life insurance death benefit proceeds

A. 1 and 2

B. 3

C. 1 and 3

D. 2 and 3

9-3. Gordon creates an irrevocable trust into which he transfers income-producing property. The trust provides income to his children for life, remainder to the grandchildren. Gordon has appointed his wife Sophia as the trustee of the trust. Sophia, as the trustee, is given the power to apply trust income to purchase life insurance on Gordon's life. Who is responsible for the payment of the income tax liability attributed to the trust income?

A. Sophia, as an individual.

B. The children and grandchildren as trust beneficiaries.

C. Sophia, as the trustee, and the children and grandchildren based upon the DNI calculation.

D. Gordon, as the grantor of the trust.

9-4. Which of the following accurately describes the tax ramifications associated IRD assets?

A. The decedent's estate will receive a deduction for the income tax attributed to the item of IRD.

B. The decedent's estate will receive a credit for the income tax attributed to the item of IRD.

C. The beneficiary of the item of IRD receives a deduction for the estate tax attributed to the item.

D. The beneficiary of the item of IRD receives a credit for the estate tax attributed to the item.

9-5. Which of the following income tax considerations is correct with respect to a trust beneficiary?

A. If the asset is held by the trust, the basis of the asset will have no impact on the tax consequence to the beneficiary.

B. When income is distributed to a trust beneficiary, it will be taxed to the trust beneficiary.

C. The income tax consequence on the sale of an asset will be the same whether it is owned by a trust or owned by a beneficiary.

D. If a trust contains a provision that allows the trustee to make income distributions to the grantor of the trust, but no income is distributed, income tax will be paid by the trust.

Notes

1. Treas. Reg. §1.642(b)-1.
2. I.R.C. §642(b)(2).
3. Treas. Reg. §1.642(b)-1.
4. I.R.C. §661; Treas. Reg §1.661(a)-1.
5. I.R.C. §662(b); Treas. Regs. §§1.662(b)-1–2.
6. I.R.C. §673(a).
7. *Id.*
8. I.R.C. §675(a)(1).
9. I.R.C. §675(a)(2).
10. I.R.C. §675(a)(4)
11. I.R.C. §677(a).
12. I.R.C. §§6012; 6072(a); Treas. Reg. §1.6072-1(b).
13. I.R.C. §451.
14. I.R.C. §6012(a).
15. I.R.C. §67(e).
16. I.R.C. §642(g); Treas. Reg. §1.642(g)-1.
17. I.R.C. §661.
18. I.R.C. §642.
19. I.R.C. §451(a).
20. I.R.C. §691(a)(3).
21. I.R.C. §1014(c).
22. I.R.C. §691(c).

Chapter 10

Gifting Strategies

CFP® CERTIFICATION EXAMINATION PRINCIPAL TOPICS COVERED IN THIS CHAPTER:

Gifting Strategies

- Inter-vivos gifting
- Gift-giving techniques and strategies
- Appropriate gift property
- Gifts of present and future interests
- Applicable credit amount
- Gift, estate, and income tax implications

Basis

- Basis of property received by gift
- Basis of inherited property

Learning Objectives

To ensure that you have a solid understanding of the various gifting techniques and strategies available, the following learning objectives are addressed in this chapter:

- Recognize the tax and non-tax advantages of gifting.

- Identify the best property interests to gift, according to a client's objectives.

- Explain the purpose and nature of the gift tax law.

- Recognize when a completed transfer has occurred.

- Define direct, indirect, present, and future-interest gifts.

- Describe the unified transfer tax system and how taxable gifts affect the estate tax.

- Understand how the unified credit shelters gift and estate taxes.

- Calculate the income tax basis of gifted property.

Chapter Contents

OVERVIEW

When someone gives property to another person or transfers the property into an irrevocable trust, the person has made an **inter-vivos** (lifetime) **gift**. Inter-vivos gifting is a very important estate planning technique because it transfers wealth to others and reduces the value of a person's estate, which may consequently reduce estate tax liability. Therefore, an inter-vivos gift is not a bequest, which transfers property at death according to provisions in the decedent's will.

Financial planners need to work together with their clients to determine whether gifting strategies are warranted based on each client's personal and financial goals, current and future liquidity needs, available assets and resources, and tax situation. Lifetime gifting should be considered as part of a client's overall estate plan, and it should be coordinated with a client's retirement, tax, and investment planning objectives within the framework of a comprehensive financial plan. The planner should review the client's assets and liabilities and all sources of income—including life insurance policies—and then project the growth rate of these assets before recommending the best property interests to gift to others.

Practice Standard 300-1

Analyzing and Evaluating the Client's Information

A financial planning practitioner shall analyze the information to gain an understanding of the client's financial situation and then evaluate to what extent the client's goals, needs and priorities can be met by the client's resources and current course of action.

GIFTING STRATEGIES

Under common law, a **gift** is defined simply as a voluntary transfer without adequate consideration. To escape the **gift tax**, there must be "adequate and full consideration" equal in value to the property transferred. For example, a $100,000 building that is transferred from a mother to her daughter for $100,000 in cash clearly does not constitute a gift. If that same building was given outright to the daughter with no cash in exchange, or, if the daughter gave her mother less than $100,000, then the transfer would constitute a gift.

Parties to a Gift

A person who gifts property to another person or entity is known as a **donor**, and the recipient of a gift is the **donee**. Almost anyone can be a donee, including spouses, children, other relatives, partners, beneficiaries of a trust, and corporate shareholders. Donees can also be entities such as charities, organizations, foundations, and others. A donee does not pay any income or gift taxes when a gift is received, but the donee could pay income taxes if the property earns income or is subsequently sold. Furthermore, if the donee still owns the gifted property at the time of his death, the property could be subject to estate taxes and probate costs.

Non-tax Advantages of Gifting

Individuals give property away during their lifetimes for many different reasons. Some of the non-tax advantages of lifetime gifting may include:

- the vicarious enjoyment of seeing the donee use and enjoy the gift;

- to provide for the education, support, and financial well-being of the donee;

- to provide an opportunity for the donor to see how well, or how poorly, the donee manages the business or other property;

- to maintain privacy that would be impossible to obtain through a testamentary gift;

- to potentially reduce probate and administrative costs and avoid delays; and

- to protect the donor from the claims of his creditors.

Tax-oriented Advantages of Gifting

Gifting can potentially reduce a person's estate tax liability and provide the donor with some distinct tax advantages that are available only for lifetime gifts.

- A donor can give up to $14,000 gift tax free to an unlimited number of donees in 2015.

- Married couples can "gift-split" so that $28,000 can be given gift tax free to an unlimited number of individuals in 2015.

- The value of the gifted property is removed from the donor's estate, along with any appreciation on the property accruing between the time of the gift and the date of the donor's death.

- Any gift taxes paid more than three years before the donor's death remove that money from the donor's gross estate, which further reduces the value of the donor's estate.

Best Property to Gift

The type of property to gift requires careful consideration with the client's integrated estate plan. A number of factors must be examined when selecting the types of property that are appropriate for gifts. Be sure also to consider the age, maturity, and experience of the donee before selecting a gift.

In general, the best types of property to gift include:

- **Property that is likely to appreciate in value.** Other things being equal, planners generally try to pick property that will appreciate substantially in value from the time of the transfer. Some examples include common stock, antiques and art, and real estate. The removal from the donor's estate of the appreciation in the property, as well as the removal of any income from the property, could save a meaningful amount of estate and income taxes.

- **Property that has a low gift tax value and a high estate tax value.** Life insurance, for example, is property with a low present value but a high appreciation potential. If held until the date the insured dies, its appreciation in value is guaranteed. Life insurance policies are often transferred to individuals or trusts to avoid inclusion of the death benefit in the owner-insured's estate.

- **Income-producing property when the donee is in a lower income tax bracket than the donor.** Income splitting between the donor and a donee aged 18 or older can be obtained by transferring high-income-producing property to a family member in a lower bracket. High-dividend participating preferred stock in a closely held business or stock in a successful S corporation is a good example of high-income-producing property. Kiddie tax rules will apply when a donee is younger than age 19, or age 19–23 and attending college.

- **Property that has already appreciated in value** should be given away **if a sale of such property is contemplated and the donee is in a lower income tax bracket than the donor.**

- **Appreciated property as a gift to charity.** The donor could avoid a capital gains tax and receive an income tax charitable deduction, but this deduction is subject to adjusted gross income (AGI) limitations.

- **Property that is located in a state other than the owner's state of domicile.** This property makes sense to gift away or to transfer into a trust to avoid facing an ancillary probate at the time of the donor's death.

Best Property to Keep

It is extremely important to focus on the client's circumstances before making a gift. Do not give away any asset if it will reduce the client's standard of living or if it will financially or psychologically endanger his "comfort level." Planners should focus particularly on the impact of the gift on the client's income and capital needs (both present and anticipated) as well as on the client's need for liquidity.

Some of the best types of property to keep include:

- **Highly appreciated property that is likely to be sold after the owner's death.** Property included in a decedent's estate is stepped up to a new **basis** of fair market value (FMV) at death. If the property is expected to be sold immediately after the owner's death, the person who inherits the property will not have to pay a capital gains tax on the subsequent sale. If that same property was given to the beneficiaries during lifetime, then there would be no step-up in basis, and the beneficiary would have to pay income tax on the subsequent sale of property.

- **Property that, if sold, would result in a loss.** When a donor gifts property to a donee, the donee will take the lesser of the donor's basis or the FMV of the property as of the date of the transfer. Therefore, it is not a good idea to give away property that would result in a loss because the donee cannot use the donor's loss to reduce his income taxes. The donor should sell that property, take the income tax deduction for the loss himself, and then gift the proceeds of the sale to the donee.

- **Depreciating income property.** Depreciation deductions offset an owner's income tax liability so the property should be kept until it has been fully depreciated.

Pros and Cons of Gifting

To gift or not to gift is an estate planning issue that needs to be carefully considered, because there are several advantages and disadvantages to making inter-vivos gifts. Donors who make completed gifts remove the value of the properties from their gross estate, but they also lose control over their property and diminish their wealth. Property held until the donor's death is included and perhaps taxed in the donor's estate, but it will receive a step-up in basis to FMV. The heirs will inherit the property with this new basis, which is an advantage if they intend to sell the property at a later time. However, if property is gifted during the donor's lifetime, the donee generally takes the donor's adjusted basis in the property, which is often less than the FMV of the gift.

As you can see, there are some distinct tax—and non-tax—consequences to making gifts, and perhaps some competing family interests as well. A financial planner can expertly guide a client through the decision-making process to arrive at a course of action that is in the client's and the family's best interests.

Financial Planning Practice Standard 400-3

Presenting the Financial Planning Recommendation(s)

The financial planning practitioner shall communicate the recommendation(s) in a manner and to an extent reasonably necessary to assist the client in making an informed decision.

PURPOSE AND NATURE OF THE GIFT TAX LAW

The federal gift tax was introduced in 1932 to prevent taxpayers from transferring their entire estates to others during their lifetime without paying a transfer tax. For tax law purposes, neither the statutes nor the regulations specifically define what is meant by the term *gift*. For gift tax purposes, a gift can be broadly defined to include a sale, exchange, or other transfer of property from one person (the donor) to another (the donee) without adequate and full consideration in money or money's worth. The regulations dealing with the valuation of gifts provide that a gift is the difference between the value of property transferred and the consideration received.

Value of property transferred – Consideration received = Gift

Some transfers do not fall within the scope of the gift tax law.

- Services rendered for the benefit of another person

- Compensation for professional services

- A disclaimer, which is a written refusal to accept a gift

- A promise to make a gift in the future

- Bad bargains, which are sales for less-than-adequate money's worth

- Sham gifts, which shift the income tax burden to someone in a lower bracket

- The assignment of income to another person

- Payments made pursuant to a legal decree or court order

- Contributions to political parties

The Gift Tax

The gift tax is an excise tax, a tax levied not directly on the gift itself or on the right to receive the property, but rather on the right of an individual to transfer money or other property to another. The gift tax is based on the value of the property transferred. *Value*, for gift tax purposes, is defined as "the price at which the property would change hands between a willing buyer and a willing seller, neither being under any compulsion to buy or to sell, and both having reasonable knowledge of relevant facts." Therefore, value is usually the FMV of the property on the date of the transfer.

Elements of a Gift

Before a gift is subject to federal gift tax, certain requirements must be met, which are summarized here:

- The donor must be competent to make a gift, and the donee must be capable of receiving the gift.

- There must be an "intention" by the donor to make a gift.

- The donor must deliver the gift to the donee.

- The donee must take possession of the property.

Direct and Indirect Gifts

Taxable gifts can be both direct and indirect gifts. **Direct gifts** are gifts that are made outright to others, and they can consist of real and personal property. The gift tax is imposed on the shifting of property rights, regardless of whether the property is tangible or intangible. It can be applied even if the property transferred (such as a municipal bond) is exempt from federal income tax or other taxes. Direct gifts subject to a gift tax can also include transfers of cash, life insurance policies, stocks, bonds, partnership interests, and even gifts of royalty rights.

In addition to an outright transfer, **indirect gifts** are also subject to the gift tax. Some examples of indirect gifts include a transfer of money or property into an irrevocable trust, the payment of someone else's expenses, the forgiveness of a debt or a note, foregone interest on an intrafamily interest-free or below-market loan, or the assignment of benefits in an insurance policy.

Present and Future Gifts

When a gift is made to an individual or transferred into a trust, the donee may have a present or a future interest in the property. A **present-interest gift** occurs when the donee has the unrestricted right to the immediate use, possession, or enjoyment of the property or the income from the property. An example is a gift of a painting to a friend. The friend can keep the painting, sell the painting, or gift it to someone else.

With a **future-interest gift**, the donee must wait before he can use, possess, or enjoy the property or obtain the income. An example of a future-interest gift is when income-producing property is transferred into a trust and the income can accumulate for a period of time before any income or corpus is distributed to the beneficiaries. The beneficiaries (donees) in this case all have a future interest in the trust property.

Completed Transfers

A **completed transfer** is necessary before the gift tax can be applied. The term *completed transfer* implies that the gift has been put beyond the donor's recall, i.e., that he has irrevocably parted with dominion and control over the gift. Property transferred during lifetime is valued for gift tax purposes on the date the completed gift is made. No alternate valuation date is allowed.

In a number of situations it is difficult to ascertain just when a completed gift occurs because a gift can be incomplete when the transfer is initially made.

Personal Checks or Notes

No gift is made at the moment the donor gives the donee a personal check because the gift is not taxable until the check is cashed. For instance, if a check is mailed in December, received in late December, but not cashed until January of the following year, no gift is made until that year. This is because, typically, the maker of a check is under no legal obligation to honor the check until it is cashed. Likewise, a gift of a negotiable note is not complete until it is paid.

Gift Causa Mortis

An individual on his deathbed will sometimes make a **gift causa mortis** (in anticipation of his imminent death) and then quite unexpectedly recover. Neither the original gift nor the return of the property to the donor is subject to the gift tax if the donor recovers and the donee returns the property. A gift causa mortis is therefore incomplete as long as the donor is alive; it becomes complete at the donor's death.

Stock

A gift of stock is completed on the date the stock was transferred or the date endorsed certificates are delivered to the donee (or his agent) or to the corporation (or its transfer agent).

U.S. Government Bonds

A transfer is not a completed gift until the registration is changed in accordance with federal regulations. For example, if a grandmother purchases a U.S. savings bond that is registered as payable to her and to her two children as co-owners, no gift is made to the grandchildren until one of them surrenders the bond for cash.

Totten Trust

This is a bank savings account where the donor makes a deposit for the donee (Joanne Q. Donor in trust for James P. Donee) and retains possession of the savings book. Because the donor can recover the entire amount deposited, it is a revocable transfer, and no gift occurs until the donee makes a withdrawal of funds.

Joint Bank Accounts

Typically with a joint checking or savings account, the person making a deposit can withdraw all of the funds or any portion of them. Therefore, the donor has retained a power to revoke the gift, so it is incomplete. Similar to a Totten trust, when the donee makes a withdrawal of funds from the account (and thereby eliminates the donor's dominion and control), a gift of the funds occurs. For example, if a father deposited $100,000 into a bank account in November of last year, and his son withdraws $8,000 this March, the father has made a gift to his son of $8,000 this year.

Joint Brokerage Account

The creation and contribution to a joint brokerage account held in "street name" is not a gift until the joint owner makes a withdrawal for his personal benefit. At that time, the donee acquires indefeasible rights and the donor parts irrevocably with the funds. Conversely, if a person calls her broker and says, "Buy 100 shares of Texas Oil and Gas and title them in joint names, mine and my husband's, with right of survivorship," the purchase constitutes a non-taxable gift to her husband. The husband has acquired rights to a portion of the stock on the date of the purchase that he did not have before.

Real Estate

Real estate is transferred by executing a deed in favor of the donee. But if the donor retains the deed, does not record it, makes no attempt to inform the donee of the transfer, and continues to treat the property as his own, no transfer occurs.

Forgiveness of a Note

When property is transferred in exchange for an installment note, the transaction is treated as a sale for income tax purposes, but forgiveness of the note is a gift. The gift occurs when the donor marks the note "cancelled by gift."

Split-interest Gifts

When the owner of a property keeps a lifetime interest in the property for himself and gifts the remainder interest in the property away, the owner has made a gift of the present value of the remainder interest. Although the donee has to wait to own the property outright, the gift is made at the time the donor transfers the property interest into a trust or changes the title of the deed.

INCOMPLETE GIFTS IN TRUST

An **incomplete gift** in trust does not trigger a gift tax. Donors sometimes transfer property to a trust, but they retain the right to revoke the transfer. Property transferred into a revocable trust is not a completed gift. A completed gift occurs only when a donor relinquishes all control over the transferred property, i.e., when the trust becomes irrevocable. However, distributions from the trust will be treated as a completed gift.

Client Situation

Emily created a revocable trust in 2013 for the benefit of her disabled brother, Peter. She transferred $90,000 into the trust and gave a corporate trustee the discretion to make disbursements of income and corpus for her brother's health, education, maintenance, and support. Last year the trust distributed $15,000 to Peter. Only $15,000 is a completed gift subject to the gift tax, not the $90,000 that Emily initially transferred into the trust. If Emily chooses to make the trust irrevocable this year, then a completed gift will occur, and the trust corpus will be subject to a gift tax.

When property is transferred into an irrevocable trust, it is treated as a completed gift if the donor has parted with total control over the property. However, there are several instances where transfers into irrevocable trusts are treated as *incomplete* gifts and are not taxed, when the grantor retains certain powers:

 The power to alter the interest of the trust beneficiaries

- The power to name new beneficiaries of the trust

- A testamentary general power of appointment over the remainder of the trust, to dispose of the trust assets at death

---

Client Situation

Alan transferred stock to an irrevocable trust for his two children and three grandchildren. The income from the trust is payable to Alan's children for as long as they live. Then, the remainder is payable to his grandchildren or their estates. If Alan retains the power to vary the amount of income his children will receive, or to reach into the corpus to enhance their security, the gift is incomplete. But the gift becomes complete if Alan relinquishes control. If that happens when the stock has substantially increased in value, the taxable gift—and possibly the gift tax payable by Alan—may also increase substantially.

RELATIONSHIP OF THE GIFT TAX SYSTEM TO THE ESTATE TAX SYSTEM

The gift tax and the estate tax are both transfer taxes that are unified and interrelated under a federal transfer tax system. Under the Tax Relief, Unemployment Insurance Authorization, and Job Creation Act of 2010,[1] lifetime gifts and testamentary transfers became subject to the same unified gift and estate tax rate schedule as they had been in the past. This act imposes the same tax burden on transfers made during life as at death. In 2012, these provisions were made permanent under "The American Taxpayer Relief Act of 2012" (ATRA).[2]

Cumulative and Progressive

Gift and estate taxes have commonalities because both are **cumulative** and **progressive** in nature. The gift and estate tax rates are progressive and range from 18% to a maximum of 40%. The gift tax is cumulative, because all previous taxable gifts from 1932 are added to the current year's taxable gifts before a gift tax is applied. This pushes the tax into a higher rate bracket up to the maximum bracket of 40%. The estate tax is also cumulative. All taxable gifts made since 1976 are added back into the estate tax calculation to bump up the estate tax rate to a higher bracket.

Client Situation

Gary and Renee made their first gift to their daughter Kenna last year. The taxable gift for each spouse was $15,000 and the tax on the gift was $2,800. This year Gary and Renee made another taxable gift of $15,000 to their daughter Rory. The tax on this year's gift is $3,200, not $2,800. Even though Gary and Renee have made the same amount of taxable gifts each year, the gift tax is higher this year than last year, because the gift tax is cumulative and progressive.

Unified Credit

Each person can make taxable gifts up to $5,430,000 through lifetime inter-vivos gifts, or transfer $5,430,000 through bequests at death, and avoid taxation. The $5,430,000 is the **exemption equivalent** amount that escapes taxation. Each taxpayer has a **unified credit**, also called an *applicable credit*, which offsets the tax on a dollar-for-dollar basis. Based on the current year's unified gift and estate tax table, the tax on $5,430,000 is $2,117,800, but the unified credit (of 2,117,800) will offset the entire gift or estate tax liability.

The unified credit must be used to offset tax each time a taxable gift is made. As a result, the remaining unified credit is reduced with each new taxable gift, so less of the credit is available to offset future taxable gifts. The unified credit is fully depleted once taxable gifts or estates exceed $5,430,000 in 2015; at that point, a tax must be paid. The excess amount is taxed at 40%.

Client Situation

Beth gave her brother Sean a taxable gift of $430,000 this year. Last year Beth made taxable gifts totaling $5 million. Beth did not have to pay a tax on the gift she made to Sean, because she used the remaining portion of her unified credit to offset the tax. Two months later, Beth made another taxable gift worth $300,000 to her sister Irene. Because Beth had exhausted her unified credit on the gift she made to Sean, no further credit is available to reduce the tax on the additional $300,000. Therefore, Beth will have to pay a gift tax this year when she files her gift tax return.

Practitioner Tip: So far, Beth has reduced the value of her gross estate by $5,730,000 and the amount of gift tax she has to pay this year. However, the $5,730,000 will be added back into Beth's estate tax calculation as an adjusted taxable gift, which will increase her estate tax rate because of the progressive nature of the tax. Any gift taxes Beth pays will be entered as a credit on her estate tax return, which will reduce her estate tax liability. This example demonstrates how the federal unified gift and estate tax transfer systems are interrelated.

Marital and Charitable Deductions

Both the gift and estate taxes permit deductions for property transferred to spouses and qualified charities through marital and charitable deductions. The marital deduction can be claimed on the donor spouse's gift tax returns or on the decedent spouse's estate tax return. A gift made to a qualified charity or a tax-exempt organization during life can result in both an income tax and a gift tax charitable deduction, whereas a bequest to a charity will receive only an estate tax charitable deduction.

Gift and Estate Tax Differences

Some unique aspects of the federal gift tax system do not pertain to estate taxes. For example, the value of a gift can be reduced by an annual exclusion. A donor can make tax-free gifts of $14,000 to an unlimited number of donees in 2015 without reducing any portion of the donor's unified credit. Gift splitting is another gift tax reduction technique available to married couples; it reduces the value of a gift by one-half for each spouse. If a spouse consents to gift split, then a couple can gift $28,000 gift-tax-free to an unlimited number of donees in 2015.

Client Situation

John transferred $6,014,000 into an irrevocable trust for his daughter Gabrielle this year. Gabrielle can receive all of the income from this trust for life, and she can access the trust corpus without restriction. John can use an annual exclusion of $14,000 to reduce the taxable gift to $6 million. The gift tax on $6 million is $2,345,800, but John can apply his unified credit of 2,117,800 to reduce his gift tax liability to $228,000. John must pay the gift tax when he files his gift tax return, and the $228,000 tax will be paid from his personal bank account. It is not paid from the $6,014,000 million transferred into the trust because the gift tax is tax exclusive. To date, John's gross estate has been reduced by $6,242,000 (the sum of the gift and the gift tax paid).

Assets included in a decedent's gross estate are "stepped-up" in basis, which means that basis is increased to the property's fair market value at the date of death. The recipient of inherited property can avoid paying a capital gains tax if the property is sold before it appreciates in value. Therefore, if the estate is not subject to estate tax, there are clear income tax advantages for heirs if property remains in the owner's estate and transfers at death. In contrast, property that is gifted during lifetime retains the owner's carry-over basis in the property, and may be subject to a capital gains tax once the property is sold.

GIFT TAX RELATIONSHIP TO INCOME TAXES

When the gift tax law was written, one of its principal purposes was to discourage taxpayers from making gifts to family members in a lower tax bracket to reduce their taxable incomes. Income-producing property transferred into trusts or acquired by a trust may be taxed to the donor, the trust, or the beneficiaries, and if it is taxable to the beneficiary, it may be taxed at the parent's rate (for minors) or at the beneficiary's tax bracket. Donees who receive a direct gift of property acquire a carry-over basis in the property that is used to calculate a potential income tax gain on a future sale. Property transferred to a trust also retains the grantor's basis in the property. Financial planners must understand the relationship and impact of income taxes on property transfers to individuals and trusts, and they should know the basis rules for gifted property.

Determining the Basis of Gifted Property

Basis is the starting point in any computation used to determine how much gain (or loss) is incurred upon a sale of property. Gain, for example, is found by the formula:

Amount realized – Adjusted basis = Gain

Therefore, the higher the basis, the lower the reportable gain on the sale of an asset. For an asset acquired by a purchase, basis is usually the cost of the property.

When property is transferred from a donor to a donee and the donee later disposes of the property by sale or other taxable disposition, the gain depends on the donee's basis. To calculate the tax on the property sold, the donee must first determine his carry-over basis.

The Fair Market Value of a Gift Exceeds the Donor's Adjusted Basis

If the FMV of an asset on the date a gift is made is *greater* than the donor's basis, then the donee will take over the donor's basis and the donor's holding period.

Client Situation

A mother's adjusted basis in stock is $12,000, and she gifts this stock to her daughter when the stock is worth $15,000. The daughter then sells the stock for $15,000 and realizes a capital gain of $3,000.

Holding Period at Death

The holding period for inherited property that is subsequently sold is a long-term capital gain, regardless of the actual holding period.

Client Situation

A son inherited stock from his father with a stepped-up basis of $100,000. The son sold the stock five months later for $120,000; therefore, the son will have a $20,000 long-term capital gain.

The FMV of a Gift Is Less than the Donor's Adjusted Basis

In this situation, the donee's new cost basis and holding period depend on the price the donee eventually sells the property for.

1. If the FMV on the date of the gift is *less* than the donor's basis, and the donee sells the property at that price (FMV) or lower, then the donee's new basis will be the FMV of the gift at the date of transfer. Furthermore, the donee's holding period begins on the date the gift is made.

    Example 1: Ron's basis in stock is $12,000, and he gifts the stock to his son Jim when it is worth $10,000. Jim then sells the stock four months later for $8,000. Jim's carry-over basis is $10,000, and his short-term capital loss is $2,000.

2. If the donee subsequently sells the property at any price *greater* than the FMV at the time of the gift but for *less* than the donor's basis, no gain or loss is recognized on the sale.

    Example 2: Jane's basis in stock is $20,000, and she gifts the stock to her daughter, Laurie, when it is worth $16,000. If Laurie sells the stock for $18,000, her carry-over basis is $16,000, and she recognizes no capital gain or loss on the sale.

3. If a donor gifted property with an FMV of *less* than his adjusted basis and the donee subsequently sells the property for a *gain*, then the donee's basis is the donor's adjusted basis, and the donee will assume the donor's full holding period.

> **Example 3:** Ted's uncle purchased some very volatile stock several years ago for $50,000. He gifted this stock to Ted when the FMV was $30,000. When Ted sold the stock six months later for $60,000, his carry-over basis was his uncle's adjusted basis of $50,000. Ted's long-term capital gain was $10,000.

Gift Tax Paid

A donor who gifts more than $5,430,000 in his lifetime must pay gift taxes on any subsequent taxable gifts in 2015. If the donor must pay a gift tax when a gift is made and the FMV of the gift is *greater* than the donor's basis, then the gift tax is included when calculating the donee's new basis in the gifted property. However, if gift taxes were paid when the FMV of the gift was *less* than the donor's basis, then no gift tax adjustment is made to the donee's basis.

Client Situation

Suppose Ellie has stock with a basis of $24,000, which she gifts to her niece Mary Ann when the stock's FMV is $64,000. Ellie has to pay a gift tax on this gift because she used up her unified credit of 2,117,800 when making previous gifts totaling over $5,430,000. Ellie can use an annual exclusion of $14,000 to reduce the gift tax because she made no other gifts to Mary Ann this year. Therefore, her taxable gift is $50,000, for which the gift tax is calculated to be $20,000. The gift tax is tax exclusive because it will be paid from a source other than the gift.

Ellie's adjusted basis is used to determine Mary Ann's new basis in the stock. First, the appreciation of the stock is divided by the taxable gift multiplied by the gift tax paid. In this case, the appreciation of the gift is $40,000 ($64,000 – $24,000) divided by the taxable gift of $50,000, or .80, multiplied by the gift tax paid ($20,000), or $16,000. This $16,000 is added to Ellie's adjusted basis of $24,000 to determine Mary Ann's new basis in the property, which is $40,000. Because the FMV of the gift is greater than the donor's basis, the donee will assume the donor's full holding period.

If Ellie made a $14,000 gift to Mary Ann before giving her this stock, then the appreciation of $40,000 would be divided by the taxable gift of $64,000, or .625, multiplied by the gift tax paid ($25,600), or $16,000. Mary Ann's new basis in the property would be $40,000 ($24,000 + $16,000).

Bargain Sale to Family Member—Donee's New Basis

A **bargain sale** is part sale and part gift. If the sale price is below FMV, the difference between the sale price and FMV is the gift. Bargain sales can be made to charities, so the donor receives cash from the sale (gains must be reported) and a partial income tax deduction for the gift. A bargain sale to family members could result in a taxable gift.

> **Client Situation**
>
> Lucy sold her vacation home, worth $600,000, to her son Billy for $400,000. Lucy had paid $100,000 for the home many years ago, which is her basis in the property. Lucy's taxable gain is $300,000 (the $400,000 sale price minus her basis). Billy's basis in the home is his purchase price of $400,000. Lucy has also made a taxable gift of $200,000 (the difference between the sale price and FMV) minus the annual exclusion.

Reverse Gift

A donor with low-basis property may gift the property to a donee who is seriously ill to receive the property back with a full step-up in basis at the donee's death. This technique, called a **reverse gift**, will not work if the donee receives the property within one year of his death. In that case, the donor's basis would be the adjusted basis in the property that the donee held before death, including any gift taxes the donor paid upon transfer. The property may be included in both the donee's gross estate and the donor's gross estate at the date-of-death FMV. It should be noted, however, that the transfer will receive a step-up in basis to FMV at the date of death if the following conditions apply:

- The donee lives for more than one year after receiving the gift.

- The property is bequeathed to someone other than the donor or the donor's spouse.

> **Client Situation**
>
> Jerry gifted stock worth $80,000, which has a basis of $20,000, to his dying wife Connie. If Connie dies 10 months later, the stock will not receive a step-up in basis to FMV unless she bequeaths it to someone other than Jerry. If Connie dies 15 months after receiving the stock from Jerry, and she bequeaths it to Jerry, the stock will receive a step-up in basis to FMV at Connie's death.

Gift Subject to a Mortgage

A gift of property subject to indebtedness that is greater than its cost to the donor may result in a taxable gain. A gift of such property causes the donor to realize a capital gain on the excess of the debt over the basis.

> **Client Situation**
>
> Vince purchased a building many years ago for $100,000, which has appreciated to $1 million this year. Last month he gifted the building, which was mortgaged to $700,000, to his wife Audrey. This resulted in an income tax gain to Vince on the difference between the debt outstanding at the time of the transfer and his basis, or $600,000. The gain would be realized when the gift is complete.

Chapter Highlights

- Gifting is an important estate planning technique that affords a donor many tax and non-tax benefits.

- Financial planners should work with their clients to identify the best property interests to gift and the most advantageous gifting strategies to pursue.

- Planners should calculate a wealthy client's current estate tax liability to show how inter-vivos gifting will reduce the value of his estate and possibly the resulting estate tax.

- Financial planners must be aware of the ramifications of how the federal gift tax affects the estate tax, and how gifting affects the income tax basis of the property the donee receives, before making any gift and estate tax planning recommendations.

Key Terms

applicable credit	gift tax
bargain sale	incomplete gift
basis	indirect gift
completed transfer	inter-vivos gift
cumulative	present-interest gift
direct gift	progressive
donee	reverse gift
donor	stepped-up basis
exemption equivalent	tax exclusive
future-interest gift	tax inclusive
gift	unified credit
gift causa mortis	

Review Questions

10-1. Tony has a gross estate of $5.5 million. He wants to gift some property to his daughter Paula to reduce the value of his gross estate at death. Which property should Tony gift?

A. A vacation home worth $600,000 that Tony inherited from his father at a basis of $100,000. Paula and her family vacation there every year and would never sell the home.

B. Four lakefront cottages that Tony bought for $150,000, which he owns and manages. The cottages were recently appraised at $600,000. Paula and her husband do not want to manage the cottages after Tony dies, and they plan to sell them soon after his death.

C. An investment in undeveloped land valued at $600,000 that Tony purchased for $700,000.

10-2. From the following options, identify which gifts are subject to the gift tax law.

A. A father established a revocable trust five years ago and last month changed the beneficiary of the trust to his daughter.

B. A mother changed the deed to her home to give her son a remainder interest in the property.

C. An author gave his right to future royalties to his daughter.

D. A father added his son as a joint owner on his brokerage account.

10-3. Grandmother (GM) is a widow. She has a bank account with $400,000 in her name. She adds granddaughter (GD) as a joint owner of this account with right of survivorship. Which of the following statements best describes the estate planning consequences associated with GM's action?

A. At GM's death, $200,000 will be included in her estate.

B. At GM's death, this account will not be subject to probate.

C. GM has made a gift of $200,000 to GD.

D. All of the above.

10-4. Which of the following statements is/are incorrect?

A. A direct gift is an outright transfer of real or personal property.

B. A transfer of $1 million into an irrevocable trust is an indirect gift made to the trust beneficiaries.

C. Transferred property is valued for gift tax purposes on the date the completed gift is made, or on the alternate valuation date.

D. When someone receives the remainder interest in an irrevocable trust, he has received a future interest gift.

10-5. A donor makes a gift to a donee. Which of the following statements is/are correct with respect to the basis of the property?

A. The donor's basis is always carried over to the donee.

B. The donor's basis is always carried over if the property is transferred at a loss.

C. The donee acquires the donor's basis as long as the property is transferred at a gain.

D. The donee's basis is equal to the FMV of the property on the date of the transfer.

10-6. Which of the following statements does/do not correctly pertain to the unified credit?

A. The credit is available to offset both inter-vivos gifts and testamentary transfers.

B. Use of the unified credit is mandatory for all taxable inter-vivos gifts.

C. The unified credit offsets the gift tax and the estate tax to reduce tax liability.

D. The unified credit is also known as the *exemption equivalent amount*.

Notes

1. Pub. L. No. 111-312, 124 Stat. 3296, H.R. 4853.

2. Pub. L. No. 112-240, 126 Stat. 2313 (Jan. 2, 2013).

Chapter 11

Gift Tax Calculation

CFP® CERTIFICATION EXAMINATION PRINCIPAL TOPICS COVERED IN THIS CHAPTER:

Gift Tax Compliance and Tax Calculation

Calculation

- Annual exclusion
- Applicable credit amount
- Gift splitting
- Prior taxable gifts
- Education and medical exclusions
- Marital and charitable deductions
- Tax liability

Gift Tax Filing Requirements

Gifting Strategies

- Gifts to non-citizen spouses

Estate Tax Compliance and Tax Calculation

- Adjusted taxable gifts

Learning Objectives

To ensure that you have a solid understanding of how to calculate gift taxes and how taxable lifetime gifts affect the estate tax calculation, the following learning objectives are addressed in this chapter:

- Calculate the gift tax value of split-interest gifts.
- List the five steps involved in determining a taxable gift.
- Identify exempt gifts.
- Explain how and when gift splitting applies.
- Identify present-interest and future-interest gifts.
- Recognize terminable interest property.

- Calculate taxable gifts.
- Calculate the current year's gift tax liability.
- Calculate the amount of unified credit that remains after a taxable gift is made.
- Calculate a net gift.
- Recognize that taxable gifts are reported as adjusted taxable gifts on the estate tax return.
- Explain gift tax filing requirements.

Chapter Contents

OVERVIEW

A person's right to transfer the title of property to others during lifetime or at death is subject to transfer taxes, which include gift taxes, estate taxes, and generation-skipping transfer taxes. The type of tax imposed on a transfer is determined by the amount transferred, when it is transferred, and to whom it is transferred.

Financial planners and other professionals who recommend gifting strategies for their clients need to understand how gift taxes are calculated and how the payment of gift taxes can affect a donor's estate tax liability. Many techniques are available to individuals who transfer property outright to others or into irrevocable trusts, and for business owners who transfer closely held stock and other business property to family members to reduce a client's gift tax liability. To take optimal advantage of such tax-saving strategies, planners must be aware of these techniques, how and when they are used, and what they can accomplish.

Practice Standard 200-1

Determining a Client's Personal and Financial Goals, Needs and Priorities

The financial planning practitioner and the client shall mutually define the client's personal and financial goals, needs and priorities that are relevant to the scope of the engagement before any recommendation is made and/or implemented.

VALUATION OF GIFTS

Valuation is the first step in the gift tax computation process. Gifts made outright to others or property that is transferred into irrevocable trusts is typically valued at the fair market value of the property on the date the gift is made. The fair market value of certain property interests is valued as follows:

- Mutual fund shares are valued at their net asset value.

- Publically traded stock, if traded on the valuation date, is valued at the average of the high and low market prices.

- Government bonds are valued at the redemption price.

- **Split-interest trusts** are separate gifts made to the income beneficiary and the remainder beneficiary(ies). The present value of both the income interest and the remainder interest is calculated to determine gift tax values. When a donee receives a life estate, IRS Valuation Table S provides the annuity, life estate, and remainder interest valuation factors for a single life and two lives, respectively. (See Appendix E.)

Client Situation

Fred and Joan transferred $1 million into a trust today to benefit Fred's father Harry, age 75, and their son Alex. Harry will receive all income annually for life, with the remainder of the trust payable to Alex at his death. The Section 7520 interest rate is 4.6% at the time of the transfer. To calculate the present value of Harry's income interest, IRS Table S must be consulted. (See Exhibit 11.1.) The value may be found in the Life Estate column for age 75 (0.36691). This factor is multiplied by $1 million, which results in a gift to Harry of $366,910. The present value of Alex's remainder interest gift is the amount left over, which is $1 million minus Harry's interest of $366,910 or $633,090.

Exhibit 11.1 Single Life Factors Based on Life Table 2000CM

TABLE S (4.6) SINGLE LIFE FACTORS BASED ON LIFE TABLE 2000CM							
4.6% INTEREST							
Age	Annuity	Life Estate	Remainder	Age	Annuity	Life Estate	Remainder
75	7.9763	0.36691	0.63309				

STEPS TO CALCULATE TAXABLE GIFTS

Once the value of a gift is determined, several gift tax reduction techniques can be applied. Consequently, the fair market value of a gift is not necessarily equal to the gift tax value of the gift. Gift tax values can be reduced by gift splitting, annual exclusions, marital deductions, charitable deductions, or possibly by a combination of these techniques. The amount of the gift that cannot be reduced any further equals the **taxable gift**.

For 2015, a donor can make up to $5,430,000 in taxable gifts in his lifetime before he will have to pay a gift tax. This $5,430,000 is the exemption equivalent amount that escapes taxation. Each donor has a unified credit of $2,117,800 that is applied against his gift and estate tax liability. A tax calculated on a taxable gift is offset by the donor's unified credit if the taxable gift does not exceed $5,430,000. The tax on $5,430,000 is $2,117,800 so the unified credit of $2,117,800 eliminates this tax in 2015.

There are five steps in the process of determining the amount of a taxable gift:

1. Is this a gift?

2. Can this gift be split?

3. Can an annual exclusion be taken?

4. Can a marital deduction be taken?

5. Can a charitable deduction be taken?

Is This Transfer a Gift?

The first question to consider when a gift is made is, "Is this transfer a gift?" Some gifts to individuals or trusts are not subject to gift tax. For example, when a person transfers assets into a revocable trust, a gift is not made to the beneficiaries in the trust because it is an incomplete transfer. In some instances, property transferred into an irrevocable trust is not considered a taxable gift if the grantor retains too much control over the trust or can influence and affect distributions made to trust beneficiaries. Other transfers not subject to gift tax law include:

- contributions to political parties

- qualified disclaimers

- property transferred between divorcing spouses for up to three years after the divorce is final

- services rendered for compensation

- loans that are expected to be paid back with proper interest

- contributions to Coverdell Education Savings Accounts, and

- court-ordered legal support for children

Exempt Gifts

Two **qualified transfers** are statutorily exempt from the gift tax. The first exemption is for tuition paid to an educational institution, regardless of the amount paid. This means that parents, grandparents, or even friends can pay private school or college tuition directly to the educational institution and not have the payment be subject to tax.

Another exempt transfer is the direct payment made to a physician or hospital for a person's medical care. This allows relatives or friends to pay for someone's medical expenses, including prescription drugs, without incurring a gift tax.

Client Situation

Carol wants to pay for her granddaughter Allison's college tuition at Boston University. If Carol makes the check out to Allison, and Allison pays BU with the funds she has received, then Carol has made a gift to Allison that is subject to gift tax. However, if Carol pays the tuition directly to Boston University, then no taxable gift has been made. Note that Carol did not use any of her unified credit to offset the tax on this gift, because a direct payment made to an educational institution is exempt from gift taxes.

Gift Splitting

The second step is to determine whether **gift splitting** is possible. A gift-splitting election is permitted only between a husband and a wife, but it is not allowed when a spouse is not a U.S. citizen at the time the gift is made. Gift splitting cuts the value of a gift in half by treating the gift as if it was made one-half by each spouse. This reduces the amount of the taxable gift attributed to each spouse.

There are two requirements for gift splitting: A gift must be made from the donor spouse's individually owned non-community property, and the other spouse must consent to split the gift with the donor spouse. Once a gift is split, all gifts made in the same calendar year must be split. Note that a gift made to a spouse is not eligible to be split: only gifts that spouses make to others can be split.

Client Situation

Bill and Diana are married and have a daughter, Isabella, who is getting married this year. Diana wants to give Isabella an extra $40,000 for her wedding from her own money market account, and she has asked Bill to split this gift with her. Bill has agreed; therefore, Bill and Diana will each make a gift to Isabella of $20,000 this year, even though Bill has not contributed financially to this gift. Diana also plans to give her mother Ida a check for $30,000 from her money market account for Ida's birthday later this year. This gift will also be split with Bill, because all gifts made in the same calendar year must be split. Therefore, both spouses will make a gift to Ida of $15,000 apiece.

Practitioner Tip: In many community property states, one spouse cannot make a gift of community property without the prior written consent of the other spouse, or the gift can be voided. There is no need to split a gift, because each spouse actually owns his or her one-half interest in the property. Gift splitting is implied when the gift is made from community property.

Annual Exclusion

The third step is to determine whether an annual exclusion is available to the donor to reduce the taxable value of a gift. Generally, the **annual exclusion** allows a donor to make tax-free gifts of up to $14,000 to any number of individuals each year. However, an annual exclusion is allowed only for *present-interest gifts*. A present interest is one in which the donee's possession or enjoyment of a property begins at the time the gift is made.

Examples of present-interest gifts include:

Outright gifts of property:

- Cash

- Real property

- Personal property

Property transferred into irrevocable trusts:

- A beneficiary receives income for life (a life estate).

- A beneficiary receives an immediate right to income for a number of years (a term certain).

- The trust must distribute all income annually to the beneficiaries.

- Trust beneficiaries are given Crummey powers (which convert their future interest in the trust to a present interest).

- Non-income-producing property is transferred to a trust and the trustee can sell the property to provide income for the trust beneficiaries.

Property transferred to minors:

- UGMA and UTMA custodial accounts

- Section 2503(c) trusts

- Section 2503(b) trusts (the income interest)

- Qualified tuition program (Section 529 plans)

Life insurance policy:

- A policy assigned to one beneficiary

- Premiums paid to individual policy owners

Client Situation

This year James made cash gifts of $4,000 to his nephew, $10,000 to his brother, and $16,000 to his father. The gifts to his nephew and brother are less than $14,000; therefore, they are not taxable gifts. The gift to his father is a taxable gift, but James's annual exclusion of $14,000 will reduce the taxable amount to $2,000. James's total taxable gifts are $2,000 this year.

Practitioner Tip: Note that the annual exclusion amount has not always been $14,000. This amount is indexed for inflation. From 1997 to 2001, the annual exclusion amount was $10,000, then from 2002 to 2005 the annual exclusion amount was $11,000, and from 2006 to 2008 the annual exclusion amount was $12,000. The annual exclusion has remained at $13,000 from 2009 to 2012 and increased to $14,000 in 2013. Annual exclusion gifts remain at $14,000 per donee in 2015.

Future-interest Gifts

Gifts of future interest do not qualify for the annual exclusion. With a future-interest gift, the donee does not gain possession or enjoyment of the gifted property until sometime after the gift has been made. When a donor makes a future-interest gift to a donee, the donor cannot take an annual exclusion of up to $14,000 to reduce the tax on the gift.

Examples of future-interest gifts include:

- a remainder interest in real property or in a trust;

- non-income-producing property transferred into a trust that cannot be sold (for example, non-dividend-paying stock or growth stocks);

- assets transferred into a trust that provides for income to accumulate for a period of time, which will be distributed to the beneficiaries in the future;

- a trust that includes a sprinkle provision; the trustee has the discretionary authority to distribute unequal shares of trust income to beneficiaries;

- a trust that includes a spray provision; the trustee has the discretion to distribute unequal amounts of trust income or principal to beneficiaries;

- a life insurance policy assigned to multiple beneficiaries; and

- a life insurance policy transferred into a trust, as well as money transferred into the trust each year to pay the premiums, unless the beneficiaries are given Crummey powers.

Client Situation

Kyle set up an irrevocable trust for his sister Jocelyn and his son Jeffrey. He transferred $150,000 of dividend-paying stock into the trust last week. Jocelyn is to receive the income from the trust for the next five years, and then Jeffrey will receive the trust's remainder interest. Kyle has made a gift to the two beneficiaries in the trust and he needs to determine the taxable amount of the gift.

The present value of Jocelyn's five-year income interest is valued at $30,200. Kyle can take an annual exclusion for the present-interest gift he gave to Jocelyn, which reduces this taxable gift to $16,200. Kyle cannot take an annual exclusion for the present value of the remainder interest ($119,800) that he gave to Jeffrey because it is a gift of future interest. The total gift tax value of the gifts he made to both Jocelyn and Jeffrey is $136,000.

Practitioner Tip: Gift splitting can be combined with annual exclusions to further reduce the taxable value of a gift. A married couple can agree to split their gifts to make tax-free gifts of $28,000 to each donee this year. This would cause the gift tax rate to be lower because the unified rates are progressive.

Client Situation

Mike and Christy are married, and Christy has a daughter, Tess, from a previous marriage. Tess is expecting her first child, and Christy intends to make a gift to Tess of $50,000 to help her out financially. If Christy writes Tess a check from her savings account, she will make a taxable gift of $36,000. The tax on the gift would be $7,320 if Christy had previously used up her entire unified credit. In this case, Christy does not have to actually pay this tax, because her unified credit is available to offset the tax.

> Christy has asked Mike to split the gift with her, and Mike has agreed. Now Mike and Christy will each make a gift of $25,000 to Tess, which is a taxable gift of $11,000 after utilizing their annual exclusions. The tax on $11,000 would be only $2,000 if they had each used up their unified credits. Gift splitting has technically saved Mike and Christy $3,320 of gift tax ($7,320 that Christy would have paid less $2,000 paid by Mike and $2,000 paid by Christy).

MARITAL AND CHARITABLE DEDUCTIONS

Techniques such as gift splitting and the use of annual exclusions can be applied only to reduce the amount of a taxable inter-vivos gift, not to reduce a transfer made at death. However, under the unified transfer tax system, both gift and estate taxes can be reduced by two deductions: the marital deduction and the charitable deduction. A gift made to a spouse can be reduced in value by the annual exclusion and the marital deduction, assuming these techniques can be applied.

Unlimited Marital Deduction

For a gift to qualify for the gift tax **marital deduction**, the following conditions must be satisfied:

- The donor's spouse must be a United States citizen at the time the gift is made.

- The recipient of the gift must be the spouse of the donor at the time the gift is made.

- The property transferred to the donee spouse must not be terminable interest property.

An unlimited marital deduction is available to the donor spouse when an outright gift in property is made to a donee spouse. The value of the gift would first be reduced by the annual exclusion if the gift is a present-interest gift, and the tax on the remaining amount would be offset by the marital deduction.

> ### Client Situation
>
> Dawn gave her husband Bruce $60,000 on his sixtieth birthday last month. The taxable value of the gift is first reduced by Dawn's annual exclusion of $14,000. The remaining taxable portion of $46,000 is offset by a marital deduction equal to the taxable amount of $46,000. Dawn's gift tax liability is zero. If Dawn gives Bruce another $20,000 before the year has ended, she cannot use an annual exclusion for this gift, but a marital deduction of $20,000 will offset the gift tax.

Another situation when a donor spouse can take an unlimited marital deduction is when a remainder interest is gifted to the donee spouse in real property or in a trust. Although the donee spouse has to wait to possess or enjoy the property, the donee spouse will eventually have complete control over the real property or the assets in the trust. This qualifies the gift for a gift tax marital deduction.

Client Situation

Mike created an irrevocable trust for the benefit of his mother Gloria, age 85, and funded it with $500,000. The income will be paid to Gloria for her life, and his wife Debbie will receive the remainder interest. The present value of Gloria's income interest is $115,000, and the present value of Debbie's remainder interest is $385,000. The gift Mike made to Gloria can be reduced by Mike's annual exclusion for a taxable amount of $101,000. The gift Mike made to Debbie cannot be reduced by Mike's annual exclusion because it is a future-interest gift. However, Mike can use a marital deduction of $385,000 to eliminate the tax on this remainder interest gift. Mike made a total taxable gift of $101,000 when he established this trust.

Non-citizen Spouse

A marital deduction is not available for property **gifted to a non-citizen spouse**. Lifetime transfers of up to $147,000 per year to a non-citizen spouse qualify for the gift tax marital deduction. The donee spouse must be given the property outright or at least have the right to income and a general power of appointment over the principal.

Client Situation

Victor's wife, Juanita was born in Costa Rica, and she is planning to become a U.S. citizen, but she has not yet applied for citizenship. Victor changed the deed to his house, worth $400,000, to tenancy-by-the-entirety with Juanita. Victor has made a gift of half of the property, and the taxable gift can be reduced by $147,000. Victor will report the taxable gift of $53,000 on his gift tax return.

Practitioner Tip: If Victor had waited to change the deed until after Juanita attained U.S. citizenship, no taxable gift would have occurred.

Terminable Interest Property

A marital deduction is not allowed for **terminable interest property (TIP)**, which is property for which the spouse/beneficiary's interest terminates at some future point and is not included in the surviving spouse's taxable estate. Following are some examples of TIP:

- A spouse is given an income interest in a trust for life (a life estate).

- A spouse is given trust income for a term of years.

- A spouse is given a life estate in real property.

In these situations, a donee spouse does not have possession or enjoyment of the remainder interest in the property and consequently does not have total control over the entire property interest. The donor spouse chooses the remainder beneficiary in the property when the property is transferred into the trust or when a deed is executed. Because the donor spouse has not given the donee spouse complete control over the property, the donor spouse cannot take a marital deduction for the property transferred to the spouse. However, the donor spouse can take an annual exclusion to reduce the taxable value of the present-interest gift.

Client Situation

Tommy owns a vacation home on the coast of Maine that has been passed down through his family for the last three generations. Tommy recently changed the deed so that his wife Elaine would have a life estate in the property, and his son Tim would receive the property after Elaine's death. The house was appraised at $600,000.

Tommy has made a present-interest gift of $450,000 to Elaine, which can be reduced by his annual exclusion, but not by a marital deduction ($450,000 – $14,000 = $436,000). Tommy has made a gift to Tim of the present value of the remainder interest, or $150,000. The taxable value of the gift to Tim cannot be reduced by Tommy's annual exclusion because it is a future-interest gift. Therefore, the total taxable amount of the gift is $586,000 ($436,000 + $150,000).

Practitioner Tip: To calculate the amount of the taxable gifts that Tommy made to Elaine and Tim, these four steps were considered in the following order:

1. **Is this a gift?** Yes. There are two gifts: the life estate to Elaine and the remainder interest to Tim.

2. **Can this gift be split?** No. Elaine is the recipient of a life estate; therefore, she cannot consent to splitting the gift with Tommy.

3. **Can an annual exclusion be taken?** Yes, for the present-interest gift to Elaine, but not for the future interest to Tim.

4. **Can a marital deduction be taken?** No. Tommy has given Elaine TIP—her interest in the property terminates at some future point.

Terminable Interest Property Exceptions

When a donor spouse gives a donee spouse TIP and gives the donee spouse a general power of appointment, the donor can take a marital deduction to offset the tax on the gift. For example, a husband can establish an irrevocable trust and give his wife a life estate in the property. He cannot take a marital deduction for the TIP he gifted to his wife unless he also gives his wife a general power of appointment over the trust property. A general power of appointment allows holders to appoint property to themselves, their creditors, their estate, and to creditors of their estate. With a general power of appointment, the wife, in this example, would receive all of the income from the trust, and she would have unrestricted access to the trust corpus as well. Because the wife now has total control over the trust property, the husband is allowed a marital deduction.

Another exception is for a gift of **qualified terminable interest property (QTIP)**. If a donor spouse gives a donee spouse a "qualifying income interest for life," it qualifies for a gift tax marital deduction. To qualify:

- The donee spouse must be entitled to all the income from the property, and it must be payable at least annually.

- The property cannot be appointed to a person other than the surviving spouse.

- The property must be taxable in the donee spouse's estate at death.

Client Situation

Jacquie inherited a substantial amount of money from her mother. She established an irrevocable trust with $3 million that gave her husband Scott all the income for life, and her daughter Amanda the remainder interest in the trust. Jacquie also gave Scott the power to invade the trust corpus without restriction, which is a general power of appointment. The gift of the income interest to Scott was valued at $2 million, but Jacquie can take an annual exclusion and a marital deduction to reduce the taxable gift to Scott to zero. The gift of the remainder interest to Amanda cannot be reduced by gift splitting or by an annual exclusion; therefore, Jacquie has made a taxable gift of $1 million when she established this trust. If Scott did not have a general power to invade the trust corpus, the marital deduction could not be applied.

Estate Tax Implications

A marital deduction is also available to reduce a decedent spouse's estate tax liability. When a donor spouse takes a marital deduction for property gifted to a donee spouse, and the donee spouse keeps the property until death, the value of the property is included in the donee spouse's estate and could be subject to an estate tax.

Client Situation

Jimmy gave his wife Jennifer a parcel of land zoned for commercial use. The land was appraised at $2 million, but it is expected to appreciate substantially over the next 10 years. Jimmy's gift tax liability was zero because an annual exclusion and a marital deduction eliminated a tax on the gift. When Jennifer dies, the appreciated value of the property will be included in her gross estate and could be subject to an estate tax.

Qualified terminable interest property that is gifted to a spouse is eligible for a gift tax marital deduction if the donor spouse makes the QTIP election on the gift tax return. However, this property will be included in the donee spouse's gross estate. Likewise, when a donee spouse is given a general power of appointment over property, a marital deduction is available to the donor, but the property will be included in the donee spouse's estate.

Client Situation

Sandi transferred $4 million into a trust that gave her husband George the income for life, and her son Ryan, the remainder interest. The present value of the income interest was calculated to be $2.5 million, and the remainder interest was valued at $1.5 million. When Sandi filed her gift tax return, she qualified the gift of the TIP for the marital deduction, which reduced the total taxable gift to $1.5 million. However, when George dies, the fair market value of this trust will be included in his gross estate even though he received only a terminable interest—the lifetime income—from the trust.

Charitable Deduction

A gift made to a qualified charity could potentially be reduced by gift splitting, an annual exclusion, and a **charitable deduction**, when applicable. The amount that can be passed to a qualified charity, gift tax free, is unlimited. A gift to a qualified charity includes gifts made to:

- a government (federal or state) for public use;

- a religious, scientific, or charitable organization;

- a fraternal society or association; and

- a veteran's organization.

Client Situation

Mary made a gift of $300,000 to the Conservancy of Southwest Florida. This present-interest gift was first reduced by an annual exclusion, and then by a charitable deduction equal to the remaining value of the gift ($286,000).

COMPUTING TAXABLE GIFTS

To compute the current year's taxable gifts, all five steps in the calculation process must be addressed in sequence (see Exhibit 11.2).

Client Situation

Walter made the following gifts this year: $160,000 to his son, $125,000 to his daughter, $8,000 to his grandson, and $25,000 to Boston University. All of these gifts can be reduced by annual exclusions, but note that the annual exclusions total $50,000, not $56,000, because the gift to his grandson is only $8,000.

Exhibit 11.2 Computing Taxable Gifts

Step 1	*List* total gifts for year.		$318,000
Step 2	*Subtract* one-half of gift deemed to be made by donor's spouse (split gifts).	$ 0	
	Gifts deemed to be made by donor:		$318,000
Step 3	*Subtract* annual exclusion(s).	$ 50,000	
	Gifts after subtracting exclusion(s):		$268,000
Step 4	*Subtract* marital deduction.	$ 0	
Step 5	*Subtract* charitable deduction.	$ 11,000	
	Taxable gifts:		$257,000

Client Situation

Assume that Walter's wife Linda has agreed to split these gifts. The value of the gifts will be reduced by half. The annual exclusion amounts for each spouse will total $44,500, as follows: $14,000 each for the gifts to their son and to their daughter; $4,000 for the gift to their grandson; and $12,500 for the gift to BU. Each spouse's annual exclusion eliminated any remaining charitable deduction. Walter and Linda will each have taxable gifts of $114,500. (See Exhibit 11.3.)

Exhibit 11.3 Computing Taxable Gifts: Gift Splitting

Step 1	*List* total gifts for year.		$318,000
Step 2	*Subtract* one-half of gift deemed to be made by donor's spouse (split gifts).	$159,000	
	Gifts deemed to be made by donor:		$159,000
Step 3	*Subtract* annual exclusion(s).	$ 44,500	
	Gifts after subtracting exclusion(s):		$114,500
Step 4	*Subtract* marital deduction.	$ 0	
Step 5	*Subtract* charitable deduction.	$ 0	
	Taxable gifts:		$114,500

Note: The calculation on the wife's return would parallel this return

> **Client Situation**
>
> Suppose that Walter made a gift to Linda of $200,000 before the end of the year. This would increase his annual exclusion amount by $14,000 and provide for a marital deduction. See Walter's gift tax computation in Exhibit 11.4.

Exhibit 11.4 Computing Taxable Gifts: Marital Deduction

Step 1	*List* total gifts for year.		$518,000
Step 2	*Subtract* one-half of gift deemed to be made by donor's spouse (split gifts).	$159,000	
	Gifts deemed to be made by donor:		$359,000
Step 3	*Subtract* annual exclusion(s).	$ 58,500	
	Gifts after subtracting exclusion(s):		$300,500
Step 4	*Subtract* marital deduction.	$186,000	
Step 5	*Subtract* charitable deduction.	$ 0	
	Taxable gifts:		$114,500

COMPUTING GIFT TAX PAYABLE

Once the current year's taxable gifts have been calculated, it is necessary to calculate the taxable gifts for each previous year that gifts were made (since 1932). Because the gift tax is both cumulative and progressive, these taxable gifts are all added together to determine the total taxable gifts the donor has made throughout his lifetime.

> **Client Situation**
>
> Ed and his wife Amy have two children, Pam and Colin. Ed has made cash gifts to their two children for the past three years and Amy has agreed to split all gifts with Ed. Gift splitting and annual exclusions reduced the taxable amount of each gift for each spouse. Therefore, the computation strategy is to divide the gift in half and subtract $14,000, the annual exclusion amount for al three years. (See Table 11.1.)

Table 11.1 Calculating Total Taxable Gifts

	Gifts to Pam	Taxable Amount	Gifts to Colin	Taxable Amount	Total Taxable Gifts
2013	$38,000	$5,000	$48,000	$10,000	$15,000
2014	$43,000	$7,500	$43,000	$7,500	$15,000
2015	$48,000	$10,000	$38,000	$5,000	$15,000
					$45,000

When the total value of taxable gifts for the reporting period is determined, the actual tax payable is computed using the method demonstrated in Exhibit 11.5.

Exhibit 11.5 Calculating Gift Tax Payable

Step 1	Compute gift tax on all *taxable* gifts regardless of when made. (Use gift tax rate schedule.)	$_____
Step 2	Compute gift tax on all *taxable* gifts made prior to the present year's gift(s). (Use gift tax rate schedule.)	$_____
Step 3	Subtract Step 2 result from Step 1 result.	$_____
Step 4	Enter gift tax credit remaining.	$_____
Step 5	Subtract Step 4 result from Step 3 result to obtain *gift tax* payable.	$_____

Step 1: Compute Tax on all Taxable Gifts

Ed and Amy have each made total taxable gifts of $45,000. The tax on $45,000 is found by using the gift tax rate schedule in effect for the year of the gift (see Appendix B.4). Note that the current rate table is used regardless of when the earlier gifts were made. The tax on $45,000 is $9,400.

Step 2: Compute Previous Years' Taxable Gifts

Ed and Amy both made taxable gifts of $15,000 in 2013 and again in 2014. Taxable gifts made prior to the present year's gifts total $30,000 for each spouse. The tax on $30,000 is $6,000.

Step 3: Compute Current Tentative Tax

To determine the amount of the current year's tentative tax, Ed and Amy must subtract $6,000 from $9,400, which results in a tentative tax of $3,400.

Now suppose that Ed and Amy had calculated only the tax on the taxable gifts made this year. The tax on $15,000 is $2,800. Because Ed and Amy have made the same amount of taxable gifts each year, why isn't the tax always $2,800? The answer is that the gift tax rate is progressive and cumulative. That is why the current tentative tax is calculated to be a higher amount ($3,400) after adding in all previous year's taxable gifts.

Step 4: Gift Tax Credit Remaining

Every time Ed and Amy made a taxable gift they had to use their respective unified credits to offset the tax. The $6,000 tax on prior taxable gifts had been offset by a portion of each spouse's unified credit. When additional gifts were made in 2015, the tentative tax was calculated to be $3,400. Ed and Amy's unified credits were reduced again in 2015 to shelter against this tax.

Practitioner Tip: If Ed and Amy wanted to know how much of their **unified credit remained** after making gifts in 2015, it can be easily calculated. Because each spouse has made total taxable gifts of $45,000 and the tax on $45,000 is $9,400, they have each used 9,400 of their unified credit to date. Therefore, Ed and Amy have $2,108,400 of their unified credits remaining in 2015 to offset tax on future taxable gifts ($2,117,800 – $9,400).

Step 5: Gift Tax Payable

Ed and Amy do not have to pay any gift tax, because they have not made taxable gifts that exceeded $5,430,000. Each spouse has unified credit available to offset future taxable gifts.

THE GIFT TAX

A donor's unified credit must be used to offset the gift tax each time a taxable gift is made. Therefore, the unified credit is continually reduced and is fully depleted when taxable gifts exceed $5,430,000. When this occurs, the donor must pay a gift tax. The tax rates for the gift tax and the estate tax are unified under the federal transfer tax system so that gifts and bequests of equal value incur the same tax liability.

Client Situation

Paton bought his son, Brandon, a sports car last year, which brought his total lifetime taxable gifts up to $5 million. Paton did not have to pay a gift tax because some of his unified credit was still available to offset the tax on the gift. This year, if Paton makes a taxable gift of $500,000, he will have to pay a gift tax because he will have used his entire unified credit.

Cumulative and Progressive

The gift tax and the estate tax are both cumulative and progressive, ranging from 18% to 40% this year. All taxable gifts are added together before the gift tax is applied, which results in a higher tax rate. The value of the donor's estate is reduced by the amount of the gifts he has made throughout his lifetime. Any gift taxes paid will further reduce the value of his estate unless the donor dies within three years of paying a gift tax.

Client Situation

Last year Joe and Tricia each made their first taxable gift of $15,000 to their daughter, Katie. The gift tax was calculated to be $2,000 in the 20% rate bracket, but neither Joe nor Tricia had to pay a gift tax, because their unified credits offset the tax. This year Joe and Tricia each made another $15,000 taxable gift to their son, Joey. The gift tax rate was higher, in the 22% rate bracket, because the taxable gift from last year was added to this year's taxable gift, which bumped them into a higher gift tax bracket. This example illustrates how the gift tax is progressive and cumulative. (See Appendix B.4.)

Estate Tax Implications

Gifting reduces the value of a donor's gross estate. Ed made total gifts of $258,000 in the past three years, which reduced his estate by $258,000. The total taxable gifts of $45,000 will be added into each spouse's estate tax calculation as an **adjusted taxable gift**. The federal estate tax is also progressive and cumulative, and adding an adjusted taxable gift increases the tentative estate tax base.

FILING A GIFT TAX RETURN

When a donor makes a taxable gift of more than $14,000, a **gift tax return** must be filed. The donor files IRS Form 709 at the same time his income tax return is due, on April 15th of the following year.

A gift tax return must be filed for any year in which a married couple elects to split gifts. The amount of the taxable gift determines whether only one or both spouses must file a gift tax return.

When the value of a split gift results in no taxable gift (the value of the gift is between $14,000 and $28,000), only one spouse must file a return. For example, a husband makes a gift of $20,000 to his nephew and his wife consents to gift split. The value of the gift for each spouse is only $10,000, which is less than the annual exclusion amount. However, the wife must consent to split the gift on the donor spouse's IRS Form 709, because there are no joint gift tax returns.

When the value of a gift exceeds $28,000 (therefore, even after splitting, both spouses have made a taxable gift), then both spouses must file a gift tax return. Suppose that a husband and wife jointly made a gift of $30,000 to their daughter. After splitting the gift, each spouse has made a taxable gift of $1,000 ($15,000 – $14,000) that would be reported on their individual gift tax returns.

Gift tax returns must be filed when future-interest gifts are made to others, regardless of amount, and when split-interest gifts are made to charities (i.e., where there are charitable and noncharitable donees of the same gift). In community property states, each spouse can give an amount equal to the annual exclusion without filing a gift tax return.

Payment of Gift Taxes

In 2015, gift taxes must be paid when taxable gifts of more than $5,430,000 are made. It is the donor's responsibility to pay the gift tax from a source other than the gift so that the value of the gift is not reduced to pay the tax. Remember, the gift tax is *tax exclusive*. If a donor fails to pay the gift tax, and the tax cannot be collected from the donor, then the donee is liable for the tax for up to one year after the assessment period.

Any gift taxes paid within three years of a donor's death are included in the donor's gross estate. This is known as the *gross-up rule*. However, a *gift tax payable credit* can be subtracted from the tentative tax to reduce estate tax liability. A gift tax paid more than three years prior to a donor's death reduces the value of a donor's gross estate.

Client Situation

Anthony, a widower, made his first taxable gift of $5.6 million in March 2015 prior to his death in May of this year. His unified credit could shelter only up to $5,430,000 in taxable gifts; therefore, Anthony paid a tax on this gift of $68,000. His executor filed his estate tax return, and under the gross-up rule, the $68,000 tax was included in his gross estate. However, a credit of $68,000 was subtracted for the gift tax paid. The taxable gift of $5.6 million was added into the *adjusted taxable gift* column of his estate tax return, which increased Anthony's estate tax liability.

Net Gift

A **net gift** occurs when a donee agrees to pay a donor's gift tax as a condition of receiving the gift. Both parties should sign a written agreement that obligates the donee to pay the tax before the gift is made. If the gift is made to a trust, the trustee should sign the agreement which obligates the trust to pay the gift tax. The advantage of a net gift is that the donee's gift tax liability is lower than the donor's, and the gift tax paid by the donee reduces the value of the taxable gift. A disadvantage is that the tax is paid from the donee's personal funds or from trust assets. Note that the donor's unified credit must be used first. The formula for calculating a donee's gift tax liability follows:

Donor's tentative tax ÷ (1 + donor's gift tax rate)

Example for 2015: David gave his daughter Marsha a family heirloom worth $6,014,000 today. Marsha agreed to pay the tax on the gift. After subtracting the annual exclusion, the taxable gift is $6 million. This is David's first taxable gift. The tentative tax is $228,000 ($2,345,800 – David's unified credit of $2,117,800). The gift tax paid by Marsha is $162,857 ($228,000 ÷ 1.40).

The adjusted taxable gift on David's estate tax return IRS Form 706 is the net amount of the gift, **$5,837,143** (gift of $6 million – $162,857 gift tax paid by Marsha).

The gift tax credit on David's IRS Form 706 is **$162,857.**

If David dies within three years of making this gift, the **$162,857** gift tax paid goes into his gross estate on IRS Form 706 under the gross-up rule.

The net value of the gift to Marsha is $6,014,000 – $162,857 = **$5,851,143.**

David would have taxable income if the gift tax Marsha paid exceeded his adjusted basis in the property. David inherited the family heirloom, so there is no taxable income to report.

Chapter Highlights

- Gifts are often valued at fair market value at the time the gift is made, with some exceptions. The taxable amount of split-interest gifts is determined by the present value of the income interest and the present value of the remainder interest.

- There are five steps in the process of calculating taxable gifts. Gift tax returns are filed for gifts that exceed $14,000.

- Exempt gifts are direct payments made for tuition or medical expenses.

- Gift splitting is permitted only between husband and wife, and it requires the donee spouse's consent. Gift tax returns must be filed when gift splitting occurs.

- A donor must ascertain whether a gift made to a donee is a present-interest gift or a future-interest gift to use an annual exclusion to offset the taxable gift.

- Marital deductions cannot be taken for TIP transferred to a spouse unless the donor spouse gives the donee spouse a general power of appointment or makes a QTIP election on the gift tax return.

- The gift tax payable is calculated by adding together all of a donor's taxable gifts from 1932 to the present. The tax on the total taxable gifts is computed. Next, the tax on the previous years' taxable gifts is subtracted from the tax on the total taxable gifts to arrive at the current gift tax payable. The donor's unified credit offsets the tax for all taxable gifts that do not exceed $5,430,000.

Key Terms

adjusted taxable gift

annual exclusion

charitable deduction

gift splitting

gift tax return

gift to a non-citizen spouse

marital deduction

net gift

qualified terminable interest property (QTIP)

qualified transfer (exempt gifts)

split-interest trusts

taxable gift

terminable interest property (TIP)

Review Questions

11-1. Identify transfers that are included when determining taxable gifts.

A. You cancelled a $1,000 debt from your brother.

B. You added your daughter's name to the deed to your house.

C. You added your son's name to your checking account.

D. You established a revocable trust and named your spouse as beneficiary.

11-2. Adrian has made the following gifts this year. Which gift qualifies for the annual exclusion?

A. Adrian paid for his nephew's tuition at a private high school.

B. Adrian established a $1 million irrevocable trust for his twin sons. The bank trustee has the discretion to distribute income to each child prior to age 35, at which time the trust corpus will be distributed to them.

C. Adrian transferred artwork valued at $500,000 into an irrevocable trust for his sister.

D. Adrian transferred $2 million of municipal bonds into an irrevocable trust for his wife, who is the sole beneficiary. His wife has unrestricted use of the trust assets.

11-3. Jonathan made the following gifts to his wife, Kristen, and son, Silas, this year. Which gift does not qualify for the gift tax marital deduction?

A. Jonathan gave Kristen a remainder interest in his Montana ranch.

B. Jonathan transferred $3 million of securities into an irrevocable trust. Kristen will receive all income for life, and Silas will receive the remainder interest. The trust gives Kristen the right to invade the corpus without restriction.

C. Jonathan established an irrevocable trust and funded it with $2,500,000.

Kristen will receive the income for 10 years, and Silas will receive the remainder interest.

D. Jonathan transferred $6 million into an irrevocable trust that gives Kristen a qualifying income interest for life. Silas will receive the remainder interest in the trust. Jonathan made a QTIP election on his gift tax return.

11-4. Martin recently inherited property from his father. Martin and his wife Regina jointly made cash gifts of $200,000 to their son this year. This is the first taxable gift they have ever made. Which of the following statements is/are correct?

A. Martin and Regina each made taxable gifts of $86,000 this year.

B. Martin, the donor spouse, will file a gift tax return, and Regina will indicate her consent to gift split on his IRS Form 709.

C. Martin and Regina each has $2,031,800 of their unified credit remaining.

D. When Martin and Regina die, $86,000 will be added into their estate tax return as an adjusted taxable gift.

11-5. Lynne transferred $1 million into a trust for the benefit of her husband Kiron, age 36, and her young daughter Beth. Kiron will receive all income for life and Beth will receive the remainder interest. Using IRS Valuation Table S for a single life with a 6% interest rate, what is the value of the taxable gift Lynne made to Kiron, assuming no election is made?

Annuity	Life Estate	Remainder
14.7060	0.88236	0.11764

A. $882,360

B. $868,360

C. $117,640

D. $0

Chapter 12

Gifts to Minors

CFP® CERTIFICATION EXAMINATION PRINCIPAL TOPICS COVERED IN THIS CHAPTER:

Inter-vivos Gifting

Types, Features, and Taxation of Trusts

- Code Section 2503(b) trust
- Code Section 2503(c) trust

Learning Objectives

To ensure that you have a solid understanding of the various ways in which cash or property can be transferred to minors, and the resulting tax ramifications, the following learning objectives are addressed in this chapter:

- Explain the tax advantages of making lifetime gifts to minors.

- Compare the tax and non-tax characteristics of a Section 2503(b) trust and a Section 2503(c) trust.

- Describe the similarities and differences between a UGMA account and a UTMA account.

- Understand when "kiddie tax" rules apply and how to compute the tax.

- Identify the income tax-shifting strategies available for families.

Chapter Contents

OVERVIEW

Gifts to minors can be made in several different ways. Minors can receive outright gifts of cash or property, or they can receive property that has been transferred into trusts. Minors can also receive property placed into custodial accounts or funds that are deposited into tax-advantaged education accounts. Parents, grandparents, and others who make gifts to minors can take advantage of some favorable gift tax and generation-skipping transfer tax provisions, and perhaps shift family wealth and income taxation to family members in a lower tax bracket.

Financial planners need to be aware of the advantages and disadvantages of the various options available for passing property to minors and how these transfers affect both the client's and the child's present and future tax situation.

Practice Standard 400-3

Presenting the Financial Planning Recommendation(s)

The financial planning practitioner shall communicate the recommendation(s) in a manner and to an extent reasonably necessary to assist the client in making an informed decision.

ADVANTAGES OF GIFTING TO MINORS

Estate Tax Advantage

In most situations, when a donor makes an inter-vivos gift, the value of his gross estate is reduced by the amount of the gift. If the gifted property has the potential to appreciate in value, then that appreciation is shifted to the donee and is never taxed in the donor's estate. Note that when a gift tax—which is tax exclusive in nature—must be paid, it reduces the value of the donor's gross estate because the tax is paid from other assets that the donor owns.

> **Client Situation**
>
> Gerald owns an asset that is worth $100,000 today. It is anticipated that the asset will appreciate at the rate of 10% per year, so that in 10 years it will be worth approximately $260,000. If the property is given away now, the gift tax is calculated on the $100,000 minus the annual exclusion. If the asset is not given away and it becomes part of Gerald's estate (10 years from today), the estate tax is computed on approximately $260,000.

Gift Tax Advantage

The IRS states in Revenue Ruling 54-400 that "an unqualified and unrestricted gift to a minor, with or without the appointment of a guardian, is a gift of a present interest."[1] Therefore, a donor and the donor's spouse can utilize annual exclusions to reduce or eliminate a tax on a gift when property is gifted outright to minors, or when a minor beneficiary has been given a present interest in trust property.

> ### Client Situation
>
> Brian transferred dividend-paying securities worth $50,000 into an irrevocable trust for his son Brad, who is 15 years old. Brad will receive all income from this trust annually, and the principal will be distributed to Brad when he reaches age 30. Brian's wife Marilyn has consented to split this taxable gift with Brian to reduce its value. Now, both Brian and Marilyn can use annual exclusions to further reduce the gift tax value of this transfer.

Generation-skipping Transfer Tax Advantage

Grandparents who make gifts to their grandchildren may be subject to a generation-skipping transfer (GST) tax. This tax is imposed in addition to a gift tax. However, the GST tax on a gift made directly to a grandchild can be reduced by the transferor's **GST tax annual exclusion** of $14,000. Any taxable portion of the gift can be further decreased by the transferor's remaining GST exemption, because a grandparent can gift up to $5,430,000 in taxable gifts in 2015 to grandchildren before a GST tax is imposed.

> ### Client Situation
>
> Ruth Ann and Al paid for their grandson Jordan's college tuition this year by writing a check to Boston University for $60,000. They also paid for their granddaughter Katrina's wedding by giving her a check for $50,000. The money paid for Jordan's college tuition is an exempt gift, which is not subject to a gift tax or to a GST tax. The money given to Katrina is subject to both gift and GST taxes. Ruth Ann and Al split the gift to Katrina so that each spouse made a taxable gift of $25,000. The gift was further reduced by each spouse's annual exclusions of $14,000. This reduced the gift tax value and the GST tax value to a taxable gift of $11,000 for each spouse. Neither Ruth Ann nor Al had to pay a tax on this gift, because each had a sufficient amount of gift tax unified credit and GST exemption available to offset both taxes.

Practitioner Tip: IRC § 2503(e) refers to "qualified" transfers, such as tuition paid directly to an educational institution, or direct payments made for medical care. These transfers are exempt from gift tax and GST tax. Donors do not have to apply annual exclusions, unified credits, or GST tax exemptions to reduce or eliminate transfer taxes on these gifts. Consequently, such tax-saving techniques remain available to the donor to offset other taxable gifts.

---

529 Plan Advantage

A Section 529 plan (or **529 plan**) is a type of education savings plan that allows funds to grow tax deferred, and allows tax-free distributions of both principal and earnings for qualified education expenses. Annual exclusions may apply to contributions made to 529 plan accounts to finance the costs of higher education. A donor can front-load a contribution by making five years' worth of annual exclusion gifts in one year, or $70,000 in 2015 and $140,000 if a married couple consents to gift split. Any additional taxable gifts made to the same donee from the donor within the ensuing five-year period would not be decreased by annual exclusions. If the donor dies within five years after making the contribution, a pro rata portion of the contribution will be included in the donor's estate.

Client Situation

Joanne contributed $70,000 to a 529 plan savings account for her son Dustin in 2015, and she made an election to treat the gift as if it were made pro rata over five years. This qualified the gift for the gift tax annual exclusion. The next year, Joanne gave Dustin a check for $15,000 for his birthday, but she could not use an annual exclusion to offset this taxable gift. Joanne can use an annual exclusion again for any gifts she makes to Dustin in 2020 and thereafter, but not before.

Practitioner Tip: Suppose that Joanne died in 2017. The $28,000 gift that was attributable to years 2018 and 2019 would be included in her gross estate. However, the $14,000 gift attributed to the year of her death would not be included. Note that only a pro rata portion of the contribution, and not the current account balance, is included in the donor's gross estate.

Income Tax Advantage

Gifts made to minors can have income tax advantages as well. Any income-producing property gifted to a person less than age 24 who is in a lower marginal tax bracket than the donor may result in income tax savings for a high-bracket donor.

Client Situation

Andrea owns $20,000 of interest-paying bonds. The bonds yield $1,100 annually. Andrea is currently in a 28% federal income tax bracket. On the advice of her financial planner, in 2015 she gives the bonds to her son Evan, who is 23 years old and a full-time student at a community college. Andrea's husband Jim consents to split the gift with her so that there is no taxable gift. This will result in shifting the income tax liability from Andrea, who would have netted only $792 [$1,100 – (28% × $1,100)] from the $1,100 interest, to Evan, who is in a 10% tax bracket. Evan has a special standard deduction of $1,050 (making only $50 taxable), and will therefore net $1,095 [$1,100 – (10% × $50)] from the interest. This gift will save the family $303 ($1,095 - $792) annually.

DISADVANTAGES OF GIFTING TO MINORS

Practical problems are often involved with making larger gifts to minors. Although minors can buy, sell, and deal with some limited types of property such as U.S. savings bonds, gifts of other types of property create difficulties. For example, some states do not give minors the legal capacity to purchase their own property, care for it, sell it, or transfer it. Some states forbid the registration of securities in a minor's name, and a broker may be reluctant to deal in securities titled in a minor's name. For example, in many states, a minor has the legal ability to disaffirm a sale of stock sold at a low price that later rises in value. Furthermore, a buyer receives no assurance of permanent title when a minor signs a real estate deed.

Minors can receive property that has been transferred to a conservator for their benefit, but legal guardianship of the minor is not a viable option in many situations. Because guardianship laws are rigid, a guardian must generally post bond, and periodic and expensive court accounting is often required. Most importantly, a parent may not want to give a legal minor control over a large amount of cash or other property.

To minimize the practical problems involved with most large gifts to minors, such transfers are generally made in trust or under some type of guardianship or custodial arrangement. There are three basic means of qualifying "cared-for gifts" to minors under IRC § 2503:

- An Section 2503(b) trust

- An Section 2503(c) trust

- The Uniform Gifts to Minors Act (or the Uniform Transfers to Minors Act).

CODE SECTION 2503(b) TRUST

A **Code section 2503(b) trust** is typically established for the benefit of minor beneficiaries. It is an irrevocable trust that can hold any type of property that is transferred into it. More than one beneficiary is permitted, and trust income and corpus can be split between different trust beneficiaries. All income from this trust must be distributed annually to the income beneficiaries.

The minor receives possession of the trust principal whenever the trust agreement specifies. A distribution does not have to be made by age 21; the corpus can be held for as long as the beneficiary lives. In fact, the principal can actually bypass the income beneficiary and go directly to the individuals whom the grantor—or even the named beneficiary—has specified.

Although the entire amount of property placed in a Section 2503(b) trust would be considered a gift, for annual exclusion purposes it would be split into two parts: income and principal. The present value of the income would be eligible for the annual exclusion. The remainder interest of the gift would not qualify for the annual exclusion. Note that an annual exclusion would be denied for a Section 2503(b) trust that permits principal to be invested in non-income-producing securities, non-income-producing real estate, or life insurance policies (because they do not produce taxable income).

> **Client Situation**
>
> Assume Ken places $10,000 into a § 2503(b) trust that is required to pay his 10-year-old daughter Margaret all income until she reaches age 25. Assume a 5.0% IRC § 7520 rate. The present value of the income that Margaret would receive over those 15 years is $5,190 ($10,000 × .518983).[2] If the income were payable for Margaret's entire life, the present value would jump to $9,417 ($10,000 × .94171.)[3] In either situation, Ken can use an annual exclusion to eliminate the tax on the gift to Margaret by the amount of the present value of Margaret's income interest.

Practitioner Tip: Rather than have the trust distribute income outright to a minor beneficiary, the income could be deposited in a custodial account and used for the child's benefit, or it could accumulate in the account until it is turned over to the child. Income would be taxed to the minor and would be subject to kiddie tax rules as discussed later in this chapter.

CODE SECTION 2503(c) TRUST

The Code **section 2503(c) trust** differs from the Section 2503(b) trust in several ways.

- Only one trust beneficiary is permitted.

- The trust does not require the trustee to distribute income currently.

- The trust requires the distribution of accumulated income and principal when the minor reaches age 21.

A gift to a § 2503(c) trust would appear to be a future-interest gift, but the donor can apply an annual exclusion if certain requirements are met.

- The trust income and principal can be expended on behalf of the beneficiary, or any accumulated income and principal will pass to the beneficiary at age 21. The rule is that age 21 is the maximum, rather than the minimum, age at which the right to trust assets can occur. Any distributed income is taxed to the minor, and accumulated income is taxed to the trust.

- If the beneficiary dies prior to age 21, income and principal pass through the beneficiary's estate, or to appointees if the donor granted the beneficiary a general power of appointment.

Practitioner Tip: A donor may not wish to distribute large sums of income or assets to a beneficiary at age 21. It is possible to provide continued management of the trust assets and, at the same time, avoid forfeiting the annual exclusion. For example, the trust may give the donee only the right, for a limited but reasonable period, to withdraw all of the trust assets at age 21. If the beneficiary fails to give the trustee written notice, the trust can continue automatically for as long as the donor provided when he established the trust.

UNIFORM GIFTS/TRANSFERS TO MINORS ACTS

The **Uniform Gifts to Minors Act (UGMA)** and the **Uniform Transfers to Minors Act (UTMA)** provide alternatives to the Section 2503(c) trust. The Uniform Acts are frequently utilized for smaller gifts because of their simplicity and because they offer the benefits of management, income and estate tax shifting and the investment characteristics of a trust with few or none of the setup costs.

UGMA and UTMA Custodial Accounts

UGMA enables a donor to make an inter-vivos gift of certain types of property to a minor, such as money, stocks, bonds, certificates of interest, a life insurance policy, or an annuity contract, by registering the property in the name of a custodian for the minor. The custodian may be the donor, another adult, a trust company, or a bank with trust powers. Many states also allow gifts of real property, personal property, and intangibles, and a few states permit transfers to custodians from other sources, such as trusts and estates, as well as lifetime gifts.

UTMA allows any kind of property, real or personal, tangible or intangible, to be gifted to a minor. In addition, it permits property transfers from trusts, estates, and guardianships, so that transfers are not limited to lifetime gifts. Almost all of the states have replaced their UGMA laws with the more flexible UTMA.

A custodial account is also indicated over a trust if the gift consists of stock in an S corporation. Generally speaking, a trust cannot hold S corporation stock without causing a loss of the election privilege. The result might be double taxation of corporate profits and forfeiture of the S corporation election, which allows the passing through of profits (and losses) to shareholders.

Under both the UGMA and the UTMA, the minor immediately acquires both legal and equitable title to the gift held by the custodian. Therefore, property in a custodial account counts as the child's asset for financial aid purposes.

Requirements

- Property must be transferred to a custodian who holds it for the minor.

- A separate account must be established for each child.

- Once made, a custodial gift is irrevocable.

- The property must be distributed to the child when the child reaches the age specified by state statute—generally 18 or 21.

> **Client Situation**
>
> Tony transferred his 10 shares of IBM stock to his wife as custodian of their son Marco by having the stock registered as follows: "Ginny Arcangelo as custodian for Marco Arcangelo under the Pennsylvania Uniform Transfers to Minors Act." The gift is a present-interest gift and would therefore qualify for the gift tax annual exclusion. Future appreciation in the value of the stock, as well as the original gift value of the stock, would be out of Tony's estate. Any dividend income or capital gains from the sale of the stock would be taxed to Marco.

Tax Implications of Custodial Accounts

Income Tax: Income from any custodial property is taxed to the minor as it is earned, whether distributed or not. The income will be subject to kiddie tax rules. When income produced by a custodial gift relieves an individual such as a parent of a legal obligation, the income is taxed to the parent. A parent's duty to support minor children varies among states.

Gift Tax: The gift is one of a present interest and qualifies for the gift tax annual exclusion. The exclusion is allowed even though custodial property will not be distributed to the donee until age 18 or 21, depending on the state.

Estate Tax: The value of property in the custodial account is generally included in the minor's estate if the child dies before the account terminates. Likewise, custodial property is included in the estate of the donor if the donor serves as custodian and dies while serving in that capacity. Under UTMA, if the custodian has not chosen a successor, the minor can do so if the minor is at least 14 years old. If the minor does not choose a successor or the minor is younger than 14, the minor's guardian will be appointed, or the courts will select a successor.

Practitioner Tip: If income from the account is used to satisfy a donor parent's support obligations, the value of the property could be included in the donor parent's estate. A parent's duty to support minor children varies among states.

Advantages of Trusts over Custodial Accounts

A Section 2503(c) trust and a Section 2503(b) trust have a number of advantages over the type of custodianship found in UGMA or UTMA.

Table 12.1 Comparison of Gifts to Minors

Factor	Section 2503(b)	Section 2503(c) Trust	UGMA	UTMA
Type of property	Donor can make gifts of almost any type of property.	Donor can make gifts of almost any type of property.	Type of property must be permitted by appropriate statute. Gift of real estate may not be Permitted.	Donor can make gifts of almost any type of property.
Dispositive provisions	Donor can provide for disposition of trust assets if donee dies without having made disposition.	Donor can provide for disposition of trust assets if donee dies without having made disposition.	Disposition must follow statutory guideline.	Disposition must follow statutory guideline.
Investment powers	Trustee may be given broad, virtually unlimited investment powers.	Trustee may be given broad, virtually unlimited investment powers.	Custodian's authority is passive and limited to investment powers specified by statute.	Custodian has greater investment powers that are limited by statute.
Time of distribution of assets	Age specified by trust.	Trust can continue automatically even after beneficiary reaches age 21. Trustee can make distribution between state law age of majority and age 21.	Custodial assets must be paid to beneficiary upon reaching statutory age—typically age 18.	Custodial assets must be paid to beneficiary upon reaching statutory age—typically age 21.
Number of beneficiaries permitted	Multiple beneficiaries allowed. Different income and remainder beneficiaries permitted.	One.	One.	One.

Source: Adapted from Leimberg, S. R., et al. *The Tools & Techniques of Estate Planning, 16th Ed.*, p. 224. Copyright 2013 The National Underwriter Company.

KIDDIE TAX RULES

Unearned income is investment income, which includes such items as interest, dividends, capital gains, rents, and royalties. There are three situations where net unearned income is taxed to a child at the parent's marginal tax bracket. The **kiddie tax** applies to a child who has unearned income in excess of $2,100 in the following circumstances:

- An unmarried child under age 18;

- An 18-year-old child with earned income less than or equal to one half of the child's support cost; or

- Full-time students aged 19–23 with earned income that is less than or equal to one half of their own support cost.

The tax payable by a child younger than age 24 on net unearned income is essentially the additional amount of tax the parent would have had to pay if the net unearned income of the child were included in the parent's taxable income.

If parents have two or more children with unearned income to be taxed at the parent's marginal tax rate, all of the children's applicable unearned income will be added together and the tax calculated. The tax is then allocated to each child based on the child's pro rata share of unearned income. (See Table 12.2).

Table 12.2 Kiddie Tax Rates

Child's Age	Investment Income	Federal Tax Rate
Under age 19 and full-time students ages 19-23	$0.00-$1,050	Not Taxed
	$1,051-$2,100	Taxed at the child's rate
	Over $2,100	Taxed at the parent's rate
Age 18 and students under age 24 who earn more than half of their own support	$0.00-$1,050	Not taxed

Kiddie Tax Calculation

The Kiddie tax is calculated in three stages (numbers are indexed for 2015):

1. There is no tax on the first $1,050 of unearned income because of the child's standard deduction. The standard deduction offsets *unearned* income first, up to $1,050. Any remaining standard deduction is then available to offset earned income.

2. The next $1,050 of unearned income is taxed to the child at the child's bracket.

3. Unearned income in excess of the first $2,100 is taxed to the child at the appropriate parent's rate.

A dependent child younger than age 24 with $2,100 of unearned income is taxed as follows:

Unearned income	$2,100
Standard deduction	- 1,050
Net unearned income	$1,050
Taxed at child rate	x 10%
Tax	$105.00

Client Situation

Garrett is 20 years old and a full-time student at the state university. His UTMA account earned interest of $2,500 this year. Garrett has no other sources of income, and his parents pay for his full support. The first $1,050 will not be taxed because of his standard deduction; the next $1,050 will be taxed in Garrett's tax bracket; and $400 will be taxed at his parent's tax bracket this year.

Earned Income

The kiddie tax does not apply to any earned income a dependent child receives. This gives business owners an opportunity to shift income to their children if they are hired for a legitimate business purpose.

Standard Deduction

The standard deduction is the greater of $1,050 or earned income plus $350, not to exceed $6,300 in 2015. Earned income in excess of the standard deduction is taxed at the child's income tax bracket.

Client Situation

JoAnn is 17 years old and earned $4,000 this summer from a part-time job. In addition, she has $3,000 of interest income from a bond fund. Any amount of *unearned* income over $2,100 will be taxed at the parent's marginal tax rate. In this case, $900 will be taxed at her parent's tax rate ($3,000 – $2,100). The earned income as well as any remaining unearned income not reduced by the standard deduction will be taxed at the child's rate. Assume that the parent's marginal tax rate is 35%.

JoAnn's unearned income	$ 3,000
JoAnn's earned income	$ 4,000
Total income	$ 7,000
Less standard deduction	$ (4,350)
JoAnn's taxable income	$ 2,650

> ### Tax Liability
>
> Of the taxable income, $900 will be taxed at the parent's rate of 35%. The remaining $1,750 of the taxable income will be taxed at the child's rate of 10%. Therefore, the child's liability is ($900 × 35%) + ($1,750 × 10%) = $315 + $175 = $490.

INCOME SHIFTING TECHNIQUES

Even for children younger than age 24, there are many ways to shift both wealth and income and avoid kiddie taxes. Following is a listing of some **income shifting techniques**.

- Give a Series EE U.S. Savings Bond that will not mature until after the child is age 18. No tax will be payable until the bond is redeemed. At that time, the gain will be taxed at the child's relatively lower tax bracket.

- Give growth stocks (or growth stock mutual funds) that pay little or no current dividends. The child will therefore pay no tax currently and can hold the stock until reaching age 24. Upon a sale after reaching age 24, the child will be taxed at the child's bracket.

- Give *deep discount* tax-free municipal bonds that mature on or after the child's 24th birthday. The bond interest will be tax free to the child and the discount (face less cost basis) will be taxed to the child at the child's bracket when the bond is redeemed at maturity.

- Employ your children. Pay them a reasonable salary for work they actually perform. Regardless of how much is paid to the child, the business will have a deduction at its tax bracket, and the amount will be taxable to the child at the child's bracket. Furthermore, the child could establish an IRA to shelter income further.

- Judicious use of a Section 2503(c) trust will allow significant income shifting. The trust can accumulate income while the beneficiary is less than 18 years old (or in some cases 24) while avoiding the kiddie tax.

- Concentrate on gift and estate tax saving devices such as the annual exclusion. Parents should consider giving $14,000 to $28,000 of non-income-producing assets annually to a minor's trust or custodial account; the assets can be converted into income-producing assets slowly after the child turns age 24. The fund can be self-liquidating and exhaust itself by the time the child finishes college or graduate school.

Income shifting can be very successful when a child is age 24 or older. (See Table 12.3 for an illustration of this practice.)

Table 12.3 Advantage of Income Tax Shifting

Advantage of Income Shifting for a Child 24 or Older

Investment..	$20,000
Rate of return	10%
Parent's tax rate	39.6%
Parent's after-tax rate of return	6%
Child's tax rate...	15%
Child's after-tax rate of return	8.5%

Accumulated Value

Years	Parent (6%)	Child (8.5%)	Advantage of Gift
5	$26,765	$30,073	$3,308
10	$35,817	$45,220	$9,403
15	$47,931	$67,995	$20,064
20	$64,143	$102,241	$38,098

Source: Adapted from Leimberg, S. R., et al. *The Tools & Techniques of Estate Planning, 16th Ed.*, p. 276. Copyright 2013 The National Underwriter Company.

Chapter Highlights

- Transferring property to minors offers many estate tax advantages for donors. The value of the gross estate is reduced and the appreciation on gifted assets is not taxed in the donor's estate.

- Donors can use gift-splitting techniques and annual exclusions to reduce taxable gifts to minors when property is transferred into Section 2503(c) trusts and custodial accounts. Annual exclusions apply to the income interest of a Section 2503(b) trust.

- Donors can reduce income taxes by means of income shifting techniques, but kiddie tax rules can render some techniques less attractive than others.

- Donors can take advantage of transfer vehicles such as Section 2503(b) trusts, Section 2503(c) trusts, custodial accounts, and 529 plans when making gifts to minors.

Key Terms

529 plan/front-load contributions	income shifting techniques
IRC Section 2503(b) trust	kiddie tax
IRC Section 2503(c) trust	Uniform Gift to Minors Act (UGMA)
generation-skipping transfer tax (GST) annual exclusion	Uniform Transfer to Minors Act (UTMA)

Review Questions

12-1. Craig owns an apartment building that has appreciated substantially in the last several years. He wants to remove this property and all future appreciation from his sizeable estate by transferring the building to his eight-year-old son, Tucker. Craig does not want the income from the apartment rentals distributed to Tucker now, but he wants Tucker to take ownership of the building and the undistributed income when he turns 21. Their state's statutory age of majority is age 18.

How should Craig transfer the building to Tucker?

A. Transfer the building into a § 2503(b) trust.

B. Transfer the building into a § 2503(c) trust.

C. Transfer the building into a UGMA account.

D. Transfer the building into a UTMA account.

12-2. Elliot and Jean jointly established a trust for their children: Rachael, age 18; and Greg, age 21. All income will be distributed to Rachael for the next six years to pay for her undergraduate and graduate school expenses. Greg will receive the remainder interest in the trust. Which of the following statements is/are correct?

A. Elliot and Jean can take annual exclusions to offset the taxable gifts they made to both Rachael and Greg.

B. Elliot and Jean have established a § 2503(b) trust.

C. Elliot and Jean have established a § 2503(c) trust.

D. Elliot and Jean have established a sprinkle trust.

12-3. Which of the following statements concerning the estate tax and estate transfers to minors is incorrect?

A. Parents who gift their children appreciating assets remove the value of the assets and the future appreciation from their gross estates.

B. Taxable gifts made to minors are included in the donor's estate as an adjusted taxable gift.

C. A parent who front-loads a 529 plan with a $70,000 contribution and dies four years later will have the plan's entire account balance included in his gross estate.

D. A decedent's executor can transfer property from the estate into a UTMA account.

12-4. Which of the following techniques are available to parents to shift wealth and income to their children?

A. Transfer growth stock mutual funds into a UGMA account.

B. Make an outright gift of a Series EE bond to a child that will not mature until after the child attains age 18.

C. Transfer non-income-producing assets into a Section 2303(b) trust for the benefit of several minor beneficiaries.

D. Transfer tax-free municipal bonds to a minor that will mature after the child's 24th birthday.

12-5. Tara is 18 years old and a senior in high school. Her parents' marginal tax bracket is 25%, and Tara's tax bracket is 10%. Suppose that Tara earned $3,000 of interest income in her UTMA last year. What is Tara's total tax liability for 2015?

A. Tara would pay nothing and her parents would pay $750 in tax.

B. Tara would pay $205 in tax.

C. Tara would pay $330 in tax.

D. Tara would pay $950 in tax.

Notes

1. Revenue Ruling 54-400, 1954-2CB 319, Internal Revenue Service, (Jan. 1, 1954), UIL No. 2503.00-00 Taxable gifts, Letter Ruling 5402181630A, (Feb. 18, 1954), Internal Revenue Service, (Feb. 18, 1954).

2. See term-certain valuation tables in Appendix E.

3. See single-life valuation tables in Appendix E.

Chapter 13

The Gross Estate

CFP® CERTIFICATION EXAMINATION PRINCIPAL TOPICS COVERED IN THIS CHAPTER:

The Gross Estate

- Inclusions
- Exclusions
- Valuation techniques and the federal gross estate
- Alternate valuation date

Income in Respect of a Decedent (IRD)

- Assets qualifying as IRD
- Calculation for IRD deduction

Learning Objectives

To ensure that you have a solid understanding of which property interests are included in the gross estate, the following learning objectives are addressed in this chapter:

- Explain when the fair market value of an asset or the alternate valuation date should be used to value property included in a decedent's estate.

- Identify which separately owned property interests are included in a decedent's gross estate.

- Explain how IRD assets affect a decedent's estate tax and a recipient's income tax.

- Determine the value of jointly held property in a decedent's estate.

- Identify property interests that are subject to the three-year rule.

Chapter Contents

OVERVIEW

The federal estate tax is a tax on the transfer of property when a person dies. It is measured by the value of the property rights that are shifted from the decedent to others. In essence, it is a tax on the right to transfer property or an interest in property rather than a tax on the right to receive property, which is characteristic of an inheritance tax.

An essential step in the estate planning process is to determine whether a client has a current estate tax liability or the client will be subject to an estate tax in the future. This step informs the financial planner, the attorney, and other members of the financial planning team whether strategies should be developed and implemented to minimize this transfer tax when formulating a client's overall estate plan. A financial planner must first identify which assets are included in a client's gross estate and then establish the value of the assets before the estate tax can be calculated. This step begins with an accounting of the client's assets through an examination of his deeds, documents, and contracts to discern the types of property interests owned, and how that property is titled and transferred to others.

Practice Standard 200-2

Obtaining Quantitative Information and Documents

The financial planning practitioner shall obtain sufficient quantitative information and documents about a client relevant to the scope of the engagement before any recommendation is made and/or implemented.

THE GROSS ESTATE

The **gross estate** is a tax concept that represents the total of all property in which a decedent had an interest and that must be included in the estate. The gross estate includes property the decedent owned outright and the share of property the decedent owned jointly with others. It also includes property that the decedent previously gifted to others or transferred into trusts if the decedent retained certain interests, powers, or control over that property once it was transferred.

Fair Market Value

Property included in the gross estate is typically valued at **fair market value (FMV)** at the time of the owner's death. Fair market value is defined in the regulations as the price that a willing buyer would pay a willing seller.[1]

Frequently, a taxpayer's valuation differs widely from the value established by the IRS. Courts are asked to resolve the valuation question. The use of appraisals by qualified experts, documentation of sales of similar property recently sold, and arm's length agreements are effective tools for substantiating property values.

Generally, when an organized market for an item exists, the market price will prevail. In the absence of an established market, the IRS position is that the price at which the item or a comparable item would have been sold at retail determines its value.

Assets owned by a decedent receive a new federal income tax basis equal to the property's FMV for federal estate tax purposes. When the fair market value of the asset is higher than the pre-death basis, the old basis is "stepped-up" to the fair market value. A sale of the inherited property results in no taxable gain if the new adjusted basis is equal to the amount realized on the sale.

A step-down in basis is also possible at death. Where assets have lost value since their acquisition, so that the estate tax value is lower than the property's basis, the loss inherent in the property disappears at death and the beneficiary will receive the property with a lower basis than had the decedent. Thus in a steadily declining market, it may be better to gift loss property prior to death to preserve the higher tax basis, even though the recipient's basis will be limited to the FMV of the property on the date of the transfer, (plus any gift tax paid).

Alternate Valuation Date

Federal estate taxes are based either on the FMV of the transferred property as of the date of the owner's death, or the value of the property six months after the decedent's death. The latter date is known as the **alternate valuation date**. If the alternate valuation date is elected, then all property in the estate is valued as of this date.

The executor may elect the alternate valuation date when the decedent's property has depreciated in value after death. To qualify for the alternate valuation date, there must be a decrease in the total value of the gross estate and a decrease in the decedent's estate tax liability six months after death.

If the alternate valuation date is elected and the property is distributed, sold, exchanged, or otherwise disposed of within six months of a decedent's death, it will be valued as of the date of transfer rather than the alternate valuation date. Certain types of property diminish in value as time goes on; for example, the present value of an annuity decreases each time a payment is made. Any property interest whose value is affected by the mere passage of time is ineligible for the alternate valuation date, and the asset is valued as of the date of the owner's death.

Client Situation

Kasper, a bachelor, died on New Year's Day in Miami. The value of his gross estate at death was $6 million, and he did not make any testamentary bequests to charity. Soon after Kasper's death, the value of his real estate holdings and stock in his investment portfolio began depreciating, and by July 1 his gross estate was valued at $5.5 million. This decline in value also reduced the amount of estate tax that Kasper owed, and his executor elected the alternate valuation date on his estate tax return.

Practitioner Tip: If Kasper had been married and bequeathed all of his property to his wife, the unlimited marital deduction would have eliminated his entire estate tax liability upon his death. Therefore, the alternate valuation date could not have been elected because there would have been no decrease in Kasper's estate tax liability six months after his death.

PROPERTY OWNED OUTRIGHT (IRC § 2033)

All property owned by an individual at the time of death is includable in the gross estate at the proper estate tax value. Property is includable if it was owned by the decedent at the time of his death and it was transferred at death by the decedent's will or by state intestacy laws.

The estate tax is levied on the transmission of property at death from a decedent to others. Property interests are includable in the gross estate only to the extent that such interests and rights are passed on to some other party at the estate owner's death. The property is not included in the decedent's estate if he did not have the right to transfer the property to others.

All types of property— real or personal—owned outright by a decedent at death are includable. This means that intangible personal property such as stocks and bonds, as well as tangible personal property such as a decedent's jewelry and other personal effects, are included. Consequently, all property included in a decedent's probate estate is also included in the decedent's gross estate.

Tangible Property

Following are some examples of tangible property.

- Cash

- Real estate owned solely by the decedent

- Cars, boats, and other vehicles

- Collectibles such as art and antiques

- Household furnishings and goods

- Business real and personal property

Intangible Property

Here are some examples of intangible property.

Investment and business assets:

- Cash equivalents

- Stocks—the mean between the high and low selling price on the date of valuation, which is typically the date of the owner's death. For example, a stock's high is $120.50, the low is $118.63, and the close is 120. The date-of-death value is $119.57.

- Decedent's share of closely held stock with voting rights

- EE or HH bonds—the redemption value of the bonds

- Publicly traded bonds—the mean between the high and low selling price as valued on the date of valuation

- Bank or investment accounts

- Partnership interests

- Promissory notes and installment sale payments

Income in Respect of a Decedent

Income in respect of a decedent (IRD) is the right to future income earned but not received prior to a decedent's death. Examples of IRD include rents, dividends, unpaid salary, insurance renewal commissions, bonuses, IRAs, deferred compensation, interest payments, royalties, patents, etc. Such rights, as of the date of death or the alternate valuation date (whichever is applicable) are generally considered property owned outright and must be included in a decedent's gross estate. The income will not receive a step-up in basis in the decedent's estate.

This income is taxable when it is distributed to a decedent's estate to pay taxes and estate administrative expenses, or when it is distributed to a beneficiary or a trust. The income may also be subject to an estate tax because it is included in the decedent's gross estate. Any estate tax paid that is attributed to an IRD item is allowable as an income tax deduction to the recipient of the income. This deduction is taken as a miscellaneous itemized deduction, which is not subject to the 2% adjusted gross income (AGI) floor.

Client Situation

Terry had a gross estate of $6.5 million and bequeathed his IRA, valued at $600,000, to his nephew Kurt. The value of Terry's IRA was included in his gross estate. Terry's net federal estate tax was $428,000 after applying his unified credit ($2,117,800) to offset the tentative tax.

Suppose, however, that the IRA had not been included in Terry's estate. His gross estate would have been worth only $5.9 million, with a net federal estate tax of $188,000.

The difference between the estate tax that included the IRA ($428,000) and the estate tax without the IRA ($188,000) is $240,000. If Kurt received a taxable distribution of $300,000 this year from the IRA, he would report income of $300,000 and receive a deduction of $120,000 ($300,000 divided by $600,000 IRA × $240,000).

Retirement Benefits

Individuals can have their pension benefits paid out as a single-life benefit, or they can choose a survivorship option, which pays a reduced benefit amount to the survivor upon the retiree's death. Single-life pension benefits cease at death, so there is nothing to include in a decedent's gross estate. For retirement plans with survivorship benefits, the present value of a survivor's future income stream is included in the decedent's estate.

Client Situation

Nate retired 10 years ago with a joint and survivor pension; his wife Cheryl was the beneficiary. When Nate died, Cheryl was 72 years old. The amount of the retirement benefit included in Nate's gross estate was the present value of the annuity that Cheryl would receive for the remainder of her life. This amount can be calculated actuarially from a single-life valuation table, using the surviving spouse's age and the IRC § 7520 interest rate in effect at the time of the decedent spouse's death.

Annuities (IRC § 2039)

Similar to retirement benefits, a **single-life annuity** whether private or commercial, ceases at an annuitant's death and is not included in a decedent's gross estate. However, with a single-premium-refund life annuity, the beneficiary receives a lump sum cash refund amount, which is included in the decedent's estate.

A portion of the value of annuities with survivorship benefits is included in a decedent's gross estate. For example, a **private annuity** can be arranged between a buyer and a seller of business, real, or personal property so that the buyer will make regular payments to the seller for the seller's lifetime. With a survivorship private annuity, the present value of the survivor's future income stream, as determined by government valuation tables, is included in the decedent's gross estate.

Client Situation

Steve purchased a private annuity that would pay him $20,000 a year for life and upon his death pay his wife Jayne $10,000 a year for as long as she lives. Steve died when Jayne was age 55. Using the government valuation tables reproduced in Appendix E (Table S), if a 5% IRC § 7520 rate applied at the time of Steve's death, the annuity would have a present value of $133,935 (13.3935 × $10,000), which would be included in Steve's gross estate.

For a **commercial annuity**, the value of the survivorship interest is the amount that the same insurance company would charge for a single annuity on the survivor at the time of the first annuitant's death. If the survivor paid for a portion of the annuity, then a comparable amount of the value of the annuity is excluded from the decedent's gross estate.

Client Situation

Randy and Wendy purchased a joint and survivor annuity together many years ago. Wendy paid one third of the $90,000 annuity, and Randy paid the remaining $60,000. When Randy died, the value of the **survivorship annuity** was $45,000. The amount included in Randy's estate was the value of the annuity at his death ($45,000) multiplied by his cost basis of $60,000, divided by the cost of the annuity ($90,000), or $30,000.

Life Insurance (IRC § 2042)

Several situations can cause the death benefit amount of a life insurance policy to be included in a decedent's gross estate.

- The decedent was the owner and the insured of a life insurance policy.

- The decedent was not the owner of the policy but retained an incident of ownership, such as the right to name policy beneficiaries; surrender, assign, or revoke the policy; borrow cash values; receive policy dividends; or use the policy itself as collateral for a loan.

- The life insurance policy names the owner and insured's estate or executor as the beneficiary of the policy, to pay the decedent's debts, taxes, and estate administration expenses.

- The decedent owner/insured was the trustee of an irrevocable life insurance trust.

A life insurance policy can have an owner who is different from the insured. For example, a brother can own a policy on his sister's life. When the owner dies before the insured, then the value of the policy—not the death benefit amount—is included in the owner's gross estate. The value of the policy will depend on the type of life insurance policy the decedent owned.

- Single-premium policy: The value included in the gross estate is the replacement cost value of the policy.

- Whole life policy: The value included is the interpolated terminal reserve plus any unearned premiums, or the approximate cash value of the policy.

- Term policy: The value in the estate is the unused premium amount.

Client Situation

Gwen purchased a $100,000 term life insurance policy on her husband Joe's life in January. The policy had an annual premium of $2,000. Gwen died in June, six months later. The unused premium amount of $1,000 (in this case, half of the annual premium) was included in her gross estate.

General Power of Appointment (IRC § 2041)

Powers of appointment are granted by a donor, typically the grantor of a trust, to a holder, who is often a trust beneficiary. A donor can give a holder a **general power of appointment** over trust property, to use for the holder's benefit without restriction. Any property over which a decedent held a general power of appointment at the time of death is included in his gross estate. A holder with a general power of appointment over trust property will include the entire FMV of the trust assets in his gross estate at death.

A donor can grant a holder a **special or limited power of appointment**. A holder cannot appoint the property to himself without first obtaining the donor's consent, or the consent of the other trust beneficiaries, unless the holder is permitted to use the property for his health, education, maintenance, and support. None of the property subject to the limited power is included in a holder's gross estate, because restrictions are placed on the holder's ability to use or appoint the property to himself or others.

A donor can also give a holder the right to withdraw the greater of $5,000 or 5% of the trust corpus each year. This is known as a **5-and-5 power**. A decedent with a 5-and-5 power will include the greater of $5,000 or 5% of the trust property in his gross estate, reduced by any amount the holder exercised in the year of his death.

Client Situation

Douglas was the beneficiary of a trust established by his father and was given the right to appoint the greater of $5,000 or 5% of the trust corpus every year. When Douglas died in May, the FMV of the trust was $1 million. Douglas had withdrawn $35,000 from the trust in April to buy his son a new car. At his death, the entire $50,000 (5% of the trust corpus) was not included in his gross estate, only the $15,000 remaining that Douglas had not exercised prior to his death.

TRUSTS

A decedent must possess more than the legal title to property before it can be includable in his gross estate. A trustee has legal title to trust property, but if the trustee did not establish the trust and derived no benefit from the trust property, then the FMV of the trust is not included in his estate.

Revocable Trust

A grantor who creates a revocable trust and transfers property into that trust will include the FMV of the trust assets in his gross estate at death. It does not matter whether the grantor had named himself the trustee or a beneficiary of his revocable trust; what matters is the extent of control the grantor had over the trust property while he was alive. The grantor of a revocable trust has complete control over trust assets and the trust itself. For example, the grantor can change the terms of the trust or even revoke it at any time.

Irrevocable Trust

In most situations, the FMV of the assets held in an irrevocable trust are not included in a grantor's gross estate at death. The grantor cannot change the terms of an irrevocable trust or revoke the trust once it has been established, and he has no control over distributions of the trust income or corpus. However, if a grantor is sole trustee of his irrevocable trust, then the FMV of trust assets is included in his gross estate in the following circumstances:

- The grantor could distribute trust income, accumulate income, or distribute principal to the income beneficiaries.

- The grantor could change the trustee to another person, other than an institutional trustee such as a bank.

- The grantor could change the trust beneficiaries or name new beneficiaries.

- The grantor could use trust income or corpus to discharge his legal obligations of child support.

JOINTLY OWNED PROPERTY (IRC § 2040)

The decedent's gross estate includes the value of his share of property held jointly with others.

Tenancy by the Entirety

This form of property ownership applies only to a married couple. When the first spouse dies, 50% of the FMV of the property is included in the decedent spouse's gross estate. The amount each spouse contributed to acquire the property has no bearing on the amount included in the decedent spouse's gross estate.

Client Situation

Louie and Janis bought a home together after they were married and titled the property as tenancy by the entirety. The house cost $100,000; Louie paid $60,000, and Janis paid $40,000. When Janis died 40 years later, the FMV of the home was $800,000. Her accountant included $400,000 of the value of the home in her gross estate. The home automatically passed to Louie by operation of law, and Louie is now the sole owner of the home.

Practitioner Tip: Louie received a $400,000 step-up in basis for the value of the property included in Janis's estate, which was added to his original basis of $50,000. Note that Louie's new basis is not $460,000, because each spouse's original basis is one half of the acquisition cost.

Community Property

Community property can be held only by a husband and wife. The value of the decedent's share of community property, which is 50% of the FMV of the property, will be included in his gross estate.

Dower and Curtesy (IRC § 2034)

These property rights derive from English common law, and they give a widow (**dower**) and widower (**curtesy**) the right to a life estate in all of a decedent spouse's property. This is similar to elective share statutes that provide surviving spouses with a share of a decedent's property to prevent them from being disinherited. The value of the life estate is included in a decedent's gross estate.

Joint Tenancy with Right of Survivorship (JTWROS) with Spouses

When spouses title their property jointly, then 50% of the FMV of the property is included in the decedent spouse's gross estate. Similar to a tenancy by the entirety, the amount each spouse paid for the property does not affect the amount included in the decedent spouse's gross estate.

Client Situation

Stan and his wife Shelley purchased 100 shares of AT&T for $50,000, and they hold the property as JTWROS. Stan made the entire contribution from his salary, but only 50% of the stock will be included in his gross estate. If the stock is worth $120,000 at that time, $60,000 will be included in Stan's estate.

JTWROS with Nonspouses

For property owners who are not married, the **percentage-of-contribution rule** applies. The rule is that 100% of jointly held property is includable in the estate of the first joint owner to die, except to the extent that the survivor can prove contribution with funds that were not acquired by gift from the decedent. If the survivor paid a portion of the acquisition cost, then only a percentage of the FMV of the property is included in the decedent's gross estate.

Client Situation

Jim and Riley are brothers who purchased a small duplex together near a ski resort in Vermont and titled it as JTWROS. They paid $120,000 in cash for the property; Jim contributed $48,000, and Riley contributed $72,000 toward the purchase price. Riley died in a tragic ski accident six years later. At the time of his death, the duplex was appraised at $160,000. Because Riley had contributed 60% of the acquisition cost, then $96,000 (60% of $160,000) was included in Riley's gross estate.

Joint Bank Accounts

Fifty percent of a bank account held jointly by a husband and wife is included in the decedent spouse's gross estate. The contribution rule also applies to joint bank accounts for nonspouses. Therefore, 100% is included in the decedent's gross estate unless it can be proven that the surviving owner contributed to the account.

Practitioner Tip: With nonspouses, if one joint owner bought the property or received it by gift or inheritance, then 100% is included in the decedent owner's gross estate. It is the responsibility of the executor and the surviving owner to prove that the surviving owner of the jointly held property did not furnish any consideration when the property was acquired.

Tenancy in Common

When a person holds property as a tenant in common with one or more individuals, then at death a fractional share of the tenant's property is included in his gross estate.

> **Client Situation**
>
> Anne and her two daughters Phyllis and Rosemary bought a condo together at the Jersey shore for $600,000. They titled the property as tenants in common and contributed unequal amounts toward the purchase price. Anne paid $300,000, and Phyllis and Rosemary each paid $150,000. Anne died several years later when the condo was valued at $700,000. Her executor included $350,000 in her gross estate, which represents Anne's fractional share (one-half) of her ownership in the property.

TRANSFERS WITH RETAINED PROPERTY INTERESTS

When a donor makes a gift of property to a donee but keeps some degree of control over the gifted property, the value of that property is added back into the donor's gross estate at his death.

Life Estate (IRC § 2036)

When a decedent retains a lifetime interest in gifted property it is included in the decedent's gross estate. When a donor transfers property to another person or to a trust but retains the income or control over the income for life, then the FMV of the property is included in the donor's gross estate at death. This can occur when the donor:

- Creates a life estate;

- Retains possession, enjoyment, or right to income from the property; or

- Retains the right to specify who will possess or enjoy either the property itself or the income it produces.

The rationale for including a life estate in a decedent's gross estate is that the right to enjoy or control property or designate who will receive the property or its income is characteristic of ownership. Since a donor's possession or enjoyment does not end—and the donee's possession or enjoyment of the property cannot begin—until the decedent dies and "transfers" the retained interest, the donor will continue to be treated as if he owned the property.

Client Situation

Carolyn transfers stock in Texas Electric Company to a trust. She provides that the income from the trust is payable to herself for life and that the corpus will then pass to her daughter. The Texas Electric Company stock is includable in Carolyn's estate, because she has retained a life estate.

Client Situation

Ruth changed the deed on her home to give herself a life estate in her property and designated her son, Marty, as the remainder beneficiary. This gift was subject to a gift tax for the present value of the remainder interest of the home, but Ruth did not have to pay any tax because her unified credit was available to offset the tax on this gift. The FMV of the home will be included in Ruth's estate when she dies because she retained the right to possess and enjoy the property until her death.

Taxable gifts are included in a decedent's estate tax return, IRS Form 706, as an **adjusted taxable gift.** In the preceding example, the FMV of Ruth's home will be included in her gross estate when she dies. However, the taxable gift she made to Marty will not be added into her estate tax return as an adjusted taxable gift. The amount of the taxable gift and the FMV of the home cannot be added into the estate tax return twice in two different categories, the gross estate category and the category for adjusted taxable gifts. Therefore, a tax "adjustment" will be made for this taxable gift, and the gift will not be included in the category for adjusted taxable gifts.

Practitioner Tip: See Appendix 13A, Federal Estate Tax Calculation, to view the steps in the estate tax calculation process and the placement of these entries on the worksheet.

An individual can also *receive* a life estate in a property or a trust from a donor. The life tenant's interest in a property ends at his death and passes directly to another beneficiary selected by the donor, not by the life tenant. Because the life tenant has no control over the property, other than the enjoyment of the life interest or the right to receive income, the property is not included in the life tenant's gross estate under IRC § 2036.

Reversionary Interest (IRC § 2037)

When a donor makes a lifetime gift of property but retains a reversionary interest—for example, if the gift is contingent upon the donee surviving the donor—the property is includable in the donor's gross estate at death. If the donee can obtain ownership of the property only by being alive at the time the donor dies, and the donor retained a significant right (more than 5% chance) to regain the property or dispose of it by will, then the value of the transferred property is includable in the donor's estate. The right to regain a property is called a *reversionary interest,* which causes the value of a gifted property to be included in a donor's gross estate. The right to regain or dispose of the property must actuarially be worth more than 5% of its value. A reversionary interest of less than 5% would not be included in a donor's estate.

Client Situation

During his lifetime, Stuart transferred property to his wife Mona for her lifetime. Upon Mona's death, the property was to return to Stuart if he was living. If he was not living, the property was to go to Stuart's daughter Ellen. Stuart dies before Mona. Stuart's daughter can obtain possession or enjoyment of the property only if she survives Stuart. If she is not alive when Stuart dies, neither she nor her heirs will receive any interest in the property. Stuart retained a reversionary interest under the original transfer. If Stuart's reversion is worth more than 5% of the value of the property that he placed in trust, the value of the remainder interest will be includable in his estate. Such a transfer is includable because it is considered a substitute for disposing of the property by will.

Revocable Gifts (IRC § 2038)

If a decedent made a transfer of property during his lifetime but retained the power to alter, amend, or revoke the gift, the value of property subject to that power is included in the decedent's gross estate. A gift causa mortis is an example of a revocable gift.

Client Situation

Five years ago, Rob created a revocable trust and funded it with $80,000. At the time of Rob's death, the trust was valued at $100,000. The FMV of the trust, or $100,000, was included in Rob's gross estate.

PROPERTY TRANSFERRED WITHIN THREE YEARS OF DEATH (IRC § 2035)

When a donor makes a completed gift to a donee, the value of that gift is removed from the donor's gross estate because the donor has not retained any further interest in the property.

However, when a donor makes gifts of certain property interests to others yet retains some rights or power over that property until his death, then the value of the transferred property is added back into his gross estate when he dies. For example, a donor can transfer property to others and still keep a life estate in that property (IRC § 2036); or he can keep a reversionary interest in the property he has gifted away (IRC § 2037); or he can retain the power to alter, amend, or revoke the gift (IRC § 2038). Because the donor retained these rights or powers over the transferred property until his death, the value of the property is included in the donor's gross estate.

Code section 2035 addresses property interests that are included in a decedent's gross estate based on a three-year time frame. The general rule is that gifts made within three years of death are not, with certain exceptions, includable in a decedent's gross estate, regardless of their size or the manner in which they are made. For example, an individual could give away property worth millions, even days before his death, and it would not be included in his estate. (The property would be subject to a gift tax instead).

The Three-year Rule

Under IRC § 2035, the value of certain property interests can be included in a decedent's gross estate if the decedent gave up his rights, powers, and interests in the property within three years of his death. This is known as the *three-year rule.* Property subject to the three-year rule includes property previously transferred under the following IRC sections:

- IRC § 2036 (transfer with a retained life estate)

- IRC § 2037 (transfer with a retained reversionary interest)

- IRC § 2038 (revocable transfer)

- IRC § 2042 (transfer of a life insurance policy)

The three-year rule is intended to prevent a person with retained property rights from benefitting from a much lower gift tax if he transfers his complete interest in the property right before his death. The three-year rule ensures that the value of the property is included in the decedent's gross estate at its date-of-death value and is therefore subject to an estate tax.

The value of property is not included in the owner's gross estate when he has given up his rights, powers, or interests in the property *more* than three years before death. However, if a person surrendered these rights to the property *within* three years of his death, the value of the property would be included in his gross estate under Code section 2035, rather than under Sections 2036, 2037, and 2038. The transfer of a life insurance policy is subject to the three-year rule under IRC § 2035 when the owner of the policy is also the insured. The owner must outlive the transfer for more than three years or the death benefit amount will be included in the decedent's gross estate.

Client Situation

Five years ago, Christina created a revocable trust and funded it with $200,000. Two years ago, when the trust was worth $220,000, Christina made the trust irrevocable. Christina died four months ago when the trust was worth $230,000. Consequently, $230,000 was included in Christina's gross estate.

Client Situation

Candace, a widow, created a life estate in her home five years ago so she could live there for the rest of her life. She gifted the remainder interest to her son, Blake. The FMV of the home was $1.6 million on the date of the gift, with Candace's retained life estate interest valued at $700,000. Soon afterwards, Candace began dating a man she met at the local senior center. They married two years ago and bought an apartment together in an assisted living center. Candace gave up the life estate in the home when she remarried and she died last month. The FMV of the home was $1.8 million at her death, and this amount was included in Candace's gross estate under the three-year rule. The gift to Blake of the remainder interest in the home ($900,000) was not included in her estate tax return as an adjusted taxable gift because the FMV of the home was included in her gross estate.

Practitioner Tip: If Candace had given up her interest in the home more than three years before she died, then the FMV of the home would not have been included in her gross estate. Instead, the $900,000 remainder interest gift to her son would have been included on her estate tax return as an adjusted taxable gift.

Client Situation

Perry owned a $1 million whole-life insurance policy on his own life. Perry's attorney established an irrevocable life insurance trust and transferred ownership of the policy to the trust two years before Perry died. The $1 million proceeds were paid to the trust, and this death benefit amount was included in Perry's gross estate under the three-year rule.

Practitioner Tip: The three-year rule does not apply to a life insurance policy owned by someone who is not the insured. The owner could gift the policy to the insured or transfer it to another person or trust to remove the proceeds from his gross estate anytime before he dies to avoid inclusion in his gross estate.

Client Situation

Ross owned a single-premium life insurance policy on his wife's life that had a death benefit of $2 million. The replacement cost of the policy was $150,000. Last year Ross transferred the policy to his wife, Valery, prior to his death. Because Ross was the owner of the policy but was not the insured, the three-year rule did not apply, and neither the death benefit amount nor the replacement cost of the policy was included in his gross estate.

Practitioner Tip: If Ross had not transferred the policy to Valery, then the replacement cost of the policy ($150,000) would have been included in his gross estate. The death benefit amount is included in the gross estate only when the decedent was the owner and the insured of the policy.

The Gross-up Rule

When a donor makes a gift, he must determine whether the gift is taxable. A taxable gift can be reduced by gift-splitting, annual exclusions, and marital and charitable deductions, if any of these techniques apply. The amount that remains is the taxable gift. The tax on a taxable gift can be offset by the donor's unified credit, which can shelter against taxes on gifts made throughout the donor's lifetime that do not exceed $5,430,000. When taxable gifts made by a donor exceed $5,430,000, then a gift tax must be paid.

All taxable gifts from 1976 to the present are added into a decedent's estate tax return as an adjusted taxable gift. This serves to increase an estate's tentative tax base before a tentative estate tax is computed.

When a gift is made, a donor's estate is reduced by the amount of the gift. Likewise, when a gift tax is paid, a donor's estate is also reduced by the amount of the tax. Under Section 2035, the amount of gift taxes paid within three years of a donor's death are added back into the donor's gross estate. This provision is known as the **gross-up rule.** Any gift taxes actually paid by the donor are subtracted as a credit from the estate's tentative tax to reduce the overall amount of the estate tax.

Client Situation

Four years ago, Derek made several taxable gifts that required him to pay $60,000 in gift taxes. Derek made another taxable gift one year ago and paid $26,000 in gift taxes. When Derek died last month, his executor included the $26,000 he paid in gift taxes within three years of his death in his gross estate. A "gift tax payable credit" for $86,000 was subtracted from his estate's tentative tax on Derek's estate tax return, IRS Form 706.

Practitioner Tip: Note that the gross-up rule applies only to gift taxes, not to generation-skipping transfer taxes, paid by the decedent within three years of his death.

Chapter Highlights

- Property included in the gross estate is valued either at FMV at the date of death or at the alternate valuation date six months later. To elect the alternate valuation date, the gross estate and the estate tax liability must both be less than the date-of-death value.

- Individually owned property is included in a decedent's estate. Property owned jointly with spouses includes 50% of the value in the decedent spouse's gross estate, whereas property owned with nonspouses includes a percentage based on contribution.

- IRD assets are included in a decedent's gross estate and are taxable as income to the beneficiary. An income tax deduction is available to the recipient of the income if the IRD asset was taxed in the decedent's estate.

- Annuities and retirement benefits that end at the decedent's death are not included in the gross estate, but survivorship benefits are included.

- The death benefit amount of a life insurance policy is included in the gross estate of a decedent who was both the owner and the insured. Only the value of the policy is included in an owner's gross estate if he was not the insured.

- Decedents who have a general power of appointment over property include the value of that property in their gross estates. Decedents with a 5-and-5 power include the greater of $5,000 or 5% of the value of the trust in their gross estates. Decedents holding a special or limited power of appointment over property do not include that property in their gross estates.

- A life estate under Code section 2036 is included in the life tenant's estate if that person created the life estate for himself. A person who receives a life estate from another person does not include that property in his gross estate.

- A reversionary interest under Code section 2037 is included in a person's estate if he retains a reversionary interest of more than 5%.

- Property included in a revocable trust under Code section 2038 is included in the grantor's gross estate. Property held in an irrevocable trust generally is not included unless the grantor retains control or rights over the trust.

- The three-year rule applies to life estates, reversionary interests, revocable transfers, transfers of life insurance policies, and gift taxes paid within three years of death.

Key Terms

5-and-5 power	incident of ownership
adjusted taxable gift	income in respect of a decedent (IRD)
alternate valuation date	percentage-of-contribution rule
commercial annuity	private annuity
curtesy	reversionary interest
dower	single-life annuity
fair market value (FMV)	special or limited power of appointment
general power of appointment	survivorship annuity
gross estate	three-year rule
gross-up rule	

Review Questions

13-1. Roger died last month. Which of the following assets is not included in Roger's gross estate at death?

A. A vacation home Roger owns in another state.

B. A home Roger inherited from his grandfather and later retitled as JTWROS with his brother, who was alive at Roger's death.

C. Roger was the beneficiary of a trust created by his father, who gave him the right to invade the trust corpus without restriction.

D. In the week before Roger died, he transferred $500,000 worth of closely held stock in his business to his four children.

13-2. Patti died two months ago with the following assets. Which asset will be included in Patti's gross estate?

A. A life estate in a trust that Patti received from her father that distributed all income to Patti for life.

B. A life insurance policy Patti owned on her brother's life that she gifted to him two years before she died.

C. Ten years ago, Patti created an irrevocable trust for her two children and funded it with $400,000 worth of rapidly appreciating stock. Patti, as trustee, retained the right to accumulate or distribute the income to her children as she wished.

D. Patti was the beneficiary of a trust that allowed her to withdraw money from the trust only for her son's education.

13-3. Glenn was the holder of a 5-and-5 power of appointment over trust assets worth $500,000 at his death. Glenn did not withdraw any income or principal from the trust in the year he died. How much of the value of this trust was included in Glenn's estate at his death?

A. $500,000

B. $25,000

C. $5,000

D. $0

13-4. Simon and Kate met at a local support group for divorced parents, and they were married last year. Simon has two daughters from a previous marriage, and Kate has one son. They bought a house together after they were married and titled the property as tenants in common. Simon contributed 75% toward the price of the home, and Kate paid 25%. If Kate dies when the value of the home is $600,000, how much will be included in Kate's estate?

A. $600,000

B. $300,000

C. $150,000

D. $0

13-5. Polly inherited a home from her husband worth $4.8 million. She created a life estate in her home six years ago and named her daughter, Gemma, as the remainder beneficiary. At that time, the home was appraised at $5.3 million. Last year, Polly became terminally ill and moved to Minnesota to receive better medical care. Before she moved, she relinquished her interest in her home, worth $6 million, and died four months later. The value of her home was $6.1 million at the time of her death. How much of the value of the home is included in Polly's gross estate?

A. $4.8 million

B. $5.3 million

C. $6 million

D. $6.1 million

Notes

1. Treas. Reg. § 25.2512–1.

Federal Estate Tax Calculation

Gross Estate $_____

    Funeral and Administration Expenses

    Debts and Taxes

    Casualty and Theft Losses

                                                    Total Deductions _____

Adjusted Gross Estate $_____

    Marital Deduction

    Charitable Deduction

    State Death Tax Deduction

                                                    Total Deductions _____

Taxable Estate $_____

    + Adjusted Taxable Gifts $_____

Tentative Tax Base $_____

Tentative Tax (Compute tax.) $_____

    Gift Tax Paid or Payable (Credit) $_____

Estate Tax Payable before Credits $_____

Tax Credits

    Unified Credit

    Prior Transfer Credit

    Foreign Death Tax Credit   Total Credits _____

Federal Estate Tax Payable $_____

Chapter 14

Estate Tax Calculation

CFP® CERTIFICATION EXAMINATION PRINCIPAL TOPIC COVERED IN THIS CHAPTER:

Estate Tax Compliance and Tax Calculation

- Deductions
- Adjusted gross estate
- Deductions from the adjusted gross estate
- Taxable estate

- Adjusted taxable gifts
- Tentative tax base
- Tentative tax calculation
- Credits
  - Gift tax payable
  - Unified credit amount
  - Prior transfer credit
- Estate tax filing requirements

Learning Objectives

To ensure that you have a solid understanding of how to calculate the estate tax, the following learning objectives are addressed in this chapter:

- Identify which deductions may be taken from the gross estate.

- Explain when a marital deduction is available to the decedent's estate.

- Compute a tentative estate tax using the unified tax table.

- Determine which credits are available to a decedent to reduce the estate tax.

- Explain when an estate tax return must be filed and identify the parties responsible for payment.

- Demonstrate how to compute an estate tax for different client situations.

Chapter Contents

OVERVIEW

There are five stages involved in calculating the federal estate tax liability. After the gross estate has been calculated, the remaining stages mostly involve subtracting allowable deductions and credits that reduce the amount of estate tax owed. These four stages consist of determining the decedent's adjusted gross estate, the taxable estate, the estate tax payable before credits, and federal estate tax liability. (See Exhibit 14.1.)

Exhibit 14.1

Federal Estate Tax Calculation

Gross Estate $_____

    Funeral and Administration Expenses

    Debts and Taxes

    Casualty and Theft Losses

                           Total Deductions _____

Adjusted Gross Estate $_____

    Marital Deduction

    Charitable Deduction

    State Death Tax Deduction

                           Total Deductions _____

Taxable Estate $_____

    + Adjusted Taxable Gifts $_____

Tentative Tax Base $_____

Tentative Tax (Compute tax.) $_____

    Gift Tax Paid or Payable (Credit) $_____

Estate Tax Payable before Credits $_____

Tax Credits

    Unified Credit

    Prior Transfer Credit

    Foreign Death Tax Credit   Total Credits _____

Federal Estate Tax Payable $_____

Financial planners must understand when these deductions and credits can be used and how they are applied when estimating a client's potential estate tax. A common objective of most married couples is to minimize their combined estate tax liability. Once current and projected estate tax is estimated, planning to reduce the federal estate tax in each spouse's estate can begin.

Practice Standard 300-1

Analyzing and Evaluating the Client's Information

A financial planning practitioner shall analyze the information to gain an understanding of the client's financial situation and then evaluate to what extent the client's goals, needs and priorities can be met by the client's resources and current course of action.

THE GROSS ESTATE

The gross estate is the first entry on the estate tax return, IRS Form 706; it includes all property in which a decedent retained any ownership, rights, or interests. The property is usually valued at fair market value at the time of the owner's death or at the alternate valuation date, six months later.

DETERMINING THE ADJUSTED GROSS ESTATE

Certain deductions are allowed from the gross estate to arrive at the **adjusted gross estate**, which is calculated primarily to determine whether certain IRC sections that are favorable to business owners can be applied. The adjusted gross estate can also provide an estimate of how much money is available to the estate to pay for any estate taxes owed. (See Exhibit 14.2.)

Exhibit 14.2

Federal Estate Tax Worksheet

Gross Estate

Funeral Deduction	$_____
Administration Expenses Deduction	$_____
Debts and Taxes Deduction	$_____
Losses Deduction	$_____
Adjusted Gross Estate	$_____

Deductions allowed fall into three categories:

1. funeral and administrative expenses;

2. debts (including certain taxes), mortgages, and liens; and

2. casualty and theft losses.

Funeral Expenses

Funeral expenses are deductible, subject to certain limitations. Such expenses include interment, burial lot or vault, grave marker, perpetual care of the gravesite, and transportation of the person bringing the body to the place of burial. Deductions are generally limited to a "reasonable" amount.

Administrative Expenses

Administrative expenses encompass the costs of administering property that is includable in the decedent's gross estate. Essentially, this means expenses incurred in the collection and preservation of probate assets, the payment of estate debts, and the distribution of probate assets to estate beneficiaries. Such expenses include court costs, accounting fees, appraisers' fees, brokerage costs, executors' commissions, and attorneys' fees. These expenses vary widely from location to location and depend on the size of the estate and the complexity of the administration problems involved.

Certain administrative costs can be deducted from either the federal estate tax return (IRS Form 706) or from the estate's income tax return (IRS Form 1041). The executor of the estate has the option of claiming these expenses on either return.

Practitioner Tip: Generally, the executor elects to deduct attorneys' fees and executors' commissions from the return for which the tax rates are higher. This results in an overall tax savings. But note that a deduction on the income tax return as opposed to the estate tax return, or vice versa, can result in favoring one beneficiary or group of beneficiaries over another.

Client Situation

Wayne died with a gross estate worth $15 million, which he left to his wife in his will. Wayne had extensive real estate holdings, and appraisers were needed to determine the fair market value of his properties for inclusion in his gross estate. Wayne's executor elected to deduct the substantial administrative expenses from the estate's income tax return (IRS Form 1041) because the marital deduction eliminated the estate tax payable on his estate tax return.

Debts, Mortgages, and Liens

Debts are deductible if they were the personal obligations of the decedent at the time of death (together with any interest accrued up to the date of death). Debts can include credit card balances, lease payments, and promissory notes. Mortgages and liens are deductible if the decedent was personally liable and the full value of the property was includable in the estate. But if the decedent had no personal liability for the payment of the mortgage or lien, yet the full value of the property was included in his estate, then these debts would also be deductible.

In the case of community property, only the claims and expenses that were the decedent's personal obligations are deductible in full. This means that an allocation of claims and expenses must be made. Because only one-half of the total community property is includable in the decedent spouse's estate, only one-half of community property debts such as the mortgage on community real property can be deducted for federal estate tax purposes.

Client Situation

Regina and her husband Cliff owned their primary home together as tenancy by the entirety in Virginia. Regina also owned a one-half interest in a condo in Hawaii with her sister Mia, which they had titled as a tenancy in common. Both states are common law states. Regina died with a gross estate valued at $2 million. The balance on the mortgages for both properties totaled $500,000 at her death; therefore, $250,000 was deducted as a debt from Regina's gross estate.

Taxes

Certain taxes unpaid at the time of a decedent's death are considered debts. Three common deductible taxes are:

1. income taxes unpaid but reportable for some tax period prior to the decedent's death;

2. gift taxes that were not paid on gifts the decedent made some time prior to death; and

3. property taxes that accrued but remained unpaid at the time of the decedent's death.

Casualty and Theft Losses

Casualty and theft losses are deductible by the estate if they arose from fire, storm, shipwreck, another casualty, or theft. To be deductible, a loss must have occurred while the estate was in the process of settlement and before it was closed. Such deductions are limited in two respects: the deduction is reduced to the extent that insurance or any other compensation is available to offset the loss and to the extent that a loss is reflected in the alternate valuation.

Practitioner Tip: At the executor's option, losses can be deducted from either the estate tax return or the estate's income tax return. Typically, they are taken on the return that produces the highest deduction.

DETERMINING THE TAXABLE ESTATE

Once the adjusted gross estate is calculated, other deductions are taken to calculate the taxable estate. (See Exhibit 14.3.)

Exhibit 14.3

Adjusted Gross Estate		$_____
Marital Deduction	$_____	
Charitable Deduction	$_____	
State Death Tax Deduction	$_____	
Taxable Estate		$_____

The adjusted gross estate can be reduced by three deductions:

1. A marital deduction

2. A charitable deduction

3. A state death tax deduction

Marital Deduction

A **marital deduction** is allowed for property that is included in the decedent's gross estate and that passes at death to a surviving spouse "in a qualifying manner," which is defined as a way that gives the surviving spouse control and enjoyment over the property—essentially tantamount to outright ownership. For example, when property passes to a surviving spouse through a bequest from a decedent's will, the spouse has been given total control over the inherited property, and a marital deduction equal to the value of the property is allowable in the decedent's estate.

Property transferred to a surviving spouse does not qualify for a marital deduction in the decedent spouse's estate if the property is terminable interest property. A surviving spouse who is not given complete control over the property and who cannot transmit the property to others has **terminable interest property** (TIP). However, the executor can make a **QTIP election** on the decedent's estate tax return to qualify the property for the marital deduction.

> **Client Situation**
>
> Todd bequeathed a life estate in his townhouse to his second wife Angie. When Angie dies, the home will pass to Todd's daughter from his previous marriage. Angie was given a terminable interest in the home because her interest in the property ends at her death, and she cannot direct whom the property will pass to when she dies. A marital deduction was unavailable for this property in Todd's estate because his executor did not make a QTIP election.

The marital deduction applies only if the surviving spouse is a U.S. citizen. The maximum amount allowable as a marital deduction for federal estate tax purposes is the net value of the property passing to the surviving spouse in a qualifying manner. Otherwise, there is no limit to the marital deduction. An individual could conceivably transfer his entire estate to his spouse estate tax free.

Charitable Deduction

A **charitable deduction** is allowed for the fair market value of any type of gift to a "qualified charity" at a decedent's death. The deduction is limited to the net value of the property includable in the gross estate that is transferred to the charity. In other words, a decedent could conceivably leave his entire estate to charity and receive a deduction for the entire amount if permitted by state law. States that have adopted **mortmain statutes** allow heirs to contest the decedent's will if property was bequeathed to charities or religious organizations, or if the amounts bequeathed exceeded the limits established by state law.

State Death Tax Deduction

A **deduction for state death taxes** is allowed for any death taxes paid to a state because of any tangible, intangible, or real property includable in the decedent's gross estate. This deduction includes payment to a state for estate, inheritance, or generation-skipping transfer taxes.

The **taxable estate** is the result of subtracting deductions that were available to the decedent from the adjusted gross estate

DETERMINING THE TENTATIVE TAX BASE

Once the taxable estate has been determined, **adjusted taxable gifts** are added to arrive at the **tentative tax base**. (See Exhibit 14.4.)

Exhibit 14.4

Taxable Estate	$_____
+ Adjusted Taxable Gifts	$_____
Tentative Tax Base	$_____

Adjusted taxable gifts are defined as the taxable portion of all post-1976 gifts. A gift is taxable to the extent that it exceeds the sum of any allowable gift tax annual exclusion, gift tax marital deduction, or gift tax charitable deduction. Gift splitting can be used to reduce the amount of a taxable gift, if applicable, and gifts that are exempt from taxation such as qualified transfers for educational or medical expenses are not considered taxable gifts.

Client Situation

Harrison and his wife Anna jointly made a gift of $40,000 to their daughter Jodie to help her purchase her first condo. After gift splitting ($20,000) and further reducing the taxable portion of their gift by an annual exclusion ($14,000), Harrison and Anna each made a taxable gift of $6,000.

Practitioner Tip: A surviving spouse can make an election to split gifts with the decedent spouse if gifts were made before the decedent's death and no gift tax return had been filed. A split gift would decrease the value of a decedent's gross estate, which could decrease the estate tax owed and transfer more to estate beneficiaries.

Gifts that are already includable in a decedent's gross estate for any reason, such as a gift with a retained **life estate** or a gift with a retained **reversionary interest** greater than 5%, are not considered adjusted taxable gifts. An asset included in the gross estate is "adjusted" from this category of taxable gifts to avoid double taxation, and it is not included here in the estate tax calculation. That is why this entry on IRS Form 706 is called "adjusted" taxable gifts.

Client Situation

Rebecca created a life estate in her home that permitted her to live there for the rest of her life, and she gifted the remainder interest to her son Jacoby. The fair market value of the home at the time of the gift was $600,000, and the present value of the remainder interest she gifted to Jacoby was valued at $365,000. This taxable gift could not be reduced by gift splitting, an annual exclusion, or any other gift tax deductions. Rebecca died 10 years later when the value of the home was $800,000. The $800,000 was included in her gross estate under IRC § 2036, but the $365,000 taxable gift was not entered on IRS Form 706 as an adjusted taxable gift. An adjustment was made in this category so the home was not taxed twice.

Adding adjusted taxable gifts to the taxable estate makes the estate tax computation part of a unified transfer tax calculation. The process is cumulative and progressive. This means that taxable gifts since 1976 are added back into the estate tax calculation as adjusted taxable gifts to increase the tax, which is progressive, with tax rates ranging from 18% to 40%. The net effect of adding in adjusted taxable gifts is generally to subject the taxable estate at death to rates that are higher than if the computation did not consider lifetime gifts.

When adjusted taxable gifts are combined with the taxable estate, the result is the tentative tax base, the amount upon which the tax rates are based.

Client Situation

Tracey, a single woman, made her first taxable gift last year of $1 million. She did not pay a gift tax because her unified credit offset the tax on this gift. When Tracey died this year her taxable estate was $10 million, and the $1 million gift was added to her estate tax return as an adjusted taxable gift. Tracey's tentative tax base was $11 million.

Practitioner Tip: Planners should ensure that their clients understand that taxable gifts are pulled back into the estate tax calculation and that the value of the taxable estate plus taxable gifts will be combined before the tentative tax is calculated.

COMPUTING THE TENTATIVE TAX

At this point, the **tentative tax** is computed by applying the appropriate rates to the tentative tax base. (See Exhibit 14.5.)

Exhibit 14.5

Tentative Tax Base	$_____
Tentative Tax	$_____
- Gift Tax on Adjusted Taxable Gifts	($_____)
Tax Payable Before Credits	$_____

Different tax rate schedules apply depending on the year of death. These rates are progressive: the greater the estate, the higher the tax rate. For example, the tax on a computation base of $1,000 is $180. On $100,000, the tax is $23,800. On $1 million, the tax is $345,800. (See Appendix B.4.)

When calculating the tax in excess of $1,000,000, note that the highest tax rate is fixed at 40%. The portion in excess of $1,000,000 is taxed at a flat rate of 40%. For the initial $1,000,000, progressive tax rates still apply. Under these rates, the tax on the initial $1,000,000 of the computation base is $345,800.

To calculate a tax on an amount that exceeds $1,000,000, $345,800 is added to the tax. For example, a tax on $2 million is computed as adding $345,800 for the first $1 million together with the 40% flat tax on the second $1,000,000 ($1,000,000 × 40%) or $400,000, for a total tax of $745,800.

Client Situation

Tracey's tentative tax base was $11 million. The tax on the first $1 million was $345,800. The tax on the remaining $10 million at 40% was $4 million. Tracey's tentative tax is $4,345,800 ($4,000,000 + $345,800).

Gift Taxes Paid or Payable

Because the taxable portion of gifts made after 1976 has already been added back in as adjusted taxable gifts, the gift tax generated by such gifts is subtracted at this point to arrive at the tax payable before credits. A gift tax is payable for any lifetime gifts that exceed $5,430,000 in 2015. This amount is known as the **exemption equivalent**.

The tax liability on taxable gifts under $5,430,000 is offset during a donor's lifetime by a *unified credit*. The term unified credit was adopted because it is a credit used as an offset against gift as well as estate taxes. A unified credit of $2,117,800 is available to shelter gift taxes and must be used against each taxable gift. As additional taxable gifts are made, the unified credit is reduced and finally eliminated once gifts total more than $5,430,000. At that point, a gift tax must be paid.

DETERMINING FEDERAL ESTATE TAX PAYABLE

Certain tax credits are allowed as a dollar-for-dollar reduction of the estate tax. (See Exhibit 14.6.)

Exhibit 14.6

Tax Payable before Credits		$_____
Unified Credit	$_____	
Pre-1977 Gift Tax Credit	$_____	
Previously Taxed Property Credit	$_____	
Foreign Death Tax Credit	$_____	
Total Credits		($_____)
Federal Estate Tax		$_____

These credits are:

- the unified credit;

- the credit for pre-1977 gift tax;

- the credit for taxes on prior transfers; and

- the credit for foreign death taxes.

The Unified Credit

A unified credit is allowed to reduce the estate tax. To the extent the unified credit has been used against gift taxes, the credit available against the estate tax is, in effect, lowered. However, in the estate tax computation, the full unified credit of $2,117,800 was restored for 2015.

Client Situation

Marian, a widow, died in 2015 with a $6 million taxable estate. In 2014 she made only one taxable gift of $20,000 after using an annual exclusion. The tax on the gift ($3,800) was not paid because Marian used $3,800 of her unified credit to offset the tax. Therefore, when Marian's executor added back $20,000 of adjusted taxable gifts on her IRS Form 706, it restored the $3,800 of unified credit. That is why a unified credit (of $2,117,800 in 2015) can be subtracted on IRS Form 706 to reduce the estate tax regardless of the amount of taxable gifts made in a donor's lifetime. See Exhibit 14.7 for Marian's estate tax liability in 2015, ignoring other tax credits.

Exhibit 14.7

2015	Taxable Estate	$6 million
Plus:	Adjusted taxable gifts	$20,000
	Tentative Tax Base	$6,020,000
	Tentative Tax on $6,020,000	$2,353,800
Minus:	Gift taxes paid on lifetime transfers	$0
Minus:	Unified Credit	$2,117,800
	Estate Tax Due	**$236,000**

Practitioner Tip: No refund is available if the unified credit exceeds the amount of the estate tax owed.

Other Tax Credits

A credit is available for gift tax paid on gifts made before 1977 when the property is included in the donor's gross estate because of retained interests in the gifted property.

A credit for foreign death taxes is intended to prevent double taxation. It is allowed for death taxes paid to a foreign country or a U.S. possession on property that is included in the decedent's gross estate and situated (and subject to tax) in that country or possession. The credit is available only to U.S. citizens or resident aliens.

A credit for estate taxes paid on prior transfers is available to reduce the estate tax on property owned by two decedents. When a prior decedent (the transferor) transferred property (which was taxed at death) to the present decedent and the property is includable in the present decedent's estate, a credit is allowed for all or part of the estate tax paid by the transferor's estate on the transferred property. The present decedent must have inherited the property while he was alive. The transferor must have died within 10 years before or two years after the present decedent.

As long as the property was includable in the transferor's estate and passed from the transferor to the present decedent, the method of transfer is irrelevant; it can be by will, by intestacy, by election against the will, by lifetime gift, as life insurance proceeds, or as joint property with right of survivorship.

The credit is the lower of

- the federal estate tax attributable to the transferred property in the transferor's estate, or

- the federal estate tax attributable to the transferred property in the estate of the present decedent.

The credit is reduced by 20% increments every two years, and at the end of 10 years after the transferor's death no credit is allowable. For example, between years two and four only 80% of the credit is allowable.

Client Situation

Robin died in 2012 with a taxable estate of $7 million. He bequeathed his entire estate to his partner, Calvin. Calvin died in 2015 and the property he inherited from Robin was included in his gross estate. A credit for 80% of the estate tax paid by Robin's estate was taken on Calvin's estate tax return.

The total of all allowable credits is subtracted from the tax payable before credits to determine the net federal estate tax payable.

ESTATE TAX CALCULATIONS

Example 1: Estate with No Lifetime Taxable Gifts

Joseph, recently divorced, died in 2015. His gross estate was $5,740,000. Funeral and administrative costs totaled $25,000. Debts and taxes totaled $15,000. Joseph made no taxable gifts during his lifetime. The estate tax liability and the estate's cash requirements were computed as shown in Exhibit 14.8.

Exhibit 14.8

Federal Estate Tax Worksheet with Cash Requirements

	1. Gross Estate		$5,740,000
minus	2. Funeral and Administration Expenses	$25,000	
	3. Debts and Taxes	$15,000	
	4. Losses	$0	
	Total Deductions	**$40,000**	
equals	5. Adjusted Gross Estate		$5,700,000
minus	6. Marital Deduction	$0	
	7. Charitable Deduction	$0	
	8. State Death Tax Deduction	$0	
	Total Deductions	**$0**	**$0**
equals	9. Taxable Estate		$5,700,000
plus	10. Adjusted Taxable Gifts		$0
equals	11. Tentative Tax Base		$5,700,000
compute	12. Tentative Tax	$2,225,800	
minus	13. Gift Taxes Payable	$0	
equals	14. Tax Payable Before Credits		$2,225,800
minus	15. Tax Credits		
	a. Unified Credit	$2,117,800	
	b. Credit for Tax on Prior Transfers	$0	
	c. Credit for Foreign Death Taxes	$0	
	Total Reductions	**$2,117,800**	
equals	16. Net Federal Estate Tax Payable		$108,000
plus	17. Total Cash Bequests		$0
equals	18. **Total Cash Requirements** [(sum of lines 2 + 3) + Estate Tax Payable] = $40,000 + $108,000		**$148,000**

Example 2: Estate with Lifetime Taxable Gifts

Tina, a single woman, had a gross estate of $6.8 million at the time of her death in 2015. Assume funeral and administrative expenses were $60,000, and that debts and taxes totaled $40,000. Tina made her first taxable gift of $100,000 in 2013 (a $114,000 gift to her niece minus the annual exclusion of $14,000). The computation of Tina's estate tax and estate cash requirements is presented in Exhibit 14.9.

Exhibit 14.9

Federal Estate Tax Worksheet with Cash Requirements

	1. Gross Estate		$6,800,000
minus	2. Funeral and Administration Expenses	$60,000	
	3. Debts and Taxes	$40,000	
	4. Losses	$0	
	Total Deductions	**$100,000**	
equals	5. Adjusted Gross Estate		$6,700,000
minus	6. Marital Deduction	$0	
	7. Charitable Deduction	$0	
	8. State Death Tax Deduction	$0	
	Total Deductions	**$0**	**$0**
equals	9. Taxable Estate		$6,700,000
plus	10. Adjusted Taxable Gifts		$100,000
equals	11. Tentative Tax Base		$6,800,000
compute	12. Tentative Tax	$2,665,800	
minus	13. Gift Taxes Payable	$0	
equals	14. Tax Payable Before Credits		$2,665,800
minus	15. Tax Credits		
	a. Unified Credit	$2,117,800	
	b. Credit for Tax on Prior Transfers	$0	
	c. Credit for Foreign Death Taxes	$0	
	Total Reductions	**$2,117,800**	
equals	16. Net Federal Estate Tax Payable		$548,000
plus	17. Total Cash Bequests		$0
equals	18. **Total Cash Requirements** [(sum of lines 2 + 3) + Estate Tax Payable] = $100,000 + $548,000		**$648,000**

Example 3: Gross-up Rule

Russell made his first taxable gift in 2013 of $5.8 million. The exclusion amount was $5,250,000 in 2013, so Russell had to pay a gift tax of $220,000 after using his unified credit to offset the tax. Russell died in 2015. Funeral and administrative expenses totaled $25,000. Russell's estate had $40,000 of expenses. The gift tax he paid in 2013 was included in his gross estate per the **gross-up rule**, (IRC § 2035), because the gift tax was paid within three years of his death. His gross estate in 2015 was valued at $3.5 million. See Exhibit 14.10 for how this was determined.

Exhibit 14.10

Federal Estate Tax Worksheet with Cash Requirements

	1. Gross Estate (includes gift tax paid within 3 years of death)			$3,720,000
minus	2. Funeral and Administration Expenses	$25,000		
	3. Debts and Taxes	$40,000		
	4. Losses	$0		
	Total Deductions	**$65,000**		
equals	5. Adjusted Gross Estate			$3,655,000
minus	6. Marital Deduction		$0	
	7. Charitable Deduction		$0	
	8. State Death Tax Deduction		$0	
	Total Deductions		**$0**	**$0**
equals	9. Taxable Estate			$3,655,000
plus	10. Adjusted Taxable Gifts			$5,800,000
equals	11. Tentative Tax Base			$9,455,000
compute	12. Tentative Tax	$3,727,800		
minus	13. Gift Taxes Payable	$220,000		
equals	14. Tax Payable Before Credits			$3,507,800
minus	15. Tax Credits			
	a. Unified Credit	$2,117,800		
	b. Credit for Tax on Prior Transfers	$0		
	c. Credit for Foreign Death Taxes	$0		
	Total Reductions	**$2,117,800**		
equals	16. Net Federal Estate Tax Payable			$1,390,000
plus	17. Total Cash Bequests			$0
equals	18. **Total Cash Requirements** [(sum of lines 2 + 3 = $65,000) + Estate Tax Payable] = $1,390,000			**$1,455,000**

Example 4: Transfer under IRC § 2036

In 2013, Shirley created a life estate in a home she inherited from her husband Rufus. She gifted the remainder interest in her home to her son Reggie. The present value of the remainder interest was valued for gift tax purposes at $500,000. When Shirley died unexpectedly in 2015, the fair market value of her home was appraised at $4 million. Shirley also had $2.5 million in cash at the time of her death. Her funeral and administrative expenses totaled $30,000 and debts and taxes totaled $30,000. (See Exhibit 14.11.)

Exhibit 14.11

Federal Estate Tax Worksheet with Cash Requirements

	1. Gross Estate (includes cash and the FMV of Shirley's home)		$6,500,000
minus	2. Funeral and Administration Expenses	$30,000	
	3. Debts and Taxes	$30,000	
	4. Losses	$0	
	Total Deductions	**$60,000**	
equals	5. Adjusted Gross Estate		$6,440,000
minus	6. Marital Deduction	$0	
	7. Charitable Deduction	$0	
	8. State Death Tax Deduction	$0	
	Total Deductions	**$0**	**$0**
equals	9. Taxable Estate		$6,440,000
plus	10. Adjusted Taxable Gifts (The $500,000 gift of the remainder interest in her home is not included because retained life estates are included in the decedent's gross estate per IRC §2036.)		$0
equals	11. Tentative Tax Base		$6,440,000
compute	12. Tentative Tax	$2,521,800	
minus	13. Gift Taxes Payable	$0	
equals	14. Tax Payable Before Credits		$2,521,800
minus	15. Tax Credits		
	a. Unified Credit	$2,117,800	
	b. Credit for Tax on Prior Transfers	$0	
	c. Credit for Foreign Death Taxes	$0	
	Total Reductions	**$2,117,800**	
equals	16. Net Federal Estate Tax Payable		$404,000
plus	17. Total Cash Bequests		$0
equals	18. **Total Cash Requirements** [(sum of lines 2 + 3) + Estate Tax Payable] = $60,000 + $404,000		**$464,000**

FILING AN ESTATE TAX RETURN

The estate tax is due at the time the estate tax return is to be filed, nine months after a decedent's death. An executor must file an estate tax return, IRS Form 706, if the gross estate exceeds the exemption equivalent amount of $5,430,000. A return must also be filed if the gross estate is less than $5,430,000, but this threshold amount is exceeded when adjusted taxable gifts are added back into the return. Therefore, in some estates, filing is required even if the taxable estate is far less than the exemption equivalent.

An executor or administrator can request that the IRS grant an extension of time for paying the tax—up to 12 months from the date fixed for the payment—if there is reasonable cause. Furthermore, upon the executor's showing of reasonable cause, the IRS could, at its discretion, grant a series of extensions that could run as long as 10 years from the due date of the original return. There is no definition of *reasonable cause* in the IRC or regulations. However, the regulations provide examples of situations where reasonable cause will be found.

- A substantial portion of the estate consists of rights to receive future payments such as annuities, accounts receivable, or renewal commissions and the estate cannot borrow against these assets without incurring substantial loss. The gross estate is unascertainable at the time the tax is normally due, because the estate has a claim to substantial assets that cannot be collected without litigation.

- An estate has insufficient funds to pay claims against the estate (including estate taxes when due) and at the same time provide a reasonable allowance during the period of administration for a decedent's surviving spouse and dependent children, because the executor, despite reasonable efforts, cannot convert assets in his possession into cash.

Payment of the Tax

The estate tax is **tax inclusive**, which means that the money used to pay the tax is also included and taxed in the decedent's estate.

Practitioner Tip: The estate tax is different from the gift tax, which is **tax exclusive**. Gift taxes paid do not reduce the amount of the property gifted to the donee, but they do reduce the value of the donor's gross estate, unless the gift tax amount is brought back into the decedent's gross estate under the gross-up rule.

The executor is personally liable to pay the tax from assets the decedent owned. If the tax cannot be collected from the executor, then the heirs are responsible for paying the portion of the tax that is attributed to their inheritance. An executor can waive any executor fees he has the right to receive to avoid reporting taxable income on his personal income tax return. This makes sense if the executor is a beneficiary of the estate and would therefore receive a tax-free inheritance.

Chapter Highlights

- The gross estate is the starting point for the estate tax calculation. Deductions for funeral expenses, administrative expenses, debts, mortgages, liens, and casualty losses can be taken to arrive at the adjusted gross estate.

- Deductions can be taken from the adjusted gross estate for marital and charitable deductions and for state death taxes paid.

- A marital deduction is available to the decedent spouse's estate if property was included in the gross estate and transferred to the spouse in a qualifying manner. Property passing to the surviving spouse through intestacy, will contents, nuptial agreements or elective share statutes also qualifies for the marital deduction in the decedent spouse's estate.

- The executor can make a QTIP election on the decedent's estate tax return to qualify terminable interest property that passes to the surviving spouse for a marital deduction.

- Taxable gifts made since 1976 are added back into the taxable estate as adjusted taxable gifts, which results in a higher tentative tax base.

- A unified tax table is used to compute the tentative tax base for gifts and estates. The tax rate is cumulative and progressive with a top rate of 40%.

- Gift taxes actually paid by the decedent or that would have been generated by lifetime gifts are subtracted from the tentative tax to arrive at the tax payable before credits.

- The unified credit eliminates an estate tax for estates that do not exceed $5,430,000 in 2015. The unified credit is always restored in full. The credit amount for 2015 is $2,117,800.

- It is the executor's responsibility to pay the decedent's estate tax, due nine months after death.

Key Terms

adjusted gross estate	reversionary interest
adjusted taxable gifts	state death tax deduction
charitable deduction	tax exclusive
exemption equivalent	tax inclusive
gross-up rule	taxable estate
life estate	tentative tax
marital deduction	tentative tax base
mortmain statutes	terminable interest property (TIP)
QTIP election	unified credit

Review Questions

14-1. Burt died with an estate of individually owned property valued at $20 million, which he left to his wife Claire in his will. He did not own any property jointly with Claire other than their home. His estate had funeral and administrative expenses of $100,000, a mortgage on the home for $800,000, a mortgage on an office building in Charlotte for $1.2 million, and $400,000 in unpaid property taxes on the office building. What is the amount of the adjusted gross estate reported on Burt's estate tax return?

A. $17,500,000

B. $17,900,000

C. $18,300,000

D. $18,500,000

14-2. Identify which gifts will be included as an adjusted taxable gift on the donor's IRS Form 706.

A. Thomas made his first gift to his son for $10,000 this year.

B. Mitch and Arlene split a gift they made to their daughter for $60,000.

C. Theresa created a life estate in an irrevocable trust to receive the income for life and gifted the remainder interest to her son. The present value of the remainder interest on the date the gift was made was valued at $200,000.

D. Martha paid the community rehab center $15,000 for expenses related to her mother's care.

14-3. Christopher made cash gifts to his two children for the past three years totaling $250,000 and his wife consented to split the gifts with him. Total taxable gifts were reduced to $45,000 for each spouse after gift splitting and annual exclusions were applied. The gift tax was computed as $9,400 prior to the unified credit. Assume Christopher died this year. Which of the following statements are correct?

A. Christopher's gross estate has been reduced by $250,000 through gifting.

B. The unified credit amount on Christopher's estate tax return is reported as $2,108,400 because the total tax on the gifts ($9,400) reduced the amount of his unified credit.

C. Christopher's executor must add $45,000 of total taxable gifts to the "adjusted taxable gift" entry on his estate tax return.

D. The gift tax that Christopher paid was added to his gross estate under the gross-up rule.

14-4. Which of the following statements pertaining to the estate tax is incorrect?

A. The estate tax is tax inclusive because the money used to pay the tax is taken from a separate account.

B. The executor is personally liable to pay the tax from assets the decedent owned.

C. The estate tax is due nine months after death unless an extension is granted.

D. An estate tax return must be filed for a widow with a gross estate of $3 million who made taxable gifts of $4 million 10 years ago.

14-5. Dean had a gross estate of $6.6 million. His funeral, administrative expenses, and debts totaled $100,000. He made two taxable gifts last year totaling $2.5 million. Which of the following statements pertaining to Dean's estate tax return are correct?

A. Dean's adjusted gross estate was $6.5 million.

B. Dean's tentative tax base was $9 million.

C. The gross-up rule did not apply to Dean's estate.

D. Although Dean's unified credit was reduced when he made two taxable gifts, the full credit amount of $2,117,800 was subtracted from the tentative tax.

Chapter 15

The Marital Deduction

CFP® CERTIFICATION EXAMINATION PRINCIPAL TOPICS COVERED IN THIS CHAPTER:

Marital Deduction

- Requirements
- Qualifying transfers
- Terminable interest rule and exceptions
- Qualified domestic trust (QDOT)

Learning Objectives

To ensure that you have a solid understanding of the requirements and applications of the marital deduction, the following learning objectives are addressed in this chapter:

- Describe the appropriate use of the marital deduction for estate planning purposes.

- Define the requirements for a qualified transfer.

- Identify property interests subject to the terminable interest rule and when exceptions apply.

- Recognize the estate tax implications of terminable interest property for each spouse.

- Determine the amount of a marital deduction for all property interests included in a decedent spouse's estate.

- Explain the requirements of a qualified domestic trust.

- Evaluate when the use of a qualified disclaimer is appropriate.

Chapter Contents

OVERVIEW

Marital deduction planning is of fundamental importance in planning for wealth transfers between spouses. The marital deduction is a deduction for gift or estate tax purposes for property passing to a spouse. An unlimited marital deduction eliminates a transfer tax that a couple would otherwise have to pay at the time a gift or bequest is made. However, this transferred property may be taxed at a later time. For example, property gifted to a spouse that remains in the recipient spouse's possession at death is included in that spouse's gross estate. Similarly, with an estate tax marital deduction, assets transferred to the surviving spouse are not diminished by the payment of an estate tax at the first spouse's death, but any remaining assets may be taxed in the surviving spouse's estate.

Financial planners should know whether a marital deduction is available given a particular client situation before estimating a client's estate tax liability. A planner should always work with a client's estate planning attorney to determine the best way to leave an inheritance to a spouse and others and to ensure that the estate plan is coordinated with the couple's financial planning objectives and tax situation.

Practice Standard 200-1

Determining a Client's Personal and Financial Goals, Needs and Priorities

The financial planning practitioner and the client shall mutually define the client's personal and financial goals, needs and priorities that are relevant to the scope of the engagement before any recommendation is made and/or implemented.

MARITAL DEDUCTION QUALIFICATIONS

An unlimited marital deduction is available for gifts and bequests made to spouses in a qualifying manner. A spouse must have complete control and enjoyment over property for the property to pass in a qualifying manner. In addition, to qualify for the gift or estate tax marital deduction the following conditions must be satisfied at the time the property is transferred.

- The recipient spouse must be a U.S. citizen.

- The recipient must be the donor's legal spouse at the time the gift is made or the property is inherited.

- The transferred property must not be terminable interest property, unless a **qualifying terminable interest property (QTIP) election** is made.

- Property transferred at death must have been included in the decedent's gross estate.

ESTATE TAX MARITAL DEDUCTION

The maximum amount allowable as a marital deduction for federal estate tax purposes is the net value of the property passing to the surviving spouse in a qualifying manner. The net value is the amount included in a decedent's gross estate reduced by debts, taxes, and administrative expenses.

Client Situation

Bryce died last month with a gross estate of $8 million, which passed directly to his wife Stephanie under his will. His funeral, administrative expenses, and debts totaled $700,000, which included a mortgage balance of $600,000 for Bryce's $2 million country estate. Bryce's adjusted gross estate is $7.3 million; therefore, the amount that qualifies for the marital deduction in Bryce's estate is $7.3 million.

There is no limit to the marital deduction, and it can eliminate an estate tax liability regardless of the value of an estate. But the marital deduction defers only the estate tax because a tax may be payable on the couple's assets when the second spouse dies. This can result in a greater estate tax if the assets appreciate in value after the first spouse's death and the surviving spouse does not remarry, spend down the assets, or gift some of the assets away.

WHEN A MARITAL DEDUCTION IS AVAILABLE

The marital deduction is available in a decedent's estate when certain property interests are included in the gross estate and transferred to the surviving spouse. The net amount the surviving spouse receives through these transfer methods determines the amount that qualifies for the marital deduction in the decedent spouse's estate. The marital deduction rules apply to community property states as well as common law or separate property states. Examples of property interests that qualify for marital deductions include:

- individually owned property bequeathed to a spouse through the decedent's will;

- property that passes to the beneficiary spouse from a decedent's revocable trust;

- fractional shares of tenancy-in-common property bequeathed outright to the surviving spouse through the will;

- property transferred to the spouse by state laws of intestacy or through a successful challenge to the will by a will contest;

- property awarded to the surviving spouse through the state's elective share statute;

- property transferred to the surviving spouse by a dower or a curtesy (life estate);

- property transferred to the surviving spouse through a valid nuptial agreement;

- property transferred to a surviving spouse when the couple is legally separated;

- property that passes to the surviving spouse's estate under a **presumption-of-survivorship clause** in the will when it cannot be determined which spouse died first;

- Property appointed to the surviving spouse by a power of appointment exercised by the decedent, or if the surviving spouse is a **taker in default** when a decedent did not exercise a **general power of appointment** at death.

Client Situation

Karen was the owner of a successful business but she never made the time to meet with an estate planning attorney to write a will or create other essential estate planning documents. When she died unexpectedly her estate went into probate, and her business and personal property interests were divided among her husband and children according to her state's law of intestacy. Her husband received one-half of her net estate, and her three children received the remaining one-half of her property. A marital deduction was available to Karen's estate for the value of her property that passed to her husband through intestacy.

Jointly Owned Property

Property that is jointly owned by spouses through a joint tenancy with right of survivorship (JTWROS), a tenancy by the entirety, and community property passing to the surviving spouse is includable in the decedent spouse's gross estate at one-half of the property's value. A marital deduction equal to the net value in the adjusted gross estate is available to the decedent spouse's estate.

Client Situation

Darren and Hayley owned a home together JTWROS and it was appraised at $1.8 million at Darren's death. Darren and Hayley had paid off the mortgage on the home several years ago. Although $900,000 was included in Darren's gross estate, a marital deduction of $900,000 was available to offset any estate tax attributed to the home in Darren's estate. The entire $1.8 million value of the home now belongs to Hayley.

Survivorship Benefits

When a surviving spouse is the beneficiary of a joint and survivor pension or annuity (private or commercial), the value of the survivorship benefit in the decedent's estate is eligible for a corresponding marital deduction.

> ### Client Situation
>
> Sherry had purchased an annuity that paid her $30,000 a year for life and that would pay her husband, Bruno, $15,000 a year for his life when Sherry died. The present value of the annuity's lifetime payments to Bruno was calculated to be worth $120,000 when Sherry died. The $120,000 was included in Sherry's gross estate but this amount was subtracted from her adjusted gross estate because it qualified for the marital deduction.

Life Insurance Owner/Insured

A marital deduction is available to offset the death benefit amount of a life insurance policy included in the deceased policy owner's estate if the surviving spouse is named the beneficiary of the policy.

> ### Client Situation
>
> Evelyn was the owner and the insured of a $3 million whole-life insurance policy. Her husband, Bill, was the beneficiary of the policy. When Evelyn died the death benefit amount of $3 million was included in her gross estate, but a marital deduction was available to completely offset the estate tax on this policy.

Policy Owner Is Not the Insured

When a life insurance policy was owned by a decedent who was not the insured, then the policy's value, which is different from the death benefit amount, is includable in the owner's estate. If the surviving spouse is named the new owner of the policy in the insurance contract or in the will, then a marital deduction is available for the value of the policy included in the deceased owner's estate.

> ### Client Situation
>
> Corey was the owner and beneficiary of a $1 million single-premium whole-life insurance policy on his wife's life. When Corey died, the replacement cost of the policy was valued at $210,000, and this amount was included in Corey's gross estate. Corey left the policy to his wife in his will; therefore, a marital deduction for $210,000 was available to Corey's estate.

WHEN A MARITAL DEDUCTION IS NOT AVAILABLE

For property to qualify for a marital deduction, the spouse must be given outright ownership of the property or sufficient control over it during lifetime and/or at death. A marital deduction would be disallowed for property transferred to a trust when the spouse merely serves as trustee. If property is transferred to a trust, and the recipient spouse is both trustee and a trust beneficiary, certain requirements must be met for the marital deduction to be allowed.

A marital deduction is not available to a donor spouse when a donee spouse is given a **special or limited power of appointment** over the donor's property. The donee spouse, as holder of the special or limited power of appointment, is restricted with respect to appointing property to himself or to others. Therefore, the donor spouse is not entitled to a marital deduction unless, perhaps, the donor spouse elects QTIP treatment.

Terminable Interest Property

A marital deduction is not available for terminable interest property (TIP) passing to a spouse. **Terminable interest property** is property gifted or bequeathed to a recipient spouse that will pass to someone else after the recipient's interest ends. When the decedent spouse has not given the surviving spouse complete control over the property, and the surviving spouse cannot direct whom the property will pass to upon death, then a marital deduction is not allowed in the decedent spouse's estate.

Client Situation

Ronnie's will establishes a testamentary trust that will pay his wife Sarah all income annually for her life. The trust stipulates that when Sarah dies, the trust corpus will be distributed to Ronnie's two children from a previous marriage, the remainder beneficiaries of the trust. Ronnie has given Sarah a terminable interest in this trust because her income interest ends at her death, and because she cannot determine who will receive the trust corpus. A marital deduction will not be allowed in Ronnie's estate for the income interest he bequeathed to Sarah. As a result, the property will not be included in Sarah's gross estate at her death because her interest in the trust ends at her death.

QTIP Exception

Most terminable interests can qualify for the marital deduction if the executor makes the appropriate **QTIP election** in a timely manner. A qualifying terminable interest is one that satisfies the following requirements:

- Property passes directly from the decedent to the surviving spouse.

- The surviving spouse receives a "qualified income interest" for life.

- The decedent's executor makes an irrevocable election on his estate tax return.

A qualified income interest must meet the following criteria:

- The surviving spouse must be entitled to all of the income for life.

- Income must be distributed at least annually; therefore, no income is permitted to accumulate in the trust.

- The spouse must be the only trust beneficiary during his or her lifetime, and trust income and principal cannot be distributed to any beneficiary other than the surviving spouse while the spouse is alive.

- The remaining value of the property will be included in the surviving spouse's gross estate.

Client Situation

In the preceding example, when Ronnie died five months ago, his executor made a QTIP election on his estate tax return that qualified the trust for a marital deduction in Ronnie's estate. Because a marital deduction was available to Ronnie's estate, the value of the remaining trust corpus will be included in Sarah's gross estate when she dies, as if she were the ultimate recipient instead of the children. Sarah's executor is entitled to recover from Ronnie's two children the share of estate taxes generated in her estate by the inclusion of that property—unless Sarah chooses to exonerate Ronnie's children in her will.

Practitioner Tip: For estate tax purposes, the property transferred into the trust must be included in either Ronnie's estate now or in Sarah's estate in the future. If the trust assets are expected to appreciate substantially over time, it may be prudent not to make the QTIP election at Ronnie's death because the estate tax could be significantly greater for Sarah's estate. If the trust assets are expected to diminish over time, the QTIP election will defer the estate tax, and the value of the property that remains in trust at Sarah's death, presumably less than the value at Ronnie's death, would be subject to the tax.

General Power of Appointment Exception

A marital deduction is also available for a life estate bequeathed to a surviving spouse if the spouse is given a general power of appointment over the real property or trust corpus. To avoid a terminable interest in the property, the surviving spouse must have unrestricted access to the property for life or be given the right to appoint the property to others at death, including her estate or the creditors of her estate. The decedent spouse would obtain a marital deduction for the present value of the property transferred to the surviving spouse, but the value of the property or the trust would be included in the surviving spouse's gross estate.

Client Situation

Marie's will established a testamentary trust that was funded with $2 million at her death. Marie's husband Dale was given the right to receive all of the income from this trust for his life, and their daughter, Debra, as the remainder beneficiary, was given the right to receive the trust assets after her father's death. A power of appointment clause in the trust gave Dale the power to invade the trust corpus without restriction. Therefore Dale was given a general power of appointment over this trust. For that reason, Marie's estate could take a marital deduction for the present value of the income interest bequeathed to Dale in trust.

Practitioner Tip: When a surviving spouse is granted the power to invade trust corpus without restriction during his lifetime, the surviving spouse may dispose of property however he wishes. In this case, Dale could spend all of the trust assets without restriction, or he could take trust assets and give them to another person, not Debra! Financial planners should pay close attention to the powers of appointment that are granted in an estate planning document not only to understand the tax implications, but also to understand the potential unintended consequences of the named remainder beneficiaries who are not inheriting assets.

Client Situation

Jack's will established a testamentary trust that was funded with $500,000 following his death. His wife Christy was entitled to trust income during her lifetime. At death, Christy had a general power to appoint assets. If Christy does not exercise this power of appointment, assets will pass to their two children, Ian and Leia. Because Christy has the ability to appoint assets to whomever she wishes at death, including her estate or the creditors of her estate, the marital deduction will be available for Jack's estate and assets will be included in Christy's estate.

Other Terminable Interest Property Exceptions

Additional statutory exceptions to the terminable interest rule qualify for a marital deduction in a decedent's estate.

- A bequest to the surviving spouse that is conditional upon the spouse living longer than six months after the decedent spouse's death. However, if the spouse dies within six months of the decedent, no marital deduction is available in the decedent spouse's estate.

- Life insurance proceeds or annuity payments that are payable to the surviving spouse for life when the spouse is given a general power of appointment over the payments.

- A testamentary charitable remainder trust that pays the surviving spouse income for life.

Client Situation

Vickie's will established a testamentary **charitable remainder annuity trust** (CRAT) that benefitted her husband Danny and her favorite charity, the Whale and Dolphin Conservation Society. The trust will pay Danny income for life in the form of a fixed annual annuity payment. Upon Danny's death, the remaining assets in the trust will pass to the charity. Although Danny was given a terminable interest in the trust, lifetime income from a CRAT or a CRUT (**charitable remainder unitrust**) is an exception to the terminable interest rule. Therefore, Vickie's estate received a marital deduction for the present value of the lifetime income passing to Danny, and her estate received a charitable deduction for the value of the remainder interest passing to charity.

NON-CITIZEN SPOUSE

A marital deduction is available only for gifts or bequests made from one U.S. citizen spouse to another citizen spouse and is not available for transfers made to a non-citizen spouse. A non-citizen spouse can be either a **resident alien** who lives in the U.S. or a nonresident alien who does not reside in this country.

Gifts made to a non-U.S. citizen spouse that are in excess of the exemption amount are taxable. However, there is a higher gift tax annual exclusion available to the donor spouse to reduce the amount of the taxable gift than gifts made to other donees. The annual exclusion for gifts made to a non-U.S. citizen spouse is $147,000 in 2015. This annual exclusion can be applied only to reduce the tax for a gift of a present interest or a gift that would generally qualify for the marital deduction.

Client Situation

Stacey is a U.S. citizen who married Damien, an Irish citizen. This year Stacey bought Damien a power boat for $100,000 and transferred the remainder interest in her home in the Florida Keys to him. An annual exclusion reduced the gift tax on the power boat to zero but the remaining annual exclusion of $47,000 could not offset the gift tax on the home because it was a future-interest gift.

If the surviving spouse is not a U.S. citizen, the estate tax marital deduction is available only if the bequest ends up in a **qualified domestic trust** (**QDOT**). This trust, created under the decedent's will or living trust, meets the requirements for the estate tax marital deduction for transfers made to the trust. Note that a decedent spouse could still transfer $5,430,000 directly to a nonmarital trust for the benefit of the non-citizen spouse because this exclusion amount is independent of the marital deduction.

A marital deduction only postpones the time when an estate tax must be paid. If a resident alien spouse were to leave the United States and return to his native country after inheriting a spouse's assets, then there is no certainty that the IRS would ever collect the estate tax on those assets. The purpose of the marital deduction is to defer estate tax rather than to allow assets to escape estate tax. Therefore, the estate tax must be paid either by the decedent spouse's estate, from lifetime distributions made from a QDOT to the non-citizen spouse, or when the QDOT terminates at the non-citizen spouse's death.

A QDOT must meet the following requirements:

- The trustee must be a U.S. citizen or a bank or trust company with a domestic presence.

- The non-citizen spouse must receive all income annually for life.

- The trustee has the right to withhold the decedent's estate taxes from corpus distributed to the non-citizen spouse during life or at death.

- The executor must elect that the trust be treated as a QDOT on the estate tax return.

If the surviving non-citizen spouse becomes a U.S. citizen before the decedent's estate tax return is filed and the surviving spouse was a resident of the U.S. at all times after the decedent's death and before becoming a citizen, the usual marital deduction is available to the surviving spouse (i.e., a QDOT is not required). If the surviving spouse becomes a U.S. citizen after the QDOT is established, the spouse may still be able to treat the balance of the QDOT assets as a conventional marital deduction.

Practitioner Tip: It makes sense to gift property to a non-citizen spouse throughout his lifetime to take advantage of the greater annual exclusion amounts. The non-citizen spouse could also establish a QDOT before the decedent's estate tax return is filed to have the marital deduction available to the decedent spouse's estate. The best strategy, however, is to have the resident alien become a U.S. citizen to have the marital deduction available to the decedent spouse's estate.

QUALIFIED DISCLAIMER

A disclaimer is an irrevocable refusal by a potential beneficiary (a **disclaimant**) to accept an inter-vivos gift or a bequest under the terms of a will or trust. For federal tax purposes, the disclaimant is regarded as never having received the property and treated as if he had predeceased the transferor. As a result, no transfer is considered to have been made by the disclaimant for federal gift, estate, or generation-skipping transfer (GST) tax purposes when the property passes to a different beneficiary or trust.

When a surviving spouse disclaims property she is treated as having predeceased her spouse. If the asset was to pass to the surviving spouse by will, it is returned to the decedent's estate and passes to the contingent beneficiaries or a disclaimer trust established by the will. Similarly, if assets pass to a surviving spouse per the terms of a trust, the survivor is treated as if she predeceased the beneficiaries and the contingent beneficiaries will inherit. With respect to life insurance or retirement benefits, if a surviving spouse is the primary beneficiary and disclaims assets, the contingent beneficiary named in the beneficiary designation will take the proceeds or benefits. Property disclaimed by the surviving spouse does not qualify a marital deduction in the decedent spouse's estate.

Requirements

- There must be a written refusal by the disclaimant to accept an interest in property. This must be received by the transferor, his legal representative, or the holder of legal title to the property.

- The disclaimer must be made no later than nine months after the transfer or before the day the disclaimant attains the age of 21.

- The interest must pass without any direction from the disclaimant. The interest will pass to the next beneficiary in line, which may include a trust in which the disclaimant has an interest.

- All or a portion of a property interest may be disclaimed.

- The disclaimer must comply with applicable state laws.

Disclaimer Trust

A couple must consider using a disclaimer and plan for this contingency prior to the first spouse's death. The couple may want the disclaimed property to pass to a **disclaimer trust**, which is a trust that will function only in the event the surviving spouse (or his or her estate representative) disclaims the bequest under the will or trust. The trust can be for the benefit of the surviving spouse and children, or the children only. If, at the death of the first spouse, the combined estate of the deceased and the surviving spouses would exceed the unified credit exemption equivalent ($5,430,000), then the surviving spouse can disclaim into the trust to take advantage of all or part of the unified credit exemption equivalent of the estate of the deceased spouse. When the surviving spouse dies, the trust created by the disclaimer will bypass his or her taxable estate and the corpus will pass to the remainder beneficiaries.

Strategies Using a Qualified Disclaimer

Qualified disclaimers are used as an appropriate estate planning tool in the following situations.

- When a beneficiary of property under a will or trust wishes to make a tax-free transfer to the person who would be the next recipient of such property under the will or trust. This transfer would not count as a gift for tax purposes.

Client Situation
Raymond's will left his entire estate to his sister Carla, assuming she survives him. However, if Carla predeceases Raymond, then his estate is left to Carla's daughter Julia. When Raymond died four months ago, Carla disclaimed her inheritance in favor of Julia. Because Carla never took possession of Raymond's property, she did not make a gift to Julia when she disclaimed the property.

- When an individual with children and a large estate in his own right is left a bequest by another individual and this bequest would compound the recipient's potential estate tax problem. The first recipient may wish to disclaim the bequest in favor of the next recipients under the will or trust. By making the disclaimer, the disclaimed property will not be included in the disclaimant's estate at his death because he did not own the property.

Client Situation

Mick, a wealthy client, has four children. Mick's aunt just died and, under the terms of her will, Mick was named as the sole beneficiary of her entire estate if he is alive. If Mick is deceased when she dies, his four children are named equally as contingent heirs. Mick has adequate assets and income to live comfortably and does not need additional property to compound his significant estate tax. By filing a qualified disclaimer within nine months of his aunt's death (and before accepting the assets), Mick will be deemed to have predeceased his aunt for federal estate tax purposes, and his interest in her estate will be distributed to his children under the terms of her will without any federal gift, estate, or GST tax liability to him.

Practitioner Tip: The aunt's property will be distributed to Mick's children pursuant to the terms of his aunt's will. This will constitute a **direct skip** for GST tax purposes. The transfers may or may not be subject to a GST tax, depending upon how much property is involved and the extent to which the aunt's GST tax exemption ($5,430,000) is allocated to the transfers.

- When an individual who is in a high income tax bracket is left a bequest "if he is living, otherwise to his children" and his children are age 18 or older (or in the case of a full time student, age 24 or older) and are in lower income tax brackets. In this case, a disclaimer can shift the income taxation attributable to the property to the children's lower tax brackets if the children are the next recipients of the bequest under the will or trust.

- When the decedent wishes property to pass to a charity using the most effective tax strategy.

Client Situation

Ed specifically leaves $100,000 to his son with a gift over to his favorite charity if his son disclaims. After Ed's death, his son can decide whether to accept the bequest and donate it to charity and receive an income tax deduction on his personal income tax return, or to disclaim the property in favor of the charity and have Ed's estate receive the charitable deduction.

Disclaimer Planning for Spouses

Disclaimer planning is a common strategy that offers great flexibility to spouses. There are a number of situations where disclaimer planning is appropriate.

- Property may be left to a surviving spouse who does not need or want it. The surviving spouse could disclaim the portion he does not want and avoid including the assets in his taxable estate at his death.

- One of the more common disclaimer strategies is to provide that the surviving spouse is the primary beneficiary of an asset or under a will, and to name the bypass trust as the contingent beneficiary. Using disclaimer planning, the surviving spouse can determine whether he wishes to keep the assets for his own use during his lifetime or disclaim the assets and have them pass to the bypass trust. The surviving spouse can disclaim up to the amount that would cause an estate tax liability in the decedent's estate. The surviving spouse can also be a beneficiary of the bypass trust, and the assets may still be available for his use.

Client Situation

Laura had a gross estate of $16 million in solely owned assets. She bequeathed $5 million to a qualified charity and $11 million to her husband Howard. Laura did not have an estate tax liability because a marital deduction and a charitable deduction were available to her estate to eliminate the tax. This was not an effective estate planning strategy because Laura "overqualified" her estate for the marital deduction by not utilizing her estate's unified credit. On the advice of his attorney, Howard disclaimed $5,430,000 back to Laura's estate. This property passed to a bypass trust established by Laura's will, which allows the trustee to distribute assets to Howard during his lifetime and will keep any assets remaining in the trust at Howard's death out of his estate. This transfer enabled Laura's estate to fully utilize her unified credit because the property passing to the terminable interest trust did not qualify for the marital deduction.

Practitioner Tip: A disclaimer by the surviving spouse can be used to increase the deceased spouse's estate to an amount that will be fully offset by the unified credit and keep the property out of the estate of the surviving spouse. Attorneys frequently advise clients to disclaim only a portion of the property up to the amount that would cause an estate tax to the bypass trust of which the spouse is a trust beneficiary.

- When the bequest to the surviving spouse is insufficient to take advantage of the optimum marital deduction, a disclaimer by other beneficiaries in favor of the surviving spouse can be used to qualify a transfer for the marital deduction.

Client Situation

Jules thought that, at his death, his wife would have ample funds and his son very few. Therefore, he left most of his property to his son, with a contingent gift to his wife in the event his son predeceased him. At the time of Jules's death, the son was financially well off, but the surviving spouse was in more difficult financial straits. By disclaiming his share and permitting the surviving spouse to take, the son not only allowed a better distribution of assets but also may have qualified Jules's estate for a marital deduction because of the transfer of the assets to the surviving spouse. This could result in a substantial saving on federal estate taxes. The surviving spouse could then make gifts to her son using the gift tax annual exclusion and her unified credit, if she desired.

Chapter Highlights

- An unlimited marital deduction is available for gifts and bequests made to spouses "in a qualifying manner."

- The maximum amount allowable as a marital deduction for federal estate tax purposes is the net value of the property included in the decedent's estate passing to the surviving spouse.

- A marital deduction is available for certain property interests transferred in a qualifying manner that pass through probate, by operation of law, or by contract if the spouse is a named beneficiary.

- A marital deduction is not available for TIP passing to a spouse unless the spouse is given a general power of appointment over the property or has the right to the income interest in a CRAT or a CRUT. The donor spouse or the decedent's executor can also make an election to qualify the lifetime income interest in TIP for the marital deduction.

- A marital deduction is not available for gifts or bequests made to a non-citizen spouse. A greater annual exclusion is available to the donor spouse to offset the tax on taxable gifts, and a QDOT can be established to obtain a marital deduction in the decedent spouse's estate.

- Property disclaimed by a surviving spouse at the decedent's death passes to other beneficiaries or a disclaimer trust under the will and does not qualify for the marital deduction in the decedent's estate.

Key Terms

charitable remainder annuity trust	QTIP election
charitable remainder unitrust	qualified disclaimer
direct skip	qualified domestic trust (QDOT)
disclaimant	qualifying manner
disclaimer trust	resident alien
general power of appointment	special or limited power of appointment
generation-skipping transfer tax exemption	taker in default
presumption-of-survivorship clause	terminable interest property

Review Questions

15-1. Which of the following property interests does not qualify for a marital deduction from the deceased wife's adjusted gross estate?

A. A terminable interest trust that paid the husband all income annually for life. The executor elected to qualify the trust for the marital deduction on the wife's estate tax return.

B. The lifetime income interest the husband received from a testamentary trust with a power to invade the trust corpus.

C. Property the husband received through the state's elective share statute.

D. A vacation home the husband received from his wife that allows him to use the property for life. At his death, the property will pass to his wife's son from a previous marriage, as she directed.

15-2. Skip was married to Libby when he died three months ago. Which of the following property interests qualifies for the marital deduction in his estate?

A. The value of Skip's revocable trust that named Libby as the trust beneficiary after Skip's death.

B. Skip was the owner of a whole-life insurance policy on Libby's life. The life insurance policy named Libby as the contingent owner upon Skip's death.

C. A painting that Skip and his former wife, Olivia, purchased on their honeymoon that Skip bequeathed to Olivia.

D. Skip was the recipient of a life estate that his father gave him in the family cottage in Maine. The residuary clause in Skip's will left the rest and residue of his estate to his wife, Libby.

15-3. Which of the following statements regarding a QDOT is incorrect?

A. A U.S. citizen spouse cannot gift property to a non-citizen spouse unless a QDOT is established before the gift is made.

B. The estate tax attributed to the deceased spouse's property can be paid by withholding a portion of the tax from lifetime distributions made to the non-citizen spouse from the QDOT.

C. The non-citizen spouse must receive all income annually for life.

D. The non-citizen spouse can establish a QDOT if the citizen spouse did not establish the trust prior to his death.

15-4. All of the following statements regarding a qualified disclaimer are correct except:

A. For federal tax purposes, the disclaimant is regarded as never having received the property and is treated as if he predeceased the transferor.

B. Disclaimed property that is transferred to a person who is two or more generations below the decedent may be subject to a GST tax, depending on the amount of GST tax exemption allocated to the transfer.

C. A Disclaimer Trust will bypass inclusion in the surviving spouse's taxable estate.

D. Property that is disclaimed by the surviving spouse receives a marital deduction in the decedent spouse's estate.

15-5. Louise died and left her entire estate of $20 million to her husband, Dirk. Dirk disclaimed $5,430,000 of her property that was directed into a Disclaimer Trust established in Louise's will. Dirk will receive all the income from this trust for life and the corpus will pass to their son at Dirk's death. Based on this information, which of the following statements are correct?

A. The property in the Disclaimer Trust will not be taxed in Dirk's estate at death.

B. Dirk must disclaim the entire $20 million of Louise's property for the qualified disclaimer to be effective.

C. A marital deduction for the $5,430,000 transferred into the trust is not available to Louise's estate.

D. Louise's executor must qualify the property for the qualified disclaimer technique on IRS Form 706.

Chapter 16

Marital Trusts

CFP® CERTIFICATION EXAMINATION PRINCIPAL TOPICS COVERED IN THIS CHAPTER:

Types, features, and taxation of trusts

- Bypass trust
- Marital trust
- Qualified terminable interest property (QTIP) trust

Deferral and minimization of estate taxes

- Marital deduction and bypass trust planning

Learning Objectives

To ensure that you have a solid understanding of marital trusts and estate planning techniques for married couples, the following learning objectives are addressed in this chapter:

- Understand the concept of "over-qualifying" a decedent's estate for the marital deduction and know which trusts and techniques are available to rectify this problem.

- Describe the tax and nontax characteristics of the bypass trust.

- Evaluate when a particular marital trust should be used to meet clients' estate planning objectives.

- Explain the relationship between the marital deduction and the qualified terminable interest property trust.

- Determine when estate equalization should be used to minimize tax on a couple's combined estates.

- Describe the benefits and disadvantages of portability.

Chapter Contents

Overview

The Unified Credit

The Bypass Trust

    Bypass Trust and the Marital Deduction

Marital Trusts

    Power of Appointment Trust
    QTIP Trust
    Estate Marital Trust

Portability

    Drawbacks of Portability

Marital Planning Techniques

    Estate Equalization
    Bypass Trust with Estate Equalization
    Bypass Planning versus Portability

Chapter Highlights

Key Terms

Review Questions

OVERVIEW

One of the most common estate planning goals couples have is to give the surviving spouse full use of the family's economic wealth while minimizing the total federal estate tax payable at the death of both spouses. Married couples can easily eliminate federal estate taxes entirely at the death of the first spouse through a plan that capitalizes on the unlimited marital deduction, but the challenge is to minimize estate taxes in the couple's combined estates.

The marital deduction is a deduction for gift or estate tax purposes for property passing to a spouse either outright or into a qualifying trust. The unified credit is provided to each taxpayer and can be applied against either gift taxes or estate taxes. Planning for married couples involves coordinating the marital deduction with the unified credit so that the credit can reduce or eliminate the decedent spouse's estate tax liability. The marital deduction can offset and defer any remaining tax in the decedent's estate.

Financial planners must know how to evaluate the pros and cons of various estate planning trusts and tax-saving techniques that are available to transfer marital property to surviving spouses. Planners should work closely with the client's attorney and estate planning team to choose the most appropriate trusts and strategies to meet their client's estate planning objectives.

Practice Standard 400-2

Developing the Financial Planning Recommendation(s)

The financial planning practitioner shall develop the recommendation(s) based on the selected alternative(s) and the current course of action in an effort to reasonably meet the client's goals, needs and priorities.

THE UNIFIED CREDIT

A unified credit is available to each person's estate to reduce his estate tax liability. Married couples often have simple wills that leave all of their property to the surviving spouse at death, and this arrangement will avoid an estate tax on the first spouse's estate. But if all of the decedent's property is entitled to a marital deduction, then the spouse may have "**over-qualified" his estate for the marital deduction** and "under-utilized" the unified credit. If all assets were to pass outright to the surviving spouse, then the assets included in the surviving spouse's gross estate could be needlessly taxed. Therefore, married couples with significant wealth should plan their estates so that each spouse takes advantage of his own unified credit.

Individuals can transfer up to $5,430,000 in 2015 either during their lifetime or at their death before a transfer tax is due. Married couples have the advantage of both spouses' unified credits to offset the tax on transfers from their combined estates of up to $10,860,000 in 2015.

Couples who do not have such a sizable estate may not need to engage in sophisticated planning techniques because they can transfer property to each other outright, or in trust, without triggering a federal estate tax in either spouse's estate.

THE BYPASS TRUST

When a married couple has a sizeable estate, each spouse can establish a **bypass trust** to take advantage of his available estate tax exemption. The bypass trust is often called the "B" Trust, the **credit shelter trust**, or the **family trust**. The surviving spouse is typically the beneficiary of this trust; however, children or other beneficiaries are permitted.

An amount equal to the estate tax exclusion of $5,430,000 (assuming no lifetime taxable gifts were made) is carved from the decedent's estate and passes to the bypass trust. The trust property is included in the decedent's gross estate, but the unified credit is used to offset the estate tax on this property. The result is that the decedent's estate is not over-qualified for the marital deduction. The property also bypasses inclusion in the surviving spouse's estate—hence, the name "bypass" trust. Therefore, the trust property is not subject to an estate tax in either spouse's estate.

It is common for bypass provisions to be included in either a testamentary trust or an inter-vivos revocable trust. The trust is funded with property that the decedent owned individually, or with the decedent's interest in property owned as a tenant in common.

Practitioner Tip: It is imperative that asset ownership be coordinated with a couple's estate plan. Property the couple owned as joint tenants with right of survivorship or as tenants by the entirety may need to be retitled or the asset will pass to the survivor and not to the bypass trust. The financial planner should ensure that the client understands the need to retitle his assets, and that he understands the potential risks of doing so. For example, the couple will lose joint creditor protection for property titled as a tenancy by the entirety if the property is divided and retitled for individual ownership.

The spouse as beneficiary of a bypass trust has a lifetime interest in the trust but does not have direct control over the trust income or assets. Unlike a marital trust, there is no requirement that all trust income must be paid annually to the surviving spouse.

Although the trustee can be directed to distribute the net income of this trust to the surviving spouse during the spouse's lifetime, income can also accumulate in the trust. Furthermore, income can be directed to other beneficiaries at the trustee's discretion through a "sprinkle" or "spray" clause in the trust instrument. The income produced by the trust assets will be taxable to the trust if the income is accumulated or to the income beneficiary if it is paid out.

Practitioner Tip: A client's future income needs and tax rates should be examined first to determine the appropriate distribution provisions. Allowing large amounts of income to accumulate in this trust can result in adverse income taxation because the top income tax rate of 39.6% kicks in at $12,301 for trusts in 2015. To put that in perspective, the 39.6%

rate generally does not apply to individuals until income exceeds $413,200. By allowing the trustee to distribute trust income, the income and the tax liability may be shifted to beneficiaries in lower income tax brackets.

Client Situation

Adam and Maureen have two children. Each spouse has an estate of $7 million. Their attorney established a revocable trust for each spouse that included bypass planning. Per the terms of the trust, an amount equal to the remaining estate tax exemption ($5,430,000 in 2015) would be carved from their respective estates to fund each bypass trust. Assume that Maureen dies in 2015. Adam could receive income from the trust, if needed, but he will not receive mandatory income distributions every year. The $5,430,000 is included in Maureen's gross estate, but her unified credit offsets the estate tax on this property. When Adam dies the trust will terminate, and each child will receive one-half of the trust assets. The trust corpus will "bypass" inclusion in Adam's gross estate because of the terminable interest he has in this trust.

To give the surviving spouse greater control over the ultimate disposition of trust assets without causing later estate taxation, the surviving spouse can be given a **special or limited power of appointment** under this bypass trust. For example, a surviving spouse (the holder) might be given the right to appoint all or any part of the assets in the bypass trust to a limited class of beneficiaries, such as the children of the grantor. This means that the surviving spouse can appoint the assets in this trust only to the specified beneficiaries, but can do so in any proportion or amount the spouse desires. Such a power of appointment will not be classified as a **general power of appointment** and will not subject the corpus of the trust to federal estate taxes at the death of the holder so long as the power cannot be exercised in favor of the holder of the power, his estate, his creditors, or the creditors of his estate.

The spouse may also be given the right to exercise the power according to an **ascertainable standard** for the holder's health, education, maintenance and support. This limited power would prevent the trust corpus from being included in the spouse's estate but would give the surviving spouse some control over the disposition of the property.

Practitioner Tip: The inclusion of a limited power of appointment gives the survivor flexibility to determine how assets should be appropriately distributed. This is particularly attractive when the children are very young at the first spouse's death. Although many parents believe that age 25, 30, or even 40 are appropriate ages for distribution when children are young, as those ages approach, many parents do not think their children can handle the financial responsibility of inheriting the trust assets. That is why allowing the surviving spouse discretion to determine the appropriate age or method of distribution through a limited power of appointment may be more beneficial than outright distribution of the assets at predetermined ages.

> **Client Situation**
>
> When Maureen died, the trustee of the bypass trust could make discretionary income distributions to Adam. A trust provision also included an ascertainable standard so that Adam could appoint additional trust property to himself or others to pay for expenses relating to health, education, maintenance, and support. Adam has a limited power of appointment, not a general power of appointment, and the trust property will not be included in his gross estate.

The bypass trust can also safely provide the surviving spouse a noncumulative limited right of withdrawal. Usually, the surviving spouse is provided with a "noncumulative" (use it or lose it) right to withdraw each year the greater of 5% of the trust corpus or $5,000. Although this **5-and-5 power** will not cause the entire corpus to be subject to estate tax, the amount subject to withdrawal in the year of the surviving spouse's death will be included in the surviving spouse's estate.

> **Client Situation**
>
> If Maureen's bypass trust also gave Adam the right to withdraw the greater of $5,000 or 5% of the trust corpus each year, then in the year that Adam dies, his estate will include either $5,000 or 5% of the trust corpus, whichever amount is greater. However if Adam had withdrawn an amount subject to this power in the year he died, then the greater of $5,000 or 5% of the trust corpus would be not included in his gross estate.

At the death of the surviving spouse, the bypass trust can continue to function for the benefit of the grantor's family or, more commonly, the trust can be terminated and the appropriate amounts paid to the remainder trust beneficiaries, who are typically the couple's children.

Bypass Trust and the Marital Deduction

A bypass trust will give the surviving spouse limited access to the trust income and corpus. Couples with large estates may want the surviving spouse to have direct access and control over more of the marital assets without paying an estate tax at the first spouse's death. This goal can be accomplished by combining the bypass trust with the marital deduction in the decedent spouse's estate. The bypass trust is funded first and the balance of the decedent's assets are passed outright to the surviving spouse or transferred to a marital trust. The decedent spouse will not have an estate tax liability because the marital deduction and the unified credit are both used to offset the tax. But assets not consumed by the spouse or that remain in the marital trust will be subject to estate tax at the death of the surviving spouse because of the broad powers the survivor is given in the trusts.

Practitioner Tip: A decision must be made as to how much of the marital deduction property should be subject to the surviving spouse's power to say where it goes at the survivor's death. This is particularly true in second or late-life marriages.

MARITAL TRUSTS

Three common marital trusts provide a decedent's estate with a marital deduction. Recall that when a marital deduction is available to a decedent's estate the property is included in the surviving spouse's estate. Often, the decedent's will establishes two separate trusts: a marital trust (known as the "A" trust) and a bypass trust or "B" trust. This is referred to as **A-B trust planning**. A marital trust, the "A" Trust, may be a power of appointment trust, a QTIP trust, or an estate trust.

Power of Appointment Trust

A **power of appointment trust** gives the surviving spouse a right to all of the trust income for life, payable at least annually. The trust gives the surviving spouse a power to appoint the property during lifetime or by will at death to anyone the surviving spouse wishes, including to the surviving spouse's estate.

This gives the spouse a general power of appointment over the trust assets and qualifies the trust property for the marital deduction in the decedent spouse's estate. Consequently, the value of the trust property will be included in the spouse's estate unless it is consumed or given away before the survivor's death. The power must be exercisable by the surviving spouse in all events, and no person can have any power to appoint any part of the trust assets to someone other than the surviving spouse.

Client Situation

Brett and Natalie were married for 60 years when Brett died in 2015. Brett had an estate worth $12 million comprised of individually owned assets at his death. Brett's will established a bypass trust and $5,430,000 was transferred into the trust for the benefit of Natalie and the children. Brett left the rest of his estate to Natalie in a power of appointment trust, and named her co-trustee of the trust. Natalie had the right to spend the income and corpus from this trust without restriction and could determine the beneficiaries of this trust in her will.

There was no estate tax due at Brett's death, but Natalie's estate will pay a tax on the $6,570,000 she inherited from Brett's estate when she dies. If the assets in the power of appointment trust appreciate in value, this will increase the amount of estate tax that Natalie's estate would owe. Natalie should spend down the assets from the power of appointment trust before taking any distributions from the bypass trust, because the assets in the bypass trust will not be included in her estate. Natalie's estate can use her unified credit to offset the estate tax from the power of appointment trust at her death.

Practitioner Tip: Married couples living in a community property state could have separate property as well as community property; both kinds of property must be considered in determining the amount that will be optimal for the marital deduction.

QTIP Trust

A **qualified terminable interest property (QTIP) trust** allows the decedent spouse's estate a marital deduction for property passing to a trust for the benefit of the surviving spouse, even though the decedent controlled the passing of trust property at the surviving spouse's death. The QTIP trust ensures that at least some or all of the marital deduction property passes to the decedent's chosen beneficiaries at the surviving spouse's death. This is particularly appealing in second and late-life marriages.

A marital deduction is not available to a decedent's estate for terminable interest property that passes to the surviving spouse unless the executor makes an election to have the trust treated as a QTIP trust on the decedent's estate tax return. In a QTIP trust the surviving spouse must receive all of the trust income for life, payable at least annually. The grantor can determine whether trust principal is distributable to the surviving spouse, but it is not required. The spouse can be given a 5-and-5 power to appoint the greater of $5,000 or 5% of the trust corpus each year. No other beneficiary has a right to receive trust income or principal during the surviving spouse's lifetime. The spouse must have the power to require the trustee to make the assets produce income if the trust is funded with non-income-producing assets.

If the executor elects to take a marital deduction at the first spouse's death for assets going into the QTIP trust, then the assets remaining in the trust at the death of the surviving spouse will be included in the surviving spouse's estate. Thus, the marital deduction has merely deferred the tax on any assets in this trust that are not used up for the benefit of the surviving spouse.

Any assets remaining in this trust at the survivor's death will be distributed to the beneficiaries that the grantor has named, and the surviving spouse cannot choose the trust beneficiaries. The remainder beneficiaries are likely to be the grantor's children or other beneficiaries. Trust corpus can be distributed outright or remain in trust as the grantor stipulated. The spouse's executor can seek reimbursement for estate taxes assessed on this property from the trust beneficiaries because the spouse's estate has a "right of recovery."

Client Situation

Leo had an estate valued at $20 million when he died in 2015. Leo had been married to Brenda, his second wife, for 20 years. Leo had three children from his first marriage. Leo's estate was structured so that the exclusion amount at the time of his death ($5,430,000 in 2015) would be transferred into a bypass trust. An additional $5 million was transferred into a power of appointment trust, which gave Brenda complete access to the assets during her life and enabled her to appoint the property to whomever she desired at her death. The remaining $9,570,000 was placed into a trust that would pay Brenda all of the trust income every year and distribute the trust corpus to Leo's children at Brenda's death. Leo's executor made an election to treat the assets in this trust as qualified terminable interest property.

Leo's estate paid no estate tax because the property transferred into the power of appointment trust and the QTIP trust was entitled to a marital deduction in Leo's estate, and because the tax on the nonmarital property in the "B" trust was offset by Leo's unified credit. Assuming the assets in all of these trusts did not appreciate at the time of Brenda's death, the amount included in Brenda's estate would be $5 million from the power of appointment trust and $9,570,000 from the QTIP trust. Brenda's unified credit would be available to offset the tax in her estate.

Practitioner Tip: If a couple's objective is for the survivor to be given a testamentary power of disposition over only a portion of the assets, then a power of appointment trust should be used for that purpose, and the balance of the assets can go into a QTIP trust. Both trusts will qualify for the marital deduction and be included in the survivor's estate, but only the beneficiary of the power of appointment trust can appoint property to others at death.

Estate Marital Trust

The **estate trust** (also called the *estate marital trust*) is another trust that provides for a marital deduction in the decedent spouse's estate for property transferred into the trust. This trust is indicated when:

- there is a need or desire to invest in non-income-producing property;

- the survivor will not need trust assets or income during the survivor's lifetime; and

- the property placed in trust is not likely to appreciate substantially in value.

The surviving spouse has a right to receive all or part of the income earned by the trust for life, but distributions are made to the spouse at the trustee's discretion. The remainder of the trust, both corpus and accumulated income, must be payable to the surviving spouse's estate at death. This entitles the decedent's estate to a marital deduction for property placed in this trust. The surviving spouse will determine the ultimate beneficiaries of this trust under his or her will.

An estate trust falls outside the terminable interest rules because no income or corpus passes to anyone other than the spouse and the spouse's estate. This enables the trustee to accumulate income or invest in non-income-producing property. However, accumulations will be taxed as part of the surviving spouse's estate at death along with the original corpus.

Client Situation

Neil and Betsy were married without children and had amassed a fortune in their separate investment and real estate portfolios. Betsy funded a revocable bypass trust prior to her death this year and arranged for the remainder of her estate to pass into a power of appointment trust and an estate trust for Neil, the sole beneficiary of each trust. Betsy's appreciating investments were placed in the power of appointment trust and the real estate holdings that were not expected to appreciate were placed in the estate trust. Betsy's estate was not subject to an estate tax because of the marital deduction and unified credit that were available to her estate to eliminate the tax. Neil neither needed nor wanted the property placed in the estate trust, but the value of this trust and the power of appointment trust will be included in Neil's gross estate when he dies.

Table 16.1 summarizes some of the features of marital and nonmarital trusts.

Table 16.1 A Comparison of Marital and Nonmarital Trusts

	Bypass Trust	"A" Trust	QTIP Trust	Estate Trust
Qualifies for marital deduction in decedent's estate	No	Yes	Yes	Yes
Included in survivor's estate	No	Yes	Yes	Yes
Survivor has testamentary control over the assets	No	Yes	No	Yes
Provides income to survivor	Discretionary	Annually	Annually	Discretionary

PORTABILITY

Portability is a concept that was introduced with the Tax Act of 2010. Prior to this act, the estate tax exemption was a "use it or lose it" exemption. If a decedent did not take advantage of his available federal estate tax exemption at death, the opportunity to shelter those assets from tax was lost. Therefore, if the decedent left all assets to his surviving spouse, those assets would be subject to tax in her estate.

Under the concept of portability, a surviving spouse can increase his **applicable exclusion amount** of $5,430,000 in 2015; (now referred to as the *basic exclusion amount*) by the amount of the **deceased spousal unused exclusion amount (DSUEA)**. The DSUEA is added to a surviving spouse's basic exclusion amount to reduce gift and/or estate taxes on the married couple's combined taxable estates.

Portability can lessen the need to implement bypass trust planning for married couples with combined estates valued at less than $10,860,000.

Client Situation

Mark and Eileen were married for 45 years when Mark died in 2015. Mark had a gross estate of $2 million and adjusted taxable gifts of $1 million. His $3 million taxable estate did not incur an estate tax because it was less than the exemption equivalent of $5,430,000. Under portability, $2,430,000 of Mark's unused exclusion (DSUEA) was transferred to Eileen. Eileen currently has an exclusion of $7,860,000 (her $5,430,000 basic exclusion plus Mark's unused exclusion of $2,430,000.)

Eileen can use this $7,860,000 exclusion against taxable gifts made in her lifetime and/or she can apply it toward her taxable estate. Note that the unused portion of Mark's generation-skipping transfer tax exclusion cannot be transferred to Eileen.

To take advantage of portability, an executor must:

- file a timely estate tax return or file timely extensions (no matter how small the estate);

- compute the DSUEA; and

- make an irrevocable election on the return to utilize the DSUEA.

Drawbacks of Portability

Although portability offers great flexibility within estate planning, certain drawbacks should be considered.

- Portability has been adopted only at the federal level. If a client lives in a state that applies a separate estate tax, each taxpayer should consider sheltering a minimum of the available state estate tax exemption. Otherwise the survivor's estate will be taxed on the amount of assets that remain from the predeceased spouse's estate.

- If a spouse remarries following the first spouse's death, that first spouse's exemption will remain unused as the exemption available at a survivor's death is based on the unused exemption of the *last* deceased spouse. From an administrative perspective, an estate tax return must be filed for the surviving spouse to claim this exemption. This will greatly increase the number of returns that have to be filed, because almost every estate will want the surviving spouse to take advantage of this provision.

- Although the estate tax exemption is portable, the GST exemption is not. Therefore, if a person wants to maximize generation-skipping tax planning, then trusts should be used rather than distributing assets outright to the surviving spouse.

- Trust planning also offers some asset protection benefits. A trust can shelter assets from creditors, whereas no such protection is provided if the assets pass outright to the survivor under the portability provisions. And if assets are given outright to the surviving spouse and the spouse remarries, the assets may not be used as the decedent spouse intended.

- The DSUEA, unlike the basic exclusion amount, is not adjusted for inflation. Therefore, any income and appreciation accruing after the predeceased spouse's death are not sheltered by the DSUEA.

Practitioner Tip: Portability applies in states where same-sex marriage is allowed. However, many state governments do not recognize marriages for same-sex couples. In these states, an estate or gift tax marital deduction will not be allowed for assets passing to a same-sex spouse, and portability will not apply to the surviving spouse. It is therefore important that a same-sex couple implement a bypass trust at each spouse's death to maximize state estate tax savings in states where same-sex marriage is not recognized.

MARITAL PLANNING TECHNIQUES

Savings in federal estate taxes generally occur at the survivor's death, because the estate tax can be reduced to zero in the first spouse's estate. Property inherited by the surviving spouse is included in the survivor's estate and can result in more overall tax if the spouse's estate exceeds the exemption equivalent and the spouse does not remarry or consume the assets in the trust.

Estate Equalization

The concept of equalizing an estate, or **estate equalization**, is often the most economical method of minimizing taxes over the deaths of both husband and wife when their combined estates will be more than $10.86 million in 2015. Because of progressive estate tax rates, taxes can be lessened by paying tax early, when property is increasing in value. For example, if an asset now worth $100,000 is projected to be worth $500,000 at the second death, it is usually much more economical to pay the tax based on the current $100,000 value than on the $500,000 it will be worth later. However, most couples would prefer to minimize the tax at the first spouse's death to leave more assets available for the survivor's support and take the risk of having slightly higher overall taxes.

Bypass Trust with Estate Equalization

Married couples with significantly more wealth than $10.86 million in 2015 may have unequal ownership of their marital assets. The best strategy to minimize estate taxes in both spouses' estates is to have the spouse with the most assets gift an amount to the other spouse that equalizes the taxable value of each estate. This gift would not be taxed because an unlimited marital deduction is available to the donor spouse to offset the taxable gift.

Client Situation

Michael, who was married to Kay, had a gross estate of $16 million when he died in January 2015. All of his property passed to Kay in his will. Kay died in November 2015, and her estate of $16 million consisted of all the property she inherited from Michael's estate. Kay had a taxable estate of $6,345,800 before credits. After utilizing Kay's unified credit and Michael's unused unified credit (DSUEA), Kay's taxable estate was reduced to $2,110,200.

Assume instead that Michael had gifted $8 million to Kay before he died to equalize their estates, and that Michael and Kay had previously established revocable bypass trusts. When Michael died, $5,430,000 was transferred into the bypass trust and the trustee was permitted to distribute income to Kay as needed. This property was included in Michael's estate but it was not taxed. The remainder of his estate ($2,570,000) was left to Kay in his will and qualified for a marital deduction in his estate. No estate tax was paid at Michael's death.

When Kay died, the $2,570,000 in assets she inherited from Michael was added to her estate of $8 million for a total gross estate of $10,570,000. The tax on her estate was $4,173,800 before applying her unified credit, for a taxable estate of $2,056,000.

Michael and Kay saved $54,200 on estate taxes for their combined estates when utilizing the techniques of estate equalization with bypass trusts.

The use of the bypass trust with estate equalization becomes a more valuable strategy with greater estate tax savings when it is applied to larger estates. Couples with estates of less than $5,430,000 do not have to establish trusts for estate tax saving purposes. Transferring assets into a bypass trust or a disclaimer trust would result in a loss of the step-up in income tax basis at the spouse's death when assets are finally distributed to other trust beneficiaries. Instead, there is a full step-up in basis when assets are transferred outright to the surviving spouse or transferred through the decedent's revocable trust, which is an advantage for couples with smaller estates.

Bypass Planning versus Portability

Client Situation

Sandy and Brian have two daughters, Brittany and Erica. Brian has an investment account worth $1,500,000 and owns the couple's home, which is worth $1,500,000. Brian also owns a life insurance policy with a $2 million death benefit on his life. Sandy has a $1 million stock account and owns a $1 million vacation home.

Brian's primary goal is to make sure that Sandy is well provided for during her lifetime, and that everything is left to their two children at Sandy's death. If Brian were to die today and left his property to Sandy, his estate would be distributed accordingly. (See Figure 16.1.) Assuming Brian and Sandy have not made any lifetime taxable gifts, and assuming his executor files a timely estate tax return preserving his unused exemption amount, there would be no federal estate tax following Sandy's death, because of portability.

Brian consulted with his financial planner who suggested that Brian discuss bypass trust planning with his attorney. The planner explained that at his death, rather than leaving all of his assets outright to his wife, Brain could establish a bypass trust for Sandy's benefit. This trust would provide two main benefits. First, assets that passed to the trust would be protected from any creditor claims. Because Sandy is a physician, this is attractive. Second, while Sandy is a brilliant physician, Brian is concerned with her ability to manage the assets. Brian can name a professional trustee to help manage the trust assets.

The trustee would be directed to set aside the amount that could pass free from estate tax at Brian's death, which would be transferred into the bypass trust. (See Figure 16.2.)

The trustee would be directed to pay trust principal and income to Sandy for her health, education, maintenance, or support. Following Sandy's death, these assets would pass to Brittany and Erica per the terms of Brian's trust. The assets would not be subject to tax at Sandy's death because Sandy did not own the assets, Brian's trust did.

The financial planner reminds Brian, that any assets included in a decedent's estate will get a step up in basis to the date of death value. So, if Brian leaves all assets to Sandy, assets would receive a step-up in basis at Brian's death, and, again, at Sandy's death. If, however, Brian chooses to leave assets to a bypass trust, any assets in the trust would not be included in Sandy's estate at her death, and, would not receive the second step-up in basis at her death.

Finally, the financial planner points out that Sandy and Brian currently do not live in a state that imposes a separate state-level estate tax, but that the analysis would be very different if they did.

Figure 16.1 All to Sandy at Brian's Death

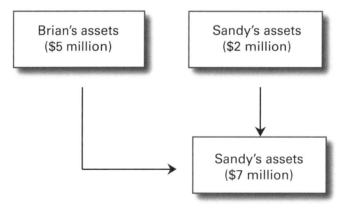

At Sandy's death, $7 million will be included in her gross estate.

Practitioner Tip: It is essential that Brian coordinate ownership of his assets with his estate planning objectives. If Sandy is named the beneficiary of Brian's life insurance policy, for example, that asset will pass to her directly rather than to the bypass trust for her benefit. (See Figure 16.2.)

Figure 16.2 Bypass Planning at Brian's Death

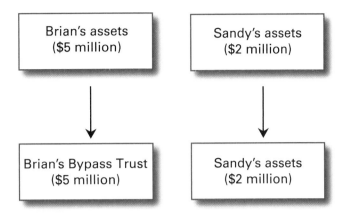

At Sandy's death, $2 million will be included in her gross estate.

Client Situation

Patty and Jim have amassed an enviable estate. Patty has a $2 million mutual fund portfolio and a $2 million bond portfolio. Jim owns the couple's primary residence valued at $1,500,000 and a stock account worth $3 million. When Patty dies, she leaves everything to Jim. At his subsequent death, he will have $8,500,000 of assets passing through his gross estate.

Due to portability and the federal estate tax exemption of remains at $5,430,000 per taxpayer, there will be no federal estate tax due at Jim's death if he dies in 2015. If they live in a state that has a separate state-level estate tax, Patty's exemption will not have been used, and all assets will be subject to a state death tax in Jim's estate. (See Figure 16.3.)

Figure 16.3 All to Jim at Patty's Death.

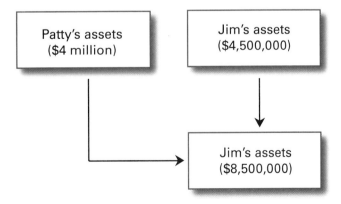

At Jim's death, $8,500,000 will be included in his gross estate.

With bypass trust planning, at Patty's death the estate would be distributed as in Figure 16.4.

Figure 16.4 Bypass Planning at Patty's Death

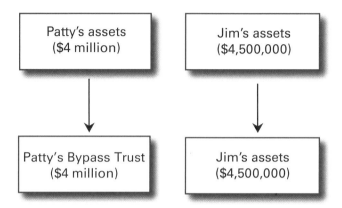

At Jim's death, $4,500,000 will be included in his gross estate because $4 million has been sheltered in Patty's bypass trust.

Practitioner Tip: Typically, only the amount that can pass free from estate tax will be transferred to the bypass trust at the first spouse's death. In the preceding example, if Patty's net worth were $9 million instead of $4 million, only $5,430,000 would pass to the bypass trust, and the remaining $3,570,000 would pass either outright to Jim or to a marital trust for his benefit. (See Figure 16.5.)

Figure 16.5 A-B Planning at Patty's Death

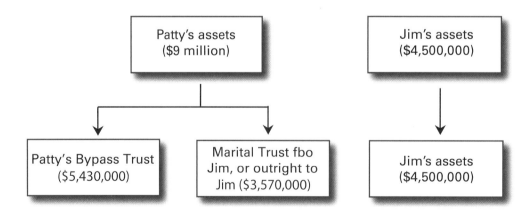

At Jim's death, $8,070,000 will be included in his gross estate because $5,430,000 has been sheltered in Patty's bypass trust.

Chapter Highlights

- Married couples with substantial wealth should equalize their estates and fund bypass trusts to make full use of each spouse's unified credit and to reduce the tax in their combined estates.

- The bypass trust is a terminable interest trust that does not qualify for the marital deduction but takes advantage of a decedent's unified credit. This trust avoids over-qualifying the decedent's estate for the marital deduction.

- The power of appointment trust gives the surviving spouse a general power of appointment over property in the trust, which entitles the decedent's estate to a marital deduction for the value of the trust property.

- A QTIP election allows a decedent's executor to obtain a marital deduction for a lifetime income interest given to the surviving spouse, even though the spouse will not have control over the distribution of the principal. Trust assets are includable in the surviving spouse's estate.

- The purpose of the estate marital trust is to provide the decedent's estate with a marital deduction, but because this property will be included in the survivor's estate, the assets should be non-income producing and not likely to appreciate in value.

- With portability, the unused portion of the decedent's exclusion amount (DSUEA) is added to the surviving spouse's basic exclusion amount to reduce or even eliminate the survivor's gift and estate taxes.

Key Terms

A-B trust planning

applicable exclusion amount

ascertainable standard

basic exclusion amount

bypass trust

credit shelter trust

deceased spousal unused exclusion amount (DSUEA)

estate equalization

estate marital trust

family trust

5-and-5 power

general power of appointment

over-qualifying the estate for the marital deduction

portability

power of appointment trust

QTIP trust

special or limited power of appointment

Review Questions

16-1. Randy and Janet have an estate worth $20 million and all of the assets are titled in Randy's name. After meeting with a financial planner, the couple established the following estate planning objectives: To give the surviving spouse lifetime and testamentary control over assets that will be professionally managed; to utilize their unified credits; and to minimize their total estate tax liability for their combined estates. Which techniques and trusts will accomplish their goals?

A. A QTIP trust

B. Bypass trusts for each spouse

C. A power of appointment trust

D. Estate equalization

16-2. Carmen and Elayna have been married for four years, and Carmen has two grown children from a previous marriage. Carmen has a successful business and a rapidly appreciating estate that is currently valued at $14 million. Carmen wants his children to be the sole beneficiaries of his estate, to prevent a new spouse from getting any of his property if Elayna were to remarry. He wants to establish two trusts, which gives Elayna all the income from one trust and some income if needed from another. Which trusts will accomplish all of Carmen's goals?

A. A bypass trust and a power of appointment trust

B. A QTIP trust and an estate marital trust

C. A bypass trust and a QTIP trust

D. A power of appointment trust and a QTIP trust

16-3. Irene was a very wealthy woman who died recently and left the following property to her husband Albert. Which property interests will not be included in Albert's estate when he dies?

A. Irene's one-third ownership in a ski resort that she owned as a tenant in common.

B. A building zoned for commercial real estate that she owned with Albert as tenants by the entirety.

C. A parcel of undeveloped land transferred into an estate marital trust.

D. Stocks disclaimed by Albert that passed through Irene's residuary estate to a disclaimer trust. Albert is the trust beneficiary and can receive discretionary income distributions from the trustee.

16-4. Max and his three children were the beneficiaries of a bypass trust established when Max's wife died. Provisions in the trust gave Max the right to income if needed, combined with a 5-and-5 power over the trust corpus. Max could also appoint all or part of the assets in the trust to his children. When Max died the trust was valued at $6 million, and Max had not exercised the power to make withdrawals from the trust that year. What amount was included in Max's gross estate at death?

A. $0

B. $5,000

C. $300,000

D. $6 million

16-5. Darnell died in February 2013 with a total gross estate of $700,000, which he left to his wife Alicia in his will. Alicia married Jesse in October 2013, but Jesse's daughter Faith did not accept Alicia, and the strain of this marriage caused Jesse to die prematurely in January 2015. Jesse had a gross estate of $4 million and had made prior taxable gifts of $1 million. He left $2 million to Faith and $2 million to Alicia in his will. Alicia died in November 2015. What was Alicia's applicable exclusion amount at her death?

A. $2 million

B. $2,430,000

C. $5,430,000

D. $7,860,000

E. $10,860,000

Chapter 17

Charitable Transfers

CFP® CERTIFICATION EXAMINATION PRINCIPAL TOPIC COVERED IN THIS CHAPTER:

Charitable Transfers

- Outright gifts
- Charitable remainder trusts
  - Unitrusts (CRUTs)
  - Annuity trusts (CRATs)
- Charitable lead trusts
  - Unitrusts (CLUTs)
  - Annuity trusts (CLATs)

- Charitable gift annuities
- Pooled income funds
- Private foundations
- Donor-advised funds
- Estate and gift taxation

Learning Objectives

To ensure that you have an understanding of the manner in which charitable transfers can be made and the tax implications of the various methods of charitable transfers, the following learning objectives are addressed in this chapter:

- Understand when a gift or bequest qualifies as a charitable transfer.

- Explain the income, gift, and estate tax consequences of charitable transfers.

- Identify and select the various charitable transfer vehicles that are appropriate

for a client based on current and future income needs and tax advantages.

- Compare and contrast the differences between charitable remainder trusts and a charitable lead trust.

Chapter Contents

Overview

What Is a Charity?

Public Charities

Direct Gifts to Charity

Income Taxation of Charitable Gifts

    Charitable Transfers at Death

Charitable Techniques

    Donor-advised Funds
    Private Foundations

Split-interest Charitable Transfers

    Charitable Remainder Trusts
        Charitable Remainder Annuity Trusts
        Charitable Remainder Unitrusts
        Net Income Makeup Charitable
            Remainder Unitrust
    Charitable Lead Trusts
    Pooled Income Funds
    Charitable Gift Annuities
    Charitable Remainders

Chapter Highlights

Key Terms

Review Questions

OVERVIEW

A charitable contribution is a gratuitous transfer of property to a charitable, religious, scientific, educational, or other specified organization. Individuals have many reasons to make a charitable transfer. Many are charitably inclined and want to benefit certain organizations, for example an organization that they might volunteer for, their church, or their alma mater. Charitable giving, during lifetime or at death, can fulfill a client's philanthropic inclinations.

There are also certain tax benefits to making charitable transfers. If the donee (recipient) of a gift falls within one of the categories designated in the Internal Revenue Code, a charitable deduction can be taken for income, gift, or estate tax purposes. Charitable contributions have tax value; therefore, they can result in a current income tax deduction, reduce federal estate taxes, and be made free of gift tax. From the charity's point of view, charitable contributions are also tax favored: the charity itself pays no tax upon receipt of either a lifetime gift or a bequest and, generally, no income tax is paid by the qualified charity on income it earns from donated property.

Numerous options are available for making charitable transfers. To make appropriate recommendations, financial planners must understand the tax and non-tax implications of the various trusts and other charitable vehicles that can be used to accomplish a client's charitable goals.

Practice Standard 200-1

Determining a Client's Personal and Financial Goals, Needs and Priorities

The financial planning practitioner and the client shall mutually define the client's personal and financial goals, needs and priorities that are relevant to the scope of the engagement before any recommendation is made and/or implemented.

WHAT IS A CHARITY?

It is important to first determine whether a donee organization is, in fact, a charity. Charitable contributions may be deductible for income, gift, and estate tax purposes if they are made to a **qualified charity**. A donee will be considered qualified only if it meets all three of these conditions:

1. It must be operated exclusively for religious, charitable, scientific, literary, or educational purposes; to foster national or international amateur sports competition; or to prevent cruelty to children or animals.

2. No part of the organization's earnings can benefit any private shareholder or similar individual.

3. The organization cannot be one disqualified for tax exemption because it attempts to influence legislation or participates in, publishes or distributes statements for, or intervenes in any political campaign on behalf of any candidate seeking public office.[1]

Certain organizations are not considered charitable organizations, and gifts made to such groups do not qualify as charitable transfers. For example, contributions to political parties are not considered charitable transfers, and a taxpayer who makes a contribution to a political party cannot deduct that contribution for income tax purposes. Contributions to political parties are not considered gifts for gift tax purposes; however, if a decedent leaves assets to a political party, they will be distributed after the estate tax has been paid.

Practitioner Tip: It is very important that a donee organization actually qualify as a charity for the taxpayer to be able to claim a deduction. If an organization purports to be a qualified charity but is not actually a qualified charity, the taxpayer will not be permitted the deduction. This can have serious implications for a client's estate, gift, or income tax liability. The client or practitioner should ascertain whether a potential donee is qualified under the Internal Revenue Code. The IRS publishes a list of qualified charities in IRS Publication 78, which can be viewed on the IRS Web site at apps.irs.gov/app/pub78. If it is not listed in IRS Publication 78, it is wise to request a determination letter from the IRS indicating whether the charity does or does not qualify.

PUBLIC CHARITIES

Charitable organizations are classified as **public charities** or **private charities**. The IRS lists a number of organizations that are considered public charitable organizations. Many public charities are very well known, such as the American Red Cross. Public charities include:

- churches;

- educational institutions (or organizations that benefit certain state and municipal colleges and universities);

- hospitals and medical research organizations;

- the U.S. government or a state or possession of the U.S. government (assuming the gift was made for public purposes);

- charities that have active fundraising programs and receive contributions from many sources (such as the Salvation Army or Big Brothers, Big Sisters);

- charities that receive income from the conduct of activities in furtherance of the organization's exempt purpose; and

- charities that actively function in a supporting relationship to one or more existing public charities.

DIRECT GIFTS TO CHARITY

A **direct gift to charity** is probably one of the simplest income tax and estate planning techniques. During lifetime, such a gift can be accomplished merely by writing a check, assigning stock, transferring life insurance policies, signing a deed to real estate, or conveying property to charity in any other standard outright manner.

Likewise, at death gifts to charity can be made by will, by life insurance contract, by employee benefit contract (i.e., the death benefits from a pension plan, IRA, 401(k) plan, or nonqualified deferred compensation plan can be paid to charity), or by trust. Generally, lifetime gifts to charity yield both higher tax and non-tax rewards.

Client Situation

Caitlin is very involved in her university's alumni organization and wishes to make a charitable contribution to her university. She plans on giving $100,000 to the university this year and leaving $1 million to the university at her death. When Caitlin transfers $100,000 to the university there is no gift tax consequence because the university is a qualified charity. Caitlin can deduct $100,000 as an itemized deduction on her income tax return, subject to certain adjusted gross income (AGI) limitations and depending on the type of property that Caitlin donates. At death, Caitlin's estate can take a $1 million deduction for the amounts left to her university.

Practitioner Tip: Charities do not pay income tax; therefore, there is an opportunity to leverage gifts. For gifts during lifetime, securities or other assets that have appreciated significantly can be an appropriate charitable gift. The donor will be able to deduct the fair market value (FMV) of the donated securities, and all of the capital gain will escape taxation because the individual never realized the gain. Since 2006, taxpayers age 70½ or older have been permitted to make charitable contributions directly from their IRAs to charity. These distributions must come directly from an IRA (and not another qualified plan) and must be distributed directly to the charity (not a donor advised fund). The annual limit has been $100,000 per taxpayer per year. The legislation has typically expired every year or every two years, but has been part of a tax extenders package. Currently, this legislation has not been extended beyond the 2014 tax year. If it is, this is another way for a taxpayer to leverage gifts to charity. The financial planner must understand the client's income tax situation in order to understand which type of lifetime charitable gift will give the taxpayer the most leverage. At death, retirement plan assets could be suitable for a charitable contribution. Individual beneficiaries would have to pay income tax on distributions from retirement plans, but a charity does not have to pay income tax.

Client Situation

Caitlin meets with her financial planner and reviews her lifetime charitable goals and estate planning goals. Aside from the charitable goals described above, Caitlin wants to leave all assets to her brother Matt. She has $5 million of securities with a basis of $250,000, a home worth $500,000 and an IRA worth $2 million. Her financial planner advises her that she could give the securities to the university while she is alive. Caitlin will be able to give her appreciated securities to the university and can deduct the full FMV of the donated securities without realizing and paying tax on the significant capital gain. At death, Caitlin can give her IRA to the university. At Caitlin's death, the remaining securities will receive a step-up in basis to the date-of-death value, so there will be no income tax liability if Matt liquidates the account. If Caitlin left her IRA to Matt, he would have to pay income tax on the distributions he receives from the IRA.

INCOME TAXATION OF CHARITABLE GIFTS

To qualify for a charitable deduction, there must be an actual transfer of property to a charitable organization. This property can be in the form of cash, securities, bonds, tangible personal property, intangible property, or real estate, just to name a few. A charitable deduction is allowed to the extent that the value of the transfer exceeds any value received by the donor. For example, if a donor purchases a ticket to a dinner and lecture at a local university for $100, the allowable charitable deduction will be $100 less the benefit that the donor received for the dinner and lecture.

The donation of time or services is ineligible for a gift tax charitable deduction. For example, if a carpenter spent 10 hours building chairs for his church, he could not deduct his normal hourly wage as a charitable contribution. However, he could deduct the cost of materials that he purchased and used in producing the finished product.

Likewise, a taxpayer who donates the use of his property to a charity has not made a contribution of property. So the rent-free use of an office—or even an office building—no matter how valuable is not considered a charitable contribution any more than a contribution of personal services.

When a donor makes a gift to a public charity during his lifetime, the donor may be entitled to an itemized deduction on his income tax return. A taxpayer can deduct the fair market value of his direct gifts to charity as an itemized deduction, subject to certain AGI limitations, described in Code section 170. The amount of the deduction is limited by the type of property contributed and the type of entity that it is given to. It is important to note that these limitations apply only to a donor's income tax deduction and not to the unlimited gift tax or estate tax deductions.

Gifts of cash can be deducted up to 50% of the donor's AGI. Gifts of appreciated securities that have been held for one year or longer can be deducted up to 30% of the donor's AGI. Other types of property could have different AGI limitations (see Table 17.1).

Practitioner Tip: If a taxpayer makes a charitable gift that exceeds AGI limitations, the excess charitable contribution can be carried forward for up to five years and be claimed as an itemized deduction in future years.

Note that the AGI Limitations that are shown in Table 17.1 also are subject to the phase-out of itemized deductions. Single Taxpayers with AGI exceeding $258,250 and Married taxpayers with AGI exceeding $309,900 will begin to realize a phase-out of itemized deductions. The total amount of certain itemized deductions (including charitable contributions) is reduced by 3% of the amount by which the taxpayer's AGI exceeds the threshold amount, with the reduction not to exceed 80% of the otherwise allowable itemized deductions.

Table 17.1 Charitable Income Tax Deduction—AGI Limitations

Property Gifted	Public Charity	Private Charity
Cash	50%	30%
Ordinary income assets (i.e., securities held for less than 1 year)	50% Limited to basis	30% Limited to basis
Appreciated long-term capital gain property (i.e., securities held for more than 1 year)	FMV up to 30% or basis up to 50%	FMV up to 20% or basis up to 30%
Tangible personal property held more than 1 year (use related)	FMV up to 30% or basis up to 50%	FMV up to 20% or basis up to 30%
Tangible personal property (unrelated use)	50% limited to basis	30% limited to basis
Life insurance	Basis up to 50% or replacement value up to 30%	Basis or replacement value up to 30%

Practitioner Tip: To claim an income tax deduction, a taxpayer must meet certain documentation requirements. For example, a taxpayer who has donated more than $250 to a qualified charity must have a receipt from that charity showing the contribution. Similar requirements apply to tangible personal property, automobiles, and securities.

Client Situation

Mary wrote a check to the ASPCA for $16,000 this year. Her AGI is $30,000; therefore, her charitable income tax deduction is limited to $15,000 (50% for cash donated to a public charity). Mary has a charitable contribution carryover of $1,000.

Client Situation

Bill was an apprentice photographer in 1960 when he purchased some of Arthur Griffith's photographs for $1,500. Today, the collection is valued at $18,000 and Bill would like to donate this work to the Chicago Institute of Art to be displayed. Because the property is being donated for a related use, he can deduct the FMV of the photographs up to 30% of his AGI, which is $8,000. Therefore, he can deduct 30% of his AGI ($2,400) for this long-term gain and carry over the excess of $15,600.

Client Situation

Susan bought stock three months ago for $15,000 and donated it today to a public charity. The FMV of the stock is $19,000, and Susan's AGI is $34,000. Because the stock was held for less than one year, Susan's charitable deduction will be limited to her basis ($15,000) up to 50% of her AGI.

Client Situation

Bobby had a stamp collection worth $50,000 with a basis of $20,000 that he donated to the American Cancer Society in honor of his late wife. His AGI is $90,000, but because the gift is unrelated to the purpose of the charity, Bobby's income tax deduction will be limited to his basis ($20,000).

Charitable Transfers at Death

An estate can deduct the FMV of any gifts made to charity at death to the extent the property was included in the decedent's taxable estate. A charitable contribution at death is deductible regardless of whether it is made by will, trust, or the terms of a life insurance policy. But to be deductible by the decedent, he must make the gift, as distinguished from a transfer made by his estate or beneficiaries. Therefore, a deduction is not allowed for a bequest to charity if the bequest requires the approval of a third party.

There is no gift tax for gifts made to qualifying charities during life because an unlimited gift tax charitable deduction is available to offset the tax on the gift. Consequently, no lifetime charitable gifts are added to a decedent's estate tax return as an adjusted taxable gift. Generally, lifetime gifts to charity yield both higher tax and non-tax rewards.

CHARITABLE TECHNIQUES

Donor-advised Funds

A **donor-advised fund** is a type of public charity to which individuals can make charitable contributions. Donor-advised funds are typically community foundations or funds overseen by mutual fund companies or brokerage firms. Typically, a donor will contribute cash, securities, or other property to a public charity or community foundation, which sets up a subaccount or fund in the donor's name. This is an irrevocable gift to the fund. The donor loses control over the asset and cannot reclaim any interest in the asset. The donor, or a person appointed by the donor, can make recommendations of grants to be paid from that fund to select charitable beneficiaries.

One of the key benefits of the donor-advised fund is that the donor obtains a current income tax deduction even though the selection of the charity to receive the donation may not happen for some time. This is accomplished by contributing a property to the donor-advised fund and letting it remain within the fund to be invested. The donor has the ability to make *suggestions* for the donor-advised fund regarding which charities shall receive distributions. Although the donor cannot require that the recommendations be followed, typically they are. This enables a current charitable deduction followed by a future benefit to the charities

---

Practitioner Tip: Gifts to donor-advised funds qualify as direct gifts to charity, and the donor will receive an income tax deduction in the year that a contribution is made to the fund, subject to AGI limitations.

> ### Client Situation
>
> Beth has realized a higher taxable income this year than in the past. She wishes to offset this income with a charitable contribution, but she has not decided which charity to benefit. Beth creates an account with her local community foundation and irrevocably gifts $75,000 to that account. She will receive an immediate income tax deduction of $75,000 (assuming that her AGI exceeds $150,000) and can determine which charities she wishes to benefit in the future.

Private Foundations

A private foundation is a separate legal entity, either a not-for-profit corporation or a tax-exempt trust. Most private foundations are established and controlled by families who make gifts to the foundation and manage its assets and charitable gifts. Unlike a public charity, private foundations typically receive their donations from one family rather than from many sources. One of the considerations in determining whether a private foundation is an appropriate vehicle is that the cost to establish and maintain a private foundation can be much higher than other charitable vehicles such as a donor-advised fund. Family members who make gifts to the foundation can take an income tax deduction limited to 30% of AGI for cash and 20% of AGI for long-term capital gains property.

The regulations governing the operation of private foundations are very strict. A foundation must distribute a minimum of 5% of its assets to public charities every year, file income tax returns each year, and not have unrelated business transaction income. Family members (or other parties) who manage the foundation can be paid for this work.

> ### Client Situation
>
> The Harper family has amassed a great fortune. They are charitably inclined and want to give back to the community and certain institutions. The Harpers decide that they want to establish a family foundation to instill in their children and grandchildren their philanthropic values. They establish the Harper Family Foundation and contribute $2 million to it. They allow their children and grandchildren to work for the foundation, selecting different charities to make annual donations to. Each year the foundation must distribute at least 5% of its assets ($100,000 in the first year) to various charities. Their children and grandchildren may be paid a salary for their work with the Harper Family Foundation.

SPLIT-INTEREST CHARITABLE TRANSFERS

Generally, split-interest charitable transfers are not permitted; however, the Code provides for several exceptions to this rule. Charitable remainder trusts,[2] charitable lead trusts,[3] and pooled income funds[4] are statutorily permitted split-interest charitable transfers. A **split-interest charitable transfer** is the transfer of a partial interest— either a current income stream or a remainder interest—to charity. A non-charitable beneficiary receives the interest that the charity does not receive.

Charitable Remainder Trusts

A charitable remainder trust is a split-interest trust that provides a current income stream to an individual beneficiary with the remainder interest passing to a charity. (See Figure 17.1) The current income stream can be either a unitrust amount (charitable remainder unitrust [CRUT]) or an annuity amount (charitable remainder annuity trust [CRAT]). With a charitable remainder trust, a grantor irrevocably transfers assets to the trust, and either the grantor or a designated beneficiary will receive annual payments for up to 20 years or for life. At the end of the income period, the remainder interest will pass to charity.

Figure 17.1 Charitable Remainder Trust

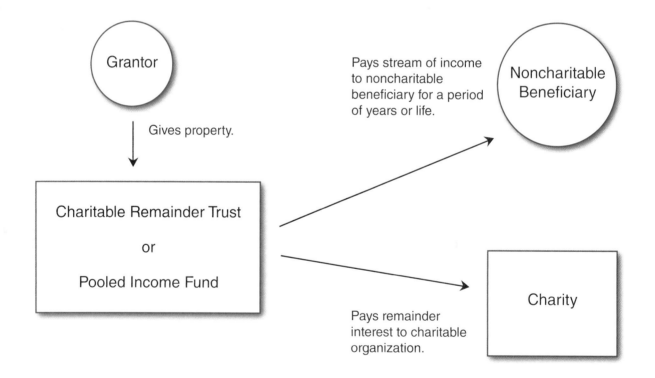

Charitable remainder trusts are often funded with appreciated securities. When the trust sells the stock, no capital gains tax is due. Consequently, more money is available in trust to produce a greater income stream for the donor or the donor's beneficiary. The annuity percentage must not be less than 5% nor more than 50% of the initial fair market value of all the property transferred in trust. The value of the remainder must equal at least 10% of the initial fair market value of all assets transferred to trust and the entire remainder must go to charity.

The donor can receive an income tax deduction in the year the trust is funded. The value of the income tax deduction is the present value of the charity's remainder interest. The value of the remainder interest is determined by a calculation using actuarial factors based on the beneficiary's age (or the specified term of the trust), the annual amount payable to the beneficiary, and the appropriate monthly section 7520 rate. If the charitable remainder trust is funded at death, the decedent's estate will be able to take an estate tax deduction for the present value of the charity's remainder interest.

Each payment to a beneficiary will be treated in the following manner:[5]

- first, as ordinary income to the extent the has trust ordinary income for the year and undistributed ordinary income for prior years;

- second, as capital gain to the extent of the trust's capital gains for the year and undistributed capital gains for prior years;

- third, as other income to the extent of the trust's other income for the year and undistributed other income for prior years; and

- fourth, as a tax-free distribution of principal.

Because trust distributions are taxed to the current non-charitable beneficiary, any income or capital gains realized are realized when the distribution is made. If, for example, a client funds the trust with highly appreciated securities, the capital gains realized by the trust are taxed to the beneficiary as part of his distribution.

Practitioner Tip: Because the donor must receive at least 5% per year, and at least 10% of the FMV of the assets must ultimately pass to charity, a young donor may not be able to qualify for this type of trust.[6]

Charitable Remainder Annuity Trusts

A **Charitable Remainder Annuity Trust (CRAT)** is a trust designed to permit payment of a fixed amount at least annually to a non-charitable beneficiary with the remainder going to charity. With a CRAT, the donor transfers money or securities to a trust that pays him (or another designated beneficiary) a fixed dollar amount (a fixed annuity) each year for life. If the actual income generated by the assets of the trust is insufficient to meet the required annual fixed payment, the shortfall is paid from capital gains or principal.

Once a CRAT is funded, no further assets can be added to the trust. This means that if the investment performance does not meet expectations, trust principal and the value of the remainder will be depleted over time. If the actual income of the annuity trust is greater than the amount to be paid out to the non-charitable beneficiary in any given year, the excess income is reinvested in the trust and becomes part of its corpus, eventually going to the charitable remainderman. Although a CRAT is an irrevocable trust and the donor cannot alter or amend it, with certain limitations, the donor can retain the right to change the charitable beneficiary.

Client Situation

AnnMarie gifted appreciating stock with a basis of $50,000 to a CRAT, which sold the stock for $300,000. The CRAT invested the proceeds in bonds paying a fixed 6% per year. This gave AnnMarie an annual income of $18,000 from the CRAT. In contrast, if AnnMarie had sold the stock outside the CRAT the sale would have been subject to a capital gains tax. For example, if AnnMarie's capital gains rate was 15%, then the tax would have been $37,500 ($300,000 minus the basis of $50,000 times 15%) and AnnMarie would net only $262,500 after the sale. If AnnMarie then bought bonds paying 6% with the proceeds, her yearly income would have been $15,750 or $2,250 less than the income generated from the CRAT. AnnMarie's contribution to the CRAT enabled her to receive an income tax deduction for the present value of the trust's remainder interest in the year the trust was established. Appreciation on the stocks will not be included in AnnMarie's gross estate when she dies.

Charitable Remainder Unitrusts

A **Charitable Remainder Unitrust (CRUT)**, like a charitable remainder annuity trust, is basically designed to permit payment of a periodic sum to a non-charitable beneficiary with a remainder to charity. The key distinction is that with a CRUT, rather than a fixed annuity amount being paid to the non-charitable beneficiary, a fixed percentage of the net fair market value of the principal will be paid to the beneficiary. This amount is revalued annually, based on the value of the trust. The amount paid to the beneficiary varies based on the trust's investment performance, which can provide an inflation hedge. Additional assets can be added to a CRUT to produce greater income, if desired.

Client Situation

Jamie just retired and has received deferred compensation that is subject to income tax this year. Jamie also has a stock portfolio that has appreciated significantly over the years, which he plans to liquidate and invest in a more conservative bond portfolio. Jamie wishes to offset the large income tax liability that he will face this year by making a charitable donation; however, he also wants to retain an income stream to supplement his retirement income. He meets with his financial planner who suggests that Jamie consider a charitable remainder trust.

The planner asks Jamie whether he prefers a fixed dollar amount each year or if he wishes to receive a percentage of trust assets that could fluctuate based on the trust's investment performance. He also asks whether Jamie plans on making charitable contributions to the trust in future years. Because Jamie prefers a fixed income stream and does not anticipate future contributions, they decide that a CRAT is the more appropriate type of trust. Jamie can fund the trust with his appreciated securities, and he will be allowed to deduct the present value of the charitable remainder interest this year. When Jamie receives distributions from the trust, they will be subject to tax first as ordinary income (to the extent the trust has ordinary income), next as capital gains, third as other income, and finally as a return of principal.

Net Income Makeup Charitable Remainder Unitrust

A **Net Income Makeup Charitable Remainder Unitrust** (NIMCRUT) is a type of CRUT in which only trust income is used to make the unitrust payment to the beneficiary. If the net income produced by the trust in any given year is inadequate to meet the unitrust payment amount, the trust can have a "make-up" provision. A beneficiary can receive the lesser of a percentage of trust assets or the actual trust income each year, plus any excess income had there been a deficiency in previous years. NIMCRUTs are typically funded with assets that will produce less income in the early years when the beneficiary's income is greater; then the trustee should convert to higher income investments in retirement years when the beneficiary is in a lower tax bracket.

Client Situation

Betsy is 60 years old and plans to continue working until she reaches age 63. She wants to make a charitable gift to her church but is concerned that once she stops working, she will need additional income. Betsy meets with her financial planner, who suggests a NIMCRUT. She can take an income tax deduction in the year that the trust is funded. The trustee can invest trust assets in securities that will not produce much income for the next 10 years and can then shift the trust investments to income-producing securities. When Betsy retires in three years, she will be able to receive distributions based on the trust's current unitrust amount, plus she can receive excess income to make up for the first 10 years when the trust produced little income.

Practitioner Tip: Such NIMCRUTs have been used as an alternative to qualified pension plans by investing in assets that produce little or no income in the early years (when the donor's income is high), and then converting to high-income investments after the donor's retirement.

Client Situation

Assume that Betsy funds the NIMCRUT with $1 million and the unitrust payment is 5% of the value of the trust, to be calculated annually. Table 17.2 illustrates the make-up provisions of her NIMCRUT over the course of the next three years

Table 17.2 NIMCRUT Makeup Example

Year	FMV	5% FMV	Income	Distribution	MU (ann.)	MU (total)
1	$1,000,000	$50,000	$40,000	$40,000	$10,000	$10,000
2	$1,200,000	$60,000	$50,000	$50,000	$10,000	$20,000
3	$1,300,000	$65,000	$90,000	$85,000	$0	$0

Charitable Lead Trusts

A **Charitable Lead Trust** (CLT) is essentially the reverse of a charitable remainder trust. With a CLT, the charity receives the present income stream and the non-charitable beneficiary receives the remainder interest. (See Figure 17.2.) The donor transfers income-producing property to a trust. The trust in turn will provide the charity with a guaranteed annuity (i.e., a **charitable lead annuity trust**), *or* annual payments equal to a fixed percentage of the FMV of the trust property as annually recomputed (i.e., a **charitable lead unitrust**). At the end of the specified period, the property is returned to the donor or goes to a non-charitable beneficiary of the donor's choice. Since the non-charitable beneficiary will receive the money in the future, the value of this future gift is reduced to an amount equal to the present value of that future gift. In some cases, the duration of the charitable interest can reduce the amount of this future gift to zero.

Figure 17.2 Charitable Lead Trust

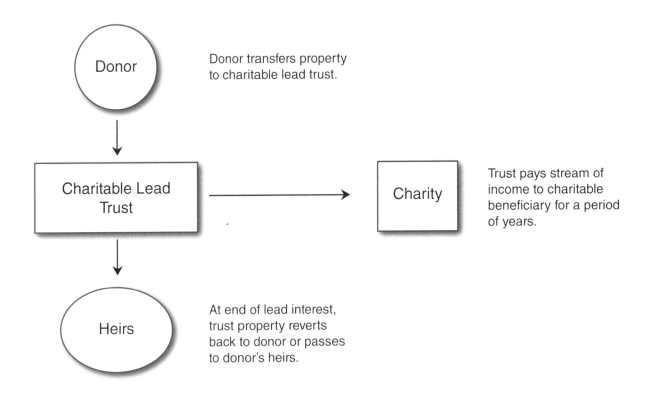

There are two types of charitable lead trusts (CLTs): the grantor CLT and the non-grantor CLT. A CLT is a **grantor CLT** if the donor has a reversionary interest in the income or the principal of the trust that is greater than 5%, or is otherwise considered the owner of the income or principal under the grantor trust rules. The grantor CLT typically allows a large up-front income tax deduction in the year it is funded; therefore, it is commonly used by taxpayers to reduce the tax burden of an unusually high-income year. The trade-off for the large up-front current deduction is that the grantor must be treated as the owner of the trust to receive the income tax deduction; therefore, under grantor trust rules, the donor is taxed on the income the trust earns each year. The income tax deduction is based on the present value of the charity's future rights to annuity or unitrust payments.

With a **non-grantor CLT**, there is no deduction at the time the CLT is funded. This type of trust is often used when the goal is to avoid percentage limitations on gifts to charities, and to avoid the amount going to charity from the CLT each year being treated as income to the donor.

Alternatively, the transfer can be made at death, in which case there is no income tax deduction, but there is a step-up in the income tax basis of the assets going into the trust.

Another use of the CLT is to permit the transfer of assets to the next generation at a very low transfer tax value (a portion of such value having been given to charity). This situation typically arises where the assets within a CLT are expected to increase in value at a rate higher than the section 7520 rate.

Client Situation

Frank is a wealthy businessman. He has a taxable estate and is in the top estate tax bracket of 40%. Frank's children also have taxable estates and will be in the top estate tax bracket. Frank meets with his financial planner to discuss estate planning strategies. Frank is charitably inclined and makes annual donations of $50,000 to a local charity. He also wishes to benefit his granddaughter Anne. His planner suggests that he consider funding a charitable lead trust at his death. Frank's will creates a $1 million trust that pays a charitable institution $60,000 a year for 20 years. The trust enables Frank's estate to take a $1 million charitable deduction (which is the present value of the charity's income interest based on IRS calculations). At the end of 20 years, the remaining trust principal will pass to Frank's granddaughter.

Pooled Income Funds

A **Pooled Income Fund** is a trust generally created and maintained by a public charity rather than a private donor and which meets certain requirements. The donor must contribute an irrevocable, vested remainder interest to the charitable organization that maintains the fund, but he will retain a lifetime income interest either for himself or another named income beneficiary. The donor's property is commingled with the property transferred by other donors. Each income beneficiary must be entitled to and receive a pro rata share of the income annually, based on the rate of return earned by the fund. Pooled income funds cannot invest in tax-exempt securities, and no donor or income beneficiary can be a trustee of the pooled income fund.

Charitable Gift Annuities

A **Charitable Gift Annuity** is an arrangement between a donor and a charity in which the donor pays the charity a certain amount and in turn the charity pays the donor (or other designated beneficiary) an annuity stream of income for life. (See Figure 17.3.) In this arrangement the donor receives a benefit in conjunction with his charitable gift. Such a contribution is deductible only to the extent that the value of the contributed property exceeds any consideration or benefit to the donor. For example, an individual might donate cash to a charity. At the time the gift is made, the donor will receive a gift tax charitable deduction for the fair market value of the property given to charity minus the actuarial value of the annuity. If the annuitant dies before recovering the initial investment in the annuity, a charitable deduction is allowed on the decedent's estate tax return for the remaining balance of the annuity.

Figure 17.3 Charitable Gift Annuity

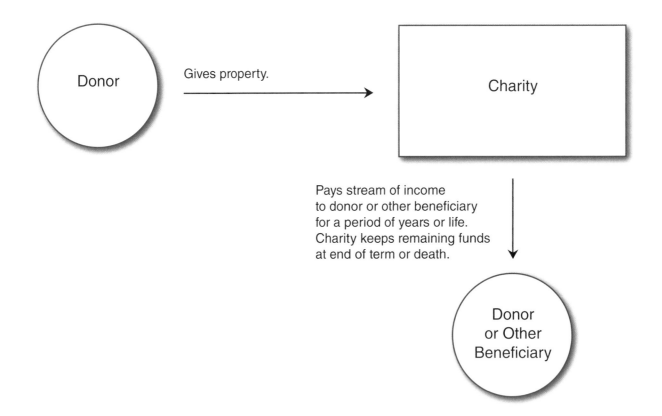

If a donor made a gift to a charity in exchange for annuity payments to his spouse, a marital deduction is available if the spouse receives all annuity payments and has a general power of appointment over annuity payments after the donor's death. When a joint and survivor annuity arrangement is made, the decedent can take a marital deduction for the value of the spouse's annuity interest included in the decedent's estate. If the beneficiary is someone other than the beneficiary or his spouse, there will be a taxable gift in the amount of the present value of the annuity payments.

Charitable Remainders

A donor can gift a personal residence or a farm to a charity and continue to live there for the rest of his life; this is called a **Charitable Remainder**. The donor is entitled to an income tax deduction for the present value of the remainder interest gifted to charity, based on the donor's age and the value of the property at the time the gift is made. The donor must continue to maintain the property and pay property taxes, but the taxes are deductible on the donor's income tax return. At the donor's death, the value of the property is included in his gross estate, but the tax is offset by an estate tax charitable deduction.

Chapter Highlights

- Charitable giving may not only fulfill a client's philanthropic goals, it can also entitle the donor to certain income, gift, and estate tax benefits. Lifetime gifts to charity are not subject to gift tax. There is an unlimited estate tax charitable deduction. Income tax deductions are limited to certain percentages of a donor's adjusted gross income based on the type of property donated and whether the charity is a public or private charity.

- A donor-advised fund is a charitable planning vehicle that allows a donor to create a subaccount with a charitable organization and make recommendations for the fund regarding which charities should receive charitable distributions.

- A private foundation is a charitable planning vehicle most often established and funded by families. Private foundations can be expensive and complex to organize and maintain, but they may be appropriate for extremely wealthy individuals.

- A direct gift to charity is one in which the donor makes a simple outright gift directly to a charity.

- A charitable remainder trust is a split-interest transfer in which a donor creates a trust and donates property to it. The donor or another beneficiary will receive an income stream for life or for a period of years, and the charity will receive the remainder interest. If the income stream is a fixed annuity, the trust is a CRAT. If the income stream is a unitrust amount calculated annually on the value of trust assets, the trust is a CRUT.

- A NIMCRUT is a type of CRUT that allows flexibility with respect to payments to the income beneficiary. The lesser of the unitrust amount or trust income is paid to the beneficiary, with the trust providing "make-up" provisions for years in which the income amount is less than the unitrust amount.

- A charitable lead trust is a split-interest transfer in which a donor creates and donates property to a trust. With a CLT, the charity receives the income stream for the life of the donor or for a period of years, and the donor or another beneficiary receives the remainder interest. If the income stream is a fixed annuity, the trust is a CLAT. If the income stream is a unitrust amount calculated annually on the value of trust assets, the trust is a CLUT. The donor receives an immediate income tax deduction if the CLT is a grantor CLT; however, he will also be taxed on any income that the trust generates annually.

- A charitable remainder is a remainder interest gift of a personal residence or farm to a charity that qualifies for an income tax deduction in the year the gift is made.

Key Terms

charitable gift annuity

charitable lead annuity trust

charitable lead unitrust

charitable remainder

charitable remainder annuity trust

charitable remainder unitrust

direct gift to charity

donor-advised fund

grantor charitable lead trust (CLT)

net income makeup charitable remainder unitrust (NIMCRUT)

non-grantor charitable lead trust

pooled income fund

private foundation

public charity

split-interest charitable transfer

qualified charity

Review Questions

17-1. Colby is actively involved with supporting his alma mater. In 2015, Colby contributed $11,000 of highly appreciated securities, $20,000 cash to an endowment appeal, and 100 hours of his time normally billed at $200/hour. If no further charitable contributions are made in 2015, what is the total value of Colby's charitable contributions for the year?

A. $20,000

B. $31,000

C. $51,000

D. Cannot determine because we have no information on Colby's AGI.

17-2. With respect to charitable contributions, all of the following are true, except:

A. Allowing the Girl Scouts to use a building rent-free for one year will not generate a charitable contribution equivalent to the FMV of the rental of the building.

B. A gift of cash to a private foundation allows an income tax deduction of up to 50% of AGI.

C. A gift of appreciated securities to a public charity allows an income tax deduction of up to 30% of AGI.

D. A gift of related-use personal property allows the donor to determine the value of the deduction based upon the FMV of the property on the date of transfer, not the donor's basis in the property.

17-3. The advantages associated with making charitable gifts of appreciated securities include

1. The capital gains tax liability is transferred to the charity.

2. The donor's income tax deduction is based on the FMV of the security.

3. The appreciated security is removed from the donor's gross estate only if the transfer was made more than three years before death.

A. 2

B. 2 and 3

C. 1 and 3

D. 3

17-4. Susan creates a charitable remainder trust into which she transfers $1 million cash. Susan retains a 20-year unitrust interest, which is valued at $500,000. When is Susan able to take her $500,000 charitable deduction?

A. A $500,000 deduction is taken in the year the trust is funded.

B. A $250,000 deduction is taken in the year the trust is funded; a $250,000 deduction is taken at the end of the 20 years.

C. A $500,000 deduction is taken at the end of the unitrust interest.

D. Cannot determine because a unitrust requires an annual valuation of the trust assets.

17-5. Joseph is 75 years old. He is very interested in making a charitable contribution of highly appreciated securities, but he cannot afford to give up the income stream generated by these securities. Given Joseph's age, he is most concerned about receiving a guaranteed amount of income; however, he would also like to provide a benefit to his favorite charity. Which of the following vehicles can best accomplish Joseph's planning objectives?

A. CLAT

B. CRAT

C. NIMCRUT

D. CRUT

17-6. Sally transfers appreciated securities into a CRUT. With respect to the gain on the securities:

A. Sally will never pay tax.

B. Sally will pay tax based on the nature of distributions from the trust subject to the trust tax tier rules.

C. The trust will pay the tax only after the securities have been sold.

D. Sally and the trust will share the tax after the securities have been sold.

Notes

1. I.R.C. §170(c)(2)(B)-(D).

2. I.R.C. §664; Treas. Reg. §1.664-1.

3. I.R.C. §2522(c)(2)(B).

4. I.R.C. §642(c)(5).

5. I.R.C. §664(b); Reg. §1.664-1(d).

6. Rev. Rul. 79-368, 1979-2 CB 109.

Chapter 18

State Death Tax Deduction

CFP® CERTIFICATION EXAMINATION PRINCIPAL TOPIC COVERED IN THIS CHAPTER:

- Deductions from the Gross Estate

Learning Objectives

To ensure that you have an understanding of the manner in which states tax a decedent's assets, and the effect that a state estate or inheritance tax has on a decedent's taxable estate, the following learning objectives are addressed in this chapter:

- Understand the difference between the state death tax deduction and the state death tax credit.

- Compare and contrast the differences between a sponge tax, inheritance tax, and estate tax at the state level.

Chapter Contents

OVERVIEW

Since 2005, one of the allowable deductions from the adjusted gross estate has been the state death tax deduction. Prior to 2005, the federal estate tax provided a state death tax credit rather than a state death tax deduction that reduced a greater amount of federal estate tax paid and diverted tax dollars to the state.

It is important for financial planners to understand the different types of state death taxes that can affect a client's total tax liability so that they can advise clients regarding how state-level planning will affect federal estate tax planning.

Furthermore, the current federal estate tax exemption of $5,430,000 ensures that many taxpayers will not be subject to the federal estate tax. The enactment of portability allows married taxpayers to shelter $10,860,000 from federal estate tax at the surviving spouse's death in 2015. Often times, clients will have to determine whether it is appropriate to implement state-level estate tax planning to reduce the overall state-level estate tax liability on a married couple's combined estates.

Practice Standard 400-2

Developing the Financial Planning Recommendation(s)

The financial planning practitioner shall develop the recommendation(s) based on the selected alternative(s) and the current course of action in an effort to reasonably meet the client's goals, needs and priorities.

HISTORY

In 2001, the Economic Growth and Tax Relief Reconciliation Act (EGTRRA) dramatically changed the federal estate tax treatment of the state death tax. Before 2001, the federal estate tax allowed a credit for state death taxes. The amount of the credit was known as the **credit for state death tax**. The maximum credit for state death taxes was calculated by subtracting $60,000 from the federal adjusted taxable estate, and the remaining amount was applied to the federal credit for state death tax table (see Appendix B.3)

Under the federal credit for state death taxes, an amount of the federal estate tax due was payable directly to the states. This allowed the states to keep a portion of the tax that would have been transferred to the federal government and allowed the states to collect an estate tax without necessarily increasing the taxpayer's amount of estate tax due.

When EGTRRA was implemented in 2001, it increased the amount of the federal estate tax exemption and slashed estate tax rates. At the same time, EGTRRA gradually reduced the amount of the state death tax credit that could be applied against the federal estate tax. In 2001, 100% of the maximum credit for state death tax was allowed. This was reduced by 25% each year from 2002 through 2004; beginning in 2005, no federal credit for state death taxes remained. A summary of the estate tax exemption amount and rates since 2000 can be found in Appendix B.2.

For federal estate tax purposes, the federal credit for state death tax was replaced with a **state death tax deduction** provided for under IRC § 2058.[1] In calculating the taxable estate, taxpayers are permitted to deduct the amount of state death taxes paid from the value of the adjusted gross estate.

As a result of the phase-out of the credit for state death taxes paid, states that relied on the federal credit no longer collected a portion of the federal estate tax paid. Consequently, some states **decoupled** or separated from the federal state death tax credit and implemented a separate estate or inheritance tax.

STATE ESTATE TAX CONSIDERATIONS

Although a client should consult his estate planning attorney with respect to the impact that state law will have on his estate plan, it is important for the financial planner to have a basic understanding of state estate tax laws. Each state's laws are unique and applicable only to that particular state. State estate taxes can affect the structure of a client's estate plan, the client's liquidity needs, and other important planning considerations.

Some of the state estate tax factors that affect a client's estate plan include:

- whether a state imposes its own estate tax;

- whether a state recognizes charitable estate tax deductions;

- whether a state allows state-level qualified terminable interest property (QTIP) planning;

- the amount of a state's estate tax exemption;

- whether a state recognizes portability;

- the rates at which tax is applied; and

- whether lifetime gifts are factored into a state's estate tax calculation.

Furthermore, the current federal estate tax exemption of $5,430,000 ($10,860,000 for a married couple relying on portability) ensures that many taxpayers will not be subject to the federal estate tax. To date, very few states have adopted portability, and many states that have imposed a federal estate tax have a much smaller exemption than the federal estate tax exemption. Therefore, if a client relies on portability to pass assets at the surviving spouse's death, or relies on the current high federal estate tax exemption, the client may miss the opportunity to take advantage of each spouse's state-level estate tax exemption, and married couples could face an increase in overall state estate tax liability on their combined estates.

Finally, many clients have homes in two states and spend time living in both states. If a client has homes in both a sponge tax state, which does not impose a separate death tax, and in a state that does impose a separate state-level death tax, the client could choose to establish a domicile in the state that does not impose a death tax. Although real property is taxable in the state where it is located, the bulk of a decedent's assets would not be subject to a state-level death tax.

Client Situation

Sarah and Brady have homes in both Rhode Island and Florida. Their legal domicile is Rhode Island; however, because they are now retired, they are considering where they might want to spend most of their time and where they should declare a domicile. Sarah and Brady meet with their financial planner, who explains that they should discuss with their attorney the implications that living in each state might have on their estate plan. He points out that Rhode Island has decoupled from the federal credit for state death tax and imposes a separate state-level estate tax, whereas Florida remains a sponge tax state. If Sarah and Brady move to Florida permanently, they may not be subject to a state-level estate tax, which can provide them with significant estate tax savings.

SPONGE TAX STATES

The majority of states have not imposed a separate state-level estate or inheritance tax. These states, known as **sponge tax states**, have not collected a state death tax since 2005 and the termination of the federal credit for state death taxes.

STATE ESTATE TAX

Many of the states that have decoupled from the federal estate tax have imposed a state-level estate tax based on the decedent's right to transfer assets at death. These states have implemented their own separate estate tax structure and might have a separate estate tax exemption, which can vary from state to state. Some states have continued to apply the estate tax rates in effect under the federal credit for state death tax, and others have applied their own separate state-level estate tax rates.

Client Situation

Kim and Rob live in Massachusetts. They have met with an estate planner and have implemented a tax-efficient estate plan. Kim and Rob have approximately $4 million of assets. Given that the value of their combined estates is less than the available federal estate tax exemption, they are less concerned with federal tax planning. However, if all of their assets were to pass outright to the surviving spouse, the decedent spouse would have missed the opportunity to take advantage of the Massachusetts estate tax exemption. To remedy this situation, each spouse's estate plan will include a credit shelter trust that will be funded up to the maximum available Massachusetts estate tax exemption, and all other remaining assets will pass outright to the survivor. This will shelter the assets from Massachusetts estate tax at the survivor's death, allowing each spouse to take advantage of his Massachusetts estate tax exemption. See Figures 18.1 and 18.2 for illustrations of this concept.

Figure 18.1 No State-level Estate Tax Planning

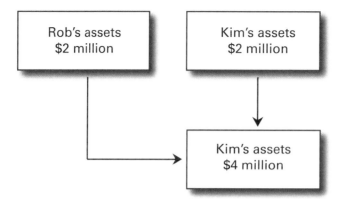

At Kim's death, $4 million will be included in her federal and Massachusetts gross estate. Although no federal estate tax is due, they have lost the opportunity to shelter Rob's Massachusetts estate tax exemption.

Figure 18.2 State-level Estate Tax Planning

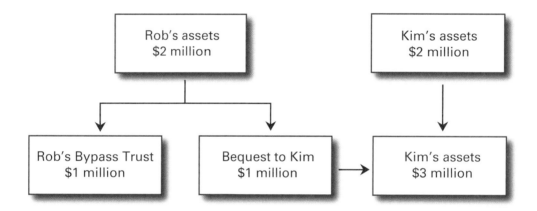

At Kim's death, $3 million will be included in her federal and Massachusetts gross estate. Because they took advantage of sheltering $1 million form Massachusetts estate tax at Rob's death, their state estate tax liability will be reduced.

INHERITANCE TAX

An **inheritance tax** is a tax assessed based on an individual's right to inherit or receive assets from a decedent. The amount of the tax is assessed based on the value of the property that passes to each individual. The individual's relationship to the decedent determines the rate of estate tax imposed. For example, assets left to a surviving spouse could be exempt from state-level estate tax, whereas assets left to a child might be subject to tax at one rate and assets left to a sibling taxed at a different rate. In some states, payment of the inheritance tax is the executor's responsibility, and in other states it is paid by the recipient of the property.

Client Situation

Bob lives in Kentucky, which is an inheritance tax state. Kentucky recognizes spouses, parents, children, grandchildren, and siblings as exempt classes of beneficiaries. Assets passing to other beneficiaries have a $200,000 exemption and a 16% estate tax. When Bob died, he left $1 million to his sister Theresa and $500,000 to his cousin Eileen. No inheritance tax will be due on the bequest to Theresa. Eileen will be responsible for paying the state inheritance tax of $48,000 on her bequest.

STATE QTIP PLANNING

One of the tax planning challenges that has resulted from decoupling is planning for different exemption amounts at the state and federal levels. For example, in 2015 the federal estate tax exemption is $5,430,000, but many states that have decoupled have lower exemption amounts. Prior to portability, typical planning for married couples who were concerned with avoiding an estate tax included the use of bypass or credit shelter trusts. Although portability may have eliminated the need for bypass trust planning at the first spouse's death, it can still make sense for many couples to implement this planning. For example, if the couple's state of domicile has an estate tax exemption that is less than the federal estate tax exemption, then the choice would be either to fully fund the credit shelter trust and pay a state estate tax or not take full advantage of the federal estate tax exemption to avoid paying a state estate tax.

As a result, a number of states have provided a mechanism using state-level QTIP planning to allow a married couple to take full advantage of the available federal estate tax exemption while deferring state-level estate tax until the second spouse's death. Rather than the full federal estate tax exemption amount passing to the credit shelter trust, the amount that can pass free from both federal and state estate tax would pass to the credit shelter trust. The difference would pass to a state-level QTIP trust. This amount would pass free from federal estate tax at the surviving spouse's death, but it would be subject to state-level estate tax at the survivor's death.

Client Situation

Doreen and Shawn have a sizeable estate valued at approximately $12 million. They have met with an estate planner and implemented an estate plan that includes credit shelter trust planning. Doreen and Shawn have divided their assets equally between them and have coordinated asset ownership with their estate planning objectives.

Doreen and Shawn live in a state that has decoupled from the federal estate tax and has a $2 million estate tax exemption. If their state did not recognize state-level QTIP planning, they would have to decide whether they wanted to shelter all of the decedent's available $5,430,000 federal estate tax exemption and pay a state-level estate tax on the $3,430,000 difference, or only shelter the $2 million state estate tax exemption and defer any state estate tax payable.

Because Doreen and Shawn live in a state that recognizes state-level QTIP planning, they can shelter the full federal estate tax exemption amount while deferring state-level estate tax until the survivor's subsequent death. Therefore, $2 million will be sheltered from both federal and state estate tax at the first spouse's death. Assume that Doreen dies in 2015. The difference, $3,430,000, will be treated as QTIP property for state purposes only. This property will pass free from federal estate tax at Shawn's death, but it will also be subject to state-level estate tax at his death. See Figure 18.3 for an illustration of this concept.

Figure 18.3 State-level QTIP Planning at Doreen's Death

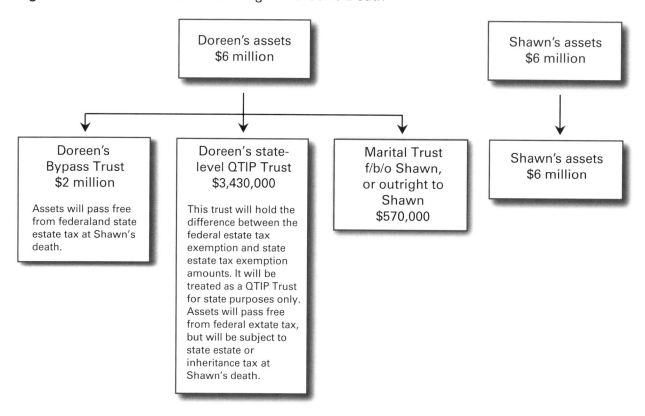

At Shawn's death, $6,570,000 will be included in his federal gross estate, and $10,000,000 will be included in his state gross estate.

Practitioner Tip: Wealthier clients with estates that exceed (or are likely to exceed) the combined federal estate tax exemption of $10,860,000, will have to consider whether they are better off funding the state-level QTIP trust, which would allow assets to pass outside of the surviving spouse's federal taxable estate, or to have those assets pass outright to the survivor, or to a marital trust for the survivor. If assets pass outright to the survivor and are included in the survivor's federal estate, there will be a second step-up in basis at the survivor's death, however, the full value, including any post-death appreciation, will be subject to estate tax. If assets pass to the state-level QTIP, all appreciation between the first spouse's death and second spouse's death will escape estate taxation in the survivor's estate, however, there will be no second step-up in basis.

Chapter Highlights

- Beginning in 2005, the federal credit for state death tax was completely phased out. Instead, taxpayers can deduct any state estate tax paid from their adjusted gross estate.

- Financial planners should understand the state estate tax laws for the states in which they practice and for any state in which a client has property so that they can explain the impact state laws may have on a client's planning.

- Some states have decoupled from the federal credit for state death tax and have implemented their own state-level estate tax.

- The amount of the state estate tax exemption can vary from state to state, and the tax rates in effect can also vary from state to state.

- Some states impose an inheritance tax rather than an estate tax. An inheritance tax is a tax on a beneficiary's right to inherit assets, as opposed to a tax on a decedent's right to transfer assets.

Key Terms

credit for state death tax

decoupled

inheritance tax

state death tax deduction

sponge tax state

Review Questions

18-1. Which of the following statements are not correct with respect to state estate tax?

1. States are able to collect a portion of the estate tax that is paid to the federal government.

2. Taxpayers can deduct on their federal estate tax return any state estate tax paid.

3. Taxpayers can deduct on their state estate tax return any federal estate tax paid.

A. 1, 2, and 3

B. 1 and 3

C. 2 and 3

D. 1 and 2

18-2. Why is it important for a financial planner to understand state estate tax planning?

A. Because all states follow the federal estate tax laws.

B. It is not important for a financial planner to understand state estate tax laws because only an estate planning attorney has access to this information.

C. Because many states have decoupled from the federal deduction for state death tax and imposed a state-level estate tax, which can affect a client's estate plan.

D. Because a federal and state estate tax will be due if the client's estate is less than $5,430,000 in 2015.

18-3. Which of the following is true with respect to state level estate tax?

A. There can be no state estate tax if there is no federal estate tax.

B. Each state calculates the estate tax due based on the federal credit for state death tax table.

C. State-level QTIP planning allows the deferral of state-level estate tax until a surviving spouse's death.

18-4. True or False: It is always best to take advantage of the full state estate tax exemption amount available at a decedent's death.

18-5. Which of the following is not correct regarding states that impose an inheritance tax?

A. The amount of the tax is assessed based on the value of property passing to each individual.

B. The relationship of the beneficiary to the decedent may affect the tax rate.

C. Payment of the tax is always the responsibility of the recipient of that property.

Notes

1. The state death tax deduction appears on line 3b of IRS Form 706 (Rev. August 2011).

Generation-Skipping Transfer Tax

CFP® CERTIFICATION EXAMINATION PRINCIPAL TOPICS COVERED IN THIS CHAPTER:

Identify transfers subject to the GST tax

- Direct skips
- Taxable distributions
- Taxable terminations

Exemptions and exclusions from the GST tax

- The GST tax exemption
- Qualifying annual exclusion gifts and direct transfers

Learning Objectives

To ensure that you have a solid understanding of the generation-skipping transfer tax, the following learning objectives are addressed in this chapter:

- Identify the circumstances that trigger the Generation-Skipping Transfer (GST) tax.

- Explain when an annual exclusion applies to a gift made to a skip person or a skip person trust.

- Recognize how the GST exemption is allocated to different transfers to reduce or eliminate the GST tax.

- Calculate the federal GST tax on a lifetime gift and on a bequest.

- Explain the use of the reverse QTIP election.

- Identify which party is responsible for paying the GST tax in a direct skip, a taxable distribution, and a taxable termination.

Chapter Contents

OVERVIEW

Whenever property is transferred to a family member of the next generation or succeeding generations, a wealth transfer tax is imposed as a gift tax or an estate tax. Prior to 1976, a **generation-skipping transfer** was traditionally used as a device to save federal gift and estate tax by keeping property out of the taxable estates of children. A grantor would establish a trust benefitting his children, grandchildren, great-grandchildren, and so on, which would last for multiple generations. The child, as beneficiary of a trust, could be trustee, have all the income, invade the principal for personal needs, and control the distribution of the property, as long as he did not have a general power of appointment. This would allow the assets to continue to pass from generation to generation without being subject to estate tax in every generation. The **Generation-Skipping Transfer (GST) tax** was instituted in 1986 to deter the wealthy from passing assets transfer-tax free to successive generations and to collect more federal tax revenue, which was previously lost through generational skips.

By making gifts to grandchildren or more remote descendants, a client can avoid paying transfer taxes in each generation. Each taxpayer has an exemption that shelters against the GST tax, called a **GST exemption**. Individuals can make lifetime gifts up to $5,430,000 in 2015 before a gift is subject to a gift tax or a GST tax. Therefore, a significant amount of property can be transferred to family members before a GST tax is incurred.

Financial planners can provide extra value to their clients by helping them understand the circumstances that trigger this tax and the trusts and techniques that are available to minimize or avoid the tax. The GST tax is imposed in addition to the gift tax and the estate tax; therefore, financial planners need to calculate their client's total transfer tax liability when gifts and bequests are made to persons who are subject to this tax. Planners should work with attorneys, accountants, and other members of the client's estate planning team to recommend the most effective GST tax planning strategies for a client given the client's particular tax situation and estate planning objectives.

Practice Standard 400-3

Presenting the Financial Planning Recommendation(s)

The financial planning practitioner shall communicate the recommendation(s) in a manner and to an extent reasonably necessary to assist the client in making an informed decision.

GST PLANNING CONSIDERATIONS

There are three situations in which GST planning is useful.

First, when a child stands to inherit a substantial estate from a parent and already has a substantial estate of his own, a generation-skipping trust would be set up to receive the parent's property for the benefit of the child and his children. A generation-skipping trust allows the child the use and enjoyment of the inherited property, together with protection against creditors, divorce courts, or bankruptcy. The amount subject to the GST exemption is also excluded from the child's already substantial estate. Although the parent might pay gift or estate tax, upon the child's death, there would be no further estate tax or GST tax on the inherited property if the assets remain in the trust and are not distributed outright to the child. Furthermore, no estate tax or GST tax is paid by the grandchildren or future issue if the assets remain in trust and are not distributed to them.

Secondly, a generation-skipping trust can be used when parents wish to minimize transfer taxes in a child's estate but still give the child the use and benefit of the property, or when the parents wish to protect the property from a spendthrift child or from being subject to loss through a child's divorce or bankruptcy. In these situations, a generation-skipping trust is beneficial. The child can be permitted trust income or discretionary payments of principal, but the remaining trust property is preserved for subsequent distribution to grandchildren. The trust can continue through the grandchildren's lives (and for great-grandchildren as well), avoiding transfer tax in each generation, subject only to the limitation on the maximum life of a trust under state law.

Thirdly, a client might wish to make gifts to a grandchild for his support or enjoyment, or to avoid tax in the child's estate. Gifts that immediately benefit grandchildren are generally subject to the GST tax unless they qualify for the generation-skipping exemption or the annual exclusion.

GENERATION ASSIGNMENT

A generation-skipping transfer is any transfer of property by gift or bequest, to any person who, under federal tax law, is assigned to a generation that is two or more generations below that of the transferor A **transferor** is the person who makes a gift or a bequest that is subject to a GST tax, and a **transferee** is the recipient of the transfer. For GST tax purposes, all persons are assigned to a generation.

A gift or bequest made to someone of the same generation as the transferor or who is one generation below the transferor is exempt from this tax. Spouses of the transferor are always assigned to the same generation as the transferor, regardless of their age.

In the case of family members, the transferor's grandchildren, great nieces, and great nephews would be assigned two generations below the transferor. Great-grandchildren are assigned more than two generations below the transferor and any transfers to them would be subject to the GST tax.

Client Situation

Norman is a retired business owner who provided money to his grandson Dax to fund his start-up business. Norman wrote Dax a check for $300,000 so that he could purchase the tools and machinery needed for his business. For GST purposes, Norman was the transferor and Dax was the transferee because Dax was two generations below Norman in family lineage. Norman's gift to Dax was subject to both a potential gift tax and a potential GST tax.

Unrelated persons are assigned to the transferor's generation if they are not more than 12½ years younger than the transferor. Otherwise, unrelated persons are assigned to succeeding generations on the basis of 25 years for each generation. For example, the first younger generation would be 12½ to 37½ years younger than the transferor. Gifts or bequests made to transferees in this age group would not be subject to the GST tax. However gifts or bequests made to nonrelatives who are more than 37½ years younger than the transferor are subject to a GST tax. When the transferee is an entity such as an estate, trust, partnership, or corporation, then individuals who own beneficial interests in the entity are assigned to specific generations.

Client Situation

Josephine, age 84, is in poor health and is confined to her home. She has employed Courtney to provide her with homecare assistance several times a week. Josephine is very fond of Courtney and she recently gave her a gift of $15,000 for her 40th birthday. This gift is subject to a GST tax because Courtney is more than 37½ years younger than Josephine.

The **predeceased parent rule** applies if an individual's parent who is a lineal descendant of the transferor or transferor's spouse is deceased at the time of transfer. Under this rule, the individual and all succeeding generations move up one generation for purposes of applying the GST tax. This rule applies when gifts are made directly to the individual or for transfers into trusts for the individual's benefit.

Client Situation

Rodney's family had included a daughter, Heidi, and her son Toby, age 16. Heidi died unexpectedly last year. Rodney established an irrevocable trust for his grandson Toby and transferred $500,000 of dividend-paying securities to the trust. This transfer was not subject to a GST tax per the predeceased parent rule because Toby was deemed to have moved up one generation at his mother's death.

This predeceased parent rule also applies to collateral relatives such as nephews and nieces if the transferor had no living lineal descendants at the time of the transfer.

Client Situation

Dana never married but she was very close to her nephew Mario and his two children, Vinnie and Marissa. Although Mario died four years ago, Dana continues to give generous checks to her grandnephew and grandniece every year at the holidays. The taxable gifts that Dana makes to Vinnie and Marissa are not considered to be generation-skipping transfers under the predeceased parent rule.

Skip Persons

A person who is two or more generations below that of the transferor is defined as a **skip person**. Any direct transfer of property to a skip person by gift or bequest can trigger the GST tax.

A trust can also qualify as a skip person if all beneficiaries holding interests in the trust are skip persons; this is known as a **skip person trust**. For example, a trust qualifies as a skip person if all of the beneficiaries are the grantor's grandchildren. Assets transferred into a trust that benefits only skip persons are subject to the GST tax.

A disclaimer is a written refusal by a potential beneficiary to accept a gift or a bequest. A disclaimer that results in property passing to a person at least two generations below that of the original transferor will result in a GST tax.

> ### Client Situation
>
> Julie died and left $50,000 to her son Conrad in her will. Conrad disclaimed the bequest from his mother. As a result of that disclaimer, the money passed to Julie's granddaughter Mindy. Mindy is a skip person because she received the disclaimed property that was transferred from Julie's estate. The GST tax would be imposed on the transfer—in addition to the federal estate tax.

DIRECT SKIPS

A **direct skip** is a direct transfer subject to an estate or gift tax made to a skip person. For example, a gift from an individual to his grandchild is a direct skip that could be subject to a GST tax.

A direct skip can also occur when an individual makes a transfer to a trust if all the beneficiaries of the trust are skip persons. Therefore, an individual who creates an irrevocable trust for the benefit of his grandchildren would be making a direct skip upon funding the trust.

Examples of direct skips occur when a transferor:

- gifts cash or other property directly to a skip person;

- transfers assets into an irrevocable trust and a skip person is the sole beneficiary of the trust income and corpus;

- transfers assets into an irrevocable trust with multiple skip person beneficiaries who are the only income and remainder beneficiaries; and

- transfers assets into a UGMA or UTMA account, or a 529 plan to benefit a skip person.

A transfer to a trust that includes skip persons and beneficiaries who are not two or more generations below the transferor is not a direct skip, it is an **indirect skip**.

Client Situation

Cindy transferred $2 million into an irrevocable trust for the benefit of her son Nathan and his two sons. Nathan will receive all of the trust income for life, and at his death Cindy's grandsons will receive the remainder interest. This is not a skip person trust because all of the beneficiaries are not two or more generations younger than Cindy. The transfer to the trust is an example of an indirect skip.

GST taxes are calculated differently for direct and indirect skips. GST taxes for direct and indirect skips are reported on different tax forms and are due at different times, depending on when the taxable GST transfer event occurs.

GST Taxes for Lifetime Direct Skips

A generation-skipping transfer occurs at the time a gift is made or when property is bequeathed to a skip person. Therefore, a direct skip that is a gift could be subject to two potential taxes, the gift tax and the GST tax. Many of the same tax-reducing techniques that apply to the gift tax apply to the GST tax as well, with the net amount of the gift subject to both taxes. When property is bequeathed to a skip person, the estate tax and GST tax both apply.

Each person, and therefore each spouse, has a GST exemption of $5,430,000 in 2015. A gift subject to the GST tax which is "split" by the spouses will be treated as having been made half by each spouse and each spouse can use some or all of his or her GST exemption to avoid the tax. In 2015, married couples can gift up to $10.86 million to skip persons through gift splitting before a GST tax must be paid. Transfers that exceed this amount are taxed at a flat 40% tax rate, which is equal to the highest estate tax rate.

It appears that in many cases the total cost of making a property transfer can exceed or approach the value of the gift.

Client Situation

Assume a grandfather in a 40% gift tax bracket makes a gift in 2015 of $2 million, and it is made to a trust for his grandchild. Assume he has used his GST tax exemption and he has already used his gift tax unified credit. The GST tax is $800,000 ($2,000,000 × .40). If grandfather pays the GST tax of $800,000, for gift tax purposes, the amount of the taxable gift is $2,800,000 ($2,000,000 + $800,000). The gift tax on the total deemed gift is $1,065,800. The total tax therefore is $1,865,800, which almost equals the value of the gift. Grandfather will have spent $3,865,800: $2 million for the gift to his grandson and $1,865,800 in taxes.

Transfers made by gift that would qualify as direct payments for the skip person's educational or medical expenses are not subject to either the gift tax or the GST tax. Gifts that are not taxable by reason of the gift tax annual exclusion are also exempt for GST tax under most circumstances. However, transfers in trust will not qualify for this exemption unless:

- the trust has a single beneficiary who is a skip person, and

- no portion of the trust's income or principal can be distributed to or used for the benefit of anyone other than the skip person, as long as that person is alive, and

- if the beneficiary dies before the trust terminates, the trust assets will be included in his estate.

Therefore, for purposes of the GST tax, annual exclusions are not available for

- trusts with multiple skip person beneficiaries unless separate trust shares are created for each beneficiary, and

- discretionary distributions made to a trust beneficiary through sprinkle or spray provisions included in the trust instrument.

Client Situation

Arnold and Vanessa have an estate currently valued at $12 million, which is expected to appreciate in value. On the advice of their financial planner, they decided to begin making gifts to their son and two grandchildren this year to reduce the value of their combined estates. Both Arnold and Vanessa's full unified credits remain available for gifting purposes.

Gifts made in 2015

1. They gave their son Andy a check for $200,000.

2. They paid University of Georgia $50,000 for their grandson Jamie's college tuition.

3. They contributed $50,000 to a 529 plan for their granddaughter Carrie.

4. They established an irrevocable trust funded with $100,000 for Jamie and Carrie, who will receive all of the income from the trust each year and will receive the corpus when Jamie turns 30.

Result:

1. The gift of $200,000 that Arnold and Vanessa made to Andy was reduced by gift splitting and annual exclusions for a taxable gift of $86,000 for each spouse. No gift tax is due for either spouse because each spouse will apply his own unified credit against the gift tax. The gift was not subject to the GST tax because Andy is not a skip person.

2. Neither the gift tax nor the GST tax applied to the direct payment of tuition to the university.

3. The GST tax and the gift tax did apply to the contribution the couple made to the 529 plan for Carrie. With gift splitting and annual exclusions, the taxable gift was reduced to $11,000 for each spouse. No gift tax was paid because Arnold and Vanessa's unified credits were available to offset the tax on this gift. Likewise, for GST purposes, the taxable portion of the gift was reduced to $11,000. Arnold and Vanessa each allocated $11,000 of their GST exemption to the transfer to offset the GST tax on their respective gift tax returns.

4. The money transferred into the trust was subject to both gift and GST taxes. Gift splitting and two annual exclusions reduced the transfer to a taxable gift of $22,000 for each spouse ($50,000 – $28,000), but the gift tax was offset by Arnold and Vanessa's unified credits. Gift splitting was used to reduce the taxable amount of the gift subject to GST taxes to $50,000 each, but neither spouse could reduce the tax further by annual exclusions because the trust was established with two skip person beneficiaries. Arnold and Vanessa did not have to pay a GST tax because each spouse's GST exemptions were available to offset the tax.

Calculating the GST Tax for Lifetime Transfers

The GST tax on a direct skip made during a transferor's lifetime can be reduced by gift splitting and annual exclusions if either or both of these techniques can be applied. The remaining amount is the taxable gift, which is subject to a GST tax.

In 2015, each taxpayer has a total GST exemption of $5,430,000 to offset GST tax liability. The GST exemption or a portion of it can be allocated to an outright gift or to a trust in an amount equal to the value of the property transferred. This can reduce or eliminate any current or future GST tax on the transferred property.

The amount of the GST exemption allocated to the transfer is divided by the taxable amount of the gift to determine the **applicable fraction.**

The applicable fraction is subtracted from 1, resulting in the **inclusion ratio.**

The GST tax rate in effect at the time the gift is made is multiplied by the inclusion ratio to arrive at the **applicable rate.**

The applicable rate is then multiplied by the taxable amount of the gift to determine the total GST tax due.

Client Situation

Troy, a widower, transferred $1 million into an irrevocable trust this year. The trust stipulated that the income would accumulate for five years. At the end of this period, the income would be distributed to his daughter Melissa, and the corpus would be distributed to his grandson Gabe. Troy allocated $400,000 of his remaining GST exemption to the trust on his gift tax return for 2015 when the trust was funded.

The applicable fraction: .40 $\dfrac{\$400,000 \text{ exemption}}{\$1,000,000 \text{ taxable gift}}$

The inclusion ratio: 1.0 – .40 = .60

After applying the GST tax rate of 40%, the applicable rate totaled .24 (40% × .60 inclusion ratio).

Troy's GST tax liability in 2015 is: $240,000 (.24 × $1,000,000).

See Exhibit 19.1 for a more comprehensive treatment of calculating the GST tax.

Exhibit 19.1

Part A – Use to calculate GST tax for direct skips.

Part B – Use to calculate the new inclusion ratio for a trust whenever a transfer is made to the trust or GST exemption is allocated to the trust. It is generally preferable to keep the inclusion ratio for a trust at either one (no protection from GST tax) or zero (fully protected from GST tax). Apply ETIP and CLAT rules, if appropriate.

Part C – Use to calculate GST tax for taxable distributions and taxable terminations. Generally, use the inclusion ratio from Part B. If there were no other transfers to the trust and no other allocations of GST exemption to the trust, the inclusion ratio from Part A could be used for the trust.

Part A – GST Direct Skip

1	Transfer	_____
2	Federal estate or state death taxes borne by transfer	_____
3	Federal gift or estate tax charitable deduction	_____
4	Nontaxable gift portion (GST exclusions)	_____
5	Total reductions [(2) + (3) + (4)]	_____
6	Net transfer (denominator) [(1) - (5)]	_____
7	GST exemption allocated (numerator)	_____
8	Applicable fraction [(7) / (6)]	_____
9	Inclusion ratio [1 - (8)]	_____
10	Maximum tax rate	_____
11	Effective maximum tax rate	_____ *
12	Applicable rate [(9) x (11)]	_____
13	GST tax [(6) x (12)]	_____

* If lifetime transfer, or GST tax is borne by other property, enter (10); otherwise, use formula [(10) / (1 + (10)]

Part B – GST Inclusion Ratio for Trust

1	Prior applicable fraction	_____ *
2	Prior value of trust	_____ *
3	Nontax portion [(1) x (2)]	_____ *
4	Current transfer	_____
5	Federal estate or state death taxes borne by transfer	_____
6	Federal gift or estate tax charitable deduction	_____
7	Nontaxable gift portion (if transfer is direct skip)	_____
8	Total reductions [(5) + (6) + (7)]	_____
9	Net transfer [(4) - (8)]	_____
10	Current GST exemption allocation	_____
11	Numerator [(3) + (10)]	_____
12	Denominator [(2) + (9)]	_____
13	New applicable fraction [(11) / (12)]	_____
14	New inclusion ratio [1 - (13)]	_____

* If no prior transfers have been made to this trust, enter 0

Part C – GST Taxable Termination/Distribution

1   Transfer _____

2   Inclusion ratio _____

3   Maximum tax rate _____

4   Applicable rate [(2) x (3)] _____

5   Gross-up rate _____ *

6   Grossed-up transfer [(1) x (1 + (5))] _____

7   GST tax [(6) x (4)] _____

* If transfer is taxable distribution and donee pays GST tax, use formula [1 / (1 - (4)) - 1]; otherwise enter 0%

Allocation of the GST Exemption

Given the severity of the GST tax, probably the most important planning decision is how to allocate the $5,430,000 GST exemption.

The amount of GST exemption allocated to a transfer is typically equal to the fair market value of the property transferred to an individual or trust. The effective date of allocation for direct skips during the transferor's lifetime is the date of transfer. When all or a portion of a person's GST exemption is allocated to a generation-skipping transfer, this has the effect of exempting the property transferred and all future appreciation on the property from the GST tax. Once made, the election is irrevocable. The GST exemption will be automatically allocated to a direct skip during life and to an indirect skip unless the donor elects otherwise. The GST exemption can be allocated by the transferor or the executor among any property that is transferred. If the GST exemption amount increases in the future, additional GST gifts can be made without incurring a GST tax.

Client Situation

Jackson, a divorced man, transferred $1 million in trust for his children and grandchildren. To eliminate the GST tax, Jackson allocated $1 million of GST exemption to the trust and avoided any GST tax liability. All the property in that trust will always be exempt from the GST tax, no matter how much it appreciates.

The applicable fraction: $\dfrac{\$1,000,000 \text{ exemption}}{\$1,000,000 \text{ taxable gift}}$

The inclusion ratio: $1.0 - 1 = 0$

An inclusion ratio of *zero* means that no GST tax is due. When an exempt trust is established with an inclusion ratio of zero, that trust generally maintains 100% immunity from GST tax as long as there are no later additions of nonexempt property to the trust.

An inclusion ratio of *one* means that the entire future value of all taxable terminations and taxable distributions from a trust to skip person beneficiaries is subject to a GST tax.

Practitioner Tip: The client's exemption should be allocated so that each trust is given an inclusion ratio of one or zero. A client should either allocate an exemption amount that equals the value of the property transferred to the trust for an inclusion ratio of zero, or he should not allocate any portion of the exemption to the trust for an inclusion ratio of one. That way no trust is partially exempt and partially nonexempt from GST tax.

In the preceding client situation, if Jackson allocates only half of his exemption, then one-half of all future distributions from the trust to his grandchildren would be subject to the tax as taxable distributions, and one-half of the value of the assets remaining in the trust would be subject to the GST tax when his children die (as taxable terminations).

Practitioner Tip: For optimal results, it is best to fund a GST exempt trust with assets that have the greatest growth potential. This allows the maximum amount of assets to pass to future generations without transfer tax because, once the exemption is allocated to the trust, all future growth and appreciation of those assets will be exempt from GST tax.

Calculating the GST Tax for Transfers at Death

The transfer of a decedent's property at death to a skip person is a direct skip that is subject to a GST tax. Any death taxes, funeral or administrative expenses, or mortgages that are payable from this GST transfer are deducted first. The GST tax is then calculated by subtracting the amount of the decedent's GST exemption that is allocated to the transfer from the net amount of the property transferred. This amount is multiplied by the GST tax rate in effect in the year of the transferor's death.

Client Situation

Claudia died this year and bequeathed $1 million to her granddaughter Emma in her will. Claudia had previously established a trust that named Emma as the remainder beneficiary, and another trust that provided Emma with all of the trust income and corpus. When Claudia died, she only had $600,000 left of her $5,430,000 GST exemption. After subtracting the remaining exemption from the $1 million bequest, the taxable amount of Claudia's bequest for GST purposes was $400,000. This amount was multiplied by a flat tax rate of 40% for a GST tax of $160,000. Claudia's will addressed how the GST tax would be paid, which was either from Claudia's estate or from the bequest to Emma.

At the transferor's death, when the executor or other person making the allocation fails to allocate the exemption, it is allocated automatically according to a statutory formula. The statute allocates any unused exemption first to direct skips occurring at the individual's death on a pro rata basis, and then to any trusts from which a taxable distribution or termination could occur after the transferor's death.

Payment of the GST Tax for Direct Skips

The GST tax is paid by the transferor when a direct skip gift is made, or paid by the trustee when a lifetime transfer is made to a skip person trust. The GST tax is reported on the transferor's federal gift tax return, IRS Form 709. The GST tax is imposed only once per generation. Certain transfers that have already been subject to the GST tax in which the transferee was in the same or lower generation as the present transferee are excluded from GST tax.

At the transferor's death, the executor is responsible for payment of the GST tax in the case of a direct skip. The value of the property for GST tax purposes is the same as its value for federal estate tax purposes, including elections for the alternate valuation date or special-use valuation. The GST tax would be reported on the decedent's federal estate tax return, IRS Form 706, which is due nine months after the decedent's date of death.

The tax in a direct skip is *tax exclusive*. In other words, the tax is paid by the transferor or the estate and the taxable amount does not include the amount of generation-skipping tax.

Client Situation

Luke made a gift of $1 million to his granddaughter Nichole this year. He had previously made gifts that totaled more than $6 million to his grandchildren in the past. Luke has to pay a gift tax and a GST tax because he has no further unified credit or GST exemption available to offset the taxes on this new gift. Both transfer taxes are tax exclusive and are paid from other assets or accounts that Luke owns. The value of the gift to Nichole is not reduced by payment of these taxes and Nichole will net the full $1 million.

INDIRECT SKIPS

An indirect skip is made when property is transferred into a trust for the benefit of a skip person and a non-skip person in the same trust. For example, when a grandfather funds a trust for his daughter and grandchildren, this is not a direct skip because all of the beneficiaries are not two or more generations below the grandfather. The daughter in this example is a not a skip person. Assume the daughter will receive all of the income from the trust for life and the grandchildren will receive the remainder interest. A generation-skipping transfer will not occur until the daughter's interest in the trust ends at her death, and the grandchildren receive the remainder interest. This is an example of a taxable termination.

Another example of an indirect skip occurs when a transferor gives a child a life estate in real property and gifts the remainder interest to a grandchild. Two gifts are made for gift tax purposes, one to the child and one the grandchild. However, a GST tax is not paid until the child's interest in the property ends (at the child's death) and the property is transferred to the grandchild. This is also an example of a taxable termination.

An indirect skip defers the GST tax until a later time, as opposed to a direct skip, where the GST tax is payable at the time a generation-skipping transfer is made. The GST exemption will be automatically allocated to an indirect skip unless the donor elects otherwise. Elections can be made with respect to a transfer or for all transfers to a trust. There are separate tax returns to report the GST tax depending on whether the indirect skip is a taxable distribution or a taxable termination.

Taxable Distributions

A **taxable distribution** is any distribution of income or corpus from a trust to a skip person that is not otherwise subject to estate or gift tax. For instance, a distribution from a trust to a grandson of the grantor would be to a skip person. Likewise, if a mother creates a trust providing distributions of income or principal to her daughter or granddaughter at the discretion of the trustee, a distribution from that trust to the granddaughter is a taxable distribution. A distribution from one trust to a second trust would be considered a transfer to a skip person if all interests in the second trust were held by skip persons.

When a grantor allocates a GST exemption that matches the amount initially transferred into the trust, then no GST tax is due when a distribution is made to a skip person. However, if the grantor had no further GST exemption available to allocate to the trust when the trust was funded, then any distributions made to skip person beneficiaries would be subject to the GST tax.

Trust distributions are subject to the tax regardless of whether they are made from income or from corpus. The taxable amount is the net value of the property received by the skip person less any consideration paid by that transferee. In other words, the taxable amount is what the skip person received, reduced by (1) any expenses incurred by the skip person in connection with the determination, collection, or refund of the GST tax, and (2) any consideration paid for the distribution.

The skip person is obligated to pay the GST tax in a taxable distribution. Recipients of income subject to the GST tax can take an income tax deduction for the GST tax imposed on the distribution. If the trust itself pays the tax, the payment will be treated as an additional taxable distribution. The GST tax is reported on Form 709, and the return is due on April 15 following the year in which the taxable distribution was made.

The tax levied on a taxable distribution is tax inclusive. That means the amount subject to tax includes the property and the GST tax itself.

Client Situation

Klista transferred $2 million to an irrevocable trust for the benefit of her son Jason and her grandson Trevor. Klista had used up the entire amount of her GST exemption in previous gifts made to her grandchildren over the years. Consequently, no GST exemption was allocated to this trust and the trust had an inclusion ratio of one. The trustee made a taxable distribution of $100,000 of trust income to Trevor this year. Trevor will have to include this amount on his income tax return. The GST tax, at a tax rate of 40%, was $40,000. Assuming Trevor pays the tax from this distribution, he will net only $60,000 less income tax.

Taxable Termination

A **taxable termination** is essentially the termination by death, lapse of time, release of a power, or otherwise of an interest in property held in a trust resulting in skip persons holding all the interests in the trust.

Client Situation

If Brady leaves a life income to his son Wes with a remainder to his granddaughter Gwen, the son's death terminates his life interest in trust property and it then passes to Gwen, a skip person. A taxable termination occurs on the date of the son's death.

A taxable termination cannot occur as long as at least one non-skip person has a present interest in the property. Furthermore, there is no taxable termination if an estate or gift tax is imposed on the non-skip individual (the son, Wes, in the example above) at termination.

When a grantor allocates his GST exemption to the trust, then no GST tax is due when the non-skip person beneficiary dies. However, if the grantor had no GST exemption available to allocate to the trust when the trust was established, then the trust has an inclusion ratio of one, and a GST tax is due when the taxable termination occurs.

Client Situation

Ellie transferred $3 million into an irrevocable trust, which will pay her son Daniel all income for life and will give her granddaughter Lindsay the remaining assets in the trust at Daniel's death. Ellie allocated $3 million of her GST exemption to the trust, which has an inclusion ratio of zero. A taxable termination will occur when Daniel dies; however, the property passing to Lindsay will not be subject to a GST tax.

The taxable amount is the value of all property involved less a deduction for expenses attributable to the property. The trustee is responsible for the payment of the tax in a taxable termination. The GST tax return is reported on Form 709 and due on April 15 following the year in which the taxable termination occurred.

The tax payable upon a taxable termination is tax inclusive because, as with the taxable distribution, the property subject to the transfer includes the GST tax itself.

Client Situation

Assume $1 million is placed into an irrevocable trust for the benefit of the grantor's daughter for life with remainder to his granddaughter. At the daughter's death in 2015, a taxable termination occurs. Assume no exemptions were claimed and the trust has an inclusion ratio of one. The tax is 40% of $1 million, or $400,000. It must be paid out of property passing to the granddaughter. Therefore, the granddaughter nets only $600,000.

Practitioner Tip: Taxable distributions and taxable terminations are tax inclusive, whereas direct skips are tax exclusive. Therefore, it makes sense to use the GST exemption to minimize the tax on taxable distributions and terminations.

When persons are initially assigned to generations it is possible that subsequent events will result in generation reassignment. For example, upon a taxable transfer to succeeding generations of skip persons, such as grandchildren and great-grandchildren, each transfer is subject to tax, but upon each successive transfer, the transferor is assigned to a lower generation. This is to prevent the imposition of the GST tax twice on transfers to persons in the same generation.

MULTIGENERATIONAL PLANNING

Portability does not apply to GST tax and the GST exemption is not freely transferable between spouses. If all assets are titled in one spouse's name, the spouse without assets may not be able to take advantage of his available GST exemption. Therefore, financial planners should ensure that sufficient assets are titled in each spouse's name to take advantage of their respective GST exemptions. Where community property is involved, it is unnecessary for one spouse to consider a transfer to the other so that both can use their full GST exemption.

Some clients might also want to consider direct skip transfers for grandchildren or more remote descendants. Compare the result when a trust provides for distributions to a child for life, then grandchildren for life, and the remainder to great-grandchildren. There will be three taxable events: when the trust is created (estate or gift tax); when the child dies (taxable termination); and when the last surviving grandchild dies (taxable termination). Allowing distributions directly to great-grandchildren while the child is still alive eliminates one level of tax. Also, direct transfers to grandchildren after a child is deceased eliminate one level of tax, because the grandchildren move up a generation.

To take advantage of the GST exemptions of a client and spouse, a common approach to multigenerational planning is the establishment of a **dynasty trust**, which is intended to continue through succeeding generations as long as the law will permit. The actual distribution of these trust assets is postponed as long as possible, to avoid estate tax as long as possible. Such trusts could last many years. For example, if a trust with a present value of $2 million continues in existence for at least 75 years and grows at an annual rate of only 4%, it will increase to more than $37 million. This kind of planning might appeal to clients who have a tradition of preserving wealth in a family through succeeding generations.

Client Situation

Jeremy and Fran have an estate of $2,200,000 and plan to use life insurance and leveraging to maximize the utilization of their GST tax exemptions for the benefit of their five children and their issue. The transferors make annual gifts to the trust to pay the life insurance premiums. Those annual gifts are exempt from gift tax under the annual exclusion. In addition, GST exemption is allocated to the annual gifts. The premiums are $25,000 per year for 16 years, for a total of $400,000 of premium (assume $200,000 given by each spouse). The insurance is the "survivorship" type that only pays when the survivor dies.

In this situation, although only $400,000 of GST exemption was allocated to the life insurance trust premiums, all of the $1 million of insurance proceeds paid at the second spouse's death will be sheltered from GST tax.

Practitioner Tip: Clients should protect irrevocable life insurance trusts from the GST tax by allocating a portion of the GST exemption to each transfer made to the trust. Keep in mind that the use of a portion of the GST exemption to shield, for example, 16 $25,000 annual premiums protects not only that $400,000, but also the future trust corpus generated by the policy proceeds. Leveraging the GST exemption this way can be the single most effective long-term means of keeping wealth within a family.

Reverse QTIP Election

When one spouse makes a gift to the other—either during lifetime or at death—in a form that qualifies for the marital deduction, there is a danger that all or part of the available GST exemption of the transferor spouse will be lost.

A bypass trust provides that income and/or principal be payable to a decedent's surviving spouse and other family beneficiaries. When grandchildren are included as beneficiaries of this trust, the decedent's GST exemption can be allocated to the bypass trust to exempt the trust from all future GST taxes.

If a married couple intends to transfer assets to grandchildren at the surviving spouse's death, and the value of the assets exceeds the amount of GST exemption the surviving spouse has available at death, then a GST tax must be paid. To avoid this situation, the decedent's estate can be arranged so that a marital deduction is available to the decedent's estate through a QTIP trust rather than a power of appointment trust. The surviving spouse would receive all income from the trust annually, and the skip person beneficiaries would receive the remainder interest. On the federal estate tax return, the executor would make a **reverse QTIP election** so that the decedent is treated as the transferor, not the surviving spouse. Now the decedent's GST exemption can be fully utilized to offset future GST taxes from this trust. The surviving spouse's GST exemption was not used in this trust and remains available to offset future taxable gifts or bequests to skip persons. This reverse QTIP election is irrevocable and provides maximum leverage of the couple's GST exemptions if the decedent spouse did not use his full GST exemption while he was alive.

Practitioner Tip: This problem has become less of a concern for many because the GST exemption equals the estate tax unified credit equivalent amount of $5,430,000 in 2015. However, if the decedent makes gifts or transfers during lifetime that make the amounts of estate tax unified credit and GST exemption remaining at death unequal, a reverse QTIP election could still be useful.

Chapter Highlights

- A GST is any transfer of property by gift or at death to any person who is assigned to a generation that is two or more generations below that of the transferor. This person is known as a *skip person*. A trust can also be a skip person if all beneficiaries are skip persons.

- A direct skip is a transfer subject to an estate or gift tax made to a skip person. The transferor is responsible for paying the GST tax on a direct skip. The tax is tax exclusive.

- A transfer to a trust that includes other beneficiaries who are not two or more generations below the transferor is an example of an indirect skip.

- The generation-skipping tax can be imposed *in addition to* any estate or gift tax that could also be due because of the transfer.

- The GST exemption is $5,430,000 in 2015, which can be allocated to generation-skipping transfers to reduce or eliminate the tax. Transfers that exceed this amount are taxed at a flat 40% tax rate, which is equal to the highest estate tax rate.

- GST tax annual exclusions are unavailable for trusts with multiple skip person beneficiaries or for discretionary distributions made to a single trust beneficiary.

- The GST tax on an inter-vivos direct skip is determined by dividing the amount of GST exemption allocated to the transfer by the taxable amount of the gift. This applicable fraction is subtracted from one to arrive at the inclusion ratio, which is multiplied by the GST tax rate. This applicable rate is multiplied by the taxable amount of the gift to determine the total GST tax due.

- The GST exemption should be allocated to obtain an inclusion ratio of either zero or one. An inclusion ratio of zero means no GST tax is ever due, and a ratio of one means all the property subject to a GST taxable distribution or a taxable termination is taxed.

- The GST tax for bequests is calculated by subtracting the amount of the decedent's GST exemption allocated to the transfer from the net amount of the property transferred, multiplied by 40% in 2015.

- A taxable distribution is any distribution of income or corpus from a trust to a skip person. The skip person is responsible for paying the GST tax. The tax is tax inclusive.

- A taxable termination occurs after a non-skip beneficiary dies and property is passed to skip persons. The trustee is responsible for paying the GST tax. The tax is tax inclusive.

- An executor can make a reverse QTIP election so that the decedent is treated as the transferor for GST purposes, not the surviving spouse.

- A dynasty trust can take advantage of both the client and spouse's GST exemptions to preserve family wealth throughout succeeding generations.

Key Terms

applicable fraction

applicable rate

direct skip

dynasty trust

generation-skipping transfer (GST)

generation-skipping transfer tax

GST exemption

inclusion ratio

indirect skip

predeceased parent rule

reverse QTIP election

skip person

skip person trust

taxable distribution

taxable termination

transferee

transferor

Review Questions

19-1. Jeanette has two children and four grandchildren. She inherited an estate from her husband worth $15 million and began making gifts to reduce the value of her estate. To date, she has made the following transfers and has allocated her GST exemption to all of them:

1. She created an irrevocable trust funded with $2 million that provides her children with income for life. The corpus will be distributed to her grandchildren at the last child's death.

2. Last year she gave her children, grandchildren, and two great nephews $15,000 for their birthdays.

3. She established separate irrevocable trusts for each of her grandchildren, which she funded with $500,000. The income in these trusts will accumulate until each child attains age 35.

How much of Jeanette's GST exemption remains to offset taxes on future gifts?

A. $1,000,000

B. $1,030,000

C. $1,166,000

D. $1,424,000

19-2. Which of the following GST transfers is not made to a skip person?

A. A gift made from a grandfather to his great-granddaughter.

B. A gift made from a great aunt to her great niece.

C. A gift made from a grandmother to her granddaughter after the granddaughter's parent died.

D. A transfer of $100,000 to an irrevocable trust for the sole benefit of the transferor's grandson, who is the only trust beneficiary.

19-3. Which of the following transfers are examples of an indirect skip?

A. Dion funded an irrevocable trust with $1 million, which gave his daughter Sasha income for life, and his grandchildren the remainder interest.

B. Ivan's will established a life estate in his mountain cabin for his daughter Sophia, with the remainder passing to his grandson at Sophia's death.

C. Bobby died and bequeathed $80,000 to his son Justin. Justin disclaimed this property, which then passed from Bobby's estate to his daughter Kaylee.

D. Lenny placed $600,000 in an irrevocable trust for his three grandsons to fund their future college education.

19-4. Which statement regarding the payment of GST tax is incorrect?

A. Annual exclusions are not available to reduce the GST tax when property

is transferred into an irrevocable trust for multiple skip person beneficiaries, or when a trustee has the discretion to make distributions to a skip person beneficiary.

B. The GST tax for direct skips is tax inclusive.

C. When an exempt trust is established with an inclusion ration of zero, that trust generally maintains total immunity from GST tax.

D. If a trust has an inclusion ratio of one, then a GST tax is due for a taxable distribution or a taxable termination.

19-5. Which of the following statements concerning allocation of the GST exemption is incorrect?

A. The GST exemption offsets the gift tax, the estate tax, and the GST tax when a transfer subject to a GST tax is made.

B. The GST exemption will be automatically allocated to a direct skip during life and to an indirect skip unless the donor elects otherwise.

C. The client's exemption should be allocated so that each trust is given an inclusion ratio of either one or zero, so that a trust is not partially exempt and partially nonexempt from GST tax.

D. The executor can make a reverse QTIP election so that the decedent is considered the transferor for the remainder property passing to skip person beneficiaries in a QTIP trust.

Chapter 20

Powers of Appointment

CFP® CERTIFICATION EXAMINATION PRINCIPAL TOPICS COVERED IN THIS CHAPTER:

Powers of Appointment

- Use and purpose
- General powers
- Special (limited) powers
- Distributions for an ascertainable standard

- 5-and-5 power
- Crummey powers
- Tax implications
- Lapse of power

Learning Objectives

To ensure you have a solid understanding of the types of powers of appointment, including Crummey powers, and the resulting tax implications, the following learning objectives are addressed in this chapter:

- Distinguish general powers of appointments from special powers.

- Understand the gift and estate tax implications of powers of appointment.

- Recognize when property is subject to an ascertainable standard.

- Describe the gift and estate tax consequences of 5-and-5 powers.

- Recognize when it is appropriate to use Crummey powers.

- Understand how Crummey powers affect gift and estate taxes for grantors and trust beneficiaries.

Chapter Contents

OVERVIEW

Powers of appointment (POAs) are rights that are given in a will, trust, or other instrument that grant a *donee* or a **holder of a power of appointment** the right to dispose of a portion of the donor's property. When the holder appoints the donor's property to someone else, that recipient is known as the **appointee**, who is usually a trust beneficiary. There are many reasons why a donor would want to allow someone else to make decisions concerning property interests, because powers of appointment afford the holder some measure of flexibility:

- A donor wants to avoid family conflict or confrontation by giving an objective, unrelated person the right to dispose of the donor's property.

- A donor does not know what the future needs of his intended beneficiaries will be—or even who or how many beneficiaries he will have.

- A holder of the power will likely survive the donor and can make informed decisions about who should receive the trust property, how much income or principal should be allocated to beneficiaries, and when principal or income should be paid out.

The donor might decide to give trust beneficiaries powers of appointment to take advantage of certain gift and estate tax benefits:

- A donor wants to reduce the gift tax value of assets transferred into a trust. Beneficiaries who are given Crummey withdrawal powers have a present interest in a trust; therefore, a donor can take an annual exclusion for each Crummey beneficiary.

- The donor wants a gift or estate tax marital deduction for terminable interest property transferred to his spouse.

Financial planners should be aware of any powers of appointment their clients have acquired because there are gift and estate tax implications for holding, exercising, or releasing these powers.

POWERS OF APPOINTMENT

There are no required or magic words or phrases for creating a POA. In fact, it is possible to create such a power without even using the word *appoint*. The courts examine whether the words used in the will or trust manifest the intent to create a power. Thus, a power to invade or consume trust corpus is a power of appointment. For purposes of trust law, a power of appointment is "general" if there are no restrictions on the holder's choice of appointees. When there are certain restrictions, then the power is termed a "limited" power of appointment or a "special" power of appointment. It is the planner's responsibility to identify what kind of powers of appointment a client may hold and to recognize how these powers can affect the client's estate plan.

Practice Standard 200-2

Obtaining Quantitative Information and Documents

The financial planning practitioner shall obtain sufficient quantitative information and documents about a client relevant to the scope of the engagement before any recommendation is made and/or implemented.

GENERAL POWERS OF APPOINTMENT

A **general power of appointment** grants broad powers to a holder to dispose of a donor's property, or to appoint it to anyone he wants, including:

- the holder;

- the holder's estate;

- the holder's creditors; and

- creditors of the holder's estate.

Powers of appointment can be granted by a donor to a holder during the donor's life, which would impose a gift tax, or at death, which would be subject to an estate tax.

A donor who grants a general power of appointment while he is alive can use annual exclusions, marital deductions, and the unified credit, if applicable, to reduce or eliminate any taxable gifts. Likewise, if a general power of appointment is created at a donor's death by will or trust, the transfer is subject to estate taxes. Both transfers could also be subject to a **Generation-Skipping Transfer (GST) tax** if the power is granted to a holder who is two or more generations below the donor.

A holder must **exercise the power of appointment** in the precise manner the donor has specified. For example, if the power can be exercised only during the holder's lifetime, then it cannot be exercised by the holder's will. The power can be exercised by the holder's will only if there is explicit language in the will that allows the exercise of the power. If a donor has not stated how the power is to be exercised, the holder can use any normal method by which the property subject to the power can be transferred. For example, real property could be appointed by deed and stock certificates by endorsement.

Client Situation

Jackie's mother Rose transferred $300,000 into an irrevocable trust and named Jackie as the beneficiary. Jackie has the right to receive all of the trust income for her life, and a power of appointment clause in the trust gives Jackie the power to invade the trust corpus without restriction. Consequently, Jackie has a general power of appointment over the trust corpus.

Tax Implications for the Holder of a General POA

When a donor grants a general POA, he can be subject to gift or estate tax, and possibly a GST tax in addition to the gift or estate tax. The holder of the power can also be subject to gift, estate, or GST taxes when he or she transfers the donor's property to others.

Estate Tax

At death, the holder must include any property subject to the general POA in his gross estate. Although the holder has not been given title to the donor's property, the holder has complete control over the property, which causes it to be includible in his estate under Code section 2041. A holder can also receive a testamentary general POA that allows him to appoint property through his will. This property would also be included in the holder's gross estate but it would not be part of his probate estate.

The holder of a general power can choose to take the following actions.

- The holder can exercise the power to demand money from a trust. This is known as a *withdrawal right*, a *demand right*, or a *power to invade* the trust corpus.

- The holder can release a power, which surrenders all rights over the designated property.

- The holder can decide to let the power lapse by not exercising it within a specified period of time.

These three situations could subject the holder to a gift tax at the time they occur.

Gift Tax

When a holder exercises a POA in favor of someone else, a gift is made of the fair market value of the property transferred. When the holder releases the power, the holder is making a gift to the remaindermen in the trust. And when the holder does not exercise the power within the allotted time frame, the withdrawal right expires and the holder has let the power lapse. The **lapse of a power** is also a gift from the holder to the remaindermen in the trust. With a release or lapse of the power, the power passes to a "taker in default," who is the ultimate recipient of the property, usually the remaining trust beneficiaries.

Client Situation

Virginia is the holder of a general power of appointment over a trust that her mother left her. The trust allows her to appoint trust property during her lifetime, or at her death, to whomever she wishes. If she does not exercise the power of appointment, the trust property will pass to her brother Joseph. If Virginia exercises the power of appointment in favor of her son Richard while she is still alive, she has made a gift to Richard that is subject to gift tax. Virginia can exercise the power of appointment by will, appointing the property to whomever she wishes at her death, including her estate. If she does not exercise the power of appointment by will, the property will pass to Joseph. Either way, the property will be included in her gross estate because she has the ability to dispose of it in the trust.

Practitioner Tip: If the holder exercised or released the general power during life but kept an interest in the property that would have been subject to Code sections 2036, 2037, and 2038, then the entire value of the property would be included in the holder's gross estate.

Example: Eric exercised a general power by appointing rental property to his sister Kate, but Eric retained the right to receive all of the rental income for the rest of his life. Under Code section 2036, the fair market value of the rental property will be included in Eric's gross estate.

SPECIAL OR LIMITED POWERS OF APPOINTMENT

A **special or limited power of appointment** is one that typically does not allow the holder to appoint property to himself, his estate, his creditors, or creditors of his estate. Rather, the holder can appoint property either to a specified class of beneficiaries, such as his children or a charity, or to anyone other than himself, his creditors, his estate, or creditors of his estate.

However, there are exceptions to this rule. The donor could permit the holder to demand income or corpus from the trust by restricting the holder's authority to exercise the power in the following ways:

- The holder must obtain the donor's consent.

- The holder must obtain approval from the other trust beneficiaries. These beneficiaries have an "adverse interest" because any trust property the holder appoints to himself will reduce the amount available for them.

- The holder can exercise the power according to an ascertainable standard.

Ascertainable Standard

An **ascertainable standard** gives a holder the right to consume, invade, or appropriate trust income or principal only for very specific purposes. An ascertainable standard can be spelled out in many ways, but the most common definition allows for the distribution or invasion of trust corpus for the holder's "health, education, maintenance, and support"; the acronym to remember is *HEMS*. Maintenance and support are synonymous and represent the holder's accustomed standard of living, which is not limited to the bare necessities of life. The holder must be given any one or a combination of these uses for an ascertainable standard to apply.

A trust clause that uses the terms "welfare," "comfort," or "well-being" do not represent an ascertainable standard. These terms create a general POA over trust property even though they are similar in meaning to "maintenance and support." Examples of acceptable phrases that create ascertainable standards are:

- "Support in reasonable comfort or accustomed manner of living";

- "Education including college and professional education"; and

- "Medical, dental, hospital, and nursing expenses and expenses of invalidism."

Estate Tax

Special powers of appointment are not included in a holder's gross estate, and the exercise, release, or lapse of a special power will not cause any estate tax liability for the holder. Someone can be named both the trustee and beneficiary of a trust, and trust property is not included in his gross estate if he can appoint property only to himself according to an ascertainable standard.

Practitioner Tip: If a client is named both the trustee and beneficiary of a trust, he should be very careful to ensure that the standards set out in the trust are carefully adhered to. The trust must be maintained as a trust rather than used as a personal account, and property can be distributed only for the specific purposes allowed by the trust. The trustee-beneficiary cannot use property for any other purposes or the entire value of the trust will be included in his estate.

Gift Tax

There is no gift tax liability when special powers of appointment are exercised, released, or allowed to lapse.

Client Situation

Carolyn created a $500,000 irrevocable trust to benefit her father Tom and her husband Nigel. Tom will receive the trust income for life and he is permitted to withdraw $30,000 from trust corpus each year to pay for his medical expenses. Tom has a special power of appointment; therefore, no portion of the trust will be included in his estate at death. Nigel is the remainder beneficiary of the trust, and the value of the trust's assets will be included in his estate when he dies.

5-AND-5 POWERS

A **5-and-5 power** is a commonly used technique that provides flexibility and financial security for a beneficiary with little or no tax consequence. A donor can give a holder a **noncumulative right of withdrawal**, which allows the greater of $5,000 or 5% of the trust corpus to be withdrawn each year. *Noncumulative* means that if the money is not withdrawn this year, it cannot be withdrawn in subsequent years. The importance of this withdrawal right is that it gives the beneficiaries a present interest in the trust, which allows the donor to take annual exclusions against the property placed in trust. The holder of a 5-and-5 power is taxed differently for gift and estate taxes than a holder of a general power of appointment.

Gift Tax

A taxable gift can occur when a holder of a 5-and-5 power does not withdraw any money from a trust within a certain period of time, and his withdrawal right lapses accordingly. When a lapse occurs, a gift is made to the other beneficiaries in the trust. The question is, is this a taxable gift? There is a **de minimis rule** that says, in essence, that the tax law will ignore small amounts. A lapsed amount that is equal to or less than $5,000 or 5% of the trust corpus is not taxed.

Client Situation

Monica funded an irrevocable trust with $50,000. She gave her husband Bill and her son Jake a noncumulative right to withdraw the greater of $5,000 or 5% of the trust corpus each year. Bill and Jake could have withdrawn $5,000 from the trust this year but instead they let their withdrawal rights lapse. As a result, they did not make any taxable gifts to each other.

The *excess* above $5,000 or 5% of the trust corpus is treated as the release of a general power and is taxed accordingly. The excess can be treated as a gift subject to gift tax or as a transfer that could be subject to estate tax. To ensure that the preceding limits are not breached, the right of invasion must be made noncumulative.

Client Situation

Ted established an irrevocable trust with $1 million and gave his daughter, Peggy a life estate in the trust. Ted named his grandson Drew the remainder beneficiary. Ted also gave Peggy a noncumulative right to withdraw $60,000 from the trust each year. If Peggy does not withdraw any money from the trust this year, she has made a taxable gift to the trust for the amount that exceeds 5% of the trust corpus. In this case, Peggy has made a taxable gift of $10,000, which is the amount that exceeds 5% of the trust corpus of $50,000.

CRUMMEY POWERS

A trust provision included in irrevocable trusts that provides gift tax benefits for the grantor is known as a **Crummey power**. A grantor can take annual exclusions to reduce taxable gifts when trust beneficiaries have a present interest in the trust, but not when they have a future interest. Beneficiaries have future interests if a trust can accumulate income or if a life insurance policy is transferred into the trust. A Crummey power converts a future interest to a present interest, which allows the grantor to take an annual exclusion for each trust beneficiary that holds the power.

Each time a grantor transfers money into a Crummey trust, the beneficiary has a legal right to withdraw an amount equal to the value of the gift. This right of withdrawal gives the beneficiary a present interest in the trust property, even if the beneficiary does not exercise the power by withdrawing funds from the trust.

The Crummey power is not a "demand" or "invasion" right, which gives a beneficiary the right to demand payment of existing trust corpus or income. Instead, the Crummey power is a right to withdraw money that has been recently transferred into the trust. For example, suppose no deposit was made to a trust in the second year, but the trust corpus appreciated and generated some income. Crummey beneficiaries could not receive distributions from the trust because no assets were gifted into the trust that year.

Crummey Notice

The trustee must notify in writing every Crummey beneficiary—even minors—that they have an immediate right to withdraw the funds transferred into the trust within a specific period of time, typically 30 days. This is known as a **Crummey notice.** The withdrawal right cannot be illusory but must be an actual right to withdraw the gift made on the beneficiary's behalf. Implicit in every Crummey trust is the notion that the beneficiary will not exercise the right to withdraw and the gifts to the trust will remain in the trust until termination.

Crummey Withdrawal Amounts

A donor's gift to trust is eligible for the annual exclusion only to the extent the trust has assets sufficient to satisfy the beneficiary's demand rights. Generally, the Crummey withdrawal amount is limited to the *lesser* of:

- the annual exclusion of $14,000, or $28,000 if gift splitting occurs;

- the amount the beneficiary can withdraw in proportion to the amount contributed to the trust; and

- the *greater* of $5,000 or 5% of the amount transferred into the trust. Note that with a 5-and-5 power the holder has a noncumulative right to withdraw the greater of $5,000 or 5% of the trust corpus annually.

Client Situation

Tim established an irrevocable trust for his four young children this year and funded it with $20,000. Tim intends to transfer $20,000 into the trust each year for the next 10 years to fund his children's education. The money in the trust will accumulate until his oldest son is ready to attend college in 10 years. The trust document gives each child a 30-day right to withdraw the greater of $5,000 or 5% of the money Tim transfers into the trust every year.

> **Result:** Ordinarily, beneficiaries have a future interest in a trust if they cannot receive annual distributions. If Tim did not give his children Crummey powers, then Tim could not take any annual exclusions when he transferred money into the trust. But in this case, Tim's children have been given the right to withdraw $5,000 from the trust this year, which gives them a present interest in the trust instead. The children are too young to read and understand the Crummey notice sent to them by the trustee, so Tim as their guardian has allowed their withdrawal rights to lapse. As a result, Tim can take an annual exclusion of $5,000 per child and the $20,000 transferred into the trust is not a taxable gift. When the children are older and are able to understand their Crummey rights of withdrawal, Tim will explain the purpose of the trust to them.

Practitioner Tip: An irrevocable trust with a Crummey power can provide for a discretionary stream of income for one beneficiary and allow for the distribution of trust corpus to another non-income beneficiary. This is more advantageous than a Section 2503(b) trust, which must distribute all income annually to the trust beneficiaries.

Crummey Lapses

Parents, as grantors of irrevocable trusts, want to use annual exclusions to reduce the value of taxable gifts made to these trusts, but they do not actually want their children to withdraw the money transferred into the trust each year. In compliance, Crummey beneficiaries will not exercise their withdrawal rights, thereby letting their withdrawal rights lapse. A **Crummey lapse**, or the **release of a general power of appointment**, results in a gift to the other beneficiaries in the trust. This is a future-interest gift because beneficiaries must wait until the trust terminates before the assets are divided and distributed to them. The lapse of a Crummey power could cause adverse gift and estate tax consequences.

Gift Tax

A Crummey beneficiary, as holder of a general POA, is subject to gift taxes when his right of withdrawal is allowed to lapse. Only the lapsed amount that *exceeds* the greater of $5,000 or 5% of the trust corpus is taxed. Amounts in excess of the safe harbor of $5,000 or 5% are treated as the release of a general POA, and they are taxable.

> ### Client Situation
>
> Dad sets up an irrevocable trust with Crummey powers for his two children, Brian and Brittany. Dad transfers $22,000 into the trust, allowing Brian and Brittany each to withdraw one-half of the gift. The children do not exercise their withdrawal rights within 30 days and the $22,000 remains in the trust. Brian and Brittany have made gifts to each other of the $11,000 they chose to leave in the trust. However the entire $11,000 is not subject to a gift tax.
>
> Here, $6,000 is considered a taxable gift because the amount that Brian or Brittany could have withdrawn ($11,000) minus $5,000 (the greater of $5,000 or 5%) is $6,000. Brain and Brittany would report these future-interest gifts on their gift tax return, IRS Form 709, but their unified credits would eliminate any gift tax liability.

Gift tax with limited withdrawal rights. Crummey beneficiaries who cannot withdraw more than $5,000 or 5% of the trust corpus will not make any taxable gifts to the other trust beneficiaries when they let their withdrawal rights lapse.

Client Situation

An irrevocable trust owns a life insurance policy with an annual premium of $18,000. The grantor, who is the insured, must transfer $18,000 into the trust each year so that the trustee can pay the insurance premiums. The trust beneficiaries consist of three children and one grandchild, which makes four gift tax annual exclusions available to the grantor. In this trust, withdrawal rights equal $4,500 per beneficiary, which is less than $5,000 or 5% of the trust corpus. When the beneficiaries let their withdrawal right lapse there are no taxable excess lapses. If the facts are changed so that the grandchild was not named a beneficiary of the trust, withdrawal rights would be more than $5,000 for each beneficiary and taxable lapses would occur.

Practitioner Tip: Under a court case known as *Estate of Cristofani* v. *Commissioner*,[1] annual exclusions can also be taken for grandchildren who are Crummey beneficiaries, although they are remote contingent remaindermen of the trust who will receive trust benefits only if their parent dies—a per stirpes distribution. Adding grandchildren as trust beneficiaries is beneficial because it increases the number of annual exclusions available to a grantor—and the grantor's spouse, if gift splitting is used. Note that in the example above, the GST annual exclusion does not apply because this trust is not a direct skip trust (i.e., there are two generations of beneficiaries in the same trust). Therefore, a portion of the grantor's $5,430,000 GST exemption must be used to offset the GST taxable gift when premium payments are transferred into the trust each year.

Estate Tax with Limited Withdrawal Rights

Beneficiaries who are given Crummey powers restricted to withdrawing the greater of $5,000 or 5% of the trust corpus each year have a portion of the trust included in their gross estate if they die before the trust has terminated. If a beneficiary exercised his withdrawal right and took money from the trust in the year he died, then nothing is included in his gross estate. However, if the beneficiary's withdrawal right was unexercised at the time of his death, then only the greater of $5,000 or 5% of the trust corpus is included in his gross estate. Note that this amount is not included in the beneficiary's probate estate.

Client Situation

Sue was given a Crummey right of withdrawal over a trust that allowed her to withdraw 5% of the trust assets every year. When Sue died the trust was valued at $1 million. Sue did not withdraw any money from the trust in the year she died; therefore, $50,000 was included in her gross estate.

Estate Tax with Cumulative Releases

Lapses that exceed $5,000 or 5% of the trust corpus are treated as the release of a general power of appointment and the excess amount is transferred to the trust. A release is similar to a retained life estate under Code section 2036 because the Crummey beneficiary, holder of the general power of appointment, retains the use or enjoyment of the excess income or principal in the trust. If a lapse occurs due to a holder's death, then the total value of the property that could have been appointed is included in the holder's gross estate. In addition, all lifetime lapses that resulted in taxable gifts are calculated based on the value of the property subject to the released power over the fair market value of the trust. The resulting annual percentages are then added together and multiplied by the fair market value of the trust at the holder's death to determine the amount included in the holder's gross estate.

Client Situation

Sam's mother funded a trust with $300,000, which gave Sam a noncumulative general power of appointment to withdraw $15,000 from the trust each year. Sam's children were named the remainder beneficiaries of the trust. Sam never exercised his withdrawal rights. Sam also had the right to decide how the money in trust would be divided among his children at his death. This right gave Sam the power to control who would possess or enjoy the property under IRC § 2036. Therefore, lifetime lapses must be brought back into Sam's gross estate when he dies.

In the first year the trust was established, no taxable gift was made to the other trust beneficiaries when Sam did not withdraw $15,000 (5% of $300,000 = $15,000).

At the end of the second year, the trust corpus decreased to $260,000 (5% of $260,000 = $13,000). Sam's withdrawal right of $15,000 exceeded 5% of the trust corpus by $2,000 (2,000 ÷ 260,000 = .77%).

By the end of the third year, the trust corpus further declined to $240,000 (5% of $240,000 = $12,000), resulting in an excess lapse of $3,000 or 1.25%

Sam died in the fourth year when the trust assets totaled $280,000.

Sam's estate will include lapses of .77% + 1.25% = 2.02% × $280,000 = $5,656.

Sam's estate will also include the amount he could have withdrawn in the year he died ($15,000).

The total amount included in Sam's gross estate subject to this withdrawal right is $20,656.

Practitioner Tip: Because most Crummey trusts are intended to be paid out during a beneficiary's lifetime, and many Crummey beneficiaries' estates are well below the estate tax unified credit amount, this is usually not a problem.

Solving the Excess Lapse Problem

There are several ways to establish irrevocable trusts to avoid making taxable gifts to the other trust beneficiaries when a Crummey right of withdrawal has lapsed. (See Table 20.1.)

Table 20.1 Crummey Lapses

	Gift Tax	**Estate Tax**
Limited to 5-and-5	No taxable gift	>$5,000 or 5% of trust corpus
Unlimited withdrawal right	Taxable gift is excess over 5-and-5	Withdrawal amount in year of death plus % of annual lapses over 5-and-5

Establish Separate Trusts for Each Beneficiary

Mom can establish a Crummey trust for her daughter Jen, the only trust beneficiary. Mom can use an annual exclusion to reduce or eliminate a taxable gift of up to $14,000. If Jen does not withdraw the money, she is not making a gift to another trust beneficiary and Jen's unified credit remains intact.

Limit the Crummey Right of Withdrawal to the Greater of $5,000 or 5%

Beneficiaries who are limited to withdrawing the greater of $5,000 or 5% of the trust corpus each year do not make taxable gifts to the other trust beneficiaries when they let their withdrawal rights lapse. Only withdrawal amounts that exceed the safe harbor of $5,000 or 5% are taxed.

Practitioner Tip: Be aware of the resulting gift tax consequence to the grantor. When a Crummey beneficiary's withdrawal right is limited to taking out the greater of $5,000 or 5%, then the grantor's annual exclusion is also limited to matching the beneficiary's withdrawal amount.

Client Situation

Dad created an unfunded irrevocable life insurance trust (ILIT) with annual premium payments of $30,000. His children Jared and Lisa are Crummey beneficiaries who can withdraw $5,000 from the trust this year, but they have let their withdrawal rights lapse. Dad's annual exclusion is limited to $5,000 for each child, or $10,000. Dad's taxable gift is $20,000 offset by his unified credit. If Mom agrees to gift split with Dad, then each parent has made a gift of $15,000 minus two annual exclusions of $5,000 for a taxable gift of $5,000 each. Both Mom and Dad will have to file a gift tax return this year, but their unified credits will offset the tax.

Gift $5,000 per Beneficiary (or $10,000 If Gift Splitting) into the Trust Each Year until the Value of the Trust Surpasses $100,000

Once the trust has accumulated more than $100,000, annual gifts can be increased to 5% of the trust value (or the cash surrender value of an insurance policy), thereby increasing the grantor's annual exclusion amount. When the trust has $280,000 in assets, the grantor can take a full annual exclusion of $14,000 per trust beneficiary.

Transfer $280,000 into Trust and Use the Grantor's Unified Credit to Offset the Taxable Gift

To avoid having Crummey beneficiaries make taxable gifts when they let their withdrawal rights lapse, the trust document should limit any subsequent Crummey gifting to 5% of the value of the trust assets. This way the grantor can take a $14,000 annual exclusion for each trust beneficiary in an unfunded ILIT or $28,000 if gift splitting is used to reduce the taxable amount of the premium.

Subtrusts

Separate trusts, or **subtrusts**, can be created within the ILIT for each Crummey beneficiary. The grantor can take full annual exclusions for the money allocated to each separate trust and gift taxes are avoided when beneficiaries let their withdrawal powers lapse. When the insured dies the trustee pays back each separate trust for the gifts that have lapsed over the years, which funds the separate trusts.

Hanging Power

A **hanging power** allows a beneficiary to withdraw more than the $5,000 or 5% safe harbor amount and make full use of the grantor's annual exclusions. The power to withdraw lasts all year, and then the excess over the 5-and-5 is carried forward until such time as the lapse of the hanging power is no longer treated as a taxable gift. The beneficiary can draw against the excess but the withdrawal power diminishes over time, which alleviates the adverse gift tax consequences. If the trust has not terminated when the beneficiary dies, then the beneficiary is in possession of the power at death, which is includible in the powerholder's estate. If the trust terminates before the powerholder dies, there is no adverse estate tax result. The IRS does not view this technique favorably.

Chapter Highlights

- A donor or *principal* grants a *donee* or a *holder of the power* the right to dispose of a portion of the donor's property.

- There are several types of powers of appointment: general powers, special or limited powers, and 5-and-5 powers, which are often used in Crummey trusts.

- Powers of appointments are taxed differently when they are exercised, released, or allowed to lapse. The release of a general power of appointment results in a gift to the remainder beneficiaries in trust. The lapse of a power is also a gift made by the holder to the remaindermen in the trust.

- An ascertainable standard gives the holder the right to consume, invade, or appropriate trust income or principal solely for the holder's "health, education, maintenance, and support."

- The Crummey power is not a "demand" or "invasion" right, which gives the beneficiary the right to demand payment of existing trust corpus or income. Instead, the Crummey power is a right to withdraw money that has been recently transferred to the trust.

- Crummey powers give beneficiaries a present interest in a trust, which permits the grantor and perhaps a spouse to use annual exclusions to reduce taxable transfers to a trust.

- Generally, the Crummey withdrawal amount is limited to the *lesser* of the annual exclusion of $14,000, or $28,000 if gift splitting occurs, or the *greater* of $5,000 or 5% of the amount transferred to the trust.

- A Crummey beneficiary is subject to gift taxes for the lapsed amount that *exceeds* the greater of $5,000 or 5% of the trust corpus. Therefore, Crummey beneficiaries who cannot withdraw more than $5,000 or 5% of the trust corpus do not make any taxable gifts to the other trust beneficiaries when they let their withdrawal rights lapse.

- Powers of appointment are important estate planning techniques often used in irrevocable life insurance trusts and in marital trusts to fulfill specific estate planning objectives.

Key Terms

appointee

ascertainable standard

Crummey lapse

Crummey notice

Crummey power

de minimis rule

exercise a power of appointment

5-and-5 power

general power of appointment

generation-skipping transfer tax

hanging power

holder of a power of appointment

lapse of a power

noncumulative right of withdrawal

powers of appointment

release a general power of appointment

special or limited power of appointment

subtrusts

Review Questions

20-1. Identify whether the power of appointment described is a general power of appointment or a special power of appointment.

  A. A holder can exercise the power to appoint property to himself with the consent of the other trust beneficiary.

  B. A holder can exercise the power in favor of her creditors.

  C. A holder was given a testamentary power to exercise the power in favor of his children.

  D. A holder can exercise the power for her comfort and support.

20-2. Paul established a trust for Elaine that gave her a life estate with a general power to appoint the greater of $5,000 or 5% of the trust corpus to herself each year. When Elaine died, the trust was valued at $700,000 and she had not yet withdrawn money from the trust that year. What amount was included in Elaine's estate from this trust?

  A. $700,000

  B. $35,000

  C. $5,000

  D. $0

20-3. Adele established an irrevocable trust and funded it with $1.5 million in securities. Her three married children are the beneficiaries of the trust, and each child can withdraw $50,000 of the trust corpus each year. Her daughter Liz did not withdraw money from the trust this year. Did Liz make a taxable gift to her brother and sister who are the other beneficiaries of the trust?

  A. No, because the amount of the power that lapsed was less than 5% of the trust corpus.

  B. Yes, because Liz allowed her general power of appointment over the trust property to lapse.

  C. No, because Liz had a limited power of appointment over the trust corpus, which is not taxable.

  D. Yes, because the right to make a withdrawal is considered a taxable gift to the other beneficiaries when the withdrawal right is not exercised.

20-4. Charlie created a trust for his daughter Chelsea and his son Jonathan. A POA clause gives each child a noncumulative right to withdraw the greater of $5,000 or 5% of the value of the trust each year. Charlie transferred $120,000 into the trust this year; how much of his annual exclusion can be used to offset the taxable gift for each donee?

  A. $5,000 per donee

  B. $6,000 per donee

  C. $14,000 per donee

  D. $28,000 per donee

20-5. Spiros and Nicki have established a trust to benefit their two children and five grandchildren. Spiros transferred a $2 million single premium insurance policy on his life into the trust, which had a gift tax value of $340,000. The beneficiaries of the trust can withdraw the greater of $5,000 or 5% of the trust corpus each year. Which of the following statements are correct?

A. With gift splitting, each parent can take seven annual exclusions to reduce the taxable gifts by $98,000.

B. For GST tax purposes, Spiros and Nicki can take five annual exclusions for their grandchildren because this is a direct skip trust.

C. The beneficiaries of the trust were given an ascertainable standard to make withdrawals from the trust corpus.

D. Spiros and Nicki can each use a portion of their unified credit to offset the gift tax when the policy is transferred into the trust, and they can allocate a portion of their GST tax exemption on their individual gift tax return to shelter any future GST taxes whenever distributions are made to the grandchildren.

20-6. Pam has a general POA over her mother's assets. Which of the following statements are correct regarding the power?

1. Pam can appoint her mother's money to pay for her children's education.

2. Pam can appoint her mother's money to pay her bills.

3. Pam must only appoint money using an ascertainable standard (health, education, maintenance, support).

4. If Pam were to die before her mother, Pam's gross estate would include her mother's assets although not previously appointed by Pam.

A. 1 only

B. 1 and 3

C. 1, 2 and 4

D. 1, 2 and 3

E. 1, 2, 3 and 4

Notes

1. Estate of *Cristofani v. Commissioner.* 97 T.C. 74 (1991).

Chapter 21

Life Insurance Planning

CFP® CERTIFICATION EXAMINATION PRINCIPAL TOPICS COVERED IN THIS CHAPTER:

Life Insurance (Individual)

- Policy types

Use of Life Insurance in Estate Planning

- Incidents of ownership
- Ownership and beneficiary considerations
- Estate and gift taxation

Learning Objectives

To ensure you have a solid understanding of the use of life insurance in estate planning, the following learning objectives are addressed in this chapter:

- Identify the most appropriate types of insurance policies to meet specific client objectives.

- Evaluate how policy ownership and beneficiary designations affect a client's estate plan.

- Recognize when incidents of ownership are retained after a policy is transferred.

- Evaluate the estate, probate, and gift tax consequences of owning and transferring a life insurance policy.

- Analyze a policy transfer to determine if the three-year rule applies.

Chapter Contents

OVERVIEW

Life insurance planning is an integral part of estate planning. Life insurance policies are used for many different purposes to meet client objectives that can change over time. Financial planners should understand the characteristics and types of insurance policies available and how ownership affects their client's estate tax situation. Planners should periodically review their client's insurance policies, risks, and exposures to ensure they have adequate coverage to meet their needs, to determine whether proper beneficiary designations are in place, and to evaluate how new or existing policies should be owned.

LIFE INSURANCE NEEDS

Younger clients often need life insurance to provide income protection for their families in the event of premature death. Life insurance proceeds can be used to:

- replace lost wages to maintain a family's standard of living;

- retire or reduce liabilities such as home mortgages, credit card balances, car loans, personal debts, and medical expenses; and

- fund future education expenses, retirement savings, and other large capital needs a family might have.

In later years clients can withdraw cash value amounts from life insurance policies through policy loans to:

- pay for education expenses;

- supplement their retirement income;

- retire their mortgage;

- make gifts to family members; and

- fund their personal goals.

Wealthier clients with large estates could need liquidity (cash) to:

- pay for estate and inheritance taxes and estate settlement expenses;

- generate family wealth for current and future generations; and

- make bequests to specific individuals and charities, and fund family foundations.

Business owners and corporations often purchase life insurance to:

- fund business continuation agreements;

- finance certain corporate obligations such as nonqualified deferred compensation or salary continuation plans;

- indemnify a corporation for the lost services of a key employee; and

- provide work incentives and rewards to valuable employees.

All of these estate planning objectives and others can be accomplished through proper planning with life insurance. Financial planners should be aware of the advantages and disadvantages of using life insurance policies to meet a client's objectives. Many different types of insurance policies are available and financial planners should be aware of the characteristics, differences, and taxation of these policies when evaluating which policies are best for their clients.

Practice Standard 200-1

Determining a Client's Personal and Financial Goals, Needs and Priorities

The financial planning practitioner and the client shall mutually define the client's personal and financial goals, needs and priorities that are relevant to the scope of the engagement before any recommendation is made and/or implemented.

TYPES OF POLICIES FOR INDIVIDUALS

Life insurance policies provide cash to a beneficiary equal to the death benefit amount when the policy owner dies. The death benefit amount is the face value amount of the policy, which is usually significantly greater than the premiums paid for the policy. Life insurance contracts are governed by state law and typically offer the policy owner and beneficiary some creditor protection, which varies from state to state. Policies can be held until maturity, sold to others, or gifted to individuals or trusts. An unconditional sale or gift of all ownership rights in a life insurance policy is known as an *absolute assignment*.

Practice Standard 500-2

Selecting Products and Services for Implementation

The financial planning practitioner shall select appropriate products and services that are consistent with the client's goals, needs and priorities.

Term Insurance

Term insurance is a type of life insurance purchased for a set period of time or term. With this type of insurance policy, the insured must die before the term expires for benefits to be paid. At the expiration of the term, the insurance protection terminates and if the insured is still alive, the death benefit is not paid. Initially, the cash outlay for insurance protection is relatively low so that the policy owner receives the maximum short-term protection for the minimum cash outlay. However, because the cost of term coverage depends largely on the insured's age, the cost of insurance coverage increases as the insured ages. There is no cash value savings component to term insurance.

Several types of term insurance are available:

1. *Annual renewable term.* This type of policy is renewable each year (regardless of the insured's physical condition) at an increasing premium.

2. *Convertible term.* This type of policy can be exchanged without evidence of insurability for a whole-life, universal life, variable life, or endowment type of policy.

3. *Decreasing term.* A familiar kind of decreasing term is often referred to as mortgage insurance. The death benefit decreases over the specified period of time, but the premium generally remains level.

4. *Level term.* Here the death benefit remains the same for the entire term of the policy. Generally the premium also remains level. Common term periods are 5, 10, 15, 20, and 30 years.

Client Situation

Matt and Leah are married and expecting their first child. Matt obtained his Ph.D. last year and teaches part-time at a university, and Leah works as a medical technician in a local clinic. Leah plans to go back to work soon after their baby is born because both incomes are needed to pay for their living expenses. They each purchased a $100,000 term life insurance policy on their own lives to cover living expenses and school loans in the event that one of them dies prematurely. They intend to purchase more coverage over time when they can afford to pay for the increased protection.

Permanent Insurance

Permanent insurance can be either whole-life insurance or universal life insurance, and either traditional or variable. Permanent insurance combines life insurance coverage with a savings element in the form of cash value. Premiums are typically higher for permanent insurance than for term insurance because the policy builds cash value. Over time, cash value builds up tax-deferred within the policy, which increases annually.

Most insurance policies allow the insured to access the cash value during his lifetime through policy loans. The interest earned on cash values typically is not taxable unless the policy is surrendered for cash and the cash value exceeds the amounts that have been paid in policy premiums. The policy owner can borrow against the cash value in the form of interest-bearing loans or as surrender proceeds.

Whole-life Insurance

A **whole-life insurance** policy is typically designed to be a permanent policy, with coverage lasting for the insured's lifetime. Whole-life insurance coverage is guaranteed to remain level throughout the life of the contract.

There are basically two types of whole life insurance. The first is known as *straight whole-life* and the second is known as *limited-payment life*. With a straight whole-life policy, premiums are payable for the lifetime of the insured. With a limited-payment life policy, premiums are payable over a shorter period of time and are significantly higher. *Single premium whole life insurance* is a type of limited-pay insurance policy which develops immediate cash value.

Universal Life Insurance

A **universal life** policy is interest-sensitive life insurance in which the investment, expense, and mortality elements are separately and specifically defined. A contract owner selects a death benefit that either increases over time, coinciding with the increased cash value of the policy, or alternatively, remains level regardless of underlying value changes. The insurer deducts certain expenses and mortality charges from the premium paid. The remaining premium is then credited toward the contract owner's cash values.

There is no "standard" universal life policy because each contract owner can choose the level of premium, the death benefit, and the length of the premium-paying period. This provides significant flexibility in premium payments. Usually a minimum premium must be paid the first policy year, but after that the contract owner can vary the amount, the payment date, or the frequency of subsequent premiums. As long as there is enough cash value to pay the expense charges and mortality costs, the policy remains in force. If the cash value falls below that level, the policy will terminate.

Interest earned on the cash value is credited at rates based on current investment earnings. Typically, there is a minimum contractual guarantee for interest credited. Loans can be taken against cash values subject to an interest charge. Unlike most traditional whole-life policies, it is permissible to make partial withdrawals of cash value while the insured is alive. Because withdrawals are not loans, no interest charges are incurred.

Client Situation

Steve and Jen have two young children and would like to have one more child. Steve is a commercial real estate broker and his income depends on the local real estate market. He bought a universal life policy several years ago when his first child was born because he wanted permanent insurance and the premiums were less expensive than whole-life insurance. As real estate sales improved, Steve paid higher premiums every year to increase the cash values within his policy. Steve is reassured that he will not lose his insurance coverage if his income dips and he cannot pay the premiums next year as long as his cash reserves are sufficient to keep the policy in force.

Variable Life Insurance

A **variable life insurance** policy is a permanent insurance policy that has an investment component. Unlike traditional whole-life insurance or traditional universal life insurance, the insured can select different subaccounts offered by the insurance company for the purpose of investing the cash value. The types of subaccounts offered can include money market accounts, stock accounts, bond accounts, and other types of investment accounts. The policy owner allocates the premium among various subaccounts after deductions for mortality costs and expenses. Owners can reallocate their investments several times a year. The cash value is adjusted on a daily basis, whereas the death benefit typically is adjusted once a year.

Neither the death benefit nor the surrender value payable during life is guaranteed: both can increase or decrease depending upon the investment performance of the assets underlying the policy. Generally, the death benefit cannot decrease below the initial face amount of the policy as long as all required premiums have been paid.

Premiums are fixed and always remain the same. Unlike some other types of insurance, the sale of a variable life insurance product must be accompanied or preceded by a prospectus approved by the Securities and Exchange Commission, because variable life is treated as a security. It can be sold only by agents registered as broker-dealers with FINRA.

Client Situation

Mark is a 50-year-old engineer who enjoys managing his own investments. He owns a whole-life insurance policy, which is sufficient for his family's needs, but he wants to build up greater cash reserves at a faster rate. He recently purchased a variable life insurance policy to invest the cash values in stock funds and to obtain additional death benefit protection, although he plans to reduce the death benefit amount as his children get older. He understands the investment risks involved and he wants his investments to grow tax-deferred within this policy.

Survivorship Life Insurance

Survivorship insurance, sometimes called joint-and-survivor life or second-to-die life, insures two or more people. The policy can be either a whole-life, term, universal, or variable type of policy. The death benefit under a survivorship policy is not payable to a beneficiary until the last insured dies; therefore, no money is available to pay expenses at the first insured's death. The policy can insure any two individuals as long as there is an insurable interest. Its use is typically confined to husband-wife, parent-child, or two related business people, such as business owners or key employees. Premiums are generally less expensive for a survivorship policy than for a policy that insures an individual's life, because benefits are not paid out until the survivor's death.

This type of policy is commonly used to provide estate liquidity to relieve the federal estate tax burden for wealthier couples who have elected to take maximum advantage of the marital deduction. Although no federal estate tax is due upon the first spouse's death, there may be an estate tax due at the survivor's death, and the proceeds can be used to pay this tax.

Client Situation

Chuck and Judy are active retirees in good health, and they enjoy playing golf and tennis every week. They jointly own their two homes and investment accounts and they both have simple wills that leave their personal assets to each other. None of their property will be taxed in the decedent spouse's estate because the marital deduction will shelter these assets from the estate tax. The assets will pass to the surviving spouse and be taxed in that estate, but their second-to-die life insurance policy will provide the surviving spouse's executor with enough money to pay for debts, estate taxes, and probate expenses.

Practitioner Tip: Many types of life insurance policies and products are available to meet specific client needs. It is the financial planner's responsibility to help clients determine their goals, priorities, and insurance needs, and then identify the right types of policy to match their client's objectives. Financial planners also must understand the tax ramifications of how a policy is owned and how the ownership of insurance policies can affect a client's overall estate plan.

PARTIES TO A LIFE INSURANCE POLICY

There are three parties to a life insurance contract: the owner, the insured, and at least one beneficiary. The owner has title to the policy and legal rights of ownership. The owner is often the insured, but a policy can be owned by someone other than the insured. For example, a wife can own a policy on her husband's life to maintain control of the policy and the cash values. The beneficiary is the person named in the policy to receive the death benefit when the insured dies. Policy proceeds received by the beneficiary are generally free from state and federal income tax unless the policy has been sold from one individual to another.

Incidents of Ownership

Financial planners should become familiar with policy ownership provisions and how ownership affects a decedent's gross and probate estates.

The basic ownership rights or **incidents of ownership** in a policy are:

- the right to name and change the beneficiary;

- the right to cash in a policy;

- the right to receive dividends;

- the right to borrow against policy cash values or to make partial withdrawals;

- the right to pledge the policy as collateral for a loan—a *collateral assignment*; and

- the right to dispose of some or all of the policy ownership rights mentioned above.

LIFE INSURANCE POLICY VALUATIONS

The value of a life insurance policy depends upon its type. When an owner of a policy makes a gift of that policy during life, the value of the gift will depend upon the type of policy transferred. Likewise, when the owner of a policy is not the insured, the value of the policy is included in the owner's gross estate and probate estate at death. Notice how valuations are determined for different types of life insurance policies:

1. *Single-premium policy.* The value is the new issuance charge for a comparable contract of equal face value. The value of the policy is based on the age of the insured at the date of the gift or at the owner's death.

2. *Whole-life policy.* The value is the interpolated terminal reserve plus any unearned premiums (approximately the cash value amount). If the cash surrender value is greater, then it is used to determine the gift tax value.

3. *Term policy.* The value is the unused premium amount. For example, if an owner purchased a term policy on another person's life in January that had a premium of $1,200 per year, and the owner died in June, the value of the policy included in the owner's estate is $600.

4. *New policy bought for another person.* The value is the gross premium paid by the donor.

Practitioner Tip: The policy owner's insurance company should be contacted to obtain the value of the policy at the date of the gift or at the date of death for transfer tax purposes.

ESTATE AND PROBATE CONSEQUENCES OF OWNERSHIP

The estate and probate consequences of being an owner *and* the insured of a life insurance policy in a common law state are very different from owning a policy on another person's life. Following is an examination of the differences in ownership.

Owner-insured

When a policy owner is the insured, the face value of a policy is included in the owner's gross estate at death. The death benefit amount avoids probate if the owner has named a beneficiary in the contract. The type of beneficiary named in the policy affects the taxation of benefits in an owner-insured's estate.

In a community property state, when community funds are used to purchase an insurance policy and there has been no agreement otherwise affecting the ownership of the policy, the policy belongs one-half to each spouse.

Spouse as Beneficiary

Married couples who name their spouse as beneficiary receive an unlimited estate tax marital deduction for the death benefits included in the decedent owner's estate. When spouses own a second-to-die policy, if the policy value is included in the decedent spouse's estate, and passes to the living spouse, the estate tax is offset by a marital deduction.

The estate tax marital deduction may not apply in two situations.

- If a spouse disclaims the proceeds then they do not qualify for a marital deduction in the decedent's estate because the spouse has forfeited all rights to the proceeds.

- If the surviving spouse receives a terminable interest from a life settlement payout option, as opposed to a lump sum payment, then the proceeds do not qualify for the marital deduction in the decedent spouse's estate.

Client Situation

Chris is the owner and the insured of a $3 million whole-life insurance policy. His wife Ginny is the beneficiary. When Chris dies, $3 million will be included in his gross estate, which will avoid taxation because of an offsetting marital deduction of $3 million for the insurance proceeds that pass to his wife. The death benefit is not subject to probate at Chris's death because he has named a policy beneficiary. Ginny will receive the insurance proceeds income tax free, and any portion of the proceeds she has not spent at the time of her death will be included in her gross estate.

Nonspouse as Beneficiary

When the beneficiary is a nonspouse such as a child, the policy's death benefit is subject to a potential estate tax in the owner's estate. If a minor child is named beneficiary, the insurance company will not transfer the proceeds until a guardian has been appointed by a court. As a result, delays and costs are associated with this process.

> **Client Situation**
>
> If Chris had named their 10-year-old daughter Sally as the beneficiary of the policy, the $3 million death benefit would be included in his gross estate. The court would have to appoint a guardian for Sally before the proceeds could be distributed because she is a minor.

Estate as Beneficiary

If the owner has listed the estate or the estate's executor as beneficiary of the policy, then the proceeds will be included in the owner's gross estate. The proceeds will also go through probate at the owner's death, which increases probate costs and could expose the proceeds to creditor claims. The owner must have a will to distribute the insurance proceeds to others or they will be subject to intestacy.

> **Client Situation**
>
> If Chris had named his estate as the beneficiary of this policy, the $3 million death benefit would be included in his gross estate and the amount would be subject to probate.

Revocable Trust as Beneficiary

An owner can name a revocable trust to receive life insurance proceeds to pay estate taxes, debts, and expenses; to care for the surviving spouse and dependent beneficiaries; or to fund the Credit Shelter Trust, but the proceeds will be included in the owner's gross estate.

> **Client Situation**
>
> If Chris had named his revocable trust as the beneficiary of this policy, the $3 million death benefit would be included in his gross estate. However, the assets would not be subject to probate.

Practitioner Tip: Financial planners should review beneficiary designations on all of their clients' insurance policies, annuities, pension plans, IRAs, and investment accounts to ensure that proper beneficiaries and contingent beneficiaries are named. The beneficiary's ability to manage and invest insurance proceeds paid as a lump sum should also be considered. Alternatively, a trust or a settlement option could provide greater financial security for the beneficiary and peace of mind for the insured.

Owner Is Not the Insured

The value of a life insurance policy whose policy owner is not the insured but who dies before the insured will be included in the owner's gross estate. The value of the policy is different from the death benefit amount of the policy, and the value depends on the type of policy owned. The value of the policy is also included in the owner's probate estate. Note that the beneficiary of the policy does not receive any benefits when the owner dies because the insured is still alive at that time. Couples might choose this form of ownership with the expectation of lowering their estate tax, but this ownership arrangement can potentially present problems for a couple's estate.

Client Situation

Assume that Ray is the owner and beneficiary of a policy on his wife Nancy's life. If Ray predeceases her, the value of the policy will be included in his gross estate and could be taxed unless a marital deduction is available to offset his estate tax. How can a planner determine whether a marital deduction is available? That depends on who the new owner of the policy is.

If Ray's policy names Nancy as contingent owner of the policy, then she becomes the new owner and the insured at Ray's death. As a result, the value included in Ray's gross estate would be offset by the marital deduction. When Nancy dies, the death benefit will be included in her gross and subject to probate if she has not named a beneficiary before her death.

If Ray's policy does not name a contingent owner, then Ray's will should be examined to determine whether Nancy is named as the new owner of the policy or she becomes the new owner through provisions stated in the will's residuary clause. In both situations, a marital deduction would be available in Ray's estate.

But what happens if Ray has no will? Then his state's intestate succession statute would determine the new owner of the policy at his death. If Ray's state of domicile grants 50% of a husband's property to his wife, then a marital deduction for only that portion (50%) of the value of the policy can be realized by Ray's estate. Nancy would own only one-half of the insurance policy and the other heirs would own the other half after Ray's death.

Practitioner Tip: Couples can own life insurance policies on each other's lives to avoid significant estate taxes at the first spouse's death. This could be appropriate because only the value of the policy, not the death benefit amount, is included in the gross estate. However, it is important to name a contingent owner in the insurance policy or the spouse's will; otherwise, the decedent's estate would be subject to partial intestacy. Table 21.1 shows the effects of policy ownership on the decedent's estate.

Table 21.1 A Comparison of Policy Ownership When Spouse is Beneficiary

	Estate	Probate	Marital Deduction
Owner-insured	Death benefit	No	Yes
Owner (not the insured)	Policy value	Yes	Yes (if spouse is new owner)

Children as Owners

Parents can transfer ownership of a policy to their adult children to keep the death benefit out of their estates. This could create unintended problems if a child dies; if a child does not want to pay the premiums to keep the policy active; or if the cash value is the asset of a child who gets divorced, files for bankruptcy, has creditor problems, or is subsequently sued. Parents who want to pursue this ownership option might consider having their children purchase umbrella policies on their homeowners and auto insurance policies to mitigate a portion of this creditor risk.

Practitioner Tip: A better solution might be to have an **irrevocable life insurance trust (ILIT)** own a life insurance policy instead. A major benefit of an ILIT is that a trustee can be chosen who understands the importance of providing liquidity for the payment of taxes, debts, and other estate-related cash needs, and it provides greater assurance that the proceeds will be used for the intended purpose.

Three-year Rule

A person who is the owner and the insured of a life insurance policy must include the death benefit amount of this policy in his gross estate at death. To avoid this situation, a client could give his policy to others or to an ILIT to remove the death benefit amount from his gross estate. This strategy will work if he outlives the transfer by three or more years. However, if the owner dies within three years of gifting the policy, then the death benefit amount is brought back into his gross estate for estate tax purposes. This is known as the **three-year rule** under Code section 2035.

When a person retains any incidents of ownership over a policy on his life, or on another person's life, the policy's death benefit will be included in his gross estate when he dies. The three-year rule will also apply if the decedent retained incidents of ownership over a policy on his own life, yet transferred the policy to another person or trust within three years of his death.

The three-year rule does not apply if an owner who is not the insured transfers this policy to another person or to an ILIT. The owner could die the day after gifting the policy and would not have the value of the policy brought back into his gross estate. Also note that a life insurance policy sold to another person is not subject to the three-year rule.

> **Client Situation**
>
> Alice, age 63, was the owner and the insured of a whole-life insurance policy with a death benefit of $4 million. Alice's financial planner advised her to transfer the policy into an ILIT to remove the death benefit from her gross estate. Alice died tragically two years after the policy was transferred into the trust. The $4 million death benefit was included in her gross estate because she did not live longer than three years from the date the policy was placed into the trust.

> **Client Situation**
>
> Eduardo was the owner and beneficiary of a $1 million life insurance policy that he purchased on his brother's life. The policy had a death benefit amount of $1 million. One year after owning the policy, Eduardo gifted it to his brother Gus because he could not afford the premiums. When Eduardo died six months later, the value of the policy was not included in Eduardo's estate because the three-year rule did not apply.

GIFT TAXATION FOR POLICIES TRANSFERRED DURING LIFETIME

Clients with significant wealth (i.e., individuals with estates exceeding $5,430,000 or couples with estates exceeding $10,860,000 in 2015) are subject to federal estate taxes on their combined taxable estates. Furthermore, state estate or inheritance taxes can also apply. Life insurance policies owned by the insured increase a client's estate by the death benefit amount when the owner dies. When reviewing a wealthier client's insurance policies, a financial planner should discuss transferring ownership of these policies to children or to an ILIT to remove the death benefit from the client's gross estate.

Practice Standard 400-1

Identifying and Evaluating Financial Planning Alternative(s)

The financial planning practitioner shall consider sufficient and relevant alternatives to the client's current course of action in an effort to reasonably meet the client's goals, needs and priorities.

Transfers of life insurance policies to individuals or trusts can be subject to gift taxes. The face value of a policy is typically many times greater than the gift tax value. One way to leverage the donor's gift tax annual exclusions, unified credit, and/or generation-skipping exemption is by making gifts of life insurance policies that have a low current gift value in relation to their value at the insured's death.

Calculating the Taxable Gift

When a policy has been gifted, the first step is to determine the gift tax value of the policy, which depends upon the type of insurance policy transferred. Gift taxes can be reduced by gift splitting, annual exclusions, marital deductions, and charitable deductions, and these techniques also apply when transferring insurance policies to individuals, trusts, and charities. Once the gift tax is reduced, the donor must apply any remaining unified credit to offset the tax on the gift. If there is no remaining unified credit, then the donor will pay a gift tax on the policy transfer.

Owner-insured

When the owner is the insured and the policy is gifted outright to another person, the donor can take an annual exclusion against the gift tax value because it is a present-interest gift. The new owner has a present interest because he can keep the policy, sell it, or gift it to someone else. But be aware that such a transfer is subject to the three-year rule.

Client Situation

Joe and Sandy are married and have a combined estate worth $12 million. To reduce the value of his rapidly appreciating estate, Joe recently transferred a whole-life insurance policy with a face value of $2 million and a cash value of $500,000 to Sandy. Sandy is the new owner and beneficiary of the policy and Joe remains the insured. Joe did not pay any gift tax when he gave the policy to Sandy because he used an annual exclusion and a marital deduction to reduce the taxable gift to zero. If Joes dies more than three years after the transfer, the $2 million death benefit will be removed from his gross estate. However, if Joe dies sooner than three years from the date he transferred the policy to Sandy, then the $2 million death benefit will be included in his gross estate.

If the $2 million is effectively removed from Joe's estate, any amount that Sandy has not spent during her lifetime will be included in her gross estate at her death. Joe and Sandy could consider gifting the policy to an ILIT or to their children to reduce the value of their overall taxable estate.

Owner Is Not the Insured

In a situation where the owner of a policy is not the insured, and he gifts the policy to another person or transfers the policy into a trust, the donor can use an annual exclusion or a marital deduction, if applicable, to reduce the value of the taxable gift. Note that the three-year rule would not apply in this situation because the policy owner is not the insured.

Different Owner, Insured, and Beneficiary

Problems can arise when the owner-insured of a policy gifts the policy to another person who is not the beneficiary, or when the owner, insured, and beneficiary of the policy are three different parties. When the insured dies, the beneficiaries will receive the death benefit as intended, but this entire amount is deemed to be a gift from the owner of the policy, which is subject to gift taxes.

Client Situation

Barry, who has substantial wealth, is the owner and insured of a $1 million term life insurance policy. He recently transferred ownership of the policy to his wife Kelly and named their two adult children as beneficiaries. If Barry dies next year, the children will receive the $1 million insurance proceeds, but this will be construed as a gift to the children from Kelly. If Barry had named Kelly as the owner and the beneficiary of the policy, then Kelly could gift the proceeds to the children up to the maximum amount of the annual exclusion each year to avoid making any taxable gifts.

Client Situation

If Kelly had purchased a policy on Barry's life and named her children as beneficiaries of the policy at any point in time, the same unintended gift tax situation would apply.

In a community property state, if a policy on the husband is community property and the beneficiary is someone other than the wife, a transfer subject to gift tax occurs when the insured dies and the proceeds are payable to that third person. The amount of the gift will be one-half of the proceeds, which represents the wife's one-half community interest in the policy.

Client Situation

Gayle and Rich live in Texas, a community property state. Rich is the owner and the insured of a $200,000 whole-life insurance policy and he has named his nephew Adam as the beneficiary of the policy. When Rich dies, one-half of the $200,000 payment that Adam receives is considered a gift from Gayle.

Premium Payments

When premiums are paid on behalf of a policy owner, the premium payments are gifts subject to gift taxes. For example, a son owns a $500,000 policy on his father's life and his father pays the $1,500 premium to the insurance company every year. The gift made by the father is not a taxable gift because the premiums are less than the annual exclusion amount. However, if the premiums were $15,000 per year, the father's payment of the premium would result in a taxable gift.

Gifting Policies to Grandchildren

Grandparents can make a gift of a life insurance policy they own directly to their grandchild or great-grandchild, but this transfer will be subject to both gift taxes and generation-skipping transfer (GST) taxes. And if the transferor (a grandparent) continues to pay the policy premiums for the grandchild, then additional gift and GST taxes could apply. The transferor can use the techniques of gift splitting and annual exclusions to reduce any taxable gifts and GST taxes, and they can use their unified credit against the gift tax and the GST tax exemption to shelter any taxable gifts.

Client Situation

Linda, a widow, had transferred a $1 million life insurance policy to her granddaughter Grace four years ago. This was the first taxable gift that Linda had made in her lifetime. The transfer of the policy was subject to both GST tax and gift tax. But Linda did not have to actually pay any taxes on the transfer because she used an annual exclusion to reduce the amount of the taxable gift and applied her unified credit against the gift tax, which was based on the value of the policy. Linda also allocated a portion of her GST exemption on her gift tax return four years ago when the gift was made to offset the GST tax. If Linda were to die today, this policy would be excluded from her gross estate, because she lived longer than three years from the date of the gift.

Practitioner Tip: Keep in mind that if Linda had transferred the policy to both of her granddaughters, Grace and Lara, the generation-skipping and gift tax annual exclusions could not be used to offset the gift tax, because the policy was gifted to multiple beneficiaries. However, Linda's unified credit and GST tax exemption could be applied to reduce the taxable gift to zero.

Chapter Highlights

- There are many types of life insurance policies. Term insurance is purchased for a set period of time and has no cash value. Permanent insurance can be either whole-life insurance or universal life insurance, and it can be either traditional or variable.

- There are two types of whole-life insurance policies. In a straight whole-life policy, premiums are payable for the lifetime of the insured. In a limited payment life policy, premiums are payable over a shorter period of time and are significantly higher. An example is a single-premium whole-life policy.

- A universal life policy is interest-sensitive life insurance in which the investment, expense, and mortality elements are separately and specifically defined.

- A variable life insurance policy is a permanent insurance policy that has an investment component.

- Survivorship life insurance, sometimes called *joint and survivor life or second-to-die life*, insures two or more people.

- The estate and probate consequences of being the owner and the insured of a life insurance policy in a common-law state are very different from owning a policy on another person's life.

- The owner of a policy who transfers it to another person or to an irrevocable life insurance trust must outlive that transfer for three years or the policy proceeds will be included in the insured's estate. The three-year rule does not apply if the owner who is not the insured transfers this policy to another person or a trust.

- A gift of life insurance policies is a way to leverage the donor's gift tax annual exclusion, unified credit, and/or generation-skipping exemption by making gifts of policies that have a low current "gift value" in relation to their value at the insured's death.

- The gift tax value of an insurance policy depends on the type of policy transferred.

- When the owner, insured, and beneficiary of a policy are three different parties, then when the insured dies, the proceeds are deemed to be a gift from the owner of the policy to the beneficiary and are subject to gift taxes.

- When premiums are paid on behalf of a policy owner the premium payments are gifts subject to gift taxes.

Key Terms

incidents of ownership

irrevocable life insurance trust (ILIT)

permanent insurance

survivorship life insurance

term insurance

three-year rule

universal life insurance

variable life insurance

whole-life insurance

Review Questions

21.1. Rick and Barbara are married with two children. Four years ago, Barbara bought a $75,000 life insurance policy on her mother's life and named her children as policy beneficiaries. Barbara did not name a contingent owner of the policy. Barbara died this year and the insurance policy was valued at $18,000. Which of the following statements is/are correct?

A. The death benefit of $75,000 will be included in Barbara's gross estate.

B. The $18,000 value of the policy will be included in Barbara's gross estate.

C. The value of the policy will be included in Barbara's probate estate.

D. Following Barbara's death, the children will receive the life insurance proceeds income tax free.

21-2. Assume that Barbara did not have a will and that her state's intestacy succession laws grant 50% of her estate to her husband and the other half of her estate is divided equally between her children. Which of the following statements is/are correct?

A. Rich will own one-half of the policy and each child will own one-quarter of the policy.

B. The marital deduction in Barbara's estate is equal to one-half of the value of the policy.

C. No marital deduction is available to offset Barbara's estate tax because her mother is the insured.

D. Barbara's mother, who is the insured, will become the new owner of Barbara's policy.

21-3. Five years ago, Don bought a $600,000 life insurance policy on his own life and named his estate as the beneficiary. Four years ago, Don irrevocably assigned all incidents of ownership in the policy to his wife Betty. Don died this year after a brief illness. The insurance company placed a value on the policy of $400,000. Which of the following statements is/are correct?

A. When Don dies the death benefit amount of $600,000 is included in his gross estate.

B. Betty is the new owner of the policy; therefore, a marital deduction of $600,000 is available to Don's estate.

C. The life insurance policy is not included in Don's estate at death because he transferred the policy to Betty more than three years ago.

D. The $400,000 value of the policy will be included in Don's estate at his death.

21-4. Six years ago, Philip bought a life insurance policy on his own life worth $1,250,000 and he named his wife Anita the beneficiary. Two years ago Philip created an unfunded ILIT and transferred the policy to the trust. The trust gives Anita a lifetime income interest with a general power of appointment over the trust corpus. At Anita's death, the remainder interest in the trust will pass to Philip's favorite charity. Which of the following statements is/are correct?

A. The death benefit will be included in Philip's gross estate.

B. Because Anita is entitled only to receive income for her lifetime, Philip's estate will not have a marital deduction available to offset the estate tax for the value of the policy included in his gross estate.

C. Philip's estate will receive a charitable deduction for $1,250,000 if Anita should predecease Philip.

D. The death benefit will not be included in Philip's estate because he purchased the policy more than three years ago.

21-5. Ronnie was the owner of a $2 million whole-life insurance policy and her husband Brad was the insured. Ronnie transferred ownership of the policy to Brad last year, and died three months later. Which of the following statements is/are correct?

A. The death benefit amount of $2 million is included in Ronnie's gross estate.

B. The value of the policy is included in Ronnie's gross estate.

C. Neither the death benefit amount nor the value of the policy is included in Ronnie's gross estate.

D. If Brad disclaims the death benefit proceeds, then $2 million is included in Ronnie's gross estate.

Chapter 22

Irrevocable Life Insurance Trusts

CFP® CERTIFICATION EXAMINATION PRINCIPAL TOPICS COVERED IN THIS CHAPTER:

Sources for Estate Liquidity Use of Life Insurance in Estate Planning

- Irrevocable life insurance trust (ILIT)
- Estate and gift taxation

Learning Objectives

To ensure you have a solid understanding of the sources for estate liquidity and the characteristics of irrevocable life insurance trusts, the following learning objectives are addressed in this chapter:

- Identify sources for estate liquidity.

- Recognize the different types of irrevocable life insurance trust (ILIT).

- Compare and contrast the characteristics and tax aspects of a funded ILIT with an unfunded ILIT.

- Recognize the advantages and tax implications of dynasty trusts.

Chapter Contents

OVERVIEW

When a person dies, money is often needed to pay for the decedent's final expenses, taxes, and debts, and to provide for the financial security of remaining family members. Estate taxes are due nine months after death, and money must be readily available to the estate to pay for these taxes and other estate settlement costs, without delay.

Life insurance is frequently purchased to provide sufficient capital at the insured's death to meet the family's financial and liquidity needs. **Irrevocable life insurance trust**s (ILITs) are one means of owning life insurance policies, and these trusts have attractive tax and nontax advantages. For example, wealthier policy owners who are concerned about having life insurance proceeds taxed in their estates can establish an ILIT to remove the death benefit from their estates. Other clients who are concerned that their beneficiaries may not make the life insurance proceeds available to their estate can establish an ILIT instead. Finally, ILITs can provide professional management of life insurance proceeds for beneficiaries who lack the investment skills needed to manage the proceeds, especially if the beneficiaries are minors.

Financial planners should review a client's assets, liabilities, and will to determine whether enough cash or other liquid assets are available to the estate to cover expenses when the client dies. Planners can also recommend estate tax reduction or deferral techniques that are intended to improve the liquidity position of the estate. Financial planners should become familiar with several types of ILITs, because each type of trust has very different estate and gift tax implications for grantors and beneficiaries.

Practice Standard 200-2

Obtaining Quantitative Information and Documents

The financial planning practitioner shall obtain sufficient quantitative information and documents about a client relevant to the scope of the engagement before any recommendation is made and/or implemented.

ESTATE LIQUIDITY

Money is often needed soon after a client's death to pay for:

- funeral expenses;

- medical bills;

- federal and state estate taxes, inheritance taxes, and income taxes;

- a decedent's debts;

- estate settlement costs; and

- probate administration expenses.

A client's estate must have sufficient liquidity to cover these postmortem costs; otherwise, the executor might have to borrow money or sell some assets to make up the shortfall. Keep in mind that the best price may not be obtained for an asset if a forced sale is required. Assets that are difficult to value such as artwork, collectibles, antiques, and jewelry must be appraised, and buyers could be difficult to locate or might not be willing to pay full price. Estates that have illiquid assets that are hard to sell, such as real estate in a down market, might have to sell these assets at a loss in the absence of proper planning.

Business owners might have a significant portion of their wealth tied into their business in the form of illiquid assets, and they would not want company assets sold at their death to pay for any estate-related expenses. Code section 6166 defers payment of the estate tax and generation-skipping transfer (GST) tax for a sole proprietorship, partnership, or closely held corporation if certain requirements are met. Executors must determine whether this estate reduction technique and others can be applied to a business owner's estate to improve the estate's liquidity position.

Sources for Estate Liquidity

A life insurance policy is one of the best sources of **estate liquidity**. Proceeds can be used to provide the estate with sufficient funds to pay for taxes and estate-related expenses. However, a disadvantage of owning a life insurance policy in one's own name is that the death benefit can be taxed in the estate. And if the estate is named the beneficiary of the policy, then in addition to possible estate taxes, the proceeds would be subject to probate costs and administrative delays.

The best way to provide an estate with tax-free liquidity and avoid the preceding pitfalls is to have the trustee of an irrevocable trust own a life insurance policy on the insured. A policy owned by an ILIT can provide the trust with money at the grantor-insured's death. The trust can allow the trustee to make loans for adequate interest and security to the estate, or purchase assets at fair market value from the estate. This can be accomplished as long as the trustee is not obligated to use the funds for these purposes; otherwise, the proceeds will be included in the insured's gross estate. Estate assets sold to the trust can be professionally managed by the trustee, and the trustee can invest and manage the remaining funds to provide greater financial security for the trust beneficiaries. The trust can also allow the trustee to distribute property to the beneficiaries, which the beneficiaries may use to cover expenses and use for other purposes.

IRREVOCABLE LIFE INSURANCE TRUST

An attorney is needed to draft and execute an inter-vivos ILIT. The grantor-policy owner can either transfer the policy to the trust by signing an irrevocable assignment of the policy to the trustee of the trust, or can make a cash gift to the trust to enable the trustee to purchase a new policy. The trustee becomes the owner and the primary beneficiary of the grantor's insurance policy to ensure that the proceeds are paid to the trust at the grantor's death. The grantor should not be the trustee of the ILIT to avoid having any incidents of ownership in the trust that would bring the death benefit back into the grantor's gross estate. This would defeat the purpose of the trust. The beneficiaries of the ILIT are not named as the beneficiaries of the insurance policy because the trustee collects the proceeds and makes distributions to them according to the instructions and terms of the trust.

Advantages of an ILIT

The primary advantage of an ILIT is that it removes the death benefit from the grantor-insured's estate, but the trust can also shelter the proceeds and any future appreciation from the surviving spouse's gross estate if the trust is structured properly. Another advantage is that the insurance proceeds paid to the trust are protected from the claims of creditors, including the decedent's creditors. If the grantor-insured has any concerns about the beneficiaries' ability to manage life insurance proceeds, or if the beneficiaries are minors, an ILIT will enable the grantor-insured to name a trustee who can handle these matters. Because the grantor can dictate the terms of the trust, the trustee can be given the authority to distribute the proceeds on a discretionary basis over time to multiple beneficiaries.

Disadvantages of an ILIT

A disadvantage of an ILIT is that the grantor's life insurance policy is irrevocably assigned to the trust and the grantor has no further control or interest over the policy because the trust holds all incidents of ownership. The grantor should not be the trustee of the ILIT or the death proceeds could be brought back into the gross estate. The grantor cannot change the beneficiaries of the policy if circumstances change, even in a situation where the spouse is a trust beneficiary and the spouses eventually divorce! An ILIT can also be costly to establish and maintain because of legal fees and trustee fees.

Practitioner Tip: A younger client could establish a revocable bypass trust with the trust as beneficiary of the insurance policy. This allows the grantor the flexibility to respond to any personal circumstances that might change in the future, such as divorce, remarriage, additional children, or if a child has special needs that qualify for government benefits. A professional trustee could be chosen to manage the proceeds for the surviving spouse and children, but there are no estate tax advantages because the proceeds are still included in the client's estate.

TYPES OF ILITS

Irrevocable life insurance trusts can be established and structured in several different ways. The grantor-insured can transfer an existing life insurance policy into the trust so that a trustee, other than the grantor, becomes the new owner and beneficiary of the policy with the spouse and/or other family members as trust beneficiaries. The grantor could also transfer money into the trust with the expectation that the trustee will purchase a new policy on the grantor's life. In both situations the trustee must pay the annual premiums to keep the policy active; there are various ways to arrange this.

Funded ILIT

A **funded ILIT** is one that holds a life insurance policy and income-producing property that will generate sufficient income to pay for future premiums. The grantor would gift income-producing property into the trust. This eliminates the need for the grantor to transfer money into the trust each year to pay for any future insurance premiums. The grantor could either transfer an existing policy to the trust, or the trustee can purchase a new life insurance policy on the grantor's life. Transfers of both the policy and the property into the trust are subject to gift taxes, and the grantor must determine whether he has made any taxable gifts when the transfers are made.

Unfunded ILIT

An **unfunded ILIT** is a trust that contains only a life insurance policy. The grantor-insured either assigns ownership of an existing life insurance policy to the trust or the trustee purchases a new policy on the grantor's life. The transfer of an existing policy to the trust, or money to purchase a new policy would constitute a gift, which could be subject to gift tax.

GIFT TAX CONSIDERATIONS

When an existing life insurance policy is transferred into an ILIT, the grantor has made a gift to the trust. The gift tax value of the policy is determined by the type of policy transferred. The transfer is considered a future interest gift because the beneficiaries will not receive any distributions from the trust until the grantor-insured dies.

If the life insurance policy has ongoing premiums, the trustee must pay those premiums each year. Assuming the trust holds no other assets (unfunded trust) there are no other income-generating assets in the trust that can be used to pay those premiums. As a result, the grantor must transfer enough money into the trust each year to cover the premiums, and these transfers are considered gifts.

Finally, when a grantor transfers income-producing property to a funded ILIT, the transfer of that property would also constitute a gift.

In these situations, the grantor must determine whether a taxable gift has been made, and if so, depending on the terms of the trust, the grantor may use several techniques to reduce the amount of the taxable gift.

Gift Splitting

If the grantor's spouse is not a beneficiary of the trust, the grantor can use gift splitting to divide the taxable gift in half. Gift splitting can be used to reduce the taxable amount of an existing policy transferred to the trust and for premiums payments transferred to an unfunded ILIT each year. The grantor must obtain the consent of his spouse to split the gift and a gift tax return must be filed.

Annual Exclusions and Crummey Powers

Crummey powers give beneficiaries the right to make withdrawals from the trust each year. Crummey powers may be used to qualify the initial gift in trust of the grantor's life insurance policy, income producing property, and any subsequent gifts of premiums for the gift tax annual exclusion. Typically, contributions to an ILIT are intended to secure life insurance, which will not be distributed to the beneficiaries until after the grantor's death, making it a future interest. If the trust contains Crummey powers, the grantor can take annual exclusions for each beneficiary because the beneficiaries are deemed to have a present interest. When the beneficiaries do not withdraw the money, they have allowed their withdrawal right to lapse, and the trustee may use the money in the trust to pay the life insurance premiums.

Client Situation

Joe transferred his life insurance policy to an irrevocable trust for the benefit of his two children and a grandchild. All of the beneficiaries have been given Crummey rights of withdrawal. The premiums are $60,000 each year, and Joe can use his annual exclusion to reduce the value of the gift by $14,000 for each beneficiary in the trust. But this only reduces the taxable gift by $42,000 and Joe will have to use his unified credit to offset the tax on the remaining $18,000 of premium payments every year. To fix this problem, Joe asked his wife Ellen to split the gifts with him on his gift tax return (IRS Form 709) and she agreed. Now both spouses can use annual exclusions, which reduces the taxable gift to zero, and neither spouse has to use any of their unified credits to offset a gift tax when transferring money into the trust each year.

Based on the court case *Estate of Cristofani* v. *Commissioner,* annual exclusions can also be taken for grandchildren who are Crummey beneficiaries, even though they are remote contingent remaindermen of the trust who will receive trust benefits only when their parent dies. As trust beneficiaries, grandchildren increase the number of annual exclusions available to a grantor—and the grantor's spouse, if gift splitting is used.

Crummey Not Limited to 5-and-5

In an ILIT a substantial portion of the trust corpus can be included in the income beneficiary's gross estate if the beneficiary's Crummey withdrawal right is not limited to a 5-and-5 power, because cumulative releases are brought back into the gross estate under Code section 2036.

Client Situation

George established an irrevocable trust in 2013 and the trustee purchased a $600,000 whole-life insurance policy on his life. The premium payments totaled $9,000 each year. George named his son Jim as the lifetime income beneficiary and his granddaughter Michelle as the remainderman of the trust. George died two years after creating the trust in 2015.

George's estate: The death benefit was not included in George's estate since an existing policy was not transferred into the trust in 2013, thus the three-year rule was avoided.

Jim's Estate: Jim never exercised his withdrawal rights when money was transferred into the trust to pay the premiums in 2013, 2014 and 2015. The lapsed amounts over the safe harbor of $5,000 represented a release of $4,000 each year that was transferred to the trust. Consequently, when Jim dies, a portion of the trust will be included in his gross estate as follows:

- Jim as transferor/grantor released $4,000 in 2013 or $4,000/$9,000 = 0.444

- Jim released $4,000 again in 2014 when the trust totaled $14,000 ($9,000 gift to trust plus a $5,000 cash surrender value of the policy). $4,000/$14,000 = 0.285

- Jim released $4,000 in 2015 out of total trust assets of $21,000 based on the policy's cash surrender value of $12,000. $4,000/$21,000 = 0.190

The cumulative lapses equaled $12,000 over three years, but 91.9% of the trust assets will be included in Jim's estate at death.

ESTATE TAX CONSIDERATIONS

An existing life insurance policy transferred to an ILIT is subject to the **three-year rule**, wherein if the grantor dies within three years of transferring the policy to the trust, then the death benefit amount will be included in his gross estate.

When the trustee of an ILIT purchases a new life insurance policy on the grantor or the grantor's spouse, the trustee will become the owner and the beneficiary of the insurance policy. As long as the trustee is not required to purchase insurance with the funds contributed by the grantor, the three-year rule can be avoided and the policy proceeds will not be included in the grantor or his spouse's estate.

Client Situation

John, age 45, is unmarried and in good health. He owns a thriving business and wants to leave a substantial inheritance to his niece and nephew someday. John's attorney recently established an ILIT that allows, but does not direct, the trustee to invest in life insurance on John's life, and the trust does not require payment of premiums. John transferred money into the trust that was more than sufficient to purchase a $4 million policy on his life, and he will continue to transfer money into the trust each year to keep the policy in force. John's niece and nephew were given Crummey powers that enable them to make annual withdrawals of the premium payments from the trust each year. Their present interest in the trust allows John to use two annual exclusions to reduce the taxable gifts made to the trust every year. If John were to die one year after establishing the trust, the insurance proceeds would not be included in John's estate because the three-year rule would not apply.

Avoiding the Three-year Rule

A grantor-insured can purchase an additional term insurance policy or term insurance rider lasting three years, which is equal to the potential estate tax should the policy be included in his estate. Another solution is to have the ILIT structured as a grantor trust for income tax purposes. The trust could purchase the policy from the grantor to avoid inclusion in the grantor's estate under the three-year rule since the policy was never gifted to the trust. ILITs are structured as a grantor trust for income tax purposes therefore the transfer-for-value rule would not apply.

Grantor as Trustee

Be aware that if the grantor is the trustee of the ILIT or retains any incidents of ownership over the policy, then the entire death benefit will be included in the owner's estate whenever the grantor dies.

INCOME TAX CONSIDERATIONS

Under **grantor trust rules**, if income in the trust can be used to pay for life insurance premiums on the grantor's life or on the spouse's life, then the trust income, to the extent it is used to pay the premiums, is taxable to the grantor. Typically, ILITs do not have significant trust income therefore this is usually not a problem.

Client Situation

Frank and Lauren are married without children and have a combined estate worth $7 million. Frank also owns a whole-life insurance policy with a face value of $2 million. Lauren recently discovered that she will inherit $3 million dollars from her ailing father, which prompted them to meet with their financial planner. The planner, working with their attorney, advised Frank to transfer ownership of his insurance policy into an ILIT with Lauren as the trust beneficiary. Frank will also transfer interest-bearing bonds into the trust to pay for the premiums each year. Frank will use up some of his unified credit when he transfers the policy and the bonds into the trust, but the bonds will be removed from his estate and the policy's death benefit will not be included if he survives the transfer for three years. Lauren will receive discretionary payments from the trust throughout her lifetime so that the trust assets will not be included in her gross estate when she dies. Crummey powers were not drafted into this trust because Lauren is the sole beneficiary of the ILIT and the income from the bonds is sufficient to pay for the insurance premiums every year. Under grantor trust rules, Frank is taxed on the trust income.

SPOUSE AS BENEFICIARY OF AN ILIT

When a spouse is the beneficiary of an ILIT, no gift tax marital deduction is available to offset the initial transfer of the policy into the trust or the subsequent premium payments made to the trust. The reason is that the spouse's interest in the trust is at the discretion of the trustee and contingent upon surviving the insured.

Gift Tax

Gift splitting with the spouse is impossible because the spouse is a beneficiary of the trust. However, the grantor can take annual exclusions when money is transferred in to pay the premiums each year if all the trust beneficiaries, including the spouse, are given Crummey powers.

Estate Tax—Surviving Spouse

The trust is typically structured so that the trustee can make only discretionary distributions of income to the surviving spouse and the other trust beneficiaries after the insured dies. The spouse can also be given a life estate in the trust, which is a terminable interest, with the children named as remainder beneficiaries. In either case, the spouse would not have any control over the trust corpus, and the death benefit and any subsequent appreciation of the assets in the trust would not be included in his gross estate. The surviving spouse could also be given an ascertainable standard to use the trust corpus for expenses related to health, education, maintenance, or support, and this would not cause any inclusion of the trust corpus in the spouse's estate.

Practitioner Tip: If the surviving spouse is given a limited invasion power over the trust corpus, such as a 5-and-5 power, then only the greater of $5,000 or 5% of the trust corpus is included in the spouse's gross estate at death.

Estate Tax Exceptions

Two situations will cause all of the trust assets to be included in the surviving spouse's estate.

- The spouse is given a general power of appointment over the trust corpus.

- The spouse is given a life estate and the trust's remainder interest is payable to the spouse's estate.

Estate Tax—Decedent Spouse

In the preceding situations, the trust can qualify for the marital deduction in the decedent spouse's estate, or the executor can make a QTIP election to qualify the trust for the marital deduction if the grantor dies within three years of transferring the policy to the trust.

Furthermore, the ILIT could be drafted to include a provision that the proceeds be paid to the surviving spouse or to another trust that qualifies for the marital deduction if the decedent dies within three years of the initial policy transfer. The death benefit would be included in the decedent spouse's estate but it would not be taxed because the proceeds would qualify for the estate tax marital deduction.

Credit Shelter Trust Buys a Life Insurance Policy on the Surviving Spouse's Life

A credit shelter trust can be the beneficiary of a life insurance policy when the first spouse dies. If trust principal is not needed for lifetime distributions to the surviving spouse or children, then the trust can purchase a new life insurance policy on the surviving spouse's life. When the spouse dies, the proceeds paid to the trust are income and estate tax free, which is better than if the trust principal was invested primarily for growth, because the appreciation would be subject to capital gain. The surviving spouse must be insurable, and should not be the trustee or a co-trustee of the trust. Instead, a disinterested trustee should purchase the policy to avoid any incidents of ownership that would cause the proceeds to be payable to the spouse's estate. The spouse should also release any testamentary limited power of appointment held over the credit shelter trust.

DYNASTY TRUSTS

Dynasty trusts are created to provide families with substantial wealth that will last throughout future generations. Many states have rules against perpetuities that restrict a trust's existence to 90 years, but other states permit the creation of Dynasty Trusts that can last for 360 years or longer. Dynasty trusts are generation-skipping transfer trusts that can avoid estate, gift and generation-skipping transfer taxes. A **spendthrift provision** in a trust protects the income and assets from the claims of the beneficiaries' creditors, divorce, and bankruptcy. Life insurance is often used to fund dynasty trusts, which can create tremendous wealth for multiple generations.

Practice Standard 500-2

Selecting Products and Services for Implementation

The financial planning practitioner shall select appropriate products and services that are consistent with the client's goals, needs and priorities.

Avoiding GST Tax

An ILIT that has two or more generations of beneficiaries can be exempt from GST tax by having the grantor/transferor allocate a portion of his GST exemption to the trust equal to the amount of money transferred in to purchase a policy on the grantor's life. This exemption removes the life insurance proceeds and any resulting appreciation from GST taxes for the life of the trust. The grantor and the grantor's spouse could use gift splitting to reduce any taxable gifts of premium payments transferred into the trust each year, and each spouse would allocate a portion of their GST exemption to the premium payments to avoid paying a GST tax. Beneficiaries should be limited to a 5-and-5 power with a maximum withdrawal right of $14,000 per beneficiary.

Estate Tax

Beneficiaries are entitled to receive income at the discretion of the trustee for their health, education, maintenance, and support, and some corpus, if needed. Therefore, money in the trust is not included or taxed in the beneficiary's estate.

Client Situation

Charles and Roberta established an ILIT with their bank as trustee. The trust purchased a $3 million second-to-die life insurance policy and each spouse allocated $1.5 million of their GST exemption to the trust. This gives the trust an inclusion ratio of zero, which will not be subject to any current or future GST taxes. Charles and Roberta named their two children and five grandchildren as beneficiaries of the trust and gave them all Crummey powers limited to the 5-and-5 withdrawal amounts. This allows the parents, with gift splitting, to transfer in a maximum of $196,000 gift tax free to pay for the premiums each year. Charles and Roberta will allocate a matching portion of their GST exemption to each premium payment transferred to the trust. Once the last parent has died, $3 million is available to the trustee to invest, and the children will receive discretionary income with a limited power of appointment over the trust corpus. A taxable termination will not occur once the last child has died, and trust assets will not be included in either child's gross estate. The grandchildren will receive discretionary income from the trustee until the trust terminates when the youngest grandchild reaches age 35. At that time the assets will be divided equally and distributed to the grandchildren.

Chapter Highlights

- The client's estate must have sufficient liquidity to cover postmortem costs; otherwise, the executor might need to borrow money or sell assets to make up the shortfall.

- A policy owned by an ILIT can provide financial security for trust beneficiaries and can purchase estate assets for liquidity purposes upon the insured's death.

- An ILIT removes the death benefit from the grantor-insured's estate and can shelter the proceeds and any future appreciation from the surviving spouse's gross estate if the trust is structured properly.

- A funded ILIT is one that holds a life insurance policy and income-producing property that will pay for future premiums.

- An unfunded ILIT is a trust that contains only a life insurance policy. The grantor must transfer funds to the trust each year to pay the premiums; therefore, beneficiaries are given Crummey powers to acquire a present interest in the trust.

- An ILIT can purchase a life insurance policy on the grantor's life. A benefit is that the insured is not subject to the three-year rule after the policy is acquired.

- Life insurance is often used to fund dynasty trusts, which are created to provide families with substantial wealth that lasts for several generations.

Key Terms

Crummey power

dynasty trust

estate liquidity

funded ILIT

grantor trust rules

irrevocable life insurance trust (ILIT)

spendthrift provision

three-year rule

unfunded ILIT

Review Questions

22-1. Robert, a widower, created an ILIT four years ago and transferred his $3 million whole-life policy into the trust. Robert established the trust to remove the death benefit from his gross estate and to provide his estate with liquidity to pay his estate tax. The trust explicitly directs the trustee, his bank, and the co-trustee, his brother Larry, to purchase assets from Robert's estate at his death. The bank will professionally manage the estate assets purchased by the trust for the benefit of Robert's two children, the trust beneficiaries. Which of the following statements is correct?

A. When Robert dies, the $3 million proceeds will not be included in his gross estate because he survived the three-year term.

B. When Robert dies, the $3 million proceeds will be included in his gross estate because the trustee was obligated to use the proceeds to purchase assets from his estate.

C. The assets in the trust will be included in Larry's gross estate at death because he is the trustee.

D. The children, as beneficiaries of the trust, have incidents of ownership in the life insurance policy.

22-2. Carlos recently established an ILIT and transferred his life insurance policy with a death benefit of $1,250,000 into the trust. Carlos named his wife, Susanne, and his two children from a previous marriage as Crummey beneficiaries; they are entitled to withdraw the greater of $5,000 or 5% from the trust each year. Carlos wants to reduce the gift tax value of the $50,000 premiums transferred to the trust this year. What gifting techniques are available to Carlos to reduce the taxable gift? Circle all that apply.

A. Annual exclusions of $14,000 for each beneficiary.

B. Gift splitting, if Susanne consents.

C. A marital deduction for a portion of the gift tax attributed to Susanne.

D. Annual exclusions of $5,000 for each beneficiary.

22-3. Marcy transferred $40,000 into a trust two years ago. She named her bank as trustee, her husband Marshall as the income beneficiary, and their son Russ as the remainder beneficiary. A trust provision also gave Marshall a right to appoint property to himself for his support in his accustomed manner of living. The bank purchased a $1 million life insurance policy on Marcy's life soon after the money was transferred into the trust. When Marcy died this year, the value of the policy was $200,000. How much of the trust assets will be included in Marcy's gross estate?

A. $1 million death benefit.

B. $200,000 value of the policy.

C. $40,000 that was transferred into the trust two years ago.

D. None of the trust assets will be included in her estate.

22-4. Using the same facts in Question 3, how much of the trust will be included in Marshall's gross estate if the trust grows to $1.2 million in the year he dies?

A. $1.2 million.

B. The $1 million death benefit amount.

C. The value of the assets that are subject to his general power of appointment.

D. The present value of his income interest in the trust based on his date of death.

E. None of the trust assets will be included in Marshall's gross estate.

22-5. In 2011, Daryl bought a life insurance policy on his life with a death benefit of $200,000. He named his wife Melanie the beneficiary of this policy. In 2014, Daryl created an ILIT with Melanie as beneficiary, and transferred all incidents of ownership in the policy to the trust. The ILIT gives Melanie a lifetime income interest and a general power of appointment over the trust corpus. The value of the policy was $60,000 at Daryl's death in 2015. Which of the following statements are correct?

A. The death benefit amount is included in Daryl's estate but a marital deduction is available to offset the tax.

B. The value of the policy is included in Daryl's estate and a marital deduction is not available to offset the tax.

C. When Melanie dies, the value of the trust will be included in her estate.

D. When Melanie dies, the value of the trust assets will not be included in her estate.

Chapter 23

Estate Planning with Retirement Benefits

CFP® CERTIFICATION EXAMINATION PRINCIPAL TOPICS COVERED IN THIS CHAPTER:

Methods of Property Transfer at Death

- Transfers by contract

Distribution rules, alternatives and taxation

- Election of distribution options
- Required minimum distributions
- Beneficiary considerations
- Taxation of distributions

Learning Objectives

To ensure that you have a solid understanding of the manner in which retirement assets pass at a client's death and the potential income tax consequences for beneficiaries, the following learning objectives are addressed in this chapter:

- Understand the distribution options available to different classes of beneficiaries of retirement plans.

- Recognize the income tax implications that a beneficiary faces upon receiving retirement plan assets.

Chapter Contents

OVERVIEW

For clients who have worked for many years, retirement assets can be a significant portion of their net worth. Retirement assets such as 401(k)s, 403(b)s, IRAs, and Roth IRAs have specific rules that affect the income tax treatment of plan distributions. These assets pass to others by beneficiary designation. Depending on the relationship of the beneficiary to the decedent, the beneficiary is required to take distributions from the account over a certain period of time. Depending on the type of retirement account the client has, there may be significant income tax consequences for taking account distributions.

It is important that financial planners understand the importance of structuring a proper beneficiary designation that accomplishes a client's estate planning goals. In addition, the financial planner must understand and be able to explain the income tax consequences of retirement plan distributions to a client.

Practice Standard 400-2

Developing the Financial Planning Recommendation(s)

The financial planning practitioner shall develop the recommendation(s) based on the selected alternative(s) and the current course of action in an effort to reasonably meet the client's goals, needs and priorities.

INCOME TAXATION OF RETIREMENT PLAN BENEFITS

Traditional retirement plans such as IRAs, 401(k)s, and 403(b)s are funded with pre-tax assets, which grow on a tax-deferred basis. When an account holder takes distributions from a traditional retirement account, he must pay income tax on the amount of the distribution. Roth plans are funded with post-tax dollars; however, all growth is tax deferred and qualified withdrawals from Roth IRAs are tax free. The focus of this discussion is traditional retirement plans.

The IRS has imposed requirements and restrictions on the withdrawal of assets from traditional retirement plans in exchange for allowing tax-deferred growth on retirement plan assets. One of these restrictions is that account holders cannot begin taking withdrawals from a plan before age 59. If the owner of a retirement account takes withdrawals prior to age 59, unless the withdrawal falls within one of a few exceptions, the owner will pay income tax penalties. Alternatively, owners of retirement accounts are required to begin taking withdrawals from traditional retirement accounts at age 70½, unless they are still working. If a client is still working after age 70½, he can defer distributions from his employer's plan until he retires. In that case, the client will have to take distributions from any IRAs or non-active employer plans at age 70½. Withdrawals from retirement accounts are typically calculated as **required minimum distributions**, or RMDs. RMD amounts are based on the account owner's life expectancy, which is factored into IRS actuarial tables. Roth IRAs do not require the account owner to begin taking distributions at age 70½, rather no RMDs are required from Roth IRAs.

Practitioner Tip: A client is required to take an RMD for the year that he turns 70½ or stops working; however, that distribution can be deferred until the following tax year. If the distribution is deferred to the next tax year, there will be two distributions in one year—one for the year that he turned 70½ and one for the current tax year.

Client Situation

Jason turned 70½ in 2015. He has not needed retirement assets in order to meet living expenses but has to start taking RMDs. Jason must begin taking RMDs based on when he turns 70½, however, he can postpone his 2015 distribution and take a distribution for both 2015 and 2016 in 2016.

When an account holder dies, retirement plan assets pass directly to a new account owner by beneficiary designation. Just as there are rules that restrict an account holder's ability to access retirement assets, there are rules that dictate when a beneficiary must begin to take plan distributions. Generally a beneficiary's relationship to the decedent determines when distributions must begin and how they can be taken. The beneficiary of a retirement account must pay income tax on non-Roth distributions he receives from an inherited retirement plan in much the same way as an account holder who receives distributions from his own plan.

Practitioner Tip: Income taxes can greatly reduce the value of retirement plan assets and perhaps other assets that a beneficiary might receive. Financial planners should discuss with clients not only the impact that estate taxes will have on their estates, but also how income taxes could affect the value of specific bequests. The financial planner should also ensure that a client has carefully considered options for planning with retirement assets, and the income tax consequences of selecting different beneficiary designations.

One of the major benefits of retirement plans is the tax-deferred growth of assets. Clients often defer taking plan distributions for as long as possible to take advantage of this. For example, a client may choose not to take a distribution until he needs the money for living expenses or until he is required to by law. Likewise, beneficiaries of retirement assets often choose to stretch payments out for as long as permissible to take full advantage of this tax-saving feature.

BENEFICIARY DESIGNATIONS

When a person dies owning retirement plan assets, those assets must be paid out over a period of no more than five years from the date of his death, unless the decedent leaves them to a **designated beneficiary**.[1] A designated beneficiary is any individual that has been identified as a beneficiary either by the terms of the plan or by the employee's beneficiary designation form.[2] The designated beneficiary need not be specified by name, but he must be identifiable. For example, an individual could name "my wife" or "my children" as the beneficiaries of his retirement plan.[3] The identification of a designated beneficiary is important for purposes of determining the rules that apply to the distribution of retirement plan assets. Different rules apply for a decedent's surviving spouse than for other plan beneficiaries.

Client Situation

Vicky has a 401(k). She has completed the beneficiary designation and indicated that "my husband" is the primary beneficiary of her account. At Vicky's death, her husband Robert will inherit the assets, even though she did not identify Robert by his legal name.

If a person older than 70½ had been taking annual distributions from his retirement plan and died before he was able to take a distribution that year, then the distribution for that year must be taken by the designated beneficiary of the retirement plan, regardless of who that beneficiary might be. The amount that must be distributed to the beneficiary is the amount the decedent would have been required to take in the year he died.[4]

Surviving Spouse as Beneficiary

When a decedent names his surviving spouse as the beneficiary of his retirement plan, the surviving spouse is able to execute a **spousal rollover** and roll assets into an IRA in her own name. The spouse can then treat the IRA as if it were her own account and defer any distribution of assets until she attains age 70½, if desired. At the surviving spouse's subsequent death, she can designate her own beneficiaries for the rollover IRA. If a surviving spouse requires proceeds from the retirement assets to meet living expenses, he can create an inherited IRA and take distributions over his life expectancy, using single life expectancy uniform table. A spousal beneficiary is not required to take distributions from a deceased spouse's Roth IRA. A client's financial needs must be closely examined before a distribution option is selected.

Practitioner Tip: The ability to continue income tax deferral of retirement benefits and to name new plan beneficiaries is a major advantage of spousal rollovers. Wealthier clients who do not rely on distributions from retirement assets to supplement their living expenses benefit the most by allowing retirement assets to remain in the account and continue to grow on a tax-deferred basis for as long as possible.

Non-spousal Beneficiary

When a nonspouse is the designated beneficiary of retirement assets, he can create an **inherited IRA**. The distributions from an inherited IRA are based on the beneficiary's life expectancy, or the entire balance must be distributed within five years of the date of the decedent's death. The beneficiary must begin taking distributions from the plan by September 30 of the year following the decedent's year of death. Distributions are required from both traditional, as well as Roth plans.

Client Situation

Doug has an IRA and he named his wife Maggie the beneficiary of the account. After Doug's death, Maggie can create a spousal rollover IRA and hold off on taking distributions until she reaches age 70½. Maggie can name her children, Paul and Ashley, as beneficiaries of the rollover IRA, and following Maggie's death, Paul and Ashley can create inherited IRAs in their own names. Paul and Ashley will have to begin taking distributions from their inherited IRAs by September 30 of the year following Maggie's death using their respetive life expectancies.

Practitioner Tip: When a retirement plan has a designated beneficiary, distributions are based on the actuarial life expectancy of that beneficiary. If a single beneficiary is named, his individual life expectancy can be used for calculating distributions. However, if a class of beneficiaries such as "my children" is listed, distributions will be paid out over the life expectancy of the oldest member of the class, rather than over each person's life expectancy. When the beneficiaries in a class have a difference in age, which is often the case, this can affect the length of time over which distributions are paid out and taxed. Therefore, it is advisable to name each beneficiary as a proportional owner of the account rather than simply listing the beneficiaries as members of a particular class.

Practitioner Tip: If a decedent had reached age 70½ and was already taking RMDs at the time of his death, in addition to the options available for a spousal rollover or an inherited IRA, his beneficiaries could elect to continue receiving distributions based on his (the deceased account holder's) life expectancy. If the decedent was older than the beneficiary, the RMDs would be larger than if the beneficiary's life expectancy were used as the measuring life for calculations.

Estate as Beneficiary

Clients sometimes name their estate as the beneficiary of their retirement assets. Other times, the estate can end up as the beneficiary of a retirement plan by default. Although each employee benefit plan has its own rules, in most cases if an employee does not complete a proper beneficiary designation form, the plan default provisions provide that the beneficiary will be the employee's estate. The IRS has indicated that the estate is not a designated beneficiary.[5] Even if assets pass through the estate and are distributed to an individual by the terms of a decedent's will or trust there is no designated beneficiary for purposes of calculating RMDs. This means that assets will have to be distributed from the retirement plan—and income tax will have to be paid—within five years of the date of the decedent's death.

Client Situation

When Gail started her new job, she received a packet of information to fill out on her first day of work but quickly got swept up in the tasks of her new position. One of the forms in the packet was a beneficiary designation form for her 403(b) plan—which she never filled out. At Gail's death, her 403(b) plan benefits will be paid to her estate. Gail's two children, Ryan and Lauren, will inherit all assets under Gail's will. Even though Ryan and Lauren are the identified beneficiaries of Gail's will, they will be required to take distributions from her 403(b) plan within five years of the date of Gail's death and will be unable to stretch RMDs out over their own life expectancies.

Practitioner Tip: Often, clients mistakenly believe that naming the estate as a beneficiary of their retirement plans will ensure that their intended beneficiaries receive the retirement assets. Although this may be the correct disposition, clients do not understand that there are adverse income tax consequences for the plan beneficiaries. Other times, for whatever reason, clients fail to name a beneficiary for their retirement assets. Although each employer's plan has its own rules, this often means that retirement assets default to the estate.

Trust as Beneficiary

Under certain circumstances an individual might wish to name a trust as the beneficiary of his retirement assets. Although this is a more complicated strategy, it may be appropriate for clients in certain situations. A trust qualifies as a designated beneficiary if certain technical requirements are met. One is that the IRS must be able to *look through* the trust to determine who the trust beneficiaries are. If the beneficiaries are all identifiable, and all would qualify as designated beneficiaries had they been named beneficiaries outside the trust, then retirement assets can be distributed to the trust over the oldest beneficiary's life expectancy. This is referred to as a **look-through trust**.

Practitioner Tip: For beneficiaries to qualify as designated beneficiaries, they must all be individuals, not organizations. If an organization, such as a charity, is named as a beneficiary of the trust, then the trust might not qualify as a look-through trust and retirement plan assets will have to be distributed within five years of the decedent's death. This could be the case even if the organization or charity is named as a successor or contingent beneficiary of the trust.

> ### Client Situation
>
> Dan has established a bypass trust, which names his wife Maura as the sole trust beneficiary during her lifetime, and following her death assets are to be held in trust for their son Alex. At the time of Dan's death, Maura is age 63 and Alex is 30. Because Maura and Alex are the only trust beneficiaries, the trust qualifies as a look-through trust. Retirement plan assets can be paid to the trust over Maura's life expectancy.

The terms of the trust determine whether RMDs received by the trust are paid out to beneficiaries. If the trust requires that all of the minimum distributions are to be paid to trust beneficiaries, the trust is a **conduit trust**. If the trust allows the trustee to accumulate RMDs within the trust, it is known as an **accumulation trust**. Planning with a conduit trust is often simpler, because all RMDs are distributed outright to the trust beneficiaries. However, it is important to consider a client's planning objectives when determining which type of trust is most appropriate. For example, if one of the trust beneficiaries is receiving government benefits, such as a special needs beneficiary, the receipt of RMDs could disqualify the beneficiary from receiving the government benefits.

Practitioner Tip: There are many very specific rules to qualify a trust as a designated beneficiary. For this strategy to be effective, it is imperative that a client work with a qualified estate planning attorney who understands these rules and is able to draft a trust that will meet IRS requirements.

BYPASS PLANNING WITH RETIREMENT ASSETS

To the extent possible, it is preferable to fund a bypass trust with non-retirement assets rather than retirement assets. When retirement assets are left to a surviving spouse, he can create a rollover IRA. Distributions from the rollover IRA are based on the surviving spouse's life expectancy, and at his death the surviving spouse can name additional beneficiaries, such as children. The additional beneficiaries would then be able to create an inherited IRA and could take distributions from the retirement plan assets over their presumably longer life expectancies. When retirement assets are used to fund a bypass trust, however, if the surviving spouse and children were both beneficiaries of the bypass trust, retirement assets would be paid to the trust over the surviving spouse's life expectancy, even after the surviving spouse has passed away. This reduces the duration of the retirement benefits.

However, there are circumstances where it might make sense to use retirement assets to fund a bypass trust. If an individual does not have adequate non-retirement assets with which to fund his bypass trust, he will have to decide between not fully funding the bypass trust and using retirement plan assets to fund the trust. Much of this planning will be affected by federal and state tax laws in effect at the time of the client's death; therefore, these options should be carefully examined. If this strategy is used, the trust must be a look-through trust to qualify for the extended payment of retirement plan distributions.

Practitioner Tip: In 2015, with a $5,430,000 federal estate tax exemption for each taxpayer and the advantage of portability, married couples can shelter up to $10,860,000 from federal estate tax. Many clients are unconcerned with federal estate tax because the value of their combined estates is below this combined exemption amount. However, portability has not been adopted at the state level; therefore, for those interested in sheltering assets from state estate tax, bypass planning remains an important planning technique.

Client Situation

Brad and Christine have a net worth of $4 million. They live in a state that has a separate state-level estate tax with an exemption of $2 million per taxpayer. They wish to implement a tax-efficient estate plan to ensure that the survivor is well taken care of and to leave any remaining assets to their children Jenny and Andy. Brad and Christine each have a $1 million IRA and a $1 million investment account. They meet with their financial planner, who explains that they could consider using their IRA assets to fund their bypass trust. The planner explains that if Brad leaves his retirement assets to Christine, she would be able to create a spousal rollover IRA and to name Andy and Jenny as beneficiaries following her death. Andy and Jenny could then take distributions from the retirement plan over their longer life expectancies.

The downside to this strategy is that Brad will not have taken full advantage of his state estate tax exemption and the state estate tax at Christine's death will be greater than if he had implemented bypass planning. Their planner further explains that Brad could name his bypass trust as the beneficiary of his IRA. Christine, Jenny, and Andy are all beneficiaries of the bypass trust. Retirement assets would be paid out to the trust over Christine's life expectancy, even after Christine died. Jenny and Andy would lose the advantages of extended IRA distributions, but the state-level estate tax liability at Christine's death would be less because of this planning strategy.

CHARITABLE PLANNING WITH RETIREMENT ASSETS

Clients who are charitably inclined may wish to consider using retirement assets to satisfy any charitable bequests. Because charities are not required to pay income tax, this can increase the amount that can be left to both charitable and non-charitable beneficiaries. Any charitable beneficiary should be designated directly through a beneficiary designation on the plan account rather than through the terms of a will or trust. If a client's estate or trust is named as the beneficiary of retirement assets, the assets will be subject to income taxation in the client's estate or trust despite that fact that the assets will ultimately be distributed to charities.

Client Situation

Kim has an estate consisting of a $1 million investment account and a $1 million IRA. She wishes to leave half of her estate to her daughter Katie and half to her church. Kim meets with her financial planner. He explains that Kim could consider leaving the investment account to Katie and the IRA to her church. Katie would receive a step-up in basis to the date-of-death value of the investment account. Because Kim's church is a qualified charity, it would not have to pay income tax on the retirement assets and would receive the full $1 million. However, if Kim leaves half of each asset to her church and to Katie, then Katie would have to pay income tax on the amount she received from the retirement assets, which would reduce the amount she actually inherited.

Chapter Highlights

- The IRS has specific rules with respect to distributions from retirement assets. One of the benefits of retirement assets is that these accounts grow tax deferred.

- Retirement assets must be distributed from the account and income tax must be paid within five years of a decedent's death, unless the decedent had a designated beneficiary. An estate is not a designated beneficiary.

- If the surviving spouse is named the beneficiary of a decedent's retirement plan, he can create a spousal rollover IRA and treat the IRA as his own. This allows him to defer distributions until attaining age 70½; he can also name additional account beneficiaries.

- If a non-spousal beneficiary is named as the beneficiary of a decedent's retirement plan, he can create an inherited IRA and take distributions over his life expectancy.

- A trust may qualify as a designated beneficiary if it qualifies as a look-through trust. All beneficiaries must be identifiable and qualify as designated beneficiaries. Retirement assets are distributed over the oldest trust beneficiary's life expectancy.

Key Terms

accumulation trust

conduit trust

designated beneficiary

inherited IRA

look-through trust

required minimum distribution (RMD)

spousal rollover

Review Questions

23-1. Tom names his wife Lisa as the beneficiary of his IRA. Which of the following is correct?

A. Lisa must take distributions from the IRA within five years.

B. Lisa can take distributions from the IRA over their son John's life expectancy.

C. Lisa can create a spousal rollover, defer distributions until she is age 70½, and name additional IRA beneficiaries.

D. Lisa can create a spousal rollover and take distributions over her life expectancy beginning September 30 of the year following the year of Tom's death.

23-2. Which of the following statements is/ are correct regarding the use of retirement assets to fund a bypass trust?

1. When a trust is named as the beneficiary of retirement assets, distributions must be paid to the beneficiaries each year.

2. When a trust is named as the beneficiary of retirement assets, the assets will be distributed to the trustee based on the life expectancy of the oldest trust beneficiary.

3. When a trust is named as the beneficiary of retirement assets, the retirement assets will be included in the surviving spouse's estate.

A. 1 and 2

B. 1 and 3

C. 2 only

D. 3 only

23-3. Blake has named his wife Miranda as the primary beneficiary of his 401(k) and their daughter Christina as the contingent beneficiary. Miranda predeceased Blake; however, he never updated his beneficiary designations. Which of the following statements is incorrect?

A. Christina will inherit the 401(k) at Blake's death and will be able to create an inherited IRA.

B. Christina must take 401(k) distributions beginning September 30 of the year following the year of Blake's death.

C. Christina can defer distributions until she turns 70½.

D. Christina can take distributions based on her life expectancy.

23-4 Beth's will provides that all assets pass to her son James following her death. Is this statement true or false: There is no difference between Beth naming James the beneficiary or her estate as the beneficiary of her 401(k) since James is the sole beneficiary of Beth's estate.

23-5 Which of the following statements is not correct regarding beneficiary designations of retirement assets?

A. The beneficiary of a retirement account will have to pay income tax on distributions from that account, just as the account owner would.

B. When a trust is the beneficiary of a retirement account, all minimum distributions must pass through to the trust beneficiaries.

C. When a client is charitably inclined, leaving retirement assets to a charity may be a way to minimize income taxation of retirement assets.

D. Generally speaking, a surviving spouse will have more alternatives with respect to taking distributions from retirement assets than a non-spouse beneficiary.

Notes

1. IRC §401(a)(9)(B)(ii).
2. Treas. Reg. §§1.401(a)(9)-4., A-1.
3. Id.
4. Treas. Reg. §§1.401(a)(9)-5., A-4(a).
5. Treas. Reg. §§1.401(a)(9)-4., A-3.

Chapter 24

Estate Freeze Strategies

CFP® CERTIFICATION EXAMINATION PRINCIPAL TOPICS COVERED IN THIS CHAPTER:

Estate freezes

- Corporate and partnership recapitalizations (Code section 2701)
- Transfers in trust

Qualified interest trusts

- Grantor retained annuity trusts (GRATs)
- Grantor retained unitrusts (GRUTs)
- Qualified personal residence trusts (QPRTs or House-GRITs)
- Valuation of qualified interests

Learning Objectives

To ensure that you have a solid understanding of advanced estate planning techniques such as estate freezes and grantor retained trusts, the following learning objectives are addressed in this chapter:

- Define an estate freeze.

- Know when and how to apply the preferred stock recapitalization technique.

- Compare and contrast the differences between GRITs, GRATs, and GRUTs.

- Recognize the circumstances when a qualified interest trust is appropriate for clients.

- Evaluate the gift and estate tax ramifications of using GRITs, GRATs, GRUTs, and QPRTs.

Chapter Contents

OVERVIEW

Wealthier taxpayers may wish to employ advanced estate planning strategies to reduce their gift and estate tax liabilities. **Estate freeze** techniques are strategies that allow the owner of a property or business interest to retain much of the present value of the asset or control of the asset while shifting future appreciation of that asset to others. A freeze ensures retention of the enterprise in a family with minimal transfer tax costs.

To recommend the most appropriate techniques for meeting clients' gift and wealth transfer goals, financial planners should become familiar with the characteristics of each of these strategies and what they can accomplish.

Practice Standard 400-2

Developing the Financial Planning Recommendation(s)

The financial planning practitioner shall develop the recommendation(s) based on the selected alternative(s) and the current course of action in an effort to reasonably meet the client's goals, needs and priorities.

IRC CHAPTER 14 REQUIREMENTS

The IRS enacted Chapter 14 of the Internal Revenue Code to restrict the transfer of partial interests in an asset to certain family members. These family members include the grantor's spouse, ancestors (i.e., parents and grandparents), lineal descendants (children and grandchildren), siblings, and the spouses of these beneficiaries. The IRS determined that when a transferor transfers a partial interest to these family members, and retains a partial interest, the value of the retained interest equals zero. Therefore, the value of the gift will be the full fair market value of the property. There are several exceptions to this rule. Code sections 2701 and 2702 allow a donor to make a gift of a partial interest in property at a reduced gift tax value. Certain requirements must be met to allow the reduced gift tax valuation. First, these strategies are available only when the beneficiaries are the grantor's spouse, lineal descendants (parents, grandparents, children or grandchildren, siblings, or the spouses of these family members.

Next, the donor must retain a qualified interest. For purposes of sections 2701 and 2702, qualified payments are payments that are fixed in time and amount. When a donor transfers a partial interest in an asset and retains a qualified interest, the value of the taxable gift is based on the fair market value (FMV) of the property transferred less the value of the owner's retained interest. If the donor does not retain a qualified interest, the value of the gift is based on the entire FMV of the asset.

Qualified transfers include preferred stock recapitalization, grantor retained annuity trusts (GRATs), grantor retained unitrusts (GRUTs), and qualified personal residence trusts (QPRTs). Under these strategies, an owner or family member gifts a partial interest in property to a family member and retains some ownership in the property after the gift is made.

Chapter 14 does not apply to:

- sales;

- gifts to third parties who are not defined as related family members under sections 2701 and 2702;

- gifts of an entire business or property interest; or

- transfers made at death.

Therefore, certain strategies, such as grantor retained income trusts (GRITs) will remain a planning strategy for transferring assets at a reduced gift tax value to nieces, nephews or other unrelated beneficiaries.

SECTION 2701 PREFERRED STOCK RECAPITALIZATION

Preferred stock recapitalization is a strategy that can be employed when a business owner wants to transfer some of his closely held stock to his children to reduce the value of his estate, freeze the value of the remaining shares in his estate, and allow his children to benefit from the future appreciation of the stock. This strategy allows him to receive income from the corporation and retain control of his business. Preferred stock recapitalization is governed by Code section 2701.

To employ this strategy, a business owner recapitalizes his stock into voting preferred shares and non-voting common shares. He would then gift the non-voting common shares to his children. The business owner's retention of cumulative preferred shares provides a qualified payment because he retains the right to receive dividends at a fixed par value. When he gifts some of the common stock to his children, the value of the gift is the value of the stock reduced by annual exclusions and applicable discounts. Without a qualified payment, the business owner would have a retained interest of zero and the value of the gifted stock would be the FMV of the closely held business. Recapitalization also freezes the value of the preferred shares at par value no matter how much the business grows, which further reduces the value of the stock in the owner's gross estate at death.

The owner must retain the right to receive dividends at a fixed par value on cumulative preferred stock at least annually. Therefore, the gift tax will be applied only to the amount of common stock transferred, not to the entire value of the company stock. General valuation principles can apply. With this strategy, the qualified payment requirement is met because the owner has retained a distribution right to receive qualified payments because preferred stock is structured so that payments are fixed in time and amount. The cumulative nature of preferred stock guarantees that payments will be made at liquidation of the corporation, if not sooner. Payments must be fixed in amount, meaning that values can be readily determined, because payments are not subject to a declaration of dividends by the directors of the corporation.

Because the value of the gift is determined by subtracting the value of the retained qualified payment from the value of the entire entity, it is possible the result could be a small amount when the value of the qualified payment is large. However, regardless of the results of the subtraction method, the minimum value that can be assigned to the transfer of a junior equity interest is 10% of the total value of all equity interests in the partnership or corporation, plus the total indebtedness of the entity to the transferor, or an applicable family member.

An interest is not considered qualified if the dividends are noncumulative or if the owner retains extraordinary payment rights, such as the right to exercise puts or calls, and the rights to covert shares or compel liquidation. An "unqualified interest" would cause the gifted shares to be taxed at the full FMV of the business interest, not on the partial amount of stock gifted. The IRS would consider the business owner to have a retained interest of zero in the stock, even though the owner did not gift it all away.

The cumulative preferred shares satisfy the owner's income needs while providing him with a qualified payment under Chapter 14 in the form of fixed dividends. However, any appreciation in the value of the corporation will occur outside of the owner's estate. The non-voting common shares are removed from the owner's estate, which avoids estate taxation on the value of the common stock and on its future appreciation as well. The value of the corporate interest retained by the owner is frozen because the preferred shares are measured at par value. Note that the minimum value rule applies, so the gift tax value of the common stock must be at least 10% of the total value of the business owner's stock. This technique allows the owner to retain total control of the business, receive income from the preferred shares, freeze the preferred shares at par value, and give family members direct ownership in the business with the benefit of future appreciation on their common shares.

Client Situation

Gary owns a carpet cleaning company worth $1 million, and after recapitalizing the stock, he gifts $400,000 of his non-voting common stock to his children, keeping $600,000 of cumulative preferred shares. He pays gift taxes on the $400,000 and income taxes on the fixed dividends he receives annually on the preferred shares. When he dies, his company might be valued at $3 million, but only the original $600,000 of retained preferred stock is included in his gross estate.

GRANTOR RETAINED INCOME TRUSTS (GRITs)

Before the enactment of the Revenue Reconciliation Act of 1990 and Code section 2702, **grantor retained income trusts (GRITs)** were a popular strategy for transferring wealth to others. In a GRIT transaction, the grantor transfers property to a trust and retains an income interest in the trust and/or a reversionary interest in the trust for a period of years. Assuming the grantor survives the initial trust term, the grantor would have no further retained interest in the property and the property would pass to the trust beneficiaries.

When the trust is funded, there are essentially two interests: the grantor's current interest and the remainder beneficiary's interest. The value of these interests is calculated based on the grantor's life expectancy and the section 7520 rate at the time the trust is created. The grantor makes a taxable gift of the remainder interest when the trust is funded. Because the gift is a future-interest gift, the grantor is not permitted to apply an annual exclusion against the taxable gift.

Transfers into GRITs are now considered unqualified interests for the purposes of section 2702. Examples of qualified interests are **annuity payments**, which are fixed payment amounts, and **unitrust payments**, which can fluctuate annually. Because the grantor's interest in a GRIT is not structured as an annuity or a unitrust income payment, and the grantor can receive all of the trust income, the grantor's retained interest is valued at zero for gift tax purposes if the remainder beneficiary is a spouse or lineal descendant. Therefore, the gift tax is assessed on the total FMV of the assets transferred into the trust rather than to only the remainder interest. GRITs remain a useful estate planning strategy when the remainder beneficiary is a niece or nephew or other relative, or an unrelated party.

Client Situation

Francis created an irrevocable trust funded with $2 million of appreciating securities. The trust will distribute all income to Francis for five years and the remainder interest will pass to his two sons after his income interest ends. Francis did not structure this split-interest trust to receive a qualified payment, such as an annuity or unitrust payment. Instead, Francis will receive all of the trust income each year. Francis has created a GRIT, and for gift tax purposes, Francis has a retained an interest of zero. The gift of the remainder interest is taxed on the full $2 million transferred to the trust, not on the present value of the remainder interest.

With a GRIT, because the grantor retains an income interest, he will pay income tax on income received by the trust. Although the initial FMV of the property is subject to gift tax, any appreciation on the property will pass to the beneficiaries' estate gift tax free.

Advantages of a GRIT

A GRIT, which was commonly used for income property, is now generally limited to transfers of a personal residence or certain tangible property such as artwork in situations where the grantor retains the use of the property during the term of the trust. For example, a grantor can use a GRIT for a work of art that he wants to display in his own home and then have the artwork pass to a trust beneficiary when his term ends. Assuming the grantor survives the term, the artwork would not be included in the grantor's estate and it would also avoid probate.

Because GRITs are not governed by section 2702, the remainder beneficiary can be a non-family member, niece, nephew, or other individual who is not defined under the IRC. This makes the GRIT an attractive strategy for transferring property in many situations. GRITs with non-family member beneficiaries such as friends, life partners, nieces, and nephews retain favorable gift tax treatment; only the present value of the remainder interest is subject to tax.

> **Client Situation**
>
> Danny owns a factory. He is 50 years old and wants to give the factory to his nephew John when he retires. Danny met with his financial planner, who recommended a GRIT. Danny retains the right to use the factory for the next 10 years, and he retains a reversionary interest for the next 10 years. At the end of the 10-year term, the factory becomes John's property. The value of Danny's taxable gift to John will depend on the term of the trust and the section 7520 rate in effect on the date of transfer. Assuming the trust term is 10 years, and the section 7520 rate is 2.0%, Danny's taxable gift would be $767,790. If the section 7520 rate is 5.0%, his taxable gift would be $574,580. At the end of the trust term, the factory will pass to John. If the value of the factory has appreciated during the 10-year term, all appreciation will pass to John tax free.

QUALIFIED TRANSFERS IN TRUST

A grantor retained trust is an irrevocable trust into which a grantor places assets and retains an income interest for a fixed period of years. Principal and any trust appreciation at the end of the term pass to a noncharitable beneficiary.

The purpose of a grantor retained trust is to:

- transfer property to family in trust at a reduced gift tax value;

- pass appreciation to beneficiaries without triggering an additional gift tax; and

- reduce the value of the grantor's estate.

Under section 2702, if a grantor transfers assets to a trust and retains either a qualified annuity interest, qualified unitrust interest, or qualified remainder interest, certain favorable valuation treatments might be allowed for gift tax purposes. Non-contingent remainder interests are qualified interests if other interests in the trust are annuity or unitrust interests. At the end of the grantor's income interest, the remainder passes to trust beneficiaries. The initial trust term can be for a specific number of years or the grantor's lifetime.

Certain restrictions under section 2702 limit the applicability and success of these trusts. First, only certain family members can be trust beneficiaries. Next, the grantor must survive the initial trust term or the entire value of the trust property is includible in his estate. If the grantor survives the initial trust term, his interest in the trust terminates, and upon his death the assets in the trust are not included in his estate. No beneficiary other than the stated income beneficiary can receive payments from the trust.

Practitioner Tip: When grandchildren are beneficiaries of grantor retained trusts, the grantor's generation-skipping transfer tax exemption cannot be allocated to the trust until after the grantor's income period ends. By that time, the grandchildren's interest in the trust could be much greater than it was at the time the trust was established.

GRATs AND GRUTs

Grantor retained annuity trusts (GRATs) and **grantor retained unitrusts (GRUTs)** receive favorable gift tax treatment for remainder interests passing to family beneficiaries, but GRITs do not. The difference in taxation is because of the type of payments the grantor receives.

An annuity or unitrust payment in a split-interest trust (GRAT or GRUT) is considered a qualified interest under Chapter 14 of the Internal Revenue Code, and all income distributed annually from a GRIT is not.

Qualified payments are fixed in time and amount. For example, an annuity payment is a level payment amount distributed annually to an income beneficiary throughout the income term. With a unitrust payment, the grantor retains a right to a distribution of income based on a fixed percentage of the value of the trust property, which is revalued annually.

Client Situation

Leslie transferred $1 million into a grantor retained trust that retains a 5% income stream. With a GRAT, Leslie receives a fixed payment of $50,000 per year for a specified number of years. With a GRUT, Leslie would also receive an initial distribution of $50,000 in the first year. However, the next year's payout of 5% of trust assets would depend on the investment performance of the assets in the trust. Leslie might receive more or less than $50,000 each year, throughout her income term.

With GRATs and GRUTs, only the present value of the remainder interest of the trust is subject to gift taxes, not the FMV of the assets transferred into the trust. The gift tax value for the remainder interest is less than the FMV of the assets transferred into the trust, because the beneficiaries do not have current use of the trust assets and cannot receive the assets until the grantor's income term has ended.

Practitioner Tip: The grantor can reduce the gift tax even more by selecting a longer income payout period or increasing the annuity rate.

The Income Term

Because the trust is irrevocable, the concept of distributable net income (DNI) applies. DNI provides that any income earned by a trust will be deemed first distributable from a trust, regardless of whether trust income or principal is actually distributed. To the extent the trust has income, it will be distributed first. The grantor pays income tax on the income received.

Practitioner Tip: Payment of income taxes reduces the value of the grantor's estate, but income distributions increase the value of the estate. This income can be gifted to others or to charities to further reduce the value of the grantor's estate.

If the grantor survives the income term, the beneficiaries receive the trust property and any appreciation with no additional gift taxes imposed on the transfer. Furthermore, the trust corpus is removed from the grantor's estate. A beneficiary's basis is the grantor's carryover basis in the trust assets rather than a stepped-up basis at the grantor's death.

If the grantor does not survive the specified income period, then the trust assets will be included in the grantor's estate. These assets will still pass to trust beneficiaries as part of the trust. Consequently, the remainder interest gift would not be added back as an adjusted taxable gift on the grantor's estate tax return, IRS Form 706.

Practitioner Tip: The best assets with which to fund a qualified trust are assets that are expected to appreciate at a greater rate than the **section 7520 rate**. This is because the section 7520 rate is the bar by which a grantor's interest is measured. For example, the lower the section 7520 rate, the easier it is for trust investments to outperform that rate and pass along excess appreciation to trust beneficiaries.

Qualified Annuity Interests

A qualified annuity interest is an irrevocable right to receive a fixed amount at least annually, payable to or for the benefit of the holder of the term interest (i.e., the transferor or an applicable family member). Note that an applicable family member other than the grantor can be the income beneficiary of a GRAT. In that situation, the grantor would have made a gift of both the present value of the income interest and the remainder interest. The annuity can be based on a fixed dollar amount or a percentage of the value of the trust, and it cannot vary except to the extent that the amount (or percentage) in any year does not exceed 120% of the amount (or percentage) from the preceding year.

Once a trust has been funded, no additional contributions are allowed to the GRAT. Therefore, if trust income does not produce adequate cash to pay the annuity stream, the trust principal must be invaded to fund the annuity payment.

Client Situation

Kay wishes to transfer assets to her daughter Terry. Kay has $1 million invested in a stock portfolio that has decreased in value over the past year; however, Kay expects the assets to appreciate significantly over the next several years. Kay met with her financial planner and they discussed using a GRAT to transfer the stock portfolio to Terry. Kay put the $1 million in a GRAT with a five-year term. Kay is 63 years old and the section 7520 rate is 2.0%. Kay structures a 10% annuity payment ($100,000 annually) from the GRAT for the initial trust term. The value of Kay's annuity interest is $471,350 and the value of Terry's remainder interest is $528,650. Kay has made a taxable gift of $528,650. If trust assets appreciate by 8% over the course of the next five years, the value of the assets remaining in trust that Terry will receive will be $887,668. Effectively, Kay will have removed $887,668 from her estate by making a taxable gift of $528,650, assuming she survives the five-year term. All of the trust's appreciation will pass to Terry free from gift tax.

Zeroed-out GRAT

A client can create a GRAT that has no remainder interest by creating an annuity stream of income that pays out the entire principal of the trust. This is referred to as a **zeroed-out GRAT**. With a zeroed-out GRAT, the grantor typically creates a trust that provides a short-term annuity with a high payout to eliminate most of the gift tax on the computed remainder interest. The success of the GRAT depends on the appreciation of trust assets. If the assets appreciate at a rate exceeding the section 7520 rate used to calculate the remainder interest, then the excess growth is transferred gift tax free. The value of the income and remainder interests for gift tax calculations are determined using Table B of the Treasury Tables, using the current section 7520 rate.

Client Situation

Assume that Kay has used all of her available lifetime gift tax exemption and does not wish to incur a gift tax liability. She could create a zeroed-out GRAT. Assuming the same five-year term, the annuity payment that would zero-out the GRAT would be $212,156.57. Kay's annuity interest would be $1 million (the full value of the property placed in the trust) and the remainder interest would be $0. Assuming the same 8% rate of return, at the end of the initial trust term Terry would receive $225,000, which will be transferred gift tax free.

Qualified Unitrust Interests

A qualified unitrust interest is an irrevocable right to the annual payment of a fixed percentage of the net FMV of the trust assets, to be determined annually. A unitrust payment provides an inflation hedge. Rather than receiving a fixed dollar amount annually, payments are based on the FMV of the trust each year. This amount is affected by investment performance of the assets managed in the trust. Unlike the GRAT, additional contributions are permitted to the GRUT to give the grantor additional income, if needed.

Practitioner Tip: Because the GRUT must be revalued annually, it is not advisable to fund the GRUT with hard-to-value assets such as closely held stock or real estate that is expected to appreciate in value.

Client Situation

Bill wishes to transfer assets to his son Joe, but Bill is concerned that given rising inflation, he may need some of the assets to live on. Bill has $1 million invested in mutual funds. Bill decides to create a GRUT, retaining a 10-year interest in the trust. Bill funds the trust with $1 million and retains a 5% unitrust payment. The initial payment will be $50,000. The next year's payment will be equal to 5% of the trust's FMV, which depends on the performance of the underlying investments in the GRUT. Assuming Bill is 75 years old and the section 7520 rate in effect at the time the trust is funded is 3.6%, the present value of Joe's remainder interest is $598,737. At Bill's death, the remaining trust principal, including all of the trust's appreciation exceeding the section 7520 rate, will pass to Joe gift tax free. Assuming the trust has outperformed the annuity payment amount, Joe will be left with an amount greater than the amount of Bill's gift.

PERSONAL RESIDENCE TRUSTS (PRTS)

A grantor retained income trust (GRIT) can still be used effectively when the transferor transfers an interest in a personal residence to a trust and retains the right to use the property for residential purposes for a term of years. Section 2702 carves out an exception for a personal residence trust (PRT). The regulations require that such a trust be limited to holding a single residence or a fractional interest in a residence, such as a tenancy in common.

The residence cannot be occupied by any person other than the grantor, a spouse, or dependent; must be available at all times for such use; and cannot be sold or used for any other purpose. The residence can include appurtenant structures and adjacent land reasonably appropriate for residential purposes and be subject to a mortgage, but that does not include any personal property such as furnishings.

Qualified Personal Residence Trusts (QPRTs)

The Treasury regulations carve out a safe harbor called a **qualified personal residence trust**. A QPRT should contain provisions substantially the same as those required for personal residence trusts, but they can be more flexible in certain situations.

A QPRT is an irrevocable trust that holds a person's residence, allowing couples or individuals to live in the house rent free for a fixed period of time. At the end of the term, the home passes gift tax free to the trust beneficiaries and will be removed from the grantor's estate. A home transferred to trust is taxed at the present value of the home's remainder interest, rather than at its FMV. If the grantor dies before the term of residence ends, then the FMV of the home is included in the grantor's estate. A QPRT allows the grantor to "freeze" the value of the home when it is placed in trust and pass along any future appreciation to trust beneficiaries. A beneficiary's basis in the home is the grantor's original basis increased by a portion of any gift taxes paid.

Grantors can have two homes subject to a QPRT, a primary residence and a vacation home, or a fractional interest in either. A home subject to a mortgage can also be transferred into the trust. Grantors must continue to pay property taxes and home maintenance expenses, and the trust can hold cash strictly limited to these purposes. Grantors can continue to live in the home after their term ends by paying rent to the trust.

Client Situation

Harvey is a 70-year-old widower with a $14 million estate. Harvey transferred his personal residence, appraised at $6 million, to a QPRT for the benefit of his son Joel. Harvey will continue to live in the home for the next six years. Harvey has made a taxable gift to Joel of the present value of the home's remainder interest, but because it is less than the FMV of the home, Harvey's unified credit was available to offset the gift tax. If Harvey outlives the six-year term, he intends to remain in the home and pay rent to the trust, which will benefit Joel. The rent payments would not be considered gifts to Joel and will reduce Harvey's taxable estate. The home, and any appreciation in the home, will not be taxed in Harvey's estate.

Although the regulations seem to require that no assets other than an interest in a personal residence can ever be held in a PRT, and the interest in the residence cannot be sold during the term of the trust, the QPRT permits both under limited circumstances. It is conceivable this trust could have income. If it does, it must be distributed to the term holder; no distributions can be made to any other person.

The QPRT must prohibit the holding of any property other than the personal residence and contain the following provisions:

- No distributions to other persons are permitted.

- Cash can be held for the initial purchase of the residence within three months, or purchase of a replacement residence within three months of the date the cash is added to the trust.

- Cash can also be held for up to six months for payment of trust expenses, including mortgage payments, and for improvements.

- If the property is sold or insurance proceeds are received, a two-year replacement period is permitted. Excess cash must be distributed at least quarterly or at the termination of the trust to the term holder.

- If the property is no longer used as a personal residence, the trust must terminate and its assets must be distributed to the term holder within 30 days, unless it is converted into a GRAT.

In the case of a QPRT, it is possible to sell a residence, reinvest only part of the proceeds in a new residence, and convert the rest to an annuity if there is no prepayment of the term interest.

ADVANTAGES OF GRATs, GRUTs, AND QPRTs

GRATs, GRUTs, and QPRTs are the closest thing to a no-lose situation; they are a "What have we got to lose?" technique. If the GRAT, GRUT, or QPRT is successful, the client will have transferred assets to his beneficiaries at a fraction of the FMV.

GRATs, GRUTs, and QPRTs should be considered only when there is a strong probability that a client will outlive the trust term and that the assets transferred into the trust will not compromise the grantor's financial security. These trusts are particularly useful when the grantor is single and could have a substantial federal estate tax liability. Wealthy widows or widowers, divorced individuals, or other unmarried persons can use these trusts to transfer appreciating property to others at a reduced gift tax value and possibly avoid paying estate taxes and probate expenses at their death.

If the client does not use a GRAT, GRUT, or QPRT and retains property in his or her sole name, the property plus any appreciation on the property is includible in his estate. If the client who sets up a GRAT, GRUT, or QPRT dies during the specified term, the result is that an amount not in excess of the value of the property plus any appreciation on the property will be includible in his or her estate (the same result as if the client had done nothing). Even if the grantor dies and the property is includable in his estate, the property will pass per the terms of the trust to trust beneficiaries as the grantor intended.

DISADVANTAGES OF GRATs, GRUTs, AND QPRTs

There are some potential disadvantages with respect to GRATs, GRUTs, and QPRTs. If the strategy is unsuccessful, although there will be no disadvantage from an estate tax perspective, the client will have incurred attorney fees and other transaction costs, such as appraisal fees and the property titling costs of establishing the trust.

If the grantor dies during the specified trust term, his executor could be liable for tax on the includible assets—but the property itself might not be available to pay that tax. One possible solution to this problem is to purchase sufficient term life insurance that will last for the duration of the grantor's income term.

When the grantor survives the specified term of the trust, no step-up in basis for the property is allowed. This is because the property was not acquired from a decedent but from a gift at the time the trust was funded.

One additional consideration is that if appreciated property is transferred to a GRAT, GRUT, or QPRT, the tax on any gain will eventually be paid by:

- the grantor (so long as the trust is a grantor trust);

- the trust (when the trust ceases to be a grantor trust); or

- the beneficiaries (if the property is distributed outright to them on termination of the trust).

Practitioner Tip: The payment of taxes by the grantor might not be a disadvantage, however, because the purpose of the trust is to "defund" the grantor's estate and shift as much wealth as possible to the remainder beneficiary with minimal gift taxes.

Chapter Highlights

- Split-interest trusts such as GRITs, GRATs, GRUTs, and QPRTs are tax-efficient methods of transferring wealth to family members or other trust beneficiaries.

- A GRIT is a strategy that has become less common since the enactment of Code section 2702. It is typically used to transfer property to nonfamily beneficiaries. The grantor retains an income interest in the trust, and perhaps a reversionary interest. The grantor makes a taxable gift when the trust is funded. If the grantor survives the term, remaining trust assets pass to the beneficiary free from further estate or gift tax.

- A GRAT is a qualified transfer in which the grantor retains the right to receive an annuity stream of income over a period of time. At the end of the annuity period, trust property passes to the beneficiaries free from further estate or gift tax.

- A GRUT is a qualified transfer in which the grantor retains a unitrust payment from a trust for a period of time. At the end of the unitrust period, property passes to the beneficiaries free from further estate or gift tax.

- A GRAT or GRUT can be created only for certain family members including a spouse, lineal ancestors and descendants, siblings, or the spouses of these family members. A GRIT can be created for any beneficiary.

- A QPRT is a qualified trust used to transfer a donor's primary residence or vacation home to trust beneficiaries. When a donor creates a QPRT, he retains the right to live in the home for a number of years. Following the initial trust term, the home passes outright to, or remains in trust for, trust beneficiaries. If the donor wishes to use the property following the initial trust term, he must pay rent to the beneficiaries who now own the property.

Key Terms

annuity payment

Code section 7520 rate

estate freeze

grantor retained annuity trusts (GRATs)

grantor retained income trusts (GRITs)

grantor retained unitrusts (GRUTs)

preferred stock recapitalization

qualified personal residence trust (QPRT)

unitrust payment

zeroed-out GRAT

Review Questions

24-1. Enzo owns a tailoring business that he wishes to transfer to his son Paulo. He wishes to retain an income stream from the business but wants any future appreciation from the business to occur outside of his taxable estate. Which of the following strategies would be appropriate?

A. GRAT

B. QPRT

C. Preferred stock recapitalization

D. GRIT

24-2. For purposes of Code section 2701, in the context of the estate freeze, applicable retained interests are given a value of zero. Examples of applicable retained interests include which of the following rights retained by the older generations?

   1. Liquidation rights

   2. Puts

   3. Conversion rights

A. 1

B. 1 and 3

C. 2

D, 1, 2, and 3

24-3. The grantor, age 70, is interested in removing an income-producing asset with significant appreciation potential from her estate. However, she also wants to retain payments from this asset for a specific period of time but is concerned about inflation eroding her payments. Given these

two objectives, which of the following estate planning strategies would allow her to accomplish both objectives?

A. 10-year GRAT

B. 10-year QPRT

C. 10-year ILIT

D. 10-year GRUT

24-4. In 2005, Joe, who is 75 years old, created a 10-year QPRT into which he transferred his $200,000 residence. Joe's basis in the residence is $50,000. At the time Joe transferred the residence into the QPRT, the section 7520 rate was 5%. Therefore, Joe's interest was valued at $77,217. At the end of the 10 years, the assets within the trust transfer to Joe's niece and nephew. When the QPRT was created, what was the value of the taxable gift?

A. $0

B. $100,783

C. $122,783

D. $200,000

24-5. Joe dies in 2006 when the value of the residence is $225,000. What amount of the trust assets will be included in Joe's gross estate?

A. $0

B. $50,000

C. $200,000

D. $225,000

24-6. Which of the following statements concerning GRUTs is incorrect?

A. The trust assets are valued annually.

B. No additional contributions to the trust can be made.

C. The payments from the trust will not be the same every year.

D. The annual distributions from the trust will fluctuate.

Chapter 25

Intra-family and Other Business Transfer Techniques

CFP® CERTIFICATION EXAMINATION PRINCIPAL TOPICS COVERED IN THIS CHAPTER:

Intra-family and Other Business Transfer Techniques

- Characteristics
- Techniques
  - Installment note
  - Self-cancelling installment note (SCIN)
  - Private annuity

- Intra-family loan
- Bargain sale
- Gift or sale leaseback
- Intentionally defective grantor trust

Federal income, gift, estate and generation-skipping transfer tax implications

Learning Objectives

To ensure that you have a solid understanding of the types of intra-family and other business transfer techniques, the following learning objectives are addressed in this chapter:

- Compare and contrast the different types of business transfer techniques.

- Know the gift and estate tax implications of each business transfer technique.

- Recommend appropriate business transfer techniques such as installment sales, private annuities, SCINs, gift and sale leasebacks, or IDGTs.

Chapter Contents

OVERVIEW

Clients who own family businesses or other significant assets might be looking for ways to transfer wealth to their children or grandchildren. A number of strategies and techniques are available to accomplish these goals. The strategies appropriate for a given situation depend on the client's financial needs; the financial resources of the intended beneficiaries; and the income, estate, and gift tax consequences of these strategies.

Financial planners must understand the various intra-family transfer techniques available to meet a client's goals, and must be able to ascertain which strategy is the most appropriate for a client's situation. The financial planner must work with a client's accountant, lawyer, and other financial professionals to implement a plan that accomplishes the client's objectives.

Practice Standard 400-1

Identifying and Evaluating Financial Planning Alternative(s)

The financial planning practitioner shall consider sufficient and relevant alternatives to the client's current course of action in an effort to reasonably meet the client's goals, needs and priorities.

INSTALLMENT SALES

The **installment sale** is a device for spreading out the taxable gain on the sale of an asset and thereby deferring income tax on the gain from the sale of the property. The sale must be for the fair market value (FMV) of the asset, proper interest must be charged, and the agreement must be formal, as evidenced by a secured promissory note.

An installment sale is a transaction in which an owner sells property to a buyer, but instead of receiving payment outright, payments are spread over a set term of years. The seller must receive at least one payment after the taxable year in which the sale occurs. For example, if a seller sells property in 2015, at least one payment must be due in 2016 or beyond to qualify as an installment sale. After that, payments can begin and end whenever both parties choose, or they can vary and even be skipped in subsequent years. This technique affords great flexibility for family members or others who purchase a business interest, because payments can be made as profits are generated.

An installment sale is appropriate in a number of situations:

- When a taxpayer wants to sell property to another individual or family member who might not have enough capital to purchase the property outright or provide a down payment for the sale. Employees with minimal capital can buy out a business owner who, in return for allowing a long-term payout, might receive a higher price for his business. This device is often used to create a market for a business where none previously existed.

- When an individual in a high income-tax bracket holds substantially appreciated real estate or securities other than marketable securities. In certain cases, all or a portion of the tax on the sale of such property can be spread over the period of installments. It is important to note that installment sales are not available for the sale of marketable securities.

- An installment sale can be an effective estate freezing device when the sale is between family members and involves rapidly appreciating, closely held stock, real estate, or other assets. Used in this manner, the installment sale can serve to freeze the size of an estate subsequent to the sale and thus stabilize the value of the seller's estate for federal estate tax purposes. This technique also shifts future appreciation of the property to a younger generation. An installment sale to a grandchild at full FMV avoids the generation-skipping transfer tax.

Income Tax Consequences

One of the major advantages of the installment sale is that taxable gains are prorated over the payment period. This means that the seller pays the tax due only as actual payments from the sale are received. The seller might be able to shift most of the profit from a high-income (high-tax) year to a year or years in which he is in a lower bracket.

Practitioner Tip: Note that if the buyer of property is related to the seller, and the buyer sells the property within two years of the purchase, the seller must recognize the entire gain. If the sale results in a loss, the installment method cannot be used, and the loss deduction must be taken in the tax year of the sale.

For income tax purposes, the installments must be broken into three parts: (1) a return of basis; (2) gain; and (3) interest income. The taxpayer must report the parts of the payment that represent gain and interest income. Interest is segregated from principal payments and taxed as ordinary income. The profit percentage (the difference between the sale price and adjusted basis) is applied to each installment payment of principal to determine the amount taxed as a capital gain. The balance of the payment is considered a tax-free return of the seller's basis.

Client Situation

Betty would like to sell land that she purchased for $100,000. The land is now worth $250,000. Her accountant has explained that a high tax on the gain in the property could consume a substantial portion of her profit. If she receives all of the sale proceeds ($250,000) in the year of sale, the result is that her entire profit ($150,000) will be taxed in one year. Betty would like to find a way to reduce or minimize the impact of taxes, or defer those taxes. The installment sale is a possible solution to this problem. The title to the property would pass immediately from Betty to the buyer, but Betty would *not* receive a lump sum payment outright. Instead, Betty would receive the sale price in installments spread out over two or more tax years (although a lump sum payment in a later year will qualify for installment reporting).

Betty agrees to accept $25,000 a year for 10 years, and she will not have to report the $150,000 gain in the year of the sale. Instead, because her ratio of gross profit ($150,000) to contract price ($250,000) is 60%, she will report $15,000, or 60% of each $25,000 payment she receives, as capital gain. (Interest has been ignored here for simplicity.) This approach allows Betty to spread the payment of the tax over a number of years during which she is receiving payments.

If the interest rate in effect at the time of the installment sale was 4.0%, then the buyer would also pay Betty interest. Betty would receive a total payment of $30,822.74 a year for the next 10 years. Betty would report $15,000 as capital gain and $5,822.74 in interest each year ($30,822.74 - $25,000), which is taxed at her marginal tax bracket.

Practitioner Tip: The buyer's basis is the price paid for the property, and this amount is used to calculate the gain on a future sale.

Gift Tax Consequences

When an installment sale is based on the full FMV of the property transferred, the seller has not made a gift to the buyer of the property. The holder of an installment note can choose to forgive all or a portion of the payments made by the buyer and apply his gift tax annual exclusion to offset the tax.

Client Situation

If Betty had sold the land to her sister, Sheila, as an installment sale, Betty could forgive any of the future payments from Sheila. For example, if Betty made a gift of $30,822.74 to Sheila, the first $14,000 would be offset by Betty's gift tax annual exclusion and the remaining $16,822.74 would be a taxable gift. If Betty's husband Jim elected to split the gift, then $28,000 would qualify for gift tax annual exclusions and the remaining amount of the payment, or $42,822.74, would be considered a taxable gift offset by Betty and Jim's unified credits. The monies gifted could be used to make the note payment, or the payment could simply be forgiven.

Practitioner Tip: Installment note payments can be canceled by the holder during his lifetime as payments are received, using the holder's gift tax annual exclusions and unified credit to offset the tax. However, any income tax gains must be reported in the year payments are received.

Estate Tax Consequences

An installment sale removes property from a seller's estate and passes appreciation in the property along to the buyer. However, the present value of any remaining installment payments due at the seller's death is included in the gross estate.

If the seller dies during the term of the note, the entire unrealized gain on the balance of the note is accelerated and must be recognized to the extent that its value exceeds the seller's basis. The right to receive payments on the installment obligation is treated as income in respect of a decedent (IRD). Thus, payments are taxable income to the person or entity that receives those payments, as they are received. Because the note is considered IRD, there is no step-up in basis at death. The estate or other testamentary beneficiary of the installments due would report the payments in the same manner that the decedent would have reported them had he lived. However, the testamentary beneficiary of the installments would be entitled to an offsetting income tax deduction to the extent of the estate tax attributable to the installment sale balance that was taxed in the estate.

Practitioner Tip: If the holder of the note outlives the term of the sale, then only the proceeds of any payments that have not been spent or otherwise used prior to his death are included in his estate.

> ### Client Situation
>
> If Betty survives the term of the sale, neither the property nor the promissory note will be included in her estate at her death. If Betty does not survive the term of the note, the present value of any installments due will be included in her estate. Any income or capital gains will be recognized on her estate's income tax return, IRS Form 1041. The estate will be allowed an income tax deduction for any estate tax attributable to the inclusion of the note in her estate.

SELF-CANCELLING INSTALLMENT NOTES

The **self-cancelling installment note**, or SCIN, is a variation of the installment sale, typically used among family members if the property owner has a short life expectancy. When it is used, the note contains a provision under which the balance of any payments due at the date of death will be automatically canceled. The term of the SCIN must be less than the actual life expectancy of the seller; otherwise, it will be taxed as a private annuity.

A SCIN is appropriate in a number of situations:

- When the seller wants to retain a payment stream that will not continue beyond his or her death and could end at an earlier date.

- When the estate tax benefits exceed the income tax cost that results from the buyer paying a premium for the cancelation-at-death feature.

Tax Consequences of a SCIN

All of the tax rules applicable to the installment sale apply to the SCIN. However, there are some exceptions to consider. With a SCIN, the note is canceled upon the note holder's death; therefore, the value of the note is not included in the holder's gross estate.

Furthermore, when an installment note is canceled or becomes unenforceable, it is treated as a taxable disposition of the note. The gain is taxable to the decedent's estate as IRD, and the estate can take a deduction for IRD. However, no IRD deduction is allowed for a SCIN.

It is important to ensure that at least the Code section 7520 rate is applied when the SCIN is established because interest rates below this amount are deemed a partial gift to the buyer. Further, because the risk of death is a factor that clearly affects the value of the note, the sale price must exceed the actual FMV of the asset to reflect this risk. Otherwise, the transaction will be treated as a bargain sale, with adverse gift tax consequences to the seller. If the selling price is increased to include consideration of the risk of death, and the seller lives to receive all payments, the seller will have to report gain in excess of the actual gain that would have been realized had the property been sold at FMV.

Client Situation

Gene wants to sell his interest in the family business to his son Carmen. The FMV of the business is $500,000, and Gene's basis in the business is $100,000. Carmen does not have sufficient funds to purchase the business outright, and Gene does not want to recognize the full capital gain on the sale of the business in one year. They both decide that an installment note is the best technique to transfer the business to Carmen. Gene plans to use the income from the promissory note for his living expenses, but he has decided that if he dies before Carmen has paid the note the remaining balance will be forgiven. Gene and Carmen enter into a SCIN with a 15-year term. The applicable federal rate (AFR) at the time of the agreement is 2.6%. Because the note will be forgiven should Gene die before the end of the note term, they decide that an appropriate sale price is $550,000. Carmen agrees to pay $44,750 per year for the next 15 years. This includes interest, which Gene will claim as income; capital gain on the business, which is taxed at his capital gains tax rate; and a tax-free return of principal. At Gene's death, the remaining balance of the note will not be included in his estate, but any remaining capital gain on the sale of the business will be included as IRD in Gene's estate. Gene's estate will not be allowed to deduct the estate tax attributable to the inclusion of the gain in his estate.

PRIVATE ANNUITIES

A **private annuity** functions similarly to a commercial annuity; however, the arrangement is between two private parties, neither of whom is an insurance company. The seller of the annuity **(annuitant)** conveys complete ownership of a property to a buyer who is obligated to make periodic payments to the annuitant for a specified period of time. Usually this period of time is the annuitant's lifetime, but in some cases the annuity is set to last for the annuitant's life plus the life of his or her spouse or some other designated party. The payments are structured as an annuity, which is a fixed payment, and are calculated using IRS valuation tables based on the annuitant's life expectancy and current IRS interest rates.

Practitioner Tip: When a private annuity is set to last for the lifetime of the transferor and his spouse (or other designated party), payments generally continue for a longer period of time than payments under a single-life annuity; however, the amount paid each year will be less than that payable under a single-life annuity.

A private annuity is appropriate in a number of situations:

- When a client wishes to retire and shift control of a business to a family member or to a key employee.

Client Situation

Randy is the sole shareholder of a closely held corporation. Randy has no heir other than his wife. He has two key employees in the business who are capable of managing it and who are interested in owning it. Randy would like to sell them the business, but he is concerned about adequate income upon his retirement. The key employees tell Randy they would like to buy the business but cannot afford to pay him in a lump sum or in relatively few installments. Randy could sell all of his stock to the two key employees, and in return they could promise to pay him an income for his life (and perhaps for his wife's life). This should yield a higher income than if he sold the business in an installment sale. The annuity income stream would be based on the FMV of the business as well as on Randy's age and the section 7520 rate at the date the transaction is executed.

- When a client wishes to remove a sizable asset, such as a business, from his estate for estate tax purposes.

Client Situation

Abe is the sole shareholder of a closely held real estate corporation. He has two daughters who currently work in the business. He could sell the business to his daughters in return for their agreement to pay an annuity that lasts as long as he lives. This would result in a reduction in Abe's estate (and thus save estate taxes) because the value and appreciation of the business would be removed from his estate for federal estate tax purposes. At Abe's death, the daughters' annuity payments cease and neither the corporation stock nor the promised payments will be included in his estate.

The daughters' income tax basis in the stock, will be the amount of annuity payments they made to him during his lifetime. When the daughters initially purchased the annuity, their basis was equal to the FMV of the property transferred—assuming no gift was built into the transaction. Once payments commence, until Abe's death, their basis will be the greater of the amount they paid him or the amount paid plus the present value of all the future payments that will be paid if Abe lives to his life expectancy.

- When a client owns a large parcel of non-income-producing property and wants to make it income producing.

Client Situation

Andrea is a widow. She owns real estate that is currently not producing any income, but because of its choice location it is increasing substantially in value. It is expected that the property might double or triple in value over the next 10 years. Her married son is currently providing $7,000 a month to support her because her wealth derives primarily from this illiquid asset. A possible solution is for her son to discontinue gifts to his mother and, instead, she could transfer the real estate to him in exchange for a monthly lifetime income (say, $7,500 a month, assuming the present value of the land will support this payment). This will minimize Andrea's estate, substantially reduce estate taxes at her death, and at the same time, give her financial independence. The son becomes the immediate owner of the real estate. The growth in value (and increase in gross estate for tax purposes) will occur in the son's hands and not further increase his mother's estate. This concept of removing the appreciation from the donor's estate is one of the primary objectives of making lifetime transfers.

- When the client's estate is very large and the major or sole heir is a grandchild (or other beneficiary two or more generations below that of the client). Because the private annuity is a sale and not a gift, it will not be subject to the generation-skipping transfer tax.

- When the family's objective is to keep certain property in the family or direct it to specified family members (or the purchaser's objective is to bar others from obtaining the property in question) and the current owners do not want it to be subject to a will contest or any statutory rights that might thwart their directive wishes.

There are some potential risks associated with private annuities. All payments cease at the annuitant's death—even if only one payment has been made at that point. This, of course, is an advantage to the buyer, who is required to pay the annuity, but a disadvantage to the annuitant's heirs. Conversely, if an annuitant outlives his life expectancy, the buyer might pay much more than anticipated. Finally, if the buyer predeceases the annuitant, his estate must continue to make any remaining annuity payments throughout his lifetime.

Practitioner Tip: A private annuity is an unsecured contract that avoids immediate income tax on the gain when the property is initially sold. The annuitant should ensure that the buyer has adequate income or resources, such as the cash value of a life insurance policy, to make the annuity payments.

Tax Consequences of the Private Annuity

Each annuity payment a buyer makes to an annuitant is treated partially as a tax-free return of capital, partially as a capital gain, and the balance as ordinary income. Once the annuitant has recovered his basis, the entire payment is taxed as ordinary income. The buyer is not allowed a deduction for any payments made to the annuitant.

There will be no gift if the buyer's annual payments to the annuitant are actuarially equal to the FMV of the property sold. However, if the value of the promise made by the buyer is less than the value of the property transferred, the difference will constitute a gift by the annuitant.

For federal estate tax purposes, because the annuitant has sold his interest in the property before his death, it is not includable in his taxable estate. When private annuity payments are structured to terminate at the death of the annuitant, the annuity is not included in his estate either. If the annuity is a joint annuity, payments continue until the death of the last survivor. If the joint annuitant survives, the present value of future payments to him will be includable in the transferor-annuitant's estate (assuming he was sole owner of the property that was transferred in return for the joint and survivor annuity payments). However, because of the unlimited estate tax marital deduction, there would be no federal estate tax if the joint annuitant was the annuitant's spouse.

The buyer's basis in the property purchased by private annuity is a "temporary (or floating) basis" in the property equal to the value for calculation of the annuity. This provides a means for immediately increasing the basis for depreciation or depletion and can be a very significant benefit. The same basis is used to calculate gain if the transferred property is sold by the buyer. In many cases the property can be immediately resold for its FMV and because of the high basis, little if any gain is realized. However, upon the annuitant's death, the buyer's basis is adjusted to what the buyer actually paid in annuity payments.

INTRA-FAMILY LOANS

An **intra-family loan** is an interest-free or below-market-rate loan. Money is lent at either below-market interest rates or, in some cases, with no interest. Intra-family loan agreements must be actual loan agreements and should be put in writing. The loan terms, including the interest rate, should be clearly stated. This strategy is typically employed in loans between family members, such as from a parent to a child, but it can also be used in situations where corporations lend money to a non-shareholder employee. When a loan has no interest or the interest charged is below market rates, the difference between what should have been charged and what in fact was charged is deemed forgone interest. There are tax consequences to both the lender and the person to whom the loan is made.

Client Situation

Michelle and Allen want to help their son Jack buy a house. They lend Jack $400,000, which he uses to purchase the house. Jack agrees to pay his parents back over the course of the next 15 years. Michelle and Allen do not charge Jack interest on this loan.

Intra-family loans of less than $10,000 or $20,000 from a married couple are exempt from gift and income tax rules, unless the borrower uses the loan to buy income-producing property. Loans that exceed $10,000 (or $20,000 if borrowed from a married couple) must have a minimum interest rate of the applicable federal rate or there will be gift tax consequences (in the amount of the forgone interest).

Tax Consequences of Intra-family Loans

There are few tax advantages to interest-free or below-market-rate loans; however, such strategies are often used to allow the person borrowing the funds to achieve a certain goal. For example, a parent may lend funds to a child so that he can purchase a house or start a business.

Intra-family loans have both income and gift tax consequences for the lender. When a lender makes an interest-free loan or charges below-market-rate interest, he may have to pay income tax on the imputed interest that he should have received. The **forgone interest** is deemed a gift and will also be subject to income tax by the lender.

Tax law creates a fiction; for income and gift tax purposes, tax law treats interest-free and below-market loans as if a specified level of interest were charged and paid—even if it was not paid. In other words, interest is imputed (fictionally treated as if charged) on interest-free loans and other below-market-rate loans. The amount subject to gift and income taxation in most cases is the difference between (a) the applicable federal rate (AFR) and (b) the interest actually payable (if any) under the agreement between the parties. This difference is the "forgone interest."

Under this legal fiction, the borrower is treated as paying the forgone interest to the lender and can therefore take an income tax deduction for the "payment" (but only to the extent the borrower is deemed to have investment income if the interest is considered investment interest; no deduction is allowed for personal interest). The lender is treated as having received the forgone interest and therefore must report the income "received."

Client Situation

Because Michelle and Allen have not charged Jack interest on the loan, they will be deemed to have given Jack a gift in the amount of the forgone interest. This is calculated by applying the AFR at the time of the loan to the loan amount. Michelle and Allen will have to report this amount as income on their tax returns, and the amount will be deemed a gift from Michelle and Allen to Jack. They can split this gift and apply their gift tax annual exclusion amounts.

If the value of the loan is less than $100,000 and the net investment income (from the loan proceeds) is less than $1,000, there will be no tax on imputed interest. However, if the net investment income earned by the borrower exceeds $1,000, the lender will pay income tax on the imputed income up to the amount of the borrower's net investment income. When the value of the loan exceeds $100,000, income tax is due on the imputed interest.

Furthermore, if the borrower forgives the loan or payments under the loan, the amount forgiven is considered a taxable gift, but this could be offset by the lender's annual gift tax exclusion.

Client Situation

Jack lost his job and was unemployed for one year. During this time, he was unable to make the agreed-upon payments to his parents. Michelle and Allen forgave these payments. The forgiven payments, as well as the interest that should have been charged on them, are considered a gift from Michelle and Allen to Jack. They can split this gift and apply their gift tax annual exclusions.

BARGAIN SALES

A **bargain sale** is a transaction in which a donor sells property at a price below the FMV. Typically bargain sales occur between family members or to a charity. The difference between the FMV and the actual sales price is deemed a taxable gift, which can be offset by the donor's annual exclusion. The donor will realize income and pay capital gains tax to the extent that the sale price exceeds his basis in the asset. For a bargain sale to charity, the donor receives an income tax deduction for the gifted portion, not for the portion sold to charity.

Client Situation

Sally and Damon own a farm in New York and land in Florida. Sally and Damon decide that they no longer wish to own these properties and want to sell them. The FMV of the farm is $500,000; they purchased it for $200,000. They sell the farm to their son Jake for $300,000. Sally and Damon have made a gift of $200,000 (FMV of $500,000 less sale price of $300,000) to Jake. They can split this gift and apply their annual exclusions to reduce the value of the taxable gift. Sally and Damon must recognize the gain of $100,000 (difference between their basis of $200,000 and the sale price of $300,000) and pay a capital gains tax.

The value of the land in Florida is $150,000. They purchased the land 10 years ago for $125,000. Sally and Damon sell the land to a local land conservancy for $125,000. Sally and Damon will receive an income tax charitable deduction of $25,000 (difference between the FMV and sale price) on their income tax return.

SALE- OR GIFT-LEASEBACK

The purpose of the sale-leaseback and gift-leaseback transfer techniques is to remove property from an owner's estate and provide income to family members in the form of lease payments. A **sale-leaseback** involves one party selling property to another party and then leasing back the same property. In the case of a **gift-leaseback**, a gift of property to an individual or to a trust is subsequently leased back. In the case of a sale-leaseback, the purchase can be either by lump sum payment or installment payments. There are certain requirements for this to be a valid transaction. First, there must be a legal transfer of property, either by sale or gift, for the full FMV of the property. The amount of the lease payments must be reasonable and also at FMV.

Client Situation

Kristy and Shawn own a manufacturing business. The business has been incredibly successful; however, many of their assets are tied up in the business, which has significant value but has not been producing much cash flow. Kristy and Shawn decide to sell the building to their daughter Abby to remove its value from their estates. Abby pays them $500,000 through an installment sale, which is the FMV of the building. Kristy and Shawn, in turn, lease the building back from Abby and deduct the lease payments as a business expense. Abby now has the means to make an installment payment on the building, and her parents can gift back up to $28,000 of the payment to Abby through gift splitting and the use of their annual exclusions.

A sale- or gift-leaseback is appropriate in a number of situations:

- When a client has significant assets but poor cash flow, the sale of the assets will provide the client with cash, without causing the client to lose the use of the asset.

- When a client is in a high income tax bracket and wants to divert highly taxed income to a member of his family in a lower tax bracket.

- When a client owns rapidly appreciating property and would like to shift that future wealth to a family member to save estate taxes on that appreciation. By gifting the property to the younger generation and leasing the property back, the client not only removes the value of the property and any appreciation from his estate, but he transfers additional assets, in the form of the lease payments, free from gift tax. Consequently, lease payments made to the younger generation further reduce the value of the client's estate.

Tax Consequences of the Gift- or Sale-leaseback

A number of tax considerations are involved in sale- or gift-leasebacks. In the case of a sale-leaseback, the corporation that sells an asset must pay tax on any gain realized just as for any other sale. In the case of a gift-leaseback, the property owner/donor has made a taxable gift to the beneficiary or trust and may have to use a portion of the unified credit to offset the tax. By making an irrevocable gift of the property, future growth is removed from the client's estate. Note that even in a sale-leaseback transaction there may be gift tax implications if an outright gift is made or if the sale price is less than the FMV of the property.

The new property owner's basis depends on whether the asset was acquired by sale or gift. In the case of a sale-leaseback, the purchase price is the new owner's basis. In the case of a gift-leaseback, the donee or trust retains the original owner's basis.

> **Client Situation**
>
> In the preceding example, Kristy and Shawn purchased the building 20 years ago for $300,000. They will recognize a $200,000 gain on the sale of the building. Abby's basis will be $500,000. Alternatively, if Kristy and Shawn had gifted the property to Abby, there would have been no taxable gain; however, Abby's basis would be Kristy and Shawn's basis of $300,000.

Just as any partnership or corporation that rents property is allowed to take a tax deduction for the cost of the rental, when a sale-leaseback occurs, the fair rental paid by the seller for the use of its previously owned property is completely deductible as an ordinary and necessary business expense. The rent paid to the donee or new owner is recognized as taxable income to the donee.

Practitioner Tip: Often, these transactions occur between a parent and child. If the child's income tax bracket is lower than the parent's, the payment of rent allows the parents to shift income to the child in a lower tax bracket.

> **Client Situation**
>
> Kristy and Shawn will pay rent to Abby for continued use of the building in their manufacturing operation. Kristy and Shawn will be able to deduct the value of the rent as an ordinary and necessary business expense. Abby will recognize the amount of rent received as taxable income. Abby is in a lower income tax bracket than Kristy and Shawn, which will result in a shifting of family income.

INTENTIONALLY DEFECTIVE GRANTOR TRUSTS

An **intentionally defective grantor trust** (IDGT) is an irrevocable trust designed to preserve family wealth by transferring appreciating property and income to family members, which reduces the value of the grantor's estate. An IDGT is ideal for a business owner who wants to transfer his business to a trust for the benefit of his family at a low gift-tax cost and receive an income stream that can be used to supplement or fund his retirement.

Transfers to an IDGT are treated as completed gifts for federal gift tax purposes; however, they are defective for income tax purposes. A sale of assets or a business to the trust would eliminate a gift tax if the assets are sold at fair market value in exchange for a promissory note. Although trust assets are not included in the grantor's taxable estate, the trust is considered defective because the trust income is taxed to the grantor, who is treated as the "owner" of the trust for federal income tax purposes. Therefore, the sale of assets to the trust does not trigger a capital gains tax because the grantor is essentially selling assets to himself.

Practitioner Tip: IDGTs are created by intentionally violating one or more of the grantor trust rules so that the trust assets will not be included in the grantor's estate. For example, the grantor could allow someone who has no beneficial interest in the trust—a "nonadverse party"—to add trust beneficiaries, or the grantor could be permitted to reacquire trust assets by substituting assets of equal value.

With an IDGT, the grantor can either sell or transfer assets to an irrevocable trust. Because the trust contains one of the grantor trust provisions, the grantor will continue to pay tax on income generated by the assets. Because the grantor pays the income taxes incurred by the trust, the assets held in the trust grow, in essence, tax free. In addition, by paying the income tax on the income that will pass to the beneficiaries, the grantor is reducing his estate without making a taxable gift to the beneficiary.

Client Situation

Alicia establishes an IDGT for the benefit of her children, Max and Ava. Alicia owns a business that she expects will significantly increase in value over the next 10 years. She wants to sell this business to the defective trust to remove the anticipated increase in value from her estate, but she does not wish to incur any income tax consequences on the sale.

Alicia obtains an appraisal of the business and, thereafter, makes a gift of 20% of this value to the trust to serve as seed money for the anticipated purchase. Alicia then sells the business at its appraised FMV to the defective trust in exchange for a 20-year promissory note. Depending on Alicia's need (or desire) for income, the note can be structured to be interest-only (at the current AFR) with a balloon payment at the end of the term, or principal and interest can be amortized over the 20-year term. The trust income produced by the initial gift and the purchased business will be used to make the note payments to Alicia.

During the term of the note, Alicia receives a stream of interest income that is not taxable to her. At the end of the term, neither the business nor its increased value will be included in Alicia's estate. If, however, Alicia dies before the note is paid off, the value of the promissory note at the time of her death will be included in her estate.

Practitioner Tip: An IDGT allows a grantor to reduce his estate by paying income tax attributable to assets earned by the trust. The attribution of taxes to the individual rather than to the trust can actually reduce the amount of income tax owed. The top income tax bracket of 39.6% will not be reached until a single taxpayer has more than $413,200 of income or a married taxpayer has more than $464,850 of income in 2015, whereas that rate is reached at only $12,300 of income for trusts and estates.

The use of IDGTs has become increasingly popular as an estate planning technique. Because estate tax inclusion rules are applied separately from and independently of the income tax rules, unique opportunities are available to shift assets to a succeeding generation at no transfer or income tax cost and to otherwise reduce the grantor's estate.

Practitioner Tip: IDGTs can be combined with a number of other estate planning strategies. By using a defective trust, appreciating assets can be sold to the trust in exchange for an installment note without a gift being made.

Tax Consequences of IDGTs

The grantor trust is designed to allow the grantor to pay income tax on any income earned by the trust. When property is transferred to an IDGT by gift, the grantor will have made a taxable gift to the trust. If property is transferred to the IDGT by sale, assuming the asset was sold to the trust for the full FMV, no taxable gift will have been made. Because all trust income is taxed to the grantor, the sale of an asset to the trust does not result in recognition of capital gain. Note, however, that if the trust subsequently sells the underlying asset, the gain is taxed to the grantor.

Practitioner Tip: Many grantor-retained powers that cause a grantor to be treated as owner for income tax purposes will also cause the trust to be included in the grantor's taxable estate. For example, the trust will be included in the grantor's taxable estate if the grantor retains a reversionary interest valued at more than 5% of the trust corpus; the grantor personally retains control over the enjoyment of the trust; the grantor retains certain administrative powers, such as the power to vote stock transferred to the trust; or the grantor retains the income.

Chapter Highlights

- A number of advanced estate planning techniques are available to transfer business interests or other assets to family members.

- An installment sale is a transaction in which property is transferred in exchange for a series of payments (versus one lump sum payment). The realization of taxable gain is spread over each payment, which consists of a return of principal, gain, and interest. If the buyer dies during the term of the note, the remaining balance is included in his estate. If the buyer survives the term of the note, the underlying asset is not included in the seller's estate. No gift will have been made because this transfer is a bona fide sale.

- A SCIN is very similar to an installment sale, except that payments cease at the seller's death and remaining payments are not included in the seller's estate. The tax consequences of SCINs are similar to those of an installment sale because unrealized gain is taxable to the decedent's estate as IRD; however, no deduction is available for a SCIN because the note is not included in the decedent's estate.

- A private annuity is similar to a commercial annuity except that it is between two private parties. The annuitant transfers property to the buyer, who in turn pays an annuity stream of income to the annuitant. Annuity payments received by the annuitant consist of a tax-free return of capital, capital gain, and ordinary income. Private annuities structured to provide payments equal to the actuarial FMV of the property sold are neither subject to gift tax nor included in the annuitant's estate.

- Intra-family loans are loans between family members with either no interest charged or below-market interest charged. The lender includes the amount of forgone interest as taxable income and any forgone interest plus any forgiven payments are considered a gift. If the value of the loan is less than $100,000 and the net investment income is less than $1,000, the lender does not pay tax on imputed income.

- A bargain sale is the sale of an asset for less than full FMV. The difference between the sale amount and the FMV is considered a taxable gift. If the bargain sale is made to a charity, the seller/donor could be entitled to an income tax deduction (of up to the difference between the sale price and the FMV).

- A sale-leaseback is a transaction in which one party sells property to another party and subsequently leases it back. In a gift-leaseback, instead of a sale of property, property is gifted and then leased back. Lease payments are taxed as income to the lessor and could be deductible by the lessee, which shifts income to family members in lower income tax brackets.

- IDGTs are irrevocable trusts designed to increase family wealth through the sale of property or business interests to trusts. An IDGT includes one or more of the grantor trust powers, which enables the grantor to pay income tax attributable to trust assets and exclude trust property from the grantor's taxable estate at death.

Key Terms

annuitant

bargain sale

forgone interest

gift-leaseback

installment sale

intentionally defective grantor trust (IDGT)

intra-family loan

private annuity

sale-leaseback

self-cancelling installment note (SCIN)

Review Questions

25-1. Tim has a family business that he wants to transfer to his son Greg. Greg does not have the cash to pay Tim for the FMV of the business, and Tim needs income to live on for the rest of his life. Which of the following strategies would be *most* appropriate?

A. Installment sale

B. Sale-leaseback

C. Bargain sale

D. Private annuity

25-2. Steve and his son Andrew are joint business owners. Steve wants to retire, but Andrew does not have enough money to buy the business outright. Steve also does not want to recognize the capital gain all in one year if the business is sold. They agree to enter into an installment sale. Which of the following statements is/are incorrect?

A. Andrew must make his first payment within one year of the sale.

B. The sale must be for full fair market value.

C. Payments will cease at the sooner of the set period or upon Steve's death.

D. A portion of each payment received by Steve will be classified as capital gain.

25-3. Which of the following statements is/are correct concerning the taxation of installment payments under an installment note?

　1.　The basis recovery portion is subject to ordinary income tax.

　2.　The interest portion of the payment may be subject to capital gains tax.

　3.　The gain portion of the payment may be subject to capital gains tax.

A. 1

B. 2

C. 3

D. 1 and 3

25-4. Which of the following statements is/are correct concerning the tax treatment of interest-free and/or below-market-interest loans?

　1.　The forgone interest is treated as income by the borrower.

　2.　The forgone interest is treated as transferred to the borrower.

　3.　The forgone interest is income to the lender.

A. 1 and 3

B. 2

C. 3

D. 2 and 3

25-5: Sal and his wife Stella own a bakery. Their daughter Priscilla is a divorced parent who is struggling to make ends meet. Sal and Stella want to give Priscilla $30,000 a year for her support, but they are "cash poor" because their wealth is tied into their business. Which of the following statements is/are incorrect?

A. If Sal and Stella were to gift the bakery and the land to Priscilla and then lease the property back, it would remove the property and appreciation from their gross estates.

B. Using a sale-leaseback technique, Sal and Stella can sell the bakery equipment to Priscilla through an installment sale and lease it back, taking a business deduction for the lease payments made to Priscilla.

C. Using the gift-leaseback technique, Sal and Stella can transfer the bakery equipment into a trust with Priscilla as beneficiary and transfer lease payments to the trust each year for Priscilla's support.

D. Lease payments made to Priscilla are subject to income tax at her parent's marginal tax brackets.

Chapter 26

Family Limited Partnerships and Limited Liability Companies

CFP® CERTIFICATION EXAMINATION PRINCIPAL TOPIC COVERED IN THIS CHAPTER:

Family Limited Partnership (FLP) or Limited Liability Company (LLC)

- Federal income, gift, estate and generation-skipping transfer tax implications

- Valuation discounts for business interests
  - Minority discounts
  - Marketability discount
- Valuation techniques and the federal gross estate

Learning Objectives

To ensure that you have a solid understanding of family limited partnerships and limited liability companies, the following learning objectives are addressed in this chapter:

- Evaluate how family limited partnerships and limited liability companies might apply to a client's situation.

- Understand gift and estate tax implications for FLPs and LLCs.

Chapter Contents

OVERVIEW

Family limited partnerships (FLPs) and limited liability companies (LLCs) are two advanced estate planning strategies often used to accomplish income tax shifting and estate and gift tax planning within families. FLPs are often used to fractionalize the ownership of business assets or real estate to take advantage of gift and estate tax valuation discounts that significantly reduce transfer taxes. In most cases, an FLP is used to facilitate the transfer of limited partner interests from parents to children and other family members without divesting control of the assets. In other cases, an FLP is used to ensure continuous ownership of assets within the family for succeeding generations.

LLCs offer the same income tax advantages as FLPs while offering a higher degree of asset protection than the FLP. LLC management can be controlled by family members who are actively involved in the business, whereas family members who are not actively involved in the business can have ownership interests in an LLC.

Financial planners should become familiar with the characteristics of these two intra-family transfer techniques to understand the tax advantages and business opportunities that could be available to clients.

Practice Standard 400-1

Identifying and Evaluating Financial Planning Alternative(s)

The financial planning practitioner shall consider sufficient and relevant alternatives to the client's current course of action in an effort to reasonably meet the client's goals, needs, and priorities.

FAMILY LIMITED PARTNERSHIPS

A **family limited partnership (FLP)** is a limited liability entity created under state law. Family limited partnerships are so named because ownership of partnership interests typically is limited to members of the same family. If a partnership among family members is a genuine partnership, it is treated tax-wise the same as any other partnership and the same partnership rules apply.

An FLP is typically used when parents want to transfer wealth to their children in a tax-efficient manner but also want to retain control of their assets and continue to manage their property. Children might lack the maturity or business skills required to manage their parents' assets, and an FLP can provide parents with the time and opportunity to educate their children about managing and investing their assets, and even involve them in the management process.

General and Limited Partners

Upon formation, family members contribute property in return for an ownership interest in the capital and profits of the FLP. Partnership interests are divided into **general partnership interests** and **limited partnership interests**. For most FLPs, parents retain a general partnership interest and assume management and control of the partnership assets. General partners can include one or both parents, either individually or as trustees of a family living trust, an S corporation, or an LLC controlled by one or more persons. The general partner(s) typically retain(s) only a very small interest—as little as 1 or 2% of the value of the partnership. Despite retaining such a small ownership interest, the general partners retain complete management and control of partnership assets and can control the flow of income to family members.

General partners are compensated for services rendered to the FLP and receive a percentage of the FLP profits, which is allocated based on each general partner's percentage of ownership. General partners assume personal liability for debts and other liabilities that are not satisfied by FLP assets.

Limited partners receive partnership interests with the potential for appreciation on their interests. Income does not have to be distributed to limited partners unless specified in the FLP agreement. The personal liability of the limited partners is typically limited to the amount of capital they contribute to the FLP because they have given up their rights of management and control over the underlying assets.

Practitioner Tip: Almost any asset—cash, securities, bonds, real estate, even life insurance—can be transferred to an FLP as long as there is a legitimate family business purpose. However, FLPs have been subject to IRS scrutiny and certain requirements must be met. The FLP must be run as an actual business entity. A general partner must manage the assets of the FLP for the benefit of all of the partners and cannot use the assets for his own personal use. The IRS has been successful in challenging FLPs funded with the general partner's assets when the general partner has retained sole use and control of the assets. For that reason, the primary residence of a general partner may not be a suitable asset for transfer to an FLP if the general partner lives alone and no business purpose is connected with the residence.

Client Situation

Ryan and Erin Collins are each age 70. They have four children and six grandchildren and their estate consists of the following assets:

Asset	Value
Marketable securities	$1,500,000
Ryan's IRA	$750,000
Erin's IRA	$500,000
Joint checking account	$100,000
Apartment complex	$1,000,000
Other real estate	$1,500,000
Residence	$500,000
Total	$5,850,000

Ryan and Erin met with their attorney and agreed to implement an FLP to maintain ownership of their property within the family. The securities, apartment, and other real estate were contributed to an FLP, constituting a total value of partnership assets of $4 million. They did not put their residence, IRAs, or checking account into the FLP because the IRAs and checking account provide them with current income, and the couple lives in the residence alone without other family members.

In return for their capital contributions, Ryan and Erin each receive a 1% general partner interest and each receives a 49% limited partner interest. The FLP agreement gives the general partners the discretion to accumulate partnership income for future business needs and restricts the partners' ability to transfer their interests to persons outside the Collins family.

At the end of the year, the Collins' implement a gifting program whereby each spouse transfers a 2.5% limited partner interest to each of their 10 children and grandchildren, thereby transferring a total of 50% of the partnership and $2 million of the underlying asset value.

Benefits of an FLP

Control of Assets

One of the major benefits of an FLP is the ability to retain control over assets without having to own a majority interest in the FLP. This permits parents to transfer their assets to an FLP and then give or sell a majority interest (50% or more) to their children while retaining control over the assets. Although the children, as limited partners, can hold a majority interest in the FLP, control of the assets remains in the hands of the general partner, who can retain as little as a 1% general partner interest.

A parent who makes a direct gift of property to his children runs the risk that they may not manage the gift wisely. This pitfall can be avoided by placing the assets into an FLP and transferring a limited partner interest to the child. Thus, the parent retains control of the assets until the child is mature and has achieved sufficient financial acumen to manage the property.

An FLP can also enable parents to implement a succession plan for the ownership, management, and control of assets so that undesirable beneficiaries do not gain access to the assets.

Client Situation

As general partners, Ryan and Erin maintain control over the underlying assets. They can make investment decisions regarding the securities and determine how to manage the apartment complex or other real estate within the FLP. The limited partnership interest has no control over management decisions and thus has a minority interest in the partnership.

Continuity of Family Ownership

Continuous family ownership of an FLP is guaranteed by restricting each partner's ability to sell or transfer his interest to non-family members. The existence of rights of first refusal, buy-sell provisions, or other restrictions on transfers is of paramount importance to family members.

In almost all instances, the FLP agreement should prohibit partners from selling or transferring their interests in a manner that disrupts the family asset arrangement plan or family harmony. To achieve this, the FLP agreement typically provides partners and/or the partnership a right of first refusal to deal with a partner who wishes to sell or transfer his interest to a non-family member. The non-selling partners usually have the right to purchase the interest of the selling partner for cash or with an unsecured long-term promissory note that bears an interest rate favorable to the buyer. The interest in the FLP can be sold to a non-family member only if the partners or the partnership itself fails to exercise these purchase rights.

If the family members do not want the new partner to possess any voting rights, then the agreement should permit them to treat the new partner as a mere assignee, who is entitled to receive only income distributions and a proportionate share of partnership income, expenses, deductions, and credits. This provides family members with protection from the influence of unwanted active partners and ensures continued family ownership of partnership assets.

> **Client Situation**
>
> The Collins Family Limited Partnership provides partners, who are family members, with the right of first refusal to purchase shares that another partner wants to sell. Shares can be sold to a non-family member only if the family does not elect to purchase them, and the FLP interest would be limited to distributions of income without voting rights. These provisions practically guarantee that the FLP remains in the Collins family and is not transferred to any non-family members.

Asset Protection

Another benefit of FLPs is that they provide a limited degree of asset protection to the partners because FLP assets generally cannot be attached to satisfy the personal debts of limited partners. Under the Uniform Limited Partnership Act, the remedy of a personal creditor is to obtain a "charging order" from a court against the interest of the limited partner. The charging order entitles the creditor to receive the distributions that would normally be paid to the limited partner until the debt is fully paid. This allows the creditor access only to the limited partner's income interest, and not to the underlying assets of the FLP. The creditor cannot:

- obtain stock or seize partnership assets;

- participate in management decisions of the FLP;

- force liquidation of the limited partner's interest; nor

- attach the interest of the other limited partners.

Practitioner Tip: If a family member works in a high-risk profession that is vulnerable to lawsuits such as a doctor, engineer, or builder, an FLP can effectively shield personal assets by placing them in the hands of other family members, away from the reach of the partner's future creditors. In most cases, a judgment creditor is unable to attach partnership assets to satisfy the debt of an individual partner. As a further protection, most jurisdictions do not award limited partnership assets to ex-spouses.

Client Situation

Ryan and Erin are concerned that two of their children could have creditor protection issues. Their son Finn is an obstetrician. This is a profession frequently subject to professional liability, and although Finn does not currently have any malpractice claims against him, there is a high probability that at some point in his career he will face this issue. Their son Rory is in the midst of a nasty divorce from his second wife and has a gambling problem. Rory's two wives were "gold diggers" in Erin's opinion, and were interested in Rory only for his parents' money. Rory squanders money in casinos and has spent every dollar Ryan and Erin have ever given him. By giving their children limited partnership interests rather than making direct gifts of their assets, the assets are protected against any future creditor claims.

VALUATION CONSIDERATIONS

The FLP is frequently used as a means of shifting the income tax burden and future appreciation of the underlying assets from parents to children or other family members. Significant gift and estate tax valuation benefits are also associated with FLPs that result from several valuation discounts available when parents transfer limited partnership interests to their children.

As a general rule, the value of an FLP interest is worth less than direct ownership of a percentage of the assets. The sum of each of the FLP interests combined does not equal the sum of the assets themselves. This is because ownership of a limited partner interest in an FLP does not convey any rights of management or control over underlying assets, and the FLP agreement prohibits the partners from freely transferring their interests to non-family members. This reduction in value is commonly referred to as a **valuation discount.** Accordingly, to reflect these restrictions, gift and estate tax values are reduced by the application of discounts.

Because FLPs can be used to transfer limited partnership interests to lower-generation family members, reduced transfer tax values allow for:

- shifting a greater amount of limited partnership interests by percentage from parents to subsequent generations through gifting, and

- lower overall estate tax liability on the interests retained by a deceased partner.

For the majority of FLPs, combined discounts in the range of 25 to 35% are typically achieved by appraisal. Lower discounts in the range of 5 to 10% should generally be expected when the underlying assets are themselves readily marketable. Even with a modest discount, potential gift or estate tax savings can be considerable compared to taking no action.

Despite the reduction in the value of FLP interests, the real income production and growth potential of FLP assets remain available to the partners because control remains within the family.

Practitioner Tip: The IRS has scrutinized the valuation discounts that have been taken with respect to the gift or estate tax value of FLPs. For this reason, a qualified appraiser should be retained to provide a valuation of the FLP interest. The appraisal should be obtained from a full-time, accredited, independent, and experienced (preferably court-tested) valuation professional who creates reports based on specific FLP facts rather than a "fill-in-the-blanks" type of report. Realistic and justifiable assumptions should be used to develop valuation discounts, and the reasons for the types and amounts of discounts should be documented.

Minority Discounts

Transfers of limited partnership interests are subject to gift taxes. Gift taxes can be reduced by two discounts, a minority discount and a lack-of-marketability discount, which leverages the general partner's annual exclusion when FLP interests are gifted to limited partners.

A **minority discount**, or a discount for lack of control, is routinely applied to establish the estate and gift tax values of minority limited partner interests. This discount reflects the inability of a limited partner to control the operations of the FLP and to invest its assets in a manner that is advantageous to the limited partner. The minority interest discount principle refers to the fact that the owner of less than a majority interest in an enterprise cannot by himself control day-to-day or long-range managerial decisions, impact future earnings, control efforts for growth, establish executive compensation, or access corporate assets through liquidation. Because the owner of a minority interest lacks control over the business, an acquiror of a minority interest pays less for that interest, on a pro-rata basis, than if he were acquiring a controlling interest in the business. In instances where the owner lacks the ability to exercise control over the operations of the enterprise, the owner's interest can be worth significantly less than its liquidation value.

Practitioner Tip: The IRS has closely scrutinized and challenged the minority discounts applied to FLPs. The courts, the IRS, and taxpayers all agree that a minority interest is worth less than a controlling interest on a pro-rata basis. Thus, the issue is not whether a minority interest discount is allowable, but rather the amount of the minority interest discount. Typical discounts for minority interests generally range from 20 to 30%.

Marketability Discounts

A **marketability discount** is also applied to the value of limited partnership interests that do not offer a readily available market for trading. Such a discount reflects the fact that a partner who contributes assets to an FLP in return for a limited partnership interest generally has difficulty finding a buyer (if one exists).

Because a central purpose of most FLPs is to maintain ownership of assets for the benefit of family members, FLP documents generally contain specific provisions to ensure that ownership interests remain within the family. Each of these provisions, by design, reduces the marketability and therefore the value of an interest to a hypothetical buyer.

Factors that typically influence the level of the discount for lack of marketability include the nature of the FLP asset mix (e.g., real property, securities, equipment), the availability and accuracy of information relating to the FLP and its owners, the existence of transfer restrictions against ownership interests, the willingness of the partners to accept new partners, whether income is currently distributed to the partners, and the expected date on which capital contributions will be returned to the partners.

The inclusion of rights of first refusal and other transfer restrictions in the FLP agreement reduce the marketability of an FLP interest for transfer tax valuation purposes, further reducing values for estate tax and gift tax purposes. Based on the number and severity of the transfer restrictions and the factors cited previously, lack of marketability discounts can be as high as 30% or more.

Client Situation

Before making the gifts to the Collins Family Trust, Ryan and Erin hired a qualified appraiser to determine the value of the gifts of limited partner interests. The appraiser concluded that a combined 25% discount for lack of control and lack of marketability was appropriate for the limited partner gifts.

After applying these discounts to the proportionate value of FLP assets, Ryan and Erin each gave $75,000 of limited partner interests to the 10 trust beneficiaries this year. After applying their annual exclusions, each spouse made a taxable gift of $61,000 to each trust beneficiary, totaling $610,000 of taxable gifts for the year. Because their gift tax unified credits and generation-skipping transfer (GST) exemptions were still available to offset taxable gifts, no cash payment of gift tax or GST tax was required. At the end of the year, ownership of the Collins FLP is as follows:

	General Partner	Limited Partner
Ryan	1.00%	24.00%
Erin	1.00%	24.00%
Children and grandchildren (10)	0.00%	50.00%
Total	2.00%	98.00%

Income, Gift, and Estate Tax Considerations

Although FLPs are strictly scrutinized by the IRS, assuming the FLP complies with all regulations, it affords a number of income, estate, and gift tax benefits.

From an income tax perspective, the FLP allows income to be shifted from the general partners to the limited partners. The FLP allows income, expenses, and deductions to be passed through to the partners based on their percentage of ownership interest. If limited partners are in a lower tax bracket than the general partners, this allows some income shifting within the family. Of course, kiddie tax rules apply.

> **Client Situation**
>
> Over the next five years, the FLP produces $200,000 of income each year. If Ryan and Erin had not formed the FLP and gifted shares to their children and grandchildren, this income, combined with their other sources of income, would have been taxed at their marginal income tax rate, which is the highest tax bracket. Because they transferred 50% of the limited partnership interests to their children and grandchildren, Ryan and Erin will each report $50,000 of income, and each child and grandchild will report $10,000 of income. Kiddie tax rules will apply to some of their grandchildren in the current tax year.

Transfers of FLP interests during lifetime are subject to gift tax, and bequests of FLP interests are subject to estate tax. The value of the interest for both gift and estate tax purposes is reduced from fair market value for any marketability or minority interest discounts applied.

The estate tax is based on the original appraised value of the general and limited partnership interests owned at death. The FLP is an estate freeze technique because appreciation on FLP interests is not taxed in the general partner's estate.

When FLP assets are transferred at the death of either a general or limited partner, the persons inheriting the interest receive a step-up in basis to the date-of-death value of the underlying assets. If FLP assets are transferred by gift, however, the donee receives the donor's basis.

> **Client Situation**
>
> Over the course of the next several years, Erin and Ryan continued to make annual gifts of limited partner interests worth $28,000 to each of their children and grandchildren. The same 25% discount to value was applied to the gifts. Several years later, Ryan was struck with a sudden illness and died. At that time, the underlying value of the FLP assets was $7 million and ownership was as follows:
>
> | | General Partner | Limited Partner |
> |---|---|---|
> | Ryan | 1.00% | 9.00% |
> | Erin | 1.00% | 9.00% |
> | Children and grandchildren (10) | 0.00% | 80.00% |
> | Total | 2.00% | 98.00% |

In determining the value of the FLP interests includable in Ryan's estate, a 25% discount was applied on the estate tax return. As shown on the return, the estate tax value of Ryan's interest in the FLP after adding back his $610,000 in adjusted taxable gifts in prior years is as follows:

	Value
General partner (1.00%)	$52,500
Limited partner (9.00%)	$472,500
Total	$525,000
Prior taxable gifts	$610,000
Total gifts and interests	$1,135,000

Had the Collins' chosen not to form their FLP, and if no discounts to value had been applied on the estate tax return, the value of Ryan's one-half interest in the apartments, real estate, and marketable securities would have been $3,500,000 at his death. However, by implementing a gifting program using an FLP, his taxable estate was reduced by $2,365,000 and, assuming a 40% tax rate, $946,000 in estate tax was saved.

Practitioner Tip: Although family partnerships have sometimes been attacked by the IRS as mere tax avoidance schemes that should not be recognized for tax purposes, if the rules for establishing and operating such partnerships are carefully followed, the IRS currently recognizes the validity of this income-shifting device.

LIMITED LIABILITY COMPANIES (LLCS)

The **limited liability company** (LLC) is a form of business organization intended to obtain for investors the same advantages of limited liability as in the corporate form of business while at the same time avoiding corporation income tax rules. All 50 states and the District of Columbia have adopted LLC statutes, although they vary widely from state to state.

In an LLC, participants are called *members*. Generally, there must be at least two members, but some states permit LLCs with only one member. Individuals as well as various entities such as corporations, partnerships, trusts, and estates can be members.

Practitioner Tip: Although an LLC is typically used when multiple individuals want to operate a business together, it is also possible to form a one-person LLC, which allows an individual to operate a business and have limited liability protection. This approach is also possible with a corporation. However, when a one-person LLC is formed, it is treated as a sole proprietorship for tax purposes, and provided there are no employees it generally will not need a separate tax identification number or have to file a separate federal income tax return. Note that it may still be necessary to file a separate return for state income tax purposes.

An LLC has an operating agreement, which governs management of the entity. The LLC can have officers, like a corporation, if specified in the operating agreement. The agreement should also provide for the entity to be managed by delegation to "managers," who are elected in somewhat the same manner as a board of directors, or all of the members can retain the right to manage. Unlike partnerships, voting in an LLC is generally proportionate to capital contributions. However, it can also be based on profit participation. To the extent that an LLC is "manager managed," it operates like a traditional limited partnership where the general partner runs the entity and the limited partners are passive investors.

In a family setting, management of the LLC can be controlled by family members who are actively involved in the business, and other members can have ownership interests that entitle them to receive distributions from profits. These interests are typically divided between **voting interests**, which enable participation in the management of the LLC, and **non-voting interests**, which do not but they enable participation in the profits.

Client Situation

Amy and Dan have a family business that they run with their son Will. Their other two children, Nolan and Ian, are not involved in the family business. They decide to create an LLC. Amy, Dan, and Will are managing members of the LLC, and Ian and Nolan are non-managing members. Amy, Dan, and Will make the management decisions pertaining to the operation of the business. When profits are distributed, all five members of the LLC are entitled to distributions.

LLCs Compared to FLPs

The LLC can also be considered an alternative to the FLP. The transfer of family business, real estate, or other investments to a family partnership has become a major estate planning technique. It seems that the LLC can function just as well in many cases, with the additional advantage that no family member must function as a general partner and assume liability for the debts of the entity.

Most FLPs are formed by parents or members of a senior generation who transfer business or investment assets to a partnership in which they retain general partnership interests. They then make gifts of limited partnership interests to children or members of a younger generation. One drawback of the FLP is the fact that senior generation members, by acting as general partners, assume personal liability for any debts or obligations of the venture. The LLC could be used in this situation and it has the great advantage of allowing the senior family members to avoid personal liability. They can still retain management of the business or investments by providing in the articles or operating agreement that they will be the managing members.

A major problem with the use of an LLC in place of an FLP is that, under state law, the LLC dissolves on the death, withdrawal, etc., of any member for any reason. This enables transferees to force the dissolution of the entity unless there is either a unanimous or majority vote (depending on state law) by the remaining members to continue the entity. Many senior family members would not be willing to confer that power on the younger generation. In an FLP, only the withdrawal of the last remaining general partner triggers dissolution.

Practitioner Tip: In most jurisdictions, the LLC or its counterpart, the limited liability partnership (LLP), can also be used as a form of organization for a professional practice. Its advantage is that, although a professional remains liable for his own errors or omissions in the practice or business, he can generally avoid liability for the acts of any of the other owners. In an ordinary professional partnership, each partner can be held liable for the errors or omissions of any other partner.

Income, Estate, and Gift Tax Considerations

LLCs are used to obtain the advantages of limited liability for investors and participants (i.e., they cannot be liable for debts of the entity beyond their investment) while being classified as partnerships for federal income tax purposes. The result is avoidance of the corporate double tax on income, and in many situations, avoidance of any tax on liquidation.

Another significant reason for the use of the LLC is that under partnership rules any losses incurred by the entity are passed through and deductible by the members provided the LLC is classified as a partnership for income tax purposes. No such pass-through is permitted in the case of a C corporation.

Membership interests can be gifted from managing or voting members to non-voting members. Although valuation discounts might be available, they are typically less than for FLPs because the members can force liquidation of the LLC.

From the estate planning standpoint, a major advantage of either a partnership or an LLC classified as a partnership over a C or S corporation is that upon the death of a partner or member, the partnership or LLC can elect to adjust the basis of its assets to fair market value to the extent of the decedent's interest.

Chapter Highlights

- The FLP is an entity used to transfer wealth, typically from parents to children.

- The FLP allows parents to retain general partnership interests that control the management of underlying assets, and to give or bequeath to their children limited partnership interests. The general partnership interest can be as small as 1 or 2% of the partnership, allowing the majority of partnership assets to be given to the children.

- The FLP has many benefits, including allowing the senior generation to maintain control of the underlying assets, and allowing continuous family ownership of the assets. This allows parents to ensure that children are mature and fiscally responsible before they relinquish control of assets to them.

- The underlying assets of the FLP are protected from a limited partner's creditor claims, and only the income interest of the limited partner can be attached. An FLP can be advantageous for clients whose children work in potentially libelous professions or who could be subject to other creditors or divorce.

- Valuation discounts can reduce the value of partnership interests for gift or estate tax purposes. Such discounts include a minority discount because limited partners do not have control of the underlying asset, and a marketability discount reflecting the lack of marketability of limited partnership interests.

- The FLP allows income to be distributed based on ownership interests. If limited partners are in a lower income tax bracket than the general partners, this provides income shifting within the family.

- Transfers of partnership interests are subject to gift tax and estate tax. Partnership interests transferred by gift retain the donor's original basis, and interests transferred at death receive a step-up in basis to their value as of the decedent's date of death.

- An LLC is another form of business entity. It offers greater protection than the FLP because no member of the LLC has personal liability beyond his membership interest.

- The LLC is often used in families to transfer family business interests.

- LLC members can be voting or non-voting members. Voting members participate in the day-to-day management of LLC assets, and non-voting members are permitted to vote in profit distributions but not in the management of the LLC.

Key Terms

family limited partnership (FLP)

general partnership interests

limited liability company (LLC)

limited partnership interests

marketability discount

minority discount

non-voting interests

valuation discount

voting interests

Review Questions

26-1. From an estate planning perspective, the benefits of an FLP include:

1. Reducing the value of the estate for estate tax purposes.

2. Leveraging the value of lifetime gifts.

3. Maintaining control over gifted assets during lifetime.

A. 1 and 2

B. 2

C. 2 and 3

D. 1, 2, and 3

26- 2. Which of the following is not a benefit associated with a family limited partnership?

A. Retention of assets within the family through rights of first refusal.

B. Ability to shift income to a family member in a lower income tax bracket.

C. Greater IRS scrutiny.

D. Protection of partnership assets from the creditors of individual partners.

26-3. A limited liability company

1. Can be taxed as a partnership.

2. Is a business entity alternative to a family limited partnership.

3. Is a business entity limiting the liability of the members of the enterprise.

A. 2

B. 3

C. 2 and 3

D. 1, 2, and 3

26-4. Molly and Andrew have established an FLP. They each retain a 1% general partnership interest and a 10% limited partnership interest. They have used annual exclusion gifts to give 78% of the value of the FLP to their five children. The value of the underlying assets is $1 million. A qualified appraiser has provided a valuation of the FLP and indicated that a 30% discount applies. At Andrew's death, what is the value of FLP assets included in his taxable estate?

A. $10,000

B. $110,000

C. $7,000

D. $77,000

26-5 Which of the following valuation discounts may be available for FLP interests?

A. Income Tax Discount

B. General Interest Discount

C. Family Discount

D. Minority Discount

Chapter 27

Business Planning Strategies

CFP® CERTIFICATION EXAMINATION PRINCIPAL TOPICS COVERED IN THIS CHAPTER:

Business Uses of Insurance

- Buy-sell agreements

- Key employee life insurance

- Split-dollar life insurance

Postmortem Estate Planning Techniques

- Deferral of estate tax (Code section 6166)
- Corporate stock redemption (Code section 303)
- Special use valuation (Code section 2032A)

Learning Objectives

To ensure you have a solid understanding of the types and uses of business insurance and postmortem estate planning techniques available for business owners, the following learning objectives are addressed in this chapter:

- Identify the different types of insurance policies and ownership arrangements available to business owners and employees.

- Describe the considerations involved in business succession planning.

- Understand the purpose and structure of business continuation agreements.

- Identify the various types of postmortem planning techniques available to business owners and recognize when they can be implemented.

Chapter Contents

OVERVIEW

Business owners must plan for the continuation or sale of their businesses and for the security of their families in the event they become disabled or die prematurely. Families often depend on the income, salary, and other forms of revenue generated by a closely held business, and they might suffer financial hardship if the owner was suddenly unable to run the business. A closely held business could be the largest asset in an owner's estate, and it could also be the most illiquid. Therefore, planning is essential to reduce the owner's estate tax liability and to obtain adequate liquidity for the estate through the transfer or sale of the business entity.

Business owners need to work with financial planners, attorneys, and other advisers to properly plan for their estates and to protect their families, because there are many planning issues they have to address. Estate planning for business owners generally involves succession planning, liquidity planning, business continuation agreements, insurance planning, business valuations, trusts, and estate tax reduction techniques. An estate plan must be coordinated with an owner's business plan, succession plan and the owner's personal estate planning objectives. The financial planner must work with a team of professionals such as attorneys, insurance agents, and accountants to develop and implement the client's estate plan and determine with the client how the plan will be monitored.

Practice Standard 500-1

Agreeing on Implementation Responsibilities

The financial planning practitioner and the client shall mutually agree on the implementation responsibilities consistent with the scope of the engagement.

Practice Standard 600-1

Defining Monitoring Responsibilities

The financial planning practitioner and client shall mutually define monitoring responsibilities.

PLANNING WITH LIFE INSURANCE

Life insurance is an essential component of business planning because it provides the owner's estate with the funds needed to continue the operation of the business after the owner dies. Employers can offer several types of life insurance policies in employee benefit packages that have advantages for both the business owner and the company's employees. Financial planners should be aware of the tax and nontax characteristics of these policies.

Key Person Life Insurance

A **key person life insurance** policy is owned by a business to insure the life of a particularly valuable employee, such as the business owner. The business should be the premium payer, owner, and beneficiary of the policy. Proceeds, when received, can be used to offset reduced profits and help pay for the replacement of the key individual. In the case of an uninsurable stockholder, a sinking fund can be established by using fixed or variable annuities, mutual funds, or other securities.

Premiums are not deductible by the corporation or other business entity, but death benefit proceeds are free from income tax with the possible exception of a corporate-level alternative minimum tax (AMT). The premiums paid by the corporation are not taxable income to the insured.

Estate Tax

For federal estate tax purposes, if the insured is a stockholder, the death proceeds will be considered in determining the value of the decedent's stock interest and could enhance the value of the stock. If the business owner controls only 60% of the business, only 60% of the value of the corporate stock will be includable in his estate for federal estate tax purposes.

The insurance proceeds will not be included in the insured's estate if the corporation is the owner and the beneficiary of the policy. Note that if the death proceeds are payable to a personal beneficiary of an insured controlling shareholder (one who owns more than 50% of the corporate stock) the proceeds will be fully includable in the insured's estate.

Practitioner Tip: The owner and beneficiary of any key person policy should be carefully reviewed to ensure that death benefit proceeds are not inadvertently included in a deceased employee's gross estate.

Client Situation

Travis works for Naples Boatworks, Inc., a closely held marine repair business. Travis started working for the company eight years ago after completing vocational school, and he has received extensive training and mentoring from the owner. Travis is a valuable employee to the business who cannot easily be replaced. Therefore the company purchased a life insurance policy on his life and it pays the annual premiums. Naples Boatworks is the owner and beneficiary of the policy. Now the company can afford to hire another experienced mechanic in the event that Travis dies. The death benefit would not be included in Travis's gross estate because Travis is not the owner of the insurance policy.

Split-dollar Life Insurance

Split-dollar life insurance is an arrangement, typically between an employer and an employee, under which the cash values, death benefits, and cost (premiums) of the policy can be split between the parties. This provides an incentive to key employees, a way by which an employer can reward key individuals on a selective basis, and a means to provide stockholder-employees with substantial insurance coverage at a minimal cost. This arrangement can also be effective when a significant amount of insurance is needed for the business owner's estate. A private split-dollar arrangement can also be used between relatives, such as between a father and a son.

Under the classic arrangement, ownership and benefits of the policy are often split between employer and employee. For example, the employer can own the cash value portion of the policy and the employee can name a beneficiary of the death benefit of the policy. The owner can pay the part of the annual premium that equals the current year's increase in the cash surrender value of the policy and invest the cash value. The employee who owns the death benefit protection pays the balance, if any, of the premium. This is typically the cost of the annual term insurance premium associated with the death benefit. Under another version of split-dollar, known as an *employer pay-all* plan, the corporation pays the entire premium, and the employee will be taxed on the value of the death benefit coverage.

In another form of split-dollar arrangement, the employee owns the policy, pays the premiums with monies given to him by the employer, and assigns the policy to the employer. This is known as *collateral assignment split-dollar*.

In the event of the insured employee's death or separation of employment, the cash value of the premiums paid by the corporation typically is returned to the corporation. The insured employee or his beneficiary receives the balance of the proceeds.

At death, the result of the arrangement is that the employer will have an increasing death benefit and the employee's beneficiary will have a decreasing death benefit amount. To maintain the insured-employee's death benefit on a level basis, dividends can be used to purchase an amount of term insurance equal to the cash surrender value of the contract; or if a universal life policy is used, the death benefit can increase.

If the employee separates from employment, the employer recoups his outlay from the cash value and transfers any remaining benefit of the policy to the employee.

Estate Tax

When an employee owns a portion of the policy outside of a trust, the death benefit will be included in his gross estate; therefore, the proceeds will be available to pay for estate taxes and administrative expenses. However, if the employee's spouse or an irrevocable trust purchases a policy on his life and then enters into a split-dollar agreement with the corporation, the death benefit can be excludable from the employee's estate as long as the corporation's rights are limited to a recovery of the death proceeds equal to its contributions.

Client Situation

Kathryn owns a custom upholstery business, Bedford Upholstery. Donna, an employee, was a skilled seamstress who worked in the business for more than 20 years. Kathryn had purchased a $100,000 whole-life policy on Donna's life many years ago to reward her for her work and the contributions she made to the company. Kathryn paid the cash value portion of the premiums every year, and Donna paid a small amount toward the mortality and expense portion of the premiums. When Donna died last year, the business was repaid the $15,000 it contributed toward the premiums. Donna's husband, Hank, received the remaining death benefit amount of $85,000.

Salary Increase or Selective Pension Plan

A **salary increase** or **selective pension plan** provides an employee—or a business owner—with additional deferred compensation. This enables the employer to reward highly compensated employees by supplementing their qualified pension plan beyond the maximum compensation limits. The employer can purchase a whole-life, universal life, or variable life insurance policy, which is designed to have a high cash value. The employer pays all the premiums, which are a deductible expense. The employee has all rights of ownership, including the right to name the beneficiary of the policy. One disadvantage is that the employee is taxed on the amount of the premiums paid by the employer as additional compensation.

Transfer Taxes

The death benefit is included in the employee's estate unless the policy is assigned to another person or transferred into a trust more than three years before the employee's death. If the policy is transferred, the current value of the policy, plus any future premium payments the employer will make, are considered a gift from the employee to the new owner of the policy.

Practitioner Tip: A salary continuation plan is usually a defined benefit type of plan. Payments can be based on average earnings over the employee's final three years of service, the number of years of service, or even the achievement of specified business goals.

BUSINESS SUCCESSION PLANNING

The transition of ownership in a closely held business must be planned in advance or the business entity could terminate soon after the owner's death. In fact, many family businesses do not survive the transition to the next generation. Owners of family businesses typically want to leave the business to the children who actively participate in it, but they also want to distribute their wealth fairly to other family members who are not involved. When the closely held business is not a family business, the surviving business owners rarely want the deceased's family members involved in the day-to-day operations of the business. Succession planning is essential to accomplish the business owner's objectives and to address the legal and tax ramifications of a business transfer.

Business succession planning involves having the client work with his team of advisers to plan for the orderly transition of his closely held business. The purpose of a succession plan for a family-owned business is often to keep the business within the family in a manner that meets the owner's personal and financial goals. A succession plan is likely to consider the following issues:

- Who will be responsible for managing the business?

- Will the owner retain any financial benefit or control over the business after the transfer?

- Who will own the business after the transfer?

- When and how will the business be transferred?

- How will taxes and estate settlement costs be paid at the owner's death?

- In a family-owned business, will children who are not involved in the business inherit business stock or other non-business assets?

The answers to these questions—and many others—significantly affect the business owner's overall estate plan and the lives of all family members. A business succession plan often includes a business continuation agreement, which is a legal contract that provides the terms for transferring an owner's business interest to other co-owners.

BUSINESS CONTINUATION AGREEMENTS

A **business continuation agreement** is an arrangement for the orderly disposition and continuation of a business interest in the event of the owner's death, disability, retirement, or withdrawal from the business. The agreement can also provide contingency plans that address other potential events such as divorce, insolvency, bankruptcy, or the loss of a co-owner's professional license.

Corporations and partnerships use three basic types of buy-sell agreements known as stock redemption (entity purchase) agreements, cross-purchase agreements, and hybrid agreements. The business or partnership purchases life insurance, and perhaps disability insurance, to buy the owner's stock or partnership interest in the event of the owner's disability or death. This provides the remaining shareholders, or the business itself, with a greater share of ownership and control, and facilitates a smoother transition after an owner's death. Without a buy-sell agreement, the estate might not have enough liquid assets available to pay estate settlement costs and taxes. Thus, the business might have to take out loans or be sold before the estate tax is due, which is only nine months after the business owner's death.

Advantages of a Buy-sell Agreement

There are many advantages to a having a **buy-sell agreement** in place.

- It provides a guaranteed market for the sale of the business.

- It provides the owner's estate with certain liquidity.

- It values the business for federal and state death tax purposes.

- It prevents the owner's stock from passing through probate.

- It allows for the continuity of a family business without outsider control.

- It prevents family members from suddenly owning a portion of the business with other unrelated co-owners.

Establishing the Value of a Business

A properly drawn stock redemption agreement and cross-purchase agreement are generally effective in helping to establish the value of a business for federal estate tax purposes, providing:

- the estate is obligated to sell at the decedent-shareholder's death, or the estate is obligated to offer the decedent's shares at his death at the agreement price;

- there is a lifetime "first offer" provision prohibiting a shareholder from disposing of his stock interest without first offering it to the other shareholders at no more than the contract price;

- the price was fair and adequate when made and resulted from a bona fide arm's length transaction; and

- the price is fixed by the terms of the agreement or the agreement contains a formula or method for determining the price.

Stock Redemption Plan

In a **stock redemption plan** the company purchases life insurance on the shareholder's life. The corporation is the owner and beneficiary of the policy and pays all of the insurance premiums. The insurance will provide the company with the necessary funds to purchase (redeem) the stock of the withdrawing or deceased shareholder, at a future time. The shareholder's estate is obligated to sell all of the deceased owner's stock to the corporation, and this arrangement guarantees a market for the stock in the shareholder's estate, at a predetermined price. The cash received by the shareholder's estate provides some liquidity for the estate, which the executor can use for any purpose.

Client Situation

Deceased shareholder. Herb and Steve are equal stockholders in a business valued at $5 million. The business purchases $2,500,000 of life insurance on both men. At Herb's death, his stock passes to his estate. The life insurance proceeds on Herb's life are paid to the business. Then the business pays the agreed-upon amount or formula price to Herb's estate according to the agreement. In return for the cash, Herb's executor transfers the stock to the business. Steve, therefore, ends up with ownership of all the outstanding voting stock (the stock owned by the business itself is not entitled to vote).

Client Situation

Disabled shareholder. Under the buy-sell agreement, should Herb become totally disabled prior to retirement, he would receive his full salary for one year. At the end of a year of total disability, Herb's interest would be sold to the business. The business would pay at least $250,000 (10% × $2,500,000) as a down payment to Herb. The business would also issue Herb a 10-year note (secured by his stock, which is placed in an escrow account) for the remaining value of the stock. The business would pay interest on the note. The rate would be the safe harbor rate needed to avoid the unstated interest rules. To help pay off the note, the business would apply for, pay for, and name itself beneficiary of a disability income insurance policy.

Client Situation

Retired shareholder. In the event Herb retired, he would sell his stock to the business. The business would pay Herb at least $250,000 (10% × $2,500,000) as a down payment, plus it would give Herb a 10-year note (secured by his stock) for the remaining amount. The business would pay interest on the note at the safe harbor rate needed to avoid the unstated interest rules. The cash value of the life insurance policy on Herb's life could be used to help finance the down payment. One limiting factor, in general, is that in many states, the corporation can redeem its stock only to the extent that it has earned a surplus.

Tax Implications of a Stock Redemption Plan

1. Assuming the corporation is sole owner and sole beneficiary of the policy, the value of the insurance on the decedent's life will not be includable in his gross estate. However, the value of the stock will be included in his gross estate.

2. The decedent's estate will not realize any taxable gain for income tax purposes because the stock purchased from the estate obtains a stepped-up basis. The corporation generally pays a price equal to the stock's value, so no gain is realized by the estate.

> ### Client Situation
>
> On January 1 Doug and Kenny, who are unrelated, each invested $50,000 in a corporation that was worth $500,000 ($250,000 each) at Doug's death. If the corporation paid Doug's estate $250,000 in complete redemption of his stock, there would be no income tax consequences to his estate. This is because the estate's basis in the stock is stepped up from $50,000 to $250,000 (the value for death tax purposes), which is the same amount received by the estate under the redemption. The amount realized ($250,000) by the estate did not exceed the estate's basis ($250,000), so there is no taxable gain.

Practitioner Tip: Note that Kenny, the surviving shareholder, does not receive an increase in his stock's basis because the corporation is redeeming only the stock owned by Doug.

3. Premiums paid by the corporation will not be taxable income to its shareholders.

4. Life insurance or disability income premiums used to fund the agreement are not deductible by the corporation. The corporation receives the insurance proceeds income tax free, but they may be subject to a corporate AMT.

5. The biggest potential problem in a corporate stock redemption agreement is the possibility that the redemption will be treated as a dividend distribution, i.e., taxed as ordinary income to the extent of the corporation's earnings and profits rather than as a sale or exchange, which is treated as a capital gain. This can be avoided with a redemption of all of a shareholder's stock, a complete termination of the stockholder's interest.

Cross-purchase Agreement

A **cross-purchase agreement** is an agreement made by individual shareholders, not the corporation, to purchase a shareholder's stock upon the death or disability of a fellow shareholder. Life insurance policies are typically used to fund the cross-purchase agreement, and each shareholder purchases a policy on the other participants' lives. Each shareholder is the beneficiary of the various policies he owns and is also responsible for paying the premiums. The death benefit amount of each policy is equal to the amount each shareholder needs to purchase a percentage of the stock from a deceased shareholder's estate. The formula for determining the number of policies is $N \times (N - 1)$ with N being the number of shareholders. For example, if there were 5 shareholders, 20 separate policies would be required.

> **Client Situation**
>
> Jerry, Sharon, and Lorraine are equal shareholders in an airport limousine service, which they formed as a closely held corporation. Each owns 100 shares of company stock. They recently entered into a cross-purchase agreement to buy all of the stock from a deceased shareholder's estate. Jerry, Sharon, and Lorraine purchased a whole-life insurance policy on the lives of the two other shareholders and have named themselves beneficiaries of the policies they own. As a result, the shareholders have purchased a total of six insurance policies to fund this agreement.
>
> Assume that Lorraine dies this year. Jerry and Sharon will use the proceeds from their respective insurance policies on Lorraine's life to buy the stock from Lorraine's estate. In return for the cash, Lorraine's executor will transfer 50% of Lorraine's stock to Jerry and 50% to Sharon. Jerry and Sharon will each own 150 shares of stock, and Lorraine's estate will have the cash it needs to pay its debts and expenses and to pay off the mortgage on her condo. Jerry and Sharon can also buy back the policies that Lorraine's executor owns on their lives without triggering future income taxes under the transfer-for-value rule.

Transfer-for-value Rule

The **transfer-for–value rule** provides that if insurance policies are transferred for value (sold) then the owner-beneficiary of the policy will have taxable income when the insured dies. The amount the new owner-beneficiary paid for the policy plus the total premiums paid after the policy was purchased is subtracted from the proceeds, and the remainder will be taxable as ordinary income. However, there are exceptions to the rule when the transfer for value is made to the insured, as in the preceding example, to the insured's partner, to a partnership or corporation in which the insured is a shareholder or officer, to the insured's spouse, or when the new owner's basis (cost) is determined in whole or in part by reference to the transferor's basis.

> **Client Situation**
>
> Patrick sold his $200,000 life insurance policy to his son Cody for $8,000. Cody became the new owner and beneficiary of the policy, and he continued to pay the $1,500 premiums until Patrick's death five years later. Cody received the death benefit of $200,000; however, $184,500 was includable in his income and taxed at his marginal rate. The amount that was not subject to income tax included the $8,000 he paid for the policy and the total premiums he paid, or $7,500.

Tax Implications of a Cross-purchase Agreement

- The value of life insurance owned on a decedent-shareholder's life by a surviving shareholder is not included in the decedent's estate for federal estate tax purposes because the insured had no incidents of ownership in the policy. Note that the value of the shares, however, is included in the decedent-shareholder's estate.

- The value of the life insurance policies the decedent owned at the time of death on the lives of the surviving co-shareholders is includable in the decedent's estate. Generally, the includable amount is equivalent to the policy's value, depending on the type of policy owned, which is not the death benefit amount.

- Life insurance or disability income premiums paid to fund the agreement are not deductible by the co-shareholders. The respective shareholders will receive death proceeds or disability benefits income tax free. There will be no AMT regardless of the size of the policy.

- The sale of stock to the surviving shareholders is treated as a capital gain, but it is not taxed in the decedent shareholder's estate because the value of the shares is stepped up to fair market value at the date of death. There is no possibility under a cross-purchase agreement that the purchases of stock by the remaining shareholders will be treated as dividends. By definition, in a cross-purchase plan the entire transaction is between co-shareholders, not between the corporation and its shareholders, so there can be no attribution problems because there are no redemptions.

- The surviving shareholder has the advantage of increasing his basis in the company for income tax purposes by the amount of money he or she pays for the stock. This advantage is not available under a stock redemption plan, which results in a reduced gain to the surviving shareholders in the event of a subsequent lifetime sale.

Client Situation

Steve, Roberta, and Lee each own an interest in the SRL Corporation worth $100,000. Each invested $10,000 in 1977 when the corporation was formed. If Lee dies and the corporation (pursuant to a fully funded buy-sell agreement) pays his executor $100,000 for his stock, Steve's basis and Roberta's basis remain at $10,000. But if Steve and Roberta had been the purchasers and had each *personally* paid $50,000 to Lee's executor, their individual basis would have increased by that $50,000 amount. The distinction is important because, in this simplified example, the taxable gain on a future sale of Steve's stock or Roberta's stock could be as much as $50,000 less using a cross-purchase arrangement.

Practitioner Tip: It is important to recognize that this does not mean a cross-purchase plan is always better than a stock redemption.

Hybrid Business Continuation Agreements

Hybrid business continuation agreements, also known as "wait and see" agreements, postpone the decision of whether to use a cross-purchase agreement or a stock redemption agreement until after the shareholder's death. Similar to a cross-purchase agreement, shareholders purchase life insurance on the lives of the other participants. The corporation has a first option to purchase any or all of a deceased shareholder's interest, and surviving shareholders have a secondary option to purchase any stock remaining. If a stock redemption is chosen, the shareholders could use the proceeds of the life insurance to make interest-bearing loans or capital contributions to the corporation to effectuate a stock redemption.

BUSINESS CONTINUATION PLANS FOR PARTNERSHIPS

Planning is essential for the continuation of a partnership upon a partner's death. Unlike a corporation, if more than 50% of the total partnership capital *and* profits are sold within a 12-month period, the partnership is dissolved under Code section 708. However, if the interest of a partner is liquidated rather than sold, the partnership will not terminate. Partnership liquidation plans prevent termination of the partnership as long as at least two partners remain after the liquidation is complete.

If life insurance is used to provide funding in the case of the liquidation plan, the partnership is the owner and the beneficiary of the policies taken out on the partners' lives, and the partnership pays the premiums. The insurance proceeds are used to make liquidation payments to a deceased partner's estate. Note that the receipt of the insurance proceeds increases the income tax basis of the partnership interests of all partners, including the interest owned by the decedent. Any gain or loss realized by the selling partner is treated as a gain from sale or exchange of a capital asset, and the stepped-up basis at death eliminates most of this gain.

When insurance on the life of each partner is owned by the other partners under a cross-purchase plan, the partners are the beneficiaries and the premium payers of each policy. Partners agree to purchase a predetermined amount of the partnership interest from a deceased partner's estate, similar to a corporate cross-purchase plan. The decedent's estate can transfer life insurance policies back to the surviving partners, which is not subject to taxes under the transfer-for-value rule.

POSTMORTEM ELECTIONS FOR BUSINESS OWNERS

After an estate owner dies, the estate's personal representative must make a number of tax elections or tax decisions. A business owner's executor can take several elections that will reduce or delay taxes paid by the estate, thereby improving the liquidity position of the estate. The financial planner and the client should review the various postmortem elections available to see how they fit into a client's estate plan and how they can be made.

Practice Standard 400-2

Developing the Financial Planning Recommendation(s)

The financial planning practitioner shall develop the recommendation(s) based on the selected alternative(s) and the current course of action in an effort to reasonably meet the client's goals, needs and priorities.

CODE SECTION 303 STOCK REDEMPTION

Code section 303 allows the purchase of a portion of a decedent shareholder's stock by his corporation to be treated as a sale or exchange rather than as a dividend. This is important because a sale can be taxed as a long-term capital gain, whereas a dividend is taxed as ordinary income, possibly at higher rates. A section 303 partial redemption can provide cash and/or other property from the decedent shareholder's corporation to the decedent shareholder's executor, to pay death taxes and other death-related expenses. A **section 303 stock redemption** is used when:

- there is a desire to keep control of a closely held or family corporation within the decedent-shareholder's family after death;

- the corporate stock is a major estate asset and a forced sale or liquidation of the business to pay death taxes and other costs is a threat; or

- a tax-favored withdrawal of funds from the corporation at the death of the stockholder would be useful.

A closely held corporation can use the proceeds from a key person life insurance policy, or other corporate assets, to redeem (buy) the closely held stock from the decedent owner's estate. The decedent's stock is purchased from the person who is obligated to pay both federal and state taxes and settlement expenses at the shareholder's death. This person could be the executor, a trustee of an irrevocable trust, the surviving spouse, or another beneficiary whose share of the decedent's estate is reduced by these expenses.

The estate then transfers the decedent's closely held stock to the corporation in exchange for an amount equal to the death taxes, funeral expenses, and estate administrative costs. The funds received in the redemption do not have to be used directly to pay estate settlement costs if the executor does not need the cash for liquidity purposes.

The stock will receive a stepped-up basis upon the owner's death and, assuming the redeemed shares qualify for special capital gains tax treatment, no gain will be recognized on the sale.

Client Situation

Aaron, a widower, owns 75% of a corporation. His son Joshua owns the remaining 25%. Aaron's portion of the stock is valued at $6 million. The value of his estate, after subtracting allowable deductions, is $10 million. Assume there is little cash in Aaron's estate. Aaron's estate and inheritance taxes and other death-related expenses are projected to be about $4 million. The corporation will purchase $4 million of life insurance on Aaron's life.

Step 1: At Aaron's death, his stock will pass to his estate.

Step 2: The corporation then receives the insurance proceeds on Aaron's life.

Step 3: The corporation uses the life insurance proceeds to pay Aaron's estate for stock qualifying for the section 303 redemption.

Step 4: The estate transfers stock with a value equal to the money it receives to the corporation.

Step 5: Aaron's estate uses the cash to pay federal and state death taxes and administrative and funeral expenses.

Practitioner Tip: The closely held corporation transfers enough cash to the estate to pay for death-related taxes such as the estate tax, inheritance tax, and GST tax, funeral expenses, and estate administrative costs that do not include debts. Be aware that the value of the redeemed stock should not exceed these costs, or the excess amount could be taxed as a dividend to the person from whom the stock is being redeemed.

Qualifications for Section 303 Redemptions

Stock to be redeemed by the corporation must have been included in the decedent's gross estate for federal estate tax purposes. The business must be an incorporated business or an S corporation, because Code section 303 does not apply to unincorporated businesses. The value of this stock must comprise *more than* 35% of the deceased owner's adjusted gross estate, which is determined after subtracting estate administrative expenses, debts, funeral expenses, casualty losses, and death taxes from the decedent's gross estate. The stock of two or more corporations can be aggregated for purposes of meeting the "more than 35% of adjusted gross estate" test if 20% or more of the outstanding stock of *each* corporation is included in the decedent's gross estate.

Client Situation

Jay owns a closely held business, Coastal Media, Inc. Assume that Jay's gross estate is $1,250,000 and that administrative and funeral costs are $250,000. There are no other deductible expenses. To qualify for a section 303 redemption, the value of the stock in question must exceed $350,000 because they must be more than 35% of ($1,250,000 – $250,000).

Practitioner Tip: Gifts of *all* property the business owner has made within three years of death that exceeded the gift tax annual exclusion amount are added back into the owner's gross estate before the percentage test is applied. This makes it more difficult for the owner's estate to meet the adjusted gross estate percentage test and qualify for section 303 redemption.

To determine whether an estate qualifies for section 303 stock redemption, see Exhibit 27.1.

Exhibit 27.1 Determination of Qualification for section 303 Stock Redemption

Determination of whether an Estate Qualifies for a Section 303 Stock Redemption

Federal estate tax value of corporate stock in gross estate ....(1) $1,200,000

Gross estate less allowable deductions..(2) $2,000,000

35% of gross estate less allowable deductions..(3) $700,000

Qualifies if (1) is greater than (3)

Redemption under Section 303 Protected to Extent of

Funeral and administration expenses.. $90,000

Federal Estate and Generation-Skipping taxes $200,100

State death taxes $24,900

Generation-skipping transfer taxes...$0

Interest collected as part of above taxes $0

Maximum allowable Section 303 redemption $315,000

Computations Courtesy – NumberCruncher Software available at Leimberg.com

INSTALLMENT PAYMENT OF ESTATE TAXES

Generally, the federal estate tax is payable in full within nine months of the date of death. The Internal Revenue Code does provide relief under certain circumstances by allowing an executor to pay the federal estate taxes attributable to the decedent's business over a period of years. An installment payment of the estate tax is indicated when:

- The estate has insufficient liquidity to pay the estate taxes when due without selling assets at a substantial loss.

- The estate can earn a greater after-tax rate of return on its money or other investments than it spends in interest for the deferral privilege.

- Future profits or cash flow from the decedent's business are expected to pay all or part of the deferred tax.

If the requirements of Code section 6166 are met, the executor can elect to pay the federal estate tax and GST tax attributable to the decedent's interest in a closely held business or farm in installments over a period of up to 14 years. Note that the balance of the estate tax or GST tax must be paid at the regular payment date.

During the first four years, the executor pays only interest on the unpaid tax. Interest with respect to the deferral is payable at 2% on the tax generated by the first $1,470,000 of business value in 2015 and at 45% of the regular underpayment rate on the balance. The underpayment rate varies quarterly. Interest calculated using these special rates is not deductible for estate or income tax purposes.

The executor pays off the principal of the unpaid tax, together with interest on the unpaid balance in equal annual increments over the next 10 years. The first installment of principal is due not later than five years and nine months from the date of death. Each succeeding installment must be paid within one year after the previous installment.

Qualifications for Code Section 6166

The requirements for qualifying for **Code section 6166 installment payments of the estate tax due** are as follows:

1. The decedent must be a U.S. citizen or resident at the time of his or her death.

2. The gross estate must include a closely held business interest, which can be in a sole proprietorship, a partnership, a corporation, or a farm that was actively managed at the time of the owner's death. Unlike section 303, an unincorporated business qualifies for this special tax treatment.

Practitioner Tip: A partnership interest will qualify if 20% or more of the total capital interest in the partnership is included in the gross estate, or if the partnership has 45 or fewer partners. Stock in a corporation qualifies if 20% or more in value of the voting stock is included in determining the gross estate of the decedent, or the corporation has 45 or fewer shareholders.

---

3. The value of the closely held stock included in the estate must exceed 35% of the adjusted gross estate. Aggregation of various business interests of the decedent is allowed for purposes of meeting the percentage requirement, provided the decedent owned at least 20% of the total value of each closely held business.

4. If the decedent made a gift of property within three years of death, the estate is treated as meeting the more-than-35% requirement only if the estate meets such requirement both with and without application of the three-year rule.

Client Situation

When Andrea died, the value of her wholly owned, closely held business, a computer center, was $3,600,000. Her gross estate was $8 million. Administrative costs, debts, and expenses totaled $300,000. Federal estate taxes totaled $1,910,000. Qualification for section 6166 is determined as follows.

Section 6166 Installment Payout (up to 14-years)

(1)	Estate tax value of closely held business included in gross estate..........	$3,600,000
(2)	Adjusted gross estate.............................	$7,700,000
(3)	35% × adjusted gross estate.................	$2,695,000

Line 1 exceeds Line 3; estate qualifies

Because the estate qualifies for the section 6166 deferral, the executor can elect to pay that portion of estate taxes attributable to the inclusion of the business in installments over a maximum of 14 years. For the first four years no tax is due, only interest on the tax owed. For up to the next 10 years, equal annual installments of tax owed and declining interest on the unpaid balance are due.

Practitioner Tip: There is an overall limitation on the portion of the tax that qualifies for the 2% interest rate. This amount varies because the interest payable at 2% is adjusted periodically for inflation, and the estate tax exemption and the unified credit amounts will change in the future.

SPECIAL USE VALUATION

Code section 2032A special use valuation allows for certain farm or real property in a closely held business to be valued at less than fair market value in the business owner's estate, with the objective of reducing the estate tax. An executor can elect to value qualifying real property on the basis of its actual "special" use rather than its "highest and best" use. This special use valuation rule—especially useful when the price of farmland is artificially increased by, or has not kept up with, the price per acre of encroaching housing developments—enables an executor to value the farmland at its value for farming purposes. The maximum reduction of the decedent's gross estate under this provision is $1,100,000 in 2015.

Qualifications for Code Section 2032A

Four initial qualifications should be reviewed to see whether an estate qualifies for special use valuation. If one criterion is not met, then this estate tax reduction technique does not apply. Following are the qualification requirements:

- The decedent is a U.S. citizen or resident, and the real property is located within the U.S.

- On the date of the decedent's death, the property must be involved in a "qualified use." This is defined as a farm used for farming purposes or property used in a trade or business other than farming.

- The real property must have been owned by the decedent or a member of his family and used as a farm or in a closely held business for an aggregate of five years or more of the eight-year period ending on the date of the decedent's death. During this period, the decedent or a member of his family must have been a material participant in the operation of the farm or other business.

- Such property must pass to a "qualified heir." This term is defined to include the decedent's immediate family plus his ancestors or lineal descendants.

Two additional qualification tests must be met for an estate to qualify for special use valuation:

1. The value of the real and personal property (less debts or unpaid mortgages) in the decedent's estate must equal at least 50% of the decedent's gross estate (less debts or unpaid mortgages).

2. At least 25% of the gross estate (less debts and unpaid mortgages on all property in the gross estate) must be qualified farm or closely held business real property.

Client Situation

Robert Brooks died with an estate valued at $6 million. He owned 70% of the voting common stock in Brooks Industries, Inc., which was valued at $3.8 million at his date of death. His share of the real property owned by the corporation was valued at $1 million. To determine whether his estate qualifies for special use valuation, both tests must be applied and met.

50% Test: $3.8 million stock ÷ $6 million estate = 0.63, which exceeds 50%.

25% Test: $1 million real property ÷ $6 million estate = 0.167, which does not exceed 25%. Therefore, Robert Brooks' estate does not qualify for special use valuation.

Practitioner Tip: Remember to subtract out any debts or unpaid mortgages from the gross estate and from the property values used in calculating the 50% and 25% tests. Also note that any gifts of property made within three years of the business owner's death must be added back into the gross estate for the purpose of this calculation before the 50% and 25% tests are applied.

If all of the qualifying tests are met, the value of the real estate in the decedent's gross estate will be reduced based on its actual current use. The decedent's heirs must keep the property and continue to use it in the same qualified manner for up to 10 years after the business owner's death or a tax will be imposed that recaptures all or part of the tax reduction amount.

Chapter Highlights

- A key person life insurance policy is owned by a business to insure the life of a particularly valuable employee, such as the business owner.

- Split-dollar life insurance is an arrangement, typically between an employer and an employee, under which the cash value, death benefits, and cost (premiums) of a policy can be split between the parties.

- A salary increase or a selective pension plan provides an employee or business owner with additional deferred compensation.

- Business succession planning involves having a client work with a team of advisers to plan for the orderly transition of his closely held business.

- A business continuation agreement is an arrangement for the orderly disposition and continuation of a business interest in the event of the owner's death, disability, or retirement, or upon withdrawal from the business.

- In a stock redemption plan, the company purchases life insurance on the shareholder's life to purchase (redeem) his stock at death. The shareholder's estate is obligated to sell all of the deceased owner's stock to the corporation, and this provides a guaranteed market for the stock at a predetermined price.

- A cross-purchase agreement is made by individual shareholders, not the corporation, to purchase a shareholder's stock upon the death or disability of a fellow shareholder.

- Hybrid agreements postpone the decision of whether to use a cross-purchase agreement or a stock redemption agreement until after a shareholder's death.

- Code section 303 allows the purchase of a portion of a decedent shareholder's stock by his corporation to be treated as a sale or exchange rather than as a dividend.

- If the requirements of Code section 6166 are met, the executor can elect to pay the federal estate tax and GST tax attributable to the decedent's interest in a closely held business or farm in installments over a period of up to 14 years.

- Special use valuation, Code section 2032A, allows for certain farm or real property in a closely held business to be valued at less than fair market value in the business owner's estate, with the objective of reducing the estate tax.

Key Terms

business continuation agreement

business succession planning

buy-sell agreement

cross-purchase agreement

hybrid business continuation agreement

key person life insurance

salary increase or selective pension plan

section 303 redemption

section 2032A special use valuation

section 6166 installment payment of estate tax

split-dollar life insurance

stock redemption plan

transfer-for-value rule

Review Questions

27-1. Carter is the owner and CEO of Wordsworth Industries, Inc. The corporation has purchased a $4 million key person life insurance policy on Carter's life and is the beneficiary of the policy. Which of the following statements are correct?

A. The $4-million death benefit will be included in Carter's gross estate.

B. At Carter's death his beneficiaries will receive the cash value of the policy and Wordsworth Industries will receive the remaining death benefit amount.

C. Wordsworth Industries will receive the $4-million death benefit, which could be subject to a corporate-level alternative minimum tax.

D. Wordsworth Industries will have an increasing death benefit and Carter will have a decreasing death benefit amount.

27-2. Gil and Nick are equal partners in a pest control business they started after high school. Their company, Bug-B-Gone, is an unincorporated business that has been in operation for 28 years. Both partners are married, and neither Gil nor Nick wants any ownership or control of the business from the other partner's family when one of them dies. Which technique is best suited for this purpose?

A. A section 6166 plan

B. A section 303 redemption

C. A selective pension plan

D. A cross-purchase agreement

27-3–5. William was the owner of Lyndhorst Farms, Inc., located in Pennsylvania. William had owned and operated the farm for more than 30 years prior to his death several months ago. The family-operated business was recently appraised at $2.6 million, which included the farmland, valued at $1.2 million. The farm will pass equally to William's three sons, who will continue to operate the farming business. William's gross estate, including the value of the farm, is $3.4 million. William's estate settlement costs, funeral expenses, and outstanding debts total $400,000.

27-3. Does William's estate qualify for special use valuation?

27-4. Does William's estate qualify for a section 303 stock redemption?

27-5. Does William's estate qualify for installment payment of estate taxes under Code section 6166?

Chapter 28

Estate Planning for Non-traditional Relationships

CFP® CERTIFICATION EXAMINATION PRINCIPAL TOPIC COVERED IN THIS CHAPTER:

Estate Planning for Non-traditional Relationships

- Children of another relationship
- Cohabitation

- Adoption
- Same-sex relationships

Learning Objectives

To ensure that you have a solid understanding of the estate planning techniques and strategies available to individuals in non-traditional relationships, the following learning objectives are addressed in this chapter:

- Understand the federal benefits afforded to same-sex married couples and the impact of state of celebration and state of residence.

- Identify the impact of divorce and/or remarriage on an estate plan, including asset titling and distribution, changes in beneficiary status, and selection of heirs.

- Explain how asset ownership, tax laws, and government policies affect estate planning for same-sex or unmarried couples.

- Identify the legal documents, agreements, and trusts that benefit individuals in non-traditional relationships.

Chapter Contents

OVERVIEW

Non-traditional households are becoming more common. They include single parents, blended families, unmarried couples, and same-sex partners. In the 2010 Census, married couples represented only 48% of all households—they were in the minority for the first time. The Census revealed that in the United States there are 7.5 million opposite-sex unmarried couples living together, 131,729 same-sex married couple households, and 514,735 same-sex unmarried partner households. This amounts to more than 16 million people living as **domestic partners** without the legal benefits afforded to spouses. It is, therefore, important that domestic partners design their estate planning to allow each other to manage assets in the event of incapacity and to benefit each other during life and after death.

In June 2013, the United States Supreme Court's ruling in *U.S. v. Windsor*[1] struck down the section of the Defense of Marriage Act (DOMA) that limited the legal definition of marriage to opposite sex couples.   Since this landmark ruling, planning for same-sex couples is evolving at a rapid pace.

Financial planners who work with non-traditional families must be conversant with the federal tax code, trusts, government benefits, state laws, and the various forms of property ownership that can accomplish a client's estate planning goals. Non-traditional couples need written agreements, legal documents, and expert advice to handle the property, tax, and domestic issues unique to their situations. Financial planners must work with a client's estate planning team to ensure that the proper documents and estate planning strategies are in place.

Practice Standard 100-1

Defining the Scope of the Engagement

The financial planning practitioner and the client shall mutually define the scope of the engagement before any financial planning service is provided.

ESTATE PLANNING FOR SAME-SEX COUPLES

Planning for same-sex couples will depend on two factors; the first is whether the couple was legally married in a state that recognizes same-sex marriage (**state of celebration**). The second is where the couple lives (**state of residence**). If a couple was married in and lives in a state that recognizes same-sex marriage, state law will afford that couple the same legal rights as a traditional married couple.

Alternatively, if a couple was married in a state that recognizes same-sex marriage but lives in a state that does not recognize same-sex marriage, for purposes of state law, that couple will not be deemed married for state purposes, but will be deemed married for federal purposes. In this case, planning will be slightly more complex.

Federal Planning Considerations

The Supreme Court's ruling in Windsor extended hundreds of federal benefits to same- sex couples, while some federal benefits remain unavailable.

State of Celebration

Some of the federal rights that have been extended to same-sex married couples based on the state of celebration that will affect their estate planning include:

- US Citizenship and Immigration Services allows same-sex spouses to apply for visas or green cards.

- The US Department of Labor has extended Family Medical Leave Act benefits and benefits afforded under ERISA to same-sex married spouses. This includes benefits under retirement plans, including beneficiary rights afforded to spouses.

- The Internal Revenue Service recognizes same-sex marriage in determining filing status for income and estate tax returns. Same-sex married couples will be required to file their federal income tax returns as a married couple. Further, they will be allowed the unlimited federal estate and gift tax marital deductions, to split gifts and to elect portability. Planning for a married same-sex couple will be the same as planning for a traditional married couple at the federal tax level. This is regardless of where they reside. State tax filing requirements will be determined by state law. One important note, however, is that the couple – whether same-sex or traditional –must be legally married. For example, if a couple is in a registered domestic partnership or civil union, they will not be deemed married for IRS (and many other) purposes.

Practitioner Tip: For federal income tax purposes, married same-sex couples have the option of amending their income tax returns filed in the three years preceding the Windsor ruling. In order to amend the returns, the couple must have been married at the time they filed the tax return. Clients should work with their accountants to determine if this would result in an income tax refund. This strategy tends to benefit couples where one spouse has high income and the other spouse has lower income. Note, however, that for some, this may increase their income tax liability.

State of Residence

Certain federal agencies will look to the laws of a couple's state of residence for determining eligibility. The Social Security Administration, for example, will afford benefits to same-sex married couples only if they live in a state that recognizes same-sex marriage. If a couple resides in a state that does not recognize their marriage, or if the couple is not legally married, their spouse will not receive Social Security retirement, survivor, or disability benefits on their partners' earnings record, or veteran and military benefits.

Medicaid might cover a nursing home stay for a spouse living in a state that recognizes same-sex marriage but not for a spouse in a state that does not recognize the marriage or for a domestic partner. Long-term care insurance could be considered as an alternative to the assistance normally afforded to married couples because a lien can be placed on a jointly owned home if a partner requires Medicaid assistance.

Client Situation

Ben and Jerry have been in a domestic partnership for 40 years. Ben has always worked outside of the home, and Jerry always stayed home, taking care of their house and pets. When Ben retires, he can collect Social Security based on his earnings record. If Ben and Jerry had a legally recognized marriage and lived in a state that recognized that marriage, Jerry would be able to collect Social Security retirement benefits based on Ben's earnings record, even though he never worked outside of the home.

State Planning Considerations

State law determines many rights for same-sex married couples. If a same-sex couple lives in a state that does not recognize their marriage, then inheritance, hospital visitation and other rights will be affected. Planning for same-sex married couples at the state-level will be the same for domestic partners or other unmarried couples.

ESTATE PLANNING FOR DOMESTIC PARTNERS

Without adequate planning, domestic partners cannot properly care for each other in the event of incapacity or death, or take advantage of legal protections and favorable tax strategies available to them. Although estate planning is important for all clients, because many of the legal rights afforded to married couples are not available to domestic partners, estate planning is especially important in the following situations:

- When a same-sex couple celebrated a marriage in a state that recognizes their marriage but lives in a state that does not.

- When, in the absence of planning, a partner will likely be excluded from inheriting, unlike a legal spouse.

- When two unmarried people are in a committed relationship and consider themselves to be domestic partners, regardless of their gender, and wish to provide for each other in the event of incapacity or death.

- When the net worth of two domestic partners differs substantially.

- When one or both domestic partners have children from a prior relationship.

- When domestic partners co-parent a child, but the child is related by blood or law to only one of the partners.

Components of a Comprehensive Estate Plan

Unmarried cohabitants and married same-sex couples living in states that do not recognize their marriage need to protect their interests while living together, in the event their relationship ends or if one partner dies. A comprehensive estate plan for a non-traditional family often includes:

- legal documents such as wills, durable powers of attorney, and health care proxies;

- property ownership plans;

- trusts;

- domestic partnership agreements;

- insurance policies; and

- gift and estate tax strategies.

A comprehensive estate plan should also address how each of the following applies to a non-traditional couple's circumstances:

- Child support, custody, and adoption agreements

- Divorce settlement agreements

- Retirement and employee benefits

- Health insurance

Accurate and complete records that show the extent to which partners contributed to property interests and financial assets must be kept, including:

- Purchases of real property

- Mortgage payments

- Savings and investment accounts

- Personal property items

LEGAL DOCUMENTS

Everyone needs legal documents such as a will, a durable power of attorney, and a health care power of attorney to protect themselves and their property interests. Domestic partners should also consider creating a domestic partnership agreement to address financial, property, and relationship issues.

Wills

A common estate planning goal is to ensure that property will pass to whoever a person wishes to at his death. Wills are especially important for domestic partners because in the absence of a will, state laws of intestacy determine which heirs and next of kin receive property, and nothing will be left to a spouse (if not recognized by state law), partner, stepchild, or special friend. Furthermore, domestic partners do not have the option of taking an elective share that legally married spouses have if property is not bequeathed to them.

A surviving spouse or domestic partner can inherit from a deceased partner in states that recognize their marriage, or recognize formally registered domestic partnerships or **civil unions** and grant domestic partners the same inheritance rights as spouses. Depending on the state, registered domestic partners can receive protections under state law similar to those provided to spouses in a marriage (e.g., inheritance rights, elective shares, divorce protection, and the ability to make medical decisions). Just as with spouses, however, the share passing to the surviving partner can be reduced in certain circumstances (e.g., if the deceased partner had surviving children or parents). If domestic partners have not formally registered their union, or if state law does not allow or recognize such unions, then the surviving partner will not be entitled to any share of the deceased partner's estate because the surviving partner does not fall within the definition of an "heir."

It is essential that guardians and contingent guardians for minor children be appointed in a parent's will, and custody arrangements should be explicitly addressed. Couples in non-traditional relationships might consider writing letters to family members to express their wishes and explain their decisions concerning child care, custody arrangements, and the disposition of property upon a partner's death. Families may not agree with the reasoning or the arrangements, but such letters can serve to document a couple's decisions in the event of child custody battles or court challenges to the will.

Practitioner Tip: Wills are revocable instruments that can be changed. It may be prudent for one partner to make a testamentary bequest rather than an irrevocable lifetime gift to the other partner to safeguard solely owned property interests against a changing relationship.

Client Situation

Matt and Paul have been together for many years, but they do not live in a state that recognizes their relationship. Each has a primary estate planning goal of ensuring that the other is provided for following one of their deaths. Matt and Paul each execute reciprocal wills, leaving all property to the other. If they did not have valid wills, property would pass per their state's law of intestacy to their heirs.

Durable Powers of Attorney

In the absence of proper estate planning documents, if one partner becomes incapacitated, the other partner might have no voice in handling the incapacitated partner's affairs. This is especially important for partners who have children in their lives, whether born prior to or during the partners' relationship, legally adopted by one or both partners, or born to one partner through artificial means where the other partner serves in a parenting role but is not legally related to the child.

A durable power of attorney and a health care power of attorney are legal documents that allow partners to choose who will make financial, business, and medical decisions for them if they become incapacitated. Without a durable power of attorney, probate courts would appoint a guardian and a conservator to care for the individual and their property, with resulting delays, expenses, and public court proceedings. The law presumes that biological family members should be given the right to make business and personal care decisions for an incompetent person, thus denying a partner involvement in a loved one's care.

Client Situation

Dick and Robby have been partners in a relationship for many years. Although both of their families have been very supportive of their relationship, their attorney advised each partner to obtain a durable power of attorney and a health care proxy so that hospitals and financial institutions will recognize each person's authority to act in the event one partner becomes incapacitated. This will prevent court intervention and unwanted family involvement should this situation occur.

Domestic Partnership Agreements

Domestic partnership agreements are designed to protect both partners while they are living together, and courts have recognized these agreements as binding legal contracts. Partnership agreements establish ground rules for living together. Agreements can be written to cover any situation that can affect a relationship including child raising, custody issues, and domestic responsibilities, and they can indicate how children, property, retirement assets, and financial matters should be handled in the event the couple's relationship ends. Stepparents and partners have no custody rights unless they go through formal adoption procedures, but courts will consider the custody arrangements expressed in a domestic partnership agreement.

These agreements are particularly useful when couples want to combine their financial resources because they can stipulate how the assets should be managed. Domestic partners should also consider creating a co-ownership agreement to define their respective ownership interests, rights, and obligations in relation to property that they have or acquire. For example, a co-ownership agreement could set forth the manner in which expenses related to property would be paid (e.g., a mortgage, property taxes, insurance, repairs, and capital improvements) and how the property is to be dealt with in the event that the partners terminate their relationship by death or otherwise. When real and personal property is shared, an inventory of assets is needed to list the items that each partner brought into the relationship and to document the date these assets became jointly owned.

Practitioner Tip: A domestic partnership agreement can be instrumental in avoiding a will contest in situations where family members might not be supportive of the partners' wishes. The couple should consult with an attorney and a financial planner to obtain expert advice and to understand the legal, financial, and tax consequences of their agreement.

PROPERTY INTERESTS

A person who owns property may wish to share some property interests with a partner. Property gifted to a nonspouse could be subject to gift taxes that cannot be offset by an unlimited marital deduction. Gifts of real property to nonspouses can be given outright or converted to joint tenancy with right of survivorship (JTWROS) or a tenancy in common depending on a couple's planning objectives. Gifts are irrevocable and cannot be rescinded if relationships change or income from the property is needed in the future.

Practitioner Tip: Some states allow **common-law marriages** to be contracted if state requirements are met. Couples in common-law marriages have unlimited marital deductions for property transfers, and real property is held jointly as a community property interest.

Joint Tenancy with Right of Survivorship

Property purchased as JTWROS avoids probate and provides each partner an equal interest in the property regardless of the amounts contributed to acquire it. However, the entire property could be put at risk subject to the claims of a joint owner's creditors. Although creditors can recover against only the debtor's interest, this can cause undesirable consequences, such as a forced sale of the property.

When unmarried individuals hold property as JTWROS, the entire value of the property is included in the federal gross estate of the joint tenant who is the first to die, except to the extent that the surviving tenant provided consideration to acquire or improve the property. The surviving joint tenant becomes the sole owner of the property with exclusive lifetime use and testamentary control.

> **Client Situation**
>
> Chrissy and Courtney are in a same-sex relationship. Chrissy purchases a home and titles it JTWROS with Courtney. At Chrissy's death, the home will pass by operation of law to Courtney. Because Chrissy purchased the house, the entire value will be included in Chrissy's taxable estate.

Practitioner Tip: Unmarried couples holding property in joint tenancy should keep complete and accurate records of the amount each furnishes toward the acquisition and improvement of the property. If records are not kept, the entire value of the property could be subject to tax in both taxpayers' estates.

There can be gift tax consequences to holding property in joint tenancy if a person buys property and takes title in his name and the name of another person. The purchaser has made a gift of one-half of the property to the other joint tenant with no gift tax marital deduction available to offset the tax.

There are no immediate federal gift tax consequences to the formation of a joint tenancy bank account (or a brokerage or other similar account as long as the contributor's funds can be withdrawn without the consent of the other joint owner). Instead, a gift occurs at the moment one joint tenant withdraws funds in excess of the amount that tenant contributed with no obligation to account for the proceeds to the other joint tenant. Unmarried partners can easily make unintended taxable gifts at the time of the noncontributing partner's withdrawal of funds without having the benefit of a marital deduction to offset the gift tax.

Tenancy in Common

There is a relatively simple solution to the joint tenancy gift problem. Unmarried individuals can avoid the risks of joint tenancy by holding assets as tenants-in-common. Their respective ownership interests should be proportionate to the contribution they made toward the acquisition (or improvement) of the property. Then, for estate tax purposes, only the deceased tenant's proportionate share would be included in his estate.

Client Situation

Tammy and Anita are domestic partners in a committed relationship. They purchase a piece of real property for $425,000. Tammy contributed $200,000 to the purchase price; Anita contributed $225,000. Tammy and Anita take title as tenants-in-common with Tammy holding an undivided 47% interest and Anita holding an undivided 53% interest. Tammy dies six years later when the property has appreciated in value to $600,000. Only 47% of the property's value ($600,000 × 47% = $282,000) would be included in Tammy's estate for estate tax purposes without any need for her executor to show the amounts (or source) of contributions (as would be required if Tammy and Anita held the property as joint tenants).

Practitioner Tip: For gift tax purposes, as long as the interests held as tenants in common are proportionate to the parties' respective contributions (and remain so), no gift is made.

Considerations of Home Ownership

Home ownership provides domestic partners with an opportunity to plan on a number of fronts, but it also has pitfalls. Partners who share primary residences or vacation homes may wish to shift a greater ownership share or complete ownership to the partner in the higher tax bracket, because this partner would benefit the most from taking mortgage interest and property tax deductions. Couples who own two homes could consider owning each home separately, so that if the homes are sold, each owner could take advantage of the $250,000 capital gains exclusion. Homeowners who wish to sell an equitable interest in their home to their partner could structure the transaction as an installment sale, which does not require a down payment and allows for flexible payments.

Practitioner Tip: Homeowners' insurance policies and property and liability insurance policies should list both partners' names on the policies to ensure that each person is covered in the event of a loss.

A partner with an individual bank account who pays a portion of the mortgage would have the account frozen if he or she died or became incapacitated, and the account would not be accessible to the other partner to pay the mortgage. Instead, bank accounts could be titled as JTWROS, or the partner could be given a durable power of attorney to have access to the money in the account.

Domestic partners also should be aware of property tax issues relating to the manner in which they hold property. A change in the manner in which title is held (either regarding the persons holding title or the nature of their ownership, i.e., joint tenancy, tenants in common) can cause the property to be reassessed for property tax purposes. This can cause property taxes to increase if the value of the real property has increased.

TOD and POD Accounts

For liquid assets, another alternative to ensure that property passes to the surviving partner is for the account holder to specify that an account is payable on death (POD) to the survivor. Because a POD designation is revocable and no property passes to the survivor until the partner's death, there are no gift tax consequences when the account is established. At the first partner's death assets are included in his estate and pass to the surviving partner. POD accounts are available for bank accounts like a Totten trust that name a POD beneficiary. Property can also be transferred directly to a partner at the other partner's death using a transfer on death (TOD) designation, which is available for investment accounts, mutual funds, deeds, and other property owned by the decedent.

Both TOD and POD accounts avoid probate with the added advantage that family members and others cannot contest the transfer of these assets to a designated partner. A surviving partner can receive funds from the deceased partner's account without delay after presenting transfer certificates to financial institutions.

Practitioner Tip: It is important that non-traditional couples plan for incapacity. If the depositor of a POD account or Totten trust becomes legally incapacitated, the surviving partner will not have access to the accounts without a court order or a durable power of attorney.

Client Situation

Courtney has a mutual fund account that she wishes to leave to Chrissy. Courtney executes a TOD stipulating that at her death this account will pass to Chrissy by operation of contract.

GIFT TAXES

Unmarried individuals do not have an estate tax marital deduction available to offset their estate tax. This creates a problem for domestic partners with estates that exceed $5,430,000 in 2015. One way to reduce the value of their taxable estates is by gifting to partners, charities, and others. Lifetime gifts reduce the value of a gross estate, and gifts that do not exceed the annual exclusion are not added back into the estate as an adjusted taxable gift.

Gifts from one domestic partner to the other are fully taxable unless the gifts qualify for the annual exclusion of $14,000 per donee (in 2015), or the exclusion for payment of qualified medical and educational expenses. Only legally married spouses can split gifts; therefore, domestic partners cannot take advantage of gift splitting to reduce the value of one partner's estate.

Using the annual exclusion, a person whose wealth exceeds that of his partner can systematically make gifts to increase the other partner's wealth, which allows that partner to utilize his own unified credit. Gifts can also be made to the family members of the less wealthy partner—thus providing a benefit to the family and reducing the value of the wealthier spouse's taxable estate.

In addition, payments of a donee's tuition or medical care (to the extent that the costs of such medical care are not reimbursed by insurance), if paid directly to the provider of such services, are not subject to gift tax—regardless of the amounts paid. The payment of medical insurance falls within the definition of "medical care."

The relationship of the donor to the recipient of such services on whose behalf the payment is made is irrelevant. Therefore, if one partner's wealth exceeds that of the other, the wealthier partner can pay the other's educational and medical expenses tax free. Similarly, the wealthier partner can pay such expenses on behalf of members of the other partner's family (e.g., children and siblings). The payment must be made directly to the provider of the services; reimbursing the recipient of the education/medical services for payments he previously made does not qualify.

Client Situation

Chad earns a substantial amount of money as an anesthesiologist, and Ernie earns much less as a state-employed social worker. Ernie is taking courses toward his M.B.A. and Chad is paying for Ernie's tuition. Chad makes payments directly to the college that Ernie is attending to avoid making a taxable gift to Ernie, which would be the case if he gave Ernie a check every semester to pay for his own tuition.

Unmarried partners should consider whether they wish to use their lifetime exclusion ($5,430,000 in 2015) to benefit their partner or the partner's family. Such gifts can be particularly effective if the assets that comprise the gifts are subject to a discount in valuation (e.g., fractional ownership of real property or lack of control/marketability of an interest in a business), or provide leveraging opportunities (e.g., life insurance).

Practitioner Tip: Planners should be aware that if one unmarried partner pays a larger share (or all) of the couple's living expenses, such payments could constitute taxable gifts if the cumulative total of the expenses paid on behalf of the other partner, along with any actual gifts to that partner, exceeds the annual exclusion amount available in any given year.

LIQUIDITY PLANNING WITH LIFE INSURANCE

An estate will have immediate expenses, so it is important to have funds readily available to pay for funeral and administrative expenses, probate costs, taxes, and debts. Estate taxes may be higher in non-traditional relationships because there is no marital deduction to offset them. Liquidity planning is critical to pay for these expenses, and one important source of funds is a life insurance policy.

The owner of a policy who is also the insured can name a partner as beneficiary and retain the right to change the beneficiary designation in the future if the relationship changes. However, the death benefit would be included in the owner/insured's gross estate. Another option is to have each partner purchase a life insurance policy on the other's life as owner and beneficiary. If the owner predeceases the insured, only the value of the policy at that time would be included in the owner's estate.

Practitioner Tip: It is imperative that ownership and beneficiary designations of life insurance policies be carefully examined and coordinated with estate planning objectives to avoid unintended tax consequences.

Perhaps the best alternative is to establish an irrevocable life insurance trust (ILIT) to acquire and maintain a policy. The trustee can own the policy and make premium payments. The death benefit or policy proceeds are not included in the insured's estate. If the trust purchases a new policy, it is excluded from the insured's estate immediately; whereas, if an existing policy is transferred to a trust, the insured must survive the transfer by three years for policy proceeds to be excluded from the estate.

Practitioner Tip: The ILIT would have sufficient funds at the insured's death to purchase assets from the insured's estate to provide the estate with liquidity. The trustee of the ILIT would manage trust assets for the benefit of the partner/beneficiary. The noninsured partner can be given a life income interest in the trust assets, the use of principal for ascertainable standards (health, education, maintenance, and support), and a limited power of appointment over some or all of the trust assets. Upon the partner's death, the trust assets would not be included in his gross estate.

TRUSTS

Most estate planning strategies are designed to carry out a person's objectives while minimizing tax, probate, financial, and legal costs. Trusts are often used to accomplish many of these goals. Couples in non-traditional relationships may want to consider setting up separate trusts to protect their individual interests, control their own property, and provide benefits for their partner, the trust beneficiary.

Revocable Trusts

Revocable trusts have many advantages in non-traditional relationships because they offer numerous benefits and protections that cannot be obtained from other property arrangements. A revocable trust provides privacy and flexibility, and the trust can be changed or revoked in response to changing circumstances. The grantor should transfer his individually owned property to the trust while he is alive to accomplish many of his estate planning goals.

The benefits of establishing and funding a revocable trust include:

- allowing the grantor to control his property interests;

- avoiding probate of assets at death;

- designating trust beneficiaries;

- providing for minor children in the event of death;

- naming a successor trustee to manage assets in the event of incapacity to avoid court-appointed conservators;

- observing a trustee's ability to manage assets and change trustees, if necessary; and

- preventing family members from making claims against the partner's assets at death.

Bypass (Credit Shelter) Trusts

Although bypass or credit shelter trust planning is common among married couples, the beneficiary of such trusts need not be a legally recognized spouse. In fact, unmarried partners can use bypass trusts to shelter assets from estate taxes. By having each partner fund a bypass trust, the overall amount of estate taxes paid on the couple's combined estates is reduced. To the extent that the deceased partner's generation-skipping tax exemption is allocated to the bypass trust, it may be possible to hold such assets in trust through the lifetimes of successive beneficiaries.

Bypass trusts provide the additional benefit of allowing each partner to designate the remainder beneficiaries of his assets in the trust. The use of bypass trusts has been somewhat negated by the concept of portability; however, portability does not apply to unmarried couples.

Practitioner Tip: If the value of an unmarried decedent's gross estate exceeds $5,430,000 in 2015 (including taxable gifts made during lifetime), assets not sheltered by the unified credit that remain after the payment of estate tax can also be held in trust for the benefit of the decedent's partner to avoid inclusion in the partner's gross estate. Just as with a bypass trust, trust principal and income can be available for the surviving partner's benefit and the assets will not be included in the surviving partner's gross estate.

> **Client Situation**
>
> Jacob and Edward have both been very successful in their careers; their combined estates are worth approximately $15 million. They each want to ensure that all assets are available for the survivor, but they want the assets to be transferred in a tax-efficient manner. Each partner plans to establish a bypass trust funded with $5,430,000 so that only $4,140,000 of their combined estates will be subject to tax. The survivor will be the beneficiary of the bypass trust and can access trust principal and income as limited by the terms of the trust.

Split-interest Trusts

With a grantor retained income trust (GRIT), one partner can transfer the remainder interest in property (cash, stocks, bonds, real property, or a business interest) to a trust to benefit a partner or other unrelated beneficiaries in a tax-advantaged manner. A GRIT that has certain family members as beneficiaries would result in a taxable gift equal to the value of the assets placed in the trust, but with unrelated beneficiaries, the tax is based on the value of the remainder interest. This allows domestic partners with a disparity in their personal wealth to reduce transfer taxes and increase the less wealthy partner's estate to fully utilize that partner's $5,430,000 exclusion.

Further, domestic partners can undertake a **split-interest purchase of property** wherein one purchases a term interest and the other the remainder interest. Again, normal valuation rules apply because the partners are not family. Consequently, a partner with less net worth than the other can purchase the remainder interest (at a lower value), and the wealthier partner purchases a life estate.

Or one partner can establish a qualified personal residence trust (QPRT) naming the other as the remainder beneficiary, and the grantor partner can purchase the residence from the QPRT during the retained term to move any appreciation in value to the remainder partner at no income or additional transfer tax cost.

A charitable remainder annuity trust (CRAT) or a charitable remainder unitrust (CRUT) might be appropriate for a partner who is charitably inclined and who wants the other partner to receive income for a period of years or for life. The present value of the income stream could be subject to gift taxes because a marital deduction is not available to offset the tax on the gift. The donor/partner would receive a charitable income tax deduction in the year the gift is made for the present value of the charity's remainder interest, but the donee/ partner would pay tax on the income received. Trust corpus would be distributed to the charity at the donor's death, thereby avoiding inclusion in the donor's gross estate.

Practitioner Tip: Domestic partners must be aware that these transactions are irrevocable. If there is any question regarding the desire to make a true irrevocable gift, the transaction should not be undertaken.

TERMINATING RELATIONSHIPS

When spouses divorce, no gain or loss is recognized on a transfer of property between them if the transfer is "incident to the divorce." Instead, the transfer is treated as a gift between the spouses and basis is carried over.

When nonmarried couples dissolve their relationships, the transfer of assets can result in adverse gift and income tax consequences. For example, if the value of what each partner receives is proportionate to the value he brought into the relationship, there may be a deemed "sale" or "exchange" of property that could result in taxable gain.

Or if one partner receives a payment in recognition of services rendered during the relationship, that partner could have taxable income. If the payment is not attributable to services, it can be treated as a taxable gift from the other partner (to the extent that it exceeds the available annual exclusion).

As to IRAs, when spouses divorce, the transfer of one spouse's interest in an IRA to the other spouse (or former spouse) under a divorce or separation instrument is generally not considered a taxable transfer, and such interest is thereafter treated as the other spouse's IRA. There is no such exception for nonspouses.

Practitioner Tip: Domestic partners who have formally registered their partnership must research the laws of the state in which they reside to determine whether they have any community property or other "marital property" rights under state law. These rights can have income or transfer tax consequences, as discussed above.

Client Situation

Beth and Cara were involved in a domestic partnership, but like so many of their legally married counterparts, the relationship dissolved. Beth owns the house that they live in, but they decided that Cara would keep the home. If Beth and Cara were legally married, the transfer of property from Beth to Cara would be considered "incident to the divorce" and not taxed, but because their relationship was not legally recognized, there may be income and gift tax consequences to the transfer.

PROVIDING FOR CHILDREN

Just as with couples who are legally married, planning for the children of domestic partners is a significant issue. According to the 2010 U.S. Census, 66% of children up to age 17 lived with two married parents and 7% lived with a parent or parents who were cohabitating. Depending on the particular household, a child could be the biological or adopted child of one or both partners. For example, one or both partners might have children from a prior relationship, the partners could have mutual children (adopted or biological), or a child could be born to one partner during the relationship in a situation where the other partner is not the biological parent (e.g., surrogacy, artificial insemination, or egg donation).

In many domestic partnerships, only one partner is the biological or adopted parent of a child for whom both partners serve in a co-parenting role. If the biological/adoptive parent dies while the child is a minor, issues can arise about who the child's guardian will be. This is especially true if the identity of the other biological parent is unknown (e.g., assisted reproduction techniques such as egg, sperm, or embryo donation were used).

Absent a specific nomination of the unrelated partner as the minor child's guardian, a member of the parent-partner's family could bring an action to be named the child's guardian. Therefore, domestic partners in this situation should be sure that the related parent-partner names the unrelated partner as the guardian of any minor children in his will, "Designation of Guardian in Advance of Need," or similar document. State law should be researched to determine the appropriate method by which such a nomination is made.

Divorce

Estate planning can be especially complex when divorced parents remarry because child custody issues, child support payments, and planning for blended families may have to be addressed. Planning for the death of one or both natural parents is critical to protect children and provide for their care if they are living with a stepparent or with the domestic partner of one of their biological parents. Divorced parents should select and coordinate their choice of personal and financial guardians who would care for their minor children in the event of their deaths. The security of child support payments for minor children should also be examined to ensure that adequate funds remain available for their continued financial support. When a divorced parent remarries, there is a risk that children from the first marriage could suffer financially because the noncustodial parent might be struggling to support two families.

Practitioner Tip: A person who remarries should create a new will. Otherwise, property bequeathed to a former spouse in the existing will might pass through intestacy. The new will should provide the current spouse with assets that are at least equal to the state's elective share amount to avoid a will contest upon the testator's death.

Child Support

The financial needs of children must continue to be met after their parents' divorce. Child support payments provide funds to pay for a minor's expenses—for example, education and daily living expenses—and can make a difference in the quality of the child's life, especially when a custodial parent does not earn enough to adequately provide financial support. Noncustodial parents who are obligated to make child support payments could find that several factors affect the adequacy and availability of their funds, such as:

- Death

- Disability

- Unemployment

- Financial hardship

- Inflation

- Poor investment returns

- Remarriage

Divorce decrees can mandate that child support payments be made until the children reach a specific age, that payments are annually adjusted for cost-of-living increases, and that payments are continued by the noncustodial parent's estate while the children are minors.

Meeting Support Obligations

Trusts and life insurance policies can provide financial security to support minor children. A divorced parent can establish an irrevocable **support trust** for the purpose of providing child support payments and to avoid making any direct payments to a former spouse. A grantor, who would not be the trustee, would transfer assets to the trust to secure the payments and to fulfill his support obligation. Trust income that is used to support a minor is taxed to the grantor per grantor trust rules.

The noncustodial parent can also purchase life insurance and disability insurance to provide their children with ongoing financial support in the event of his death or incapacity. Life insurance policies can be owned and arranged in several different ways:

- Children can be named as beneficiaries with the proceeds managed by a conservator.

- The former spouse can be named beneficiary to satisfy any remaining unpaid support payments.

- Ownership of the policy can be assigned to older adult children.

- Adult children can purchase life insurance directly on their parent's life.

ILITs can be established with children as trust beneficiaries. If these trusts are unfunded, meaning that only a policy on the grantor's life is held in the trust, then Crummey powers should be given to the children to reduce taxable gifts from premium payments transferred into the trust each year. At the grantor's death, the trustee would manage the insurance proceeds, and trust corpus would be distributed to the children when they reach the ages specified in the trust.

Practitioner Tip: Divorced parents can also establish custodial accounts for each child funded with cash, life insurance, or income-producing property.

Trusts

Trusts have many uses and can distribute assets to different beneficiaries within the same trust. A qualified terminable interest property (QTIP) Trust can provide all income to the current spouse for life with the remaining property distributed to children from a former marriage.

A **sprinkle trust** allows a trustee to make discretionary distributions of income to trust beneficiaries according to their needs, and a **spray trust** permits discretionary distributions of both income and corpus. For example, the trustee could distribute income to a child entering college, but he may not make any distributions to the other trust beneficiaries, such as the current spouse or children from the current and/or previous marriages.

Adoption

Stepparents and partners in non-traditional relationships have no parental or other custodial rights with respect to their partner's children unless they institute formal adoption proceedings.

If domestic partners adopt a child, both partners should be treated as parents for purposes of establishing inheritance rights. In the case of same-sex partners, however, not all states recognize joint adoptions. Domestic partners (whether the same- or opposite-sex) should be sure that their estate planning documents are extremely clear regarding who are the intended beneficiaries. For example, rather than referring to a partner's "children," "descendants," or "issue," the document should refer to the child by name.

Death of a Parent

When a parent dies, the courts generally select the natural parent as guardian, but divorced parents can name other guardians in their wills if the surviving parent is unable, unwilling, or unfit to fulfill his responsibilities. Property, death benefit proceeds from life insurance policies, and Social Security survivor benefits need to be managed for minor children by a financially competent, caring individual who is keenly aware of the children's needs. An individual and/or a financial institution could be named as trustee of a testamentary trust or an ILIT, or as a contingent trustee of a funded revocable trust. The trustee would manage, invest, and preserve assets; distribute income to minors as needed; and distribute corpus when the beneficiaries reach a certain age, as specified in the trust document.

Chapter Highlights

- The federal government recognizes same-sex marriage however, many states do not. Many rights and benefits afforded to married couples are at the state level, therefore, same-sex couples must look to state law.

- The IRS recognizes same-sex married couples as married for income, gift and estate tax purposes, regardless of where they live.

- Domestic partners need wills, durable powers of attorney, and health care powers of attorney to protect their personal, financial, and legal rights.

- Domestic partnership agreements can provide guidelines for the relationship that addresses domestic, child care, property, and financial issues.

- Unmarried partners can own property together as JTWROS and as tenants in common. If the owner of an asset changes the title of property to JTWROS to include a partner on the deed, he will have made a gift of one-half of the property's value.

- TOD and POD designations may be used to transfer assets in bank and brokerage accounts directly from a decedent to a partner.

- Unmarried couples do not have an estate tax or a gift tax marital deduction available to offset transfer taxes, because these deductions are available only to married individuals.

- An ILIT can be used to own a life insurance policy on the life of the grantor for the benefit of the grantor's partner. The proceeds cannot be taxed in either partner's estate. However, an insurable interest must exist between the policy owner and the beneficiary.

- Governmental benefits available to married couples are not available to domestic partners. Private disability insurance and long-term care insurance can provide alternative support for a domestic partner.

- Trusts can accomplish specific estate planning goals for partners in a non-traditional relationship. Trusts that have advantages for domestic partners include funded revocable trusts, bypass trusts, GRITs, QPRTs, and CRATs or CRUTs, in addition to split-interest purchases of property.

- Support trusts, child support payments, and life insurance policies can provide financial security and support for the minor children of divorced parents.

- Stepparents and partners in non-traditional relationships have no custody rights to their partner's children unless they institute formal adoption proceedings.

Key Terms

civil union	spray trust
common-law marriage	sprinkle trust
domestic partner	state of celebration
domestic partnership agreement	state of residence
split-interest purchase of property	support trust

Review Questions

28-1. Domestic partnership agreements can address all of the following issues that pertain to a relationship *except:*

A. They can designate a health care agent to care for a partner in the event of incapacity.

B. They can stipulate how a mortgage and property taxes should be paid.

C. They can establish ground rules for living together.

D. They can indicate how property should be divided if the relationship ends.

28-2. Vance and Margery live together, but they are not married or otherwise related. What tax planning techniques and benefits are available to them?

A. Marital deduction

B. Split gifts

C. Grantor retained income trust

D. QTIP Trust

28-3. Denny and Beatrice live together, but they are not married or otherwise related. Which of the following transfer methods is least likely to be effective at passing property from one of them to the other at death?

A. An IRA

B. Property owned in joint tenancy with each other

C. A TOD account

D. An election against the will

28-4. The following statements concerning home ownership are correct, *except:*

A. A partner in a higher tax bracket can be given a greater ownership share in a home to take advantage of certain tax deductions.

B. Sole ownership of a home allows a partner to take advantage of the $250,000 capital gains exclusion when the house is sold.

C. Partners can title a home as tenants by the entirety to provide creditor protection for debts incurred by both spouses.

D. The value of property owned by partners as JTWROS is included in the estate of the first tenant to die based on the contribution rule.

28-5. Which of the following statements is/are correct?

A. A spray trust can provide discretionary distributions to a beneficary from income and principal.

B. A support trust is used to provide child support, but the divorced parent is taxed on the distributed income.

C. There is no requirement that a spouse be the beneficiary of a bypass trust.

D. The grantor can change the beneficiary of a funded revocable trust.

Notes

1.   *United States v. Windsor*, 570 U.S. ___ (2013) (Docket No. 12-307).

Chapter 29

Common Estate Planning Considerations

Learning Objectives

To ensure that you have a solid understanding of common estate planning considerations, techniques and strategies, the following learning objectives are addressed in this chapter:

- Describe the various personal and financial situations that can affect an estate plan.

- Identify the legal documents that should be obtained to manage and properly transfer property interests.

- Explain how trusts, insurance policies, and legal documents are coordinated when planning for incapacity.

- Discuss how leveraged gifting is an effective tax planning strategy.

- Identify the types of trusts, techniques, and deductions that reduce the estate tax base.

Chapter Contents

OVERVIEW

Many people share some common financial planning and estate planning goals. For example, an important objective is often to accumulate and maximize wealth while protecting and preserving assets for future use. Another common goal is to transfer property to intended beneficiaries during lifetime or at death in a tax-efficient manner at the appropriate time. Although estate planning goals can be similar, most people have their own unique, personal financial and tax situations that require a customized plan. Estate plans should also be crafted with great flexibility to accommodate clients' changing needs and circumstances and to account for changes in tax laws and government policies that can affect their successful execution.

Financial planners must ascertain all the relevant facts in the context of a client's objectives and the beneficiaries' needs, abilities, and circumstances to identify any estate planning issues that must be addressed with the estate planning team. Once an estate plan has been developed, the planner, estate planning team, and client can determine the implementation and monitoring responsibilities to enact the recommendations, and the planner can coordinate periodic reviews of the plan with the client.

Practice Standard 500-1

Agreeing on Implementation Responsibilities

The financial planning practitioner and the client shall mutually agree on the implementation responsibilities consistent with the scope of the engagement.

Practice Standard 600-1

Defining Monitoring Responsibilities

The financial planning practitioner and client shall mutually define monitoring responsibilities.

ESTATE PLANNING CONSIDERATIONS

Planners must, of course, master the technical aspects of the 2012 Tax Act as well as the many "old" provisions of the law and tools and techniques that have not changed. But in the estate planning process, planners must also recognize that clients want and deserve control, certainty, compassion, flexibility, and assurance that the right recommendations have been made.

- *Control:* Consider the extent to which a given tool or technique will detract from—or enhance—a client's control over property or the goals they seek to accomplish.

- *Certainty:* Consider how likely it is that the plan will meet a client's objectives. Will the client actually carry out and accomplish his goals based on the plan's recommendations? Are the mutually agreed-upon tax, personal, and economic assumptions sufficiently realistic to meet the client's needs and expectations?

- *Compassion:* Have planners listened—really listened—to the client and client's family with care? When mutually defining goals, has the planner been able to draw out the client's needs, hopes, dreams, and fears?

- *Flexibility:* Will the tool or technique chosen as a recommendation lock the client or the client's family into a particular situation, or are sufficient options and flexibility built into the estate plan? This is especially important in an era of temporary tax laws.

- *Assurance:* Can planners assure the client that all proper steps have been taken in a timely manner by all members of the estate planning team?

Clients want to decide whom to give their property to and how assets should be transferred. Financial planners can help clients understand the schematic of their current estate plan and the taxes and costs associated with executing it to determine whether the plan is meeting the client's estate planning objectives. After consulting with the estate planning team, a financial planner can recommend alternative actions and solutions, or a modification of the client's estate planning priorities and objectives.

Practice Standard 400-1

Identifying and Evaluating Financial Planning Alternative(s)

The financial planning practitioner shall consider sufficient and relevant alternatives to the client's current course of action in an effort to reasonably meet the client's goals, needs and priorities.

Practitioner Tip: Remember that an estate plan is much more than just a proper blend of the tax aspects of tools and techniques found in estate planning. It is a plan to protect individuals, their loved ones, and their wealth now and into the future.

Changes That Can Affect an Estate Plan

Many personal and family-related issues can affect an existing estate plan.

- A client's health and anticipated longevity, and the health and competency of family members can affect the time frame for accomplishing goals and the anticipated medical costs of a financial plan, incapacity planning, and property transfers that are subject to the three-year rule.

- A death in the family, birth or adoption, marriage or remarriage, and separation or divorce of a client's family members can affect the terms of wills or revocable trusts, property ownership, or beneficiary designations on contracts such as life insurance policies, 401(k)s, and IRAs, which in turn can affect a client's overall estate plan. Copies of beneficiary designation forms and titles to client's accounts or deeds should be reviewed by the financial planner each time the client's estate plan is reviewed.

- Lifestyle changes such as a permanent move to a different state would affect documents such as wills, powers of attorney, living wills, health care proxies, deeds, and revocable trusts, and they could subject property to ancillary probate if property is owned in more than one state.

Significant changes in a client's financial situation have an immediate impact on an existing estate plan, such as:

- the acquisition or loss of property;

- changes in property values;

- the investment performance of assets;

- changes in income that cause a change in the client's tax bracket;

- changes in wealth of either the testator or the beneficiary;

- changes in living expenses; and

- the sale of a business or business property.

Personal and economic assumptions also affect the outcome of a plan and the likelihood of meeting a client's objectives. The practitioner should use client-specified, mutually agreed-upon, reasonable assumptions that may include but are not limited to the following:

- Personal assumptions, such as retirement ages, life expectancy(ies), income needs, risk factors, time horizon, and special needs; and

- Economic assumptions, such as inflation rates, tax rates, and investment returns.

Federal and state law can also influence the outcome of an estate plan or the selection of appropriate estate planning techniques, and any changes should be examined to determine their impact on a client's current estate plan. State laws can affect state inheritance and estate taxes and also determine probate proceedings, intestacy laws, community property ownership, homestead allowances, nuptial agreements, mortmain statutes, rules against perpetuities, and elective share awards. Financial planners should work together with their clients' estate planning attorneys to determine how state laws affect a client's particular situation and current financial plan.

Practice Standard 300-1

Analyzing and Evaluating the Client's Information

A financial planning practitioner shall analyze the information to gain an understanding of the client's financial situation and then evaluate to what extent the client's goals, needs and priorities can be met by the client's resources and current course of action.

Sometimes planning can favor certain individuals over others, such as when remarriage occurs. Therefore, the consequences of various tax and non-tax estate planning techniques should be examined to ensure that dependents are planned for in ways the client intends them to be.

Practitioner Tip: Estate plans should be reviewed every three to five years—more frequently when personal or financial circumstances change, and upon every major tax law change, to ensure that estate planning objectives continue to be met.

Record Keeping

Estate administration expenses can be greater if estate and financial documents are difficult or impossible to find. Important documents should be placed in a safe deposit box, and the client's executor should have access to it. Each year, clients should put an updated list of the names, phone numbers, and e-mail addresses of advisors in the box. Be aware that some safe deposit boxes are "frozen" (the state requires that the bank seal the box from entry until the inheritance tax examiner can inventory the contents) and there can be lengthy delays in getting to the papers in the box. In this case, all important information and documents should be stored in a location that the executor will be able to access it quickly and easily, in order to facilitate the estate settlement process. It is also advisable to maintain a personal inventory of important information such as account information and insurance policy schedules.

Practitioner Tip: Be sure to keep tax returns and records for at least three to six years.

PLANNING FOR DEATH

Many estate planning goals and priorities involve caring for spouses and children after a client's death, and controlling the transfer of property interests to others. These goals can be accomplished by wills, inter-vivos trusts, and/or testamentary trusts created by the decedent's will. Planning for dependents such as spouses, partners, children, and other family members, and perhaps even for pets, is essential to:

- provide for their financial welfare;

- care for their special needs; and

- maintain or improve their standards of living.

An improper disposition of assets occurs whenever the wrong asset goes to the wrong person in the wrong manner or at the wrong time. Leaving an entire estate to a surviving spouse or leaving a large or complex estate outright to a spouse unprepared or unwilling to handle it is a good example of improper planning. Leaving a sizable estate outright to a teenager or to an emotionally or mentally challenged person are also common examples of poor planning. A number of solutions help to avoid these common pitfalls. One solution is to consider a trust or custodial arrangements and to provide in the will or other dispositive instruments for young children and legally incompetent people.

"Equal but inequitable" distributions are common. If an estate is divided equally among four children who have drastically different income or capital needs, an equal distribution can be inequitable and might not accomplish a client's goals. One solution might be a sprinkle or spray provision in a trust that empowers the trustee to provide extra income or additional principal to a child who needs or deserves more or who is in an unusually low income tax bracket in a given year.

Wills

Every adult needs a will regardless of the value of his estate. In the absence of a will, the individual's state of domicile dictates the distribution of an owner's assets at death through state laws of intestacy. Distribution of property is based on the relationship the decedent has to family members, and if there are no family members, the property escheats, or reverts, to the state. Furthermore, for parents of minor children, the will is the proper legal document for choosing guardians or contingent guardians for their children. In the absence of a valid guardian designation, the court will determine which individuals will make legal, financial, and personal decisions on behalf of the children in the event of a parent's death.

Consider also the importance of a "simultaneous death" provision, so that the assets avoid needless second probates and double inheritance taxes due to loss of the marital deduction in each estate, and instead they go to the right person in the right manner.

Funeral arrangements and burial instructions should not be addressed in the will, but should be written as a separate document and given to family members.

Practitioner Tip: Revocable trusts and residuary clauses in wills should be coordinated to pay estate debts, taxes, and administrative expenses. The titling of property takes legal precedence over bequests from the will, and titles should be reviewed and coordinated with the client's objectives.

Testamentary and Revocable Trusts

A testamentary trust can be created under the will by the executor after the testator's death. Testamentary trusts can be established, for example, as bypass trusts, disclaimer trusts, and marital deduction trusts, or for other specific purposes.

An inter-vivos revocable trust can be established to accompany a will. When a revocable trust is used in an estate plan, the will pours assets into the revocable trust, and the revocable trust will provide the dispositive provisions of the estate plan. The revocable trust can establish bypass planning, allow disclaimer planning, and include marital planning. Trusts, either testamentary or revocable, can name successor trustees to provide for the continued management of a decedent's assets. The client should carefully consider the needs and capabilities of his survivors when determining the terms of the trust, including who should serve as trustee following his death.

Practitioner Tip: A revocable trust should be funded during a client's lifetime. This will avoid probate of the assets that have been transferred to the revocable trust during the client's lifetime.

Wills or revocable trusts can include a disclaimer provision that designates where property will pass if the surviving spouse disclaims an interest in the decedent's property. A spouse who does not need the assets could consider disclaiming property up to the exemption equivalent amount to fund a disclaimer trust created by will or by a previously established revocable trust. The spouse is entitled to receive an income interest in the trust, if needed, and the assets are not includable in the estate.

Practitioner Tip: Wills are revocable documents; therefore, provisions in testamentary trusts can easily be changed as the testator's personal and financial circumstances change. For example, beneficiaries can be changed in the will or the revocable trust, but they cannot be changed in an irrevocable trust.

PLANNING FOR INCAPACITY

There are many ways to plan for a client's incapacity. Many clients do not anticipate their future incapacity until it is too late. Financial planners should ensure that clients are aware of the importance of incapacity planning and that clients take the steps necessary to implement a plan.

Long-term care insurance should be considered for clients whose savings are insufficient to cover a prolonged nursing home stay, because their assets might not be available to their spouse or ultimately their heirs if the client's health were to decline substantially. Disability policies should be acquired to provide income to the spouse and family members and to pay for medical expenses in the event the breadwinner is unable to work.

Durable powers of attorney name an individual to handle an incapacitated individual's financial matters. Durable powers can be used to transfer additional assets to trusts if the principal becomes incapacitated, as long as the document is accepted by the principal's banks and investment firms. Durable powers of attorney can become "stale" after a number of years, increasing the likelihood that a financial institution will not accept the document. Also, durable powers limit the ability of the attorney-in-fact to act in certain situations and should contain adequate powers to allow the attorney-in-fact to address any anticipated needs.

Every adult should have a health care power of attorney, naming an individual to make decisions regarding health care for them. These durable powers should contain Health Insurance Portability and Accountability Act (HIPAA) provisions, or there should be a separate HIPAA authorization form. The Health Insurance Portability and Accountability Act of 1996 protects patient privacy, and without the form a health care agent may not be able to confer with the principal's health care providers. A durable power of attorney, health care directives, living will, and HIPAA authorization form should be kept at the principal's home in an accessible location, rather than in the principal's safe deposit box.

Funded revocable trusts typically provide for a client's incapacity in addition to providing for the distribution of assets following a client's death. One of the major benefits of a funded revocable trust is that a successor trustee can readily step in following a client's disability and assume management of the trust assets without delay or the use of a durable power of attorney.

An alternative to the funded revocable trust is the standby trust, which provides for the management of an individual's assets in the specific case of incapacity. The grantor can be the trustee and beneficiary of a standby trust and can name a contingent trustee to manage trust assets in the event the grantor becomes incapacitated.

Practitioner Tip: New clients might have an unfunded revocable trust; the question to ask them is, "What is its intended purpose?" If the trust is meant to be used as a standby trust, then the client needs to obtain a durable power of attorney and name a successor trustee. Financial planners can offer to help clients fund their revocable trusts by helping them transfer assets into it. This avoids probate and reduces estate administrative costs. The discussion the planner has with a client about planning for incapacity can lead to a broader conversation about the need for adequate life, disability, and long-term care insurance.

PROPERTY CONSIDERATIONS

Property ownership and titling affect the income and estate tax aspects of a current plan and can influence how real property is transferred during the owner's lifetime or at death. Valuation issues should be considered when evaluating the suitability of any transfer techniques. For example:

- The nature, condition, size, and location of the property and any zoning restrictions

- How suitable the property is for its actual or intended use and how trends of development and economic conditions affect it

- The market value of comparable properties and whether the property can be easily sold

- Whether the property can be partitioned for a partial sale to pay taxes, debts, and expenses, or whether it can be divided easily among beneficiaries

- The value of net income received from the property and how dependent the owner is on this income to pay for living expenses

- The value accepted by state probate courts for purposes of state death taxes

Jointly Held Property

Property held as joint tenancy with right of survivorship (JTWROS) with nonspouses results in taxation of the entire property in the estate of the first joint owner to die—except to the extent the survivor can prove contribution. Then, whatever the survivor receives and does not consume or give away will be included (and taxed a second time) in the survivor's gross estate.

Practitioner Tip: It is important to plan how the taxes associated with these assets are to be allocated among other beneficiaries of the estate. It is entirely possible that the joint assets pass to one person, and the taxes associated with these assets are charged to another.

Even when property is jointly owned between spouses, the surviving spouse can give away or leave the property to anyone he or she wants to at death, regardless of the wishes of the deceased spouse. The joint owner could possibly squander, gamble, give away, or lose the property to creditors, and the decedent's executor could be faced with a lack of adequate cash to pay estate taxes and other settlement expenses.

Trusts can hold and protect real property in addition to providing clients with the benefit of professional management, investment advice, and avoidance of probate. Qualified personal residence trusts (QPRTs) can be established to reduce transfer taxes when a home is initially transferred to the trust, and to keep appreciating home values out of the client's estate if the client survives the designated term.

LIFE INSURANCE

Most clients are unaware of the costs of settling an estate or how quickly taxes and other expenses must be paid after death. Worse yet, these expenses can force the sale of assets during an unfavorable market, result in the loss of control of a family business, or force liquidation of retirement assets if cash is insufficient to pay for these expenses. Advance planning is clearly needed. One solution is to acquire adequate life insurance to pay estate debts, taxes, funeral, and administrative expenses, and to provide adequate income to family members after the policy owner's death.

An insurance needs analysis conducted by a planner will reveal the proper amount of life insurance needed for the family breadwinner or for a key person in a corporation in the event of premature death. Life insurance beneficiary designations should be reviewed, and contingent beneficiaries should be named in the policy.

Be aware that whenever life insurance is paid to the insured's estate, it is needlessly subjected to probate and to the claims of the insured's creditors. In most estate planning situations, life insurance should be payable only to a named beneficiary or a trust.

When life insurance proceeds are payable outright to a beneficiary, the beneficiary might not be emotionally, legally, or financially capable of handling the money. Settlement options help ensure that payments are made over a period of years, or a trust can be named beneficiary allowing the trustee to handle the proceeds. Proceeds can also be paid to a trust for the purpose of professional management.

Practitioner Tip: A financial planner should review the beneficiary designation of any existing life insurance policy that is not held in trust to ensure that proceeds are not payable to the estate, and that any named beneficiaries are capable of handling the proceeds.

Life Insurance Policy Transfers

An irrevocable life insurance trust (ILIT) can be established to own a life insurance policy on the insured's life to remove the death benefit from the owner's gross estate. This is accomplished if the owner/insured transfers the policy to the trust more than three years before the owner's death, or if the trust purchases a new policy on the owner's life. However, when a policy is transferred to an unfunded ILIT, the transfer can be a taxable gift, and subsequent premium payments gifted to the trust could be subject to gift tax as well. An ILIT can be drafted with Crummey powers to create present interests for trust beneficiaries so that annual exclusions are available to offset the grantor's taxable gifts. If the grantor's spouse consents to split the gift, then these taxable gifts can be further reduced.

An existing ILIT should be reviewed by an attorney to ensure that the grantor is not the trustee, the trust has the flexibility to remove or replace corporate trustees, and that beneficiaries have not been given general powers of appointment that are broader than Crummey power restrictions.

Practitioner Tip: A financial planner should review the insurance policy in trust for any incidents of ownership that would cause inclusion of the death benefit in the insured's estate. When grandchildren are trust beneficiaries, the planner should ensure that the client's generation-skipping transfer (GST) tax exemption is properly allocated to the trust and to transfers of annual premiums. The planner can offer to manage the trust proceeds at the client's death, or to become a member of the investment team in the position of family advisor.

Where a husband is required by a divorce decree or separation agreement to purchase or maintain insurance on his life, he will receive no income tax deduction for premium payments if he owns the policy—even if his ex-wife is named as irrevocable beneficiary. No alimony deduction is allowed on the cash values in a policy the husband is required to transfer to his ex-wife under a divorce decree. The safest way to ensure a deduction is for the husband to increase his tax deductible alimony and for the ex-wife to purchase new insurance on his life, which she owns and on which she is the beneficiary.

Practitioner Tip: It is extremely important for a financial planner of each recently divorced spouse to immediately review the client's life, health and disability policies, and insurance situation.

MINIMIZING GIFT TAXES

There are many reasons why a client may wish to transfer or gift assets to others. These transfers should be reviewed to determine whether there are any gift tax consequences.

Gifts that are qualified transfers are not subject to gift taxes. Qualified transfers are payments made directly to an educational institution to pay for someone's tuition or to a medical facility or doctor to pay for health care expenses. These gifts are not subject to gift tax; therefore, the donor's annual exclusion and unified credit are not used against these payments and are preserved for future gifts.

Gifts made to others are not necessarily taxable gifts. Gifts that do not exceed the annual exclusion amount are not taxed. Split gifts allow a married couple to gift up to $28,000 in 2015 before a taxable gift is made. And if a taxable gift is made, the tax can be offset by the donor's unified credit.

An effective method for reducing the value of a person's estate is to gift property to others. Tax planning strategies that reduce the estate tax base reduce the amount of wealth subject to transfer taxes. For example, a gift of $10,000 to ten donees reduces a donor's estate tax base by $100,000, which lowers the estate tax by $40,000 in 2015, if the donor is in the highest marginal transfer tax bracket. Taxable gifts are added to the estate tax return as adjusted taxable gifts, but a decedent's unified credit might be available to offset an estate tax liability. It is better to add back the adjusted taxable gift, valued at the date of the gift, than to include the property and its appreciated value in the owner's gross estate.

Practitioner Tip: Techniques and strategies selected to reduce gift and estate taxes must be examined for their effect on a client's overall estate plan. Remember that the donor forfeits ownership, income, and control of the property when completed gifts are made, and the property cannot be reclaimed in the future.

Leveraged Gifts

Leveraged gifts are transfers made for a low gift tax value relative to the present or future value of the property. An example of a leveraged gift is a transfer of a life insurance policy to the policy's beneficiary or to an ILIT. What makes this gift attractive is the low gift tax value of the policy compared to the high tax-free death benefit the beneficiary will receive at the insured's death. Moreover, the death benefit will not be included in the insured's gross estate unless the policy was transferred within three years of his death.

Another leveraged gift is a contribution made to a 529 plan. The contribution qualifies for an annual exclusion because the gift is a present-interest gift. A donor can contribute

$70,000 for a beneficiary in one year and elect to spread the taxable gift over five years, or he can contribute $140,000 through gift splitting. This is a very beneficial way to leverage, or make the most of, annual exclusions and to remove the value of the gift from the contributor's estate five years after the gift was made.

Other techniques that make use of leveraged gifts are gifts of remainder interests in life estates and in split-interest trusts. A grantor retained income trust (GRIT), grantor retained annuity trust (GRAT), or grantor retained unitrust (GRUT) can pass the appreciation in trust property to remainder beneficiaries and remove the trust property from the donor's estate, assuming the donor survives the income term. GRITs must name unrelated beneficiaries as remaindermen, but GRATs and GRUTs can name family members as beneficiaries. When property is transferred to these trusts, the gift tax is not based on the property's fair market value; instead, it is valued on the property's remainder interest, which is a discounted amount. Homeowners can also transfer primary and vacation homes into QPRTs to remove the value of the property from their gross estates and pass the appreciation of the home to family members at a lower gift tax value.

An intentionally defective grantor trust (IDGT) is made "defective" by adding grantor trust powers that do not cause inclusion in the grantor's estate. A business owner can sell closely held non-voting stock to the trust at a discount via a promissory note and pay the income tax, which in essence is a tax-free gift made to the trust beneficiaries.

Another example of leveraging occurs in family limited partnerships when parents, as general partners, transfer their partnership shares to their children or other family members—the limited partners. The value of the shares is reduced by annual exclusions and two discounts, for minority interests and lack of marketability, which reduce the transfer tax costs. Properly structured family limited partnerships (FLPs) can shift taxable income to limited partners in lower tax brackets, and gifting can remove limited partnership interests and future appreciation from the general partners' gross estates.

Taxable gifts can be reduced or eliminated by annual exclusions, unified credits, and GST tax exemptions if present-interest gifts are made to skip persons. Although the gift tax and GST tax exemption equivalent is $5,430,000 in 2015, this amount is doubled when spouses consent to gift splitting. GST tax exemptions can be leveraged by allocations to trusts when trust assets are expected to appreciate over time, thereby eliminating GST taxes on future distributions. In indirect skip trusts, any funds not distributed to children are unavailable to their creditors and are not taxed in their estates.

Practitioner Tip: Practitioner Tip: An estate plan that creates a trust solely for the benefit of the grandchildren funded with the maximum generation-skipping exemption at the transferor's death can result in less money available to the estate for the children. For example, a widow with a net worth of $10 million after estate taxes who leaves an amount equal to her GST exemption in trust for her grandchildren with the remainder to her children would create a testamentary GST trust funded with $5,430,000 in 2015, leaving only $4,570,000 for her children.

The Downside of Gifting

Gifting can result in unintended consequences for the donor and the donee.

- When a property owner adds a new owner to a deed, the property is no longer held in sole ownership and the owner has made a gift that could be taxable.

- A donee receives a basis in property that is not stepped-up at the donor's death. This can subject the property to a capital gains tax if the donee sells the property in the future.

- A gift of appreciating property that produces income is ideal to transfer to others as long as the donor is not dependent on the income for financial support.

- Donors can make gifts directly to recipients because they are unwilling to establish a trust or pay the legal fees. However, gifts should be placed in trust when donees are minors or incapable of managing or unwilling to manage property on their own.

MINIMIZING ESTATE TAXES

Financial planners should periodically review the value of a client's estate to determine whether there is a current or a potential estate tax liability. For single clients with estates greater than $5,430,000 or married clients with estates more than $10.86 million there are many estate planning techniques to reduce the estate tax base that often involve the use of trusts.

Irrevocable trusts remove assets from a grantor's estate if the grantor does not retain any rights or control over the income or corpus. They can also be drafted to provide some measure of creditor protection for the surviving spouse, and they can keep family assets intact in the event of divorce. In most situations, the grantor cannot change the beneficiaries or terms of the trust, or take back trust property when personal or financial circumstances change.

A bypass trust funded with the exemption equivalent amount of $5,430,000 in 2015 is not taxed in a decedent's estate, nor is the trust corpus or appreciation taxed in the surviving spouse's estate. Children who are beneficiaries also receive trust property free of estate taxes after the parent/beneficiary's death. But an estate plan that bequeaths the exemption amount to children with the remainder to the surviving spouse could leave less of an estate for the spouse if the exemption continues to increase over time.

An *irrevocable life insurance trust (ILIT)* owns a life insurance policy on the insured's life, which can reduce the estate tax but does not allow for any changes to policy provisions.

Additional methods for reducing the estate tax base at death involve the use of:

- Estate equalization

- The marital deduction

- The charitable deduction

- The unified credit

- Special use valuation

- The alternate valuation date

Estate equalization can reduce estate taxes in both spouses' estates. The executor can prepay the estate tax when the first spouse dies, and each spouse can allocate his own GST exemptions to trusts or bequests made to skip person beneficiaries.

The unlimited marital deduction eliminates any estate taxes on property transferred to a spouse, but it merely defers the tax until that spouse's death. Reliance on the estate tax marital deduction wastes the decedent's unified credit, and the property and its appreciation will be taxed in the spouse's estate. However, with portability, the decedent spouse's unused exclusion amount (DSUEA) is transferred to the surviving spouse to shelter up to $10,860,000 in assets from taxation in the spouse's estate.

The charitable deduction is subtracted from a decedent's adjusted gross estate to reduce the taxable estate. Charitable gifts or bequests can result in income, gift, and estate tax benefits for the donor, but there will be less property available for heirs once the charitable transfer is made. Life insurance purchased for wealth replacement purposes can ensure that family members or others will receive an equitable amount of the estate at the insured's death.

The unified credit is used to offset a person's gift and estate tax liabilities and can shelter up to $2,117,800 in taxes in 2015.

Special use valuation allows for certain farm or real property in a closely held business to be valued at less than FMV in the decedent owner's estate. Certain qualifications must be met and two ratio tests applied before the executor can deduct up to $1,100,000 of the qualifying real property in 2015. A recapture tax is imposed if the heir disposes of the real property, or if it ceases to be used as "qualified use property" within 10 years of the decedent's death.

The alternate valuation date is used if there is a net decrease in the value of a decedent's gross estate and estate tax liability six months after death. The alternate valuation date cannot be used if estate taxes are eliminated through the marital deduction, so the surviving spouse could disclaim a portion of the assets to have them valued as of this date.

MINIMIZING INCOME TAXES

There is a growing concern for wealthier individuals that post-mortem federal and state income taxes could significantly affect the transfer of wealth to estate and trust beneficiaries. The high exclusion amount, which is indexed for inflation, is sufficient to shelter federal transfer taxes for most estates therefore strategies that reduce family income taxes should be examined. For example, assets included in a decedent's estate receive a step-up in income tax basis at death which could reduce or eliminate a capital gains tax when a beneficiary sells inherited property. This generates a greater income tax savings for a family than if the property had been previously gifted or transferred to a trust during the decedent's lifetime, and then subsequently sold, because there is no step-up in income tax basis for lifetime gifts.

Married couples should determine whether it is more advantageous to rely on the use of portability or to use credit shelter trust planning. Couples whose wealth is not expected to grow beyond a combined exclusion amount might want to consider relying on portability. When one spouse dies, assets included in his estate receive a step-up in basis to the decedent's date of death value. If these same assets are transferred directly to the surviving spouse, a second step-up in basis will occur at the surviving spouse's death, assuming these assets are included in the survivor's estate. Assuming portability is elected and the surviving spouse is in a lower income tax bracket than a trust, then income would be taxed at a lower rate.

There are also some clear disadvantages for relying on portability to transfer estate assets at death. Assets, and the appreciation from those assets, will be included in the surviving spouse's estate and could be subject to federal and state estate taxes or state inheritance taxes. To date, most state have not adopted portability, therefore transferring assets to the surviving spouse rather than to a credit shelter trust could result in a higher state level estate or inheritance tax on the couple's combined estate. The decedent spouse's unused exclusion amount is not adjusted for inflation, and when combined with the surviving spouse's exclusion, it may not be sufficient to shelter all estate taxes at the surviving spouse's death. Another concern is that non-tax benefits of a credit shelter trust will be lost such as creditor protection and professional asset management. Therefore, the income tax savings associated with portability must be compared with the tax and non-tax benefits of credit shelter planning.

Chapter Highlights

- Financial planners and attorneys need to work together throughout the estate planning process to provide clients with a plan that is coordinated with their objectives.

- Changing circumstances and client assumptions have a direct impact on an estate plan and its successful execution.

- Everyone needs to obtain legal documents such as a will, durable power of attorney, and health care proxy to protect themselves, their families, and their property interests.

- Debts, taxes, and administrative expenses must be paid at death, and a life insurance policy can provide the estate with the liquidity it needs, as well as financial support for the family.

- Leveraged gifts provide a greater benefit for a donee at a lower transfer tax cost to the donor.

- Estate tax reduction techniques and trusts should be examined and implemented to reduce the taxable estate.

Review Questions

29-1. Which of the following situations can affect a client's current estate plan?

A. A spousal inheritance

B. The impending divorce of a child

C. A significant loss in the value of the client's real property and investment assets

D. An investment rate of return presumed to be 10% for the next 20 years.

29-2. Techniques that reduce the estate tax base could require prior planning to be effective. Which of the following techniques does not require inter-vivos planning?

A. Estate equalization

B. Utilization of the alternate valuation date

C. A testamentary By-pass Trust

D. A Disclaimer Trust

29-3. Which documents should be kept in a client's safe deposit box?

A. Tax returns for the past 10 years

B. Durable powers of attorney, health care proxies, living wills, and HIPAA authorization forms

C. Funeral and burial instructions

D. Birth and marriage certificates, passports, deeds, and titles

29-4. What is an example of a leveraged gift?

A. Contributions to custodial accounts for minors

B. Creation of a wealth replacement trust

C. The transfer of appreciating artwork to a GRIT for a partner

D. A testamentary QTIP trust

29-5. Helen, a widow, changed the deed to her home to add her son Colton as a joint owner by changing ownership to JTWROS. Which of the following statements is/are incorrect?

A. Helen made a gift to Colton of one-half of the home, but if she predeceases him, the gift is not added as an adjusted taxable gift to her IRS Form 706.

B. Colton will receive a full step-up in the property's basis to fair market value at Helen's death.

C. Colton can change the deed to a tenancy in common without obtaining Helen's consent.

D. Helen and Colton share unequal ownership in the home because Colton did not contribute to the purchase of the home or pay any property taxes, maintenance fees, or household expenses.

Answers to Chapter Review Questions

CHAPTER 1 ANSWERS

1-1 Answer: A.

B is incorrect because all adults need estate planning regardless of the size of their estate. C is incorrect because courts will select guardians and conservators if trusts or powers of attorney are not available to manage an incapacitated person's affairs.

1-2 Answer: C.

This is known as the "general-specific" test; no violation arises from the sharing of legal knowledge that is either generally informatory or, if specific, is so obvious as to be common knowledge.

1-3 Answer: C.

It is the financial planner's role to recognize deficiencies in the client's estate plan and refer the client to an estate planning attorney, or assemble an estate planning team if other professionals with special expertise are needed to develop and implement estate planning recommendations.

1-4 Answer: All of the above.

1-5 Answer: B.

The estate planning attorney, as captain of the estate planning team, takes a leadership role in making estate planning recommendations, drafting the documents, and managing the team of professionals.

1-6 Answer: A and B.

C is incorrect because the executor collects the decedent's assets to pay for estate debts, taxes, and expenses. D is incorrect because a trustee does not necessarily specialize in estate administration and may retain an attorney that specializes in the administration of an estate.

CHAPTER 2 ANSWERS

2-1 Answer: D.

The full fair market value of the condo ($160,000) is included in Jane's estate because she bought the condo without any contribution from Keith. Keith will inherit the condo with a complete step-up in basis, so there is no capital gains tax liability if he sells the condo for $160,000. Jane made a gift to Keith of one-half the value of the property, or $75,000, when she titled the condo jointly with right of survivorship. This gift is subject to gift taxes, and the taxable portion will be included in her estate tax calculation as an adjusted taxable gift. Because Jane paid for all expenses and taxes related to the condo, and Keith did not make any financial contributions, the full value of the condo is included in her gross estate.

2-2 Answer: A.

Jill's estate will include 40% of the fair market value of the home at her death, or $144,000. Alan will inherit Jill's stepped-up basis in the property, which he will add to his original basis for a new basis of $324,000. Because the property passes to Alan by operation of law, the property will avoid probate. Alan did not make a gift to Jill because each joint tenant contributed to the purchase price of the home. Although Alan and Jill contributed disproportionate amounts to buy the home, with a JTWROS they have equal ownership of the property.

2-3 Answer: B.

When assets are held jointly with right of survivorship between two spouses, it does not matter which spouse actually purchased the property, it is presumed that each spouse owns half of the property, and one-half of the property will be included in Sal's estate. It does not matter whether Kim did not contribute to the purchase price. This is different than when an asset is held jointly with rights of survivorship with a nonspouse. The assets automatically pass to the joint property holder and cannot be bequeathed to another individual; therefore, Kim will automatically receive the house and the investment account, regardless of what Sal's will says.

2-4 Answer: B.

The following will be included in Jack's gross estate: one-half of the residence owned with Jane ($500,000), common stock ($900,000), municipal bonds ($300,000), investment real estate ($500,000), life insurance ($1,000,000), and the IRA ($550,000). Only half of the residence is included because Jane and Jack are married. Jack is the owner of the stock, municipal bonds, investment real estate, life insurance, and IRA; therefore, these assets are included. Because Jane owns the mutual funds, they will not be included in Jack's estate.

2-5 Answer: D.

Tenancy by the entirety is a form of property ownership that can be held only between spouses. When an asset is held as tenants by the entirety, during life, each spouse holds an undivided interest in the property, and neither spouse may unilaterally transfer his interest in the property. In addition, although creditors can attach a lien to the property, they cannot force the sale of the asset to satisfy one spouse's debt. At death, one-half of the value of the property will be included in the deceased spouse's estate, and the asset will automatically pass to the surviving spouse.

CHAPTER 3 ANSWERS

3-1 Answer: A.

Only 10 states have this form of ownership between spouses with each spouse owning a one-half interest in the community property.

3-2 Answers:

A. Not community property. Assets acquired by gift or inheritance are not considered community property.

B. Community property. If the joint checking account was funded with earnings after Jane and Jake married, the automobile is considered a community asset.

C. Not community property. Because the house was a separate asset and has been segregated, it will remain a separate asset after they move to Texas.

D. Not community property. Because the checking account was funded in a common-law state, it will retain its character as a separate asset when they move to Texas.

E. Community property. Because California is a quasi-community property state, and because the savings account was funded after their marriage, the savings account will be considered a community asset.

3-3 Answer: True.

Carol and Dick moved from a common-law state to a quasi-community property state. Therefore, you need to look back to see how the property was originally acquired to determine whether the property remains separate property or becomes community property after the move. Carol and Dick acquired all of their property interests in New York after their marriage. Their property would have been community property if they had originally acquired it in California. Therefore, all of their assets are considered community property after moving to California.

3-4 Answer: False.

Lester and Naomi's assets were originally acquired after they were married, thus their property was treated as community property when they moved to California. Assume, however, that Lester had titled all of the assets in his name after moving to California. When he died, 100% of the assets would have been included in his gross estate. But because the assets are community property, Naomi would have a vested right to half of the property. Lester could dispose of only half of the assets in his estate, which would also go through probate.

3-5 Answer B.

When a couple moves from a community property state to a non-community property state, any community property assets will retain the community property character. Once an asset is community property, it will always be considered community property. A and D are incorrect because, the inheritance and the investment account Shawn had before marrying Amy are not community property. C is incorrect because they funded the new investment account after moving to Florida and so it is not a community asset. Only Amy's savings account is community property.

CHAPTER 4 ANSWERS

4-1 Answer: Letters B, D, E, F, G, and J will be subject to probate.

4-2 Answer: C.

Common stock ($900,000) and municipal bonds ($300,000). The residence will automatically pass to Jane because it is owned jointly with right of survivorship. The life insurance and IRA will pass by beneficiary designation, investment real estate ($500,000), life insurance ($1,000,000), and IRA ($550,000). Only half of the residence is included because Jane and Jack are married. Jack is the owner of the stock, municipal bonds, investment real estate, life insurance, and IRA; therefore, these assets are included. Because Jane owns the mutual funds, they will not be included in Jack's estate.

4-3 Answer D.

Because their residence is titled joint (with right of survivorship) it will automatically pass to Jane. Both life insurance and IRA assets will pass by beneficiary designation, and in this case, Jack has named Jane as the beneficiary. The investment real estate titled to Jack's revocable trust will not automatically pass to Jane because it will pass per the terms of the trust.

4-4 Answer: A.

Property owned jointly with right of survivorship will pass by operation of law to the joint property holder and will not be subject to probate. Assets that are owned by a revocable trust will pass per the terms of the trust and will not be subject to probate.

4-5 Answer A.

A decedent's interest in property owned as tenants-in-common will pass per the terms of a decedent's will, or by intestate succession if there is no will and the property is subject to probate.

CHAPTER 5 ANSWERS

5-1 Answer: E.

All the above are the executor's duties.

5-2 Answer: B.

The probate process is a court proceeding to determine the validity of a will. Because it is a court proceeding, it is a public proceeding; therefore, will contests can be brought that cause the proceedings to take a great deal of time and cost a great deal of money. If a decedent dies without a will, the laws of intestacy determine the distribution of assets within the probate proceeding.

5-3 Answer: B.

Probate assets are the assets transferred under the provisions of a will. Only separately owned assets transfer under the provisions of a will. Therefore, the residence, brokerage account, and life insurance policy will pass under contractual provisions or by operation of the law, not pursuant to the provisions of the will. Therefore, there is no probate.

5-4 Answer: C.

Only assets transferred under the provisions of a will (or through intestate succession) are defined as probate assets. The assets transferring under the provisions of a will are those that were owned solely by the decedent on the date of death and they do not transfer to heirs under either operation of law or a beneficiary designation.

5-5 Answer B.

The expense and delay associated with probate can be considered one of the major disadvantages of the probate process. The remaining choices are all considered advantages of probate.

CHAPTER 6 ANSWERS

6-1 Answer: C.

The testator must have the mental capacity to sign a will. He has the requisite capacity if the testator (1) knows the nature and extent of his property, and (2) knows the natural objects of his bounty.

6-2 Answer: B.

Only half of his one-half interest in the real estate owned as a tenancy in common with his brother will pass to his wife under the provisions of his will.

6-3 Answer: C.

A codicil, executed with all of the testamentary formalities, is needed to change the will.

6-4 Answer: D.

It is appropriate to consider updating/reviewing a will in all of the aforementioned circumstances.

6-5 Answer: C.

All members of the estate planning team should be able to review a will to determine whether there is something "wrong" with it. Because each member of the estate planning team has a different relationship with the testator, all team members—not only the attorney—should have an opportunity to indicate problem areas in the will based on their knowledge of the client.

6-6 Answer: B.

A living trust is a separate document from a will. Therefore, the trustee of a living trust is appointed in the living trust, not the will.

CHAPTER 7 ANSWERS

7-1 Answer: D.

Courts do not grant a guardian legal title to a ward's property. With a durable power of attorney, legal title to the principal's property is not transferred to the attorney-in-fact. The principal retains legal title of his own property.

7-2 Answer: C.

Special needs trusts provide money for extra services not covered by government programs while preserving the beneficiary's eligibility for public assistance programs.

7-3 Answer: C.

A springing durable power of attorney is activated when an agent receives written notification from a physician that the principal is declared to be mentally or physically incompetent.

7-4 Answer: A.

A health care agent is appointed in a health care power of attorney document, not in a living will.

7-5 Answer: A.

CHAPTER 8 ANSWERS

8-1 Answer: B.

A testamentary trust is a trust created under a decedent's will. Any property passing to the trust by will is subject to probate. A testamentary trust is revocable until the testator's death; however, it becomes irrevocable at the decedent's death.

8-2 Answer: B.

Assets transferred to a revocable trust are included in a decedent's estate because the decedent has retained control and use of the assets for his lifetime. Revocable trusts are an attractive alternative to wills because any assets passing per the terms of the trust are not subject to probate and are not a matter of public record. A revocable trust may also provide for the grantor's incapacity.

8-3 Answer: C.

8-4 Answer: B.

Spendthrift provisions limit both a child's ability to squander assets and a creditor's ability to reach trust assets. Outright distribution of trust property allows children to spend assets however they wish, including gambling, or allows creditors to access the assets. Sprinkle and spray provisions or a pour-over trust may be appropriate strategies, but not the most appropriate strategies.

8-5 Answer D.

Once a decedent dies, the terms of any trusts he established in his lifetime cannot be changed. Trusts can be established to benefit both individuals and organizations, such as charities. One of the benefits of a revocable trust is that trust assets can be used by the grantor during his lifetime. An irrevocable trust is just that – irrevocable – so the grantor cannot change the terms of the trust once it is established.

CHAPTER 9 ANSWERS

9-1 Answer: A.

By definition, a simple trust requires that all income be paid to the trust beneficiary and the trust beneficiary will be subject to the income tax liability. B is incorrect because a simple trust requires that all income be paid to the beneficiary. C is incorrect because DNI does not apply to simple trusts —only income, and all income is distributed to the trust beneficiary. D is incorrect because the grantor is not responsible for the payment of income tax on a simple trust unless the grantor is the income beneficiary of the trust.

9-2 Answer: D.

If a decedent dies and is entitled to receive life insurance commissions and these commissions are paid to a beneficiary, this will be deemed to be an item of IRD because the beneficiary is responsible for the income tax liability. On death, the cash value of a life insurance policy is irrelevant, and life insurance death proceeds are not subject to income tax.

9-3 Answer: D.

This trust is a grantor trust for income tax purposes because the trustee has the power to apply trust income to purchase a life insurance policy on which Gordon is the insured. Because this is a grantor trust for income tax purposes, all income is taxed to the grantor rather than to the beneficiaries or the trust.

9-4 Answer: C.

Any estate tax attributable to the item of IRD is an income tax deduction to the beneficiary of the item of IRD.

9-5 Answer: B.

When a trust distributes income, the trust beneficiary receiving the property will be subject to income tax on that distribution. Income tax is passed through the trust to the beneficiary, based on the character of the distribution per the concept of DNI. A is incorrect because the basis of an asset is crucial in determining income tax upon the sale of that asset. An asset acquired by lifetime gift will have the donor's tax basis, while an asset acquired by bequest or at the donor's death will receive a step-up in basis to the date of death value. C is incorrect because income will be taxed either to the trust or to the beneficiary receiving the income. D is incorrect because a trust containing grantor trust provisions requires that income be taxed to the grantor, not the trust.

CHAPTER 10 ANSWERS

10-1 Answer: A.

Any one of these gifted properties would reduce Tony's gross estate by $600,000, but the vacation home will not be sold; therefore, the low basis in the property will not be subject to a capital gains tax if the property is gifted. The cottages should remain in Tony's estate to receive a complete step-up in basis at his death to reduce the capital gains tax when the cottages are subsequently sold. Tony should sell his land and use the loss to offset any investment gains and thereby reduce his income tax liability.

10-2 Answer: B and C.

B is correct because a gift of a remainder interest in property is a completed transfer, and the value of the gift is the present value of the remainder interest. C is correct because if an author gifts the right to future royalties, the gift is a single gift, not a series of gifts, and the gift is complete on the date the right to future income is assigned. A is incorrect because property transferred into a revocable trust is not a completed gift, and a change of a beneficiary designation is not considered a gift. D is incorrect. With a joint brokerage account, a gift is not complete until the noncontributing account owner makes a withdrawal for his own benefit.

10-3 Answer: B.

When GM adds GD as the joint owner on the account, no gift is made. Only when GD takes a distribution from the account for her own benefit will GM have made a gift to GD. Because GM and GD are not spouses, on the death of the first owner, 100% of the assets in this account will be included in the decedent's estate unless the survivor can prove contribution to the account. An asset owned jointly with right of survivorship will pass automatically by operation of law to the surviving owner and avoid probate.

10-4 Answer: C.

There is no alternate valuation date available for gift taxes, but an alternate valuation date is available for estate tax valuation purposes.

10-5 Answer: C.

As a general rule, when a gift is made, the donor's basis in the property is carried over to the donee as long as the property was transferred at a gain. This carry-over basis could be increased by a gift tax paid by the donor attributable to appreciation. If the FMV of the property on the date of the gift is less than the donor's basis in the property, the basis in the hands of the donee is equal to the FMV of the property on the date of the gift.

10-6 Answer: D.

The unified credit is also known as the *applicable credit*. The exemption equivalent amount this year is $5,430,000, and the tax on $5,430,000 is $2,117,800. The unified credit amount is $2,117,800, which is subtracted from the tax for a gift or estate tax liability of zero. Gifts or estates of less than $5,430,000 will leave unused a portion of the unified credit amount. The unified credit must be used to offset the tax on all taxable gifts.

CHAPTER 11 ANSWERS

11-1 Answer: A and B.

A gift is made when a debt is canceled and when the sole owner retitles a property to share its ownership. C is incorrect because a gift is not made until the son withdraws money from the account for his own use. D is not correct because a revocable trust is an incomplete transfer.

11-2 Answer: D.

The gift to Adrian's wife is a present-interest gift that can be reduced by Adrian's annual exclusion and a marital deduction to eliminate gift tax liability. A is incorrect because payment of tuition is an exempt gift. B is incorrect since the trust has a sprinkle provision; the twins will not receive mandatory distributions of income each year, so they have future interests. C is incorrect. The artwork in the trust is non-income-producing property; therefore no annual exclusion is available to Adrian.

11-3 Answer: C.

Kristen received income for a term certain, which is terminable interest property. Therefore, Jonathan cannot take a marital deduction to reduce this taxable gift, although he can take an annual exclusion. Remainder interests, qualified-income interests, and life estates with general powers of appointment do qualify for the marital deduction.

11-4 Answer: A and D.

Martin and Regina made a gift of $200,000, which is reduced by gift splitting and an annual exclusion for a taxable gift of $86,000 for each spouse. This amount will be added to their individual estate tax returns as an adjusted taxable gift. B is incorrect because each spouse will have to file a separate gift tax return this year. C is incorrect because a unified credit offsets a tax on a taxable gift. A tax on $86,000 is $19,880, so Martin and Regina's unified credit of 2,117,800 is reduced to 2,097,920.

11-5 Answer: B.

The present value of the life estate gift is $882,360, which is reduced by Lynne's annual exclusion of $14,000 for a taxable gift of $868,360. Lynne cannot reduce the value of this taxable gift by a marital deduction, because she gave Kiron terminable-interest property. Lynne's taxable gift to Beth is the present value of the remainder interest, or $117,640, which cannot be reduced by an annual exclusion. Lynne's total taxable gifts equal $986,000.

CHAPTER 12 ANSWERS

12-1 Answer: B.

A Section 2503(c) trust can accumulate income until all income and principal must be distributed at age 21. With a § 2503(b) trust, the income must be distributed every year. UGMA accounts cannot hold real estate, and although a UTMA can hold real estate, the building would be transferred to Tucker at age 18, the state's age of majority.

12-2 Answer: B.

The Section 2503(b) trust permits multiple beneficiaries, and all income must be distributed to an income beneficiary at least annually. Elliot and Jean can take only annual exclusions for the gift made to Rachael, because she has a present interest in the trust and Greg does not. A sprinkle trust would permit the trustee to make discretionary distributions of income, which is not the objective of this trust.

12-3 Answer: C.

When a donor contributes $70,000 to a 529 Plan and dies within five years of making the gift, a pro rata amount of the gift is included in the donor's estate, not a portion of the account balance.

12-4 Answer: A, B, and D

All of these techniques, except for option C, shifts wealth and income taxes to minors, who are presumably in a lower tax bracket. A Section 2503(b) trust must hold income-producing property so income can be distributed annually to all income beneficiaries.

12-5 Answer: C.

Under kiddie tax rules, the first $1,050 is sheltered by a child's standard deduction. The next $1,050 is taxed at Tara's rate of 10%, or $105. The remaining $900 is taxed at the parent's rate (25%), or $225. Tara would pay $330 ($105 + $225).

CHAPTER 13 ANSWERS

13-1 Answer: D.

The closely held stock will not be included in Roger's gross estate because he gifted it away before his death, and the transfer is not subject to the three-year rule. However, the gift is subject to gift taxes, and if a gift tax must be paid, then the tax will be included in Roger's gross estate under the gross-up rule. A is incorrect because Roger was sole owner of the vacation home, which is included in his gross estate. B is incorrect, because Roger owned 100% of the home before making a gift of one-half of the property to his brother when he retitled the property JTWROS. Per the percentage-of-contribution rule, 100% of the value of the home is included in Roger's gross estate. C is incorrect because Roger had a general power of appointment over the trust property, which is included in his gross estate.

13-2 Answer: C.

Patti was the grantor of an irrevocable trust, but because she was the trustee and retained too much control over the trust, the value of the trust will be included in Patti's gross estate under Code section 2038. A is incorrect because Patti received a life estate rather than created a life estate for herself; therefore, Section 2036 does not apply. B is incorrect because Patti was the owner but not the insured of the policy, so the transfer is not subject to the three-year rule. D is incorrect because Patti had a limited power of appointment over the trust property.

13-3 Answer: B.

Glenn could have withdrawn the greater of $5,000 or 5% of the trust assets in the year of his death, or $25,000. Because Glenn did not withdraw any money before he died, the full $25,000 was included in his gross estate.

13-4 Answer: C.

Tenancy in common permits ownership in unequal shares of a property. Kate contributed 25% of the home's acquisition cost, so 25% of the value of the home is included in her gross estate.

13-5 Answer: D.

Per Code section 2035, the three-year rule applies to a transfer of property that would have been included in the decedent's gross estate under Sections 2036, 2037, and 2038. When a life estate (§ 2036) is relinquished, the property's value at the date of a decedent's death is included in the gross estate.

CHAPTER 14 ANSWERS

14-1 Answer: B.

Funeral and administrative expenses, debts, and taxes can be deducted from the gross estate to arrive at the adjusted gross estate, from which the marital deduction is taken. All of Burt's expenses can be subtracted from his gross estate ($20,000,000) with the exception of the mortgage on the home, because that is jointly owned property. Burt's executor can deduct only $400,000 of the mortgage balance from Burt's estate for an adjusted gross estate of $17,900,000. Therefore, the amount of the marital deduction is $17,900,000.

14-2 Answer: B.

A is incorrect; the gift to the son is not a taxable gift because $10,000 is less than the annual exclusion amount. B is correct because after gift-splitting and the use of annual exclusions, Arlene and Mitch each made taxable gifts of $16,000, which will be added to their estate tax return as adjusted taxable gifts. C is incorrect because the fair market value of the trust will be included in Theresa's estate. Therefore, the $200,000 taxable gift of the remainder interest will not be included as an adjusted taxable gift. D is incorrect because a direct payment made to a medical facility for health care is exempt from gift tax law.

14-3 Answer: A and C.

A is correct because Christopher made gifts totaling $250,000; therefore, his estate is reduced by $250,000. B is incorrect because the unified credit is restored in full on the estate tax return (2,117,800) regardless of the amount of taxable gifts made in a donor's lifetime. C is correct that $45,000 of adjusted taxable gifts is added to the estate tax return. Christopher's wife will also add $45,000 of adjusted taxable gifts to her estate tax return in addition to any future taxable gifts she makes in her lifetime. D is incorrect because neither Christopher nor his wife had to pay any gift taxes on the taxable gifts they made to their children in the past three years.

14-4 Answer: A.

The estate tax is tax inclusive because the money used to pay the tax is included in the decedent's gross estate and is subject to estate taxation.

14-5 Answer: All of the above.

CHAPTER 15 ANSWERS

15-1 Answer: D.

The husband received a life estate in the vacation home, which does not qualify for a marital deduction in his wife's estate because the interest in the home will end at his death. The husband has been given terminable interest property. As a result, a marital deduction is not available to the wife's estate and the value of the vacation home will not be included in the husband's gross estate at his death.

15-2 Answer: A and B.

A. Skip's revocable trust was included in his gross estate, and the trust property passing to Libby qualifies for the marital deduction in his estate. **B.** Skip, as owner of the life insurance policy on Libby's life, transferred ownership of the policy to Libby when he died; therefore, a marital deduction is available to his estate for the value of the policy included in Skip's gross estate. **C.** Olivia is a former spouse, so a marital deduction does not apply. **D.** The life estate in the cottage is not included in Skip's gross estate.

15-3 Answer: A.

A QDOT is established to transfer marital property at death. Gifts made to a non-citizen spouse have a significantly higher exclusion amount ($147,000).

15-4 Answer: D.

All of the statements are correct except for D. When a surviving spouse disclaims the decedent's property, no marital deduction is available in the decedent spouse's estate. This enables the decedent's estate to fully utilize the unified credit to offset an estate tax on the disclaimed property.

15-5 Answer: A and C.

A is correct because the property in the disclaimer trust will bypass taxation in Dirk's estate since he has a terminable interest in the property. **C** is correct because the disclaimed property will not receive a marital deduction in Louise's estate. **B** is incorrect because Dirk can disclaim a partial interest in Louise's property. **D** is incorrect because an executor does not qualify disclaimed property. The recipient must follow IRS requirements to disclaim property in the proper manner.

CHAPTER 16 ANSWERS

16-1 Answer: B, C, and D.

Randy should gift $10 million to Janet to equalize their estates, and each spouse should establish bypass trusts to use their unified credits and reduce their overall estate tax. The remainder of their property can be transferred to a power of appointment trust at the decedent's death. This will provide the surviving spouse with lifetime and testamentary control over the assets whereas a QTIP trust would not provide the surviving spouse with a testamentary disposition over the assets.

16-2 Answer: C.

A bypass trust will provide Elayna with some income, if needed, and Carmen can name his children as the trust beneficiaries. A QTIP trust will provide Elayna with all of the income from the trust for her life, and at her death the trust assets will pass to his children, who are the beneficiaries of this trust.

16-3 Answer: D.

Property disclaimed by Albert would not receive a marital deduction in Irene's estate, and would not be included in Albert's estate because he has a terminable interest in the trust. The other property interests will be included in Albert's estate, assuming he still owns them at his death.

16-4 Answer: C.

Max had the power to withdraw the greater of $5,000 or 5% of the value of the trust corpus each year. Because Max did not exercise this power and make a withdrawal in the year he died, then 5% of the value of the trust corpus ($300,000) was included in Max's gross estate.

16-5 Answer: D.

Alicia's applicable exclusion amount is the sum of her basic exclusion amount of $5,430,000 plus Jesse's unused exclusion of $2,430,000 for a total of $7,860,000. Jesse had an exclusion of $5,430,000 at his death, but the $1 million prior taxable gift and the $2 million bequest to Faith reduced this amount to $2,430,000. Alicia could not use Darnell's DSUEA because she had remarried and could use only her most recent spouse's exclusion.

CHAPTER 17 ANSWERS

17-1 Answer: B.

The value of time or services cannot be considered a charitable contribution for deduction purposes. Therefore, the $20,000 of otherwise billable time is not a charitable contribution. Additionally, to determine the value of the charitable gifts, AGI is irrelevant. AGI is only relevant when the amount of the deduction is to be ascertained.

17-2 Answer: B.

A gift of cash to a private foundation allows for an income tax deduction of up to 30% of AGI.

17-3 Answer: A.

The charity is tax-exempt; therefore, it will not be responsible for the tax. The three-year date-of-death rule does not apply to this type of transfer. To determine the value of the deduction, the FMV of the security on the date of transfer is needed.

17-4 Answer: A.

Assuming the trust satisfies all of the remainder trust requirements, Susan has the ability to take the $500,000 deduction, subject to AGI limitations and the five-year carry-forward, in the year the trust is funded. The fact that the trust assets are valued annually in a unitrust does not affect the timing of her charitable deduction.

17-5 Answer: B.

Given that Joseph is interested in receiving a guaranteed amount of income, an annuity trust is the only vehicle that accomplishes this result. Because Joseph wants the income stream for himself and the remainder given to charity, the CRAT is the most feasible vehicle. A unitrust will create fluctuating payments to Joseph, something he is clearly not interested in receiving.

17-6 Answer: B.

Although Sally will not recognize gain when the securities are transferred into the CRUT, the distributions from the CRUT will be taxed. Therefore, if the trust sells the securities, the trust tax tier rules distribute income first, then capital gains, then tax-free income, then return of principal. The trust itself is tax-exempt so all of the tax liability will flow to Sally.

CHAPTER 18 ANSWERS

18-1 Answer: B.

1 and 3 are incorrect. Prior to 2005, states could collect a portion of the estate tax that a taxpayer paid to the federal government under the federal credit for state death tax. This was replaced in 2005 with a deduction for federal estate tax paid. Each state that imposes a state-level estate or inheritance tax has separate rules regarding exemption amounts, tax rates, and deductions.

18-2 Answer: C.

It is important for financial planners to understand state-level estate taxes, which can affect a client's overall estate plan. A planner should work together with a client's estate planning attorney to ensure that the client's documents incorporate appropriate state-level planning. Many states have decoupled from the federal estate tax and imposed a separate state-level estate or inheritance tax.

18-3 Answer: C.

State-level QTIP planning is used to allow a surviving spouse to take advantage of the full federal estate tax exemption amount when the state estate tax exemption is less than the federal estate tax exemption. The property held in the state-level QTIP will be included in the surviving spouse's taxable estate for purposes of calculating state estate tax. A is incorrect because many states have imposed an estate tax exemption amount that is less than the federal exemption amount, so there can be a state estate tax even if there is no federal estate tax. B is incorrect because several states have imposed their own tax tables and do not rely on the federal credit for state death tax table.

18-4 Answer: False.

Sometimes, a client will want to think through factors other than state estate tax planning. For example, if a married couple has $1.5 million of assets, and lives in a state with a $1 million estate tax exemption, before funding a credit-shelter trust, they will want to think through the surviving spouse's cash flow needs, whether the assets are likely to increase in value or decrease in value, and whether having those assets included in the surviving spouse's taxable estate will produce a better income tax result

18-5 Answer: C.

By nature, an inheritance tax is determined by the value of property passing to a beneficiary and the relationship of the beneficiary to the decedent. Some states provide that payment of tax is the executor's responsibility, while others provide that the recipient of the property will pay the estate tax.

CHAPTER 19 ANSWERS

19-1 Answer: D.

Jeanette has allocated $2 million of her GST exemption to the indirect skip trust, and $2 million of her GST exemption to the direct skip trusts for her four grandchildren. Because her grandchildren do not have a present interest in the trust, Jeanette cannot offset the gifts to the trust with an annual exclusion. The birthday gifts to her four grandchildren and two great nephews are direct skips that were reduced by a GST annual exclusion of $14,000 for each gift. Therefore Jeanette made GST taxable gifts of $1,000 for each of the six skip persons and used $6,000 of her GST exemption to offset the GST tax. Jeanette has $1,424,000 of her GST exemption available to offset future transfers. ($5,430,000 - $4,006,000 = $1,424,000).

19-2 Answer: C.

The predeceased parent rule applies if a parent, who is a lineal descendant of the transferor or the transferor's spouse, is deceased at the time of the transfer. In this example, the granddaughter moved up one generation and is not a skip person.

19-3 Answer: A and B.

Both transfers are indirect skips because there are skip persons and non-skip persons named as beneficiaries of the irrevocable trust and as beneficiaries of the cabin. The cabin is treated essentially as a trust for GST purposes. Both C and D are examples of direct skips.

19-4 Answer: B.

The GST tax for direct skips is tax exclusive and must be paid once the $5,430,000 GST exemption is no longer available to the transferor to offset the tax.

19-5 Answer: A.

The GST exemption is only used to offset the transferor's tax on a generation-skipping transfer. The taxpayer's unified credit is used to offset the gift tax and/or the estate tax that is attributed to the GST transfer.

CHAPTER 20 ANSWERS

20-1 Answers:

A. A holder can exercise the power to appoint property to himself with the consent of the other trust beneficiary. (special)

B. A holder can exercise the power in favor of her creditors. (general)

C. A holder was given a testamentary power to exercise the power in favor of his children. (special)

D. A holder can exercise the power for her comfort and support (general)

20-2 Answer: B.

5% of $700,000 or $35,000.

20-3 Answer: A.

No. Liz allowed her withdrawal right to lapse but this amount is less than 5% of the trust corpus, so no taxable gift was made to the other trust beneficiaries.

20-4 Answer: B.

Each child can withdraw 5% of $120,000, or $6,000; therefore, Charlie can take an annual exclusion of $6,000 per donee to reduce the value of this taxable gift.

20-5 Answer: A and D.

Each parent can take a total of seven gift tax annual exclusions, one for each beneficiary. The annual exclusion amount for each beneficiary is a maximum of $14,000 ($98,000). The parents cannot take 5% of the gift tax value of the insurance policy, or $17,000, as an annual exclusion for each beneficiary because this amount exceeds the annual exclusion limit per donee. Each parent's taxable gift is reduced from $170,000 after gift splitting and annual exclusions ($98,000) to $72,000. For GST tax purposes, they cannot take any annual exclusions for their grandchildren because this is an indirect skip trust. The beneficiaries were given a 5-and-5 power of appointment, not a limited power of appointment. Sprios and Nicki must use their unified credits to offset their taxable gifts of $72,000, and they can allocate their GST tax exemption to the trust to avoid GST taxation.

20-6 Answer: C.

All of the statements are correct except that Pam does not have a limited power of appointment with an ascertainable standard.

CHAPTER 21 ANSWERS

21-1 Answer: B and C.

Barbara is the owner but not the insured of the policy on her mother's life. Therefore, the value of the policy will be included in Barbara's gross estate and in her probate estate. The children will not receive the death benefit amount until their grandmother dies.

21-2 Answer: A and B.

Barbara died intestate, therefore Rick will own one-half of the policy and the children will own the other half of the policy. Property that passes to the surviving spouse through intestacy will receive a marital deduction in the decedent spouse's estate.

21-3 Answer: A and B.

The death benefit is included in Don's estate because his estate is the beneficiary of the policy. Don's estate can take a marital deduction for the $600,000 death benefit amount of the policy because his wife, Betty, is the owner of the policy.

21-4 Answer: A and C.

Philip died within three years of transferring the policy to the trust, therefore the death benefit is included in his gross estate. Because Anita has been given a general power of appointment over the trust corpus, Philip's estate is entitled to a marital deduction to offset the tax on the $1,250,000 included in his gross estate. If Anita dies before Philip, then the charity would receive the assets in the trust, and Philip's estate could take a charitable deduction for the proceeds passing to charity.

21-5 Answer: C.

Ronnie owned a policy on Brad's life and transferred ownership of the policy to him. This transfer is not subject to the 3-year rule because Ronnie is not the owner and the insured. Therefore, neither the death benefit amount nor the value of the policy is included in Ronnie's gross estate at her death. Brad cannot disclaim the death benefit because he is the new owner and the insured of the policy.

CHAPTER 22 ANSWERS

22-1 Answer: B.

Robert survived the transfer of the policy into the trust for more than three years, but because the trustee is obligated to use the insurance proceeds for estate liquidity purposes, the value of the trust will be included in Robert's gross estate at death. The children do not have incidents of ownership in the policy, and trust assets are not included in a trustee's estate.

22-2 Answer: D.

Carlos can take annual exclusions of $5,000 for each beneficiary for a total reduction of $15,000 in taxable gifts. Carlos cannot use gift splitting because Susanne is a beneficiary of the trust, and he cannot take a gift tax marital deduction when he transfers premium payments into the trust.

22-3 Answer: D.

None of the trust assets will be included in Marcy's gross estate. The three-year rule did not apply in this situation because Marcy did not transfer a life insurance policy into the trust.

22-4 Answer: E.

None of the trust assets will be included in Marshall's gross estate because he was given a life estate in the trust with an ascertainable standard, which is a limited power of appointment over the trust corpus.

22-5 Answers: A & C.

Daryl died within three years of transferring the policy to the ILIT therefore the death benefit is included in his gross estate. A marital deduction is available to his estate because Melanie has a general power of appointment over trust corpus. This power will cause the trust to be included in her estate at her death.

CHAPTER 23 ANSWERS

23-1 Answer: C.

One of the benefits of naming a spouse as the beneficiary of an IRA is that the spouse can create a rollover IRA. This allows the spouse to defer distributions to age 70½ and name additional beneficiaries.

23-2 Answer: C.

When a trust is named as the beneficiary of retirement assets, assets are distributed from the plan to the trustee over the life expectancy of the oldest trust beneficiary. If the trust is a conduit trust, all retirement plan distributions are distributed to the trust beneficiaries. If the trust is an accumulation trust, the trustee can accumulate distributions within the trust. When retirement assets are held in a bypass trust, they are not included in the surviving spouse's estate.

23-3 Answer: C.

Because Christina is not Blake's wife, she can create an inherited IRA. Distributions from an inherited IRA must begin by September 30 of the year following the year of the decedent's death. Distributions can be taken over the beneficiary's life expectancy. Only a surviving spouse who has created a spousal rollover can defer distributions to age 70½.

23-4 Answer: False.

An estate is not a designated beneficiary per the IRS, therefore assets payable to the estate will have to be distributed within five years of Beth's death. Alternatively, if James is named as the beneficiary of Beth's 401(k), he may create an inherited IRA and take distributions over his life expectancy.

23-5 Answer: B.

A trust that is the beneficiary of retirement assets may be an accumulation trust or a conduit trust. An accumulation trust retains or accumulates the minimum distributions as part of trust principal. A conduit trust, however, will distribute required minimum distributions to the trust beneficiary.

CHAPTER 24 ANSWERS

24-1 Answer: C.

A preferred stock recapitalization allows Enzo to retain control of his business and to receive dividends from the business after he transfers stock to his son. Any future appreciation in the value of the business will occur outside of Enzo's estate.

24-2 Answer: D.

All are examples of applicable retained interests given a value of zero. Only the right to receive dividends from cumulative preferred shares constitutes a qualified interest, which can be used to reduce the value of a taxable gift.

24-3 Answer: D.

This is an example of a client who wants to make a gift of property for estate tax purposes yet wants to retain payments from the asset. A QPRT is an inappropriate vehicle because a residence is not being transferred. The ILIT is designed to own life insurance; therefore, it is an inappropriate strategy to satisfy her objectives. Between the GRAT and the GRUT, the GRUT is more appropriate given the potential for asset appreciation. As the asset appreciates in value, the grantor's payment stream will increase as well. The 10-year period was selected because it falls within her reasonable life expectancy.

24-4 Answer: C.

The FMV of the residence less the retained interest = the value of the taxable gift. No annual exclusion applies. Therefore, $200,000 – $77,217 = $122,783.

24-5 Answer: D.

Because Joe did not survive the term, the FMV of the trust assets on the date of death will be included in his gross estate.

24-6 Answer: B.

A trust with a unitrust interest values the trust assets on an annual basis. Because the unitrust payment is based on a percentage of the assets as valued on an annual basis, naturally the payment will be different every year. Additional contributions can be made into GRUTs. No additional contributions are permitted into GRATs.

CHAPTER 25 ANSWERS

25-1 Answer: D.

Because Tim requires income for life, the private annuity is the best vehicle for meeting both of their goals. A sale-leaseback would require Tim to stay in the business rather than allowing him to transfer the business to Greg. A bargain sale would not provide a stream of income for Tim. An installment sale will provide a stream of income for a period of time but it may not be for Tim's lifetime.

25-2 Answer: C.

A, B, and D are correct. With an installment sale, payments terminate at the end of a set period of time. A self-cancelling installment note will terminate at the earlier of a set period or at Steve's death.

25-3 Answer: C.

The basis recovery is tax free. The interest portion is always subject to ordinary income tax. The gain portion of the payment may be subject to either ordinary income or capital gains tax.

25-4 Answer: D.

With these types of loans, the foregone interest will be deemed to be income received by the lender and a transfer the lender has made to the borrower.

25-5 Answer: D.

The lease payments received by Priscilla are taxed at her own marginal tax rate.

CHAPTER 26 ANSWERS

26-1 Answer: D.

All of the choices represent estate planning reasons for creating a family limited partnership.

26-2 Answer: C.

Greater IRS scrutiny is never a benefit associated with any estate planning strategy.

26-3 Answer: D.

All three of the choices are characteristics of limited liability companies.

26-4 Answer: D.

Andrew retained an 11% interest in the partnership. After applying the 30% discount, the value of this interest is $77,000. If no discount was allowed, $110,000 would be included in his estate. Both limited and general partnership interests owned by the decedent are included in his taxable estate.

26-5 Answer: D.

The minority discount is a discount for lack of control that applies to the estate and gift tax values of minority limited partner interests. This represents the inability of the limited partner to control the FLP assets and operations.

CHAPTER 27 ANSWERS

27-1 Answer: C.

Wordsworth Industries, as owner, beneficiary, and premium-payer of the policy, will receive the $4-million death benefit amount at Carter's death, which is income tax free unless subject to a corporate AMT. Under a split-dollar arrangement, an employer typically has an increasing death benefit amount and the employee has a decreasing death benefit.

27-2 Answer: D.

A cross-purchase agreement funded with life insurance guarantees that the necessary funds are available to the surviving partner to buy out the decedent's partnership interest from his family. Code section 6166 pertains to the installment payment of estate taxes. Code section 303 provides for the sale of a deceased shareholder's stock to the corporation to be taxed as a capital gain and does not apply to an unincorporated business. A selective pension plan provides an employee with additional deferred compensation.

27-3 Answer: Yes.

The initial qualifications and both percentage tests are met.

50% Test: $2.6 million ÷ $3.4 million = 76%

25% Test: 1.2 million ÷ 3.4 million = 35%

27-4 Answer: Yes.

William's adjusted gross estate is $3 million. $2.6 million ÷ $3 million = 87%

27-5 Answer: Yes.

William's adjusted gross estate is $3 million. $2.6 million ÷ $3 million = 87%

CHAPTER 28 ANSWERS

28-1 Answer: A.

A health care power of attorney is the proper form that designates a health care agent to make medical decisions for an incapacitated person.

28-2 Answer: C.

A GRIT can transfer assets from a wealthier partner to the other partner for a reduced gift tax amount. Had the beneficiaries been related to the grantor, the full value of assets transferred to the trust would have been subject to gift tax. The other techniques are available only to married couples.

28-3 Answer: D.

Elective share statutes permit spouses to elect property prescribed by state law in lieu of property left to them in a will. This state statute does not pertain to nonspouses.

28-4 Answer: C.

A tenancy by the entirety can be held only between a legally married husband and wife and only provides creditor protection for debts incurred by one spouse.

28-5 Answer: All of the above.

CHAPTER 29 ANSWERS

29-1 Answer: All of the above.

Personal, family, financial, and tax situations and economic assumptions all affect the outcome of an estate plan.

29-2 Answer: B.

The alternate valuation date is elected by the decedent's executor when the value of the gross estate and estate tax liability decreases six months after the date of death. Estate equalization could require changing property titles and gifting before a spouse's death. A testamentary by-pass trust is created under the will, which must be established prior to the testator's death. A disclaimer trust must be established before death or as a provision in the testator's will to hold any property disclaimed after the decedent's death.

29-3 Answer: D.

Important papers that are difficult or impossible to replace should be kept in a safe deposit box. Durable powers of attorney, health care proxies, living wills, HIPAA authorization forms, and funeral and burial instructions should be kept where agents, executors, and family members can easily access the documents or the information. If these individuals do not have access to the safe deposit box, it could delay or prevent timely access to these forms or information. Tax returns should be kept for a minimum of three years.

29-4 Answer: C.

A leveraged gift passes property at a low gift tax value. Artwork transferred to a GRIT is valued at the date it is transferred to the trust at the present value of the partner's remainder interest. This amount is less than fair market value, and after the grantor's term ends, the partner receives ownership of the appreciated artwork at no additional transfer tax cost.

29-5 Answer: D.

Joint tenancy with right of survivorship represents equal ownership in property, but at a tenant's death the amount included in the estate is based on the contribution rule, which can result in unequal amounts being included in the estate. The FMV of the property will be included in Helen's estate because Colton did not contribute toward the purchase price, and this amount is Colton's new basis in the property.

Appendix B

Tax Rate Schedules

APPENDIX B.1 INCOME TAX RATE SCHEDULES

	Taxable Years Beginning in 2015
STANDARD DEDUCTION:	
Married, filing jointly	$12,600
Married, filing separately	6,300
Head of Household	9,250
Single	6,300
PERSONAL EXEMPTION:	$4,000

SINGLE INDIVIDUALS					JOINT RETURNS AND SURVIVNG SPOUSES				
Taxable Years Beginning in 2015					**Taxable Years Beginning in 2015**				
Taxable Income			*Tax on Lower Amount*	*Tax Rate on Excess*	*Taxable Income*			*Tax on Lower Amount*	*Tax Rate on Excess*
$ -0-	to	$ 9,225	$ -0-	10.0%	$ -0-	to	$18,450	$ -0-	10.0%
9,225	to	37,450	922.50	15.0%	18,450	to	74,900	1,845.00	15.0%
37,450	to	90,750	5,156.25	25.0%	74,900	to	151,200	10,312.50	25.0%
90,750	to	189,300	18,421.25	28.0%	151,200	to	230,450	29,387.50	28.0%
189,300	to	411,500	46,075.25	33.0%	230,450	to	411,500	51,577.50	33.0%
411,500	to	413,200	119,401.25	35.0%	411,500	to	464,850	111,324.00	35.0%
413,200	to	......	119,926.25	39.6%	464,850	to	......	129,996.50	39.6%

MARRIED FILING SEPARATELY						HEAD OF HOUSEHOLD				
Taxable Years Beginning in 2015						Taxable Years Beginning in 2015				
Taxable Income			*Tax on Lower Amount*	*Tax Rate on Excess*		*Taxable Income*			*Tax on Lower Amount*	*Tax Rate on Excess*
$ -0-	to	$9,225	$ -0-	10.0%		$ -0-	to	$13,150	$ -0-	10.0%
9,225	to	37,450	922.50	15.0%		13,150	to	50,200	1,315.00	15.0%
37,450	to	75,600	5,156.25	25.0%		50,200	to	129,600	6,875.50	25.0%
75,600	to	115,225	14,693.75	28.0%		129,600	to	209,850	26,722.50	28.0%
115,225	to	205,750	25,788.75	33.0%		209,850	to	411,500	49,192.50	33.0%
205,750	to	232,425	55,662.00	35.0%		411,500	to	439,000	115,737.00	35.0%
232,425	to	……	64,989.25	39.6%		439,000	to	……	125,362.00	39.6%

TAX RATE SCHEDULE FOR ESTATES AND TRUSTS

Taxable Years Beginning in 2015				
Taxable Income			*Tax on Lower Amount*	*Tax Rate on Excess*
$ -0-	to	$2,500	$ -0-	15.0%
2,500	to	5,900	375.00	25.0%
5,900	to	9,050	1,225.00	28.0%
9,050	to	12,300	2,107.00	33.0%
12,300	to	……	3,197.50	39.6%

APPENDIX B.2 EXEMPTIONS AND RATES

| | Estate Tax | | | GST Tax | | | Gift Tax | | |
Year	Estate Tax Exemption Equivalent	Estate Tax Unified Credit Amount	Top Estate Tax Rate	GST Tax Exemption Amount	GST Tax Rate	Gift Tax	Gift Tax Unified Credit Amount	Annual Exclusion	Gift Tax Rate
2001	$675,000	$220,550	55%	$1,060,000	55%	$675,000	$220,550	$10,000	55%
2002	$1,000,000	$345,800	50%	$1,100,000	50%	$1,000,000	$345,800	$11,000	50%
2003	$1,000,000	$345,800	49%	$1,120,000	49%	$1,000,000	$345,800	$11,000	49%
2004	$1,500,000	$555,800	48%	$1,500,000	48%	$1,000,000	$345,800	$11,000	48%
2005	$1,500,000	$555,800	47%	$1,500,000	47%	$1,000,000	$345,800	$11,000	47%
2006	$2,000,000	$780,800	46%	$2,000,000	46%	$1,000,000	$345,800	$12,000	46%
2007	$2,000,000	$780,800	45%	$2,000,000	45%	$1,000,000	$345,800	$12,000	45%
2008	$2,000,000	$780,800	45%	$2,000,000	45%	$1,000,000	$345,800	$12,000	45%
2009	$3,500,000	$1,455,800	45%	$3,500,000	45%	$1,000,000	$345,800	$13,000	45%
2010	No estate tax or $5,000,000 exemption	None or $1,730,800	No estate tax or 35%	No GST	N/A	$1,000,000	$330,800	$13,000	35%
2011	$5,000,000	$1,730,800	35%	$5,000,000	35%	$5,000,000	$1,730,800	$13,000	35%
2012	$5,120,000	$1,772,800	35%	$5,120,000	35%	$5,120,000	$1,772,800	$13,000	35%
2013	$5,250,000	$2,045,800	40%	$5,250,000	40%	$5,250,000	$2,045,800	$14,000	40%
2014	$5,340,000	$2,081,800	40%	$5,340,000	40%	$5,340,000	$2,081,800	$14,000	40%
2015	$5,430,000	$2,117,800	40%	$5,430,000	40%	$5,430,000	$2,117,800	$14,000	40%

APPENDIX B.3 MAXIMUM CREDIT TABLE FOR STATE DEATH TAXES

The amount of any state death taxes paid may be subtracted from the federal estate tax as determined under the preceding tables, provided, however, that the maximum to be subtracted may not exceed the maximum determined under the following table:

MAXIMUM STATE DEATH TAX CREDIT*

Taxable Estate		Credit on Column 1	Rate on Excess
From	To		
$0	$100,000	$0	0%
$100,000	$150,000	$0	0.8%
$150,000	$200,000	$400	1.6%
$200,000	$300,000	$1,200	2.4%
$300,000	$500,000	$3,600	3.2%
$500,000	$700,000	$10,000	4.0%
$700,000	$900,000	$18,000	4.8%
$900,000	$1,100,000	$27,600	5.6%
$1,100,000	$1,600,000	$38,800	6.4%
$1,600,000	$2,100,000	$70,800	7.2%
$2,100,000	$2,600,000	$106,800	8.0%
$2,600,000	$3,100,000	$146,800	8.8%
$3,100,000	$3,600,000	$190,800	9.6%
$3,600,000	$4,100,000	$238,800	10.4%
$4,100,000	$5,100,000	$290,800	11.2%
$5,100,000	$6,100,000	$402,800	12.0%
$6,100,000	$7,100,000	$522,800	12.8%
$7,100,000	$8,100,000	$650,800	13.6%
$8,100,000	$9,100,000	$786,800	14.4%
$9,100,000	$10,100,000	$930,800	15.2%
$10,100,000	………..	$1,082,800	16.0%

* This table resembles the table contained in IRC Section 2011(b), but it is not the same. The IRC table is based on the adjusted taxable estate, defined as the taxable estate reduced by $60,000. This table is a modification of that table and can be used directly from the taxable estate.

The maximum state death credit calculated from the table is reduced by 25% for decedents dying in 2002, 50% for decedents dying in 2003, and 75% for decedents dying in 2004. Multiply the amount calculated above by 75% in 2002, 50% in 2003, and 25% in 2004. The state death tax credit is replaced by a deduction for state death taxes.

APPENDIX B.4 2013–2015 GIFT AND ESTATE TAX TABLE

Taxable Gift/Estate		Tax on Col. 1	Rate on Excess
From	To		
$0	$10,000	$0	18%
10,000	20,000	1,800	20%
20,000	40,000	3,800	22%
40,000	60,000	8,200	24%
60,000	80,000	13,000	26%
80,000	100,000	18,200	28%
100,000	150,000	23,800	30%
150,000	250,000	38,800	32%
250,000	500,000	70,800	34%
500,000	750,000	155,800	37%
750,000	1,000,000	248,300	39%
1,000,000	………	345,800	40%

Financial Planning Practice Standards

CFP BOARD FINANCIAL PLANNING PRACTICES STANDARDS

Practice Standard 100-1

Defining the Scope of the Engagement

The financial planning practitioner and the client shall mutually define the scope of the engagement before any financial planning service is provided.

Practice Standard 200-1

Determining a Client's Personal and Financial Goals, Needs and Priorities

The financial planning practitioner and the client shall mutually define the client's personal and financial goals, needs and priorities that are relevant to the scope of the engagement before any recommendation is made and/or implemented.

Practice Standard 200-2

Obtaining Quantitative Information and Documents

The financial planning practitioner shall obtain sufficient quantitative information and documents about a client relevant to the scope of the engagement before any recommendation is made and/or implemented.

Practice Standard 300-1

Analyzing and Evaluating the Client's Information

A financial planning practitioner shall analyze the information to gain an understanding of the client's financial situation and then evaluate to what extent the client's goals, needs and priorities can be met by the client's resources and current course of action.

Practice Standard 400-1

Identifying and Evaluating Financial Planning Alternative(s)

The financial planning practitioner shall consider sufficient and relevant alternatives to the client's current course of action in an effort to reasonably meet the client's goals, needs and priorities.

Practice Standard 400-2

Developing the Financial Planning Recommendation(s)

The financial planning practitioner shall develop the recommendation(s) based on the selected alternative(s) and the current course of action in an effort to reasonably meet the client's goals, needs and priorities.

Practice Standard 400-3

Presenting the Financial Planning Recommendation(s)

The financial planning practitioner shall communicate the recommendation(s) in a manner and to an extent reasonably necessary to assist the client in making an informed decision.

Practice Standard 500-1

Agreeing on Implementation Responsibilities

The financial planning practitioner and the client shall mutually agree on the implementation responsibilities consistent with the scope of the engagement.

Practice Standard 500-2

Selecting Products and Services for Implementation

The financial planning practitioner shall select appropriate products and services that are consistent with the client's goals, needs and priorities.

Practice Standard 600-1

Defining Monitoring Responsibilities

The financial planning practitioner and client shall mutually define monitoring responsibilities.

Documents for Incapacity Planning

APPENDIX D.1 POWER OF ATTORNEY, NEW YORK STATUTORY SHORT FORM

New York State Bar Association
New York Statutory Short Form Power of Attorney, 8/18/10, Eff. 9/12/10

POWER OF ATTORNEY
NEW YORK STATUTORY SHORT FORM

(a)   **CAUTION TO THE PRINCIPAL:** Your Power of Attorney is an important document. As the "principal," you give the person whom you choose (your "agent") authority to spend your money and sell or dispose of your property during your lifetime without telling you. You do not lose your authority to act even though you have given your agent similar authority.

When your agent exercises this authority, he or she must act according to any instructions you have provided or, where there are no specific instructions, in your best interest. "Important Information for the Agent" at the end of this document describes your agent's responsibilities.

Your agent can act on your behalf only after signing the Power of Attorney before a notary public.

You can request information from your agent at any time. If you are revoking a prior Power of Attorney, you should provide written notice of the revocation to your prior agent(s) and to any third parties who may have acted upon it, including the financial institutions where your accounts are located.

You can revoke or terminate your Power of Attorney at any time for any reason as long as you are of sound mind. If you are no longer of sound mind, a court can remove an agent for acting improperly.

Your agent cannot make health care decisions for you. You may execute a "Health Care Proxy" to do this.

The law governing Powers of Attorney is contained in the New York General Obligations Law, Article 5, Title 15. This law is available at a law library, or online through the New York State Senate or Assembly websites, www.senate.state.ny.us or www.assembly.state.ny.us.

If there is anything about this document that you do not understand, you should ask a lawyer of your own choosing to explain it to you.

(b)   DESIGNATION OF AGENT(S):

I, _____   _____
    (name of principal)   *(address of principal)*

hereby appoint:

_____   _____
(name of agent)   *(address of agent)*

_____   _____
(name of second agent)   *(address of second agent)*

   as my agent(s).

   If you designate more than one agent above, they must act together unless you initial the statement below.

(___) My agents may act SEPARATELY.

(c)   DESIGNATION OF SUCCESSOR AGENT(S): (OPTIONAL)
If any agent designated above is unable or unwilling to serve, I appoint as my successor agent(s):

_____   _____
(name of successor agent)   *(address of successor agent)*

_____   _____
(name of second successor agent),   *(address of second successor agent)*

Successor agents designated above must act together unless you initial the statement below.

(___) My successor agents may act SEPARATELY.

You may provide for specific succession rules in this section. Insert specific succession provisions here:

(d)   This POWER OF ATTORNEY shall not be affected by my subsequent incapacity unless I have stated otherwise below, under "Modifications".

(e)   This POWER OF ATTORNEY DOES NOT REVOKE any Powers of Attorney previously executed by me unless I have stated otherwise below, under "Modifications".

   If you do NOT intend to revoke your prior Powers of Attorney, and if you have granted the same authority in this Power of Attorney as you granted to another agent in a prior Power of Attorney, each agent can act separately unless you indicate under "Modifications" that the agents with the same authority are to act together.

(f)   GRANT OF AUTHORITY:
To grant your agent some or all of the authority below, either
    (1)   Initial the bracket at each authority you grant, or
    (2)   Write or type the letters for each authority you grant on the blank line at (P), and initial the bracket at (P). If you initial (P), you do not need to initial the other lines.

I grant authority to my agent(s) with respect to the following subjects as defined in sections 5-1502A through 5-1502N of the New York General Obligations Law:

(____)   (A) real estate transactions;

(____)   (B) chattel and goods transactions;

(____)   (C) bond, share, and commodity transactions;

(____)   (D) banking transactions;

(____)   (E) business operating transactions;

(____)   (F) insurance transactions;

(____)   (G) estate transactions;

(____)   (H) claims and litigation;

(____)   (I) personal and family maintenance: If you grant your agent this authority, it will allow the agent to make gifts that you customarily have made to individuals, including the agent, and charitable organizations. The total amount of all such gifts in any one calendar year cannot exceed five hundred dollars;

(____)   (J) benefits from governmental programs or civil or military service;

(____)   (K) health care billing and payment matters; records, reports, and statements;

(____)   (L) retirement benefit transactions;

(____)   (M) tax matters;

(____)   (N) all other matters;

(____)   (O) full and unqualified authority to my agent(s) to delegate any or all of the foregoing powers to any person or persons whom my agent(s) select;

(____)   (P) EACH of the matters identified by the following letters: _____.

         You need not initial the other lines if you initial line (P).

(g)   MODIFICATIONS: (OPTIONAL)

      In this section, you may make additional provisions, including language to limit or supplement authority granted to your agent. However, you cannot use this Modifications section to grant your agent authority to make gifts or changes to interests in your property. If you wish to grant your agent such authority, you MUST complete the Statutory Gifts Rider.

(h)   CERTAIN GIFT TRANSACTIONS: STATUTORY GIFTS RIDER (OPTIONAL)
      In order to authorize your agent to make gifts in excess of an annual total of $500 for all gifts described in (I) of the grant of authority section of this document (under personal and family maintenance), you must initial the statement below and execute a Statutory Gifts Rider at the same time as this instrument. Initialing the statement below by itself does not authorize your agent to make gifts. The preparation of the Statutory Gifts Rider should be supervised by a lawyer.

(____) (SGR) I grant my agent authority to make gifts in accordance with the terms and conditions of the Statutory Gifts Rider that supplements this Statutory Power of Attorney.

(i) DESIGNATION OF MONITOR(S): (OPTIONAL)

If you wish to appoint monitor(s), initial and fill in the section below:

(____) I wish to designate _____, whose address(es) is (are) _____, as monitor(s). Upon the request of the monitor(s), my agent(s) must provide the monitor(s) with a copy of the power of attorney and a record of all transactions done or made on my behalf. Third parties holding records of such transactions shall provide the records to the monitor(s) upon request.

(j) COMPENSATION OF AGENT(S): (OPTIONAL)

Your agent is entitled to be reimbursed from your assets for reasonable expenses incurred on your behalf. If you ALSO wish your agent(s) to be compensated from your assets for services rendered on your behalf, initial the statement below. If you wish to define "reasonable compensation", you may do so above, under "Modifications".

(____) My agent(s) shall be entitled to reasonable compensation for services rendered.

(k) ACCEPTANCE BY THIRD PARTIES:

I agree to indemnify the third party for any claims that may arise against the third party because of reliance on this Power of Attorney. I understand that any termination of this Power of Attorney, whether the result of my revocation of the Power of Attorney or otherwise, is not effective as to a third party until the third party has actual notice or knowledge of the termination.

(l) TERMINATION:

This Power of Attorney continues until I revoke it or it is terminated by my death or other event described in section 5-1511 of the General Obligations Law. Section 5-1511 of the General Obligations Law describes the manner in which you may revoke your Power of Attorney, and the events which terminate the Power of Attorney.

(m) SIGNATURE AND ACKNOWLEDGMENT:

In Witness Whereof I have hereunto signed my name on the ____ day of _____, 20__

PRINCIPAL signs here: ====> _____

STATE OF NEW YORK)
) ss:
COUNTY OF _____)

On the ____ day of _____, 20__, before me, the undersigned, personally appeared _____, personally known to me or proved to me on the basis of satisfactory evidence to be the individual whose name is subscribed to the within instrument and acknowledged to me that he/she executed the same in his/her capacity, and that by his/her signature on the instrument, the individual, or the person upon behalf of which the individual acted, executed the instrument.

_____

Notary Public

(n) IMPORTANT INFORMATION FOR THE AGENT:

When you accept the authority granted under this Power of Attorney, a special legal relationship is created between you and the principal. This relationship imposes on you legal responsibilities that continue until you resign or the Power of Attorney is terminated or revoked. You must:

(1)   act according to any instructions from the principal, or, where there are no instructions, in the principal's best interest;

(2)   avoid conflicts that would impair your ability to act in the principal's best interest;

(3)   keep the principal's property separate and distinct from any assets you own or control, unless otherwise permitted by law;

(4)   keep a record or all receipts, payments, and transactions conducted for the principal; and

(5)   disclose your identity as an agent whenever you act for the principal by writing or printing the principal's name and signing your own name as "agent" in either of the following manners: (Principal's Name) by (Your Signature) as Agent, or (your signature) as Agent for (Principal's Name).

You may not use the principal's assets to benefit yourself or anyone else or make gifts to yourself or anyone else unless the principal has specifically granted you that authority in this document, which is either a Statutory Gifts Rider attached to a Statutory Short Form Power of Attorney or a Non-Statutory Power of Attorney. If you have that authority, you must act according to any instructions of the principal or, where there are no such instructions, in the principal's best interest.

You may resign by giving written notice to the principal and to any co-agent, successor agent, monitor if one has been named in this document, or the principal's guardian if one has been appointed. If there is anything about this document or your responsibilities that you do not understand, you should seek legal advice.

Liability of agent: The meaning of the authority given to you is defined in New York's General Obligations Law, Article 5, Title 15. If it is found that you have violated the law or acted outside the authority granted to you in the Power of Attorney, you may be liable under the law for your violation.

(o) AGENT'S SIGNATURE AND ACKNOWLEDGMENT OF APPOINTMENT:

It is not required that the principal and the agent(s) sign at the same time, nor that multiple agents sign at the same time.

I/we, _____, have read the foregoing Power of Attorney. I am/we are the person(s) identified therein as agent(s) for the principal named therein.

I/we acknowledge my/our legal responsibilities.

Agent(s) sign(s) here: ==>   _____

                              ==>   _____

STATE OF NEW YORK   )

)   ss:

COUNTY OF _____   )

On the _____ day of _____, 20__, before me, the undersigned, personally appeared _____, personally known to me or proved to me on the basis of satisfactory evidence to be the individual whose name is subscribed to the within instrument and acknowledged to me that he/she executed the same in his/her capacity, and that by his/her signature on the instrument, the individual, or the person upon behalf of which the individual acted, executed the instrument.

_____

Notary Public

(p)   SUCCESSOR AGENT'S SIGNATURE AND ACKNOWLEDGMENT OF APPOINTMENT:

It is not required that the principal and the SUCCESSOR agent(s), if any, sign at the same time, nor that multiple SUCCESSOR agents sign at the same time. Furthermore, successor agents can not use this power of attorney unless the agent(s) designated above is/are unable or unwilling to serve.

I/we, _____, have read the foregoing Power of Attorney. I am/we are the person(s) identified therein as SUCCESSOR agent(s) for the principal named therein.

Successor Agent(s) sign(s) here: ==> _____

==> _____

STATE OF NEW YORK   )
)   ss:
COUNTY OF _____)

On the _____ day of _____, 20___, before me, the undersigned, personally appeared _____, personally known to me or proved to me on the basis of satisfactory evidence to be the individual whose name is subscribed to the within instrument and acknowledged to me that he/she executed the same in his/her capacity, and that by his/her signature on the instrument, the individual, or the person upon behalf of which the individual acted, executed the instrument.

_____

Notary Public

APPENDIX D.2 POWER OF ATTORNEY, NEW YORK STATUTORY GIFTS RIDER, AUTHORIZATION FOR CERTAIN GIFT TRANSACTIONS

 New York State Bar Association
New York Statutory Short Form Power of Attorney, 8/18/10, Eff. 9/12/10

POWER OF ATTORNEY
NEW YORK STATUTORY GIFTS RIDER
AUTHORIZATION FOR CERTAIN GIFT TRANSACTIONS

CAUTION TO THE PRINCIPAL: This OPTIONAL rider allows you to authorize your agent to make gifts in excess of an annual total of $500 for all gifts described in (I) of the Grant of Authority section of the statutory short form Power of Attorney (under personal and family maintenance), or certain other gift transactions during your lifetime. You do not have to execute this rider if you only want your agent to make gifts described in (I) of the Grant of Authority section of the statutory short form Power of Attorney and you initialed "(I)" on that section of that form. Granting any of the following authority to your agent gives your agent the authority to take actions which could significantly reduce your property or change how your property is distributed at your death. "Certain gift transactions" are described in section 5-1514 of the General Obligations Law. This Gifts Rider does not require your agent to exercise granted authority, but when he or she exercises this authority, he or she must act according to any instructions you provide, or otherwise in your best interest.

This Gifts Rider and the Power of Attorney it supplements must be read together as a single instrument.

Before signing this document authorizing your agent to make gifts, you should seek legal advice to ensure that your intentions are clearly and properly expressed.

(a) GRANT OF LIMITED AUTHORITY TO MAKE GIFTS

Granting gifting authority to your agent gives your agent the authority to take actions which could significantly reduce your property.

If you wish to allow your agent to make gifts to himself or herself, you must separately grant that authority in subdivision (c) below.

To grant your agent the gifting authority provided below, initial the bracket to the left of the authority.

(_____) I grant authority to my agent to make gifts to my spouse, children and more remote descendants, and parents, not to exceed, for each donee, the annual federal gift tax exclusion amount pursuant to the Internal Revenue Code. For gifts to my children and more remote descendants, and parents, the maximum amount of the gift to each donee shall not exceed twice the gift tax exclusion amount, if my spouse agrees to split gift treatment pursuant to the Internal Revenue Code. This authority must be exercised pursuant to my instructions, or otherwise for purposes which the agent reasonably deems to be in my best interest.

(b) MODIFICATIONS:

Use this section if you wish to authorize gifts in amounts smaller than the gift tax exclusion amount, in amounts in excess of the gift tax exclusion amount, gifts to other beneficiaries, or other gift transactions. Granting such authority to your agent gives your agent the authority to take actions which could significantly reduce your property and/or change how your property is distributed at your death. If you wish to authorize your agent to make gifts to himself or herself, you must separately grant that authority in subdivision (c) below.

(_____) I grant the following authority to my agent to make gifts pursuant to my instructions, or otherwise for purposes which the agent reasonably deems to be in my best interest:

(c) **GRANT OF SPECIFIC AUTHORITY FOR AN AGENT TO MAKE GIFTS TO HIMSELF OR HERSELF:** (OPTIONAL)

If you wish to authorize your agent to make gifts to himself or herself, you must grant that authority in this section, indicating to which agent(s) the authorization is granted, and any limitations and guidelines.

(_____) I grant specific authority for the following agent(s) to make the following gifts to himself or herself:

This authority must be exercised pursuant to my instructions, or otherwise for purposes which the agent reasonably deems to be in my best interest.

(d) **ACCEPTANCE BY THIRD PARTIES**:

I agree to indemnify the third party for any claims that may arise against the third party because of reliance on this Statutory Gifts Rider.

(e) **SIGNATURE OF PRINCIPAL AND ACKNOWLEDGMENT**:

In Witness Whereof I have hereunto signed my name on _____, 20__.

PRINCIPAL signs here: ====> _____

STATE OF NEW YORK   )
)   ss:
COUNTY OF _____)

On the ____ day of _____, 20__, before me, the undersigned, personally appeared _____, personally known to me or proved to me on the basis of satisfactory evidence to be the individual whose name is subscribed to the within instrument and acknowledged to me that he/she executed the same in her/his capacity, and that by her/his signature on the instrument, the individual, or the person upon behalf of which the individual acted, executed the instrument.

_____
Notary Public

(f) **SIGNATURES OF WITNESSES**:

By signing as a witness, I acknowledge that the principal signed the Statutory Gifts Rider in my presence and the presence of the other witness, or that the principal acknowledged to me that the principal's signature was affixed by him or her or at his or her direction. I also acknowledge that the principal has stated that this Statutory Gifts Rider reflects his or her wishes and that he or she has signed it voluntarily. I am not named herein as a permissible recipient of gifts.

_____	_____
Signature of witness 1	Signature of witness 2
_____	_____
Date	Date
_____	_____
Print Name	Print Name
_____	_____
Address	Address
_____	_____
City, State, Zip code	City, State, Zip code

(g) **This document prepared by:**

APPENDIX D.3 RHODE ISLAND POWER OF ATTORNEY FOR HEALTH CARE

Rhode Island Durable Power Of Attorney For Health Care

AN ADVANCE CARE DIRECTIVE

"A GIFT OF PREPAREDNESS"

INTRODUCTION

YOUR RIGHTS

Adults have the fundamental right to control the decisions relating to their health care. You have the right to make medical and other health care decisions for yourself so long as you can give informed consent for those decisions. No treatment may be given to you over your objection at the time of treatment. You may decide whether you want life sustaining procedures withheld or withdrawn in instances of a terminal condition.

What is a Durable Power of Attorney for Health Care?

This Durable Power of Attorney for Health Care lets you appoint someone to make health care decisions for you when you cannot actively participate in health care decision making. The person you appoint to make health care decisions for you when you cannot actively participate in health care decision making is called your agent. The agent must act consistent with your desires as stated in this document or otherwise known. Your agent must act in your best interest. Your agent stands in your place and can make any health care decision that you have the right to make.

You should read this Durable Power of Attorney for Health Care carefully. Follow the witnessing section as required. To have your wishes honored, this Durable Power of Attorney for Health Care must be valid.

REMEMBER

- You must be at least eighteen (18) years old.

- You must be a Rhode Island resident.

- You should follow the instructions on this Durable Power of Attorney for Health Care.

- You must voluntarily sign this Durable Power of Attorney for Health Care.

- You must have this Durable Power of Attorney for Health Care witnessed properly.

- No special form must be used but if you use this form it will be recognized by health care providers.

- Make copies of your Durable Power of Attorney for Health Care for your agent, alternative agent, physicians, hospital, and family.

- Do not put your Durable Power of Attorney for Health Care in a safe deposit box.

- Although you are not required to update your Durable Power of Attorney for Health Care, you may want to review it periodically.

Commonly Used Life-Support Measures Are Listed on the Back Inside Page

DURABLE POWER OF ATTORNEY FOR HEALTH CARE
(RHODE ISLAND HEALTH CARE ADVANCE DIRECTIVE)

I, _____ ,

(Insert your name and address)

am at least eighteen (18) years old, a resident of the State of Rhode Island, and understand this document allows me to name another person (called the health care agent) to make health care decisions for me if I can no longer make decisions for myself and I cannot inform my health care providers and agent about my wishes for medical treatment.

PART I: APPOINTMENT OF HEALTH CARE AGENT
THIS IS WHO I WANT TO MAKE HEALTH CARE DECISIONS
FOR ME IF I CAN NO LONGER MAKE DECISIONS

Note: You may not appoint the following individuals as an agent:

(1) your treating health care provider, such as a doctor, nurse, hospital, or nursing home,
(2) a nonrelative employee of your treating health care provider,
(3) an operator of a community care facility, or
(4) a nonrelative employee of an operator of a community care facility.

When I am no longer able to make decisions for myself, I name and appoint
_____ to make health care decisions for me. This person is called my health care agent.

Telephone number of my health care agent: _____
Address of my health care agent: _____
_____

You should discuss this health care directive with your agent and give your agent a copy.

(OPTIONAL)
APPOINTMENT OF ALTERNATE HEALTH CARE AGENTS:

You are not required to name alternative health care agents. An alternative health care agent will be able to make the same health care decisions as the health care agent named above, if the health care agent is unable or ineligible to make health care decisions for you. For example, if you name your spouse as your health care agent and your marriage is dissolved, then your former spouse is ineligible to be your health care agent.

When I am no longer able to make decisions for myself and my health care agent is not available, not able, loses the mental capacity to make health care decisions for me, becomes ineligible to act as my agent, is not willing to make health care decisions for me, or I revoke the person appointed as my agent to make health care decisions for me, I name and appoint the following persons as my agent to make health care decision for me as authorized by this document, in the order listed below:

_____ **My Initials**

My **First Alternative Health Care Agent**: _____
Telephone number of my first alternative health care agent: _____
Address of my first alternative health care agent: _____
_____

My **Second Alternative Health Care Agent**: _____
Telephone number of my second alternative health care agent: _____
Address of my second alternative health care agent: _____
_____

My health care agent is automatically given the powers I would have to make health care decisions for me if I were able to make such decisions. Some typical powers for a health care agent are listed below in (A) through (H). My health care agent must convey my wishes for medical treatment contained in this document or any other instructions I have given to my agent. If I have not given health care instructions, then my agent must act in my best interest. A court can take away the power of an agent to make health care decisions for you if your agent:

(1) Authorizes anything illegal,
(2) Acts contrary to your known wishes, or
(3) Where your desires are not known, does anything that is clearly contrary to your best interest.

Whenever I can no longer make decisions about my medical treatment, my health care agent has the power to:

(A) Make any health care decision for me. This includes the power to give, refuse, or withdraw consent to any care, treatments, services, tests, or procedures. This includes deciding whether to stop or not start health care that is keeping me or might keep me alive, and deciding about mental health treatment.
(B) Advocate for pain management for me.
(C) Choose my health care providers, including hospitals, physicians, and hospice.
(D) Choose where I live and receive health care which may include residential care, assisted living, a nursing home, a hospice, and a hospital.
(E) Review my medical records and disclose my health care information, as needed.
(F) Sign releases or other documents concerning my medical treatment.
(G) Sign waivers or releases from liability for hospitals or physicians.
(H) Make decisions concerning participation in research.

If I DO NOT want my health care agent to have a power listed above in (A) through (H) OR if I want to LIMIT an power in (A) through (H), I must say that here:

_____
_____
_____
_____

_____ **My Initials**

2

PART II: HEALTH CARE INSTRUCTIONS

THIS IS WHAT I WANT AND DO NOT WANT FOR MY HEALTH CARE

Many medical treatments may be used to try to improve my medical condition in certain circumstances or to prolong my life in other circumstances. Many medical treatments can be started and then stopped if they do not help. Examples include artificial breathing by a machine connected to a tube in the lungs, artificial feeding or fluids through tubes, attempts to start the heart, surgeries, dialysis, antibiotics, and blood transfusions. The back inside page has more information about life-support measures.

OPTIONAL -FOR DISCUSSION PURPOSES

A discussion of these questions with your health care agent may help him or her make health care decisions for you which reflect your values when you cannot make those decisions.

These are my views which may help my agent make health care decisions:

1. Do you think your life should be preserved for as long as possible? Why or why not?

_____

_____

_____

2. Would you want your pain managed, even if it makes you less alert or shortens your life?

_____

_____

_____

3. Do your religious beliefs affect the way you feel about death? Would you prefer to be buried or cremated?

_____

_____

_____

4. Should financial considerations be important when making a decision about medical care?

_____

_____

_____

5. Have you talked with your agent, alternative agent, family and friends about these issues?

_____

_____

_____

_____ **My Initials**

Here are my desires about my health care to guide my agent and health care providers.

1. If I am close to death and life support would only prolong my dying:

    INITIAL ONLY ONE:
    _____ I want to receive a feeding tube.
    _____ I DO NOT WANT a feeding tube.

    INITIAL ONLY ONE:
    _____ I want all life support that may apply.
    _____ I want NO life support.

2. If I am unconscious and it is very unlikely that I will ever become conscious again:

    INITIAL ONLY ONE:
    _____ I want to receive a feeding tube.
    _____ I DO NOT WANT a feeding tube.

    INITIAL ONLY ONE:
    _____ I want all other life support that may apply.
    _____ I want NO life support.

3. If I have a progressive illness that will be fatal and is in an advanced stage, and I am consistently and permanently unable to communicate by any means, swallow food and water safely, care for myself and recognize my family and other people, and it is very unlikely that my condition will substantially improve:

    INITIAL ONLY ONE:
    _____ I want to receive a feeding tube.
    _____ I DO NOT WANT a feeding tube.

    INITIAL ONLY ONE:
    _____ I want all life support that may apply.
    _____ I want NO life support.

Additional statement of desires, special provisions, and limitations regarding health care decisions *(More space is available on page 8)*:

_____

_____

ORGAN DONATION

_____ In the event of my death, I request that my agent inform my family or next of kin of my desire to be an organ and tissue donor for **transplant**. *(Initial if applicable)*

_____ In the event of my death, I request that my agent inform my family or next of kin of my desire to be an organ and tissue donor for **research**. *(Initial if applicable)*

4

_____ **My Initials**

RELIGIOUS AND SPIRITUAL REQUESTS

Do you want your Rabbi, Priest, Clergy, Minister, Imam, Monk, or other spiritual advisor contacted if you become sick?

INITIAL ONLY ONE:
_____ Yes _____ No

Name of Rabbi, Priest, Clergy, Minister, Imam, Monk, or other spiritual advisor:

_____

Address:_____

Phone Number: _____

DURATION

Unless you specify a shorter period in the space below, this power of attorney will exist until it is revoked.

I do not want this durable power of attorney for health care to exist until revoked. I want this durable power of attorney for health care to expire on _____
    (Fill in this space ONLY if you want the authority of your agent to end on a specific date.)

REVOCATION

I can revoke this Durable Power of Attorney for Health Care at any time and for any reason either in writing or orally. If I change my agent or alternative agents or make any other changes, I need to complete a new Durable Power of Attorney for Health Care with those changes.

PART III: MAKING THE DOCUMENT LEGAL

I revoke any prior designations, advance directives, or durable power of attorney for health care.

Date and Signature of Principal

I am thinking clearly, I agree with everything that is written in this document, and I have made this document willingly.

_____

Signature   Date signed:

_____ **My Initials**

DATE AND SIGNATURES OF TWO QUALIFIED WITNESSES OR ONE NOTARY PUBLIC

Two qualified witnesses or one notary public must sign the durable power of attorney for health care form at the same time the principal signs the document. The witnesses must be adults and must not be any of the following:

(1) a person you designate as your agent or alternate agent,
(2) a health care provider,
(3) an employee of a health care provider,
(4) the operator of a community care facility, or
(5) an employee of an operator of a community care facility.

I declare under the penalty of perjury that the person who signed or acknowledged this document is personally known to me to be the principal, that the principal signed or acknowledged this durable power of attorney for health care in my presence, that the principal appears to be of sound mind and under no duress, fraud, or undue influence, that I am not the person appointed as attorney in fact by this document, and that I am not a health care provider, an employee of a health care provider, the operator of a community care facility, or an employee of an operator of a community care facility.

OPTION ONE:

Signature: _____

Print Name: _____

Residence Address: _____

Date: _____

Signature: _____

Print Name: _____

Residence Address: _____

Date: _____

---OR---

OPTION TWO:

Signature of Notary Public: _____

Print Name: _____

Commission Expires: _____

Business Address: _____

Date: _____

6

_____ **My Initials**

Two Qualified Witnesses or One Notary Public Declaration

At least one of the qualified witnesses or the notary public must make this additional declaration:

I further declare under penalty of perjury that I am not related to the principal by blood, marriage, or adoption, and, to the best of my knowledge, I am not entitled to any part of the estate of the principal upon the death of the principal under a will now existing or by operation of law.

Signature: _____

Print Name: _____

Signature: _____

Print Name: _____

Part IV: Distributing The Document

You are not required to give anyone your Durable Power of Attorney for Health Care, but if it cannot be found at the time you need it, it cannot help you. For example, you are unable to participate in making health care decisions and your Durable Power of Attorney for Health Care is a safe deposit box, the agent, physician and other health care providers will not have access to it and they will not be able to respect your medical treatment wishes. You may want to give a copy of your Durable Power of Attorney for Health Care to some or all of the persons listed below so that it can be available when you need it.

| | **(Name)** | **(Address)** | **(Phone)** |

❑ Health Care Agent

_____

❑ First Alternative Health Care Agent

_____

❑ Second Alternative Health Care Agent

_____

❑ Physician

_____

❑ Family

_____

❑ Lawyer

_____

❑ Others

_____

7

_____ **My Initials**

ADDITIONAL SPACE FOR INFORMATION

_____
_____
_____
_____
_____
_____
_____
_____
_____
_____
_____
_____
_____
_____
_____
_____
_____
_____
_____
_____
_____
_____
_____
_____
_____
_____
_____
_____
_____
_____
_____
_____
_____
_____
_____

_____ **My Initials**

COMMONLY USED LIFE-SUPPORT MEASURES

Cardiopulmonary Resuscitation (CPR)

Cardiopulmonary resuscitation (CPR) is a group of treatments used when someone's heart and/or breathing stops. CPR is used in an attempt to restart the heart and breathing. It may consist only of mouth-to-mouth breathing or it can include pressing on the chest to mimic the heart's function and cause blood to circulate. Electric shock and drugs also are used frequently to stimulate the heart.

When used quickly in response to a sudden event like a heart attack or drowning, CPR can be life-saving. But the success rate is extremely low for people who are at the end of a terminal disease process. Critically ill patients who receive CPR have a small chance of recovering or leaving the hospital.

Rhode Islanders with a terminal condition who do not want rescue/ambulance service/emergency medical services personnel to perform CPR may join COMFORT ONE. Rescue/ambulance/emergency workers will provide comfort measures but will not perform CPR or any resuscitation. To join COMFORT ONE, speak to your physician. ONLY your physician can enroll you in the COMFORT ONE PROGRAM. Your physician writes a medical order directing rescue/ambulances service/emergency personnel not to start CPR which is filed with the Rhode Island Department of Health.

Mechanical Ventilation

Mechanical ventilation is used to help or replace how the lungs work. A machine called a ventilator (or respirator) forces air into the lungs. The ventilator is attached to a tube inserted in the nose or mouth and down into the windpipe (or trachea). Mechanical ventilation often is used to assist a person through a short-term problem or for prolonged periods in which irreversible respiratory failure happens due to injuries to the upper spinal cord or a progressive neurological disease.

Some people on long-term mechanical ventilation are able to enjoy themselves and live a quality of life that is important to them. For the dying patient, however, mechanical ventilation often merely prolongs the dying process until some other body system fails. It may supply oxygen, but it cannot improve the underlying condition.

When discussing end-of-life wishes, make clear to loved ones and your physician whether you would want mechanical ventilation if you would never regain the ability to breathe on your own or return to a quality of life acceptable to you.

Artificial Nutrition and Hydration

Artificial nutrition and hydration (or tube feeding) supplements or replaces ordinary eating and drinking by giving a chemically balanced mix of nutrients and fluid through a tube placed directly into the stomach, the upper intestine, or a vein. Artificial nutrition and hydration can save lives when used until the body heals.

Long-term artificial nutrition and hydration may be given to people with serious intestinal disorders that impair their ability to digest food, thereby helping them to enjoy a quality of life that is important to them. Sometimes long-term use of tube feeding frequently is given to people with irreversible and end-stage conditions which will not reverse the course of the disease itself or improve the quality of life. Some health care facilities and physicians may not agree with stopping or withdrawing tube feeding. You may want to talk with your loved ones and physician about your wishes for artificial nutrition and hydration in your Durable Power of Attorney for Health Care.

More copies of this form are available at: www.riag.state.ri.us

APPENDIX D.4 INSTRUCTIONS TO LIVING WILL

INSTRUCTIONS
To Living Will

A living will is a written document which directs your physician to withhold or stop life-sustaining medical procedures if you develop a terminal condition and can't state your wishes at the time a decision about those kinds of procedures must be made.

Rhode Island law suggests a form of living will but does not require its exclusive use. If you decide to sign a living will, you may use the form supplied with these instructions or make your own living will form. If you use this form, please read and follow these instructions carefully.

1. Print your name in the first line of the form.

2. Place a check mark in the third paragraph to indicate whether you want artificially-administered nutrition and hydration (food and water) to be stopped or withheld like any other life-sustaining treatment. Remember, if you do not want artificial nutrition and hydration, your living will must say so.

3. Complete the day, month and year that you sign at the bottom of this form.

4. Sign your name on the signature line (or if you are unable to do so, have someone do it for you) before two (2) witnesses who know you and are at least 18 years old.

5. Print your address on the address line.

6. Have the two (2) witnesses sign their names and print their addresses where indicated below your signature. The witnesses may not be related to you by blood or marriage.

7. Give a signed copy of your living will to your physician for your medical records.

   Remember, you may revoke your living will at any time simply by telling your physician not to follow it.

NOTE: This information is provided to make you generally aware of Rhode Island law about living wills and is not intended as legal advice for your particular situation. For legal advice about living wills or your health care rights, you should consult with an attorney.

STATE OF RHODE ISLAND

CHAPTER 23-4.11
A declaration may, but need not, be in the following form:

RIGHTS OF THE TERMINALLY ILL ACT

DECLARATION

I, _____, being of sound mind willfully and voluntarily make known my desire that my dying shall not be artificially prolonged under the circumstances set forth below, so hereby declare:

If I should have an incurable or irreversible condition that will cause my death and if I am unable to make decisions regarding my medical treatment, I direct my attending physician to withhold or withdraw procedures that merely prolong the dying process and are not necessary to my comfort, or to alleviate pain.

This authorization   includes ☐
                                 does not include ☐

the withholding or withdrawal of artificial feeding. *(check only one box above)*

Signed this _____ day of _____, _____.

_____
Signature of Declarant

_____
Address

The Declarant is personally known to me and voluntarily signed this document in my presence. I am not related to the Declarant by blood or marriage.

_____
Witness

_____
Witness

_____
Address

_____
Address

Valuation Tables

	TABLE 2000CM				
Age x	l(x)	Age x	l(x)	Age x	l(x)
0	100000	37	96921	74	66882
1	99305	38	96767	75	64561
2	99255	39	96600	76	62091
3	99222	40	96419	77	59476
4	99197	41	96223	78	56721
5	99176	42	96010	79	53833
6	99158	43	95782	80	50819
7	99140	44	95535	81	47694
8	99124	45	95268	82	44475
9	99110	46	94981	83	41181
10	99097	47	94670	84	37837
11	99085	48	94335	85	34471
12	99073	49	93975	86	31114
13	99057	50	93591	87	27799
14	99033	51	93180	88	24564
15	98998	52	92741	89	21443
16	98950	53	92270	90	18472
17	98891	54	91762	91	15685
18	98822	55	91211	92	13111
19	98745	56	90607	93	10773
20	98664	57	89947	94	8690
21	98577	58	89225	95	6871
22	98485	59	88441	96	5315
23	98390	60	87595	97	4016
24	98295	61	86681	98	2959
25	98202	62	85691	99	2122
26	98111	63	84620	100	1477
27	98022	64	83465	101	997
28	97934	65	82224	102	650
29	97844	66	80916	103	410
30	97750	67	79530	104	248
31	97652	68	78054	105	144
32	97549	69	76478	106	81
33	97441	70	74794	107	43
34	97324	71	73001	108	22
35	97199	72	71092	109	11
36	97065	73	69056	110	0

Source: S. R. Leimberg, J. H. Ellis, S. N. Kandell, R. G Miller, T. C. Polacek, M. S Rosenbloom, and G. Zwick, *The Tools & Techniques of Estate Planning*, 17th Ed. (Erlanger, KY: National Underwriter Co., 2015), App. B.

ANNUITY ADJUSTMENT FACTORS TABLE A*

FREQUENCY OF PAYMENTS

INTEREST RATE	ANNUALLY	SEMI ANNUALLY	QUARTERLY	MONTHLY	WEEKLY
3.0%	1.0000	1.0074	1.0112	1.0137	1.0146
3.2%	1.0000	1.0079	1.0119	1.0146	1.0156
3.4%	1.0000	1.0084	1.0127	1.0155	1.0166
3.6%	1.0000	1.0089	1.0134	1.0164	1.0175
3.8%	1.0000	1.0094	1.0141	1.0173	1.0185
4.0%	1.0000	1.0099	1.0149	1.0182	1.0195
4.2%	1.0000	1.0104	1.0156	1.0191	1.0205
4.4%	1.0000	1.0109	1.0164	1.0200	1.0214
4.6%	1.0000	1.0114	1.0171	1.0209	1.0224
4.8%	1.0000	1.0119	1.0178	1.0218	1.0234
5.0%	1.0000	1.0123	1.0186	1.0227	1.0243
5.2%	1.0000	1.0128	1.0193	1.0236	1.0253
5.4%	1.0000	1.0133	1.0200	1.0245	1.0262
5.6%	1.0000	1.0138	1.0208	1.0254	1.0272
5.8%	1.0000	1.0143	1.0215	1.0263	1.0282
6.0%	1.0000	1.0148	1.0222	1.0272	1.0291
6.2%	1.0000	1.0153	1.0230	1.0281	1.0301
6.4%	1.0000	1.0158	1.0237	1.0290	1.0311
6.6%	1.0000	1.0162	1.0244	1.0299	1.0320
6.8%	1.0000	1.0167	1.0252	1.0308	1.0330
7.0%	1.0000	1.0172	1.0259	1.0317	1.0339
7.2%	1.0000	1.0177	1.0266	1.0326	1.0349
7.4%	1.0000	1.0182	1.0273	1.0335	1.0358
7.6%	1.0000	1.0187	1.0281	1.0344	1.0368
7.8%	1.0000	1.0191	1.0288	1.0353	1.0378
8.0%	1.0000	1.0196	1.0295	1.0362	1.0387
8.2%	1.0000	1.0201	1.0302	1.0370	1.0397
8.4%	1.0000	1.0206	1.0310	1.0379	1.0406
8.6%	1.0000	1.0211	1.0317	1.0388	1.0416
8.8%	1.0000	1.0215	1.0324	1.0397	1.0425
9.0%	1.0000	1.0220	1.0331	1.0406	1.0435
9.2%	1.0000	1.0225	1.0339	1.0415	1.0444
9.4%	1.0000	1.0230	1.0346	1.0424	1.0454
9.6%	1.0000	1.0235	1.0353	1.0433	1.0463
9.8%	1.0000	1.0239	1.0360	1.0442	1.0473
10.0%	1.0000	1.0244	1.0368	1.0450	1.0482
10.2%	1.0000	1.0249	1.0375	1.0459	1.0492
10.4%	1.0000	1.0254	1.0382	1.0468	1.0501
10.6%	1.0000	1.0258	1.0389	1.0477	1.0511
10.8%	1.0000	1.0263	1.0396	1.0486	1.0520

*For use in calculating the value of an annuity payable at the end of each period or, if the term of the annuity is determined with respect to one or more lives, an annuity payable at the beginning of each period.

ANNUITY ADJUSTMENT FACTORS TABLE B*

FREQUENCY OF PAYMENTS

INTEREST RATE	ANNUALLY	SEMI ANNUALLY	QUARTERLY	MONTHLY	WEEKLY
3.0%	1.0300	1.0224	1.0187	1.0162	1.0152
3.2%	1.0320	1.0239	1.0199	1.0172	1.0162
3.4%	1.0340	1.0254	1.0212	1.0183	1.0172
3.6%	1.0360	1.0269	1.0224	1.0194	1.0182
3.8%	1.0380	1.0284	1.0236	1.0205	1.0192
4.0%	1.0400	1.0299	1.0249	1.0215	1.0203
4.2%	1.0420	1.0314	1.0261	1.0226	1.0213
4.4%	1.0440	1.0329	1.0274	1.0237	1.0223
4.6%	1.0460	1.0344	1.0286	1.0247	1.0233
4.8%	1.0480	1.0359	1.0298	1.0258	1.0243
5.0%	1.0500	1.0373	1.0311	1.0269	1.0253
5.2%	1.0520	1.0388	1.0323	1.0279	1.0263
5.4%	1.0540	1.0403	1.0335	1.0290	1.0273
5.6%	1.0560	1.0418	1.0348	1.0301	1.0283
5.8%	1.0580	1.0433	1.0360	1.0311	1.0293
6.0%	1.0600	1.0448	1.0372	1.0322	1.0303
6.2%	1.0620	1.0463	1.0385	1.0333	1.0313
6.4%	1.0640	1.0478	1.0397	1.0343	1.0323
6.6%	1.0660	1.0492	1.0409	1.0354	1.0333
6.8%	1.0680	1.0507	1.0422	1.0365	1.0343
7.0%	1.0700	1.0522	1.0434	1.0375	1.0353
7.2%	1.0720	1.0537	1.0446	1.0386	1.0363
7.4%	1.0740	1.0552	1.0458	1.0396	1.0373
7.6%	1.0760	1.0567	1.0471	1.0407	1.0383
7.8%	1.0780	1.0581	1.0483	1.0418	1.0393
8.0%	1.0800	1.0596	1.0495	1.0428	1.0403
8.2%	1.0820	1.0611	1.0507	1.0439	1.0413
8.4%	1.0840	1.0626	1.0520	1.0449	1.0422
8.6%	1.0860	1.0641	1.0532	1.0460	1.0432
8.8%	1.0880	1.0655	1.0544	1.0471	1.0442
9.0%	1.0900	1.0670	1.0556	1.0481	1.0452
9.2%	1.0920	1.0685	1.0569	1.0492	1.0462
9.4%	1.0940	1.0700	1.0581	1.0502	1.0472
9.6%	1.0960	1.0715	1.0593	1.0513	1.0482
9.8%	1.0980	1.0729	1.0605	1.0523	1.0492
10.0%	1.1000	1.0744	1.0618	1.0534	1.0502
10.2%	1.1020	1.0759	1.0630	1.0544	1.0512
10.4%	1.1040	1.0774	1.0642	1.0555	1.0521
10.6%	1.1060	1.0788	1.0654	1.0565	1.0531
10.8%	1.1080	1.0803	1.0666	1.0576	1.0541

*For use in calculating the value of a term certain annuity payable at the beginning of each period.

TABLE B
TERM CERTAIN FACTORS

INTEREST RATE

	4.6%				4.8%		
YEARS	ANNUITY	INCOME INTEREST	REMAINDER	YEARS	ANNUITY	INCOME INTEREST	REMAINDER
1	0.9560	.043977	.956023	1	0.9542	.045802	.954198
2	1.8700	.086020	.913980	2	1.8647	.089505	.910495
3	2.7438	.126214	.873786	3	2.7335	.131207	.868793
4	3.5791	.164641	.835359	4	3.5625	.170999	.829001
5	4.3778	.201377	.798623	5	4.3535	.208969	.791031
6	5.1413	.236499	.763501	6	5.1083	.245199	.754801
7	5.8712	.270075	.729925	7	5.8285	.279770	.720230
8	6.5690	.302175	.697825	8	6.5158	.312758	.687242
9	7.2362	.332863	.667137	9	7.1716	.344235	.655765
10	7.8740	.362202	.637798	10	7.7973	.374270	.625730
11	8.4837	.390250	.609750	11	8.3944	.402929	.597071
12	9.0666	.417065	.582935	12	8.9641	.430276	.569724
13	9.6239	.442701	.557299	13	9.5077	.456370	.543630
14	10.1567	.467210	.532790	14	10.0264	.481269	.518731
15	10.6661	.490640	.509360	15	10.5214	.505028	.494972
16	11.1530	.513040	.486960	16	10.9937	.527698	.472302
17	11.6186	.534455	.465545	17	11.4444	.549330	.450670
18	12.0637	.554929	.445071	18	11.8744	.569972	.430028
19	12.4892	.574502	.425498	19	12.2847	.589668	.410332
20	12.8960	.593214	.406786	20	12.6763	.608462	.391538
21	13.2848	.611103	.388897	21	13.0499	.626395	.373605
22	13.6566	.628206	.371794	22	13.4064	.643506	.356494
23	14.0121	.644556	.355444	23	13.7465	.659834	.340166
24	14.3519	.660187	.339813	24	14.0711	.675414	.324586
25	14.6768	.675131	.324869	25	14.3809	.690281	.309719
26	14.9873	.689418	.310582	26	14.6764	.704467	.295533
27	15.2843	.703077	.296923	27	14.9584	.718002	.281998
28	15.5681	.716134	.283866	28	15.2275	.730918	.269082
29	15.8395	.728618	.271382	29	15.4842	.743243	.256757
30	16.0990	.740553	.259447	30	15.7292	.755003	.244997
31	16.3470	.751962	.248038	31	15.9630	.766224	.233776
32	16.5841	.762870	.237130	32	16.1861	.776931	.223069
33	16.8108	.773298	.226702	33	16.3989	.787148	.212852
34	17.0276	.783268	.216732	34	16.6020	.796897	.203103
35	17.2348	.792799	.207201	35	16.7958	.806199	.193801
36	17.4329	.801911	.198089	36	16.9807	.815076	.184924
37	17.6222	.810623	.189377	37	17.1572	.823546	.176454
38	17.8033	.818951	.181049	38	17.3256	.831627	.168373
39	17.9764	.826913	.173087	39	17.4862	.839339	.160661
40	18.1418	.834525	.165475	40	17.6395	.846698	.153302
41	18.3000	.841802	.158198	41	17.7858	.853719	.146281
42	18.4513	.848759	.151241	42	17.9254	.860419	.139581
43	18.5959	.855410	.144590	43	18.0586	.866812	.133188
44	18.7341	.861769	.138231	44	18.1857	.872912	.127088
45	18.8663	.867848	.132152	45	18.3069	.878733	.121267
46	18.9926	.873660	.126340	46	18.4227	.884287	.115713
47	19.1134	.879216	.120784	47	18.5331	.889587	.110413
48	19.2289	.884527	.115473	48	18.6384	.894644	.105356
49	19.3392	.889605	.110395	49	18.7390	.899470	.100530
50	19.4448	.894460	.105540	50	18.8349	.904074	.095926

TABLE B
TERM CERTAIN FACTORS

INTEREST RATE

	5.0%				5.2%		
YEARS	ANNUITY	INCOME INTEREST	REMAINDER	YEARS	ANNUITY	INCOME INTEREST	REMAINDER
1	0.9524	.047619	.952381	1	0.9506	.049430	.950570
2	1.8594	.092971	.907029	2	1.8542	.096416	.903584
3	2.7232	.136162	.863838	3	2.7131	.141080	.858920
4	3.5460	.177298	.822702	4	3.5295	.183536	.816464
5	4.3295	.216474	.783526	5	4.3056	.223894	.776106
6	5.0757	.253785	.746215	6	5.0434	.262256	.737744
7	5.7864	.289319	.710681	7	5.7447	.298723	.701277
8	6.4632	.323161	.676839	8	6.4113	.333387	.666613
9	7.1078	.355391	.644609	9	7.0449	.366337	.633663
10	7.7217	.386087	.613913	10	7.6473	.397659	.602341
11	8.3064	.415321	.584679	11	8.2199	.427432	.572568
12	8.8633	.443163	.556837	12	8.7641	.455734	.544266
13	9.3936	.469679	.530321	13	9.2815	.482637	.517363
14	9.8986	.494932	.505068	14	9.7733	.508210	.491790
15	10.3797	.518983	.481017	15	10.2408	.532519	.467481
16	10.8378	.541888	.458112	16	10.6851	.555626	.444374
17	11.2741	.563703	.436297	17	11.1075	.577592	.422408
18	11.6896	.584479	.415521	18	11.5091	.598471	.401529
19	12.0853	.604266	.395734	19	11.8907	.618319	.381681
20	12.4622	.623111	.376889	20	12.2536	.637185	.362815
21	12.8212	.641058	.358942	21	12.5984	.655119	.344881
22	13.1630	.658150	.341850	22	12.9263	.672166	.327834
23	13.4886	.674429	.325571	23	13.2379	.688371	.311629
24	13.7986	.689932	.310068	24	13.5341	.703775	.296225
25	14.0939	.704697	.295303	25	13.8157	.718417	.281583
26	14.3752	.718759	.281241	26	14.0834	.732336	.267664
27	14.6430	.732152	.267848	27	14.3378	.745566	.254434
28	14.8981	.744906	.255094	28	14.5797	.758143	.241857
29	15.1411	.757054	.242946	29	14.8096	.770098	.229902
30	15.3725	.768623	.231377	30	15.0281	.781462	.218538
31	15.5928	.779641	.220359	31	15.2358	.792264	.207736
32	15.8027	.790134	.209866	32	15.4333	.802532	.197468
33	16.0025	.800127	.199873	33	15.6210	.812293	.187707
34	16.1929	.809645	.190355	34	15.7994	.821571	.178429
35	16.3742	.818710	.181290	35	15.9691	.830391	.169609
36	16.5469	.827343	.172657	36	16.1303	.838775	.161225
37	16.7113	.835564	.164436	37	16.2835	.846744	.153256
38	16.8679	.843395	.156605	38	16.4292	.854319	.145681
39	17.0170	.850852	.149148	39	16.5677	.861520	.138480
40	17.1591	.857954	.142046	40	16.6993	.868365	.131635
41	17.2944	.864718	.135282	41	16.8245	.874872	.125128
42	17.4232	.871160	.128840	42	16.9434	.881057	.118943
43	17.5459	.877296	.122704	43	17.0565	.886936	.113064
44	17.6628	.883139	.116861	44	17.1639	.892525	.107475
45	17.7741	.888703	.111297	45	17.2661	.897837	.102163
46	17.8801	.894003	.105997	46	17.3632	.902887	.097113
47	17.9810	.899051	.100949	47	17.4555	.907688	.092312
48	18.0772	.903858	.096142	48	17.5433	.912251	.087749
49	18.1687	.908436	.091564	49	17.6267	.916588	.083412
50	18.2559	.912796	.087204	50	17.7060	.920711	.079289

TABLE B
TERM CERTAIN FACTORS

INTEREST RATE

	5.4%				5.6%		
YEARS	ANNUITY	INCOME INTEREST	REMAINDER	YEARS	ANNUITY	INCOME INTEREST	REMAINDER
1	0.9488	.051233	.948767	1	0.9470	.053030	.946970
2	1.8489	.099842	.900158	2	1.8437	.103248	.896752
3	2.7030	.145960	.854040	3	2.6929	.150803	.849197
4	3.5132	.189715	.810285	4	3.4971	.195837	.804163
5	4.2820	.231229	.768771	5	4.2586	.238482	.761518
6	5.0114	.270616	.729384	6	4.9797	.278865	.721135
7	5.7034	.307985	.692015	7	5.6626	.317107	.682893
8	6.3600	.343439	.656561	8	6.3093	.353321	.646679
9	6.9829	.377077	.622923	9	6.9217	.387615	.612385
10	7.5739	.408991	.591009	10	7.5016	.420090	.579910
11	8.1346	.439271	.560729	11	8.0508	.450843	.549157
12	8.6666	.467999	.532001	12	8.5708	.479965	.520035
13	9.1714	.495255	.504745	13	9.0633	.507542	.492458
14	9.6503	.521115	.478885	14	9.5296	.533657	.466343
15	10.1046	.545650	.454350	15	9.9712	.558388	.441612
16	10.5357	.568928	.431072	16	10.3894	.581806	.418194
17	10.9447	.591013	.408987	17	10.7854	.603983	.396017
18	11.3327	.611967	.388033	18	11.1604	.624984	.375016
19	11.7009	.631847	.368153	19	11.5156	.644871	.355129
20	12.0502	.650709	.349291	20	11.8519	.663704	.336296
21	12.3816	.668604	.331396	21	12.1703	.681538	.318462
22	12.6960	.685583	.314417	22	12.4719	.698426	.301574
23	12.9943	.701691	.298309	23	12.7575	.714419	.285581
24	13.2773	.716975	.283025	24	13.0279	.729563	.270437
25	13.5458	.731475	.268525	25	13.2840	.743904	.256096
26	13.8006	.745232	.254768	26	13.5265	.757485	.242515
27	14.0423	.758285	.241715	27	13.7562	.770346	.229654
28	14.2716	.770669	.229331	28	13.9737	.782525	.217475
29	14.4892	.782418	.217582	29	14.1796	.794057	.205943
30	14.6957	.793566	.206434	30	14.3746	.804979	.195021
31	14.8915	.804142	.195858	31	14.5593	.815321	.184679
32	15.0773	.814177	.185823	32	14.7342	.825114	.174886
33	15.2536	.823697	.176303	33	14.8998	.834388	.165612
34	15.4209	.832730	.167270	34	15.0566	.843171	.156829
35	15.5796	.841299	.158701	35	15.2051	.851488	.148512
36	15.7302	.849430	.150570	36	15.3458	.859363	.140637
37	15.8730	.857144	.142856	37	15.4790	.866821	.133179
38	16.0086	.864463	.135537	38	15.6051	.873884	.126116
39	16.1372	.871407	.128593	39	15.7245	.880572	.119428
40	16.2592	.877996	.122004	40	15.8376	.886905	.113095
41	16.3749	.884246	.115754	41	15.9447	.892903	.107097
42	16.4848	.890177	.109823	42	16.0461	.898582	.101418
43	16.5890	.895803	.104197	43	16.1421	.903960	.096040
44	16.6878	.901142	.098858	44	16.2331	.909053	.090947
45	16.7816	.906207	.093793	45	16.3192	.913876	.086124
46	16.8706	.911012	.088988	46	16.4008	.918443	.081557
47	16.9550	.915571	.084429	47	16.4780	.922768	.077232
48	17.0351	.919897	.080103	48	16.5511	.926864	.073136
49	17.1111	.924001	.075999	49	16.6204	.930742	.069258
50	17.1832	.927894	.072106	50	16.6860	.934415	.065585

TABLE B
TERM CERTAIN FACTORS

INTEREST RATE

YEARS	5.8% ANNUITY	5.8% INCOME INTEREST	5.8% REMAINDER	YEARS	6.0% ANNUITY	6.0% INCOME INTEREST	6.0% REMAINDER
1	0.9452	.054820	.945180	1	0.9434	.056604	.943396
2	1.8385	.106636	.893364	2	1.8334	.110004	.889996
3	2.6829	.155610	.844390	3	2.6730	.160381	.839619
4	3.4810	.201900	.798100	4	3.4651	.207906	.792094
5	4.2354	.245652	.754348	5	4.2124	.252742	.747258
6	4.9484	.287006	.712994	6	4.9173	.295039	.704961
7	5.6223	.326092	.673908	7	5.5824	.334943	.665057
8	6.2592	.363036	.636964	8	6.2098	.372588	.627412
9	6.8613	.397955	.602045	9	6.8017	.408102	.591898
10	7.4303	.430959	.569041	10	7.3601	.441605	.558395
11	7.9682	.462154	.537846	11	7.8869	.473212	.526788
12	8.4765	.491639	.508361	12	8.3838	.503031	.496969
13	8.9570	.519508	.480492	13	8.8527	.531161	.468839
14	9.4112	.545849	.454151	14	9.2950	.557699	.442301
15	9.8404	.570745	.429255	15	9.7122	.582735	.417265
16	10.2462	.594277	.405723	16	10.1059	.606354	.393646
17	10.6296	.616519	.383481	17	10.4773	.628636	.371364
18	10.9921	.637542	.362458	18	10.8276	.649656	.350344
19	11.3347	.657412	.342588	19	11.1581	.669487	.330513
20	11.6585	.676193	.323807	20	11.4699	.688195	.311805
21	11.9646	.693944	.306056	21	11.7641	.705845	.294155
22	12.2538	.710722	.289278	22	12.0416	.722495	.277505
23	12.5272	.726580	.273420	23	12.3034	.738203	.261797
24	12.7857	.741569	.258431	24	12.5504	.753021	.246979
25	13.0299	.755737	.244263	25	12.7834	.767001	.232999
26	13.2608	.769127	.230873	26	13.0032	.780190	.219810
27	13.4790	.781784	.218216	27	13.2105	.792632	.207368
28	13.6853	.793747	.206253	28	13.4062	.804370	.195630
29	13.8802	.805053	.194947	29	13.5907	.815443	.184557
30	14.0645	.815740	.184260	30	13.7648	.825890	.174110
31	14.2386	.825842	.174158	31	13.9291	.835745	.164255
32	14.4033	.835389	.164611	32	14.0840	.845043	.154957
33	14.5588	.844413	.155587	33	14.2302	.853814	.146186
34	14.7059	.852942	.147058	34	14.3681	.862088	.137912
35	14.8449	.861004	.138996	35	14.4982	.869895	.130105
36	14.9763	.868624	.131376	36	14.6210	.877259	.122741
37	15.1004	.875826	.124174	37	14.7368	.884207	.115793
38	15.2178	.882633	.117367	38	14.8460	.890761	.109239
39	15.3287	.889067	.110933	39	14.9491	.896944	.103056
40	15.4336	.895149	.104851	40	15.0463	.902778	.097222
41	15.5327	.900897	.099103	41	15.1380	.908281	.091719
42	15.6264	.906330	.093670	42	15.2245	.913473	.086527
43	15.7149	.911465	.088535	43	15.3062	.918370	.081630
44	15.7986	.916318	.083682	44	15.3832	.922991	.077009
45	15.8777	.920906	.079094	45	15.4558	.927350	.072650
46	15.9524	.925242	.074758	46	15.5244	.931462	.068538
47	16.0231	.929340	.070660	47	15.5890	.935342	.064658
48	16.0899	.933214	.066786	48	15.6500	.939002	.060998
49	16.1530	.936875	.063125	49	15.7076	.942454	.057546
50	16.2127	.940335	.059665	50	15.7619	.945712	.054288

TABLE B
TERM CERTAIN FACTORS

INTEREST RATE

	6.2%				6.4%		
YEARS	ANNUITY	INCOME INTEREST	REMAINDER	YEARS	ANNUITY	INCOME INTEREST	REMAINDER
1	0.9416	.058380	.941620	1	0.9398	.060150	.939850
2	1.8283	.113353	.886647	2	1.8232	.116683	.883317
3	2.6632	.165115	.834885	3	2.6534	.169815	.830185
4	3.4493	.213856	.786144	4	3.4336	.219751	.780249
5	4.1895	.259752	.740248	5	4.1669	.266683	.733317
6	4.8866	.302968	.697032	6	4.8561	.310792	.689208
7	5.5429	.343661	.656339	7	5.5039	.352248	.647752
8	6.1609	.381978	.618022	8	6.1127	.391211	.608789
9	6.7429	.418058	.581942	9	6.6848	.427830	.572170
10	7.2908	.452032	.547968	10	7.2226	.462246	.537754
11	7.8068	.484023	.515977	11	7.7280	.494592	.505408
12	8.2927	.514146	.485854	12	8.2030	.524993	.475007
13	8.7502	.542510	.457490	13	8.6494	.553564	.446436
14	9.1809	.569219	.430781	14	9.0690	.580418	.419582
15	9.5866	.594368	.405632	15	9.4634	.605656	.394344
16	9.9685	.618049	.381951	16	9.8340	.629376	.370624
17	10.3282	.640347	.359653	17	10.1823	.651669	.348331
18	10.6668	.661344	.338656	18	10.5097	.672621	.327379
19	10.9857	.681115	.318885	19	10.8174	.692313	.307687
20	11.2860	.699732	.300268	20	11.1066	.710821	.289179
21	11.5687	.717261	.282739	21	11.3784	.728215	.271785
22	11.8350	.733768	.266232	22	11.6338	.744563	.255437
23	12.0857	.749311	.250689	23	11.8739	.759927	.240073
24	12.3217	.763946	.236054	24	12.0995	.774368	.225632
25	12.5440	.777727	.222273	25	12.3116	.787940	.212060
26	12.7533	.790703	.209297	26	12.5109	.800695	.199305
27	12.9504	.802922	.197078	27	12.6982	.812684	.187316
28	13.1359	.814428	.185572	28	12.8742	.823951	.176049
29	13.3107	.825261	.174739	29	13.0397	.834540	.165460
30	13.4752	.835463	.164537	30	13.1952	.844493	.155507
31	13.6301	.845068	.154932	31	13.3413	.853846	.146154
32	13.7760	.854113	.145887	32	13.4787	.862638	.137362
33	13.9134	.862630	.137370	33	13.6078	.870900	.129100
34	14.0427	.870650	.129350	34	13.7291	.878665	.121335
35	14.1645	.878202	.121798	35	13.8432	.885964	.114036
36	14.2792	.885312	.114688	36	13.9504	.892823	.107177
37	14.3872	.892008	.107992	37	14.0511	.899270	.100730
38	14.4889	.898312	.101688	38	14.1458	.905329	.094671
39	14.5847	.904249	.095751	39	14.2347	.911023	.088977
40	14.6748	.909839	.090161	40	14.3184	.916375	.083625
41	14.7597	.915103	.084897	41	14.3970	.921405	.078595
42	14.8397	.920059	.079941	42	14.4708	.926133	.073867
43	14.9149	.924726	.075274	43	14.5402	.930576	.069424
44	14.9858	.929120	.070880	44	14.6055	.934752	.065248
45	15.0526	.933258	.066742	45	14.6668	.938677	.061323
46	15.1154	.937155	.062845	46	14.7245	.942365	.057635
47	15.1746	.940824	.059176	47	14.7786	.945832	.054168
48	15.2303	.944278	.055722	48	14.8295	.949090	.050910
49	15.2828	.947531	.052469	49	14.8774	.952152	.047848
50	15.3322	.950595	.049405	50	14.9224	.955030	.044970

TABLE B
TERM CERTAIN FACTORS

INTEREST RATE

	6.6%				6.8%		
YEARS	ANNUITY	INCOME INTEREST	REMAINDER	YEARS	ANNUITY	INCOME INTEREST	REMAINDER
1	0.9381	.061914	.938086	1	0.9363	.063670	.936330
2	1.8181	.119994	.880006	2	1.8130	.123287	.876713
3	2.6436	.174479	.825521	3	2.6339	.179108	.820892
4	3.4180	.225590	.774410	4	3.4026	.231374	.768626
5	4.1445	.273536	.726464	5	4.1222	.280313	.719687
6	4.8260	.318514	.681486	6	4.7961	.326136	.673864
7	5.4653	.360708	.639292	7	5.4271	.369041	.630959
8	6.0650	.400289	.599711	8	6.0179	.409214	.590786
9	6.6276	.437419	.562581	9	6.5710	.446830	.553170
10	7.1553	.472250	.527750	10	7.0890	.482050	.517950
11	7.6504	.504925	.495075	11	7.5739	.515029	.484971
12	8.1148	.535577	.464423	12	8.0280	.545907	.454093
13	8.5505	.564331	.435669	13	8.4532	.574819	.425181
14	8.9592	.591305	.408695	14	8.8513	.601891	.398109
15	9.3426	.616609	.383391	15	9.2241	.627238	.372762
16	9.7022	.640346	.359654	16	9.5731	.650972	.349028
17	10.0396	.662614	.337386	17	9.8999	.673195	.326805
18	10.3561	.683502	.316498	18	10.2059	.694003	.305997
19	10.6530	.703098	.296902	19	10.4924	.713486	.286514
20	10.9315	.721480	.278520	20	10.7607	.731728	.268272
21	11.1928	.738724	.261276	21	11.0119	.748809	.251191
22	11.4379	.754901	.245099	22	11.2471	.764803	.235197
23	11.6678	.770076	.229924	23	11.4673	.779778	.220222
24	11.8835	.784311	.215689	24	11.6735	.793799	.206201
25	12.0858	.797666	.202334	25	11.8666	.806928	.193072
26	12.2756	.810193	.189807	26	12.0474	.819221	.180779
27	12.4537	.821944	.178056	27	12.2166	.830732	.169268
28	12.6207	.832969	.167031	28	12.3751	.841509	.158491
29	12.7774	.843310	.156690	29	12.5235	.851600	.148400
30	12.9244	.853011	.146989	30	12.6625	.861049	.138951
31	13.0623	.862112	.137888	31	12.7926	.869896	.130104
32	13.1917	.870649	.129351	32	12.9144	.878180	.121820
33	13.3130	.878658	.121342	33	13.0285	.885936	.114064
34	13.4268	.886170	.113830	34	13.1353	.893198	.106802
35	13.5336	.893218	.106782	35	13.2353	.899999	.100001
36	13.6338	.899829	.100171	36	13.3289	.906366	.093634
37	13.7277	.906031	.093969	37	13.4166	.912327	.087673
38	13.8159	.911849	.088151	38	13.4987	.917910	.082090
39	13.8986	.917307	.082693	39	13.5755	.923136	.076864
40	13.9762	.922427	.077573	40	13.6475	.928030	.071970
41	14.0489	.927230	.072770	41	13.7149	.932613	.067387
42	14.1172	.931735	.068265	42	13.7780	.936903	.063097
43	14.1812	.935962	.064038	43	13.8371	.940921	.059079
44	14.2413	.939926	.060074	44	13.8924	.944682	.055318
45	14.2977	.943646	.056354	45	13.9442	.948204	.051796
46	14.3505	.947135	.052865	46	13.9927	.951502	.048498
47	14.4001	.950408	.049592	47	14.0381	.954590	.045410
48	14.4466	.953478	.046522	48	14.0806	.957481	.042519
49	14.4903	.956359	.043641	49	14.1204	.960188	.039812
50	14.5312	.959061	.040939	50	14.1577	.962723	.037277

TABLE B
TERM CERTAIN FACTORS

INTEREST RATE

	7.0%				7.2%		
YEARS	ANNUITY	INCOME INTEREST	REMAINDER	YEARS	ANNUITY	INCOME INTEREST	REMAINDER
1	0.9346	.065421	.934579	1	0.9328	.067164	.932836
2	1.8080	.126561	.873439	2	1.8030	.129817	.870183
3	2.6243	.183702	.816298	3	2.6148	.188262	.811738
4	3.3872	.237105	.762895	4	3.3720	.242782	.757218
5	4.1002	.287014	.712986	5	4.0783	.293640	.706360
6	4.7665	.333658	.666342	6	4.7373	.341082	.658918
7	5.3893	.377250	.622750	7	5.3519	.385338	.614662
8	5.9713	.417991	.582009	8	5.9253	.426621	.573379
9	6.5152	.456066	.543934	9	6.4602	.465132	.534868
10	7.0236	.491651	.508349	10	6.9591	.501056	.498944
11	7.4987	.524907	.475093	11	7.4245	.534567	.465433
12	7.9427	.555988	.444012	12	7.8587	.565827	.434173
13	8.3577	.585036	.414964	13	8.2637	.594988	.405012
14	8.7455	.612183	.387817	14	8.6415	.622190	.377810
15	9.1079	.637554	.362446	15	8.9940	.647566	.352434
16	9.4466	.661265	.338735	16	9.3227	.671237	.328763
17	9.7632	.683426	.316574	17	9.6294	.693318	.306682
18	10.0591	.704136	.295864	18	9.9155	.713916	.286084
19	10.3356	.723492	.276508	19	10.1824	.733130	.266870
20	10.5940	.741581	.258419	20	10.4313	.751054	.248946
21	10.8355	.758487	.241513	21	10.6635	.767775	.232225
22	11.0612	.774287	.225713	22	10.8802	.783372	.216628
23	11.2722	.789053	.210947	23	11.0822	.797922	.202078
24	11.4693	.802853	.197147	24	11.2708	.811494	.188506
25	11.6536	.815751	.184249	25	11.4466	.824155	.175845
26	11.8258	.827805	.172195	26	11.6106	.835965	.164035
27	11.9867	.839070	.160930	27	11.7636	.846983	.153017
28	12.1371	.849598	.150402	28	11.9064	.857260	.142740
29	12.2777	.859437	.140563	29	12.0395	.866847	.133153
30	12.4090	.868633	.131367	30	12.1638	.875790	.124210
31	12.5318	.877227	.122773	31	12.2796	.884132	.115868
32	12.6466	.885259	.114741	32	12.3877	.891915	.108085
33	12.7538	.892765	.107235	33	12.4885	.899174	.100826
34	12.8540	.899781	.100219	34	12.5826	.905946	.094054
35	12.9477	.906337	.093663	35	12.6703	.912263	.087737
36	13.0352	.912465	.087535	36	12.7522	.918156	.081844
37	13.1170	.918191	.081809	37	12.8285	.923653	.076347
38	13.1935	.923543	.076457	38	12.8997	.928781	.071219
39	13.2649	.928545	.071455	39	12.9662	.933564	.066436
40	13.3317	.933220	.066780	40	13.0281	.938026	.061974
41	13.3941	.937588	.062412	41	13.0860	.942189	.057811
42	13.4524	.941671	.058329	42	13.1399	.946071	.053929
43	13.5070	.945487	.054513	43	13.1902	.949693	.050307
44	13.5579	.949054	.050946	44	13.2371	.953072	.046928
45	13.6055	.952387	.047613	45	13.2809	.956224	.043776
46	13.6500	.955501	.044499	46	13.3217	.959164	.040836
47	13.6916	.958413	.041587	47	13.3598	.961907	.038093
48	13.7305	.961133	.038867	48	13.3954	.964465	.035535
49	13.7668	.963676	.036324	49	13.4285	.966852	.033148
50	13.8007	.966052	.033948	50	13.4594	.969078	.030922

TABLE B
TERM CERTAIN FACTORS

INTEREST RATE

YEARS	7.4% ANNUITY	INCOME INTEREST	REMAINDER	YEARS	7.6% ANNUITY	INCOME INTEREST	REMAINDER
1	0.9311	.068901	.931099	1	0.9294	.070632	.929368
2	1.7980	.133055	.866945	2	1.7931	.136275	.863725
3	2.6053	.192789	.807211	3	2.5958	.197282	.802718
4	3.3568	.248407	.751593	4	3.3418	.253979	.746021
5	4.0567	.300193	.699807	5	4.0352	.306672	.693328
6	4.7082	.348410	.651590	6	4.6795	.355643	.644357
7	5.3149	.393306	.606694	7	5.2784	.401155	.598845
8	5.8798	.435108	.564892	8	5.8349	.443453	.556547
9	6.4058	.474029	.525971	9	6.3521	.482763	.517237
10	6.8955	.510269	.489731	10	6.8328	.519296	.480704
11	7.3515	.544013	.455987	11	7.2796	.553250	.446750
12	7.7761	.575431	.424569	12	7.6948	.584804	.415196
13	8.1714	.604684	.395316	13	8.0807	.614130	.385870
14	8.5395	.631922	.368078	14	8.4393	.641385	.358615
15	8.8822	.657283	.342717	15	8.7726	.666715	.333285
16	9.2013	.680897	.319103	16	9.0823	.690255	.309745
17	9.4984	.702883	.297117	17	9.3702	.712133	.287867
18	9.7751	.723355	.276645	18	9.6377	.732466	.267534
19	10.0327	.742416	.257584	19	9.8863	.751362	.248638
20	10.2725	.760164	.239836	20	10.1174	.768924	.231076
21	10.4958	.776689	.223311	21	10.3322	.785245	.214755
22	10.7037	.792075	.207925	22	10.5318	.800414	.199586
23	10.8973	.806402	.193598	23	10.7173	.814511	.185489
24	11.0776	.819741	.180259	24	10.8896	.827613	.172387
25	11.2454	.832161	.167839	25	11.0499	.839789	.160211
26	11.4017	.843725	.156275	26	11.1987	.851105	.148895
27	11.5472	.854493	.145507	27	11.3371	.861621	.138379
28	11.6827	.864518	.135482	28	11.4657	.871395	.128605
29	11.8088	.873853	.126147	29	11.5853	.880479	.119521
30	11.9263	.882545	.117455	30	11.6963	.888921	.111079
31	12.0356	.890638	.109362	31	11.7996	.896767	.103233
32	12.1375	.898173	.101827	32	11.8955	.904058	.095942
33	12.2323	.905189	.094811	33	11.9847	.910835	.089165
34	12.3206	.911722	.088278	34	12.0675	.917133	.082867
35	12.4028	.917804	.082196	35	12.1446	.922986	.077014
36	12.4793	.923468	.076532	36	12.2161	.928426	.071574
37	12.5505	.928741	.071259	37	12.2826	.933481	.066519
38	12.6169	.933651	.066349	38	12.3445	.938179	.061821
39	12.6787	.938222	.061778	39	12.4019	.942546	.057454
40	12.7362	.942479	.057521	40	12.4553	.946604	.053396
41	12.7898	.946442	.053558	41	12.5049	.950375	.049625
42	12.8396	.950132	.049868	42	12.5511	.953880	.046120
43	12.8861	.953568	.046432	43	12.5939	.957138	.042862
44	12.9293	.956767	.043233	44	12.6338	.960165	.039835
45	12.9695	.959746	.040254	45	12.6708	.962979	.037021
46	13.0070	.962520	.037480	46	12.7052	.965594	.034406
47	13.0419	.965102	.034898	47	12.7372	.968024	.031976
48	13.0744	.967507	.032493	48	12.7669	.970283	.029717
49	13.1047	.969745	.030255	49	12.7945	.972382	.027618
50	13.1328	.971830	.028170	50	12.8202	.974332	.025668

TABLE S (4.6)
SINGLE LIFE FACTORS BASED ON LIFE TABLE 2000CM

4.6% INTEREST

AGE	ANNUITY	LIFE ESTATE	REMAINDER	AGE	ANNUITY	LIFE ESTATE	REMAINDER
0	20.6611	0.95041	0.04959	55	13.9887	0.64348	0.35652
1	20.7593	0.95493	0.04507	56	13.7264	0.63141	0.36859
2	20.7249	0.95335	0.04665	57	13.4595	0.61914	0.38086
3	20.6853	0.95152	0.04848	58	13.1885	0.60667	0.39333
4	20.6421	0.94954	0.05046	59	12.9130	0.59400	0.40600
5	20.5961	0.94742	0.05258	60	12.6327	0.58110	0.41890
6	20.5474	0.94518	0.05482	61	12.3478	0.56800	0.43200
7	20.4964	0.94283	0.05717	62	12.0593	0.55473	0.44527
8	20.4426	0.94036	0.05964	63	11.7673	0.54130	0.45870
9	20.3859	0.93775	0.06225	64	11.4720	0.52771	0.47229
10	20.3264	0.93501	0.06499	65	11.1733	0.51397	0.48603
11	20.2639	0.93214	0.06786	66	10.8681	0.49993	0.50007
12	20.1986	0.92913	0.07087	67	10.5574	0.48564	0.51436
13	20.1310	0.92603	0.07397	68	10.2425	0.47115	0.52885
14	20.0620	0.92285	0.07715	69	9.9241	0.45651	0.54349
15	19.9921	0.91964	0.08036	70	9.6030	0.44174	0.55826
16	19.9217	0.91640	0.08360	71	9.2792	0.42684	0.57316
17	19.8502	0.91311	0.08689	72	8.9533	0.41185	0.58815
18	19.7775	0.90976	0.09024	73	8.6265	0.39682	0.60318
19	19.7030	0.90634	0.09366	74	8.3004	0.38182	0.61818
20	19.6258	0.90279	0.09721	75	7.9763	0.36691	0.63309
21	19.5463	0.89913	0.10087	76	7.6553	0.35214	0.64786
22	19.4640	0.89535	0.10465	77	7.3375	0.33752	0.66248
23	19.3786	0.89141	0.10859	78	7.0235	0.32308	0.67692
24	19.2891	0.88730	0.11270	79	6.7139	0.30884	0.69116
25	19.1950	0.88297	0.11703	80	6.4096	0.29484	0.70516
26	19.0961	0.87842	0.12158	81	6.1109	0.28110	0.71890
27	18.9922	0.87364	0.12636	82	5.8185	0.26765	0.73235
28	18.8833	0.86863	0.13137	83	5.5330	0.25452	0.74548
29	18.7696	0.86340	0.13660	84	5.2548	0.24172	0.75828
30	18.6514	0.85797	0.14203	85	4.9844	0.22928	0.77072
31	18.5285	0.85231	0.14769	86	4.7223	0.21722	0.78278
32	18.4007	0.84643	0.15357	87	4.4689	0.20557	0.79443
33	18.2679	0.84032	0.15968	88	4.2242	0.19431	0.80569
34	18.1306	0.83401	0.16599	89	3.9889	0.18349	0.81651
35	17.9884	0.82747	0.17253	90	3.7630	0.17310	0.82690
36	17.8411	0.82069	0.17931	91	3.5467	0.16315	0.83685
37	17.6888	0.81369	0.18631	92	3.3400	0.15364	0.84636
38	17.5311	0.80643	0.19357	93	3.1433	0.14459	0.85541
39	17.3684	0.79895	0.20105	94	2.9562	0.13598	0.86402
40	17.2005	0.79122	0.20878	95	2.7784	0.12781	0.87219
41	17.0274	0.78326	0.21674	96	2.6106	0.12009	0.87991
42	16.8490	0.77506	0.22494	97	2.4522	0.11280	0.88720
43	16.6649	0.76658	0.23342	98	2.3027	0.10592	0.89408
44	16.4752	0.75786	0.24214	99	2.1614	0.09943	0.90057
45	16.2800	0.74888	0.25112	100	2.0298	0.09337	0.90663
46	16.0788	0.73962	0.26038	101	1.9047	0.08762	0.91238
47	15.8720	0.73011	0.26989	102	1.7890	0.08229	0.91771
48	15.6593	0.72033	0.27967	103	1.6740	0.07700	0.92300
49	15.4405	0.71026	0.28974	104	1.5682	0.07214	0.92786
50	15.2150	0.69989	0.30011	105	1.4638	0.06734	0.93266
51	14.9828	0.68921	0.31079	106	1.3332	0.06133	0.93867
52	14.7439	0.67822	0.32178	107	1.1851	0.05451	0.94549
53	14.4983	0.66692	0.33308	108	0.9455	0.04349	0.95651
54	14.2464	0.65533	0.34467	109	0.4780	0.02199	0.97801

TABLE S (4.8)
SINGLE LIFE FACTORS BASED ON LIFE TABLE 2000CM

4.8% INTEREST

AGE	ANNUITY	LIFE ESTATE	REMAINDER	AGE	ANNUITY	LIFE ESTATE	REMAINDER
0	19.8956	0.95499	0.04501	55	13.6857	0.65692	0.34308
1	19.9930	0.95966	0.04034	56	13.4349	0.64488	0.35512
2	19.9630	0.95822	0.04178	57	13.1795	0.63261	0.36739
3	19.9280	0.95654	0.04346	58	12.9198	0.62015	0.37985
4	19.8897	0.95470	0.04530	59	12.6555	0.60747	0.39253
5	19.8487	0.95274	0.04726	60	12.3863	0.59454	0.40546
6	19.8051	0.95065	0.04935	61	12.1124	0.58140	0.41860
7	19.7594	0.94845	0.05155	62	11.8347	0.56806	0.43194
8	19.7112	0.94614	0.05386	63	11.5534	0.55456	0.44544
9	19.6601	0.94369	0.05631	64	11.2686	0.54089	0.45911
10	19.6065	0.94111	0.05889	65	10.9802	0.52705	0.47295
11	19.5500	0.93840	0.06160	66	10.6852	0.51289	0.48711
12	19.4908	0.93556	0.06444	67	10.3845	0.49846	0.50154
13	19.4296	0.93262	0.06738	68	10.0793	0.48381	0.51619
14	19.3670	0.92962	0.07038	69	9.7705	0.46898	0.53102
15	19.3037	0.92658	0.07342	70	9.4587	0.45402	0.54598
16	19.2398	0.92351	0.07649	71	9.1439	0.43891	0.56109
17	19.1750	0.92040	0.07960	72	8.8267	0.42368	0.57632
18	19.1091	0.91724	0.08276	73	8.5084	0.40840	0.59160
19	19.0416	0.91400	0.08600	74	8.1904	0.39314	0.60686
20	18.9716	0.91063	0.08937	75	7.8741	0.37796	0.62204
21	18.8993	0.90717	0.09283	76	7.5605	0.36290	0.63710
22	18.8245	0.90358	0.09642	77	7.2498	0.34799	0.65201
23	18.7466	0.89984	0.10016	78	6.9425	0.33324	0.66676
24	18.6650	0.89592	0.10408	79	6.6393	0.31868	0.68132
25	18.5790	0.89179	0.10821	80	6.3409	0.30437	0.69563
26	18.4883	0.88744	0.11256	81	6.0480	0.29030	0.70970
27	18.3929	0.88286	0.11714	82	5.7608	0.27652	0.72348
28	18.2927	0.87805	0.12195	83	5.4803	0.26305	0.73695
29	18.1879	0.87302	0.12698	84	5.2067	0.24992	0.75008
30	18.0787	0.86778	0.13222	85	4.9407	0.23715	0.76285
31	17.9650	0.86232	0.13768	86	4.6825	0.22476	0.77524
32	17.8467	0.85664	0.14336	87	4.4328	0.21278	0.78722
33	17.7235	0.85073	0.14927	88	4.1916	0.20120	0.79880
34	17.5960	0.84461	0.15539	89	3.9594	0.19005	0.80995
35	17.4637	0.83826	0.16174	90	3.7364	0.17935	0.82065
36	17.3265	0.83167	0.16833	91	3.5226	0.16909	0.83091
37	17.1844	0.82485	0.17515	92	3.3183	0.15928	0.84072
38	17.0371	0.81778	0.18222	93	3.1238	0.14994	0.85006
39	16.8849	0.81048	0.18952	94	2.9387	0.14106	0.85894
40	16.7277	0.80293	0.19707	95	2.7626	0.13261	0.86739
41	16.5653	0.79513	0.20487	96	2.5965	0.12463	0.87537
42	16.3978	0.78710	0.21290	97	2.4395	0.11710	0.88290
43	16.2246	0.77878	0.22122	98	2.2913	0.10998	0.89002
44	16.0461	0.77021	0.22979	99	2.1512	0.10326	0.89674
45	15.8620	0.76138	0.23862	100	2.0207	0.09699	0.90301
46	15.6721	0.75226	0.24774	101	1.8965	0.09103	0.90897
47	15.4767	0.74288	0.25712	102	1.7816	0.08552	0.91448
48	15.2754	0.73322	0.26678	103	1.6674	0.08004	0.91996
49	15.0680	0.72326	0.27674	104	1.5624	0.07499	0.92501
50	14.8540	0.71299	0.28701	105	1.4588	0.07002	0.92998
51	14.6335	0.70241	0.29759	106	1.3290	0.06379	0.93621
52	14.4061	0.69149	0.30851	107	1.1817	0.05672	0.94328
53	14.1721	0.68026	0.31974	108	0.9433	0.04528	0.95472
54	13.9318	0.66873	0.33127	109	0.4771	0.02290	0.97710

TABLE S (5.0)
SINGLE LIFE FACTORS BASED ON LIFE TABLE 2000CM

5.0% INTEREST

AGE	ANNUITY	LIFE ESTATE	REMAINDER	AGE	ANNUITY	LIFE ESTATE	REMAINDER
0	19.1799	0.95899	0.04101	55	13.3935	0.66968	0.33032
1	19.2763	0.96382	0.03618	56	13.1536	0.65768	0.34232
2	19.2501	0.96250	0.03750	57	12.9089	0.64545	0.35455
3	19.2192	0.96096	0.03904	58	12.6600	0.63300	0.36700
4	19.1851	0.95925	0.04075	59	12.4064	0.62032	0.37968
5	19.1485	0.95742	0.04258	60	12.1477	0.60739	0.39261
6	19.1095	0.95547	0.04453	61	11.8844	0.59422	0.40578
7	19.0685	0.95342	0.04658	62	11.6170	0.58085	0.41915
8	19.0251	0.95125	0.04875	63	11.3459	0.56729	0.43271
9	18.9791	0.94895	0.05105	64	11.0711	0.55355	0.44645
10	18.9306	0.94653	0.05347	65	10.7925	0.53963	0.46037
11	18.8795	0.94397	0.05603	66	10.5073	0.52536	0.47464
12	18.8258	0.94129	0.05871	67	10.2162	0.51081	0.48919
13	18.7702	0.93851	0.06149	68	9.9204	0.49602	0.50398
14	18.7133	0.93567	0.06433	69	9.6208	0.48104	0.51896
15	18.6558	0.93279	0.06721	70	9.3180	0.46590	0.53410
16	18.5978	0.92989	0.07011	71	9.0119	0.45060	0.54940
17	18.5391	0.92695	0.07305	72	8.7032	0.43516	0.56484
18	18.4793	0.92396	0.07604	73	8.3930	0.41965	0.58035
19	18.4180	0.92090	0.07910	74	8.0829	0.40414	0.59586
20	18.3543	0.91772	0.08228	75	7.7742	0.38871	0.61129
21	18.2886	0.91443	0.08557	76	7.4677	0.37339	0.62661
22	18.2205	0.91103	0.08897	77	7.1639	0.35819	0.64181
23	18.1495	0.90748	0.09252	78	6.8631	0.34316	0.65684
24	18.0749	0.90375	0.09625	79	6.5660	0.32830	0.67170
25	17.9962	0.89981	0.10019	80	6.2736	0.31368	0.68632
26	17.9131	0.89565	0.10435	81	5.9861	0.29931	0.70069
27	17.8253	0.89127	0.10873	82	5.7042	0.28521	0.71479
28	17.7330	0.88665	0.11335	83	5.4285	0.27142	0.72858
29	17.6363	0.88181	0.11819	84	5.1594	0.25797	0.74203
30	17.5354	0.87677	0.12323	85	4.8976	0.24488	0.75512
31	17.4302	0.87151	0.12849	86	4.6433	0.23217	0.76783
32	17.3205	0.86602	0.13398	87	4.3973	0.21986	0.78014
33	17.2061	0.86030	0.13970	88	4.1594	0.20797	0.79203
34	17.0875	0.85438	0.14562	89	3.9302	0.19651	0.80349
35	16.9643	0.84822	0.15178	90	3.7101	0.18550	0.81450
36	16.8364	0.84182	0.15818	91	3.4989	0.17495	0.82505
37	16.7038	0.83519	0.16481	92	3.2969	0.16485	0.83515
38	16.5661	0.82830	0.17170	93	3.1046	0.15523	0.84477
39	16.4236	0.82118	0.17882	94	2.9213	0.14607	0.85393
40	16.2762	0.81381	0.18619	95	2.7471	0.13735	0.86265
41	16.1238	0.80619	0.19381	96	2.5825	0.12912	0.87088
42	15.9665	0.79832	0.20168	97	2.4270	0.12135	0.87865
43	15.8035	0.79018	0.20982	98	2.2800	0.11400	0.88600
44	15.6353	0.78176	0.21824	99	2.1411	0.10706	0.89294
45	15.4617	0.77308	0.22692	100	2.0116	0.10058	0.89942
46	15.2823	0.76411	0.23589	101	1.8884	0.09442	0.90558
47	15.0975	0.75487	0.24513	102	1.7743	0.08872	0.91128
48	14.9069	0.74534	0.25466	103	1.6609	0.08305	0.91695
49	14.7103	0.73551	0.26449	104	1.5566	0.07783	0.92217
50	14.5071	0.72535	0.27465	105	1.4537	0.07269	0.92731
51	14.2974	0.71487	0.28513	106	1.3247	0.06624	0.93376
52	14.0810	0.70405	0.29595	107	1.1784	0.05892	0.94108
53	13.8580	0.69290	0.30710	108	0.9410	0.04705	0.95295
54	13.6286	0.68143	0.31857	109	0.4762	0.02381	0.97619

TABLE S (5.2)
SINGLE LIFE FACTORS BASED ON LIFE TABLE 2000CM

5.2% INTEREST

AGE	ANNUITY	LIFE ESTATE	REMAINDER	AGE	ANNUITY	LIFE ESTATE	REMAINDER
0	18.5097	0.96251	0.03749	55	13.1115	0.68180	0.31820
1	18.6050	0.96746	0.03254	56	12.8819	0.66986	0.33014
2	18.5821	0.96627	0.03373	57	12.6476	0.65767	0.34233
3	18.5547	0.96484	0.03516	58	12.4088	0.64526	0.35474
4	18.5243	0.96326	0.03674	59	12.1654	0.63260	0.36740
5	18.4916	0.96156	0.03844	60	11.9168	0.61967	0.38033
6	18.4566	0.95974	0.04026	61	11.6634	0.60649	0.39351
7	18.4198	0.95783	0.04217	62	11.4058	0.59310	0.40690
8	18.3807	0.95579	0.04421	63	11.1445	0.57951	0.42049
9	18.3391	0.95363	0.04637	64	10.8793	0.56572	0.43428
10	18.2952	0.95135	0.04865	65	10.6102	0.55173	0.44827
11	18.2488	0.94894	0.05106	66	10.3343	0.53738	0.46262
12	18.2000	0.94640	0.05360	67	10.0524	0.52273	0.47727
13	18.1495	0.94377	0.05623	68	9.7657	0.50782	0.49218
14	18.0977	0.94108	0.05892	69	9.4749	0.49269	0.50731
15	18.0454	0.93836	0.06164	70	9.1808	0.47740	0.52260
16	17.9927	0.93562	0.06438	71	8.8831	0.46192	0.53808
17	17.9393	0.93284	0.06716	72	8.5825	0.44629	0.55371
18	17.8850	0.93002	0.06998	73	8.2803	0.43057	0.56943
19	17.8293	0.92712	0.07288	74	7.9777	0.41484	0.58516
20	17.7714	0.92411	0.07589	75	7.6763	0.39917	0.60083
21	17.7116	0.92100	0.07900	76	7.3768	0.38360	0.61640
22	17.6495	0.91777	0.08223	77	7.0797	0.36814	0.63186
23	17.5847	0.91441	0.08559	78	6.7853	0.35283	0.64717
24	17.5165	0.91086	0.08914	79	6.4942	0.33770	0.66230
25	17.4444	0.90711	0.09289	80	6.2075	0.32279	0.67721
26	17.3680	0.90314	0.09686	81	5.9254	0.30812	0.69188
27	17.2873	0.89894	0.10106	82	5.6485	0.29372	0.70628
28	17.2021	0.89451	0.10549	83	5.3775	0.27963	0.72037
29	17.1128	0.88987	0.11013	84	5.1129	0.26587	0.73413
30	17.0195	0.88502	0.11498	85	4.8552	0.25247	0.74753
31	16.9220	0.87994	0.12006	86	4.6048	0.23945	0.76055
32	16.8202	0.87465	0.12535	87	4.3623	0.22684	0.77316
33	16.7139	0.86912	0.13088	88	4.1276	0.21464	0.78536
34	16.6036	0.86339	0.13661	89	3.9015	0.20288	0.79712
35	16.4888	0.85742	0.14258	90	3.6841	0.19157	0.80843
36	16.3695	0.85121	0.14879	91	3.4755	0.18072	0.81928
37	16.2455	0.84477	0.15523	92	3.2758	0.17034	0.82966
38	16.1167	0.83807	0.16193	93	3.0855	0.16045	0.83955
39	15.9832	0.83113	0.16887	94	2.9042	0.15102	0.84898
40	15.8450	0.82394	0.17606	95	2.7317	0.14205	0.85795
41	15.7018	0.81650	0.18350	96	2.5687	0.13357	0.86643
42	15.5539	0.80880	0.19120	97	2.4146	0.12556	0.87444
43	15.4004	0.80082	0.19918	98	2.2689	0.11798	0.88202
44	15.2419	0.79258	0.20742	99	2.1311	0.11082	0.88918
45	15.0780	0.78405	0.21595	100	2.0026	0.10413	0.89587
46	14.9084	0.77524	0.22476	101	1.8803	0.09777	0.90223
47	14.7336	0.76614	0.23386	102	1.7671	0.09189	0.90811
48	14.5530	0.75675	0.24325	103	1.6545	0.08603	0.91397
49	14.3665	0.74706	0.25294	104	1.5509	0.08065	0.91935
50	14.1735	0.73702	0.26298	105	1.4487	0.07533	0.92467
51	13.9741	0.72665	0.27335	106	1.3206	0.06867	0.93133
52	13.7679	0.71593	0.28407	107	1.1750	0.06110	0.93890
53	13.5552	0.70487	0.29513	108	0.9388	0.04882	0.95118
54	13.3363	0.69349	0.30651	109	0.4753	0.02471	0.97529

TABLE S (5.4)
SINGLE LIFE FACTORS BASED ON LIFE TABLE 2000CM

5.4% INTEREST

AGE	ANNUITY	LIFE ESTATE	REMAINDER	AGE	ANNUITY	LIFE ESTATE	REMAINDER
0	17.8813	0.96559	0.03441	55	12.8393	0.69332	0.30668
1	17.9753	0.97066	0.02934	56	12.6195	0.68145	0.31855
2	17.9552	0.96958	0.03042	57	12.3949	0.66932	0.33068
3	17.9309	0.96827	0.03173	58	12.1659	0.65696	0.34304
4	17.9038	0.96681	0.03319	59	11.9321	0.64433	0.35567
5	17.8745	0.96522	0.03478	60	11.6930	0.63142	0.36858
6	17.8431	0.96353	0.03647	61	11.4491	0.61825	0.38175
7	17.8099	0.96174	0.03826	62	11.2010	0.60486	0.39514
8	17.7746	0.95983	0.04017	63	10.9490	0.59124	0.40876
9	17.7370	0.95780	0.04220	64	10.6930	0.57742	0.42258
10	17.6972	0.95565	0.04435	65	10.4330	0.56338	0.43662
11	17.6550	0.95337	0.04663	66	10.1660	0.54897	0.45103
12	17.6106	0.95097	0.04903	67	9.8930	0.53422	0.46578
13	17.5645	0.94848	0.05152	68	9.6150	0.51921	0.48079
14	17.5173	0.94594	0.05406	69	9.3327	0.50397	0.49603
15	17.4696	0.94336	0.05664	70	9.0469	0.48853	0.51147
16	17.4217	0.94077	0.05923	71	8.7573	0.47290	0.52710
17	17.3731	0.93815	0.06185	72	8.4647	0.45709	0.54291
18	17.3237	0.93548	0.06452	73	8.1701	0.44118	0.55882
19	17.2730	0.93274	0.06726	74	7.8749	0.42524	0.57476
20	17.2203	0.92990	0.07010	75	7.5806	0.40935	0.59065
21	17.1658	0.92695	0.07305	76	7.2879	0.39354	0.60646
22	17.1092	0.92390	0.07610	77	6.9972	0.37785	0.62215
23	17.0500	0.92070	0.07930	78	6.7089	0.36228	0.63772
24	16.9876	0.91733	0.08267	79	6.4237	0.34688	0.65312
25	16.9214	0.91375	0.08625	80	6.1425	0.33170	0.66830
26	16.8512	0.90997	0.09003	81	5.8657	0.31675	0.68325
27	16.7769	0.90595	0.09405	82	5.5937	0.30206	0.69794
28	16.6983	0.90171	0.09829	83	5.3273	0.28768	0.71232
29	16.6157	0.89725	0.10275	84	5.0671	0.27362	0.72638
30	16.5293	0.89258	0.10742	85	4.8134	0.25992	0.74008
31	16.4389	0.88770	0.11230	86	4.5667	0.24660	0.75340
32	16.3443	0.88259	0.11741	87	4.3277	0.23370	0.76630
33	16.2455	0.87725	0.12275	88	4.0963	0.22120	0.77880
34	16.1427	0.87171	0.12829	89	3.8731	0.20915	0.79085
35	16.0356	0.86592	0.13408	90	3.6584	0.19756	0.80244
36	15.9242	0.85991	0.14009	91	3.4523	0.18642	0.81358
37	15.8083	0.85365	0.14635	92	3.2549	0.17577	0.82423
38	15.6877	0.84713	0.15287	93	3.0667	0.16560	0.83440
39	15.5625	0.84038	0.15962	94	2.8873	0.15591	0.84409
40	15.4328	0.83337	0.16663	95	2.7164	0.14669	0.85331
41	15.2982	0.82610	0.17390	96	2.5550	0.13797	0.86203
42	15.1590	0.81859	0.18141	97	2.4022	0.12972	0.87028
43	15.0144	0.81078	0.18922	98	2.2578	0.12192	0.87808
44	14.8648	0.80270	0.19730	99	2.1211	0.11454	0.88546
45	14.7100	0.79434	0.20566	100	1.9937	0.10766	0.89234
46	14.5497	0.78569	0.21431	101	1.8723	0.10110	0.89890
47	14.3842	0.77674	0.22326	102	1.7599	0.09504	0.90496
48	14.2130	0.76750	0.23250	103	1.6481	0.08900	0.91100
49	14.0359	0.75794	0.24206	104	1.5452	0.08344	0.91656
50	13.8525	0.74804	0.25196	105	1.4438	0.07796	0.92204
51	13.6627	0.73779	0.26221	106	1.3164	0.07108	0.92892
52	13.4663	0.72718	0.27282	107	1.1717	0.06327	0.93673
53	13.2634	0.71622	0.28378	108	0.9366	0.05058	0.94942
54	13.0543	0.70493	0.29507	109	0.4744	0.02562	0.97438

TABLE S (5.6)
SINGLE LIFE FACTORS BASED ON LIFE TABLE 2000CM

5.6% INTEREST

AGE	ANNUITY	LIFE ESTATE	REMAINDER	AGE	ANNUITY	LIFE ESTATE	REMAINDER
0	17.2910	0.96830	0.03170	55	12.5764	0.70428	0.29572
1	17.3836	0.97348	0.02652	56	12.3659	0.69249	0.30751
2	17.3661	0.97250	0.02750	57	12.1506	0.68043	0.31957
3	17.3446	0.97129	0.02871	58	11.9308	0.66812	0.33188
4	17.3203	0.96994	0.03006	59	11.7061	0.65554	0.34446
5	17.2940	0.96847	0.03153	60	11.4762	0.64267	0.35733
6	17.2657	0.96688	0.03312	61	11.2414	0.62952	0.37048
7	17.2358	0.96521	0.03479	62	11.0023	0.61613	0.38387
8	17.2039	0.96342	0.03658	63	10.7592	0.60251	0.39749
9	17.1698	0.96151	0.03849	64	10.5120	0.58867	0.41133
10	17.1336	0.95948	0.04052	65	10.2607	0.57460	0.42540
11	17.0952	0.95733	0.04267	66	10.0023	0.56013	0.43987
12	17.0547	0.95506	0.04494	67	9.7378	0.54532	0.45468
13	17.0126	0.95271	0.04729	68	9.4681	0.53022	0.46978
14	16.9695	0.95029	0.04971	69	9.1941	0.51487	0.48513
15	16.9260	0.94786	0.05214	70	8.9163	0.49931	0.50069
16	16.8823	0.94541	0.05459	71	8.6346	0.48354	0.51646
17	16.8380	0.94293	0.05707	72	8.3495	0.46757	0.53243
18	16.7930	0.94041	0.05959	73	8.0623	0.45149	0.54851
19	16.7469	0.93782	0.06218	74	7.7743	0.43536	0.56464
20	16.6988	0.93513	0.06487	75	7.4868	0.41926	0.58074
21	16.6490	0.93235	0.06765	76	7.2007	0.40324	0.59676
22	16.5974	0.92945	0.07055	77	6.9163	0.38731	0.61269
23	16.5432	0.92642	0.07358	78	6.6341	0.37151	0.62849
24	16.4861	0.92322	0.07678	79	6.3546	0.35586	0.64414
25	16.4253	0.91982	0.08018	80	6.0788	0.34041	0.65959
26	16.3607	0.91620	0.08380	81	5.8070	0.32519	0.67481
27	16.2922	0.91236	0.08764	82	5.5399	0.31023	0.68977
28	16.2195	0.90829	0.09171	83	5.2780	0.29557	0.70443
29	16.1431	0.90402	0.09598	84	5.0220	0.28123	0.71877
30	16.0631	0.89953	0.10047	85	4.7723	0.26725	0.73275
31	15.9791	0.89483	0.10517	86	4.5293	0.25364	0.74636
32	15.8912	0.88991	0.11009	87	4.2937	0.24044	0.75956
33	15.7992	0.88475	0.11525	88	4.0654	0.22766	0.77234
34	15.7034	0.87939	0.12061	89	3.8451	0.21533	0.78467
35	15.6035	0.87379	0.12621	90	3.6331	0.20345	0.79655
36	15.4993	0.86796	0.13204	91	3.4294	0.19205	0.80795
37	15.3909	0.86189	0.13811	92	3.2343	0.18112	0.81888
38	15.2778	0.85556	0.14444	93	3.0481	0.17069	0.82931
39	15.1604	0.84898	0.15102	94	2.8705	0.16075	0.83925
40	15.0385	0.84216	0.15784	95	2.7014	0.15128	0.84872
41	14.9120	0.83507	0.16493	96	2.5414	0.14232	0.85768
42	14.7809	0.82773	0.17227	97	2.3900	0.13384	0.86616
43	14.6446	0.82010	0.17990	98	2.2468	0.12582	0.87418
44	14.5034	0.81219	0.18781	99	2.1113	0.11823	0.88177
45	14.3571	0.80400	0.19600	100	1.9848	0.11115	0.88885
46	14.2054	0.79550	0.20450	101	1.8643	0.10440	0.89560
47	14.0485	0.78672	0.21328	102	1.7528	0.09816	0.90184
48	13.8861	0.77762	0.22238	103	1.6417	0.09194	0.90806
49	13.7180	0.76821	0.23179	104	1.5395	0.08621	0.91379
50	13.5436	0.75844	0.24156	105	1.4388	0.08057	0.91943
51	13.3629	0.74832	0.25168	106	1.3122	0.07349	0.92651
52	13.1757	0.73784	0.26216	107	1.1685	0.06543	0.93457
53	12.9820	0.72699	0.27301	108	0.9344	0.05233	0.94767
54	12.7821	0.71580	0.28420	109	0.4735	0.02652	0.97348

TABLE S (5.8)
SINGLE LIFE FACTORS BASED ON LIFE TABLE 2000CM

5.8% INTEREST

AGE	ANNUITY	LIFE ESTATE	REMAINDER	AGE	ANNUITY	LIFE ESTATE	REMAINDER
0	16.7360	0.97069	0.02931	55	12.3225	0.71471	0.28529
1	16.8271	0.97597	0.02403	56	12.1208	0.70301	0.29699
2	16.8118	0.97508	0.02492	57	11.9142	0.69102	0.30898
3	16.7926	0.97397	0.02603	58	11.7032	0.67879	0.32121
4	16.7709	0.97271	0.02729	59	11.4873	0.66626	0.33374
5	16.7473	0.97134	0.02866	60	11.2661	0.65344	0.34656
6	16.7218	0.96986	0.03014	61	11.0400	0.64032	0.35968
7	16.6947	0.96829	0.03171	62	10.8095	0.62695	0.37305
8	16.6658	0.96662	0.03338	63	10.5748	0.61334	0.38666
9	16.6348	0.96482	0.03518	64	10.3361	0.59949	0.40051
10	16.6019	0.96291	0.03709	65	10.0931	0.58540	0.41460
11	16.5669	0.96088	0.03912	66	9.8430	0.57089	0.42911
12	16.5298	0.95873	0.04127	67	9.5867	0.55603	0.44397
13	16.4913	0.95649	0.04351	68	9.3250	0.54085	0.45915
14	16.4519	0.95421	0.04579	69	9.0589	0.52542	0.47458
15	16.4121	0.95190	0.04810	70	8.7889	0.50975	0.49025
16	16.3722	0.94959	0.05041	71	8.5147	0.49385	0.50615
17	16.3318	0.94724	0.05276	72	8.2370	0.47775	0.52225
18	16.2907	0.94486	0.05514	73	7.9570	0.46151	0.53849
19	16.2487	0.94242	0.05758	74	7.6759	0.44520	0.55480
20	16.2048	0.93988	0.06012	75	7.3951	0.42891	0.57109
21	16.1593	0.93724	0.06276	76	7.1153	0.41269	0.58731
22	16.1121	0.93450	0.06550	77	6.8370	0.39655	0.60345
23	16.0626	0.93163	0.06837	78	6.5606	0.38052	0.61948
24	16.0101	0.92859	0.07141	79	6.2867	0.36463	0.63537
25	15.9543	0.92535	0.07465	80	6.0162	0.34894	0.65106
26	15.8948	0.92190	0.07810	81	5.7494	0.33346	0.66654
27	15.8316	0.91823	0.08177	82	5.4869	0.31824	0.68176
28	15.7644	0.91433	0.08567	83	5.2295	0.30331	0.69669
29	15.6936	0.91023	0.08977	84	4.9776	0.28870	0.71130
30	15.6193	0.90592	0.09408	85	4.7317	0.27444	0.72556
31	15.5413	0.90140	0.09860	86	4.4924	0.26056	0.73944
32	15.4596	0.89665	0.10335	87	4.2601	0.24708	0.75292
33	15.3738	0.89168	0.10832	88	4.0349	0.23402	0.76598
34	15.2844	0.88650	0.11350	89	3.8175	0.22141	0.77859
35	15.1911	0.88108	0.11892	90	3.6081	0.20927	0.79073
36	15.0936	0.87543	0.12457	91	3.4068	0.19759	0.80241
37	14.9921	0.86954	0.13046	92	3.2139	0.18640	0.81360
38	14.8860	0.86339	0.13661	93	3.0297	0.17572	0.82428
39	14.7758	0.85700	0.14300	94	2.8539	0.16553	0.83447
40	14.6612	0.85035	0.14965	95	2.6864	0.15581	0.84419
41	14.5421	0.84344	0.15656	96	2.5279	0.14662	0.85338
42	14.4186	0.83628	0.16372	97	2.3779	0.13792	0.86208
43	14.2900	0.82882	0.17118	98	2.2360	0.12969	0.87031
44	14.1566	0.82108	0.17892	99	2.1015	0.12189	0.87811
45	14.0183	0.81306	0.18694	100	1.9760	0.11461	0.88539
46	13.8746	0.80473	0.19527	101	1.8564	0.10767	0.89233
47	13.7259	0.79610	0.20390	102	1.7457	0.10125	0.89875
48	13.5718	0.78717	0.21283	103	1.6354	0.09486	0.90514
49	13.4121	0.77790	0.22210	104	1.5339	0.08897	0.91103
50	13.2462	0.76828	0.23172	105	1.4339	0.08317	0.91683
51	13.0741	0.75830	0.24170	106	1.3081	0.07587	0.92413
52	12.8955	0.74794	0.25206	107	1.1652	0.06758	0.93242
53	12.7105	0.73721	0.26279	108	0.9322	0.05407	0.94593
54	12.5194	0.72612	0.27388	109	0.4726	0.02741	0.97259

TABLE S (6.0)
SINGLE LIFE FACTORS BASED ON LIFE TABLE 2000CM

6.0% INTEREST

AGE	ANNUITY	LIFE ESTATE	REMAINDER	AGE	ANNUITY	LIFE ESTATE	REMAINDER
0	16.2132	0.97279	0.02721	55	12.0771	0.72463	0.27537
1	16.3028	0.97817	0.02183	56	11.8838	0.71303	0.28697
2	16.2894	0.97736	0.02264	57	11.6855	0.70113	0.29887
3	16.2723	0.97634	0.02366	58	11.4829	0.68897	0.31103
4	16.2529	0.97517	0.02483	59	11.2753	0.67652	0.32348
5	16.2316	0.97390	0.02610	60	11.0624	0.66375	0.33625
6	16.2086	0.97251	0.02749	61	10.8445	0.65067	0.34933
7	16.1841	0.97105	0.02895	62	10.6222	0.63733	0.36267
8	16.1578	0.96947	0.03053	63	10.3958	0.62375	0.37625
9	16.1297	0.96778	0.03222	64	10.1651	0.60990	0.39010
10	16.0996	0.96598	0.03402	65	9.9301	0.59580	0.40420
11	16.0676	0.96406	0.03594	66	9.6879	0.58128	0.41872
12	16.0337	0.96202	0.03798	67	9.4395	0.56637	0.43363
13	15.9983	0.95990	0.04010	68	9.1856	0.55113	0.44887
14	15.9622	0.95773	0.04227	69	8.9271	0.53562	0.46438
15	15.9258	0.95555	0.04445	70	8.6645	0.51987	0.48013
16	15.8893	0.95336	0.04664	71	8.3976	0.50386	0.49614
17	15.8524	0.95114	0.04886	72	8.1271	0.48763	0.51237
18	15.8149	0.94889	0.05111	73	7.8540	0.47124	0.52876
19	15.7765	0.94659	0.05341	74	7.5796	0.45477	0.54523
20	15.7364	0.94418	0.05582	75	7.3052	0.43831	0.56169
21	15.6948	0.94169	0.05831	76	7.0317	0.42190	0.57810
22	15.6516	0.93910	0.06090	77	6.7593	0.40556	0.59444
23	15.6062	0.93637	0.06363	78	6.4886	0.38932	0.61068
24	15.5581	0.93349	0.06651	79	6.2201	0.37320	0.62680
25	15.5067	0.93040	0.06960	80	5.9547	0.35728	0.64272
26	15.4519	0.92712	0.07288	81	5.6927	0.34156	0.65844
27	15.3935	0.92361	0.07639	82	5.4349	0.32609	0.67391
28	15.3313	0.91988	0.08012	83	5.1818	0.31091	0.68909
29	15.2656	0.91594	0.08406	84	4.9339	0.29604	0.70396
30	15.1967	0.91180	0.08820	85	4.6918	0.28151	0.71849
31	15.1241	0.90745	0.09255	86	4.4560	0.26736	0.73264
32	15.0480	0.90288	0.09712	87	4.2270	0.25362	0.74638
33	14.9680	0.89808	0.10192	88	4.0048	0.24029	0.75971
34	14.8845	0.89307	0.10693	89	3.7902	0.22741	0.77259
35	14.7972	0.88783	0.11217	90	3.5834	0.21500	0.78500
36	14.7060	0.88236	0.11764	91	3.3845	0.20307	0.79693
37	14.6108	0.87665	0.12335	92	3.1937	0.19162	0.80838
38	14.5113	0.87068	0.12932	93	3.0115	0.18069	0.81931
39	14.4077	0.86446	0.13554	94	2.8375	0.17025	0.82975
40	14.2999	0.85799	0.14201	95	2.6716	0.16030	0.83970
41	14.1878	0.85127	0.14873	96	2.5146	0.15088	0.84912
42	14.0713	0.84428	0.15572	97	2.3660	0.14196	0.85804
43	13.9499	0.83699	0.16301	98	2.2252	0.13351	0.86649
44	13.8238	0.82943	0.17057	99	2.0918	0.12551	0.87449
45	13.6929	0.82157	0.17843	100	1.9673	0.11804	0.88196
46	13.5568	0.81341	0.18659	101	1.8486	0.11092	0.88908
47	13.4158	0.80495	0.19505	102	1.7387	0.10432	0.89568
48	13.2695	0.79617	0.20383	103	1.6292	0.09775	0.90225
49	13.1176	0.78706	0.21294	104	1.5284	0.09170	0.90830
50	12.9597	0.77758	0.22242	105	1.4290	0.08574	0.91426
51	12.7956	0.76774	0.23226	106	1.3040	0.07824	0.92176
52	12.6252	0.75751	0.24249	107	1.1619	0.06972	0.93028
53	12.4485	0.74691	0.25309	108	0.9300	0.05580	0.94420
54	12.2657	0.73594	0.26406	109	0.4717	0.02830	0.97170

TABLE S (6.2)
SINGLE LIFE FACTORS BASED ON LIFE TABLE 2000CM

6.2% INTEREST

AGE	ANNUITY	LIFE ESTATE	REMAINDER	AGE	ANNUITY	LIFE ESTATE	REMAINDER
0	15.7202	0.97466	0.02534	55	11.8399	0.73407	0.26593
1	15.8082	0.98011	0.01989	56	11.6545	0.72258	0.27742
2	15.7966	0.97939	0.02061	57	11.4642	0.71078	0.28922
3	15.7814	0.97844	0.02156	58	11.2695	0.69871	0.30129
4	15.7639	0.97736	0.02264	59	11.0698	0.68633	0.31367
5	15.7447	0.97617	0.02383	60	10.8649	0.67362	0.32638
6	15.7238	0.97488	0.02512	61	10.6549	0.66060	0.33940
7	15.7016	0.97350	0.02650	62	10.4404	0.64731	0.35269
8	15.6777	0.97202	0.02798	63	10.2218	0.63375	0.36625
9	15.6520	0.97043	0.02957	64	9.9988	0.61993	0.38007
10	15.6246	0.96872	0.03128	65	9.7715	0.60583	0.39417
11	15.5953	0.96691	0.03309	66	9.5369	0.59129	0.40871
12	15.5641	0.96497	0.03503	67	9.2960	0.57635	0.42365
13	15.5317	0.96296	0.03704	68	9.0496	0.56108	0.43892
14	15.4985	0.96091	0.03909	69	8.7984	0.54550	0.45450
15	15.4651	0.95883	0.04117	70	8.5431	0.52967	0.47033
16	15.4316	0.95676	0.04324	71	8.2833	0.51356	0.48644
17	15.3979	0.95467	0.04533	72	8.0197	0.49722	0.50278
18	15.3636	0.95254	0.04746	73	7.7532	0.48070	0.51930
19	15.3285	0.95037	0.04963	74	7.4853	0.46409	0.53591
20	15.2918	0.94809	0.05191	75	7.2172	0.44747	0.55253
21	15.2538	0.94573	0.05427	76	6.9497	0.43088	0.56912
22	15.2142	0.94328	0.05672	77	6.6831	0.41435	0.58565
23	15.1726	0.94070	0.05930	78	6.4179	0.39791	0.60209
24	15.1284	0.93796	0.06204	79	6.1547	0.38159	0.61841
25	15.0811	0.93503	0.06497	80	5.8942	0.36544	0.63456
26	15.0305	0.93189	0.06811	81	5.6371	0.34950	0.65050
27	14.9764	0.92854	0.07146	82	5.3837	0.33379	0.66621
28	14.9188	0.92497	0.07503	83	5.1348	0.31836	0.68164
29	14.8579	0.92119	0.07881	84	4.8909	0.30324	0.69676
30	14.7938	0.91721	0.08279	85	4.6525	0.28846	0.71154
31	14.7262	0.91303	0.08697	86	4.4201	0.27405	0.72595
32	14.6552	0.90863	0.09137	87	4.1943	0.26005	0.73995
33	14.5806	0.90399	0.09601	88	3.9751	0.24646	0.75354
34	14.5026	0.89916	0.10084	89	3.7633	0.23332	0.76668
35	14.4209	0.89410	0.10590	90	3.5590	0.22066	0.77934
36	14.3354	0.88880	0.11120	91	3.3624	0.20847	0.79153
37	14.2461	0.88326	0.11674	92	3.1737	0.19677	0.80323
38	14.1527	0.87746	0.12254	93	2.9935	0.18560	0.81440
39	14.0552	0.87143	0.12857	94	2.8213	0.17492	0.82508
40	13.9538	0.86513	0.13487	95	2.6570	0.16474	0.83526
41	13.8481	0.85858	0.14142	96	2.5015	0.15509	0.84491
42	13.7381	0.85177	0.14823	97	2.3541	0.14595	0.85405
43	13.6235	0.84465	0.15535	98	2.2145	0.13730	0.86270
44	13.5042	0.83726	0.16274	99	2.0822	0.12910	0.87090
45	13.3803	0.82958	0.17042	100	1.9587	0.12144	0.87856
46	13.2513	0.82158	0.17842	101	1.8409	0.11413	0.88587
47	13.1174	0.81328	0.18672	102	1.7317	0.10737	0.89263
48	12.9784	0.80466	0.19534	103	1.6230	0.10062	0.89938
49	12.8340	0.79571	0.20429	104	1.5228	0.09442	0.90558
50	12.6835	0.78638	0.21362	105	1.4242	0.08830	0.91170
51	12.5271	0.77668	0.22332	106	1.2999	0.08060	0.91940
52	12.3644	0.76659	0.23341	107	1.1587	0.07184	0.92816
53	12.1955	0.75612	0.24388	108	0.9279	0.05753	0.94247
54	12.0205	0.74527	0.25473	109	0.4708	0.02919	0.97081

TABLE S (6.4)
SINGLE LIFE FACTORS BASED ON LIFE TABLE 2000CM

6.4% INTEREST

AGE	ANNUITY	LIFE ESTATE	REMAINDER	AGE	ANNUITY	LIFE ESTATE	REMAINDER
0	15.2547	0.97630	0.02370	55	11.6105	0.74307	0.25693
1	15.3411	0.98183	0.01817	56	11.4326	0.73169	0.26831
2	15.3310	0.98118	0.01882	57	11.2499	0.71999	0.28001
3	15.3174	0.98031	0.01969	58	11.0627	0.70801	0.29199
4	15.3017	0.97931	0.02069	59	10.8706	0.69572	0.30428
5	15.2843	0.97820	0.02180	60	10.6732	0.68309	0.31691
6	15.2654	0.97699	0.02301	61	10.4708	0.67013	0.32987
7	15.2452	0.97570	0.02430	62	10.2639	0.65689	0.34311
8	15.2235	0.97430	0.02570	63	10.0526	0.64337	0.35663
9	15.2000	0.97280	0.02720	64	9.8371	0.62957	0.37043
10	15.1748	0.97119	0.02881	65	9.6171	0.61549	0.38451
11	15.1479	0.96947	0.03053	66	9.3899	0.60095	0.39905
12	15.1193	0.96763	0.03237	67	9.1563	0.58600	0.41400
13	15.0894	0.96572	0.03428	68	8.9170	0.57069	0.42931
14	15.0589	0.96377	0.03623	69	8.6730	0.55507	0.44493
15	15.0282	0.96180	0.03820	70	8.4245	0.53917	0.46083
16	14.9975	0.95984	0.04016	71	8.1716	0.52298	0.47702
17	14.9666	0.95786	0.04214	72	7.9146	0.50653	0.49347
18	14.9352	0.95585	0.04415	73	7.6547	0.48990	0.51010
19	14.9031	0.95380	0.04620	74	7.3931	0.47316	0.52684
20	14.8695	0.95165	0.04835	75	7.1310	0.45639	0.54361
21	14.8346	0.94942	0.05058	76	6.8694	0.43964	0.56036
22	14.7983	0.94709	0.05291	77	6.6084	0.42294	0.57706
23	14.7601	0.94465	0.05535	78	6.3486	0.40631	0.59369
24	14.7195	0.94205	0.05795	79	6.0904	0.38979	0.61021
25	14.6759	0.93926	0.06074	80	5.8349	0.37343	0.62657
26	14.6292	0.93627	0.06373	81	5.5823	0.35727	0.64273
27	14.5791	0.93306	0.06694	82	5.3333	0.34133	0.65867
28	14.5257	0.92964	0.07036	83	5.0886	0.32567	0.67433
29	14.4691	0.92602	0.07398	84	4.8486	0.31031	0.68969
30	14.4094	0.92220	0.07780	85	4.6138	0.29528	0.70472
31	14.3465	0.91818	0.08182	86	4.3848	0.28063	0.71937
32	14.2803	0.91394	0.08606	87	4.1621	0.26638	0.73362
33	14.2105	0.90947	0.09053	88	3.9459	0.25254	0.74746
34	14.1375	0.90480	0.09520	89	3.7367	0.23915	0.76085
35	14.0610	0.89991	0.10009	90	3.5349	0.22623	0.77377
36	13.9809	0.89478	0.10522	91	3.3406	0.21380	0.78620
37	13.8970	0.88941	0.11059	92	3.1540	0.20186	0.79814
38	13.8092	0.88379	0.11621	93	2.9757	0.19044	0.80956
39	13.7175	0.87792	0.12208	94	2.8052	0.17953	0.82047
40	13.6219	0.87180	0.12820	95	2.6425	0.16912	0.83088
41	13.5222	0.86542	0.13458	96	2.4884	0.15926	0.84074
42	13.4184	0.85878	0.14122	97	2.3424	0.14991	0.85009
43	13.3100	0.85184	0.14816	98	2.2039	0.14105	0.85895
44	13.1972	0.84462	0.15538	99	2.0727	0.13265	0.86735
45	13.0797	0.83710	0.16290	100	1.9501	0.12481	0.87519
46	12.9574	0.82927	0.17073	101	1.8332	0.11732	0.88268
47	12.8303	0.82114	0.17886	102	1.7248	0.11039	0.88961
48	12.6982	0.81268	0.18732	103	1.6168	0.10347	0.89653
49	12.5607	0.80388	0.19612	104	1.5174	0.09711	0.90289
50	12.4173	0.79471	0.20529	105	1.4194	0.09084	0.90916
51	12.2681	0.78516	0.21484	106	1.2959	0.08294	0.91706
52	12.1127	0.77521	0.22479	107	1.1555	0.07395	0.92605
53	11.9512	0.76487	0.23513	108	0.9257	0.05925	0.94075
54	11.7837	0.75415	0.24585	109	0.4699	0.03008	0.96992

TABLE S (6.6)
SINGLE LIFE FACTORS BASED ON LIFE TABLE 2000CM

6.6% INTEREST

AGE	ANNUITY	LIFE ESTATE	REMAINDER	AGE	ANNUITY	LIFE ESTATE	REMAINDER
0	14.8146	0.97777	0.02223	55	11.3886	0.75165	0.24835
1	14.8994	0.98336	0.01664	56	11.2179	0.74038	0.25962
2	14.8905	0.98278	0.01722	57	11.0423	0.72879	0.27121
3	14.8784	0.98198	0.01802	58	10.8623	0.71691	0.28309
4	14.8643	0.98104	0.01896	59	10.6775	0.70471	0.29529
5	14.8486	0.98001	0.01999	60	10.4873	0.69216	0.30784
6	14.8314	0.97887	0.02113	61	10.2920	0.67927	0.32073
7	14.8130	0.97766	0.02234	62	10.0923	0.66609	0.33391
8	14.7931	0.97635	0.02365	63	9.8882	0.65262	0.34738
9	14.7716	0.97493	0.02507	64	9.6798	0.63887	0.36113
10	14.7486	0.97341	0.02659	65	9.4668	0.62481	0.37519
11	14.7238	0.97177	0.02823	66	9.2467	0.61028	0.38972
12	14.6974	0.97003	0.02997	67	9.0201	0.59532	0.40468
13	14.6699	0.96821	0.03179	68	8.7878	0.57999	0.42001
14	14.6418	0.96636	0.03364	69	8.5505	0.56433	0.43567
15	14.6135	0.96449	0.03551	70	8.3088	0.54838	0.45162
16	14.5853	0.96263	0.03737	71	8.0624	0.53212	0.46788
17	14.5569	0.96076	0.03924	72	7.8119	0.51559	0.48441
18	14.5282	0.95886	0.04114	73	7.5583	0.49885	0.50115
19	14.4987	0.95691	0.04309	74	7.3028	0.48198	0.51802
20	14.4679	0.95488	0.04512	75	7.0466	0.46508	0.53492
21	14.4360	0.95277	0.04723	76	6.7906	0.44818	0.55182
22	14.4026	0.95057	0.04943	77	6.5351	0.43132	0.56868
23	14.3675	0.94826	0.05174	78	6.2805	0.41451	0.58549
24	14.3301	0.94579	0.05421	79	6.0274	0.39781	0.60219
25	14.2899	0.94313	0.05687	80	5.7766	0.38125	0.61875
26	14.2467	0.94028	0.05972	81	5.5285	0.36488	0.63512
27	14.2003	0.93722	0.06278	82	5.2838	0.34873	0.65127
28	14.1507	0.93395	0.06605	83	5.0431	0.33284	0.66716
29	14.0981	0.93047	0.06953	84	4.8068	0.31725	0.68275
30	14.0425	0.92681	0.07319	85	4.5756	0.30199	0.69801
31	13.9838	0.92293	0.07707	86	4.3499	0.28710	0.71290
32	13.9220	0.91885	0.08115	87	4.1304	0.27260	0.72740
33	13.8567	0.91454	0.08546	88	3.9170	0.25852	0.74148
34	13.7884	0.91004	0.08996	89	3.7105	0.24489	0.75511
35	13.7167	0.90530	0.09470	90	3.5111	0.23173	0.76827
36	13.6415	0.90034	0.09966	91	3.3190	0.21906	0.78094
37	13.5627	0.89514	0.10486	92	3.1345	0.20688	0.79312
38	13.4801	0.88968	0.11032	93	2.9581	0.19523	0.80477
39	13.3937	0.88399	0.11601	94	2.7893	0.18409	0.81591
40	13.3036	0.87804	0.12196	95	2.6282	0.17346	0.82654
41	13.2095	0.87183	0.12817	96	2.4755	0.16338	0.83662
42	13.1114	0.86536	0.13464	97	2.3307	0.15383	0.84617
43	13.0089	0.85859	0.14141	98	2.1935	0.14477	0.85523
44	12.9020	0.85153	0.14847	99	2.0633	0.13618	0.86382
45	12.7907	0.84419	0.15581	100	1.9416	0.12815	0.87185
46	12.6746	0.83652	0.16348	101	1.8255	0.12048	0.87952
47	12.5538	0.82855	0.17145	102	1.7179	0.11338	0.88662
48	12.4281	0.82026	0.17974	103	1.6107	0.10630	0.89370
49	12.2972	0.81162	0.18838	104	1.5119	0.09979	0.90021
50	12.1606	0.80260	0.19740	105	1.4146	0.09336	0.90664
51	12.0182	0.79320	0.20680	106	1.2919	0.08526	0.91474
52	11.8696	0.78340	0.21660	107	1.1523	0.07605	0.92395
53	11.7151	0.77319	0.22681	108	0.9236	0.06096	0.93904
54	11.5546	0.76261	0.23739	109	0.4690	0.03096	0.96904

TABLE S (6.8)
SINGLE LIFE FACTORS BASED ON LIFE TABLE 2000CM

6.8% INTEREST

AGE	ANNUITY	LIFE ESTATE	REMAINDER	AGE	ANNUITY	LIFE ESTATE	REMAINDER
0	14.3980	0.97907	0.02093	55	11.1739	0.75983	0.24017
1	14.4812	0.98472	0.01528	56	11.0099	0.74868	0.25132
2	14.4735	0.98420	0.01580	57	10.8412	0.73720	0.26280
3	14.4627	0.98346	0.01654	58	10.6681	0.72543	0.27457
4	14.4499	0.98259	0.01741	59	10.4901	0.71333	0.28667
5	14.4356	0.98162	0.01838	60	10.3068	0.70086	0.29914
6	14.4200	0.98056	0.01944	61	10.1184	0.68805	0.31195
7	14.4032	0.97942	0.02058	62	9.9256	0.67494	0.32506
8	14.3851	0.97818	0.02182	63	9.7283	0.66153	0.33847
9	14.3653	0.97684	0.02316	64	9.5267	0.64782	0.35218
10	14.3441	0.97540	0.02460	65	9.3206	0.63380	0.36620
11	14.3213	0.97385	0.02615	66	9.1072	0.61929	0.38071
12	14.2970	0.97219	0.02781	67	8.8873	0.60433	0.39567
13	14.2715	0.97046	0.02954	68	8.6616	0.58899	0.41101
14	14.2456	0.96870	0.03130	69	8.4309	0.57330	0.42670
15	14.2195	0.96692	0.03308	70	8.1957	0.55731	0.44269
16	14.1935	0.96516	0.03484	71	7.9557	0.54099	0.45901
17	14.1674	0.96339	0.03661	72	7.7115	0.52438	0.47562
18	14.1410	0.96159	0.03841	73	7.4639	0.50755	0.49245
19	14.1140	0.95975	0.04025	74	7.2143	0.49057	0.50943
20	14.0857	0.95783	0.04217	75	6.9639	0.47355	0.52645
21	14.0564	0.95584	0.04416	76	6.7134	0.45651	0.54349
22	14.0258	0.95375	0.04625	77	6.4632	0.43950	0.56050
23	13.9935	0.95156	0.04844	78	6.2137	0.42253	0.57747
24	13.9590	0.94922	0.05078	79	5.9654	0.40565	0.59435
25	13.9219	0.94669	0.05331	80	5.7193	0.38891	0.61109
26	13.8819	0.94397	0.05603	81	5.4757	0.37234	0.62766
27	13.8389	0.94105	0.05895	82	5.2351	0.35599	0.64401
28	13.7928	0.93791	0.06209	83	4.9983	0.33988	0.66012
29	13.7438	0.93458	0.06542	84	4.7658	0.32407	0.67593
30	13.6920	0.93106	0.06894	85	4.5380	0.30859	0.69141
31	13.6372	0.92733	0.07267	86	4.3156	0.29346	0.70654
32	13.5794	0.92340	0.07660	87	4.0990	0.27873	0.72127
33	13.5183	0.91925	0.08075	88	3.8885	0.26442	0.73558
34	13.4543	0.91489	0.08511	89	3.6845	0.25055	0.74945
35	13.3870	0.91032	0.08968	90	3.4876	0.23716	0.76284
36	13.3164	0.90552	0.09448	91	3.2977	0.22425	0.77575
37	13.2423	0.90048	0.09952	92	3.1153	0.21184	0.78816
38	13.1645	0.89519	0.10481	93	2.9407	0.19996	0.80004
39	13.0831	0.88965	0.11035	94	2.7736	0.18860	0.81140
40	12.9981	0.88387	0.11613	95	2.6140	0.17775	0.82225
41	12.9092	0.87783	0.12217	96	2.4627	0.16746	0.83254
42	12.8165	0.87152	0.12848	97	2.3192	0.15770	0.84230
43	12.7194	0.86492	0.13508	98	2.1831	0.14845	0.85155
44	12.6182	0.85804	0.14196	99	2.0539	0.13967	0.86033
45	12.5126	0.85086	0.14914	100	1.9332	0.13146	0.86854
46	12.4023	0.84336	0.15664	101	1.8179	0.12362	0.87638
47	12.2875	0.83555	0.16445	102	1.7111	0.11636	0.88364
48	12.1679	0.82742	0.17258	103	1.6046	0.10911	0.89089
49	12.0432	0.81894	0.18106	104	1.5065	0.10244	0.89756
50	11.9129	0.81007	0.18993	105	1.4098	0.09587	0.90413
51	11.7768	0.80083	0.19917	106	1.2879	0.08758	0.91242
52	11.6348	0.79117	0.20883	107	1.1491	0.07814	0.92186
53	11.4869	0.78111	0.21889	108	0.9214	0.06266	0.93734
54	11.3331	0.77065	0.22935	109	0.4682	0.03184	0.96816

TABLE S (7.0)
SINGLE LIFE FACTORS BASED ON LIFE TABLE 2000CM

7.0% INTEREST

AGE	ANNUITY	LIFE ESTATE	REMAINDER	AGE	ANNUITY	LIFE ESTATE	REMAINDER
0	14.0032	0.98022	0.01978	55	10.9660	0.76762	0.23238
1	14.0848	0.98594	0.01406	56	10.8085	0.75660	0.24340
2	14.0781	0.98546	0.01454	57	10.6463	0.74524	0.25476
3	14.0684	0.98479	0.01521	58	10.4797	0.73358	0.26642
4	14.0568	0.98398	0.01602	59	10.3083	0.72158	0.27842
5	14.0439	0.98307	0.01693	60	10.1315	0.70921	0.29079
6	14.0296	0.98207	0.01793	61	9.9498	0.69648	0.30352
7	14.0143	0.98100	0.01900	62	9.7635	0.68344	0.31656
8	13.9976	0.97983	0.02017	63	9.5728	0.67010	0.32990
9	13.9795	0.97857	0.02143	64	9.3778	0.65644	0.34356
10	13.9600	0.97720	0.02280	65	9.1781	0.64247	0.35753
11	13.9389	0.97572	0.02428	66	8.9712	0.62799	0.37201
12	13.9164	0.97415	0.02585	67	8.7578	0.61304	0.38696
13	13.8929	0.97250	0.02750	68	8.5386	0.59770	0.40230
14	13.8688	0.97082	0.02918	69	8.3142	0.58200	0.41800
15	13.8447	0.96913	0.03087	70	8.0853	0.56597	0.43403
16	13.8208	0.96746	0.03254	71	7.8515	0.54960	0.45040
17	13.7968	0.96578	0.03422	72	7.6132	0.53293	0.46707
18	13.7725	0.96408	0.03592	73	7.3716	0.51601	0.48399
19	13.7477	0.96234	0.03766	74	7.1277	0.49894	0.50106
20	13.7217	0.96052	0.03948	75	6.8829	0.48180	0.51820
21	13.6947	0.95863	0.04137	76	6.6378	0.46464	0.53536
22	13.6666	0.95666	0.04334	77	6.3927	0.44749	0.55251
23	13.6369	0.95458	0.04542	78	6.1481	0.43037	0.56963
24	13.6051	0.95236	0.04764	79	5.9046	0.41332	0.58668
25	13.5708	0.94995	0.05005	80	5.6630	0.39641	0.60359
26	13.5337	0.94736	0.05264	81	5.4236	0.37966	0.62034
27	13.4938	0.94457	0.05543	82	5.1871	0.36310	0.63690
28	13.4509	0.94156	0.05844	83	4.9542	0.34679	0.65321
29	13.4052	0.93837	0.06163	84	4.7253	0.33077	0.66923
30	13.3569	0.93498	0.06502	85	4.5010	0.31507	0.68493
31	13.3057	0.93140	0.06860	86	4.2817	0.29972	0.70028
32	13.2516	0.92761	0.07239	87	4.0681	0.28477	0.71523
33	13.1944	0.92361	0.07639	88	3.8603	0.27022	0.72978
34	13.1344	0.91941	0.08059	89	3.6590	0.25613	0.74387
35	13.0712	0.91499	0.08501	90	3.4644	0.24251	0.75749
36	13.0048	0.91034	0.08966	91	3.2767	0.22937	0.77063
37	12.9351	0.90546	0.09454	92	3.0962	0.21674	0.78326
38	12.8618	0.90032	0.09968	93	2.9234	0.20464	0.79536
39	12.7850	0.89495	0.10505	94	2.7580	0.19306	0.80694
40	12.7047	0.88933	0.11067	95	2.6000	0.18200	0.81800
41	12.6207	0.88345	0.11655	96	2.4500	0.17150	0.82850
42	12.5330	0.87731	0.12269	97	2.3078	0.16154	0.83846
43	12.4411	0.87087	0.12913	98	2.1728	0.15209	0.84791
44	12.3451	0.86415	0.13585	99	2.0447	0.14313	0.85687
45	12.2448	0.85714	0.14286	100	1.9248	0.13474	0.86526
46	12.1401	0.84980	0.15020	101	1.8104	0.12673	0.87327
47	12.0309	0.84216	0.15784	102	1.7044	0.11931	0.88069
48	11.9170	0.83419	0.16581	103	1.5985	0.11190	0.88810
49	11.7981	0.82587	0.17413	104	1.5011	0.10508	0.89492
50	11.6737	0.81716	0.18284	105	1.4051	0.09836	0.90164
51	11.5438	0.80806	0.19194	106	1.2839	0.08987	0.91013
52	11.4079	0.79856	0.20144	107	1.1459	0.08022	0.91978
53	11.2663	0.78864	0.21136	108	0.9193	0.06435	0.93565
54	11.1189	0.77832	0.22168	109	0.4673	0.03271	0.96729

TABLE S (7.2)
SINGLE LIFE FACTORS BASED ON LIFE TABLE 2000CM

7.2% INTEREST

AGE	ANNUITY	LIFE ESTATE	REMAINDER	AGE	ANNUITY	LIFE ESTATE	REMAINDER
0	13.6286	0.98126	0.01874	55	10.7648	0.77506	0.22494
1	13.7086	0.98702	0.01298	56	10.6134	0.76417	0.23583
2	13.7027	0.98660	0.01340	57	10.4574	0.75293	0.24707
3	13.6941	0.98597	0.01403	58	10.2970	0.74138	0.25862
4	13.6836	0.98522	0.01478	59	10.1318	0.72949	0.27051
5	13.6718	0.98437	0.01563	60	9.9614	0.71722	0.28278
6	13.6588	0.98343	0.01657	61	9.7859	0.70458	0.29542
7	13.6448	0.98242	0.01758	62	9.6059	0.69163	0.30837
8	13.6295	0.98132	0.01868	63	9.4215	0.67835	0.32165
9	13.6128	0.98012	0.01988	64	9.2327	0.66476	0.33524
10	13.5947	0.97882	0.02118	65	9.0393	0.65083	0.34917
11	13.5753	0.97742	0.02258	66	8.8387	0.63639	0.36361
12	13.5544	0.97592	0.02408	67	8.6315	0.62147	0.37853
13	13.5326	0.97435	0.02565	68	8.4185	0.60613	0.39387
14	13.5103	0.97274	0.02726	69	8.2003	0.59042	0.40958
15	13.4880	0.97114	0.02886	70	7.9774	0.57437	0.42563
16	13.4659	0.96954	0.03046	71	7.7495	0.55797	0.44203
17	13.4438	0.96795	0.03205	72	7.5171	0.54123	0.45877
18	13.4214	0.96634	0.03366	73	7.2812	0.52425	0.47575
19	13.3986	0.96470	0.03530	74	7.0429	0.50709	0.49291
20	13.3747	0.96298	0.03702	75	6.8035	0.48985	0.51015
21	13.3499	0.96119	0.03881	76	6.5636	0.47258	0.52742
22	13.3240	0.95933	0.04067	77	6.3235	0.45529	0.54471
23	13.2966	0.95735	0.04265	78	6.0838	0.43803	0.56197
24	13.2672	0.95524	0.04476	79	5.8449	0.42083	0.57917
25	13.2355	0.95295	0.04705	80	5.6076	0.40375	0.59625
26	13.2011	0.95048	0.04952	81	5.3725	0.38682	0.61318
27	13.1640	0.94781	0.05219	82	5.1400	0.37008	0.62992
28	13.1240	0.94493	0.05507	83	4.9108	0.35358	0.64642
29	13.0815	0.94186	0.05814	84	4.6855	0.33735	0.66265
30	13.0363	0.93862	0.06138	85	4.4645	0.32144	0.67856
31	12.9885	0.93517	0.06483	86	4.2483	0.30588	0.69412
32	12.9378	0.93152	0.06848	87	4.0377	0.29071	0.70929
33	12.8841	0.92766	0.07234	88	3.8325	0.27594	0.72406
34	12.8278	0.92360	0.07640	89	3.6337	0.26163	0.73837
35	12.7685	0.91933	0.08067	90	3.4414	0.24778	0.75222
36	12.7060	0.91483	0.08517	91	3.2559	0.23442	0.76558
37	12.6403	0.91010	0.08990	92	3.0774	0.22157	0.77843
38	12.5712	0.90513	0.09487	93	2.9064	0.20926	0.79074
39	12.4987	0.89991	0.10009	94	2.7426	0.19747	0.80253
40	12.4229	0.89445	0.10555	95	2.5861	0.18620	0.81380
41	12.3434	0.88873	0.11127	96	2.4375	0.17550	0.82450
42	12.2604	0.88275	0.11725	97	2.2964	0.16534	0.83466
43	12.1732	0.87647	0.12353	98	2.1626	0.15570	0.84430
44	12.0822	0.86992	0.13008	99	2.0355	0.14655	0.85345
45	11.9870	0.86306	0.13694	100	1.9166	0.13799	0.86201
46	11.8874	0.85589	0.14411	101	1.8030	0.12981	0.87019
47	11.7835	0.84841	0.15159	102	1.6977	0.12223	0.87777
48	11.6750	0.84060	0.15940	103	1.5925	0.11466	0.88534
49	11.5616	0.83243	0.16757	104	1.4958	0.10769	0.89231
50	11.4428	0.82388	0.17612	105	1.4004	0.10083	0.89917
51	11.3186	0.81494	0.18506	106	1.2799	0.09216	0.90784
52	11.1886	0.80558	0.19442	107	1.1428	0.08228	0.91772
53	11.0529	0.79581	0.20419	108	0.9172	0.06604	0.93396
54	10.9115	0.78563	0.21437	109	0.4664	0.03358	0.96642

TABLE S (7.4)
SINGLE LIFE FACTORS BASED ON LIFE TABLE 2000CM

7.4% INTEREST

AGE	ANNUITY	LIFE ESTATE	REMAINDER	AGE	ANNUITY	LIFE ESTATE	REMAINDER
0	13.2727	0.98218	0.01782	55	10.5698	0.78216	0.21784
1	13.3511	0.98798	0.01202	56	10.4243	0.77140	0.22860
2	13.3461	0.98761	0.01239	57	10.2742	0.76029	0.23971
3	13.3383	0.98703	0.01297	58	10.1197	0.74886	0.25114
4	13.3288	0.98633	0.01367	59	9.9605	0.73707	0.26293
5	13.3181	0.98554	0.01446	60	9.7960	0.72491	0.27509
6	13.3061	0.98465	0.01535	61	9.6266	0.71237	0.28763
7	13.2933	0.98370	0.01630	62	9.4526	0.69950	0.30050
8	13.2792	0.98266	0.01734	63	9.2743	0.68630	0.31370
9	13.2638	0.98152	0.01848	64	9.0915	0.67277	0.32723
10	13.2471	0.98029	0.01971	65	8.9041	0.65890	0.34110
11	13.2291	0.97895	0.02105	66	8.7095	0.64450	0.35550
12	13.2097	0.97752	0.02248	67	8.5083	0.62962	0.37038
13	13.1894	0.97602	0.02398	68	8.3013	0.61430	0.38570
14	13.1688	0.97449	0.02551	69	8.0890	0.59859	0.40141
15	13.1481	0.97296	0.02704	70	7.8719	0.58252	0.41748
16	13.1276	0.97145	0.02855	71	7.6498	0.56609	0.43391
17	13.1072	0.96993	0.03007	72	7.4231	0.54931	0.45069
18	13.0866	0.96841	0.03159	73	7.1927	0.53226	0.46774
19	13.0656	0.96685	0.03315	74	6.9598	0.51503	0.48497
20	13.0436	0.96522	0.03478	75	6.7256	0.49770	0.50230
21	13.0207	0.96353	0.03647	76	6.4908	0.48032	0.51968
22	12.9968	0.96177	0.03823	77	6.2556	0.46292	0.53708
23	12.9716	0.95990	0.04010	78	6.0206	0.44552	0.55448
24	12.9445	0.95789	0.04211	79	5.7862	0.42818	0.57182
25	12.9151	0.95571	0.04429	80	5.5532	0.41094	0.58906
26	12.8832	0.95335	0.04665	81	5.3222	0.39384	0.60616
27	12.8486	0.95080	0.04920	82	5.0936	0.37692	0.62308
28	12.8114	0.94804	0.05196	83	4.8681	0.36024	0.63976
29	12.7716	0.94510	0.05490	84	4.6462	0.34382	0.65618
30	12.7294	0.94198	0.05802	85	4.4285	0.32771	0.67229
31	12.6846	0.93866	0.06134	86	4.2154	0.31194	0.68806
32	12.6372	0.93515	0.06485	87	4.0076	0.29656	0.70344
33	12.5868	0.93142	0.06858	88	3.8051	0.28158	0.71842
34	12.5339	0.92751	0.07249	89	3.6088	0.26705	0.73295
35	12.4780	0.92338	0.07662	90	3.4188	0.25299	0.74701
36	12.4192	0.91902	0.08098	91	3.2353	0.23941	0.76059
37	12.3573	0.91444	0.08556	92	3.0587	0.22635	0.77365
38	12.2921	0.90961	0.09039	93	2.8895	0.21382	0.78618
39	12.2237	0.90455	0.09545	94	2.7274	0.20183	0.79817
40	12.1519	0.89924	0.10076	95	2.5723	0.19035	0.80965
41	12.0767	0.89368	0.10632	96	2.4251	0.17945	0.82055
42	11.9981	0.88786	0.11214	97	2.2852	0.16911	0.83089
43	11.9154	0.88174	0.11826	98	2.1524	0.15928	0.84072
44	11.8289	0.87534	0.12466	99	2.0263	0.14995	0.85005
45	11.7385	0.86865	0.13135	100	1.9083	0.14122	0.85878
46	11.6437	0.86164	0.13836	101	1.7956	0.13287	0.86713
47	11.5448	0.85432	0.14568	102	1.6910	0.12513	0.87487
48	11.4414	0.84666	0.15334	103	1.5866	0.11741	0.88259
49	11.3332	0.83866	0.16134	104	1.4904	0.11029	0.88971
50	11.2197	0.83026	0.16974	105	1.3957	0.10328	0.89672
51	11.1009	0.82147	0.17853	106	1.2760	0.09442	0.90558
52	10.9765	0.81226	0.18774	107	1.1397	0.08433	0.91567
53	10.8464	0.80263	0.19737	108	0.9151	0.06771	0.93229
54	10.7107	0.79259	0.20741	109	0.4655	0.03445	0.96555

TABLE S (7.6)
SINGLE LIFE FACTORS BASED ON LIFE TABLE 2000CM

7.6% INTEREST

AGE	ANNUITY	LIFE ESTATE	REMAINDER	AGE	ANNUITY	LIFE ESTATE	REMAINDER
0	12.9343	0.98301	0.01699	55	10.3809	0.78895	0.21105
1	13.0112	0.98885	0.01115	56	10.2409	0.77831	0.22169
2	13.0068	0.98852	0.01148	57	10.0964	0.76733	0.23267
3	12.9999	0.98799	0.01201	58	9.9476	0.75602	0.24398
4	12.9912	0.98733	0.01267	59	9.7941	0.74435	0.25565
5	12.9814	0.98659	0.01341	60	9.6354	0.73229	0.26771
6	12.9705	0.98576	0.01424	61	9.4717	0.71985	0.28015
7	12.9587	0.98486	0.01514	62	9.3036	0.70707	0.29293
8	12.9457	0.98387	0.01613	63	9.1310	0.69396	0.30604
9	12.9315	0.98279	0.01721	64	8.9540	0.68050	0.31950
10	12.9160	0.98162	0.01838	65	8.7724	0.66670	0.33330
11	12.8993	0.98034	0.01966	66	8.5836	0.65235	0.34765
12	12.8812	0.97897	0.02103	67	8.3882	0.63750	0.36250
13	12.8624	0.97754	0.02246	68	8.1869	0.62220	0.37780
14	12.8431	0.97608	0.02392	69	7.9803	0.60650	0.39350
15	12.8239	0.97462	0.02538	70	7.7689	0.59043	0.40957
16	12.8050	0.97318	0.02682	71	7.5524	0.57398	0.42602
17	12.7861	0.97174	0.02826	72	7.3311	0.55716	0.44284
18	12.7671	0.97030	0.02970	73	7.1061	0.54006	0.45994
19	12.7477	0.96883	0.03117	74	6.8785	0.52276	0.47724
20	12.7274	0.96728	0.03272	75	6.6493	0.50535	0.49465
21	12.7063	0.96568	0.03432	76	6.4194	0.48787	0.51213
22	12.6843	0.96401	0.03599	77	6.1890	0.47036	0.52964
23	12.6610	0.96223	0.03777	78	5.9585	0.45285	0.54715
24	12.6359	0.96033	0.03967	79	5.7285	0.43537	0.56463
25	12.6086	0.95826	0.04174	80	5.4998	0.41798	0.58202
26	12.5790	0.95600	0.04400	81	5.2727	0.40073	0.59927
27	12.5468	0.95356	0.04644	82	5.0479	0.38364	0.61636
28	12.5121	0.95092	0.04908	83	4.8260	0.36678	0.63322
29	12.4749	0.94809	0.05191	84	4.6075	0.35017	0.64983
30	12.4355	0.94509	0.05491	85	4.3930	0.33387	0.66613
31	12.3935	0.94190	0.05810	86	4.1829	0.31790	0.68210
32	12.3489	0.93852	0.06148	87	3.9779	0.30232	0.69768
33	12.3016	0.93492	0.06508	88	3.7781	0.28713	0.71287
34	12.2519	0.93114	0.06886	89	3.5841	0.27239	0.72761
35	12.1993	0.92715	0.07285	90	3.3964	0.25812	0.74188
36	12.1439	0.92294	0.07706	91	3.2150	0.24434	0.75566
37	12.0855	0.91850	0.08150	92	3.0403	0.23106	0.76894
38	12.0239	0.91382	0.08618	93	2.8728	0.21834	0.78166
39	11.9592	0.90890	0.09110	94	2.7123	0.20613	0.79387
40	11.8913	0.90374	0.09626	95	2.5587	0.19446	0.80554
41	11.8201	0.89833	0.10167	96	2.4127	0.18337	0.81663
42	11.7456	0.89266	0.10734	97	2.2741	0.17283	0.82717
43	11.6671	0.88670	0.11330	98	2.1424	0.16282	0.83718
44	11.5850	0.88046	0.11954	99	2.0173	0.15332	0.84668
45	11.4990	0.87392	0.12608	100	1.9002	0.14441	0.85559
46	11.4088	0.86707	0.13293	101	1.7882	0.13591	0.86409
47	11.3145	0.85990	0.14010	102	1.6844	0.12801	0.87199
48	11.2159	0.85241	0.14759	103	1.5807	0.12013	0.87987
49	11.1126	0.84456	0.15544	104	1.4852	0.11287	0.88713
50	11.0042	0.83632	0.16368	105	1.3911	0.10572	0.89428
51	10.8905	0.82768	0.17232	106	1.2721	0.09668	0.90332
52	10.7713	0.81862	0.18138	107	1.1365	0.08638	0.91362
53	10.6465	0.80913	0.19087	108	0.9130	0.06938	0.93062
54	10.5163	0.79924	0.20076	109	0.4647	0.03532	0.96468

PERIOD LIFE TABLE

A period life table is based on the mortality experience of a population during a relatively short period of time. Here we present the 2006 period life table for the Social Security area population. For this table, the period life expectancy at a given age represents the average number of years of life remaining if a group of persons at that age were to experience the mortality rates for 2006 over the course of their remaining life.

Exact age	Male Death probability [a]	Male Number of lives [b]	Male Life expectancy	Female Death probability [a]	Female Number of lives [b]	Female Life expectancy
0	0.007349	100,000	75.10	0.006055	100,000	80.21
1	0.000465	99,265	74.66	0.000433	99,395	79.70
2	0.000321	99,219	73.69	0.000276	99,351	78.73
3	0.000244	99,187	72.72	0.000184	99,324	77.75
4	0.000194	99,163	71.74	0.000160	99,306	76.77
5	0.000181	99,144	70.75	0.000144	99,290	75.78
6	0.000174	99,126	69.76	0.000133	99,276	74.79
7	0.000163	99,108	68.77	0.000124	99,262	73.80
8	0.000142	99,092	67.79	0.000113	99,250	72.81
9	0.000112	99,078	66.79	0.000102	99,239	71.82
10	0.000085	99,067	65.80	0.000093	99,229	70.82
11	0.000085	99,059	64.81	0.000094	99,220	69.83
12	0.000135	99,050	63.81	0.000113	99,210	68.84
13	0.000251	99,037	62.82	0.000153	99,199	67.85
14	0.000416	99,012	61.84	0.000210	99,184	66.86
15	0.000595	98,971	60.86	0.000274	99,163	65.87
16	0.000765	98,912	59.90	0.000335	99,136	64.89
17	0.000928	98,836	58.94	0.000385	99,103	63.91
18	0.001077	98,745	58.00	0.000418	99,064	62.93
19	0.001208	98,638	57.06	0.000438	99,023	61.96
20	0.001343	98,519	56.13	0.000457	98,980	60.99
21	0.001470	98,387	55.20	0.000479	98,934	60.01
22	0.001549	98,242	54.28	0.000497	98,887	59.04
23	0.001567	98,090	53.37	0.000511	98,838	58.07
24	0.001540	97,936	52.45	0.000523	98,787	57.10
25	0.001496	97,785	51.53	0.000536	98,736	56.13
26	0.001459	97,639	50.61	0.000550	98,683	55.16
27	0.001432	97,497	49.68	0.000567	98,629	54.19
28	0.001426	97,357	48.75	0.000588	98,573	53.22
29	0.001436	97,218	47.82	0.000612	98,515	52.25
30	0.001454	97,079	46.89	0.000641	98,454	51.28
31	0.001473	96,938	45.96	0.000677	98,391	50.32
32	0.001504	96,795	45.02	0.000720	98,325	49.35
33	0.001546	96,649	44.09	0.000772	98,254	48.39
34	0.001603	96,500	43.16	0.000833	98,178	47.42
35	0.001673	96,345	42.23	0.000903	98,096	46.46
36	0.001761	96,184	41.30	0.000982	98,008	45.50
37	0.001876	96,014	40.37	0.001073	97,911	44.55

Exact age	Death probability [a]	Male Number of lives [b]	Life expectancy	Death probability [a]	Female Number of lives [b]	Life expectancy
38	0.002021	95,834	39.44	0.001179	97,806	43.59
39	0.002193	95,641	38.52	0.001299	97,691	42.65
40	0.002391	95,431	37.61	0.001430	97,564	41.70
41	0.002607	95,203	36.69	0.001570	97,425	40.76
42	0.002842	94,955	35.79	0.001720	97,272	39.82
43	0.003091	94,685	34.89	0.001878	97,104	38.89
44	0.003360	94,392	34.00	0.002046	96,922	37.96
45	0.003646	94,075	33.11	0.002229	96,724	37.04
46	0.003960	93,732	32.23	0.002423	96,508	36.12
47	0.004316	93,361	31.35	0.002622	96,274	35.21
48	0.004721	92,958	30.49	0.002826	96,022	34.30
49	0.005166	92,519	29.63	0.003038	95,750	33.39
50	0.005660	92,041	28.78	0.003275	95,460	32.49
51	0.006171	91,520	27.94	0.003535	95,147	31.60
52	0.006653	90,955	27.11	0.003798	94,811	30.71
53	0.007085	90,350	26.29	0.004061	94,450	29.83
54	0.007498	89,710	25.48	0.004338	94,067	28.94
55	0.007936	89,037	24.66	0.004640	93,659	28.07
56	0.008451	88,331	23.86	0.004993	93,224	27.20
57	0.009063	87,584	23.06	0.005419	92,759	26.33
58	0.009797	86,790	22.26	0.005936	92,256	25.47
59	0.010643	85,940	21.48	0.006534	91,708	24.62
60	0.011599	85,026	20.70	0.007219	91,109	23.78
61	0.012624	84,039	19.94	0.007956	90,452	22.95
62	0.013684	82,978	19.19	0.008698	89,732	22.13
63	0.014759	81,843	18.45	0.009424	88,951	21.32
64	0.015890	80,635	17.72	0.010174	88,113	20.52
65	0.017161	79,354	17.00	0.011009	87,217	19.72
66	0.018610	77,992	16.28	0.011986	86,257	18.94
67	0.020216	76,540	15.58	0.013117	85,223	18.16
68	0.021992	74,993	14.89	0.014430	84,105	17.40
69	0.023966	73,344	14.22	0.015924	82,891	16.64
70	0.026212	71,586	13.55	0.017646	81,571	15.90
71	0.028725	69,710	12.91	0.019544	80,132	15.18
72	0.031450	67,707	12.27	0.021523	78,566	14.47
73	0.034385	65,578	11.65	0.023551	76,875	13.78
74	0.037599	63,323	11.05	0.025717	75,064	13.10
75	0.041267	60,942	10.46	0.028247	73,134	12.43
76	0.045411	58,427	9.89	0.031187	71,068	11.78
77	0.049921	55,774	9.34	0.034405	68,852	11.14
78	0.054797	52,990	8.80	0.037905	66,483	10.52
79	0.060154	50,086	8.29	0.041808	63,963	9.92

Exact age	Male Death probability [a]	Male Number of lives [b]	Male Life expectancy	Female Death probability [a]	Female Number of lives [b]	Female Life expectancy
80	0.066266	47,073	7.78	0.046337	61,289	9.33
81	0.073175	43,954	7.30	0.051587	58,449	8.76
82	0.080723	40,737	6.84	0.057503	55,433	8.21
83	0.088916	37,449	6.39	0.064135	52,246	7.68
84	0.097922	34,119	5.97	0.071587	48,895	7.17
85	0.107951	30,778	5.56	0.079984	45,395	6.68
86	0.119182	27,456	5.18	0.089431	41,764	6.22
87	0.131736	24,183	4.81	0.100009	38,029	5.78
88	0.145669	20,998	4.46	0.111773	34,226	5.37
89	0.160978	17,939	4.14	0.124745	30,400	4.98
90	0.177636	15,051	3.84	0.138938	26,608	4.62
91	0.195594	12,378	3.56	0.154348	22,911	4.28
92	0.214792	9,957	3.30	0.170963	19,375	3.98
93	0.235163	7,818	3.07	0.188761	16,062	3.69
94	0.256634	5,979	2.86	0.207711	13,030	3.44
95	0.277945	4,445	2.67	0.226885	10,324	3.20
96	0.298731	3,209	2.51	0.245997	7,982	3.00
97	0.318602	2,251	2.36	0.264731	6,018	2.81
98	0.337164	1,534	2.24	0.282754	4,425	2.65
99	0.354023	1,017	2.12	0.299719	3,174	2.49
100	0.371724	657	2.01	0.317702	2,223	2.35
101	0.390310	413	1.90	0.336764	1,516	2.20
102	0.409825	252	1.80	0.356970	1,006	2.07
103	0.430317	148	1.70	0.378389	647	1.94
104	0.451833	85	1.60	0.401092	402	1.82
105	0.474424	46	1.51	0.425157	241	1.70
106	0.498145	24	1.42	0.450667	138	1.59
107	0.523053	12	1.34	0.477707	76	1.48
108	0.549205	6	1.26	0.506369	40	1.38
109	0.576666	3	1.18	0.536751	20	1.28
110	0.605499	1	1.11	0.568956	9	1.19
111	0.635774	0	1.03	0.603094	4	1.10
112	0.667563	0	0.97	0.639279	2	1.02
113	0.700941	0	0.90	0.677636	1	0.94
114	0.735988	0	0.84	0.718294	0	0.86
115	0.772787	0	0.78	0.761392	0	0.79
116	0.811426	0	0.72	0.807076	0	0.72
117	0.851998	0	0.66	0.851998	0	0.66
118	0.894598	0	0.61	0.894598	0	0.61
119	0.939328	0	0.56	0.939328	0	0.56

[a] Probability of dying within one year.
[b] Number of survivors out of 100,000 born alive.

TABLE V – ORDINARY LIFE ANNUITIES – ONE LIFE – EXPECTED RETURN MULTIPLES

Age	Multiple	Age	Multiple	Age	Multiple
5	76.6	42	40.6	79	10.0
6	75.6	43	39.6	80	9.5
7	74.7	44	38.7	81	8.9
8	73.7	45	37.7	82	8.4
9	72.7	46	36.8	63	7.9
10	71.7	47	35.9	84	7.4
11	70.7	48	34.9	85	6.9
12	69.7	49	34.0	86	6.5
13	68.8	50	33.1	87	6.1
14	67.8	51	32.2	88	5.7
15	66.8	52	31.3	89	5.3
16	65.8	53	30.4	90	5.0
17	64.8	54	29.5	91	4.7
18	63.9	55	28.6	92	4.4
19	62.9	56	27.7	93	4.1
20	61.9	57	26.8	94	3.9
21	60.9	58	25.9	95	3.7
22	59.9	59	25.0	96	3.4
23	59.0	60	24.2	97	3.2
24	58.0	61	23.3	98	3.0
25	57.0	62	22.5	99	2.8
26	56.0	63	21.6	100	2.7
27	55.1	64	20.8	101	2.5
28	54.1	65	20.0	102	2.3
29	53.1	66	19.2	103	2.1
30	52.2	67	18.4	104	1.9
31	51.2	68	17.6	105	1.8
32	50.2	69	16.8	106	1.6
33	49.3	70	16.0	107	1.4
34	48.3	71	15.3	108	1.3
35	47.3	72	14.6	109	1.1
36	46.4	73	13.9	110	1.0
37	45.4	74	13.2	111	.9
38	44.4	75	12.5	112	.8
39	43.5	76	11.9	113	.7
40	42.5	77	11.2	114	.6
41	41.5	78	10.6	115	.5

Frequency of Payment Adjustment Table

If the number of whole months from the annuity starting date to the first payment date is	0-1	2	3	4	5	6	7	8	9	10	11	12
And payments under the contract are to be made:												
Annually	+0.5	+0.4	+0.3	+0.2	+0.1	0	0	-0.1	-0.2	-0.3	-0.4	-0.5
Semiannually	+.2	+.1	0	0	-.1	-.2	....	....	....	....	....	....
Quarterly	+.1	0	-.1	....	....	....	....	....	....	....	....	....

FIGURING COMPOUND INTEREST AND ANNUITY VALUES

The two tables that follow on the next two pages enable the estate planner to make various projections in actual cases. They show the compound interest and annuity functions at interest rates of 5 and 10 percent.

There are three functions which can be used for compound interest computations:

1. Amount of $1 (what a dollar will be worth at some date in the future if the deposit is made immediately).

_____

Example. If $1,000 is invested today and grows at a rate of 10 percent per year compounded annually, it will be worth $1,948.72 in 7 years. (Go to Form A on the following page. Find 7th year. Look under "Amount of 1" column. The value is 1.948717 multiplied by $1,000.)

_____

2. Amount of $1 per period (what a series of $1 deposits will be worth at some date in the future if the deposits are made at the end of each period).

_____

Example. If $1,000 is invested at the end of each year for 10 years and the return has been 10 percent interest compounded annually, the value of the fund is $15,937. (Go to Form A. Find 10 years. Look under the "Amount of 1 per Period" column. The value is 15.937425. Multiply this by $1,000.)

_____

3. Sinking fund payment (how much you need to deposit at the end of each period to have a given sum of money at a specified point in the future).

_____

Example. You'll need $100,000 in 5 years to pay off a debt. If you can earn 10 percent compounded annually on your money, you must deposit $16,379.74 each year for 5 years. (Go to Form A. Find 5 years. Look under the "Sinking Fund Payment" column. The value is .1637974808. Multiply that figure by $100,000.)

_____

There are three functions which enable present worth or annuity computations:

1. Present worth of $1 (the value of $1 today if it will not be received until some time in the future).

_____

Example. You are owed $1,000 and it will be paid to you in 10 years. Assuming a 5 percent interest rate, the present value of that debt is $613.91. (Go to Form B. Find 10 years. Look under the "Present Worth of 1" column. The value is 0.613913. Multiply that by $1,000.)

_____

2. Present worth of $1 per period. (How much is a future stream of dollars–payable at the end of each year–worth today?)

_____

Example. Suppose you were to receive $1,000 at the end of each year for the next 20 years. Assuming 10 percent interest, that stream of dollars would be worth $8,513.56 today. (Go to Form A. Find 20 years. Look under the "Present Worth of 1 per Period" column. The value is 8.513564. Multiply that by $1,000.)

_____

3. Periodic payment to amortize $1. (What mortgage payment must be made each year to pay off a given loan? In other words, you have a dollar now. What annuity do you have to pay each year–given a certain number of years–to pay off the loan?)

_____

Example. What is the annual payment needed to pay off a $100,000 loan over 10 years if a 10 percent interest rate is payable on the unpaid balance? Assuming payments are made annually at the end of each year and interest is compounded annually, the amount is $16,274.54. (Go to Form A. Find 10 years. Look under the "Periodic Payment to Amortize 1" column. The value is 0.1627453949. Multiply that by $100,000.)

_____

There is one measurement function: total interest (how much interest is paid over a given period of time where a loan is amortized by regular periodic payments).

_____

Example. Assume you were going to borrow $100,000 over 10 years at 10 percent interest. The total interest you'd pay on such a loan is $62,745. (Go to Form A. Find 10 years. Look under the "Total Interest" column. The value is 0.627454. Multiply that by $100,000.)

_____

FIGURING COMPOUND INTEREST AND ANNUITY VALUES 10 PERCENT

	Amount of 1	Amount of 1 Per Period	Sinking Fund Payment	Present Worth of 1	Present Worth of 1 Per Period	Periodic Payment to Amortize 1	Total Interest
	What a single $1 deposit grows to in the future. The deposit is made at the beginning of the first period.	What a series of $1 deposits grow to in the future. A deposit is made at the end of each period.	The amount to be deposited at the end of each period that grows to $1 in the future.	What $1 to be paid in the future is worth today. Value today of a single payment tomorrow.	What $1 to be paid at the end of each period is worth today. Value today of a series of payments tomorrow.	The mortgage payment to amortize a loan of $1. An annuity certain, payable at the end of each period worth $1 today.	The total interest paid over the term on a loan of $1. The loan is amortized by regular periodic payments.
YEARS							
1	1.100000	1.000000	1.0000000000	0.909091	0.909091	1.1000000000	0.100000
2	1.210000	2.100000	0.4761904762	0.826446	1.735537	0.5761904762	0.152381
3	1.331000	3.310000	0.3021148036	0.751315	2.486852	0.4021148036	0.206344
4	1.464100	4.641000	0.2154708037	0.683013	3.169865	0.3154708037	0.261883
5	1.610510	6.105100	0.1637974808	0.620921	3.790787	0.2637974808	0.318987
6	1.771561	7.715610	0.1296073804	0.564474	4.355261	0.2296073804	0.377644
7	1.948717	9.487171	0.1054054997	0.513158	4.868419	0.2054054997	0.437838
8	2.143589	11.435888	0.0874440176	0.466507	5.334926	0.1874440176	0.499552
9	2.357948	13.579477	0.0736405391	0.424098	5.759024	0.1736405391	0.562765
10	2.593742	15.937425	0.0627453949	0.385543	6.144567	0.1627453949	0.627454
11	2.853117	18.531167	0.0539631420	0.350494	6.495061	0.1539631420	0.693595
12	3.138428	21.384284	0.0467633151	0.318631	6.813692	0.1467633151	0.761160
13	3.452271	24.522712	0.0407785238	0.289664	7.103356	0.1407785238	0.830121
14	3.797498	27.974983	0.0357462232	0.263331	7.366687	0.1357462232	0.900447
15	4.177248	31.772482	0.0314737769	0.239392	7.606080	0.1314737769	0.972107
16	4.594973	35.949730	0.0278166207	0.217629	7.823709	0.1278166207	1.045066
17	5.054470	40.544703	0.0246641344	0.197845	8.021553	0.1246641344	1.119290
18	5.559917	45.599173	0.0219302222	0.179859	8.201412	0.1219302222	1.194744
19	6.115909	51.159090	0.0195468682	0.163508	8.364920	0.1195468682	1.271390
20	6.727500	57.274999	0.0174596248	0.148644	8.513564	0.1174596248	1.349192
21	7.400250	64.002499	0.0156243898	0.135131	8.648694	0.1156243898	1.428112
22	8.140275	71.402749	0.0140050630	0.122846	8.771540	0.1140050630	1.508111
23	8.954302	79.543024	0.0125718127	0.111678	8.883218	0.1125718127	1.589152
24	9.849733	88.497327	0.0112997764	0.101526	8.984744	0.1112997764	1.671195
25	10.834706	98.347059	0.0101680722	0.092296	9.077040	0.1101680722	1.754202
26	11.918177	109.181765	0.0091590386	0.083905	9.160945	0.1091590386	1.838135
27	13.109994	121.099942	0.0082576423	0.076278	9.237223	0.1082576423	1.922956
28	14.420994	134.209936	0.0074510132	0.069343	9.306567	0.1074510132	2.008628
29	15.863093	148.630930	0.0067280747	0.063039	9.369606	0.1067280747	2.095114
30	17.449402	164.494023	0.0060792483	0.057309	9.426914	0.1060792483	2.182377
31	19.194342	181.943425	0.0054962140	0.052099	9.479013	0.1054962140	2.270383
32	21.113777	201.137767	0.0049717167	0.047362	9.526376	0.1049717167	2.359095
33	23.225154	222.251544	0.0044994063	0.043057	9.569432	0.1044994063	2.448480
34	25.547670	245.476699	0.0040737064	0.039143	9.608575	0.1040737064	2.538506
35	28.102437	271.024368	0.0036897051	0.035584	9.644159	0.1036897051	2.629140

FIGURING COMPOUND INTEREST AND ANNUITY VALUES 5 PERCENT

	Amount of 1	Amount of 1 Per Period	Sinking Fund Payment	Present Worth of 1	Present Worth of 1 Per Period	Periodic Payment to Amortize 1	Total Interest
	What a single $1 deposit grows to in the future. The deposit is made at the beginning of the first period.	What a series of $1 deposits grow to in the future. A deposit is made at the end of each period.	The amount to be deposited at the end of each period that grows to $1 in the future.	What $1 to be paid in the future is worth today. Value today of a single payment tomorrow.	What $1 to be paid at the end of each period is worth today. Value today of a series of payments tomorrow.	The mortgage payment to amortize a loan of $1. An annuity certain, payable at the end of each period worth $1 today.	The total interest paid over the term on a loan of $1. The loan is amortized by regular periodic payments.
YEARS							
1	1.050000	1.000000	1.0000000000	0.952381	0.952381	1.0500000000	0.050000
2	1.102500	2.050000	0.4878048780	0.907029	1.859410	0.5378048780	0.075610
3	1.157625	3.152500	0.3172085646	0.863838	2.723248	0.3672085646	0.101626
4	1.215506	4.310125	0.2320118326	0.822702	3.545951	0.2820118326	0.128047
5	1.276282	5.525631	0.1809747981	0.783526	4.329477	0.2309747981	0.154874
6	1.340096	6.801913	0.1470174681	0.746215	5.075692	0.1970174681	0.182105
7	1.407100	8.142008	0.1228198184	0.710681	5.786373	0.1728198184	0.209739
8	1.477455	9.549109	0.1047218136	0.676839	6.463213	0.1547218136	0.237775
9	1.551328	11.026564	0.0906900800	0.644609	7.107822	0.1406900800	0.266211
10	1.628895	12.577893	0.0795045750	0.613913	7.721735	0.1295045750	0.295046
11	1.710339	14.206787	0.0703888915	0.584679	8.306414	0.1203888915	0.324278
12	1.795856	15.917127	0.0628254100	0.556837	8.863252	0.1128254100	0.353905
13	1.885649	17.712983	0.0564557652	0.530321	9.393573	0.1064557652	0.383925
14	1.979932	19.598632	0.0510239695	0.505068	9.898641	0.1010239695	0.414336
15	2.078928	21.578564	0.0463422876	0.481017	10.379658	0.0963422876	0.445134
16	2.182875	23.657492	0.0422699080	0.458112	10.837770	0.0922699080	0.476319
17	2.292018	25.840366	0.0386991417	0.436297	11.274066	0.0886991417	0.507885
18	2.406619	28.132385	0.0355462223	0.415521	11.689587	0.0855462223	0.539832
19	2.526950	30.539004	0.0327450104	0.395734	12.085321	0.0827450104	0.572155
20	2.653298	33.065954	0.0302425872	0.376889	12.462210	0.0802425872	0.604852
21	2.785963	35.719252	0.0279961071	0.358942	12.821153	0.0779961071	0.637918
22	2.925261	38.505214	0.0259705086	0.341850	13.163003	0.0759705086	0.671351
23	3.071524	41.430475	0.0241368219	0.325571	13.488574	0.0741368219	0.705147
24	3.225100	44.501999	0.0224709008	0.310068	13.798642	0.0724709008	0.739302
25	3.386355	47.727099	0.0209524573	0.295303	14.093945	0.0709524573	0.773811
26	3.555673	51.113454	0.0195643207	0.281241	14.375185	0.0695643207	0.808672
27	3.733456	54.669126	0.0182918599	0.267848	14.643034	0.0682918599	0.843880
28	3.920129	58.402583	0.0171225304	0.255094	14.898127	0.0671225304	0.879431
29	4.116136	62.322712	0.0160455149	0.242946	15.141074	0.0660455149	0.915320
30	4.321942	66.438848	0.0150514351	0.231377	15.372451	0.0650514351	0.951543
31	4.538039	70.760790	0.0141321204	0.220359	15.592811	0.0641321204	0.988096
32	4.764941	75.298829	0.0132804189	0.209866	15.802677	0.0632804189	1.024973
33	5.003189	80.063771	0.0124900437	0.199873	16.002549	0.0624900437	1.062171
34	5.253348	85.066959	0.0117554454	0.190355	16.192904	0.0617554454	1.099685
35	5.516015	90.320307	0.0110717072	0.181290	16.374194	0.0610717072	1.137510

Glossary

529 plan "front load" contributions (IRC § 529 plan). Contributions to 529 plans that equal five years of annual exclusion contributions can be made at one time. In 2015, the amount is $70,000. (Chapter 12)

5-and-5 power. A power of appointment that gives the holder the right to withdraw the greater of $5,000 or 5% of the value of the trust corpus. (Chapters 13, 16, 20, and 22)

A-B trust planning. Combining a bypass trust ("B" trust) with a marital trust ("A" trust) to take advantage of a married couple's available federal estate tax exemption and the unlimited marital deduction. (Chapter 16)

abatement. A state statute that determines an alternative distribution of assets when a decedent makes bequests of a greater amount of assets than currently exist under his will. (Chapter 5)

accumulation trust. A trust that allows the trustee to accumulate required minimum distributions within the trust. (Chapter 23)

ademption. A state statute that determines which assets can be used to satisfy a bequest when the bequeathed asset is no longer in existence. (Chapters 5 and 6)

adjusted gross estate. The amount of a gross estate calculated after subtracting debts, taxes, and administrative expenses from a decedent's gross estate. (Chapter 14)

adjusted taxable gift. A taxable gift made after 1976 that is added to a decedent's taxable estate to determine the tentative tax base before the estate tax is applied. (Chapters 11, 13, and 14)

advance directive. A legal document that enables an individual to direct his wishes regarding life-sustaining medical treatment in the event he becomes so ill that he cannot at the time communicate his wishes. Also known as a *living will* or *natural death declaration.* (Chapter 7)

agent. A person chosen by a principal to act for the principal in a fiduciary capacity under a power of attorney or a health care proxy. (Chapter 7)

alternate valuation date. The value of property in a decedent's estate six months after death. The alternate valuation date can be used only when the value of estate or generation-skipping transfer (GST) tax will be reduced by electing the alternate valuation date. (Chapter 13)

ancillary probate. A separate probate proceeding where property located outside of a decedent's state of domicile is subject to a separate probate proceeding in the state where the property is located. (Chapter 5)

615

annual exclusion. The amount that can be given to an individual donee each year gift tax free. The amount in 2015 is $14,000. (Chapter 11)

annuitant. The person receiving payments under an annuity. (Chapter 25)

annuity payment. A level payment amount distributed at set intervals, typically monthly or annually, to an income beneficiary for a set term. (Chapter 24)

applicable credit. A credit applied to offset the estate tax due on an estate. The credit has been "unified" for gift and estate tax purposes, so it is now called the *unified credit*. But prior to that the credit was referred to as the *applicable credit*. (Chapter 10)

applicable exclusion amount. The amount of property that can be sheltered from gift or estate tax because the unified credit is applied against the tax. This amount is $5.43 million in 2015.This term is also referred to as the *exemption equivalent amount*. (Chapter 16)

applicable fraction. The amount of the GST exemption allocated to the transfer that is divided by the taxable amount of the gift. (Chapter 19)

applicable rate. The GST tax rate in effect at the time of a gift is multiplied by the inclusion ratio to arrive at the applicable rate. (Chapter 19)

appointee. A person who is appointed property by the holder of a power of appointment. (Chapter 20)

ascertainable standard. A provision that permits a trustee to distribute trust income or principal to trust beneficiaries for a specified reason. The most common ascertainable standard is health, education, maintenance, and support (HEMS). (Chapters 16 and 20)

attorney-in-fact. The agent named in a power of attorney. (Chapter 7)

bargain sale. A sale of property to family members, charities, and others for less than fair market value. This transaction is part sale and part gift. (Chapters 10 and 25)

basic exclusion amount. The applicable exclusion amount or exemption equivalent amount. (Chapter 16)

basis. The value of property used to determine gain or loss for income tax purposes when the property is sold or for gift tax purposes when the property is transferred. (Chapter 10)

beneficiary. A person who receives a beneficial interest in a trust or property bequeathed from a decedent's estate. (Chapter 8)

beneficiary designation. A legal contract that names the person, trust, or other entity to receive assets. Beneficiary designations are commonly used to distribute retirement assets and life insurance contracts. (Chapter 4)

bequest. The distribution of property under a will. (Chapter 6)

business continuation agreement. An arrangement for the orderly disposition and continuation of a business interest in the event of the owner's death, disability, retirement or withdrawal from the business. (Chapter 27)

business succession planning. A plan for the orderly transition of a closely held business. (Chapter 27)

buy-sell agreement. A business continuation agreement that provides for the orderly disposition and continuation of a business interest in the event of the owner's death, disability, retirement, or withdrawal from a business. (Chapter 27)

bypass trust. A trust that utilizes a decedent's unified credit and avoids estate taxation of trust assets at the surviving spouse's death. This trust is also known as a *"B" trust, credit shelter trust,* or *family trust.* (Chapter 16)

charitable deduction. An unlimited tax deduction that applies to gifts or bequests made to qualified charities. An income tax deduction is subject to certain limitations. (Chapters 11 and 14)

charitable gift annuity. An arrangement between a donor and a charity in which the donor pays the charity a certain amount and the charity in turn pays the donor (or other designated annuitant) an annuity stream of income for life. (Chapter 17)

charitable lead annuity trust. A split-interest trust whereby a fixed annuity stream of income is distributed to a charity and the remainder of the trust interest passes to an individual when the income term ends. (Chapter 17)

charitable lead unitrust. A split-interest trust whereby a fixed percentage of income, which is revalued annually, is distributed to a charity and the remainder interest of the trust passes to an individual beneficiary or beneficiaries when the income term ends. (Chapter 17)

charitable remainder. A charitable gift that will take place at some time in the future. For example, a donor can give a gift to charity but retain the right to use property for his lifetime. (Chapter 17)

charitable remainder annuity trust. A split-interest trust whereby a fixed annuity stream of income is distributed to an individual and the remainder of the trust interest passes to a charity when the income term ends. (Chapters 15 and 17)

charitable remainder unitrust. A split-interest trust whereby a fixed percentage of income, which is revalued annually, is distributed to a beneficiary and the remainder of the trust interest passes to a charity when the income term ends. (Chapters 15 and 17)

civil union. A registered union recognized in some states that grants unmarried couples the same inheritance rights and protections under state law that legally married spouses have. (Chapter 28)

codicil. A legal document that addresses minor changes in a will. (Chapter 6)

commercial annuity. An annuity contract with an insurance company. (Chapter 13)

commingled assets. Assets that are mixed together, such as community assets and individually owned assets. (Chapter 3)

committee. The guardian of a ward's property charged with the responsibility of investing and managing the ward's estate. Also known as a *conservator* or a *curator.* (Chapter 7)

common-law state. A state that recognizes common law (in contrast to a state that recognizes community law). (Chapter 3)

common-law marriage. A union recognized by some states for couples who live together for a period of time but do not legally marry. Common-law marriage confers unlimited marital deductions for property transfers and treats jointly held real property as community property. (Chapter 28)

community asset. An asset deemed to be owned one-half by each spouse. (Chapter 3)

community property. Property deemed to be owned one-half by each spouse. In community property states, property acquired after marriage is considered community property. (Chapter 3)

completed transfer. An irrevocable transfer of property. (Chapter 10)

complex trust. A trust that can accumulate income, distribute corpus, and make gifts to charities. A complex trust qualifies as a separate tax entity that deducts income distributed and pays tax on income retained. (Chapters 8 and 9)

conduit theory. A theory pertaining to trust taxation that provides that what enters the trust or estate as ordinary income remains ordinary income when received by beneficiaries or heirs. (Chapter 9)

conduit trust. A trust that requires any minimum distributions received by the trust to be paid to trust beneficiaries. (Chapter 23)

conservator. A person chosen by the court to manage a ward's property and financial affairs. A conservator is a fiduciary. (Chapter 7)

contingent remainder interest. An interest in a trust's remainder that is contingent on the occurrence of a certain event or circumstance. (Chapter 8)

corporate fiduciary. A corporation named to serve as a fiduciary, such as guardian, executor, or trustee. (Chapter 8)

corporate trustee. A corporation, such as a bank or trust company, named to serve as a trustee. A corporate trustee can be retained to manage, invest, and distribute trust assets for the benefit of trust beneficiaries. (Chapter 1)

co-trustees. Two or more trustees serving together. (Chapter 8)

credit for state death tax. A credit that the federal government allowed to the states for death tax collected. The credit for state death tax was phased out from 2001 to 2004. (Chapter 18)

credit shelter trust. A trust that utilizes a decedent's unified credit to shelter assets from future estate tax. Assets that pass to a credit shelter trust avoid future estate tax, for example, at the surviving spouse's death. This trust is also known as a *bypass trust*. (Chapters 16 and 22)

cross-purchase agreement. A contract made by individual shareholders to own life insurance on a fellow shareholder's life and to purchase stock upon his death or disability. (Chapter 27)

Crummey notice. A notice provided by a trustee to trust beneficiaries informing them of their right to withdraw funds transferred to the trust within a certain period of time. (Chapter 20)

Crummey powers. A trust beneficiary's right to withdraw property that is added to a trust within a certain time frame. This gives the beneficiary a present interest in the trust, and the gift qualifies for an annual exclusion. (Chapters 20 and 22)

Crummey lapses. The termination of a Crummey beneficiary's right to withdraw assets because of the passing of the defined period in which the Crummey right of withdrawal is exercisable. The Crummey beneficiary makes a gift to the other trust beneficiaries. (Chapter 20)

cumulative. Increasing by successive additions. Gift and estate taxes are cumulative in nature. Taxable gifts made since 1932 must be added to current taxable gifts before the gift tax is applied. Adjusted taxable gifts made by a decedent since 1976 are added to the taxable estate to determine the tentative tax base before the estate tax is applied. (Chapter 10)

curator. The guardian of a ward's property charged with the responsibility of investing and managing the ward's estate. Also known as a *conservator*. (Chapter 7)

curtesy. A widower's right to a life estate in a deceased spouse's property. (Chapters 4 and 13)

de minimis rule. A doctrine of tax law that ignores small amounts. (Chapter 20)

deceased spousal unused exclusion amount (DSUEA). Under portability, a surviving spouse can take advantage of a prior decedent spouse's remaining unused exclusion amount to reduce gift or estate taxes. (Chapter 16)

decoupled. Separated—many states have decoupled from the federal estate tax since the phase-out of the credit for state death tax. (Chapter 18)

designated beneficiary. An individual named as a beneficiary either by the terms of a retirement plan or by the employee's beneficiary designation. (Chapter 23)

direct gift. A gift of real or personal property made outright to others. (Chapter 10)

direct gift to charity. A gift made directly to a charity accomplished by giving assets outright to a charitable institution. (Chapter 17)

direct skip. A taxable generation-skipping transfer made to a skip person outside of a trust. (Chapters 15 and 19)

disclaimant. A beneficiary who refuses to accept a gift or a bequest, who is treated as if he had predeceased the transferor. (Chapter 15)

disclaimer trust. A trust that holds property disclaimed by a decedent's heir. (Chapter 15)

discretionary provision. A provisions that gives a trustee the discretion to make distributions to trust beneficiaries for certain criteria. (Chapter 8)

distributable net income (DNI). A concept pertaining to the income taxation of trusts that provides that to the extent that a trust has income and distributes assets to beneficiaries, those distributions are deemed income first, and a return of principal to the extent the distribution exceeds the income received by the trust. (Chapter 9)

do-not-resuscitate declaration (DNR). A document that authorizes health care providers to withhold CPR or other measures to restart a patient's heart or breathing. (Chapter 7)

domestic partners. An unmarried couple involved in a committed relationship regardless of gender. (Chapter 28)

domestic partnership agreement. A legal agreement that protects both partners in a relationship by establishing ground rules for living together. (Chapter 28)

domicile. An individual's legal residence. (Chapters 1, 2 and 4)

donee. A person or entity that is the recipient of a gift. (Chapter 10)

donor. A person who transfers his own property to another person or entity. (Chapter 10)

donor-advised fund. A type of public charity such as a community foundation or funds that are overseen by mutual fund companies or brokerage firms. Donors can make contributions to a donor-advised fund and offer suggestions for the specific charity to receive funds from its account. (Chapter 17)

dower. A widow's right to a life estate in a deceased spouse's property. (Chapters 4 and 13)

durable power of attorney. A broad power of attorney that is not terminated by the subsequent disability or incapacity of the principal. (Chapter 7)

dynasty trust. A trust created by a state that can last for many generations because it is not subject to the rule against perpetuities. Also known as a *perpetual trust*. (Chapters 8, 19, and 22)

elective share. A statute that permits a surviving spouse to elect to receive an amount prescribed by state law. (Chapter 4)

estate. The rights, titles, or interests that a person, living or deceased, has in property. (Chapter 1)

estate equalization. A technique used to equalize ownership of assets between spouses to allow each spouse to take advantage of his available estate tax exemption. (Chapter 16)

estate freeze. A technique that allows the owner of property or a business interest to retain much of the present value of the asset or control of the asset while shifting future appreciation on that asset to others. (Chapter 24)

estate liquidity. Liquid assets held by an estate that are sufficient to pay postmortem costs, debts, and taxes. (Chapter 22)

estate trust. A trust that provides for a marital deduction in the decedent spouse's estate. The surviving spouse is typically given a life interest with the remaining trust assets paid to the survivor's estate at his death. (Chapter 16)

executor. The person (and/or institution) named in a valid will to serve as the personal representative of a testator when his will is being probated. (Chapters 1, 5, and 6)

exemption equivalent. The amount of a gift or bequest that escapes taxation. For 2015, the exemption equivalent amount is $5,430,000 and the tax on this amount is offset by a person's unified credit. The term is also referred to as an *applicable exclusion amount*. (Chapters 10 and 14)

fair market value (FMV). A price that a willing seller would pay a willing buyer for property. (Chapter 13)

family allowance. A statutory provision that provides a surviving spouse with money from the decedent's estate to pay for living expenses. (Chapter 4)

family limited partnership (FLP). A limited liability entity created under state law typically used when parents want to transfer wealth to their children in a tax-efficient manner but also to retain control of their assets and continue managing their property. (Chapter 26)

family trust. A trust that utilizes a decedent's unified credit and avoids estate taxation of trust assets at the surviving spouse's death. This trust is also known as a *bypass trust*, a *"B" trust*, or *credit shelter trust*. (Chapter 16)

fee simple or fee simple absolute. Outright ownership of an asset in an individual's name. This is the most comprehensive form of ownership, and there are no restrictions on how the property holder can use the asset while he is alive. (Chapter 2)

fiduciary. A person who has the authority to perform certain acts or specific duties. A fiduciary has a high level of responsibility to perform duties with utmost care and loyalty. (Chapter 1)

forgone interest. The difference between what should have been charged as interest on a loan and what was actually charged as interest on a loan. (Chapter 25)

fractional share. A partial ownership interest in property. (Chapter 2)

funded ILIT. An ILIT that holds both a life insurance policy and income-producing property to generate income to pay annual policy premiums. (Chapter 22)

future-interest gift. A gift made to someone who cannot take immediate possession of a property or who must wait to receive beneficial use, enjoyment, or income from it. (Chapter 10)

general bequest. A provision in a will that disposes of a certain amount or value of property. (Chapter 6)

general partnership interest. A partnership interest that retains control and management of FLP assets. (Chapter 26)

general power of appointment. A power of appointment allowing the holder to use a property without restriction and to appoint property to himself, his estate, his creditors, and creditors of his estate. (Chapters 7, 13, 15, 16, and 20)

generation-skipping transfer (GST). A gift or bequest made to a person two or more generations younger than the transferor. (Chapter 19)

generation-skipping transfer tax (GSTT or GST tax). A transfer tax imposed in addition to a gift tax or an estate tax. (Chapters 19 and 20)

generation-skipping transfer (GST) tax annual exclusion. GST annual exclusions are allowed for present-interest gifts to a skip person, or if a trust has only one skip person beneficiary. (Chapters 12 and 19)

generation-skipping transfer (GST) tax exemption. The amount that a transferor can transfer to grandchildren or more remote descendants during life or at death before a GST tax is imposed. In 2015, this amount is $5,430,000. (Chapters 12 and 19)

gift. A voluntary transfer without full or adequate consideration. (Chapter 10)

gift causa mortis. A revocable gift made in anticipation of the donor's death that becomes a completed, irrevocable gift at the donor's death. (Chapter 10)

gift tax. A transfer tax imposed when a donor gifts property that is subject to the tax. (Chapter 10)

gift tax return. IRS Form 709. (Chapter 11)

gift-leaseback. A transaction involving one party making a gift of property to an individual or to a trust and subsequently leasing the same property back. (Chapter 25)

gift to a non-citizen spouse. The marital deduction cannot be used for gifts made to a non-citizen spouse. (Chapter 11)

gift splitting. A gift tax reduction technique that allows each spouse to reduce a gift by one-half of its value. (Chapter 11)

grantor. A person who creates a trust. (Chapters 1 and 8)

grantor charitable lead trust (CLT). A charitable lead trust that treats the grantor as the owner for income tax purposes. A grantor CLT typically allows a large income tax deduction in the year that it is funded. (Chapter 17)

grantor retained annuity trust (GRAT). A trust that provides a qualified annuity interest based on a fixed dollar amount or percentage of the value of the trust to an income beneficiary for a set term. (Chapter 24)

grantor retained income trust (GRIT). A trust that provides a non-qualified annuity interest to the grantor with a remainder beneficiary receiving property at the end of the set term. (Chapter 24)

grantor retained unitrust (GRUT). A trust that provides a qualified annuity interest based on a fixed percentage of the net fair market value of the trust determined annually to an income beneficiary for a set term. (Chapter 24)

grantor trust rules. Provisions found in IRC §§ 671 to 677 that apply when a grantor is the owner of the trust and that qualify a trust as a grantor trust for income tax purposes. (Chapters 9 and 22)

grantor trust. A trust that is disregarded as a separate taxable entity where the trust income is taxable to the grantor. (Chapter 9)

gross estate. A tax concept that refers to the total of all property interests held by a decedent that is included in the decedent's estate. (Chapter 13)

gross-up rule. A provision under IRC § 2035 that requires that gift taxes paid within three years of a decedent's death be added back into the gross estate. (Chapters 13 and 14)

guardian. A person who is given the authority by a court to provide for a ward's personal care and to manage his property. A guardian is a fiduciary. (Chapters 1 and 7)

guardianship. A fiduciary relationship created by the law for the purpose of enabling a guardian to manage the person or estate, or both, of a ward when the law has determined that the ward is incapable of managing his person or estate himself. (Chapter 7)

hanging power. A trust provision that allows a beneficiary to withdraw more than the $5,000 or 5% safe harbor amount and make full use of the grantor's annual exclusion, which is $14,000 per donor per beneficiary in 2015. (Chapter 20)

health care proxy. A legal document that designates an individual to make decisions regarding medical treatment in the event the principal is not legally competent. Also known as a *power of attorney for health care*. (Chapter 7)

holder of a power of appointment. The person who has the right to exercise a power of appointment per the terms of a trust. (Chapter 20)

holographic will. A handwritten will. (Chapter 6)

homestead. A state statute that offers certain rights and protections to a surviving spouse. Typically, homestead statutes protect a surviving spouse's residence. (Chapter 4)

hybrid business continuation agreement. A business continuation agreement that affords the business owners the flexibility to determine after a shareholder's death whether a cross-purchase agreement or a stock redemption agreement is more appropriate for determining the disposition of the decedent's business interest. (Chapter 27)

incapacity. The legal inability to make or communicate responsible decisions regarding one's health, medical, or personal care; property or legal and financial affairs. (Chapter 7)

incident of ownership. When a person retains a measure of control over a life insurance policy. (Chapters 13, 21, and 22)

inclusion ratio. The ratio applied to generation-skipping transfers when determining the amount of property subject to GST tax. The inclusion ratio is calculated by subtracting the applicable fraction from one. (Chapter 19)

income first rule. A rule providing that the trustee's classification of a distribution as "income" or "corpus" is ignored; instead, all amounts distributed are deemed to be income to the extent of DNI. (Chapter 9)

income in respect of a decedent (IRD). The right to income earned but not received prior to a person's death. IRD could be income that was already earned, such as wages that had not yet been paid, or future income such as commissions. (Chapters 9 and 13)

income interest. An interest in a trust's income. (Chapter 8)

income shifting techniques. Available for parents who transfer income-producing property to family members in a lower income tax bracket. (Chapter 12)

incomplete gift. A gift that is not a complete transfer of property. An incomplete gift is not subject to gift tax. (Chapter 10)

indirect gift. A gift that is not made outright to a donee but benefits the donee. An indirect gift is subject to the gift tax. (Chapter 10)

indirect skip. A transfer made to a trust that includes skip persons and non-skip person beneficiaries. (Chapter 19)

individual trustee. An individual named to serve as trustee. (Chapter 8)

inheritance tax. A tax that is assessed based on an individual's right to inherit or receive assets from a decedent. (Chapter 18)

inherited IRA. An IRA that is inherited by a beneficiary. (Chapter 23)

installment sale. A transaction in which an owner sells property to a buyer, but instead of receiving payment outright, payments are spread over a set term of years. At least one payment must be received by the seller after the taxable year in which the sale occurs. (Chapter 25)

intangible property. An individual's bank, investment, mutual fund, or other accounts; assets that are not tangible. (Chapter 6)

intentionally defective grantor trust (IDGT). A trust designed intentionally so that income is taxed to the grantor rather than to the trust. (Chapters 9 and 25)

inter-vivos gift. A gift made during the donor's lifetime. (Chapter 10)

inter-vivos trust. A trust established during the settlor's lifetime. (Chapter 8)

intestacy/intestate succession. The transfer of assets per a state's laws of intestacy. (Chapters 5 and 6)

intestate. Lacking a will; a person who dies without a will is said to die *intestate*. (Chapters 4 and 6)

intra-family loan. A loan made between family members, typically at below-market interest rates. (Chapter 25)

IRC § 2032A special use valuation. Allows for certain farm or real property in a closely held business to be valued at less than fair market value. (Chapter 27)

IRC § 6166 installment payment of estate tax. Allows an executor under certain circumstances to pay federal estate taxes attributable to the decedent's business over 14 years. (Chapter 27)

IRC § 7520 rate. The interest rate set by the IRS on a monthly basis. (Chapter 24)

irrevocable life insurance trust (ILIT). A trust that is the owner of an insurance policy. When funded properly, the death benefit proceeds are not included in the insured's estate. (Chapter 21 and 22)

irrevocable trust. A trust that cannot be amended, revoked, or changed by the grantor. (Chapter 8)

joint tenancy with right of survivorship. A form of co-ownership of property where the property owners have an undivided right to the enjoyment of property. Joint tenants own property equally, even if there are more than two joint owners. At the first owner's death, property passes automatically to the surviving property owners. (Chapter 2)

joint tenants. Two or more individuals who own property together. (Chapter 2)

joint will. One will created for two individuals, typically spouses. (Chapter 6)

key person life insurance. A policy owned by a business that insures the life of a valuable employee. (Chapter 27)

lapse of a power (of appointment). A power of appointment that is not exercised by a holder within a stipulated timeframe. (Chapter 20)

laws of intestacy. State laws that provide for the disposition of a decedent's assets if he does not have a will. (Chapter 4)

legatee. A person to whom assets are bequeathed in a will. (Chapter 6)

life estate. A lifetime interest in real property or income from a trust. A person can either create a life estate in his own property or in a trust, or he can receive a life estate from a donor or a decedent. (Chapter 2 and 14)

limited liability company (LLC). A form of business organization intended to obtain for investors the same advantages of limited liability as in the corporate form of business while at the same time avoiding corporation income tax rules. (Chapter 26)

limited partnership interest. A partnership interest with limited rights and no control over management of an FLP. (Chapter 26)

limited powers of appointment. A power of appointment granting the holder the ability to appoint assets to a group of individuals or a charity that is limited by the donor. This POA is also known as a "special" power of appointment. (Chapters 13, 15, 16, 19 and 20)

living will. A legal document that enables an individual to direct his wishes regarding life-sustaining medical treatment in the event he becomes so ill he cannot at the time communicate his wishes. Also known as an *advance directive* or *natural death declaration*. (Chapter 7)

look-through trust. A trust in which all potential trust beneficiaries are identifiable. If a trust is a look-through trust, it qualifies as a designated beneficiary of retirement plan assets. (Chapter 23)

marital deduction. An unlimited tax deduction that applies to gifts or bequests made directly or indirectly to a spouse who is a U.S. citizen. (Chapters 11 and 14)

marketability discount. A discount applied to the value of limited partnership interests indicating that there is a lack of a readily available market for trading. (Chapter 26)

minority discount. A discount applied to FLP minority interests reflecting the inability of a limited partner to control the operations of the FLP and to invest its assets in a manner that is of the greatest benefit to the limited partner. (Chapter 26)

mortmain statutes. State laws that prevent a person from bequeathing significant property interests to charities or religious organizations if the person is near death. (Chapter 14)

mutual will. A will in which each party agrees to bequeath a particular property interest to the other. (Chapter 6)

natural death declaration. A legal document that enables an individual to direct his wishes regarding life-sustaining medical treatment in the event he becomes so ill he cannot at the time communicate his wishes. Also known as a *living will* or *advance directive*. (Chapter 7)

net gift. A taxable gift made to a donee, who is required to pay the gift tax. (Chapter 11)

net income make-up charitable remainder unitrust (NIMCRUT). A type of CRUT that provides that only trust income can be used to make the unitrust payment to the beneficiary and that if the net income produced by the trust in any given year is inadequate to meet the unitrust payment amount, the trust can have a "make-up" provision. (Chapter 17)

non-citizen spouse. A person who is not a U.S. citizen who is married to a U.S. citizen. (Chapter 11)

noncumulative right of withdrawal. A provision limiting the amount that can be withdrawn under a power of appointment or a Crummey power to a specific period of time. For example, if the money that can be withdrawn from a trust is not withdrawn during one year, then it can be withdrawn subject to the power of appointment or Crummey power in subsequent years. (Chapter 19)

nuncupative will. An oral will. (Chapter 6)

nondurable power of attorney. A power of attorney limited in scope that terminates at the principal's incapacity. (Chapter 7)

non-grantor charitable lead trust. A charitable lead trust where the grantor is not treated as the trust owner for income tax purposes. Typically no income tax deduction is permitted upon funding the trust. (Chapter 17)

non-voting interests. LLC interests that are not permitted to participate in the management of an LLC. (Chapter 26)

operation of law. The transfer of property by state law rather than by will or contract. (Chapter 4)

over-qualifying an estate for the marital deduction. Reliance on the marital deduction to reduce a taxable estate rather than a decedent's unified credit. (Chapter 16)

payable on death (POD). A designation on a bank account naming the individual, trust, or other entity to receive property upon the account holder's death. (Chapter 4)

per capita. Division of property per named individual or "per head." (Chapter 6)

per stirpes. Division of property by family group rather than individual. (Chapter 6)

percentage-of-contribution rule. A rule that applies to the inclusion of property in a decedent's estate when nonspouses own property as JTWROS. The first owner to die includes 100% of the property's FMV in his estate, unless the other tenant can prove a percentage of contribution toward the acquisition cost. (Chapter 13)

permanent insurance. A life insurance policy that combines a death benefit with a savings element in the form of cash value. (Chapter 21)

perpetual trust. A trust created by a state that can last for many generations because it is not subject to the rule against perpetuities. Also known as a *dynasty trust*. (Chapters 8, 19, and 22)

personal representative. A person named in a will as executor of the estate. (Chapter 6)

plenary guardianship. Guardianship of a person, taking custody of the ward, looking after his personal needs, and in general performing the duties performed by the parents of a minor (except the duty of support) and guardianship of a ward's property with the responsibility of investing and managing the estate of the ward. (Chapter 7)

pooled income fund. A trust generally created and maintained by a public charity rather than a private donor that meets certain requirements. (Chapter 17)

portability. A provision of the 2010 tax law that allows a surviving spouse to use the decedent spouse's unused estate tax exclusion and to add this amount to his own basic exclusion amount ($5,420,000 in 2015) to offset gift and estate taxes. (Chapter 16)

postnuptial agreement. A legal contract entered into after marriage that spells out each party's rights to property. (Chapter 4)

pour-over trust. A trust funded by the "pouring in" of assets from a decedent's will. (Chapter 8)

pour-over will. A will that directs property to "pour" into a revocable trust following the testator's death. (Chapters 4 and 6)

power of appointment. The power to invade or consume trust income or corpus. (Chapter 20)

power of appointment trust. A marital trust that gives the surviving spouse a general power of appointment over the trust property. (Chapter 16)

power of attorney. A document that names an agent to transact business for the principal until the principal's death. (Chapters 1 and 7)

power of attorney for health care. A legal document that designates an individual to make decisions regarding medical treatment in the event the principal is not legally competent. Also known as a *health care proxy.* (Chapter 7)

predeceased parent rule. A rule applying to GSTs that provides that if the skip person's parent who is a lineal descendant of the transferor or the transferor's spouse is deceased at the time of the transfer, the transfer will not constitute a generation-skipping transfer. (Chapter 19)

preferred stock recapitalization. A strategy whereby a business recapitalizes stock into voting preferred shares and non-voting common shares, and gifts the non-voting common shares to his children. (Chapter 24)

prenuptial agreement. A legal contract entered into in anticipation of marriage that spells out each party's rights to property. Also known as an *antenuptial agreement.* (Chapter 4)

present-interest gift. A gift giving the donee the unrestricted right to the immediate use or enjoyment of or income from a property. (Chapter 10)

presumption of survivorship clause. A clause in a will that determines the order of death for each spouse when it cannot be determined which spouse died first. (Chapter 15)

pretermitted heir. A person such as a spouse or a child who is not named in a will. (Chapter 6)

principal. A person who gives an agent authority to act on his behalf in a power of attorney or a health care proxy. (Chapters 1 and 7)

private annuity. A sale of property to a buyer who will make fixed payments to the seller for life. (Chapters 13 and 25)

private foundation. A legal entity, either a not-for-profit corporation or a tax-exempt trust, which is typically established and controlled by families who make gifts to the foundation and manage the foundation's assets and charitable gifts. (Chapter 17)

probate. The court-supervised process of settling a decedent's estate. (Chapters 4 and 5)

progressive. Increasing in rate as the base increases. Gift and estate taxes are progressive in nature. The unified transfer tax rates for gifts and estates range from 18% to 35% in 2012. (Chapter 10)

public charity. A charitable organization recognized by the IRS as a public charity. Public charities include churches, universities, hospitals, and many other organizations. (Chapter 17)

QTIP election. A gift tax or estate tax election made by a donor on IRS Form 709 or an executor on Form 706 to qualify a life estate given to a spouse for a marital deduction. (Chapters 11, 14, and 15)

QTIP trust. A trust that qualifies for a marital deduction in the decedent's estate if the executor makes a QTIP election on the estate tax return. (Chapter 16)

qualified charity. A charitable organization that meets certain IRS requirements. (Chapter 17)

qualified disclaimer. A written refusal to accept a gift or a bequest. To be a "qualified" disclaimer, the refusal must be made within nine months of a decedent's death, before any benefit from the disclaimed property has been received by the disclaimant. A disclaimer can be made with respect to all or a portion of a property interest. (Chapter 15)

qualified domestic trust (QDOT). A trust that meets the requirements for a marital deduction in the deceased spouse's estate for property passing to a non-U.S. citizen spouse. (Chapter 15)

qualified personal residence trust (QPRT). An irrevocable trust that holds a person's residence, allowing the donor to continue to live in the house for a fixed period of time and, at the end of the term, the home will pass gift-tax free to the trust beneficiaries and be removed from the grantor's estate. (Chapter 24)

qualified terminable interest property (QTIP). Terminable interest property gifted or bequeathed to a spouse that qualifies for a marital deduction if elected by the donor or the decedent spouse's executor. (Chapters 11, 15, and 16)

qualified transfer (exempt gift). A payment made directly to an educational institution to pay for someone's tuition or to a health care provider to pay for someone's medical expenses. Both gifts are exempt from gift tax. (Chapter 11)

quasi-community property. Property acquired in a common-law state that would have been deemed community property if acquired in a community property state. (Chapter 3)

reciprocal will. A will typically created by spouses in which each party agrees to leave certain property to each other; a mutual will. (Chapter 6)

release a general power of appointment. A holder of a power of appointment can give up his right to make withdrawals from a trust pursuant to the power of appointment by providing written notification to the trustee. The holder would thereby make a gift to the remainder beneficiaries. Lapses that exceed $5,000 or 5% of the trust corpus are treated as a release of a general power of appointment. (Chapter 20)

remainder interest. A split property interest in which a person's interest in property becomes effective at some future time—typically the termination of a period of years or another person's life. (Chapters 2 and 8)

remainderman. A remainder beneficiary in a split ownership property arrangement. (Chapter 2)

required minimum distribution (RMD). The amount required to be taken as a distribution from a retirement plan based on the plan owner's age and IRS actuarial tables. (Chapter 23)

res. The principal of a trust, also known as *trust corpus.* (Chapter 8)

resident alien. A non-citizen spouse who lives in the United States. (Chapter 15)

residual bequest. A provision in a will that disposes of all property that has not been disposed of through specific or general bequest. In other words, a residual bequest disposes of everything that is left after all other bequests have been satisfied. (Chapter 6)

residuary clause. A clause in a will that disposes of all property that has not otherwise been disposed of. (Chapter 6)

reverse gift. A donor gifts property in anticipation of a donee's death to receive a step-up in basis when the same property is bequeathed to the donor (at the donee's subsequent death). This scheme does not work in all situations. (Chapter 10)

reverse QTIP election. An election made by the executor on IRS Form 706 allowing a decedent to be treated as the transferor of a GST that occurs upon the surviving spouse's death. (Chapter 19)

reversionary interest. The donor retains a future interest in property that is gifted to another person. (Chapters 13 and 14)

revocable trust. A trust created by a grantor that can be amended, revoked, or changed by the grantor during the grantor's lifetime. (Chapters 4, 6, 7, and 8)

rule against perpetuities. A statutory limit on the duration of trusts that provides that the interests of a beneficiary in a trust must generally vest within the period allowed. (Chapter 8)

salary increase pension plan. Also known as a *selective pension plan*, an employee benefit plan that provides an employee or business owner with additional deferred compensation. (Chapter 27)

sale-leaseback. A transaction involving one party selling property to another party and then leasing back the same property. (Chapter 25)

Section 303 stock redemption. Allows the purchase of a portion of a decedent shareholder's stock, limited to the amount of estate tax and other related estate expenses, by his or her corporation to be treated as a sale or exchange rather than as a dividend. (Chapter 27)

Section 2503(b) trust. A split-interest trust with multiple beneficiaries. Assets can remain in trust for as long as the trust allows. All income must be distributed to trust beneficiaries with a present interest and cannot accumulate in the trust. (Chapters 12 and 20)

Section 2503(c) trust. A trust established for one trust beneficiary. Income can accumulate; however, the grantor can take an annual exclusion when assets are transferred into the trust. Assets must be distributed when the beneficiary reaches age 21. (Chapter 12)

self-cancelling installment note (SCIN). A variation of the installment sale, typically used among family members, providing that the balance of any payments due at the date of the lender's death will be automatically canceled. (Chapter 25)

separate asset. An individually owned asset that is not considered community property. (Chapter 3)

settlor. The person who creates a trust. Also known as the *trustor*. (Chapter 8)

sharing concept. A concept applied to the taxation of income earned by trusts that provides that income tax liability be shared by beneficiaries and the trust when income is distributed from the trust to beneficiaries. (Chapter 9)

simple trust. A trust where all trust income must be distributed in the year it is earned. The trustee cannot distribute trust principal or make charitable gifts. (Chapters 8 and 9)

single-life annuity. Annuity payments are calculated on the life expectancy of one individual. (Chapter 13)

situs. The physical location of property; the jurisdiction in which real property is subject to estate tax. (Chapters 5 and 8)

skip person. A person who is two or more generations below the transferor in a GST. In the event of a non-familial relationship, a skip person is anyone more than 37½ years younger than the transferor. (Chapter 19)

skip person trust. A trust where all trust beneficiaries are skip persons. (Chapter 19)

sole ownership. The simplest form of property ownership; outright ownership of an asset. A sole property owner has complete lifetime and testamentary control of property that he owns. Property that is solely owned is held in *fee simple* or *fee simple absolute*. (Chapter 2)

special needs trust. A type of trust designed to provide financial security for disabled individuals who receive government assistance. (Chapter 7)

special or limited power of appointment. A power of appointment granting the holder the ability to appoint assets to a group of individuals or a charity that is limited by the donor. (Chapters 13, 15, 16, and 20)

specific bequest. The disposition of a specific asset under a will. (Chapter 6)

spendthrift clause. A provision in a trust that protects the beneficiary's income and assets from the claims of creditors, divorce, and bankruptcy by restricting the beneficiary's right to assign income and corpus. (Chapters 8 and 22)

split-dollar life insurance. An arrangement, typically between an employer and an employee, whereby a life insurance policy's cash value, death benefits, and premiums can be split between the parties. (Chapter 27)

split-interest purchase of property. (Chapter 28) One person purchases a term interest in property and the other person purchases the remainder interest in the same property.

split-interest trust. A trust that has beneficiaries with both present and future interests. (Chapter 11)

split-interest charitable transfer. A gift or bequest to a charity with interests that are split between present-income interest and a remainder interest. Charitable lead trusts, charitable remainder trusts, and pooled income funds are examples of split-interest charitable transfers. (Chapter 17)

sponge tax. A tax designed to absorb the credit for state death tax that is allowed by the federal government. The federal government does not currently allow a credit for state death taxes; therefore, these states do not collect a state-level estate tax. (Chapter 18)

spousal rollover. An IRA that can be created by a surviving spouse who is a beneficiary of a deceased spouse's retirement plan assets. (Chapter 23)

spray provision. A trust provision that gives the trustee discretionary authority to distribute income and corpus to trust beneficiaries in equal or unequal shares. A trust that includes a spray provision can be referred to as a *spray trust*. (Chapters 8 and 28)

sprinkle provision. A trust provision that gives the trustee discretionary authority to distribute income to trust beneficiaries in equal or unequal shares. A trust that includes a sprinkle provision can be referred to as a *sprinkle trust*. (Chapters 8 and 28)

springing power of attorney. A power of attorney that becomes effective upon the occurrence of a specified event such as physical or mental incapacity. (Chapter 7)

state death tax deduction. A deduction allowed on IRS Form 706 for estate taxes paid to a state. (Chapters 14 and 18)

state laws of intestacy. State laws that determine how assets are distributed when a decedent does not have a valid will. (Chapter 1)

state of celebration. The state in which a couple celebrates their marriage. (Chapter 28)

state of residence. The state in which a married couple resides. (Chapter 28)

stepped-up basis. Assets owned by a decedent receive a new federal income tax basis equal to the property's fair market value for federal estate tax purposes. (Chapters 2, 10 and 13)

stock redemption plan. A contract made by a company to purchase stock from a deceased shareholder's estate using life insurance proceeds. (Chapter 27)

subtrusts. Separate trusts created within an irrevocable trust for each individual trust beneficiary. (Chapter 20)

support trust. A trust created for the purpose of providing child support payments to beneficiaries whose parents are divorced. (Chapter 28)

survivorship annuity. Annuity payments made for the lifetime of two annuitants that will continue after the death of the first annuitant. (Chapter 13)

survivorship life insurance. A life insurance policy that insures more than one person. (Chapter 21)

taker in default. The ultimate recipient of property. (Chapter 15)

tangible (personal) property. An individual's personal assets or "things" such as clothing, household items, etc. (Chapter 6)

taxable gift. The remaining taxable portion of a gift after tax-reducing techniques such as gift splitting, annual exclusions, and marital and charitable deductions have been applied. (Chapter 11)

tax exclusive. When the tax paid on a gift is paid from the donor's separate funds, and does not reduce the value of the gift the donee receives. (Chapters 10, 14, and 19)

tax inclusive. When estate tax liability is paid with money that was taxed in the decedent's estate. In some situations, GST taxes are paid from distributions made to a skip person beneficiary, which reduces the amount the skip person receives. (Chapters 10, 14, and 19)

taxable distribution. A distribution of income or corpus from a trust to a skip person that is not otherwise subject to estate or gift tax. (Chapter 19)

taxable estate. The value of an estate after subtracting the available marital, charitable, or state death tax deductions. (Chapter 14)

taxable gifts. The remaining taxable portion of a gift after tax-reducing techniques such as gift splitting, annual exclusions, and marital and charitable deductions have been applied. (Chapter 11)

taxable termination. The termination by death, lapse of time, release of a power, or otherwise of an interest in property held in a trust that results in skip persons holding all interests in the trust property. (Chapter 19)

tenancy by the entirety. A form of joint tenancy limited to spouses. (Chapter 2)

tenancy in common. A form of co-ownership of property. Tenants in common own an undivided right to possess property. Each tenant owns a separate fractional interest, which can be equal or unequal, in the same property. (Chapter 2)

tentative tax. Once the tentative tax base has been determined, the tentative tax can be calculated. (Chapter 14)

tentative tax base. The value of an estate after the value of adjusted taxable gifts is added to the taxable estate. (Chapter 14)

term insurance. A type of life insurance purchased for a set period of time. (Chapter 21)

terminable interest property (TIP). Property gifted or bequeathed to spouses that does not qualify for a marital deduction because the donee spouse lacks control over the property and cannot designate the remainder beneficiaries. (Chapters 11, 14, and 15)

testamentary trust. A trust established per the terms of a decedent's will. (Chapters 4 and 8)

testate. A person who dies with a will is said to die testate. (Chapter 6)

testator. The person who executes or makes a will. (Chapter 6)

three-year rule. A rule under IRC § 2035 that provides certain property interests be brought back into a decedent's estate for estate tax purposes if the decedent dies within three years of the transfer. (Chapters 13, 21, and 22)

Totten trust. A revocable arrangement whereby an individual deposits funds into a bank account in his own name as trustee for another person. The arrangement terminates upon revocation, death, or the individual relinquishing assets to the beneficiary. A Totten trust is not a true trust. (Chapter 4)

transfer on death (TOD). The designation on a stock, mutual fund, or other account that holds securities that names the individual, trust, or other entity that receives property on the account holder's death. (Chapter 4)

transferee. The recipient of a gift such as a GST. (Chapter 19)

transfer-for-value rule. A rule providing that if a life insurance policy is sold to a beneficiary, the owner-beneficiary will have taxable income when the insured dies. (Chapter 27)

transferor. The person who makes a gift such as a GST to a skip person. (Chapter 19)

trust. A legal entity that holds property for trust beneficiaries and can provide tax advantages and creditor protections. (Chapter 1)

trust corpus. The principal of a trust, also known as *res*. (Chapter 8)

trustee. A person who holds legal title to trust assets and administers those assets for trust beneficiaries. A trustee can manage and invest assets, make distributions, and file tax returns for the trust. A trustee is a fiduciary. (Chapters 1 and 8)

trustor. The person who creates a trust. Also known as the *grantor*. (Chapter 8)

trust protector. A fiduciary who may be given certain powers to provide greater flexibility in carrying out trust provisions in the future. The trust protector can adapt various trust provisions, determined when the grantor established the trust, to provide for changes in tax law or beneficiary circumstances. A trust protector can also be referred to as a *special trustee* or *trust adviser*. (Chapter 8)

unified credit. The credit available to offset gift or estate taxes. This credit is 2,117,800 in 2015. Formerly referred to as the *applicable credit*. (Chapter 10 and 14)

unfunded ILIT. An irrevocable life insurance trust that holds only title to a life insurance policy with no additional assets that could generate income to pay the annual policy premiums. (Chapters 20 and 22)

Uniform Gift to Minors Act (UGMA). A custodial account for minors. (Chapter 12)

Uniform Transfer to Minors Act (UTMA). A custodial account for minors that holds assets such as real estate, a life insurance policy, and annuities. (Chapter 12)

unitrust payment. An annual payment of a fixed percentage of the net fair market value of trust assets, to be determined annually. (Chapter 24)

universal life insurance. An interest-sensitive life insurance policy in which the investment, expense, and mortality elements are separately and specifically defined. (Chapter 21)

valuation discount. A discount applied to the value of an asset for various reasons, such as the lack of a market or lack of control. (Chapter 26)

variable life insurance. A permanent life insurance policy that has an investment component. The insured can select different subaccounts for investing the cash value. Neither the death benefit nor the surrender value is guaranteed. (Chapter 21)

vested remainder interest. An interest in a trust's remainder that is a vested or certain interest. (Chapter 8)

voting interests. Managing interest in an LLC. (Chapter 26)

ward. An individual who is legally incapable of taking care of himself or of managing his financial affairs. (Chapter 7)

whole-life insurance. A permanent policy with coverage guaranteed for the insured's life. (Chapter 21)

will contest. A challenge to a decedent's will in probate court. (Chapter 6)

will substitutes. Alternative methods of transferring property at death such as trusts, operation of law, or contracts. (Chapter 5)

zeroed-out GRAT. A GRAT with an annuity stream of income that pays out the entire principal of the trust. (Chapter 24)

Index